Seeing & Writing 2

Richard Caldicott, **Alternate Cover Sketches**
Photographer Richard Caldicott was commissioned to shoot an image for this book's cover related to the themes of *Seeing & Writing 2*. In the final version, the book's designers arranged Caldicott's photographs on the front, back, and inside covers.

Seeing & Writing 2

Donald McQuade
University of California, Berkeley

Christine McQuade

Bedford / St. Martin's
Boston • New York

FOR BEDFORD/ST. MARTIN'S

Executive Editor: Alanya Harter
Developmental Editor: Genevieve Hamilton
Production Editor: Bridget Leahy
Senior Production Supervisor: Nancy Myers
Marketing Manager: Brian Wheel
Editorial Assistant: Jeff Voccola
Text and Cover Design: 2x4
Copyeditor: Alice Vigliani
Photo Research: Naomi Ben-Shahar
Cover and Chapter Divider Photos: Richard Caldicott
Composition: Monotype Composition Company, Inc.
Printing and Binding: R.R. Donnelly & Sons, Inc.

President: Joan E. Feinberg
Editorial Director: Denise B. Wydra
Editor in Chief: Karen Henry
Director of Marketing: Karen Melton
Director of Editing, Design, and Production: Marcia Cohen
Managing Editor: Elizabeth M. Schaaf

Library of Congress Catalog Card Number: 2002112259

For information, contact: Bedford/St. Martin's,
75 Arlington Street, Boston, MA 02116
617-399-4000
www.bedfordstmartins.com

ISBN: 0-312-40004-7

ACKNOWLEDGMENTS

Introduction
Verbal Texts

Annie Dillard. "Dumbstruck." Originally titled "Heaven and Earth in Jest," excerpt from Chapter One from *Pilgrim at Tinker Creek* by Annie Dillard. Copyright © 1974 by Annie Dillard. Reprinted by permission of HarperCollins Publishers, Inc.

Robert Frost. "Design" from *The Poetry of Robert Frost*, edited by Edward Connery Lathem. Copyright © 1964 by Lesley Frost Ballantine. Copyright © 1936 by Robert Frost. © 1969 by Henry Holt and Company. "In White" by Robert Frost from *The Dimensions of Robert Frost* by Reginald L. Cook. © 1958 by Reginald L. Cook. Reprinted by permission of Henry Holt and Company, LLC.

William Carlos Williams. "The Red Wheelbarrow." From *Collected Poems: 1909–1939*, Volume 1. Copyright © 1938 by New Directions Publishing Corp. Reprinted by permission of New Directions Publishing Corp.

Visual Texts

Subway Passengers, Walker Evans. The Metropolitan Museum of Art, Gift of Arnold H. Crane, 1971. (1971.646.18) Photograph © 1999 The Metropolitan Museum of Art.

Migrant Worker. Courtesy of Dorothea Lange.

Pile of Boards. Courtesy of Freeman Patterson.

Warren Avenue at 23rd Street, Detroit, Michigan, October 1993. Copyright Joel Sternfeld. Courtesy Pace/MacGill Gallery, New York.

Children Fleeing a Napalm Strike, Vietnam 1972. © Nick Ut. AP/Wide World Photos. Reprinted by permission.

Chapter 1
Verbal Texts

K.C. Cole. "A Matter of Scale." From *The Universe and the Teacup: The Mathematics of Truth and Beauty*. Copyright © 1998 by K.C. Cole. Reprinted by permission of Harcourt Brace & Company.

Billy Collins. "Horizon." From *The Art of Drowning*, by Billy Collins. © 1995. Reprinted by permission of the University of Pittsburgh Press.

Annie Dillard. "Seeing." From *Pilgrim at Tinker Creek* by Annie Dillard. Copyright © 1974 by Annie Dillard. Reprinted by permission of HarperCollins Publishers, Inc.

Anne Fadiman. "Mail." Originally appeared in *The American Scholar*, Volume 69, Number 1, Winter 2000. Copyright © by Anne Fadiman.

Zoe Ingalls. "Teaching Architecture Students 'The Discipline of the Hand.' " From *the Chronicle of Higher Education*, November 21, 1997. Reprinted by permission of the author.

Steven Millhauser. "The Fascination of the Miniature." From *Grand Street*, Summer 1983.

Mahbabeh Sajadi

For Susanne and Marc

Richard Caldicott, **Alternate Cover Sketches**
These "outtakes" of the specially commissioned cover photograph (here and on page ii) represent iterations of the image that were not used in the final version. Which version do you prefer? How successful do you think the final cover is? Visit www.seeingandwriting.com and let us know what you think.

Preface for Instructors

The second edition of *Seeing & Writing* strengthens our commitment to helping students improve their analytic and compositional skills by treating seriously the connection between the verbal and the visual in today's culture. *Seeing & Writing* was the first composition reader to introduce the skills students need to read both kinds of texts and to write effectively about them. This new edition reflects what we have learned from student users of the book, from their instructors, and from our own students. We are encouraged by the success of *Seeing & Writing;* among first-year composition texts, it remains the most widely used collection of contemporary writing and visual material. We take this as confirmation that a steadily increasing number of instructors recognize the pedagogical benefits of exploring the interrelations of seeing and writing.

This new edition builds on that success, providing students with more to write about and more instructional assistance with their writing. We introduce engaging and compelling new selections for reading, stunning and teachable new images from high and popular culture, and broader, stronger coverage of reading and writing about *all* kinds of texts. Our goal, however, has remained the same throughout our work on both editions: to produce a teaching tool that is as instructionally useful as it is visually attractive—a text that helps students develop and practice skills as confident, articulate writers.

In developing this second edition of *Seeing & Writing*, we not only reinforce our commitment to this goal but also refine our original idea: to illustrate the principle that effective writing is a product of clear thinking, and that clear thinking begins with careful observation. Accurate and insightful observations about daily—and seemingly ordinary—experiences enable students to think and write confidently about important and complex aspects of American culture and their own lives. Learning to see well helps students to write well.

We built the first edition of *Seeing & Writing* around a simple premise: we would invite students to give words and images equal attention. We asked students to actively and critically *see* the details of each verbal and visual text, to *think* carefully about its composition and the cultural context within which it operates, and then to *write* thoughtfully and convincingly about it. *Seeing & Writing 2* sharpens its focus on the process students can follow from first sight to polished essay.

Added Emphasis on Critical Reading, Thinking, and Writing

In this second edition of *Seeing & Writing* we have made a series of determined efforts to create an even more effective writing text. Based on numerous suggestions from students and instructors across the country who have used the book, we have added the following elements to satisfy fully the expectations and requirements of the composition classroom:

A thoroughly revised and expanded general introduction to *Seeing & Writing 2* shows and tells students about the *process* of reading, thinking, and writing—ranging from practicing close reading and drafting to revising and editing. Coverage includes more visual examples, model analyses of visual and verbal texts, and opportunities for students to practice critical reading and writing skills up front.

A new **Visualizing Composition** feature in each chapter gives concrete shape to understanding and practicing key compositional strategies, including attending to details, listening carefully to tone, recognizing and developing structure, establishing a clear purpose, attending to an audience, working with metaphor, and understanding point of view. Each discussion offers a visual example of the strategy in question and concludes with a writing exercise.

A new **Visualizing Context** feature in each chapter vividly illustrates the importance of reading—and appreciating—texts in context. Each discussion connects to a selection in the book, offers a visual illustration of the context in question, and concludes with a writing exercise. A sampling of contexts includes how *the Suburb* is constructed in popular movies; how readers ought to see the whole picture before assessing a part; and how historical images—such as the American flag being raised over Iwo Jima—echo across generations and events.

The forty new reading selections—essays, short stories, and poems—invite students to read American culture even more carefully. With a greater percentage of expository essays than the first edition, *Seeing & Writing* now includes new voices such as Nick Hornby, Anne Fadiman, Billy Collins, Sarah Vowell, and Andrew Sullivan along with such perennial favorites as Tillie Olsen, Joy Harjo, and Tobias Wolf.

The one hundred new images—photographs, paintings, sculpture, and cartoons, as well as such cultural artifacts as advertisements, film posters, publicity stills, and icons—provide engaging prompts for effective writing. These new visual texts represent artists as diverse as Richard Estes, David Graham, Andreas Gursky, Barbara Kruger, Miranda Lichtenstein, and Art Spiegelman.

A new **Appendix**—"On Reading Visual and Verbal Texts"—guides students through the process of responding effectively to contemporary visual and verbal texts.

A new **Glossary** of terms for Seeing & Writing provides students with a working vocabulary to use when talking about how the book's variety of visual and verbal texts are composed and how students can read, think, and write about them.

A new **Rhetorical Table of Contents** suggests ways in which visual and verbal texts might be used to illustrate the principal rhetorical strategies for developing an essay.

Continued Emphasis on the Interrelations of the Verbal and Visual

In addition to the new features introduced in this second edition, we have strengthened and refined four chapters ("Observing the Ordinary," "Coming to Terms with Place," "Capturing Memorable Moments," and "Reading Icons") and added three new chapters ("Embodying Identity," "Producing America," and "Challenging Images"). "Embodying Identity" focuses on how we shape the identity we present to others; its "Looking Closer" section asks how the clothes, piercings, and tattoos we wear fashion our identities. "Producing America" highlights issues surrounding the manufacturing of American identity; its "Looking Closer" section zooms in on marketing "cool." "Challenging Images" illustrates how high the stakes can be when questioning the images we see; its "Looking Closer" section examines the ethics of representation in an age of easy digital manipulation. In each of these chapters we have paid special attention to analytical reading and effective writing.

Grounded in our decades of experience on both sides of the instructional desk, *Seeing & Writing 2* expresses our commitment to the pedagogical principle that instructors ought to start where students are able. And our experience suggests that undergraduates are thoroughly familiar—although often in a passive and uncritical way—with the myriad visual elements of contemporary American experience. We believe that undergraduates are sufficiently conversant with the subjects and strategies of a wide range of visual images (including advertisements, photographs, paintings, and comic art) and related nonfiction prose, short stories, and poems to want to write about them—and the questions and issues they prompt—in original, coherent, and convincing terms. We believe that providing students with opportunities to move fluently within and between these visual and verbal worlds will improve their analytic and compositional skills.

We have designed this second edition of *Seeing & Writing* to help students improve their writing by sharpening their perception. This pedagogical principle informs the book's three goals: (1) to provide opportunities for composition students to think perceptively and critically about compelling visual and verbal aspects of American culture, (2) to help students write effectively about how they perceive themselves, especially in relation to the images and words that compete for their attention, and (3) to give instructors the flexibility to work with these materials in ways best suited to the interests and abilities of their students.

The nature and range of the visual and verbal selections reprinted here, the way the selections are organized, and the supporting materials in the instructor's manual and Web site continue to make *Seeing & Writing 2* unique and timely.

A Flexible Organization

Each chapter opens with an illustration and a brief overview of the thematic scope of the chapter; this is followed by a reading and writing exercise that invites students to observe and draw reasonable, verifiable inferences from the visual material that opens the chapter. The exercise helps students relate their initial perceptions and interpretations of this material to their own life experiences and to the materials that follow in the chapter. Generally, we have designed each chapter to progress from the concrete to the abstract, from shorter to longer texts, and from a limited and readily accessible frame of reference to more wide-ranging and interconnected ones.

The overall organization of the book reflects a similar progression—from practicing the skills of observation and inference, to working with description and narration, and then to applying rhetorical forms such as exposition and argumentation. Yet, because each chapter is self-contained and begins with an exercise in observation and inference, instructors can sequence subjects and themes to best address their own instructional needs as well as the interests and backgrounds of their students.

Features of Each Chapter

In addition to the new features included in *Seeing & Writing* 2, we have strengthened and refined the core elements of each chapter in the first edition:

Chapter dividers: Striking photographs preceding each chapter serve as visual introductions to the subject under consideration. Commissioned especially for *Seeing & Writing*, these photographs function not only as engaging chapter dividers but also represent one set of interpretations of the seven thematic units of the book.

Paired visual and verbal texts: Each chapter includes visual and verbal texts that are linked. In some instances the image and the verbal text address the same topic or theme; in others one text has inspired the other. By juxtaposing two texts, we invite students to explore the similarities and differences between communicating an idea visually and verbally.

Portfolios: This feature presents several examples of the work of a selected visual artist. The intent is to illustrate that most artists, like most writers, have an individual style and focus of vision. Each portfolio of images is accompanied by a brief biographical headnote about the artist as well as insights into his or her thematic and stylistic vision. "Seeing" and "Writing" questions conclude each portfolio, encouraging students to think and write productively about the study of multiple images by a single artist.

Retrospects: These "visual timelines" demonstrate in graphic terms the fact that cultural artifacts—such as advertisements, everyday objects, portraits, and cover art for popular magazines—are products of specific historical moments. The graphic selections constitute a comparative and historical lens through which to re-examine a particular aspect of the subject or issue being studied in the chapter. It's important for students to notice that the things people take for granted haven't always been presented in the same way. For example, in the chapter on place, we show twelve photographs by Camilo José Vergara of the same street in Harlem taken over twenty years. In the chapter on icons we reprint the changing images of the American family in TV sitcoms. We let the images speak for themselves, providing simply the title and date of each one.

Looking Closer: The terms of this feature reflect its focus. We want to help students improve their writing by showing them how to take a second, more careful, and detailed look at certain aspects of American culture that may be familiar to them already. In the chapter on icons, for example, students examine their assumptions about and attitudes towards one of the most commonplace yet highly charged images in American life: the flag. "Looking Closer" invites students to do more than recognize something out of the ordinary in the ordinary. In effect, it reinforces the pedagogical aims highlighted in the title *Seeing & Writing*. It invites students to analyze images and words related to a theme without our editorial comments and guidance. It also engages them in a reflective "double take" as they re-examine the familiar from a fresh angle of vision and with a more inquiring and analytical eye. Within the context of composition, a double take consists of a purposeful delayed reaction—an intentional rereading (that is, reviewing a visual or verbal text from a different perspective) and a deliberate revising (that is, thoughtful rewriting and careful editing), especially when the text is one's own prose.

Re: Searching the Web and **Talking Pictures**: We encourage students to use the World Wide Web—and to analyze its effectiveness—as a research tool to explore further visual and verbal resources related to the subjects and issues presented in every chapter. A boxed exercise, "Re: Searching the Web" appears in every chapter; its name summarizes its purpose. The instructions and questions that appear here encourage students to learn to use the web as a research tool by directing them to web sites where they can find additional images and prose material about the subject or issue being studied. This exercise also invites students to analyze the ways in which information is presented on the web and evaluate the reliability of that information.

We have included an additional boxed exercise in each chapter—"Talking Pictures"—to sharpen students' awareness of the roles and effects of television shows and movies on American culture.

In addition, we have interspersed throughout each chapter several instructionally self-contained images that enrich and extend the scope of a given topic or theme. These photographs, cartoons, advertisements, and other visual artifacts will stimulate discussion and prompt further thinking and writing.

Supportive and Inconspicuous Apparatus

We have deliberately kept to a minimum the amount of apparatus that introduces and follows each selection. For each one, brief biographical headnotes provide background information about the writer or artist and his or her creative goals and practices. Focused discussion questions and writing exercises follow each selection under the headings "Seeing" and "Writing."

"Seeing" questions engage students in focused and sustained ways with the subject of each selection, the compositional strategies used, and the overall organization of the selection and its interconnections with other texts in the book. "Writing" exercises often invite the student to write about the subject in a personal experience essay. (We also occasionally include the opportunity for students to write a poem or story about the subject.) These writing exercises are linked to class discussion and in-class writing.

A Note about the Design

The design of Seeing & Writing 2 creates an attractive and engaging environment in which students can reflect on—and see reflections of—contemporary American culture. The double purpose of the design reinforces our goals: to prompt further inquiry into the similarities and differences between the attractions and effects of images and verbal texts, and to encourage conversation about the ways in which such texts can be more productively connected. By integrating visual and verbal texts, juxtaposing them, and giving both equal positional importance on a page, the book's design facilitates that discussion while also reflecting the complex nature of the multimedia in which we all function.

Teaching *Seeing & Writing 2*

A comprehensive instructor's manual—*Teaching* SEEING & WRITING 2—offers suggestions on how to teach the material in this new edition, paying respectful attention to different institutional settings and instructional purposes. This compendium of teaching resources includes generous attention to such elements as:

Generating Class Discussion and In-Class Writing: A thorough assessment of how to work imaginatively and productively with the text in class to stimulate discussion and in-class writing, which may motivate students to write engaging, coherent, and convincing essays about the texts and the issues and themes it articulates.

Additional Writing Topics: A group of additional topics for each selection that includes informal and personal writing, descriptive and narrative essays, expository and argumentative papers, and research assignments.

Connections with Other Texts: For each selection, suggestions for additional connections within the chapter and within the book, along with suggestions about how to encourage students to discover these interconnections on their own, thicken the range of thematic and stylistic interconnections in *Seeing & Writing 2*.

Suggestions for Further Reading, Thinking, and Writing: A compendium of supplemental material designed for classroom use—including print, video, audio, and online sources—along with recommendations on how to use them to reinforce your instructional goals.

Additionally, **Seeing & Writing 2 Online**, a book-related web site at <www.seeingandwriting.com>, includes interactive exercises on reading visual images and web-based research activities; annotated research links about the artists, writers, and thematic and compositional issues in the book; interviews with artists; and doorways to visual resources, virtual museums, and much more.

Acknowledgments

Two converging stories account for the origins of *Seeing & Writing*. The genesis of what is in several respects an unprecedented book for the teaching of writing can be traced to innumerable conversations Don McQuade has had over more than twenty years with Charles H. Christensen, an extraordinary patron and developer of teachable ideas. Throughout this long collaboration and friendship, Chuck Christensen and Don McQuade have talked about creating a book that draws on undergraduates' familiarity with the visual dimensions of American culture to develop their skills as effective readers, thinkers, and writers.

There was a more recent impetus for launching what began as a memorable five-year adventure in both *creating* this unique instructional tool and re-creating a father-daughter relationship. *Seeing & Writing* first took shape during an extended series of family dinner conversations over the course of a few evenings in late December 1996. The participants in that conversation included Don and Susanne McQuade and their two children, Christine and Marc. Christine had returned home for the holidays from New York City, where she had completed the fall season dancing with the STREB modern dance company. Marc was home for the winter holidays from the University of California, Berkeley, where he had finished his first semester.

Marc started the conversation—and what ultimately became the book— by talking about the writing course he had just completed, a course on writing about art. Marc carried from that class to the dinner table a nagging question: Which has a more powerful impact on people—an image or a word? Here's what he later wrote about the family conversation that night:

> I was annoyed because in my History of Art class people were equating images with a single word, and I thought that was a false comparison. I compared images not with a single word but rather with a paragraph or some longer text. I believe an image is a composition of a visual vocabulary. An image has a range of meaning similar to a paragraph. . . . We were discussing the idea of an image replacing text or whether images or words were more efficient at conveying an idea.

Marc's classroom experience with and thoughts on the relationship between word and image within academic settings were—and continue to be—at the center of both the impetus for and successful development of the book.

Having studied American popular culture as a history major and served as a writing tutor at Berkeley's Student Learning Center, Christine was eager to investigate and re-envision the teaching of writing in the visual age. Her ideas about relating the visual and verbal immediately drew her father's attention and encouragement. What began as an engaging conversation soon developed in a collaborative effort to create a book designed to improve the analytical and compositional skills of students by having them see, read, think, and write about the verbal and visual dimensions of American culture.

Don and Christine's work began together spontaneously and grew organically. In this sense there is another, more personal dimension to the story about *Seeing & Writing*. The working relationship that evolved between Christine and her father became a process of negotiating differences: in location, gender, age, perspective, and family role.

Begun in conversation, *Seeing & Writing* grew and developed through a series of long-distance conversations with each other, friends, colleagues, and the professional staff at Bedford/St. Martins. Behind this collaborative effort stands a large number of friends and colleagues who graciously allowed us into their already crowded lives to seek advice, encouragement, and assistance.

For helping us by asking important questions and offering generous advice, we would like to add a special note of thanks to Austin Bunn and Eileen O'Malley Callahan of the University of California, Berkeley; Beth Chimera, Mia Chung, Lee Dembart, Kathy Gin, Justin Greene, Anne-Marie Harvey, Eli Kaufman, Laura Lanzerotti, Joel Lovell, and Greg Mullins of Evergreen College; Anjum Salam, Shayna Samuels, and Darryl Stephens of the University of California, Berkeley; and Matthew Stromberg, as well as Elizabeth Streb and the dancers of STREB. Early on in our planning for this revision, Elizabeth Abrams of the University of California, Santa Cruz, kindly helped us think through rigorously how we might make *Seeing & Writing 2* a more effective tool for teaching writing. Sandra and Yuen Gin provided us an inspiring place to work.

With a rare blend of intelligence, imagination, and energy, Lee Dembart, Greg Mullins, Barbara Roether, and especially Molly Kalkstein assisted us in doing biographic research on the writers and artists and in drafting head-notes. Special thanks to Michael Hsu for his reading and re-reading of drafts, and for his general encouragement and support. His generous and rigorous intelligence as well as his energy and patience have strengthened *Seeing & Writing* 2 in innumerable ways.

Darryl Stephens has brought inestimable intelligence, writing skill, and pedagogical care to the work of preparing the second edition. A limitless source of first-rate ideas and teaching strategies, Darryl has also been an invaluable contributor to the questions following many selections. Dan Keller of Southern Illinois University, Edwardsville, has skillfully prepared *Teaching* SEEING & WRITING 2. We are grateful to have the benefit of his accomplishments as an outstanding teacher and writer as well as of his understanding of the practical applications of the book's vision.

We are also grateful not only to the instructors who offered critiques of the book during its various stages of development but also to those from around the country who have generously chronicled their experiences teaching the first edition. For their many thoughtful and helpful recommendations, we would like to thank:

Gary Bennett, Santa Ana College; Daniel Bentley-Baker, Florida International University; Jennifer Breuer, University of Florida; Angi Caster, Highline Community College; William Chamberlain, Michigan State University; J. Brian Chambley, Ohio State University; Gina Claywell, Murray State University; Thomas Clemens, Heartland Community College; Jeff E. Cravello, California State Polytechnic University; Wayne Crawford, Western Illinois University; Jim Curran, Towson University; Litasha Dennis, University of North Carolina, Greensboro; Stephen Donatelli, Harvard University; Julie E. Ewing, Boise State University; Kathryn Flannery, Indiana University; David Garrison, University of Tennessee, Chattanooga; Laurie Glover, University of California, Davis; Paul Heilker, Virginia Polytechnic Institute and State University; Carrie Heimer, University of New Hampshire; Christina A. Hitchcock, University of New Hampshire; Charles Hood, Antelope Valley College; Melanie Jenkins, Snow College; Priscilla Kanet, Clemson University; Anne Kress, Santa Fe Community College; Jon A. Leydens, California School of Mines; Thomas E. Luddy, Salem State College; Sonia Maasik, University of California, Los Angeles; Michael Mackey, Community College of Denver; Eileen R. Maguire, University of North Florida; Dave Malone, Southwest

Missouri State University, West Plains; Benjamine McCorkle, Ohio State University; Laurie McMillin, Oberlin College; J. Eric McNeil, The University of Louisiana, Monroe; Maureen Newey, California State University; David Norlin, Cloud County Community College; Kathleen Patterson, Santa Ana College; Anthony Petruzzi, Bentley College; J. Wylene Rholetter, Auburn University; David Rollison, College of Marin; Loretta Ross, Mount San Jacinto College; Dawn Skorscewski, Emerson College; Todd Taylor, University of North Carolina, Chapel Hill; and Anne Frances Wysocki, Michigan Technological University.

In addition to introducing us to Michael Rock and Susan Sellers at 2x4, Irwin Chen—someone who moves seamlessly between word and image—contributed a lively and invaluable presence in the development of this book. It quickly became clear that *Seeing & Writing* would be a book that needed a particularly sophisticated designer's eye. Michael Rock, Susan Sellers, and Katie Andresen of 2x4 have been invaluable in helping us not only to expand our imaginations of how this book could look and function but also to sharpen our own abilities to think visually. During the preparation of this second edition, Katie Andresen has once again turned a collection of chaotic materials into an elegant and useful instructional tool.

We are delighted that Richard Caldicott accepted our invitation to prepare seven distinctive and memorable photographs for *Seeing & Writing 2* to precede the chapters and to create a completely separate work of art for the cover. Commissioned specifically for this book, Richard Caldicott's photographs provide an eminently teachable series of artistic views of contemporary American culture. We are grateful to Esin Goknar for opening the door to new sources of photography and other visual media in the first edition. With great skill and patience, Naomi Ben-Shahar has widened our lenses even further as we worked with her on selecting images for *Seeing & Writing 2*. A distinguished photography teacher, an artist, and a photo-researcher, Naomi brought the best of each of these perspectives to this project as well as her passion for teaching and learning. We thank her for all that she has taught us about seeing carefully.

We'd once again like to extend special thanks to the kind people of Bedford/St. Martin's. Alice Vigliani has copyedited the manuscript of both editions with truly outstanding skill and judgment as well as with great sensitivity and respect for our instructional purposes. Sandy Schechter, Naomi Klein, and Jeff Voccola managed with great skill and determination the complex project of securing permissions to reprint the visual and verbal materials presented in the book. We'd also like to thank Jeff Voccola for his thoughtful assistance throughout and Katherine Power for her vigorous work on the Glossary. Bridget Leahy figured out and managed the logistics of producing this edition with an admirable blend of intelligence, energy, imagination, patience, and good will. We are fortunate to have worked with her. Genevieve Hamilton contributed her keen editorial eye and sensitivity to pedagogical responsibility, along with a generous dose of good judgment, to every aspect of the later stages of preparing this second edition and the new web site for *Seeing & Writing 2*. With an imaginative design from Jennifer Smith, the site was also dynamically improved with input from Nick Carbone and Katie Schooling.

We continue to be indebted to Joan Feinberg, a perceptive, encouraging, and compelling voice of reason and impeccable judgment. Her vision of the book's potential and her critiques of our work stand as models of intellectual and professional integrity. Chuck Christensen offered wise and energizing support until the day of his retirement. His thoughtful encouragement and confidence in us and what we sought to achieve made each sentence easier to write.

We would also like to thank our editor, Alanya Harter. She is a remarkably skillful and accomplished reader and writer, someone who balances good judgment, tact, and taste with knowledge and resourcefulness. She is the kind of editor every author hopes to work with and write for. Her animating and rigorous intellectual presence is everywhere evident to us in this "final," published version of *Seeing & Writing 2*; and we remain grateful for her hard work, dedication, and patience. Without her engaging intelligence, *Seeing & Writing 2* would be less than it is.

Finally, we would like to acknowledge Susanne and Marc McQuade. This project would never have been possible without their encouragement, patience, and most important, their inspiring intellectual curiosity. "Merci vu mou!"

Donald McQuade and Christine McQuade

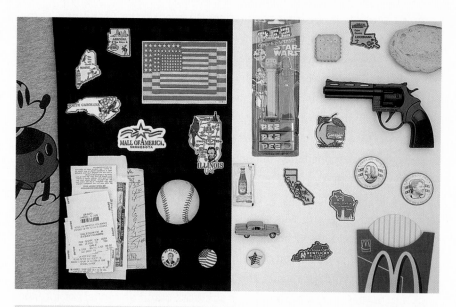

Richard Caldicott, **Two Alternate Divider Sketches**
Specially commissioned photographs by Richard Caldicott serve as visual introductions to each of the chapters in *Seeing & Writing 2*. These two sketches were presented as possibilities for Chapter 5, "Producing America." The final version appears on pages 378–79.

Contents

CHAPTER 2

126 **Coming to Terms with Place**

Introduction

Readings

CHAPTER 3

220 Capturing Memorable Moments

Introduction

Readings

287   Looking Closer: Taking Pictures

CHAPTER 4

304   # Embodying Identity

CHAPTER 5

CHAPTER 6

Introduction

Readings

Looking Closer: The Stars and Stripes

No method nor discipline can supersede the
necessity of being forever on the alert.
What is a course of history, or philosophy, or poetry,
or the most admirable routine of life,
compared with the discipline of looking always
at what is to be seen? Will you be a reader,
a student merely, or a seer?

– Henry David Thoreau

Introduction
Writing in the Age of the Image

Seeing and *writing* seem—on the surface—to have very little to do with each other. We tend to regard seeing as an effortless, reflex-level activity. Think of such common phrases as taking a "quick glance" or giving something a "look-see." They suggest speed, lightness, and ease. Writing, on the other hand, is more frequently associated with weight and labor. The idiom "writer's block" is commonly invoked; think of the classic image of a writer staring at a blank page, crumpled papers overflowing from a nearby trash can. Few writers—at any age or level of experience—have not experienced some version of this kind of frustration. In this book, we will show you that seeing and writing have more in common than you might think. They are inextricably bound; learning to see more carefully will help you to write more easily and successfully.

Seeing comes before words.
– *John Berger, 1972*

We believe that careful seeing leads to effective writing. The more your eyes are open and alert, the more you will have to write about—and the more you will write with conviction and clarity.

Snapshots of American Culture. In the following pages you will find a wide range of visual and verbal "snapshots" from American culture: words, pictures, and combinations of the two taken from our increasingly multimedia world. You will be invited to pay as much attention to, say, an episode of *The Simpsons* as to the more traditional essays and arguments you will read—and write—in most of your college courses. We hope you will consider virtually everything around you to be a potential text for serious reading, discussion, and writing—from a movie poster for the latest box-office hit to a wall with graffiti scrawled on it; from an advertisement for building a stronger body to an essay about growing up in a Korean American community; from the clothes you buy to the personal ads in your local newspaper.

The selections in *Seeing & Writing 2* reflect the texts you encounter every day while walking down the street, surfing the web, studying for your courses, visiting a museum or a gallery, watching TV, or reading a magazine or a newspaper. Some may be familiar, some unfamiliar. Some might inspire, others unsettle. Our hope is that you will use these selections to draw on your own experience with American culture and to recognize—and practice—your skills as an effective thinker and writer.

"Be a Seer." In preparing this material, we have been guided by the wisdom and encouragement Henry David Thoreau offers in *Walden* (1854), the book documenting his year-long experiment with the simple life. Today, almost a century and a half later, the distinctions he draws in the epigraph reprinted at the beginning of this introduction—between and among reader, student, and seer —endure. Following Thoreau's lead, we encourage you to be a seer, "looking always at what is to be seen."

Indeed, effective writing begins with seeing carefully—focusing your attention. When we look deliberately, we draw on all five of our senses as well as our intelligence and emotions. Effective seeing begins with noticing what is obvious and pushing beyond convenient labels and language to discover new dimensions of the world around you.

As you practice as a seer and writer what Thoreau calls "the necessity of being forever on the alert," we also urge you to think about how you see— that is, to examine how your unique point of view shapes the meaning you make from whatever passes before your eyes. We encourage you to identify to what extent—and in what ways—your background, attitudes, and personality shape what and how you see. You may well discover and learn as much about the lenses, the perspectives, through which you see as you do about the focal point of your attention. There is an old adage that says we often don't see things as they are but as *we* are.

"Cross-train." We believe that anyone interested in becoming an articulate and confident writer needs to "cross-train"—that is, to learn from the different ways in which serious thinkers see the world and express their distinct perspectives on it. You will encounter the work of some of the most

Stare. It is the way to educate your eye, and more. Stare, pry, listen, eavesdrop. Die knowing something. You are not here long.
—*Walker Evans*

"The real voyage of discovery consists of not in seeking new landscapes but in having new eye
—*Marcel Proust*

Much like the woman pictured here staring blankly into space, many of us tend to look without really noticing. For example, how carefully do you pay attention to the details of your everyday environment? How specific could you be if you were asked to describe a street corner you pass every day?

Walker Evans, **Subway Passengers, New York, New York**

accomplished writers, painters, poets, artists, and photographers of our time in the pages that follow. Each has used admirable and observable skills to articulate a unique vision through a particular medium. The strategies artists and photographers employ to capture and direct the viewer's attention, make a point, or create an effect are not very different from the strategies writers use to achieve the same effects, albeit in a different medium. For example, you might think of a writer's choice of word to be akin to a painter's brushstroke. A dot of bright color (say, red), like a single word (say, smash), doesn't do much on its own—it's the combination of different elements, the composition of a text, that gives the audience something to read, respond to, admire, and remember.

Photography can be seen as a kind of automatic writing. —W.J.T. Mitchell

Thinking carefully about visual and verbal strategies will enable you to improve your own skills as readers and writers. We seek to assist you in becoming more aware of—and developing more practiced confidence in—the skills identified with both verbal and visual literacy. These skills will enable you to learn, recognize, understand, and create compelling and convincing messages that will be understood by many people within and beyond the halls of higher education. You are already a member of several distinct communities; mastering the skills of critical reading and writing will enable you to contribute your ideas—and posit your voice—in these and other communities with which you choose to associate.

The ability to read and write in a purely visual medium; the ability to decode the meaning delivered by visual texts, as through design, typography, and images.

In the next section, we will describe a set of concrete intellectual tools that will enable you to practice the skills of seeing more clearly and writing more effectively about the world around us—the people, objects, images, events, ideas, and commercial appeals that compete for our attention and seek to gain our endorsement and loyalty.

The only thing I can say is that it takes place—
or the best of it takes place—in a sort of vacuum.
On the worst of mornings. On the least likely
of mornings. When you expect nothing to happen.
When the page is blank. When the mind is blank.
Even in a state of depression or melancholia.
And then, only with good luck. . . . Oh, don't misun-
derstand me. I think you have to be sitting there.
You have to "wait" in good faith. You have to go
to work like anyone else, or I do anyway. I have
to go to work at nine o'clock. And in that sense
you force it. You've got to start in some way. . . .
You have to have a routine and live up to it and
then hope for the best. — *Walker Percy*

See to Write; Write to See

Composing is a recursive process of seeing and writing. Taking a closer look around you not only gives you subjects and ideas to write about (which are the initial ingredients in writing) but also leads to effective writing. Such careful seeing is an intellectual equivalent of breathing in; writing is a form of intellectual exhaling—expressing an idea in clear, convincing, and memorable terms. Writing, in turn, can also help you see and understand your subject more clearly.

From the Latin *recursus,* "to run back." A term adapted from mathematics to describe a process of writing in which the writer loops back to a preceding point in order to move forward with an idea.

Why Write? We believe that you have something important to say. The motivations for writing vary widely—from the desire to earn a good grade to the need to discover more about yourself and your relation to the world. But most important, writers write because they have something to say. Perhaps the most enduring satisfaction that writing affords is gaining authority over the ideas that you value and want to express to others. Many writers have faith in their ability to surprise themselves, to be able to express something they did not previously think they knew or could say. These writers recognize the power of writing to transform the world—which in a sense has already been formed by the words and images of others—into a world of possibility, the world they create with the words they craft on a blank page.

The Composing Process. Writers usually start by searching for and then deciding on a subject to write about, developing their ideas about the subject, clarifying their purpose in writing, organizing their thoughts, and considering the audience they want to address. In the drafting phase, they usually carry out the detailed plan they have developed. In the revising phase, they shift their focus to reading and studying what they have written and determining how to improve it. These phases are not a rigid series of stages that writers work through in exactly the same manner each time. They are simply patterns of activities that describe what happens when writers write. As every writer knows, at least intuitively, writing is not a linear but a recursive process. Writing rarely proceeds neatly from one phase to the next. Rather, the phases often overlap, making the process somewhat messy. Many writers, for example, revise what they have written as soon as they see the word or sentence on the page. Others wait until they

I'm a writer. I don't cook and I don't clean. . . .
Dear child, this place is a mess—my papers are
everywhere. It would be exhausting to clean up! . . .
I can't believe I'm 87. As a child, I decided I never
wanted to be the last leaf on the tree, and now
here I am, the last leaf. I was a member of the
Harlem Renaissance, you know, and the youngest
person is the one who lives the longest. . . .
When I was seven, I said to my mother, may I
close the door? And she said, yes, but why do you
want to close your door? And I said because I
want to think. And when I was eleven, I said to
my mother, may I lock the door? And she said yes,
but why do you want to lock your door? And I said
because I want to write. – *Dorothy West*

have a complete draft and only then go back through it. Each writer participates in the writing process in a different way, at a different pace, and with a different result.

We believe that there is no single way to write, no fail-proof formula to produce successful essays. Anyone who is seriously interested in learning to write can benefit not only from listening carefully to what other writers and artists have to say about the challenges and pleasures of the composing process but also, and more important, from a willingness to practice the skills regularly. Writing is, after all, a skill; and skills develop over time with frequency of practice. Making writing a habitual, daily activity will reduce the anxiety and tension about whether you're writing correctly. Too many people focus on writing to avoid making mistakes rather than on articulating the ideas they want to convey. The best method to build confidence as a writer is to begin by seeing carefully.

Visualizing Composition

By "composition," we mean both the process of writing and the way in which a text is put together. When we talk about seeing a text, we mean reading it critically. *Critical reading* is a term you will often hear invoked in your courses. Many students think it requires them to engage in elaborate "fault-finding" exercises while reading and writing. However, the etymology of the word *critical* suggests a different kind of intellectual activity. The word derives from the Latin *criticare,* meaning "to analyze, to take apart." All your college courses will ask you to "take apart" the subject you're studying, whether it's biology, political science, literature, or any other subject. We use the phrase *critical reading* here in this sense—to take a closer look, to see actively beyond the surface of the words and images you encounter in this book, in your college courses, and in your everyday life.

Critical Reading Involves Asking Questions. Carefully analyzing a text for overall meanings and effects, as well as breaking down its structure in order to better understand each part and to explore the relationship of each part to the whole. Critical reading also involves a willingness to question what exactly in the text prompts *you* to respond in a certain way.

As you think through each question that follows, you will find yourself verifying your assertions with specific evidence. This kind of critical reading constitutes an intellectual "double take," or taking a step back—to reexamine a text from a fresh angle, with a more inquiring and analytical eye, and with sustained attention to detail. Like a double take in ordinary experience, critical reading involves a more thoughtful and purposeful delayed reaction. It consists of intentional rereading (i.e., reviewing the details of a visual or verbal text from different perspectives) and deliberate rewriting (i.e., thoughtful revising and careful editing), especially when the text is one's own prose.

What do I notice? And why?

A useful place to begin with any text is to jot down your first impressions. Answer these questions: What details do I notice? What parts of it stand out to me more than others? It is important to allow yourself to have "pure" reactions to texts before you begin analyzing them. What are your initial instincts about the text?

1. (a) The act, practice, or power of noticing. (b) Something noticed. 2. (a) The fact of being seen or noticed; the act or practice of noting and recording facts and events, as for some scientific study. (b) The data so noted and recorded. 3. A comment or remark based on something observed.

What you see in a text will depend, in part, on what you bring to it. Whenever you read anything, you bring to that experience the sum total of your past experiences and how you define yourself—in terms of race, class, gender, sexuality, and political disposition. You should also acknowledge your own predispositions to—or prejudices about—the text in question.

Once you've attended to your first impressions, look again and write down a set of more careful observations about the text. An observation is, in effect, a neutral, nonjudgmental, and verifiable statement. It's easy to make assumptions about something you're looking at or reading without taking the time to base your statements on what you can actually see.

Take a few moments to consider carefully the observations you might make about the photograph on the next page. What exactly do you see here?

We urge you to write down as many statements as possible about whatever you are observing. You might begin by writing out your thoughts—either by taking notes with pen and paper or by entering them on a keyboard—from the moment you encounter a new text. We've reprinted some observations one student made about this photograph by Joel Sternfeld, titled *Warren Avenue at 23rd Street, Detroit, Michigan, October 1993*. How do they compare with your own observations?

1 I notice that this is a photograph of a two-story building with a sidewalk and part of a street visible in front of it. The color of most of the building is light green.

2 I notice that there are three large windows on the second floor. The pane in the lower right corner of each of these three windows has the same appearance. The middle window is partially boarded up.

3 I notice that the words "When you take someones life you forfeit your own" appear under these three windows.

4 I notice that there are photos and notes on the wall on the first floor.

5 I notice that there is a "sold" sign and text on the door.

6 I notice that a brightly colored image of a person has been painted on the wall.

7 I notice that there are flowers on the sidewalk in front of the building.

8 I notice that there is a cross with flowers on it on the left side of the sidewalk.

9 I notice that there is an orange cone on the sidewalk in front of the building.

Now, think about how you might apply the same process of making careful observations to a verbal text. Take a few moments to read the following non-fiction "snapshot" from Annie Dillard's *Pilgrim at Tinker Creek* (1974), a Pulitzer Prize–winning collection of observations of nature. What do you notice about it? Here are some observations a student made about this passage:

1 I notice that Dillard uses the first person ("I") to tell the story of her experience of witnessing a frog being eaten by a "giant water bug."

2 I notice that the writer repeats the idea of being amused by the sight she sees.

3 I notice that the writer uses a metaphor in the passage "Frogs were flying all around me."

4 I notice that the writer repeats the phrase "he didn't jump" in paragraphs 1 and 2.

5 I notice that the writer uses several similes to describe the frog: "like a schematic diagram of an amphibian," "like a kicked tent," "like a deflating football," "like bright scum on top of the water."

6 I notice that the writer shifts her attention—and her readers'—from the frog to the giant water bug in paragraph 3.

7 I notice that the writer doesn't reveal until paragraph 3 the information that the frog is being eaten alive by the giant water bug.

Annie Dillard

DUMBST

C K

A couple of summers ago I was walking along the edge of the island to see what I could see in the water, and mainly to scare frogs. Frogs have an inelegant way of taking off from invisible positions on the bank just ahead of your feet, in dire panic, emitting a froggy "Yike!" and splashing into the water. Incredibly, this amused me, and, incredibly, it amuses me still. As I walked along the grassy edge of the island, I got better and better at seeing frogs both in and out of the water. I learned to recognize, slowing down, the difference in texture of the light reflected from mudbank, water, grass, or frog. Frogs were flying all around me. At the end of the island I noticed a small green frog. He was exactly half in and half out of the water, looking like a schematic diagram of an amphibian, and he didn't jump.

He didn't jump; I crept closer. At last I knelt on the island's winter-killed grass, lost, dumbstruck, staring at the frog in the creek just four feet away. He was a very small frog with wide, dull eyes. And just as I looked at him, he slowly crumpled and began to sag. The spirit vanished from his eyes as if snuffed. His skin emptied and drooped; his very skull seemed to collapse and settle like a kicked tent. He was shrinking before my eyes like a deflating football. I watched the taut, glistening skin on his shoulders ruck, and rumple, and fall. Soon, part of his skin, formless as a pricked balloon, lay in floating folds like bright scum on top of the water: it was a monstrous and terrifying thing. I gaped bewildered, appalled. An oval shadow hung in the water behind the drained frog; then the shadow glided away. The frog skin bag started to sink.

I had read about the giant water bug, but never seen one. "Giant water bug" is really the name of the creature, which is an enormous, heavy-bodied brown beetle. It eats insects, tadpoles, fish, and frogs. Its grasping forelegs are mighty and hooked inward. It seizes a victim with these legs, hugs it tight, and paralyzes it with enzymes injected during a vicious bite. That one bite is the only bite it ever takes. Through the puncture shoot the poisons that dissolve the victim's muscles and bones and organs—all but the skin—and through it the giant water bug sucks out the victim's body, reduced to a juice. This event is quite common in warm fresh water. The frog I saw was being sucked by a giant water bug. I had been kneeling on the island grass; when the unrecognizable flap of frog skin settled on the creek bottom, swaying, I stood up and brushed the knees of my pants. I couldn't catch my breath.

Making initial comments when responding to any text will enable you to build confidence in your ability to read it carefully and insightfully. Reading with an eye on making observations also best prepares you to write effectively about what you see in a text.

What can I infer from my observations?

One of the most productive ways to approach understanding and appreciating any text is to employ a two-step process: Make observations, and then draw reasonable and verifiable inferences from those observations. This pattern of observing and inferring—what we regard as the cornerstone skills of careful reading and writing—can be applied to any question you ask about a text in terms of its purpose, occasion, audience, structure, point of view, tone, or the context within which it was written or produced. Yet, how can you know whether the inferences you have drawn from your observations are reasonable?

inferences An intellectual leap—from what one sees to what those details might suggest.

What makes an inference reasonable is whether specific evidence in the text warrants the intellectual leap you've made. When drawing an inference, be careful not to rush to judgment and formulate a conclusion, even if it's provisional, before you have carefully examined the details of the evidence under consideration.

Here are some inferences a student drew based on her observations about Joel Sternfeld's photograph.

— Based on the observations I have made, I infer that this is a place where someone has been killed.

— An event has provoked public expression in this particular place.

— The inscription written on the wall—"When you take someones life you forfeit your own"—sends a direct message to anyone who sees it.

— The arrangement of flowers as well as the cross on the sidewalk function as a memorial to the person killed.

— The person whose image is painted on the wall of the building is depicted with a celestial background.

These are a few observations and inferences the same student made about the prose passage by Annie Dillard:

— Based on the observations I made, I infer that Dillard brings her readers closer to (1) her state of mind when she experienced the event she describes, than to (2) the event as she relived it through writing about it.

— Dillard's use of simile in paragraph 2 conveys a powerful sense of her fascination with the horror of witnessing the death of a frog.

— Dillard doesn't say that the frog was killed by a giant water bug; instead she tells us that the frog "crumpled and began to sag. The spirit vanished from his eyes as if snuffed. His skin emptied and drooped; his very skull seemed to collapse and settle like a kicked tent."

— It's almost as if the experience and the abstract knowledge of the frog's death exist independently until they merge in a moment of memorable inference.

Please remember to verify each interpretive claim you make with specific detail from the text in question. Providing ample—and detailed—evidence to support each of your assertions also ensures that you don't develop the habit of believing you are entitled to say whatever you want about a text and that you can read, as one student put it, "almost anything *into* a text."

What does this text say?

Every text or image is communicating something to the reader or viewer. American culture is often driven by narrative, by a desire to draw connections and tell stories. Scholars who study literacy and visual perception refer to people as *homo significans*—"meaning makers." One of the easiest and most effective ways to respond to a verbal text or an image is to determine its message, the "story" it tells.

—What are the denotative and connotative meanings of the objects, people, and places within the text or image?

— Where are the parts of the text or image placed in relation to each other? In our drive to make meaning, we often connect elements that are in close proximity and establish relationships between or among them.

This is just as true for objects as it is for people. Viewers, like readers, seek to articulate an interpretation that offers closure.

Because viewers and readers come from different backgrounds and read with different perceptions, the story or narrative of an image may be perceived differently by different viewers. In some cases, such as with images we think of as "art," these varying perspectives add depth to a reading. However, in other cases, such as with images we think of as "ads," the varying perspectives can subvert a product. For example, Duane Hanson might have been quite pleased if different people read different stories in his *Tourists* (p. 295). But if some viewers were to read the Mercedes-Benz ad (p. 464) as a parody of the power of symbols rather than as a paean to them, the Mercedes ad agency might soon find itself without an important client.

What strategies does the author or artist use?

Once you've had a chance to look closely at an image or text, to examine the details, you should establish a wider lens for viewing and look at the overall composition of the text—focus on how the details and the elements of the work are put together to form a whole composition. All texts and images are composed. What techniques or strategies do authors and artists use to construct meaning?

What is the author's or artist's purpose?

What compositional purpose does this particular text serve? Does the text explain? describe? tell a story? entertain? convince you of an argument? persuade you to engage in an action? move you to laughter or tears? Something else? These questions may be difficult to answer quickly, and you will no doubt need to work closely with details in the text and then infer some reasonable answers. Likewise, when you sit down to write your own text, we hope that you'll be motivated to draft a paper with a clear purpose in mind—rather than aiming solely at earning a decent grade.

Determining your purpose means making decisions about what to say and how to say it. The first of these concerns establishes the general content and overall goal of the essay. The second focuses on the writer's style, on choices in such aspects of writing as structure, diction, and tone. For many writers, the principal purpose can be as simple as wanting to narrate or describe an experience, recall a concert, remember a family story, advocate a certain social cause, argue on behalf of freedom of speech, or recount the pleasure of reading a book or seeing a film or a play. Just as there is no sure-fire way to succeed at writing, there is no single definition of an appropriate subject or purpose in writing.

What is the structure of this text?

What observations can you make and what inferences can you draw from the way in which the text is put together? How important is the relationship of the parts to the whole? Whether you're looking at a photograph of Hillary Clinton or reading an academic essay about the dangers of smoking, every text has a shape of its own. Images are built through subject, use of color, texture, light, line, and focus, to name just a few structural variables; written texts use ideas, words, details, and narrative voice as their structural building blocks, among others. The most polished texts are hard to pull apart, and if you're having trouble you might want to try to make a list of the constituent parts and only then think about how they contribute to the whole. (See p. 266 for more on structure.)

page 177

When you are working carefully with images, try breaking the image into *visual fields*. Effective images capture a viewer's attention and draw the viewer's eyes toward specific focal points. In doing so, some aspects of the image hold our attention, whereas others recede. Our initial impulse is to focus on the center of an image because it offers balance, but often an artist shifts the viewer's focus through the use of color, light, or line. If the viewer can locate the composition's *focal point* (or points), this can help to interpret the image.

It might prove useful first to divide an image by finding its horizontal or diagonal line. Sometimes this line is self-evident, as in Richard Misrach's *Waiting, Edwards Air Force Base,* shown above, where it is an actual horizon. Such lines direct the viewer's attention, leading it up or down or across; they also provide smooth movement within an image, which is important for the visual perception of most viewers.

Freeman Patterson, **Pile of Boards**

Familiar things offer excellent picture possibilities and a chance to exercise your imagination. A pile of boards behind my house reminded me of some sand dunes that I had photographed only three days earlier in an African desert. The similarities between the boards and the dunes helped me to remove the labels from both, and to realize that their expressive power was in their tones, shapes, lines, textures, and hues—the real subject matter of this photograph.

– Freeman Patterson, from *Photography and the Art of Seeing*

Another strategy is to look for *patterns* of color, shape, or shadow in the image. Viewers organize information by establishing relationships of similarity, by looking for patterns. Patterns may be established by repeating a color, a shape, or the use of light or dark. Just as a writer might use alliteration or rhyming to draw a reader's attention to connections in a poem, a visual artist uses repetition to draw a viewer's eye. The question is, Why is my eye being drawn in this way? The pattern may hint at the image's meaning—or part of that meaning—or it may be a pattern wholly imposed by a viewer longing for closure.

Who is imagined as the audience for this text?

Identifying the assumed *audience* for a specific text is important because certain audiences bring certain expectations to it. For example, a television show such as *Buffy the Vampire Slayer* is written and performed for one group of people, and the *NBC Nightly News with Tom Brokaw* is produced for a different group. Both shows reflect elements of the larger contexts of the networks on which they appear: the UPN network with its youth-geared programming, and the more serious National Broadcasting Company with its assertions of public-spiritedness.

Trying to picture the intended audience helps writers articulate what they want to say and how to say it. Student writers invariably speak of the problems and pleasures of struggling to convey a clear sense of their ideas to an audience, principally because they are uncertain about who will read their writing, other than their instructor. This narrow conception of—or uncertainty about—who will read their work sometimes leads inexperienced writers to try to please only their instructor and to ignore a wider range of readers, including their classmates.

More experienced writers usually ask some version of the following questions: Who is my reader? What do I have to do to help that person understand what I want to say about my subject? The first question addresses the knowledge, background, and predispositions of the reader toward the subject. The second points to the kinds of information or appeals to which the reader is most likely to respond.

Thinking about their readers helps writers make decisions about appropriate subjects, the kinds of examples to include, the type and level of diction and tone to use, and the overall organization of the essay. Every writer wants to be clear and convincing.

Dorothea Lange,
Migrant Mother
(three views)

What point of view is established in the text?

Point of view is a term used to describe the angle of vision, the vantage point from which the writer or artist presents a story or a description or makes a point. The term also applies to the way in which the writer or artist presents readers with material.

How is the image or text framed? What's included within the frame? What's been left out? What is the point of view from which the subject is seen? It can be difficult to determine what is not included in an image or an essay, but occasionally what is excluded can be more important than what you see. Consider, for example, Dorothea Lange's famous photograph of a migrant mother and her children. Notice what happens when the same subject is framed in a different way. What are the effects of Lange's decision to focus on the faces of her subjects rather than to take their picture from farther away? How do these framing choices change Lange's point of view ?

You should frame choices when you read a verbal text as well as a visual one. For example, if you are reading a classmate's essay about going to college that talks about the friendship she developed with her roommate, you might reasonably ask how using this event to describe her university days rather than, say, the classes she took or what she learned in them, contributes to the overall effect of the essay.

The angle of vision, the perspective, from which writers and artists see—and present—a subject. This perspective may be expressed—simply and literally—as the physical stance they establish in viewing a subject. In writing, point of view may also be revealed through the tone of voice, or attitude, that the writer expresses in addressing a subject.

To construct by fitting parts into a whole; to design, shape, construct; to put into words, to formulate; to contrive the evidence against an innocent person; to enclose in a frame, or as if in a frame.

How would you characterize the tone of the text?

Tone is a widely used term that has slightly different meanings when used in different disciplines. In its simplest sense, tone refers to the quality or character of sound. As such, tone usually describes the sound of one's voice,

what in composition and literature classes we call tone of voice. In music, tone refers to the sound of a distinct pitch, of a certain quality, and over a specific duration. In art, tone indicates the quality of color or the general effect of light in a painting or photograph. In everyday language, the word also can invoke images of the muscles in the body.

In speaking and writing, tone indicates the manner the writer uses to convey his or her expression. Tone is the feeling conveyed in the sentences you read and write. You could be described, for example, as speaking or writing in an angry or skeptical tone of voice. Similarly, you could be said to use a formal or informal tone in your essay. (Tone is often confused with accent, which refers to the emphasis placed on a particular syllable or work through modulating one's voice. Accent is often associated with a specific geographical area. For example, the words *park* and *water* can be said and heard with different accents.)

In order to understand and appreciate tone, we might want to read with what the poet Robert Frost calls "the hearing imagination." Frost refers to our natural ability to detect the tone of voice a person uses in a conversation, even if that conversation were to occur behind closed doors and we were not able to hear precisely what is being said. Regardless of the subject you are writing about, please remember that it is important to maintain a consistent tone throughout your essay. Continuity is maintained by the word choices you make.

In what ways—and with what effects—is metaphor used in the text? Visual artists employ many of the same devices that verbal artists use. Thus, when a viewer examines an image, he or she should look for metaphor, metonymy, and symbol. Whereas readers frequently find metaphor, viewers frequently find metonymy. The concept of "part for whole" is particularly well suited to a visual medium. For example, an artist might show only a fragment of a larger object in order to send a message to a reader.

A figure of speech in which one word or phrase substitutes for another closely associated with it—for example, Washington for the U.S. government.

Viewers should also look for symbolic images, often referred to as cultural icons. A culture often has a visual shorthand language, and within this language certain images have shared meanings: for example, the American flag, a cowboy, Elvis Presley, Marilyn Monroe. These symbolic images may be used in a way that is true to their accepted cultural currency or in a way that subverts this cultural meaning. For example, the Graphis image entitled *Man*

Visualizing Composition 21

Turning into a Barcode (see p. 21) plays on our cultural understanding of the bar code. Such codes mark commercial products, track inventory, and encode prices. So, when a person turns into a bar code, what happens to him? He is now a product, a piece of inventory just like, say, a bottle of mouthwash.

Visualizing Context

Context is an essential aspect of both understanding and practicing the art of composition—whether what is being composed is an essay, a painting, a photograph, or a film. In its simplest sense, context refers to the circumstances, the setting, within which an event occurs. The context is also the part of a text or statement that surrounds a particular word, passage, or image and helps determine its meaning. Asking questions about the relation between a text and its context—or the relation of a part to the whole—is another way to see clearly and write well.

The part of a text or statement that surrounds a particular word or image and helps to determine its meaning; the interrelated conditions within which something exists or occurs (environment or setting).

What are the cultural assumptions behind the text?

Asking questions about the larger cultural context of a particular text or image means recognizing the assumptions that are made about a shared body of knowledge on the part of the audience. For example, the spoof ad created by Adbusters shown here draws on a number of assumptions about American culture. Talking about the cultural context of this "anti-ad" might mean

page 459

talking about the real ad campaign it parodies in style and layout. It might mean discussing the fashion industry and the critique hidden in the copy, "follow the flock." It could mean addressing issues of patriotism and branding by focusing on the ad's suggestion that it is ridiculous to use the American flag (a symbol of individuality) as part of a campaign for a brand of clothing.

What are the historical circumstances behind the text?

Asking questions about the historical circumstances that led to the creation of an image means knowing or learning something about what was happening at the time a text was created, as well as what relationship certain historical events or circumstances had with its creation. For example, the

Nick Ut, **Children Fleeing a Napalm Strike**

photograph by Nick Ut, *Children Fleeing a Napalm Strike,* is rooted in a specific historical context. You could use the image to talk about the Vietnam War as a conflict that became increasingly associated with innocent victims. You could use the image to talk about the Vietnam War era as a time when the American media wielded power as never before to disseminate a political message different from official propaganda. You could talk about the antiwar movement of the 1960s in general, or about Kim Phuc (the little girl in the photograph) in particular.

Where was this text published, and where was it placed in that publication?

Texts do not appear in a vacuum. They function within specific contexts. The next time you encounter a text in its original publication, ask yourself how that text would read if you were to see it somewhere else—for example, on a billboard, on the wall of a museum, on a computer screen, or on the pages of a literature anthology.

Or you might examine the front page of your local newspaper. Be aware that editors rank news reports by virtue of their overall importance. Accordingly, the stories the editors want most people to read are placed on or near the front page. The most important stories or images of the day usually appear on the front page and above the fold.

What comes before and after a text can make a difference too. Placing an article about nuclear weapons next to an advertisement for the latest action movie, for example, might prompt you to read the essay differently than if it were placed next to a photo of the victims of war. Each of the seven chapters in *Seeing & Writing 2* focuses on a theme in American culture. How does reading a text within a particular thematic grouping affect your response to it? If, for example, Joel Sternfeld's photograph were included in Chapter 2, "Coming to Terms with Place," how might you read it in light of your response to David Guterson's essay on the manicured streets of a master-planned community in suburbia?

Different publications have different personalities. If you're not sure of the identity a certain publication has established for itself, you might work your way through it and characterize the articles, photos, and overall look of the publication. You might also do some research on the publication in the library or examine its home page for a statement of the scope of its interests and editorial content. This information will help you infer something about the kind of publication you're looking at and who the assumed audience might be.

Who wrote this text or produced it?

The more you know about the person who produced a particular text and the occasion for its production, the more information you'll have about it to inform your analysis and interpretation. For example, knowing that William Carlos Williams was a doctor who was treating a seriously ill child when he looked out the window and saw the now much-celebrated red wheelbarrow might make a difference in how you read his poem.

What response does the image or text seek to invoke in me in relation to its announced subject?

In what ways does the text attempt to convince you of an argument or summon you to action? What kind of person does the text want you to be as you approach it? as you leave it? What value(s) and code(s) of conduct does the writer of the text encourage his or her readers to adopt? Likewise, what kind of ideological theory and practice does the text promote?

Re-Seeing and Re-Writing

Once you've asked—and answered—questions about text and context, you've laid the groundwork for writing as you move from carefully observing what you see to making reasonable inferences about what is not necessarily shown.

THE RED
WHEELBARROW
(1923)

William Carlos Williams

so much depends
upon

a red wheel
barrow

glazed with rain
water

beside the white
chickens.

Getting Started

In the first phase of the writing process, a writer usually chooses a subject to write about (or one may be assigned), identifies a purpose for writing about that subject, develops observations and inferences about the text(s) in question, generates a thesis—a controlling idea—about the subject, considers the audience to be addressed, and then expands that idea in brainstorming or freewriting exercises, in an outline, or in some other form that provides the basis for a first draft of the essay.

Exercises like freewriting and brainstorming help writers search for and then decide on a subject to write about. These exercises are excellent confidence builders, especially if you are a relatively inexperienced writer, because they can help you produce a great deal of writing in a short time. They also enable you to see rather quickly just how much you have to say about a subject while resisting the urge to edit your work prematurely.

Also called nonstop writing, a strategy in which the writer puts pen or pencil to paper (or hands on a computer keyboard) to write without pausing between words or sentences to worry about grammar, sentence structure, word choice, and spelling.

Brainstorming involves recording thoughts as they occur, with no regard for their relation to each other. When writers brainstorm, they often leap from one thought to another without stopping to explore the connections between what may be two completely unrelated ideas.

Drafting an Essay

It would not be practical for us to enumerate each of the strikingly different ways writers work during the second phase of the writing process—completing a full draft of an essay. Instead, we'd like to present a few general observations about how writers view their different styles of drafting. Some writers write to discover what they want to say. In one sense, they must see their ideas on paper in order to explore, develop, and revise them. In effect, they must write in order to discover and shape their own meaning.

Some writers proceed at a very deliberate pace. They think carefully about what they are going to say before they commit themselves to writing it out. These writers generally are more comfortable composing in their heads than on paper. They usually regard thinking and writing as separate and, in fact, sequential intellectual activities. Many other writers feel most comfortable creating their own distinctive blends of the write/rewrite and the think/write approaches to drafting an essay.

Revising an Essay

Many writers appreciate the power and permanence that revision can give to the act of writing. When writers revise, they reexamine what they have written with an eye to strengthening their control over ideas. As they revise, they expand or delete, substitute or reorder. In some cases they revise to clarify or emphasize. In others they revise to tone down or reinforce particular points. And more generally, they revise either to simplify what they have written or to make it more complex. Revising gives writers an opportunity to rethink their essays, to help them accomplish their intentions more clearly and fully. Revising also includes such larger concerns as determining whether the essay is logically consistent, whether its main idea is supported adequately, whether it is organized clearly, and whether it satisfies the audience's needs or demands in engaging and accessible terms. Revising enables writers to make sure that their essays are as clear, concise, precise, and effective as possible.

Revising also allows writers to distance themselves from their work and to see more clearly its strengths and weaknesses. This helps them make constructive, effective decisions about the best ways to produce a final draft. Some writers revise after they have written a very quick and very rough draft. Once they have something on paper, they revise for as long as they have time and energy. Still other writers require more distance from their first draft to revise effectively.

Thinking about an audience also helps writers revise, edit, and proofread their essays. When writers proofread, they reread their final drafts to detect any errors—misspellings, omitted lines, inaccurate information, and the like. In general, more experienced writers concentrate on the larger concerns of writing—purpose, ideas, evidence, and structure—before they give attention to such matters as strengthening syntax and looking for exactly the right word.

Finally, we hope you enjoy the work of seeing and writing that this text offers. We have designed *Seeing & Writing* 2 to help you improve your writing by improving your perception. We have created opportunities for you to think and write perceptively and critically about compelling visual and verbal aspects of American culture, and we have designed exercises to enable you to write more effectively about how you perceive yourself and your relations to the visual images and words that compete for your attention.

Rewriting is when playwriting gets to be fun. . . . In baseball, you only get three swings and you're out. In rewriting, you get almost as many swings as you want and you know, sooner or later, you'll hit the ball.
– *Neil Simon*

The study of the rules whereby words or other elements of sentence structure are combined to form grammatical sentences. Also, the pattern of formation of sentences or phrases in a language. Syntax implies a systematic, orderly arrangement.

Reprinted here are two versions of a poem by Robert Frost. The first, "In White," was written in 1912; the second, "Design," was published in 1936. Write an essay in which you discuss the differences between these two poems. How does the speaker's tone of voice lead the reader to have a different response to each poem? Point to specific changes in diction and metaphor that help characterize the change in voice the second poem has undergone. Why do you think Frost preferred the second version?

IN WHITE

A dented spider like a snow drop white
On a white Heal-all, holding up a moth
Like a white piece of lifeless satin cloth—
Saw ever curious eye so strange a sight?—
Portent in little, assorted death and blight   5
Like the ingredients of a witches' broth?—
The beady spider, the flower like a froth,
And the moth carried like a paper kite.

What had that flower to do with being white,
The blue prunella every child's delight.   10
What brought the kindred spider to that height?
(Make we no thesis of the miller's plight.)
What but design of darkness and of night?
Design, design! Do I use the word aright?

DESIGN

I found a dimpled spider, fat and white,
On a white heal-all, holding up a moth
Like a piece of rigid satin cloth—
Assorted characters of death and blight
Mixed ready to begin the morning right,   5
Like the ingredients of a witches' broth—
A snow-drop spider, a flower like a froth,
And dead wings carried like a paper kite.

What had that flower to do with being white,
The wayside blue and innocent heal-all?   10
What brought the kindred spider to that height,
Then steered the white moth thither in the night?
What but design of darkness to appall?—
If design govern in a thing so small.

How the Book Works

Each of the selections and exercises included in this book asks you to take a closer look at the objects, people, places, identities, ideas, and experiences that make up the varied expressions of American culture—to pay closer attention to, interpret, and then write about what you see.

The seven chapters that follow are filled with images and words that will help you think critically and write convincingly about increasingly complex themes and issues: observing the "ordinary" objects in everyday life; making a space a place; using technology to record personal and public memory; understanding the relationship of the physical body to identity; examining what it means to be American, seen through the lenses of race, class, and the media; assessing the cultural impact of American icons; and trying to formulate a convincing argument about images at a time when the visual aspects of our culture seem to dominate public attention.

Verbal Text

SARAH VOWELL

Author and social observer Sarah Vowell (b. 1969) is best known for the "funny, querulous voice and shrewd comic delivery" of the monologues and documentaries she delivers for National Public Radio's *This American Life*. A contributing editor for the program since 1996, she has written about everything from her father's homemade cannon and her obsession with the *Godfather* films to the New Hampshire primary and her Cherokee ancestors' forced march on the Trail of Tears. *Newsweek* magazine named her Rookie of the Year for nonfiction in 1997 for her first book, *Radio On: A Listener's Diary* (1998). *People* magazine called her second book—an essay collection entitled *Take the Cannoli: Stories from the New World* (2001)—"wise, witty and refreshingly warm-hearted." The essays in *Cannoli*, which include "Shooting Dad," look at American history, pop culture, and Vowell's own family and "reveal the bonds holding together a great, if occasionally weird, nation."

Vowell's writing has appeared in numerous newspapers and magazines, including *Esquire, GQ, Artforum, The Los Angeles Times, The Village Voice, Spin,* and *McSweeney's*. She has covered education for *Time;* American culture for *Salon.com;* and pop music for the *San Francisco Weekly,* for which she won a 1996 Music Journalism Award. She is at work on her third book, *Partly Cloudy Patriot* (2002). A native of Oklahoma and Montana, and a long-time resident of Chicago, Vowell currently lives in New York City.

Shooting Dad

Sarah Vowell

IF YOU WERE PASSING BY THE HOUSE WHERE I grew up during my teenage years and it happened to be before Election Day, you wouldn't have needed to come inside to see that it was a house divided. You could have looked at the Democratic campaign poster in the upstairs window and the Republican one in the downstairs window and seen our home for the Civil War battleground it was. I'm not saying who was the Democrat or who was the Republican—my father or I—but I will tell you that I have never subscribed to *Guns & Ammo,* that I did not plaster the family vehicle with National Rifle Association stickers, and that hunter's orange was never my color.

About the only thing my father and I agree on is the Constitution, though I'm partial to the First Amendment, while he's always favored the Second.

I am a gunsmith's daughter. I like to call my parents' house, located on a quiet residential street in Bozeman, Montana, the United States of Firearms. Guns were everywhere: the so-called pretty ones like the circa 1850 walnut muzzleloader hanging on the wall, Dad's clients' fixer-uppers leaning into corners, an entire rack right next to the TV. I had to move revolvers out of my way to make room for a bowl of Rice Krispies on the kitchen table.

I was eleven when we moved into that Bozeman house. We had never lived in town before, and this was a college town at that. We came from Oklahoma—a dusty little Muskogee County nowhere called Braggs. My parents' property there included an orchard, a horse pasture, and a couple of acres of woods. I knew our lives had changed one morning

In each of the seven chapters we've gathered an assortment of verbal and visual texts. We encourage you to read each of these selections as a text in its own right or in conjunction with other selections in the chapter. These texts include essays, short stories, poems, cartoons, photographs, paintings, sculpture, and graphic art as well as a generous blend of advertisements, film posters, and publicity stills.

Accompanying each selection are a headnote that provides background information about the writer or artist and text, and suggested questions for "Seeing" and "Writing." The Seeing and Writing questions will help you focus carefully on each of the selections. Seeing questions help you generate careful observations and think through—and beyond—your initial response; writing questions help you identify compositional issues such as how the author or artist has chosen to assemble the elements of the piece.

We have designed each page to help you see more clearly and write more effectively. In addition to full-color elements and scores of "stand-alone" verbal and visual texts, there are several recurring features in every chapter:

Chapter Divider

Coming to Terms with Place

Chapter dividers

Striking photographs that precede each chapter serve as visual introductions to the subject being studied. Commissioned especially for *Seeing & Writing*, these photographs represent one artist's interpretation of the seven thematic units in the book.

Paired visual and verbal texts

Each chapter opens with a visual and verbal text that are linked. In some cases the text and image deal with exactly the same topic; in others they address the same theme; and in still others one text has inspired the other. By presenting two texts back to back, we're inviting you to focus on the differences and similarities between communicating an idea visually and verbally.

Portfolios

This feature shows several examples of the work of a selected visual artist, reinforcing the fact that few artists have a single take on a topic or issue and that sometimes artists create images in groups or series. We provide insights

Pair

BATO CON KHAKIS
Jacinto Jesús Cardona

Too bold for my mother's blood,
bato was not a household word.
Oh, but to be a bato con khakis
waiting to catch the city bus,

my thin belt exuding attitude,
looking limber in a blue vest,
laid-back in my dark shades.

Alas! I'm the bifocals kid;
cool bato I am not,
but I could spell gelato.
Could I be the bookish bato?

Oh, but to be a bato con khakis
deep in the Hub of South Texas,
blooming among bluebonnets.

César A. Martínez, **Bato Con Khakis, 1982**

310 EMBODYING IDENTITY

Pair: Cardona & Martínez 311

into each artist's particular thematic and stylistic vision in a biographical headnote. Seeing and Writing questions following each Portfolio prompt you to think and write productively about reading multiple works by a single artist.

Retrospects

These "visual timelines" demonstrate in graphic terms the fact that cultural artifacts—such as advertisements, everyday objects, portraits, and pages of popular magazines—are products of particular historical moments. The things people take for granted haven't always been presented in the same way. You'll find the images in each Retrospect set on a black background. We let the images speak for themselves, providing you simply with the title and date of each one.

When you encounter a Retrospect, you might ask yourself the following questions: How is each image a product of a specific historical period? What patterns can be inferred from the series of images? Each Retrospect provides an opportunity for outside research. What examples might you put on a timeline that would complicate your reading of change?

Portfolio

Retrospect

Talking Pictures and Re: Searching the Web

Two boxed writing exercises appear in a dark column in every chapter. These exercises provide you with the opportunity to explore how some of the chapter's issues are treated online or on screen. In Talking Pictures we invite you to sharpen your awareness of the roles and effects of television shows and movies in American culture. In Re: Searching the Web we offer you the opportunity to use the Internet as a research tool to enhance not only your understanding of particular questions, issues, or themes but also your ability to analyze the ways in which information is presented on the web.

Every page of *Seeing & Writing 2* has been designed to help you see more clearly and write more effectively. Given the fact that we're asking you to look closely at verbal and visual texts within and beyond this book, we also invite you to turn your attention to the content and design of the pages of this book. What choices have the editors and designers made in presenting the material in this way? We encourage you to view this book as a text to be studied. What do you make of its visual and verbal "landscape"? Please

Re: Searching the Web   Talking Pictures

Re: Searching the Web

"In the age of the Internet, people are able to construct themselves," said Sherry Turkle, sociologist and author of *Life on the Screen: Identity in the Age of the Internet* (1997). "Virtual communities can be seen as a new genre of artistic endeavor, a new form of performance art or improvisational theater. What distinguishes the virtual are the new genres developed through computer-aided design." In chat rooms, MUDs (multi-user domains), message boards, and instant Messaging, computer users are free to assume screen names, personalities, and even virtual appearances that may bear little resemblance to their off-line identities.

At the same time, the issue of maintaining online privacy and protecting personal information is under increasing scrutiny. Although it is now easier than ever to become someone else in virtual space, it's less difficult for others to find critical personal information (e-mail address, credit card information) and track online habits. Draft an essay in which you explore how identity is constructed and contested in virtual space. How do online environments help shape our sense of self? As an alternative writing exercise, you might draft an argumentative essay in which you support or refute the assertion that technology, and especially the Internet, has made anonymity increasingly difficult to maintain.

PETER ROSTOVSKY
Peter Rostovsky was born in St. Petersburg, Russia, in 1970. He was educated at Cornell University and attended the Cooper Union School of Art and the Parson School of Design; he also was a Whitney Museum Independent Study program scholar and studio resident in 1995–1996. His sculptures and paintings reexamine the overused symbols produced throughout history by putting them into modern contexts to explore personal nostalgia and hope for human society. His group exhibitions in New York include *The Project; Untold Stories; Local Color;* and *Summer Carnival.* Rostovsky has had solo exhibitions at The Project, New York (1999), at the Olive Tjaden Gallery, Ithaca, New York (1995), and at the Rockville Center Public Library, Rockville Center, New York (1994).

A recent recipient of a Public Art Fund commission and a participant in the annual show at the MetroTech Commons in Brooklyn, Rostovsky is also a participant in the first quadrennial of contemporary art held in Ghent, Belgium. He is an artist-in-residence in the graduate program at the Mount Royal School of Art, part of the Maryland Institute College of Art.

The three paintings from the *Portrait Connection* were first published in the Winter 2001 issue of *Cabinet* magazine. The editors solicited personal descriptions from *Cabinet* readers, which Rostovsky then used to image this portrait series.

SEEING
1. What are the steps in the process Sue Ferguson Gussow uses to teach her course on freehand drawing, a process that enables students to "examine the world around [them] more closely" (para. 3)? What more specific purpose does Zoe Ingalls identify for training students to do two-minute freehand sketches? What benefits does Ingalls identify for encouraging students to do freehand sketches? What figurative language (simile and metaphor) does she use to enable her readers to envision the benefits of such exercises in looking closely?
2. What skills does Gussow teach in her freehand drawing class? What does Richard Henderson mean when he talks about "the discipline of the hand" (para. 7), and what is the rationale behind—as well as the evidence to support—the assertion that "Once you have learned the discipline of the hand, you don't have to slow down your mind"? In what ways might the process of learning freehand drawing help students learn to write more effectively? Be as specific as possible.

WRITING
1. Ingalls reports that Sue Ferguson Gussow has her students draw—freehand—a picture of a pea pod from memory. "Half an hour later, she hands out pods from a grocery store and asks them to try again. The lesson sinks in right away. 'What I drew from memory was so different from the actual reality'" (paras. 2, 3). Draw—from memory—what a penny looks like. After you have completed this activity, compare and contrast your description of the penny with the actual appearance of the coin. Write a paragraph or two comparing and contrasting the differences between your initial drawing and the actual appearance of the penny. What inadvertent omissions mark your efforts to describe the penny?
2. What do you find most engaging in Sue Ferguson Gussow's method of teaching? What do you find least engaging and least helpful about her advice on drawing—and, by extension, on writing? Write an expository essay in which you compare and contrast the similarities and differences between drawing and writing as a means of "putting your thoughts down on paper." Which technique—freehand drawing or freewriting—do you find more helpful as you try to articulate your ideas about various subjects? Explain why.

Talking Pictures

Few of us are as relentlessly attentive to observing the details of everyday life as the drawing students in Sue Ferguson Gussow's classroom are asked to be (p. 84). Yet each of us inevitably spends a great deal of time dealing with the mundane. In *Seinfeld*, one of the most popular television series in history, the routines of daily life preoccupy the characters of this self-described "show about nothing."

Choose an episode of *Seinfeld* to watch, or locate a script on one of the numerous web sites devoted to the show. As you watch or read the episode, list the aspects of everyday life that are portrayed. What does the episode reveal about the daily life of these single, "30-something" New Yorkers? What strategies do the writers and director use to achieve these effects? What approach do the characters in *Seinfeld* take to daily life? What details of ordinary life do you find more or less convincingly portrayed?

Now choose an episode of another television sitcom, and list as many observations as you can about its portrayal of everyday objects and tasks. How does *Seinfeld* differ from other sitcoms in this regard? Write an essay in which you compare and contrast the portrayal of the mundane in *Seinfeld* with that of another sitcom. To what extent does either show represent your own life?

share your responses and experiences of working with *Seeing & Writing 2* by writing to us at our web site.

Looking Closer

These units at the end of each chapter consist of a carefully selected collection of materials that invite you to think about a specific, more focused aspect of the theme or issue presented in that chapter. Looking Closer units pose such questions as: How does changing one's scale of vision change what one sees? What does it mean to go home? How does the nature of photography shape one's private histories? How do people use fashion to announce their identities? What is the impact of the American flag as a national icon? To what extent can you believe what you see?

We have deliberately kept our editorial presence to a minimum in these Looking Closer units because we want you to look closely at the materials and think about the issues before shifting your focus to the author headnotes and the Seeing and Writing questions about selections.

Looking Closer

NEW Visualizing Composition

This exercise gives concrete shape to key verbal and visual strategies and stages of the writing process, including close reading, drafting, organizing, revising, comparing, and arguing. Each brief discussion links to a selection in the book, models the concept in question, and ends with a writing assignment.

NEW Visualizing Context

Each chapter includes a vivid illustration of the importance of reading texts in context. Each brief discussion links to a selection in the book, offers a visual illustration of the context in question, and ends with a writing assignment. A sampling of contexts includes how the idea of the suburb is constructed in popular movies and how historical images—like the flag being raised over Iwo Jima—echo across future images and events.

Visualizing Composition   Visualizing Context

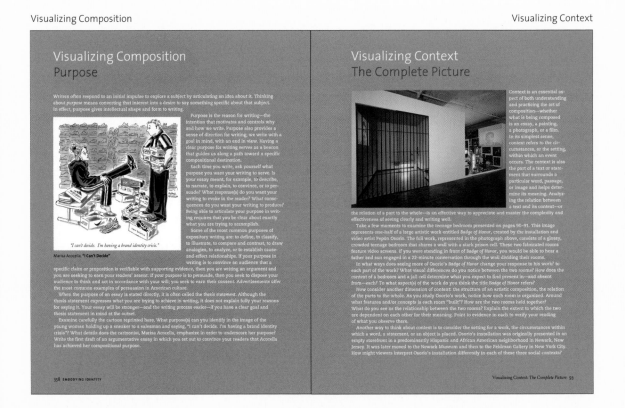

NEW Glossary

A glossary at the back of the book gives students a vocabulary to use when talking about how the variety of visual and verbal texts in the book are put together and the ways in which we can read, think, and write about them.

NEW Alternate Rhetorical Table of Contents

The alternate rhetorical table of contents suggests ways that visual and verbal texts might be used to illustrate the main rhetorical strategies of development.

Seeing & Writing Online

Our book related web site can be reached at <www.seeingandwriting.com>. This site allows you to practice observation and inference with guided visual exercises, and offers tips and links for each chapter's Re: Searching the Web activity. It also provides links to other visual resources and virtual museums, and to annotated research links for the many authors, artists, and issues in this book.

Homepage

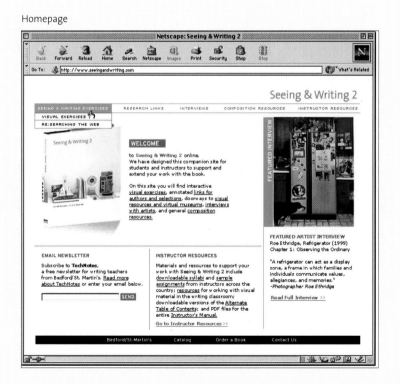

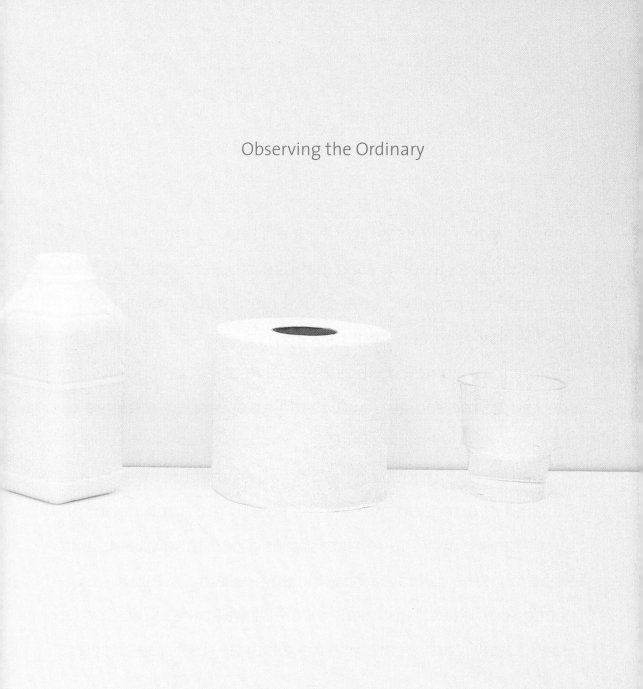

Observing the Ordinary

Chapter 1
Observing the Ordinary

Imagine the following scene: It's Thanksgiving, well into the second night of a long holiday weekend visiting your parents. You have two papers due on Monday and an exam on Tuesday. It's been only two hours since you savored the delights of a home-cooked alternative to dorm food. Yet for the third time tonight, you stand at the open refrigerator door and stare blankly inside.

Such moments involve looking without actually noticing, the kind of attention many of us give to the ordinary in our lives. Staring into the refrigerator is a common example of what might be called passive looking—seeing without recognizing, looking without being aware of what we're looking at. How clearly, and accurately, for example, can you describe

Roe Ethridge, **Refrigerator,** 1999

the objects most familiar to you: a penny; your favorite pair of shoes; the blanket on your bed; the food you ate this morning for breakfast? Most of us need to have such ordinary things physically in front of us in order to give a detailed, accurate description. Even if we all had the same object before us, each of our descriptions of it would likely be different, depending on who we are, the perspective from which we view the object, and the details we find important in it. The photograph included here, *Refrigerator*, provides an occasion to practice examining the messages ordinary objects can convey, messages read by photographer Roe Ethridge as a family's "values, allegiances, and memories." If we practice examining commonplace objects with attention to both careful observation and an awareness of what makes every individual's perspective unique, we can begin to characterize more precisely for ourselves and others who we are and what we're like. By *actively seeing* the details of the ordinary we hone our skills of observation, the first step toward becoming a confident writer.

We see things as we are, not as they are.
– *Jennifer Stone, 1997*

Observing the ordinary with fresh eyes not only sharpens our skills of description, it also helps develop our ability to draw inferences. Indeed, drawing reasonable inferences from accurate observations involves seeing more than what is actually visible. Inferences are discoveries—of something we can't immediately see from what we can see. Imagine, for example, the following scene: Two men sitting on a couch watching an NFL game on television at the same time that each is having considerable difficulty maneuvering the chips and salsa along a less-than-manicured path between bowl and mouth. By observing the men carefully, we can push beyond the stereotype they are projecting and reasonably infer from the clothes they are wearing or from other details some reliable information about what they do when they are not watching football on television.

Observing the ordinary is both the simplest skill to start exercising as a writer and a practical means of training ourselves to think and write analytically. When we are actively looking at the "ordinary," we realize it is a more complicated concept than we might at first have recognized. What might be regarded as ordinary by some of us may well be viewed as exceptional by others. Consider, for example, a car. Some people take owning a car for granted; others regard it as a luxury they can't afford. (Can you identify things that you view as ordinary in your own life that certain classmates would likely regard as exceptional?) We also invest ordinary objects with private and public meanings. Each of us might personally relate to an ordinary object —a toothbrush, a coffee cup, a pencil—in different ways, yet we are likely to share at least some of the public significance attributed to ordinary objects in American culture such as a nickel, a cell phone, a hamburger, or a television set.

As you practice writing descriptions that will make your readers see what is extraordinary in your everyday life, you'll also be practicing active seeing—that is, seeing the world around you more carefully. To be an effective thinker and writer, you need to bring all of your sight—and insight—to bear on what is around you. If you notice and attend to the ordinary, if you devote focused and sustained attention to it, you increase the likelihood that you will become one of those on whom, as the novelist Henry James once said, "nothing is lost."

Each of the selections in this chapter presents the ordinary in some extraordinary way. The work of Roe Ethridge and of other photographers throughout the chapter conveys the clarity of attention a photographer gives an object through the lens of a camera; the paintings by Tim Gardner and others show what can result when high art meets mundane subjects; and the essays by Larry Woiwode, Anne Fadiman, K. C. Cole, and Annie Dillard demonstrate how writing can make us clearly see something that we would not otherwise have noticed.

All objects, all phases of culture are alive. They have voices. They speak of their history and interrelatedness. And they are talking at once!
– Camille Paglia, 1992

ROE ETHRIDGE

The photograph on page 39 was shot in Atlanta, Georgia; it records the kitchen of the artist's childhood home. To photographer Roe Ethridge, this refrigerator in particular was the perfect example of an object as "display zone," a frame in which "families and individuals communicate values, allegiances, and memories." Ethridge took the photograph with the help of his assistant, who ran back and forth in front of the camera with Lucky, the family dog.

Refrigerator was commissioned by the *New York Times Magazine* for an issue on domestic spaces, but the piece never ran. The photo was later used, in altered form, for an advertisement on organizing kitchen clutter. Still later, the photo was included in a gallery exhibition. In a recent interview, Ethridge noted that he found it interesting that a single image could be used in such disparate contexts: documentary, commercial, and artistic.

Ethridge was born in 1969 in Miami, Florida, and received his B.F.A. degree in photography from the Atlanta College of Art. He currently lives in New York City. His work has appeared in numerous magazines and advertisements and on album covers.

SEEING

1. How would you describe *Refrigerator* to someone who has not seen it? What specific words and phrases would you use to characterize what you see in this photograph? Which details—textures, colors, objects, and shapes—stand out the most to you? Why? What relationship do you see between and among the objects placed on the refrigerator door? What story (or stories) do the photographs on the refrigerator suggest to you?

2. How does Ethridge frame the refrigerator? What patterns link the items on the refrigerator door to what can be seen in the rest of the kitchen? What are the effects of Ethridge's having taken this picture as the family dog crosses his line of sight? In what ways does the appearance of the dog add to—or detract from—the overall image captured in this photograph? What might have been the advantages—and the disadvantages—of waiting for the dog to be fully visible in the picture?

WRITING

1. Consider Ethridge's photograph as an artistic statement of a family's "values, allegiances, and memories." Choose two or three words that you think accurately describe what is being communicated by this photograph. Write a descriptive paragraph on each of these words, using evidence from this photograph to illustrate your choice. How would seeing *Refrigerator* in a different context—such as an advertisement—change the way you read it?

2. Look through any two popular magazines, and make notes about the kinds of ordinary objects presented in each. Which images of the ordinary do you find there? How are the images of these objects presented, and for what purpose? Write an essay comparing and contrasting the methods these two magazines use to present the experience of observing the ordinary.

HORIZON
Billy Collins

You can use the brush of a Japanese monk
or a pencil stub from a race track.

As long as you draw the line a third
the way up from the bottom of the page,

the effect is the same: the world suddenly   5
divided into its elemental realms.

A moment ago there was only a piece of paper.
Now there is earth and sky, sky and sea.

You were sitting alone in a small room.
Now you are walking into the heat of a vast desert   10

or standing on the edge of a winter beach
watching the light on the water, light in the air.

Michael Collins, **Seascape,** 2000

BILLY COLLINS

Known for the elegant simplicity of his poems, Billy Collins is celebrated for his ability to sustain the attention of even the most reluctant readers. "I think a lot of readers are frustrated with the obscurity and self-indulgence of most poetry," Collins said during a recent interview. "I try very assiduously to court the reader and engage him. I am interested more in a public following than a critical one."

Collins was born in New York City in 1941. His poetry collections include *Pokerface* (1977); *Video Poems* (1980); *The Apple That Astonished Paris* (1988); *Questions about Angels* (1991), which was selected by Edward Hirsch for the National Poetry Series; *The Art of Drowning* (1995); *Picnic, Lightning* (1997); and *Sailing Alone around the Room* (2001). He recorded a spoken-word CD, *The Best Cigarette*, in 1997, and his poems have appeared in journals and magazines such as *The New Yorker, The Paris Review, The American Scholar,* and *Harper's.* Collins has also received fellowships from the National Endowment for the Arts and the Guggenheim Foundation.

A distinguished professor of English at the City University of New York, Collins was named U.S. Poet Laureate in 2001. In that role he launched "Poetry 180," a national campaign to "have a poem read each day to the students of American high schools across the country."

HORIZON
Billy Collins

You can use the brush of a Japanese monk
or a pencil stub from a race track.

As long as you draw the line a third
the way up from the bottom of the page,

the effect is the same: the world suddenly
divided into its elemental realms.

A moment ago there was only a piece of paper.
Now there is earth and sky, sky and sea.

You were sitting alone in a small room.
Now you are walking into the heat of a vast desert

or standing on the edge of a winter beach
watching the light on the water, light in the air.

MICHAEL COLLINS

Writer and photographer Michael Collins often chooses landscapes as the subject of his pictures. This particular photograph is from a series entitled *The Sea,* photos taken between West Bay and Eype, West Dorset, England. It is one of seven photographs by Collins that appeared in the Winter 2001 issue of *Granta,* a magazine of fiction, essays, and photography.

Michael Collins was born in India in 1961 and grew up in England, where he spent much of his life. He studied political science at the University of Sussex and later worked as a photographic editor in London. In 1997, Collins moved to Mangerton, West Dorset, with the intention of writing a book of short stories. While there, he found himself focused on photography and became particularly interested in capturing landscapes.

Collins's photographs utilize a technique called record photography, where the purpose is to create images without a certain effect or meaning in mind. This straightforward method avoids the creation of an idealized landscape that would elicit a certain response. Instead, Collins's photographs give an accurate depiction of "what the landscape looks like, nothing more," so the viewer is free to explore the photograph and make his or her own judgments as to meaning and effect.

1. What is your first impression of Michael Collins's photograph *Seascape*? As you examine the photograph more carefully, what additional details do you observe? What inferences can you reasonably draw about Collins's artistic vision? What features of this natural scene does he seem to emphasize? with what effect? In what ways is your overall impression of the photograph different from your initial reaction? What senses—in addition to sight—does the photograph evoke?

2. Now turn your attention to the poem "Horizon" by Billy Collins. (Although Billy Collins and Michael Collins seem to share an artistic sensibility, they are not related.) To what extent does the poem give an effective definition of a horizon? What do the opening lines mean to you? What do they refer to? What is the function of the colon in line 5? What does the phrase "elemental realms" (line 6) refer to in the context of the poem? What is the effect of line 7 on establishing the significance of the poem?

3. Compare and contrast the effectiveness of the photograph by Michael Collins and the poem by Billy Collins as descriptions of a natural scene. Which artistic vision of nature do you find more engaging and appealing? Why? What can descriptive writing accomplish that photography cannot? Alternatively, what can a photograph do that writing cannot?

1. Michael Collins's photograph and Billy Collins's poem offer two very different renditions of a similar scene. Choose an object or a scene in nature—a ripe avocado, a succulent blueberry, a snow-capped mountain top, a rose-lined path—that has roused your senses of sight and smell. Write the first draft of an essay in which you make as many observations as possible, using description as a basis for drawing inferences about its distinctive character.

The combination of features or qualities that distinguishes a person, group, or object from another.

2. Michael Collins and Billy Collins use different artistic tools to re-create a sense of a scene from the natural world. What artistic "tools" can Michael Collins draw on in his photograph that Billy Collins cannot rely on in achieving particular artistic effects in his poem? Write an expository essay in which you analyze the nature and extent of the different effects produced by a photograph and a poem. Use these two texts as the basis for your comparison.

LARRY WOIWODE

Larry Woiwode (b. 1941) grew up in North Dakota and Illinois. After moving to New York City in his twenties, he began to publish poems and stories in *The New Yorker, Atlantic Monthly, Harper's,* and other prestigious magazines. Among his books are the highly acclaimed novels *What I'm Going to Do, I Think* (1969) and *Beyond the Bedroom Wall* (1975). In 1978 he moved back to North Dakota, where he lives on a small farm and continues to write.

Woiwode uses precise observation and a sense of place to open up his fictional worlds. He notes that there "seems to be a paradox in writing fiction. For some reason the purest and simplest sentences permit the most meaning to adhere to them. In other words, the more specific a simple sentence is about a place in North Dakota, let us say, the more someone from outside that region seems to read universality into it." Although "Ode to an Orange" focuses on an object rather than a place, the same principle applies. In engagingly detailed sentences, Woiwode remembers specific experiences but evokes a universal romance with an ideal orange. This selection first appeared in *Paris Review* in 1985.

Ode to an Orange

Larry Woiwode

OH, THOSE ORANGES ARRIVING IN THE MIDST OF the North Dakota winters of the forties—the mere color of them, carried through the door in a net bag or a crate from out of the white winter landscape. Their appearance was enough to set my brother and me to thinking that it might be about time to develop an illness, which was the surest way of receiving a steady supply of them.

"Mom, we think we're getting a cold."

"*We?* You mean, you two want an orange?"

This was difficult for us to answer or dispute; the matter seemed moved beyond our mere wanting.

"If you want an orange," she would say, "why don't you ask for one?"

"We want an orange."

"'We' again. '*We want an orange.*'"

"May we have an orange, please."

"That's the way you know I like you to ask for one. Now, why don't each of you ask for one in that same way, but separately?"

"Mom . . ." And so on. There was no depth of degradation that we wouldn't descend to in order to get one. If the oranges hadn't wended their way northward by Thanksgiving, they were sure to arrive before the Christmas season, stacked first in crates at the depot, filling that musty place, where pews sat back to back, with a springtime acidity, as if the building had been rinsed with a renewing elixir that set it right for yet another year. Then the crates would appear at the local grocery store, often with the top slats pried back on a few of them, so that we were aware of a resinous smell of fresh wood in addition to the already orangy atmosphere that foretold the season more explicitly than any calendar.

And in the broken-open crates (as if burst by the power of the oranges themselves), one or two of the lovely spheres would lie free of the tissue they came wrapped in—always purple tissue, as if that were the only color that could contain the populations of them in their nestled positions. The crates bore paper labels at one end—of an orange against a blue background, or of a blue goose against an orange background— signifying the colorful otherworld (unlike our wintry one) that these phenomena had arisen from. Each orange, stripped of its protective wrapping, as vivid in your vision as a pebbled sun, encouraged you to picture a whole pyramid of them in a bowl on your dining room table, glowing in the light, as if giving off the warmth that came through the windows from the real winter sun. And all of them came stamped with a blue-purple name as foreign as the otherworld that you might imagine as their place of origin, so that on Christmas day you would find yourself digging past everything else in your Christmas stocking, as if tunneling down to the country of China, in order to reach the rounded bulge at the tip of the toe which meant that you had received a personal reminder of another state of existence, wholly separate from your own.

The packed heft and texture, finally, of an orange in your hand—this is it!—and the eruption of smell and the watery fireworks as a knife, in the hand of someone skilled, like our mother, goes slicing through the skin so perfect for slicing. This gaseous spray can form a mist like smoke, which can then be lit with a match to create actual fireworks if there is a chance to hide alone with a match (matches being forbidden) and the peel from one. Sputtery ignitions can also be produced by squeezing a peel near a candle (at least one candle is generally always going at Christmastime), and the leftover peels are set on the stove top to scent the house.

And the ingenious way in which oranges come packed into their globes! The green nib at the top, like a detonator, can be bitten off, as if disarming the orange, in order to clear a place for you to sink a tooth under the peel. This is the best way to start. If you bite at the peel too much, your front teeth will feel scraped, like dry bone, and your lips will begin to burn from the bitter oil. Better to sink a tooth into this greenish or creamy depression, and then pick at that point with the nail of your thumb, removing a little piece of the peel at a time. Later, you might want to practice to see how large a piece you can remove intact. The peel can also be undone in one continuous ribbon, a feat which maybe your father is able to perform, so that after the orange is freed, looking yellowish, the peel, rewound, will stand in its original shape, although empty.

The yellowish whole of the orange can now be divided into sections, usually about a dozen, by beginning with a division down the middle; after this, each section, enclosed in its papery skin, will be able to be lifted and torn loose more easily. There is a stem up the center of the sections like a mushroom stalk, but tougher; this can be eaten. A special variety of orange, without any pits, has an extra growth, or nubbin, like half of a tiny orange, tucked into its bottom. This nubbin is nearly as bitter as the peel, but it can be eaten, too; don't worry. Some of the sections will have miniature sections embedded in them and clinging as if for life, giving the impression that babies are being hatched, and should you happen to find some of these you've found the sweetest morsels of any.

If you prefer to have your orange sliced in half, as some people do, the edges of the peel will abrade the corners of your mouth, making them feel raw, as you eat down into the white of the rind (which is the only way to do it) until you can see daylight through the orangy bubbles composing its outside. Your eyes might burn; there is no proper way to eat an orange. If there are pits, they can get in the way, and the slower you eat an orange, the more you'll find your fingers sticking together. And no matter how carefully you eat one, or bite into a quarter, juice can always fly or slip from a corner of your mouth; this happens to everyone. Close your eyes to be on the safe side, and for the eruption in your mouth of the slivers of watery meat, which should be broken and rolled fine over your tongue for the essence of orange. And if indeed you have sensed yourself coming down with a cold, there is a chance that you will feel it driven from your head—your nose and sinuses suddenly opening—in the midst of the scent of a peel and eating an orange.

And oranges can also be eaten whole—rolled into a spongy mass and punctured with a pencil (if you don't find this offensive) or a knife, and then sucked upon. Then, once the juice is gone, you can disembowel the orange as you wish and eat away its pulpy remains, and eat once more into the whitish interior of the peel, which scours the coating from your teeth and makes your numbing lips and tip of your tongue start to tingle and swell up from behind, until, in the light from the windows (shining through an empty glass bowl), you see orange again from the inside. Oh, oranges, solid o's, light from afar in the midst of the freeze, and not unlike that unspherical fruit which first went from Eve to Adam and from there (to abbreviate matters) to my brother and me.

"Mom, we think we're getting a cold."

"You mean, you want an orange?"

This is difficult to answer or dispute or even to acknowledge, finally, with the fullness that the subject deserves, and that each orange bears, within its own makeup, into this hard-edged yet insubstantial, incomplete, cold, wintry world.

SEEING

1. Larry Woiwode takes great pleasure in lingering on the special qualities of what most of us would view as an altogether ordinary piece of fruit. What impression of an orange does Woiwode create? When, how, and why does he draw on each of the five senses to create this overall effect?

2. In addition to description, what other techniques does Woiwode use to evoke such a vibrant orange? What does he mean when he says that the oranges of his youth signified "the colorful otherworld"? What range of associations do the oranges of his youth evoke in Woiwode now? He was a child in the 1940s and 1950s, the same time that labels such as "Have One" (p. 52) were used to promote the fruit. If you consider the essay and the crate label together, does the way you see each one change? Why or why not?

WRITING

1. Consider Woiwode's title: "Ode to an Orange." How does his essay satisfy the expectations usually associated with the word ode? Write your own creative ode to a piece of fruit; the goal is to evoke longing in your readers.

2. Woiwode uses each of the five senses—touch, sound, sight, smell, and taste—to convey the appeal of an orange. Imagine that you have to give up one of the five senses and that it will be taken away arbitrarily if you cannot argue convincingly for one over the others. Write the first draft of an essay that uses examples from Woiwode for support, arguing about which of the five senses is least important to you.

Formal lyric poem, usually written in an elevated style and voice, usually praising a person or thing.

Sequoia Citrus Association, **Have One**

California Orange Growers, **Orange Crate Labels**

SEQUOIA CITRUS ASSOCIATION

From the late 1880s through the 1950s, California citrus growers and farmers relied on colorful paper labels to promote the fruits and vegetables they shipped in wooden crates throughout the United States. Designed primarily to attract wholesale buyers in distant markets, these distinctive examples of commercial art also helped to promote idealized images of California and to transplant seekers of sunshine and fortune. Many early labels accentuated the image of California as a land of plenty, innocence, and beauty; but such pastoral images and allegorical scenes soon yielded to the accelerated pace and more sophisticated look of urban life: bolder typography, darker colors, and billboard-like graphics associated with automobile advertisements.

The use of paper labels ended when corporate interests overshadowed individual and family enterprises, when small private groves were consumed by cooperatives or plowed into sites for tract-home communities, and when cardboard cartons replaced wooden crates.

The orange crate label for the Have One brand, which appeared in the 1920s, and the other labels reprinted here from the early twentieth century offer striking examples of the graphics and themes used to identify brand names through easily remembered images.

have: (1) to possess a thing or a privilege, as in *to have permission*; (2) to receive, as in *I had some news*; (3) to feel an obligation to do, as in *to have a deadline*; (4) to aquire or get possession of a person or thing, as in *I had him where I wanted him*; (5) to be characterized by a certain quality, as in *I have blue eyes*; (6) to use or exercise a quality, as in *to have pity*; (7) to trick or fool, as in *I was had*; (8) to be forced to do something, as in *I have to go*.

SEEING

1. The label used by the Sequoia Citrus Association to identify its oranges looks simple: a hand, an orange, a statement. But as you examine the label more carefully, do you notice anything that makes the image more complicated? What about the hand makes it distinct? How does its placement reinforce—or subvert—the invitation to "have" an orange? What are the advantages—and the disadvantages—of using an imperative in the headline ("Have One")? Is anything being sold here besides an orange?

2. Look at each of the graphic elements in the label. What do you notice about the placement of the hand and forearm? What effects does the artist achieve by superimposing the forearm and hand on the image? What aspects of the appearance of the orange does the artist highlight in order to call attention to the orange? What other graphic elements help to focus the viewer's attention on the orange and its succulence? In what ways does the typography used in the name of the brand reinforce—or detract from—the effectiveness of this graphic design?

WRITING

1. What products are most often identified with the community in which you live or attend college? Choose one product that interests you, and conduct some preliminary research on the earliest commercial representations of it. (You might check the holdings in the periodical and rare book sections of your library, or you might visit the local historical society.) Focusing on one example of commercial art used to promote this product, write an analytical essay in which you show how the graphic elements and language borrow from or help reinforce the identity of this particular community.

2. Cryptic advertising imperatives that never explicitly name the product they are promoting (e.g., "Just do it" or "Enjoy the ride") are used in many contemporary ads and commercials. What is more effective—the image or the language—in ads like these? Choose one such advertisement or commercial—whether the product is an orange, an automobile, or a sneaker—and write an expository essay about why you think the ad or commercial does or does not "work."

Visualizing Composition
Close Reading

As you read each text in *Seeing & Writing*, visual or verbal, we encourage you to engage in the act of reading closely. Doing so involves making a series of observations about details in a text that you find engaging and memorable and drawing reasonable inferences from these observations. Reading closely means focusing your attention on details—that is, on specific aspects of technique, content, or style. Close reading is a part of the composition process that marks the beginning of analyzing a text and figuring out exactly why and how it works. The painter Richard Estes uses precise detail in creating the painting *Central Savings*. He evokes a concrete sense of what it is like to observe such a seem-ingly ordinary experience as walking past a storefront diner and encountering a reflection of a street scene in the window. Below you see an example of how one student highlighted every detail she could identify in Estes's painting, along with the comments she made in the margin.

Practice reading closely. For this exercise, assume you have been asked to write an essay on how Richard Estes evokes the senses in his paintings—to establish contrasts between perception and reality in his work. Pencil in hand, examine his painting carefully a second or even a third time with your specific question in mind, marking every example you find.

Richard Estes, **Central Savings,** 1975 (Oil on canvas.)

1. When I first looked at this image, I couldn't tell whether it was a photograph or a painting.

2. If it was a photograph, I thought it must have been a double exposure.

3. I first noticed the counter top and the bar stools in what looks like a coffee shop or diner. I also noticed the reflection of the word "Burger" in the window of the restaurant. The counters are empty, and they seem to reflect images that seem to repeat themselves over and over.

4. Then I noticed the phrase "Central Savings" over the word "Burger" and that the phrase was reversed in the window, just like the word "Burger."

5. Then I noticed the clock, but I couldn't tell whether it also was a reflection in the window.

6. As I looked more carefully at the image, I saw that there were outlines or shadows of people in the foreground. They appeared to be walking past the window.

7. Then I noticed the silver metal strip at the bottom of the picture, which led my eye to the silver metal border on the left of the image.

8. My attention was then drawn to the different colors in the picture—to the red counter tops, the yellow colors of the buildings seen in the window, and to the dark-colored figures walking by. And finally to the tiny triangle of blue sky that appears between the buildings.

9. I wasn't sure it was a painting until I read the caption saying "Oil on canvas."

 Re: Searching the Web

Choose a common commercial product that you would be likely to find in anyone's home: An orange, a carton of milk, a jar of peanut butter or jelly, a vacuum cleaner, a toaster, a radio, a CD player are a few examples. (Please do not restrict yourself to these examples. You might, for instance, choose one of the products represented by the fruit labels on p. 43.)

What ordinary object piques your interest in knowing about its origins? Using a search engine to explore the World Wide Web, gather as much information as possible on the history of this product's origins and commercial development. At what point—and in what circumstances—was an image (a drawing or a photograph) of this product important to its gaining corporate and, eventually, public acceptance? Spend some time analyzing the drawing or photograph. Then use it as the focal point for a first draft of a narrative essay that weaves together details of the history and commercial development of this ordinary object, one that remains a testament to individual ingenuity and technological progress.

ANNE FADIMAN

"The most important thing when starting out with essay writing," offered Anne Fadiman in a 1998 interview, "is to find a voice with which you're comfortable. You need to find a persona that is very much like you, but slightly caricatured . . . a distilled version of you. Once you've found that voice, you'll discover that the essay is something you can be serious or funny with, or both. And once you feel comfortable, you can write about issues that are very important to you, or about things that are very minor, and the genre will accommodate both."

Fadiman's career as an author, essayist, and editor had roots in her early childhood. For the daughter of renowned critic Clifton Fadiman and *Time-Life* correspondent Annalee Jacoby Fadiman, intellectual exercises were an integral part of family life. "When I was growing up, not only did my family walk around spouting sesquipedalians [long words], but we viewed all forms of intellectual competition as a sacrament, a kind of holy water . . . to be slathered on at every opportunity with the largest possible aspergill."

Fadiman won the National Book Critics Circle Award for her first book, *The Spirit Catches You and You Fall Down* (1997), a chronicle of the life of an epileptic Hmong child and her family living in Merced, California. "Mail" originally appeared in the literary quarterly *The American Scholar*, which Fadiman currently edits.

Mail

Anne Fadiman

SOME YEARS AGO, MY PARENTS LIVED AT THE top of a steep hill. My father kept a pair of binoculars on his desk with which, like a pirate captain hoisting his spyglass to scan the horizon for treasure ships, he periodically inspected the mailbox to see if the flag had been raised. When it finally went up, he trudged down the driveway and opened the extra-large black metal box, purchased by my mother in the same accommodating spirit with which some wives buy their husbands extra-large trousers. The day's load—a mountain of letters and about twenty pounds of review books packed in Jiffy bags, a few of which had been pierced by their angular contents and were leaking what my father called "mouse dirt"—was always tightly wedged. But he was a persistent man, and after a brief show of resistance the mail would surrender, to be carried up the hill in a tight clinch and dumped onto a gigantic desk. Until that moment, my father's day had not truly begun.

His desk was made of steel, weighed more than a refrigerator, and bristled with bookshelves and secret drawers and sliding panels and a niche for a cedar-lined humidor. (He believed that cigar-smoking and mail-reading were natural partners, like oysters and Muscadet.) I think of it as less a writing surface than a mail-sorting table. He hated Sundays and holidays because there was nothing new to spread on it. Vacations were taxing, the equivalent of forced relocations to places without food. His homecomings were always followed by day-long orgies of mail-opening—feast after famine—at the end of which all the letters were answered; all the bills were paid; the outgoing envelopes were affixed with stamps from a brass dispenser heavy enough to break your toe; the books and manuscripts were neatly stacked; and the empty Jiffy bags were stuffed into an extra-large copper wastebasket, cheering confirmation that the process of postal digestion was complete.

"One of my unfailing minor pleasures may seem dull to more energetic souls: opening the mail," he once wrote.

Living in an advanced industrial civilization is a kind of near-conquest over the unexpected. . . . Such efficiency is of course admirable. It does not, however, by its very nature afford scope to that perverse human trait, still not quite eliminated, which is pleased by the accidental. Thus to many tame citizens like me the morning mail functions as the voice of the unpredictable and keeps alive for a few minutes a day the keen sense of the unplanned and the unplannable. The letter opener is an instrument that has persisted from some antique land of chance and adventure into our ordered world of the perfectly calculated.

What chance and adventure might the day's haul contain? My brother asked him, when he was in his nineties, what kind of mail he liked best. "In my youth," he replied, "a love letter. In middle age, a job offer. Today, a check." (That was false cynicism, I think. His favorite letters were from his friends.) Whatever the accidental pleasure, it could not please until it arrived. Why were deliveries so few and so late (he frequently grumbled), when, had he lived in central London in the late seventeenth century, he could have received his mail between ten and twelve times a day?

We get what we need. In 1680, London had mail service nearly every hour because there were no telephones. If you wished to invite someone to tea in the afternoon, you could send him a letter in the morning and receive his reply before he showed up at your doorstep. Postage was one penny.

If you wished to send a letter to another town, however, delivery was less reliable and postage was gauged on a scale of staggering complexity. By the mid-1830s,

the postage on a single letter delivered within eight miles of the office where it was posted was . . . twopence, the lowest rate beyond that limit being fourpence. Beyond fifteen miles it became fivepence; after which it rose a penny at a time, but by irregular augmentation, to one shilling, the charge for three hundred miles. There was as a general rule an additional charge of a half penny on a letter crossing the Scotch border; while letters to or from Ireland had to bear, in addition, packet rates, and rates for crossing the bridges over the Conway and the Menai.

So wrote Rowland Hill, the greatest postal reformer in history, who in 1837 devised a scheme to reduce and standardize postal rates and to shift the burden of payment from the addressee to the sender.

Until a few years ago I had no idea that if you sent a letter out of town—and if you weren't a nobleman, a member of Parliament, or other VIP who had been granted the privilege of free postal franking—the postage was paid by the recipient. This dawned on me when I was reading a biography of Charles Lamb, whose employer, the East India House, allowed clerks to receive letters gratis until 1817: a substantial perk, sort of like being able to call your friends on your office's 800 number. (Lamb, who practiced stringent economies, also wrote much of his personal correspondence on company stationery. His most famous letter to Wordsworth, for instance—the one in which he refers to Coleridge as "an Archangel a little damaged"—is inscribed on a page whose heading reads "Please to state the Weights and Amounts of the following Lots.")

Sir Walter Scott liked to tell the story of how he had once had to pay "five pounds odd" in order to receive a package from a young New York lady he had never met: an atrocious play called *The Cherokee Lovers*, accompanied by a request to read it, correct it, write a prologue, and secure a producer. Two weeks later another large package arrived for which he was charged a similar amount. "Conceive my horror," he told his friend Lord Melville, "when out jumped the same identical tragedy of *The Cherokee Lovers*, with a second epistle from the authoress, stating that, as the winds had been boisterous, she feared the vessel entrusted with her former communication might have foundered, and therefore judged it prudent to forward a duplicate." Lord Melville doubtless found this tale hilarious, but Rowland Hill would have been appalled. He had grown up poor, and, as Christopher Browne notes in *Getting the Message*, his splendid history of the British postal system, "Hill had never forgotten his mother's anxiety when a letter with a high postal duty was delivered, nor the time when she

sent him out to sell a bag of clothes to raise 3*s* for a batch of letters."

Hill was a born Utilitarian who, at the age of twelve, had been so frustrated by the irregularity of the bell at the school where his father was principal that he had instituted a precisely timed bell-ringing schedule. In 1837 he published a report called "Post Office Reform: Its Importance and Practicability." Why, he argued, should legions of accountants be employed to figure out the Byzantine postal charges? Why should Britain's extortionate postal rates persist when France's revenues had risen, thanks to higher mail volume, after its rates were lowered? Why should postmen waste precious time waiting for absent addressees to come home and pay up? A national Penny Post was the answer, with postage paid by the senders, "using a bit of paper . . . covered at the back with a glutinous wash, which the bringer might, by the application of a little moisture, attach to the back of the letter." After much debate, Parliament passed a postal reform act in 1839. On January 10, 1840, Hill wrote in his diary, "Penny Postage extended to the whole kingdom this day! . . . I guess that the number despatched to-night will not be less than 100,000, or more than three times what it was this day twelve-months. If less I shall be disappointed." On January 11 he wrote, "The number of letters despatched exceeded all expectation. It was 112,000, of which all but 13,000 or 14,000 were prepaid." In May, after experimentation to produce a canceling ink that could not be surreptitiously removed, the Post Office introduced the Penny Black, bearing a profile of Queen Victoria: the first postage stamp. The press, pondering the process of cancellation, fretted about the "untoward disfiguration of the royal person," but Victoria became an enthusiastic philatelist, and renounced the royal franking privilege for the pleasure of walking to the local post office from Balmoral Castle to stock up on stamps and gossip with the postmaster. When Rowland Hill—by that time, *Sir* Rowland Hill—retired as Post Office Secretary in 1864, *Punch* asked, "SHOULD ROWLAND HILL have a Statue? Certainly, if OLIVER CROMWELL should. For one is celebrated for cutting off the head of a bad King, and the other for sticking on the head of a good Queen."

The Penny Post, wrote Harriet Martineau, "will do more for the circulation of ideas, for the fostering of domestic affections, for the humanizing of the mass generally, than any other single measure that our national wit can devise." It was incontrovertible proof, in an age that embraced progress on all fronts ("the means of locomotion and correspondence, every mechanical art, every manufacture, every thing that promotes the convenience of life," as Macaulay put it in a typical gush of national pride), that the British were the most civilized people on earth. Ancient Syrian runners, Chinese carrier pigeons, Persian post riders, Egyptian papyrus bearers, Greek *hemerodromes,* Hebrew dromedary riders, Roman esquestrian relays, medieval monk-messengers, Catalan *troters,* international couriers of the House of Thurn and Taxis, American mail wagons—what could these all have been leading up to, like an ever-ascending staircase, but the Victorian postal system?

And yet (to raise a subversive question), might it be possible that, whatever the profit in efficiency, there may have been a literary cost associated with the conversion from payment by addressee to payment by sender? If you knew that your recipient would have to bear the cost of your letter, wouldn't courtesy motivate you to write an extra-good one? On the other hand, if you paid for it yourself, wouldn't you be more likely to feel you could get away with "Having a wonderful time, wish you were here"?

I used to think my father's attachment to the mail was strange. I now feel exactly the way he did. I live in an apartment building and, with or without binoculars, I cannot see my mailbox, one of thirteen dinky aluminum cells bolted to the lobby wall. The mail usually comes around four in the afternoon (proving that the postal staircase that reached its highest point with Rowland Hill has been descending ever since), which means that at around three, *just in case,* I'm likely to visit the lobby for the first of several reconnaissance missions. There's no flag, but over the years my fingers have become postally sensitive, and I can tell if the box is full by giving it the slightest of pats. If there's a hint of convexity—it's very subtle, nothing as obvious, let us say, as the bulge of a can that might harbor botulism—I whip out my key with the same excitement with which my father set forth down his driveway.

There the resemblance ends. The thrill of the treasure hunt is followed all too quickly by the glum realization that the box contains only four kinds of mail: (1) junk; (2) bills; (3) work; and (4) letters that I will read with enjoyment, place in a folder labeled "To Answer," leave there for a geologic interval, and feel guilty about. The longer they languish, the more I despair of my ability to live up to the escalating challenge of their response. It is a truism of epistolary psychology that, for example, a Christmas thank-you note written on December 26 can say any old thing, but if you wait until February, you are convinced that nothing less than *Middlemarch* will do.

In October of 1998 I finally gave in and signed up for e-mail. I had resisted for a long time. My husband and I were proud of our retrograde status. Not only did we lack a modem, but we didn't have a car, a microwave, a Cuisinart, an electric can opener, a cellular phone, a CD player, or cable television. It's hard to give up that sort of backward image; I worried that our friends wouldn't have enough to make fun of. I also worried that learning how to use e-mail would be like learning how to program our VCR, an unsuccessful project that had confirmed what excellent judgment we had shown in not purchasing a car, etc.

As millions of people had discovered before me, e-mail was fast. Sixteenth-century correspondents used to write "Haste, haste, haste, for lyfe, for lyfe, haste!" on their most urgent letters; my "server," a word that conjured up a delicious sycophancy, treated *every* message as if someone's life depended on it. Not only did it get there instantly, caromed in a series of analog cyberpackets along the nodes of the Internet and reconverted to digital form via its recipient's modem. (I do not understand a word of what I just wrote, but that is immaterial. Could the average Victorian have diagrammed the mail coach route from Swansea to Tunbridge Wells?) More important, I *answered* e-mail fast—almost always on the day it arrived. No more guilt! I used to think I did not like to write letters. I now realize that what I didn't like was folding the paper, sealing the envelope, looking up the address, licking the stamp, getting in the elevator, crossing the street, and dropping the letter in the postbox.

At first I made plenty of mistakes. I clicked on the wrong icons, my attachments didn't stick, and, not having learned how to file addresses, I sent an X-rated message to my husband (I thought) at gcolt@aol.com instead of georgecolt@aol.com. I hope Gerald or Gertrude found it flattering. But the learning curve was as steep as my father's driveway, and pretty soon I was batting out fifteen or twenty e-mails a day in the time it had once taken me to avoid answering a single letter. My box was nearly always full—no waiting, no binoculars, no convexity checks, no tugging—and when it wasn't, the reason was not that the mail hadn't *arrived,* it was that it hadn't been *sent.* I began to look forward every morning to the festive green arrow with which AT&T WorldNet welcomed me into my father's "antique land of chance and adventure." Would I be invited to purchase Viagra, lose thirty pounds, regrow my thinning hair, obtain electronic spy software, get an EZ loan, retire in three years, or win a Pentium III 500 MHz computer (presumably in order to receive such messages even faster)? Or would I find a satisfying little clutch of friendly notes whose responses could occupy me until I awoke sufficiently to tackle something that required intelligence? As Hemingway wrote to Fitzgerald, describing the act of letter-writing: "Such a swell way to keep from working and yet feel you've done something."

My computer, without visible distension, managed to store a flood tide of mail that in nonvirtual form would have silted up my office to the ceiling. This was admirable. And when I wished to commune with my friend Charlie, who lives in Taipei, not only could I disregard the thirteen-hour time difference, but I was billed the same amount as if I had dialed his old telephone number on East 22nd Street. The German critic Bernhard Siegert has observed that the breakthrough concept behind Rowland Hill's Penny Post was "to think of all Great Britain as a single city, that is, no longer to give a moment's thought to what had been dear to Western discourse on the nature of the letter from the beginning: the idea of distance." E-mail is a modern Penny Post: the world is a single city with a single postal rate.

Alas, our Penny Post, like Hill's, comes at a price. If the transfer of postal charges from sender to recipient was the first great de-motivator in the art of letter-writing, e-mail was the second. "It now seems a good bet," Adam Gopnik has written, "that in two hundred years people will be reading someone's collected e-mail the way we read Edmund Wilson's diaries or Pepys's letters." Maybe—but will what they read be any good? E-mails are brief. (One doesn't blather; an overlong message might induce carpal tunnel syndrome in the recipient from excessive pressure on the Down arrow.) They are also—at least the ones I receive—frequently devoid of capitalization, minimally punctuated, and creatively spelled. E-mail's greatest strength—speed—is also its Achilles' heel. In effect, it's always December 26; you are not expected to write *Middlemarch,* and therefore you don't.

In a letter to his friend William Unwin, written on August 6, 1780, William Cowper noted that "a Letter may be written upon any thing or Nothing." This observation is supported by the index of *The Faber Book of Letters, 1578–1939.* Let us examine some entries from the *d* section:

> damnation, 87
> dances and entertainments, 33, 48, 59, 97, 111, 275
> dentistry, 220
> depressive illness, 81, 87
> *Dictionary of the English Language,* Johnson's, 61
> Diggers, 22
> dolphins, methods of cooking, 37

I have never received an e-mail on any of these topics. Instead, I am informed that *Your browser is not Y2K-compliant. Your son left his Pokémon turtle under our sofa. Your column is 23 lines too long.* Important pieces of news, but, as Lytton Strachey (one of the all-time great letter writers) pointed out, "No good letter was ever written to convey information, or to please its recipient: it may achieve both these results incidentally; but its fundamental purpose is to express the personality of its writer." *But wait!* you pipe up. *Someone just e-mailed me a joke!* So she did, but wasn't the personality of the sender slightly muffled by the fact that she forwarded it from an e-mail *she* received, and sent it to seventeen additional addressees?

I also take a dim, or perhaps a buffaloed, view of electronic slang. Perhaps I should view it as a linguistic milestone, as historic as the evolution of Cockney rhyming slang in the 1840s. But will the future generations who reopen our hard drives be stirred by the eloquence of the e-acronyms recommended by a Web site on "netiquette"?

BTDT	been there done that
FC	fingers crossed
IITYWTMWYBMAD	
	if I tell you what this means will you buy me a drink?
MTE	my thoughts exactly
ROTFL	rolling on the floor laughing
RTFM	read the f———— manual
TAH	take a hint
TTFN	ta-ta for now

Or by the "emoticons," otherwise known as "smileys"—punctuational images, read sideways—that "help readers interpret the e-mail writer's attitude and tone"?

:-)	ha ha
:-(	boo hoo
(-:	I am left-handed
%-)	I have been staring at green screen for 15 hours straight
:-&	I am tongue-tied
{:-)	I wear a toupee
:-[	I am a vampire
:-F	I am a bucktoothed vampire with one tooth missing
=l:-)=	I am Abraham Lincoln

"We are of a different race from the Greeks, to whom beauty was everything," wrote Thomas Car-

lyle, a Victorian progress-booster. "Our glory and our beauty arise out of our inward strength, which makes us victorious over material resistance." We have achieved a similar victory of efficiency over beauty. I wouldn't give up e-mail if you paid me, but I'd feel a pang of regret if the epistolary novels of the future were to revolve around such messages as

Subject: R U Kidding?
From: Clarissa Harlowe <claha@virtue.com>
To: Robert Lovelace
<lovelaceandlovegirlz@vice.com>
hi bob, TAH. if u think I'm gonna run off w/ u, :-F. do u really think i'm that kind of girl?? if you're looking 4 a trollop, CLICK HERE NOW: http://www.hotpix.html. TTFN.

I own a letter written by Robert Falcon Scott, the polar explorer, to G. T. Temple, Esq., who helped procure the footgear for Scott's first Antarctic expedition. The date is February 26, 1901. The envelope and octavo stationery have black borders because Queen Victoria had died in January. The paper is yellowed, the handwriting is messy, and the stamp bears the Queen's profile—and the denomination ONE PENNY. I bought the letter many years ago because, unlike a Cuisinart, which would have cost about the same, it was something I believed I could not live without. I could never feel that way about an e-mail.

I also own my father's old wastebasket, which now holds my own empty Jiffy bags. Several times a day I use his stamp dispenser; it is tarnished and dinged, but still capable of unspooling its contents with a singular smoothness. And my file cabinets hold hundreds of his letters, the earliest written in his sixties in small, crabbed handwriting, the last in his nineties, after he lost much of his sight, penned with a Magic Marker in huge capital letters. I hope my children will find them someday, as Hart Crane once found his grandmother's love letters in the attic,

pressed so long
Into a corner of the roof
That they are brown and soft,
And liable to melt as snow.

SEEING

1. Anne Fadiman uses the simple acts of waiting for and reading the mail as an occasion to organize an insightful essay on everyday objects and rituals. What organizing principle(s) help structure the movement of her thoughts about this ordinary experience? What themes tie her thoughts together? In what specific ways do you agree—or disagree—with her critique of e-mail as an effective means of communication? How is Fadiman's essay more than a nostalgic plea to return to mail that takes up physical space rather than cyber space and weighs a great deal? How do you think she would respond to the notion that literature is in danger of disappearing in the onrush of technology?

2. To what extent does Fadiman's use of historical information about the mail add to—or detract from—the overall points she makes in her essay? In what ways does this invocation of the past reinforce the image she creates of herself and her values? Point to specific examples to support your response. Then refocus your attention on Fadiman's opening paragraph. Notice her use of figurative language there ("like a pirate captain hoisting his spyglass," "a mountain of letters," "mouse dirt," etc.). Identify other examples of figurative language throughout the essay, and comment on the effectiveness of Fadiman's use of this compositional technique.

WRITING

1. One way to gain new insights into the ordinary is to examine objects and experiences that we take for granted, such as the mail. Writing an essay or a poem provides an opportunity to explore such objects and experiences; so do photography and painting. Choose an object or experience in your daily life that you have so taken for granted that you rarely think about it. Write an essay in which you use description to discover the overlooked significance of this object or experience. Alternatively, use narration to tell a story about how the object or experience changed your understanding of the significance of observing the ordinary.

2. In paragraph 1, Fadiman observes that it was not until her father "dumped" the mail onto "a gigantic desk" that his day had "truly begun." What rituals mark the different periods in your day? At which times do these rituals occur? What actions does each consist of? To what extent is the "success" of your day measured by your ability to preserve the traditions associated with each activity? Choose one such ritual, and write an essay in which you concentrate your attention—and your readers'—on the details of this activity (brushing your teeth, combing your hair, tying your shoes, or the like) to explain how you have personalized the commonplace experience.

Graphis Student Design,
Man Turning into a Barcode

WILLIAM EGGLESTON >
Born in 1939 in Memphis, Tennessee, not far from his family's Mississippi cotton farm, William Eggleston attended several colleges in the South. While he was a student at Vanderbilt University he was inspired by the work of Henri Cartier-Bresson, the French photographer celebrated for his spontaneously captured, black and white images of everyday life.

Like Cartier-Bresson, Eggleston focuses on the everyday and the private; in spirit his work invokes the practice of taking snapshots. In his book *A Guide*, published by the Museum of Modern Art in 1976, the photos are like those in any family album, suggesting stories or meanings seemingly visible only to those who know the subject. An Eggleston "snapshot" of objects under a bed might lead us to wonder, "What was he looking for?" or "Whose shoes are those?" However slight such images may seem on the surface, as a whole they demonstrate the possibilities of viewing domestic detail as rich material for a photographic diary. These powerfully simple images subvert our expectations of art; they document dull and ordinary aspects of our environment with wit and imagination.

Eggleston has been the recipient of a Guggenheim fellowship and a National Endowment for the Arts fellowship, among many other awards.

William Eggleston, **Untitled**

1. William Eggleston's photographs transform the most ordinary objects and scenes into inviting occasions for discovering the unrecognized dimensions of the most homely objects and locations. Identify each of the objects you see in this image. Which attracts your attention first? Which holds your attention the longest? What are the advantages—and disadvantages—of Eggleston's having chosen not to show all of the bed and what's underneath it?

2. Notice the angle from which the photograph is taken. How does this perspective enable Eggleston to create a presence for himself in the photograph without being literally present in it? Comment on the composition—the overall organization—of this image. What do you notice, for example, about the relation of the carpet to the shoes? to the bed? to the walls beyond it? What do you notice about Eggleston's use of light and shadows? Eggleston names this moment "Untitled." Given the observations you've made about the image, what would you call it?

1. One way to gain important new awareness of the ordinary is to look for those things that are most often hidden, like Eggleston's space under the bed. Photography provides an important opportunity to explore such spaces; writing offers another. Choose a hidden space in the place where you live—under the bed, inside a closet, behind a bookshelf—and write a detailed description of what you see there. Did seeking out a hidden space change how you see what's there?

2. This photograph appears in a collection entitled *The Pleasures and Terrors of Domestic Comfort.* Which emotion does this image most make you feel—pleasure or terror? or something else? Write an essay in two parts: First, explain what you think the collection title means and how it fits your own experience of "domestic comfort"; second, evaluate how well Eggleston's photograph fits that title.

1886 Columbia Bicycle

Save Money—Save Time—Save Temper

MAKE your trips to and from work a pleasure instead of a mean ride on a crowded car. Ride a bicycle. Don't wait on uncertain car schedules. Go when you're ready. Go by the shortest route. You can leave home later and get back sooner.

Think of the convenience. Think of the money saved. You will pay for your bicycle in a few months. Is it any wonder that more people are riding bicycles today than ever before?

How good it makes you feel! The red blood sings thru your veins, driving away those morning headaches and that old sluggish feeling! You get to work feeling like taking that old job and fairly "eating it up!" Health and a clear brain go a long way towards making a successful man. A bicycle goes nearly all the way towards making a healthy man!

The bicycle is the most economical mode of transportation. It is the most healthful. It is a pleasant benefit for every member of your family.

CYCLE TRADES OF AMERICA, Inc., 35 Warren Street, New York, U. S. A.

See Your Dealer Today

Ride a Bicycle

He'll always remember his dream Christmas, 1953

There it stands—his dream bicycle come true—the AMF Roadmaster Luxury
Liner. What a sturdy beauty—and with all those extra features he especially
wants! Mile-measuring Roadometer, Shockmaster coil-spring fork. Far-seeing
Searchbeam headlight and electric horn, too. And you, Mom and Dad,
can be satisfied he's safe—thanks to AMF engineering and Roadmaster experience.
He gets safety bumper bars and an electronically-welded frame. See
the full line of AMF Roadmasters at your dealer's and fine stores.

★ **ROADOMETER** automatically measures and records
the miles you ride from 1/10 mile up to 10,000 miles.

Ool for the small fry

here's the 20" De Luxe. Can be fitted
with SAF-T-RIDER attachment. Balance him while he's learning.

products

AMERICAN MACHINE & FOUNDRY COMPANY

Roadmaster

1953 Roadmaster

THE PLACE IS NOT IMPORTANT.
IT'S THE FREEDOM THAT COUNTS.

MURRAY

FOX RIVER. THE ALL-TERRAIN BIKE.

1998 Murray

TRACEY BARAN

Tracey Baran was born in Bath, New York, in 1975. She moved to New York City in 1993 and began studying at the School of Visual Arts. Since then, Baran's photographs have been featured in museums and galleries in New York, London, and Korea.

This photograph is from a series entitled *Give and Take* that focuses on the literal and emotional landscape of Baran's childhood. When asked how she came to photograph her family life, she explained, "I was trying to figure out myself and how I reacted to certain things. I noticed my reactions were like my parents'. It's all pretty much based on my family life in upstate New York. Studying them was like studying myself. I just wanted to show the relationships between each family member and how people live and the care they give to themselves and things that are important to them."

Baran's most recent exhibition, entitled *Still*, was shown at the LiebmanMagnan gallery in New York City in 2001.

Tracy Baran, **Untitled 2,** 1999

SEEING

1. Tracey Baran's *Untitled 2* illustrates her remarkable ability to portray ordinary activities and scenes as engaging and enduring subjects for artistic expression. What, in your view, happens to such a commonplace activity as ironing when it is captured in Baran's photograph? What do you notice about the activity presented here? Examine carefully the context within which the ironing occurs. What do you notice about the scene captured in this photograph? How would you characterize the relationship between and among the objects and people depicted in this photograph? Given what you see in this photograph, comment on the likelihood of effective communication between the older woman and the younger woman. What details in the photograph prompt you to draw such inferences?

2. Imagine yourself in a museum viewing Tracey Baran's *Untitled 2*. How would seeing it as part of an exhibit change your understanding and appreciation of it? How would Baran's attitude influence your reading of her artistic purpose? What do you think Baran "says" in this image? On what grounds could you argue that *Untitled 2* is a work of art? Try to anticipate the reasons that someone might claim that this photograph fails as an example of artistic expression.

WRITING

1. Make a list of commonplace activities, ones that you've performed so often that you tend to take them for granted and not think carefully about them. Choose one, and write an expository essay in which you focus your attention—and your readers'—on the details of this everyday activity or ritual. In what ways do you personalize this otherwise commonplace activity?

2. Make a list of specific points of similarities and differences between the scenes and relationships depicted in this photograph and in Tillie Olsen's story "I Stand Here Ironing." After you have reread the photograph and story carefully, several times, write the first draft of an essay in which you compare and contrast the aesthetic appeal—and effectiveness—of Baran's photograph and Olsen's story.

TILLIE OLSEN

Tillie Olsen was born in Omaha, Nebraska, in 1913, and was the second of six children of Jewish immigrants who had escaped Czarist Russia. Olsen followed in the footsteps of her working-class parents, married young, had four children, and worked at various low-paying jobs. She also took up writing. At age nineteen, influenced by Rebecca Harding Davis's *Life in the Iron Mills*, Olsen began what would be her only novel, *Yonnondio*. (The title, drawn from a Walt Whitman poem, means "a lament for the lost.")

Olsen became a pioneer among American writers, giving eloquent voice to the struggles of everyday people. The novelist Margaret Atwood observed that other women writers ought to regard Olsen not only with "respect" but with "reverence." "I Stand Here Ironing" is drawn from Olsen's widely acclaimed short story collection, *Tell Me a Riddle*. One critic summarized the significance of Olsen's work as her ability to find "characters who could fully embody her vision of hope with hopelessness, of beauty in the midst of ugliness."

Olsen has received awards for her fiction, including a Stanford University Creative Writing Fellowship, a Ford Foundation Grant in Literature, and a fellowship to the Radcliffe Institute for Independent Study. Her other books include her unfinished novel *Yonnondio* (1974), *Silences* (1979), and *Mothers and Daughters* (1987).

I Stand Here Ironing

Tillie Olsen

I STAND HERE IRONING, AND WHAT YOU ASKED ME moves tormented back and forth with the iron.

"I wish you would manage the time to come in and talk with me about your daughter. I'm sure you can help me understand her. She's a youngster who needs help and whom I'm deeply interested in helping."

"Who needs help." . . . Even if I came, what good would it do? You think because I am her mother I have a key, or that in some way you could use me as a key? She has lived for nineteen years. There is all that life that has happened outside of me, beyond me.

And when is there time to remember, to sift, to weigh, to estimate, to total? I will start and there will be an interruption and I will have to gather it all together again. Or I will become engulfed with all I did or did not do, with what should have been and what cannot be helped.

She was a beautiful baby. The first and only one of our five that was beautiful at birth. You do not guess how new and uneasy her tenancy in her now-loveliness. You did not know her all those years she was thought homely, or see her poring over her baby pictures, making me tell her over and over how beautiful she had been—and would be, I would tell her—and was now, to the seeing eye. But the seeing eyes were few or nonexistent. Including mine.

I nursed her. They feel that's important nowadays. I nursed all the children, but with her, with all the fierce rigidity of first motherhood, I did like the books then said. Though her cries battered me to trembling and my breasts ached with swollenness, I waited till the clock decreed.

Why do I put that first? I do not even know if it matters, or if it explains anything.

She was a beautiful baby. She blew shining bubbles of sound. She loved motion, loved light, loved color and music and textures. She would lie on the floor in her blue overalls patting the surface so hard in ecstasy her hands and feet would blur. She was a miracle to me, but when she was eight months old I had to leave her daytimes with the woman downstairs to whom she was no miracle at all, for I worked or looked for work and for Emily's father, who "could no longer endure" (he wrote in his good-bye note) "sharing the want with us."

I was nineteen. It was pre-relief, pre-WPA world of the depression. I would start running as soon as I got off the streetcar, running up the stairs, the place smelling sour, and awake or asleep to startle awake, when she saw me she would break into a clogged weeping that could not be comforted, a weeping I can hear yet.

After a while I found a job hashing[1] at night so I could be with her days, and it was better. But it came to where I had to bring her to his family and leave her.

It took a long time to raise the money for her fare back. Then she got chicken pox and I had to wait longer. When she finally came, I hardly knew her, walking quick and nervous like her father, looking like her father, thin, and dressed in a shoddy red that yellowed her skin and glared at the pockmarks. All the baby loveliness gone.

She was two. Old enough for nursery school they said, and I did not know then what I know now—the fatigue of the long day, the lacerations of group life in the kinds of nurseries that are only parking places for children.

Except that it would have made no difference if I had known. It was the only place there was. It was the only way we could be together, the only way I could hold a job.

And even without knowing, I knew. I knew the teacher that was evil because all these years it has curdled into my memory, the little boy hunched in the corner, her rasp, "why aren't you outside, because Alvin hits you? that's no reason, go out, scaredy." I knew Emily hated it even if she did not clutch and implore "don't go Mommy" like the other children, mornings.

She always had a reason why we should stay home. Momma, you look sick. Momma, I feel sick. Momma, the teachers aren't there today, they're sick. Momma, we can't go, there was a fire there last night. Momma, it's a holiday today, no school, they told me.

But never a direct protest, never rebellion. I think of our others in their three-, four-year-oldness—the explosions, the tempers, the denunciations, the demands—and I feel suddenly ill. I put the iron down. What in me demanded that goodness in her? And what was the cost, the cost to her of such goodness?

The old man living in the back once said in his gentle way: "You should smile at Emily more when you look at her." What *was* in my face when I looked at her? I loved her. There were all the acts of love.

It was only with the others I remembered what he said, and it was the face of joy, and not of care or tightness or worry I turned to them—too late for Emily. She does not smile easily, let alone almost always as her brothers and sisters do. Her face is closed and somber, but when she wants, how fluid. You must have seen it in her pantomimes, you spoke of her rare gift for comedy on the stage that rouses a laughter out of the audience so dear they applaud and applaud and do not want to let her go.

Where does it come from, that comedy? There was none of it in her when she came back to me that second time, after I had had to send her away again. She had a new daddy now to learn to love, and I think perhaps it was a better time.

Except when we left her alone nights, telling ourselves she was old enough.

"Can't you go some other time, Mommy, like tomorrow?" she would ask. "Will it be just a little while you'll be gone? Do you promise?"

The time we came back, the front door open, the clock on the floor in the hall. She rigid awake. "It wasn't just a little while. I didn't cry. Three times I called you, just three times, and then I ran downstairs to open the door so you could come faster. The clock talked loud. I threw it away, it scared me what it talked."

She said the clock talked loud again that night I went to the hospital to have Susan. She was delirious with the fever that comes before red measles, but she was fully conscious all the week I was gone and the week after we were home when she could not come near the new baby or me.

She did not get well. She stayed skeleton thin, not wanting to eat, and night after night she had night-

---

1. *Hashing:* Working as a short-order cook; literally, chopping meat and potatoes.

mares. She would call for me, and I would rouse from exhaustion to sleepily call back: "You're all right, darling, go to sleep, it's just a dream," and if she still called, in a sterner voice, "Now go to sleep, Emily, there's nothing to hurt you." Twice, only twice, when I had to get up for Susan anyhow, I went in to sit with her.

Now when it is too late (as if she would let me hold 25 and comfort her like I do the others) I get up and go to her at once at her moan or restless stirring. "Are you awake, Emily? Can I get you something?" And the answer is always the same: "No, I'm all right, go back to sleep, Mother."

They persuaded me at the clinic to send her away to a convalescent home in the country where "she can have the kind of food and care you can't manage for her, and you'll be free to concentrate on the new baby." They still send children to that place. I see pictures on the society page of sleek young women planning affairs to raise money for it, or dancing at the affairs, or decorating Easter eggs or filling Christmas stockings for the children.

They never have a picture of the children so I do not know if the girls still wear those gigantic red bows and the ravaged looks on the every other Sunday when parents can come to visit "unless otherwise notified"—as we were notified the first six weeks.

Oh it is a handsome place, green lawns and tall trees and fluted flower beds. High up on the balconies of each cottage the children stand, the girls in their red bows and white dresses, the boys in white suits and giant red ties. The parents stand below shrieking up to be heard and the children shriek down to be heard, and between them the invisible wall "Not To Be Contaminated by Parental Germs or Physical Affection."

There was a tiny girl who always stood hand in hand with Emily. Her parents never came. One visit she was gone. "They moved her to Rose Cottage" Emily shouted in explanation. "They don't like you to love anybody here."

She wrote once a week, the labored writing of a 30 seven-year-old. "I am fine. How is the baby. If I write my leter nicly I will have a star. Love." There never was a star. We wrote every other day, letters she could never hold or keep but only hear read—once. "We simply do not have room for children to keep any personal possessions," they patiently explained when we pieced one Sunday's shrieking together to plead how much it would mean to Emily, who loved so to keep things, to be allowed to keep her letters and cards.

Each visit she looked frailer. "She isn't eating," they told us.

(They had runny eggs for breakfast or mush with lumps, Emily said later, I'd hold it in my mouth and not swallow. Nothing ever tasted good, just when they had chicken.)

It took us eight months to get her released home, and only the fact that she gained back so little of her seven lost pounds convinced the social worker.

I used to try to hold and love her after she came back, but her body would stay stiff, and after a while she'd push away. She ate little. Food sickened her, and I think much of life too. Oh she had physical lightness and brightness, twinkling by on skates, bouncing like a ball up and down up and down over the jump rope, skimming over the hill; but these were momentary.

She fretted about her appearance, thin and dark 35 and foreign-looking at a time when every little girl was supposed to look or thought she should look a chubby blond replica of Shirley Temple. The doorbell sometimes rang for her, but no one seemed to come and play in the house or be a best friend. Maybe because we moved so much.

There was a boy she loved painfully through two school semesters. Months later she told me how she had taken pennies from my purse to buy him candy. "Licorice was his favorite and I brought him some every day, but he still liked Jennifer better'n me. Why, Mommy?" The kind of question for which there is no answer.

School was a worry to her. She was not glib or quick in a world where glibness and quickness were easily confused with ability to learn. To her overworked and exasperated teachers she was an over-conscientious "slow learner" who kept trying to catch up and was absent entirely too often.

I let her be absent, though sometimes the illness was imaginary. How different from my now-strictness about attendance with the others. I wasn't working. We had a new baby, I was home anyhow. Sometimes, after Susan grew old enough, I would keep her home from school, too, to have them all together.

Mostly Emily had asthma, and her breathing, harsh and labored, would fill the house with a curiously tranquil sound. I would bring the two old dresser mirrors and her boxes of collections to her bed. She would select beads and single earrings, bottle tops and shells, dried flowers and pebbles, old postcards and scraps, all sorts of oddments; then she and Susan would play Kingdom, setting up landscapes and furniture, peopling them with action.

Those were the only times of peaceful companionship between her and Susan. I have edged away from it, that poisonous feeling between them, that terrible balancing of hurts and needs I had to do between the two, and did so badly, those earlier years.

Oh there are conflicts between the others too, each one human, needing, demanding, hurting, taking—but only between Emily and Susan, no, Emily toward Susan that corroding resentment. It seems so obvious on the surface, yet it is not obvious. Susan, the second child, Susan, golden- and curly-haired and chubby, quick and articulate and assured, everything in appearance and manner Emily was not; Susan, not able to resist Emily's precious things, losing or sometimes clumsily breaking them; Susan telling jokes and riddles to company for applause while Emily sat silent (to say to me later: that was *my* riddle, Mother, I told it to Susan); Susan, who for all the five years' difference in age was just a year behind Emily in developing physically.

I am glad for that slow physical development that widened the difference between her and her contemporaries, though she suffered over it. She was too vulnerable for that terrible world of youthful competition, of preening and parading, of constant measuring of yourself against every other, of envy, "If I had that copper hair," "If I had that skin. . . ." She tormented herself enough about not looking like the others, there was enough of the unsureness, the having to be conscious of words before you speak, the constant caring—what are they thinking of me? without having it all magnified by the merciless physical drives.

Ronnie is calling. He is wet and I change him. It is rare there is such a cry now. That time of motherhood is almost behind me when the ear is not one's own but must always be racked and listening for the child cry, the child call. We sit for a while and I hold him, looking out over the city spread in charcoal with its soft aisles of light. "*Shoogily,*" he breathes and curls closer. I carry him back to bed, asleep. *Shoogily.* A funny word, a family word, inherited from Emily, invented by her to say: *comfort.*

In this and other ways she leaves her seal, I say aloud. And startle at my saying it. What do I mean? What did I start to gather together, to try and make coherent? I was at the terrible, growing years. War years. I do not remember them well. I was working, there were four smaller ones now, there was not time for her. She had to help be a mother, and housekeeper, and shopper. She had to set her seal. Mornings of crisis and near hysteria trying to get lunches packed, hair combed, coats and shoes found, everyone to school or Child Care on time, the baby ready for transportation. And always the paper scribbled on by a smaller one, the book looked at by Susan then mislaid, the homework not done. Running out to that huge school where she was one, she was lost, she was a drop; suffering over her unpreparedness, stammering and unsure in her classes.

There was so little time left at night after the kids were bedded down. She would struggle over books, always eating (it was in those years she developed her enormous appetite that is legendary in our family) and I would be ironing, or preparing food for the next day, or writing V-mail[2] to Bill, or tending the baby. Sometimes, to make me laugh, or out of her despair, she would imitate happenings or types at school.

I think I said once: "Why don't you do something like this in the school amateur show?" One morning she phoned me at work, hardly understandable through the weeping: "Mother, I did it. I won, I won; they gave me first prize; they clapped and clapped and wouldn't let me go."

Now suddenly she was Somebody, and as imprisoned in her difference as she had been in her anonymity.

She began to be asked to perform at other high schools, even in colleges, then at city and statewide affairs. The first one we went to, I only recognized her that first moment when thin, shy, she almost drowned herself into the curtains. Then: Was this Emily? The control, the command, the convulsing and deadly clowning, the spell, then the roaring, stamping audience, unwilling to let this rare and precious laughter out of their lives.

Afterwards: You ought to do something about her with a gift like that—but without money or knowing how, what does one do? We have left it all to her, and the gift has as often eddied inside, clogged and clotted, as been used and growing.

She is coming. She runs up the stairs two at a time [50] with her light graceful step, and I know she is happy tonight. Whatever it was that occasioned your call did not happen today.

"Aren't you ever going to finish the ironing, Mother? Whistler painted his mother in a rocker. I'd have to paint mine standing over an ironing board." This is one of her communicative nights and she tells me everything and nothing as she fixes herself a plate of food out of the icebox.

She is so lovely. Why did you want me to come in at all? Why were you concerned? She will find her way.

She starts up the stairs to bed. "Don't get *me* up with the rest in the morning." "But I thought you were having midterms." "Oh, those," she comes back in, kisses me, and says quite lightly, "in a couple of years when we'll all be atom-dead they won't matter a bit."

She has said it before. She *believes* it. But because I have been dredging the past, and all that compounds a human being is so heavy and meaningful in me, I cannot endure it tonight.

I will never total it all. I will never come in to say: [55] She was a child seldom smiled at. Her father left me before she was a year old. I had to work her first six years when there was work, or I sent her home and to his relatives. There were years she had care she hated. She was dark and thin and foreign-looking in a world where the prestige went to blondness and curly hair and dimples; she was slow where glibness was prized. She was a child of anxious, not proud, love. We were poor and could not afford for her the soil of easy growth. I was a young mother, I was a distracted mother. There were the other children pushing up, demanding. Her younger sister seemed all that she was not. There were years she did not let me touch her. She kept too much in herself, her life was such she had to keep too much in herself. My wisdom came too late. She has much to her and probably little will come of it. She is a child of her age, of depression, of war, of fear.

Let her be. So all that is in her will not bloom—but in how many does it? There is still enough to live by. Only help her to know—help make it so there is cause for her to know—that she is more than this dress on the ironing board, helpless before the iron. ○

2. *V-mail:* Special forms used to communicate with soldiers serving overseas at the end of World War II. These forms were photographed, put on film, and shipped to the soldier's location, cutting down on time and space a normal letter would take.

SEEING

1. Characterize the *narrator* in this story. To whom does she seem to be speaking? Why is this person so interested in Emily? Does it seem to you that he or she understands Emily better than the speaker does? If so, what leads you to think so? What does Emily's mother think about the way she has raised her daughter? In what ways would she have raised Emily differently? What are some of the ways she thinks Emily's upbringing went wrong? Who or what is responsible for what happened? What does this suggest about the mother's attitudes toward her own life? Does Emily's mother think her daughter has found happiness, now that she is such a popular performer? Why or why not?

2. Olsen's story ends with a dramatic appeal: "Only help her to know—help make it so there is cause for her to know—that she is more than this dress on the ironing board, helpless before the iron" (para. 56). What is the nature—and the significance—of the image here? To what extent does the speaker wish someone could have helped her to know the same thing earlier in her life? To what extent does she still seem "helpless before the iron" herself? How do you think Olsen wants us to react to the speaker? to the daughter? What, specifically, prompts your response?

WRITING

1. Imagine yourself in the role of one of your parents. Write the first draft of a personal essay about your life from either your father's or your mother's *point of view*. What went wrong, and what went right, in your upbringing? What mistakes might your parents have made? What are the effects of your upbringing on the way you are now? You may want to talk with your parents before writing your story, and you may want to address it to someone outside your family who knows you, but not too well.

2. Olsen builds her story around an ordinary object and an ordinary activity. She uses these simple devices as a way to develop a story that is far more than a string of excuses for the mother's failure—because of ignorance and circumstances—to give her daughter the upbringing that she needed. Choose an ordinary object, and use it as the central image for creating a story that defines the relationship between a parent and a child.

narrator The person telling the story.

point of view The perspective, or angle of vision, from which a story is told.

TIM GARDNER

"When I started drawing pictures it was out of boredom," commented Tim Gardner in a recent interview. He began painting from snapshots while visiting his older brother at college. "There were all these pictures of him and his friends partying." I took them home and started drawing them. It became a vicarious social life for me, drawing pictures of his friends." That impulse developed into a series of watercolors that have been shown in galleries in New York City and London, depicting aspects of young, male, middle-class collegiate life.

The remarkable realism of Gardner's paintings easily fools viewers into thinking they are photographs. As one New York art critic recalled about Gardner's brushwork, it "is so assured that from across the room the photographic illusion held perfectly; some images didn't dissolve into painted gesture until the viewer stood two feet away." Indeed, Gardner enjoys playing with the contrast between the realism associated with photography and the romanticism so often associated with painting. "There is a contrast between the delicate medium and the sort of crude subject matter," Gardner explains. "So in that sense, I'm interested in repelling and attracting at the same time."

Gardner grew up in Ontario, Canada, and received his M.F.A. degree from Columbia University in 1999. He is currently living and working in New York City.

Tim Gardner, **Untitled (Sto and Mitch: Daytona),** 2001

Tim Gardner, **Untitled (S. Rod and Nick Eating Wings),** 2001

Tim Gardner, **Untitled (Bhoadie in Hot Tub II),** 2001

Tim Gardner, **The Summit,** 1999

SEEING

1. What do you first notice when you examine the portfolio of paintings presented by Tim Gardner? Which image attracts your attention first? Which one holds your attention the longest? Explain why. How—and at what point—did you come to the realization that you were looking at paintings, not photographs?

2. Now that you've had time to observe Gardner's paintings, consider them as a group. What features do these images share? In what ways is each painting unique? Point to the similarities and differences in the way each is organized. What inferences can you draw about your observations of Gardner's subjects and style?

WRITING

1. Make a list of situations from your own experience that you think offer the most opportunities for descriptive or narrative writing. Choose one such recollection that is dependent on a painting or photograph; locate the image and write an essay in which you not only recount the circumstances that led to creating this image but also offer a descriptive and narrative account of the moment or scene depicted in it. Your goal in this essay is to re-create for your readers a sense of the immediacy of the moment depicted in the photograph or painting.

2. To which of Gardner's paintings are you most drawn? Why? Examine that image carefully—until you are reasonably confident that you understand and appreci-

ate how it works to elicit specific responses from an audience. Then write the first draft of a fictional narrative that sets the context for—and leads up to—the climactic scene depicted in this painting.

ZOE INGALLS >

Zoe Ingalls was born and raised in Montgomery, Alabama, earned an English degree at Goucher College in Baltimore, and now lives and works as a freelance writer and editor in Chapel Hill, North Carolina. While working for Baltimore's department of city planning, she volunteered as a writer and editor for a neighborhood and cultural guide to the city. It was her first writing job and she was hooked. In 1978 Ingalls became a staff writer for the Washington-based *Chronicle of Higher Education*, a venerable national weekly newspaper that specializes in issues and news relating to colleges and universities, and she ended up staying for the next twenty-four years. She began in the news department, worked her way into feature writing, and then went on to various high-profile beats.

Ingalls's favorite assignment was probably interviewing recipients of the prestigious Jefferson Lecture in the Humanities, awarded annually by the National Endowment for the Humanities. The opportunity to meet and interview talented and influential writers and scholars was a high point of Ingalls's career at the *Chronicle*. Because Ingalls had studied the works of William Faulkner while in college, meeting and interviewing Cleanth Brooks, the renowned Faulkner scholar and 1985 Jefferson recipient, was particularly memorable for her. Ingalls's last beat for the *Chronicle* was covering arts and culture, and she remains interested in the subjects, collecting art (mainly Southern) in her spare time. The following piece was first published in the November 1997 issue of the *Chronicle*.

TEACHING ARCHITECTURE STUDENTS "THE DISCIPLINE OF THE HAND"

Zoe Ingalls

THE PEA IS A HUMBLE VEGETABLE AT FIRST glance. Under closer scrutiny, it reveals a certain elegance of design. The pod unzips neatly along a seam. The pearl-like fruits line up one behind the other, each attached by a tiny green stem. "As alike as two peas in a pod" is the saying—yet they are surprisingly unlike one another. Some are round, some ovoid, others nearly square.

Which brings us to the first day of class in Sue Ferguson Gussow's freehand-drawing course at the Cooper Union for the Advancement of Science and Art. First she asks her students to sketch a pea pod from memory. Half an hour later, she hands out pods from a grocery store and asks them to try again.

The lesson sinks in right away. "What I drew from memory was so different from the actual reality," says Patricia E. Corrigan, a first-year student from Queens, N.Y. "It was very eye-opening. It suggested to me that I needed to examine the world around me more closely."

A textbook response, according to Ms. Gussow, and an apt introduction to the year's work—learning to breathe the illusion of life into two-dimensional surfaces.

This is Ms. Gussow's 22nd year teaching freehand drawing to first-year architecture—not art—students here. She began after the dean of the school of architecture decided that his students did not draw as well as they should. In time, her course became a requirement for graduation. She is the only drawing teacher in the architecture school.

Freehand drawing has been considered a basic tool of architecture since the Renaissance, according to Richard Henderson, associate dean of the school. Architects can use drawing as a way of thinking aloud—a means of getting their thoughts on paper.

"Sketching technique is of incredible value to architects," says Mr. Henderson. "Once you learn the discipline of the hand, you don't have to slow down your mind."

In that sense, drawing becomes an integral part of the design process. "It's not like you have a thought, and it's a complete thought, and then you make a diagram of it," says Ms. Gussow. "The drawing and the brain work are feeding each other back and forth. You're making marks; they're giving you more ideas."

Ms. Gussow, who also teaches advanced drawing to upperclassmen, got the idea for the peas after reading an essay about their similarities and differences in *The New Yorker*. In class, "the discussion begins with the concept of thinking how things are both alike and different," she says. "If you can do a juggling act between those two possibilities—the general and the specific—you can begin to look at things.

"In order to get the gross idea of a form down, you 10 have to generalize. Yet in order to make the drawing come alive, to become individuated and fascinating, you have to notice what is unique about this situation, what catches the eye."

Although peas in a pod open the semester, the human figure is the real focus of the class. Students draw from live models over and over again. "It's the most basic thing you can do in drawing," says Ms. Gussow.

Students learn the figure, but not isolated on a background of white paper. In this class, a well-drawn figure, like a well-designed building, must be shown resting firmly on the ground, with careful attention paid to the space surrounding it.

Learning to draw the figure entails seeing "how it occupies space, what makes it up, how it moves," says Elisa Garcia, a fourth-year student who took Ms. Gussow's course as a freshman and liked it so much that she is now taking the advanced class. "In terms of architecture," drawing figures helps a designer "understand the human condition and how you can make something for it."

Some of Ms. Gussow's students have taken drawing before. Many have not. On a recent afternoon in the studio classroom, 14 first-year students stand at easels and attempt to capture a model's pose—torso twisted, arms crossed at the waist, head tilted to the right.

The air conditioning hums in the background, 15 overlaid by the scratching sounds of charcoal on paper. When someone presses too hard, there's a clatter as the charcoal breaks and falls to the floor.

They work quickly, knowing that the model will change her position every five minutes. That's "long enough to do investigating and messing around, but not so long that they begin refining and cease to look at the model," says Ms. Gussow.

"The 20-minute poses, which are universal art-school poses, are the sort I despise. I like to be either very quick or long, at least an hour or more. That gives them time to push it, ruin it, really discover what they can do."

Later in the semester, the students will do long, studied drawings in which they zero in on heads, hands, and other parts of the human body. But now they've gone from doing five-minute to two-minute sketches. That's the best way to train students to get a sense of the whole of what they're drawing on paper before they begin fussing with details, Ms. Gussow explains.

"It's like dancing," she says. "When you are truly dancing, you don't consider each movement that you are making. Something impels you—the rhythm of the music, the rhythm of your body. I think that when you draw rapidly, a similar instinctual movement opens up."

"In some ways," she says, "I'm trying to pull the 20 architecture students out of their analytical bent."

It's early in the semester, and most students have not yet caught the rhythm of drawing. Ms. Gussow walks from student to student, looking over shoulders, making a point here, tidying up there, sprinkling her observations with an occasional "Good!" Sometimes she takes up the charcoal herself to demonstrate what she wants.

Some students drift toward what she calls "fake Matisse," concentrating on the outline of what they're drawing and ignoring the internal structure. They end up with figures that look as if they had been pasted on the paper, like crude copies of the cutouts of Henri Matisse.

She takes the charcoal from a young woman in a green T-shirt. "What you're doing is these little stingy hand movements," she says, making marks like inverted quotations. "What I want to encourage you to do is to think of the spine as an axis, an organizing principle. It's how the major masses of the torso and head are organized. You know it's there, and you better make sense of it in the drawing."

As she talks, she makes quick, bold strokes, a repetitive series of C's, as if she were sculpting the body with her charcoal. She compares the technique to "taking a Slinky toy and wrapping it around the body."

"The whole notion of structure comes from the 25 skeleton," she says later. "We talk about the skeleton of a building, the spine of a structure."

Michael W. Su, a first-year transfer student who has never studied drawing before, is beginning to see her point.

"Looking at volumes, seeing where spaces are, seeing that the arm is ahead of the socket here, taught me a great deal about looking closely and about what to observe, where to observe, and how," he says. "When we're drawing the figure, it really seems as if we're drawing a building. The only difference is the lines are curved. Otherwise, I think the correlation is very strong."

The class introduces students to options—of approach, of balance, or composition. Students gain "a spatial sense and a compositional sense that can actually be translated to architecture," says Mr. Henderson, the associate dean.

"One of the fundamental things when you approach a site or a piece of paper is to ask yourself, How big is it, what shape is it, and where are you going to put it?" says Ms. Gussow, who has paused in her circuit of the room. "That decision is made in the first minute or two of any drawing." She looks intently at one student's work. The drawing is only half-finished, but already it's clear that the head and torso are so large that there's not enough room on the page for the legs.

"And that is why," she continues, walking over to 30 the student, "as nice as this is, either you're going to

have to make her very stubby-legged, or . . ." The student sighs and turns to a fresh sheet.

Thomas K. Tsang, a fourth-year student who took Ms. Gussow's course as a freshman and is now in her advanced class, observes, "It's not a matter of creating beautiful drawings, but a way of thinking: Do you attack from the middle or the edge?"

On one wall of the classroom at Cooper Union, Ms. Gussow has tacked charcoal sketches of green peppers—"so body-ish and voluptuous," she says— that the students did as homework.

They were to draw at least two peppers, one of them cut open. The exercise has to do with relationships: between interior and exterior space as well as between objects. The goal is to help the students move away from what Ms. Gussow calls a "paint-by-numbers attitude toward the two-dimensional surface, where each piece is locked into the other piece in a flat way.

"We're aiming for the illusion of spatiality and structure in space, even though we're making marks on a two-dimensional surface," she says. "The reality of the drawing is forever flat; but the illusion of the drawing and the experience of the drawing could be dimensional and relational. That's the magic of it. Otherwise you're just copying."

When Ms. Gussow prepared to teach her first 35 drawing course, in 1976, she told the dean that she would teach "not only the figure, but the figure related into space—content and context," she says. "Because, really, it's a contextual figure—the figure as an occupant of space and the figure as a measurer of space."

She tells her students that what they'll be designing are not "walls and doorknobs, but spaces for the people."

"Can you design buildings without learning to draw the figure?" she asks. "Yes. Will they be wonderful buildings? I think not." ○

SEEING

1. What are the steps in the process Sue Ferguson Gussow uses to teach her course on freehand drawing, a process that enables students to "examine the world around [them] more closely" (para. 3)? What more specific purpose does Zoe Ingalls identify for training students to do two-minute freehand sketches? What benefits does Ingalls identify for encouraging students to do freehand sketches? What figurative language (simile and metaphor) does she use to enable her readers to envision the benefits of such exercises in looking closely?

2. What skills does Gussow teach in her freehand drawing class? What does Richard Henderson mean when he talks about "the discipline of the hand" (para. 7), and what is the rationale behind—as well as the evidence to support—the assertion that "Once you have learned the discipline of the hand, you don't have to slow down your mind"? In what ways might the process of learning free-hand drawing help students learn to write more effectively? Be as specific as possible.

WRITING

1. Ingalls reports that Sue Ferguson Gussow has her students draw—freehand—a picture of a pea pod from memory. "Half an hour later, she hands out pods from a grocery store and asks them to try again. The lesson sinks in right away. 'What I drew from memory was so different from the actual realty'" (paras. 2, 3). Draw—from memory—what a penny looks like. After you have completed this activity, compare and contrast your description of the penny with the actual appearance of the coin. Write a paragraph or two comparing and contrasting the differences between your initial drawing and the actual appearance of the penny. What inadvertent omissions mark your efforts to describe the penny?

2. What do you find most engaging in Sue Ferguson Gussow's method of teaching? What do you find least engaging and least helpful about her advice on drawing—and, by extension, on writing? Write an expository essay in which you compare and contrast the similarities and differences between drawing and writing as a means of "putting your thoughts down on paper." Which technique—freehand drawing or freewriting—do you find more helpful as you try to articulate your ideas about various subjects? Explain why.

 Talking Pictures

Few of us are as relentlessly attentive to observing the details of everyday life as the drawing students in Sue Ferguson Gussow's classroom are asked to be (p. 84). Yet each of us inevitably spends a great deal of time dealing with the mundane. In *Seinfeld,* one of the most popular television series in history, the routines of daily life preoccupy the characters of this self-described "show about nothing."

Choose an episode of *Seinfeld* to watch, or locate a script on one of the numerous web sites devoted to the show. As you watch or read the episode, list the aspects of everyday life that are portrayed. What does the episode reveal about the daily life of these single, "30-something" New Yorkers? What strategies do the writers and director use to achieve these effects? What approach do the characters in *Seinfeld* take to daily life? What details of ordinary life do you find more or less convincingly portrayed?

Now choose an episode of another television sitcom, and list as many observations as you can about its portrayal of everyday objects and tasks. How does *Seinfeld* differ from other sitcoms in this regard? Write an essay in which you compare and contrast the portrayal of the mundane in *Seinfeld* with that of another sitcom. To what extent does either show represent your own life?

Alfred Leslie, **Television Moon**

Celebrating such ordinary objects as a bowl of fruit or a vase with flowers, still-life paintings encourage us to view familiar objects in distinct new ways.

A member of a school of painting that had little interest in representing the world realistically.

ALFRED LESLIE

Alfred Leslie's eye for sharp, sometimes hyperrealistic detail and his technical mastery suggest a career steeped in the conventions of realist painting. Interestingly, Leslie first made his mark in the art world in the late 1940s, as a young member of the abstract expressionist generation. In the 1950s he turned increasingly to narrative forms, first in flim, then in his art. In fact, the stories related by many of his paintings contain a moral, in the sense that he challenges viewers to consider ethical interpretations of scenes and events. Leslie once expressed his desire to create "an art like the art of David, Caravaggio, and Rubens, meant to influence the conduct of people."

Born in New York City in 1927, Leslie studied briefly at New York University and has been an independent painter since 1946. His work has been included in numerous prestigious exhibitions, and his awards include a Guggenheim fellowship (1969). He lives and paints in New York City and is represented by the Oil and Steel Gallery.

SEEING

1. Alfred Leslie's painting *Television Moon* subtly disrupts a centuries-old artistic tradition: the still life. Traditional still-life painters use simplicity and clarity to call attention to objects their audience knows well. Make a series of observations about this painting. Where does your eye rest as you look carefully at *Television Moon*? How many objects do you see? What details do you notice about each? Look again at the television. What additional details do you now notice about it? What reasonable inferences can you draw from these details and their relation to the other objects depicted?

2. In one sense, still-life paintings simply describe objects in the material world. In another sense, the artists who create still-life scenes often do so in order to interpret and comment on them. In what ways can Leslie's painting be said to interpret or serve as a commentary on contemporary American life and culture?

WRITING

1. Using precise description, translate Leslie's *Television Moon* into a one-page, verbal still life. The goal is for your readers to be able to sketch the painting on the basis of your description. (You might want to ask someone to try this after you've finished to see how close you've come.)

2. Antidrug campaigns have used an unusual version of the still life: an egg in a frying pan to represent the dangers of drugs to our brains. Choose an object (e.g., a dollar bill, a syringe, a remote control, a mountain bike) that represents something you believe should be changed in contemporary American life. Write an essay in two parts. First, provide a description, either verbal or visual, of how you would convey a moral message about the object through a still life. Second, write an analysis of how effective you expect this approach to be, and explain why.

PEPÓN OSORIO

"My principal commitment as an artist is to return art to the community," says installation and video artist Pepón Osorio. Born in Santurce, Puerto Rico, in 1955, Osorio studied at the Universidad Inter-Americana in Puerto Rico; Lehman College, City University of New York; and Columbia University. From his experience as a social worker and his collaborations with avant-garde performance artist and choreographer Merián Soto, Osorio brings a closely intertwined social and artistic conscience to his art. The range of materials he uses to construct his installations— found objects, video, silkscreen, photography, and sound—are as rich as the experiences he draws on for inspiration.

Osorio created *Son's Bedroom* in 1995 as one section of an artistic installation entitled *Badge of Honor*. (A full view of the installation is reproduced on page 93.) *Son's Bedroom* is a fabricated rendition of the bedroom of a 15-year-old boy named Nelson Jr. The image on the right wall is a video screen that plays a 22-minute tape of the son talking to his father, Nelson Sr.

Osorio's work has been shown in galleries and museums around the United States and Puerto Rico. He was awarded the prestigious MacArthur ("genius") Fellowship and was featured in the PBS series "Art:21: Art in the 21st Century." Osorio currently lives and works in Philadelphia.

Pepón Osorio, **Badge of Honor,** 1995 (detail)

SEEING

1. Pepón Osorio has fabricated the bedroom of a teenage boy, who is depicted on the video screen on the right wall. As you examine this image, what do you first observe about the bedroom? Which object(s) draw your attention? What do you notice about each one? What cultural references does Osorio draw on to create this scene? What reasonable inferences can you make about this teenager's interests? Based on the particulars of what you observe in this ordinary scene, what generalization(s) can you make about Osorio's style?

2. To what extent has Osorio successfully captured the "look" of a teenage boy's bedroom? Point to specific examples to support your judgment. Which aspects of Osorio's depiction of the bedroom strike you as based more on fiction or fantasy than on fact? Why? What criteria would you use to help someone understand the differences between "fiction" and "fantasy"?

The poet Robert Frost defined *style* as "the way [a person] carries himself [herself] toward his [her] ideas and deeds." In effect, style is the way in which something is said, done, performed, or expressed.

WRITING

1. Imagine yourself standing in the doorway to your bedroom—either at home or on campus. Now imagine yourself composing a verbal picture of what you see as you examine your own bedroom. Which aspects of the room would you want to tell others about? Which aspects would you rather leave unmentioned? Write the first draft of a descriptive essay in which you convey—in as much detail as possible—what you think someone would see in your bedroom.

2. Consider the differences between the "look" of your bedroom at home and that of the space you call your own in your room on campus. Other than the size of the space, what differences do you notice in the ways you organize your space in these two locations? Write a comparison/contrast essay in which you discuss how these differences reflect a similar (or different) style of presenting yourself at home and on campus. If you live at home and commute to campus, you might try the same exercise with another member of the class, and then follow the same compositional instructions.

Visualizing Context
The Complete Picture

Context is an essential aspect of both understanding and practicing the art of composition—whether what is being composed is an essay, a painting, a photograph, or a film. In its simplest sense, context refers to the circumstances, or the setting, within which an event occurs. The context is also the part of a text or statement that surrounds a particular word, passage, or image and helps determine its meaning. Analyzing the relation between a text and its context—or the relation of a part to the whole—is an effective way to appreciate and master the complexity and effectiveness of seeing clearly and writing well.

Take a few moments to examine the teenage bedroom presented on pages 90–91. This image represents one-half of a large artistic work entitled *Badge of Honor*, created by the installation and video artist Pepón Osorio. The full work, represented in the photograph above, consists of a glossy, crowded teenage bedroom that shares a wall with a stark prison cell. These two fabricated rooms feature video screens. If you were standing in front of *Badge of Honor*, you would be able to hear a father and son engaged in a 22-minute conversation through the wall dividing their rooms.

In what ways does seeing more of Osorio's *Badge of Honor* change your response to his work? to each part of the work? What visual differences do you notice between the two rooms? How does the context of a bedroom and a jail cell determine what you expect to find present in—and absent from—each? To what aspect(s) of the work do you think the title *Badge of Honor* refers?

Now consider another dimension of context: the structure of an artistic composition, the relation of the parts to the whole. As you study Osorio's work, notice how each room is organized. Around what features and/or concepts is each room "built"? How are the two rooms held together? What do you see as the relationship between the two rooms? Explain the extent to which the two are dependent on each other for their meaning. Point to evidence in each to verify your reading of what you observe there.

Another way to think about context is to consider the setting for a work, the circumstances within which a word, a statement, or an object is placed. Osorio's installation was originally presented in an empty storefront in a predominantly Hispanic and African American neighborhood in Newark, New Jersey. It was later moved to the Newark Museum and then to the Feldman Gallery in New York City. How might viewers interpret Osorio's installation differently in each of these three social contexts?

ANNIE DILLARD

Annie Dillard was born Annie Doak in Pittsburgh in 1945. She attended Hollins College near Roanoke, Virginia, where she studied English, theology, and creative writing; married her writing teacher, Richard Dillard; and earned a master's degree with a thesis on Henry David Thoreau and Walden Pond. Before publishing her first book, *Pilgrim at Tinker Creek* (1974), she spent four seasons living near Tinker Creek in the Blue Ridge Mountains of Virginia and filled more than 20 volumes of journals with notes about her experiences and thoughts on the violence and beauty of nature, often in religious terms. Fearing that a work of theology written by a woman would not be successful, she was reluctant to publish the book. But she did, and it won the Pulitzer Prize in 1975.

Subsequently Dillard has published poetry, fiction, essays, memoirs, literary criticism, and autobiography, returning repeatedly to the themes of the mysteries of nature, the quest for meaning, and religious faith. *The Annie Dillard Reader,* a collection of her writing, was published in 1994.

"Seeing" speaks to Dillard's concern that a writer be "careful of what he reads, for that is what he will write . . . careful of what he learns, because that is what he will know."

Seeing

Annie Dillard

WHEN I WAS SIX OR SEVEN YEARS OLD, GROWING up in Pittsburgh, I used to take a precious penny of my own and hide it for someone else to find. It was a curious compulsion; sadly, I've never been seized by it since. For some reason I always "hid" the penny along the same stretch of sidewalk up the street. I would cradle it at the roots of a sycamore, say, or in a hole left by a chipped-off piece of sidewalk. Then I would take a piece of chalk, and, starting at either end of the block, draw huge arrows leading up to the penny from both directions. After I learned to write I labeled the arrows: SURPRISE AHEAD or MONEY THIS WAY. I was greatly excited, during all this arrow-drawing, at the thought of the first lucky passer-by who would receive in this way, regardless of merit, a free gift from the universe. But I never lurked about. I would go straight home and not give the matter another thought, until, some months later, I would be gripped again by the impulse to hide another penny.

It is still the first week in January, and I've got great plans. I've been thinking about seeing. There are lots of things to see, unwrapped gifts and free surprises. The world is fairly studded and strewn with pennies cast broadside from a generous hand. But—and this is the point—who gets excited by a mere penny? If you follow one arrow, if you crouch motionless on a bank to watch a tremulous ripple thrill on the water and are rewarded by the sight of a muskrat kit paddling from its den, will you count that sight a chip of copper only, and go your rueful way? It is dire poverty indeed when a man is so malnourished and fatigued that he won't stoop to pick up a penny. But if you cultivate a healthy poverty and simplicity, so that finding a penny will literally make your day, then, since the world is in fact planted in pennies, you have with your poverty bought a lifetime of days. It is that simple. What you see is what you get.

I used to be able to see flying insects in the air. I'd look ahead and see, not the row of hemlocks across the road, but the air in front of it. My eyes would focus along that column of air, picking out flying insects. But I lost interest, I guess, for I dropped the habit. Now I can see birds. Probably some people can look at the grass at their feet and discover all the crawling creatures. I would like to know grasses and sedges—and care. Then my least journey into the world would be a field trip, a series of happy recognitions. Thoreau, in an expansive mood, exulted, "What a rich book might be made about buds, including, perhaps, sprouts!" It would be nice to think so. I cherish mental images I have of three perfectly happy people. One collects stones. Another—an Englishman, say—watches clouds. The third lives on a coast and collects drops of seawater which he examines microscopically and mounts. But I don't see what the specialist sees, and so I cut myself off, not only from the total picture, but from the various forms of happiness.

Unfortunately, nature is very much a now-you-see-it, now-you-don't affair. A fish flashes, then dissolves in the water before my eyes like so much salt. Deer apparently ascend bodily into heaven; the brightest oriole fades into leaves. These disappearances stun me into stillness and concentration; they say of nature that it conceals with a grand nonchalance, and they say of vision that it is a deliberate gift, the revelation of a dancer who for my eyes only flings away her seven veils. For nature does reveal as well as conceal: now-you-don't-see-it, now-you-do. For a week last September migrating red-winged blackbirds were feeding heavily down by the creek at the back of the house. One day I went out to investigate the racket; I walked up to a tree, an Osage orange, and a hundred birds flew away. They simply materialized out of the tree. I saw a tree, then a whisk of color, then a tree again. I walked closer and another hundred blackbirds took flight. Not a branch, not a twig budged: The birds were apparently weightless as well as invisible. Or, it was as if the leaves of the Osage orange had been freed from a spell in the form of red-winged blackbirds; they flew from the tree, caught my eye in the sky, and vanished. When I looked again at the tree the leaves had reassembled as if nothing had happened. Finally I walked directly to the trunk of the tree and a final hundred, the real diehards, appeared, spread, and vanished. How could so many hide in the tree without my seeing them? The Osage orange, unruffled, looked just as it had looked from the house, when three hundred red-winged blackbirds cried from its crown. I looked downstream where they flew, and they were gone. Searching, I couldn't spot one. I wandered downstream to force them to play their hand, but they'd crossed the creek and scattered. One show to a customer. These appearances catch at my throat; they are the free gifts, the bright coppers at the roots of trees.

It's all a matter of keeping my eyes open. Nature is like one of those line drawings of a tree that are puzzles for children: Can you find hidden in the leaves a duck, a house, a boy, a bucket, a zebra, and a boot? Specialists can find the most incredibly well-hidden things. A book I read when I was young recommended an easy way to find caterpillars to rear: You simply find some fresh caterpillar droppings, look up, and there's your caterpillar. More recently an author advised me to set my mind at ease about those piles of cut stems on the ground in grassy fields. Field mice make them; they cut the grass down by degrees to reach the seeds at the head. It seems that when the grass is tightly packed, as in a field of ripe grain, the blade won't topple at a single cut through the stem; instead, the cut stem simply drops vertically, held in the crush of grain. The mouse severs the bottom again and again, the stem keeps dropping an inch at a time, and finally the head is low enough for the mouse to reach the seeds. Meanwhile, the mouse is positively littering the field with its little piles of cut stems into which, presumably, the author of the book is constantly stumbling.

If I can't see these minutiae, I still try to keep my eyes open. I'm always on the lookout for antlion traps in sandy soil, monarch pupae near milkweed, skipper larvae in locust leaves. These things are utterly common, and I've not seen one. I bang on hollow trees near water, but so far no flying squirrels have appeared. In flat country I watch every sunset in hopes of seeing the green ray. The green ray is a seldom-seen streak of light that rises from the sun like a spurting fountain at the moment of sunset; it throbs into the sky for two seconds and disappears. One more reason to keep my eyes open. A photography professor at the University of Florida just happened to see a bird die in midflight; it jerked, died, dropped, and smashed on the ground. I squint at the wind because I read Stewart Edward White: "I have always maintained that if you looked closely enough you could *see* the wind—the dim, hardly-made-out, fine débris fleeing high in the air." White was an excellent observer, and devoted an entire chapter of *The Mountains* to the subject of seeing deer: "As soon as you can forget the naturally obvious and construct an artificial obvious, then you too will see deer."

But the artificial obvious is hard to see. My eyes account for less than one percent of the weight of my head; I'm bony and dense; I see what I expect. I once spent a full three minutes looking at a bullfrog that was so unexpectedly large I couldn't see it even though a dozen enthusiastic campers were shouting directions. Finally I asked, "What color am I looking for?" and a fellow said, "Green." When at last I picked out the frog, I saw what painters are up against: The thing wasn't green at all, but the color of wet hickory bark.

The lover can see, and the knowledgeable. I visited an aunt and uncle at a quarter-horse ranch in Cody, Wyoming. I couldn't do much of anything useful, but I could, I thought, draw. So, as we all sat around the kitchen table after supper, I produced a sheet of paper and drew a horse. "That's one lame horse," my aunt volunteered. The rest of the family joined in: "Only place to saddle that one is his neck"; "Looks like we better shoot the poor thing, on account of those terrible growths." Meekly, I slid the pencil and paper down the table. Everyone in that family, including my three young cousins, could draw a horse. Beautifully. When the paper came back it looked as though five shining, real quarter horses had been corraled by mistake with a papier-mâché moose; the real horses seemed to gaze at the monster with a steady, puzzled air. I stay away from horses now, but I can do a creditable goldfish. The point is that I just don't know what the lover knows; I just can't see the artificial obvious that those in the know construct. The herpetologist asks the native, "Are there snakes in that ravine?" "Nosir." And the herpetologist comes home with, yessir, three bags full. Are there butterflies on that mountain? Are the bluets in bloom, are there arrowheads here, or fossil shells in the shale?

Peeping through my keyhole I see within the range of only about thirty percent of the light that comes from the sun; the rest is infrared and some little ultraviolet, perfectly apparent to many animals, but invisible to me. A nightmare network of ganglia, charged and firing without my knowledge, cuts and splices what I do see, editing it for my brain. Donald E. Carr points out that the sense impressions of one-celled animals are *not* edited for the brain: "This is philosophically interesting in a rather mournful way, since it means that only the simplest animals perceive the universe as it is."

A fog that won't burn away drifts and flows across my field of vision. When you see fog move against a backdrop of deep pines, you don't see the fog itself, but streaks of clearness floating across the air in dark shreds. So I see only tatters of clearness through a pervading obscurity. I can't distinguish the fog from the overcast sky; I can't be sure if the light is direct or reflected. Everywhere darkness and the presence of the unseen appalls. We estimate now that only one atom dances alone in every cubic meter of intergalactic space. I blink and squint. What planet or power yanks Halley's Comet out of orbit? We haven't seen that force yet; it's a question of distance, density, and the pallor of reflected light. We rock, cradled in the swaddling band of darkness. Even the simple darkness of night whispers suggestions to the mind. Last summer, in August, I stayed at the creek too late.

Where Tinker Creek flows under the sycamore log bridge to the tear-shaped island, it is slow and shallow, fringed thinly in cattail marsh. At this spot an astonishing bloom of life supports vast breeding populations of insects, fish, reptiles, birds, and mammals. On windless summer evenings I stalk along the creek bank or straddle the sycamore log in absolute stillness, watching for muskrats. The night I stayed too late I was hunched on the log staring spellbound at spreading, reflected stains of lilac on the water. A cloud in the sky suddenly lighted as if turned on by a switch; its reflection just as suddenly materialized on the water upstream, flat and floating, so that I couldn't see the creek bottom, or life in the water under the cloud. Downstream, away from the cloud on the water, water turtles smooth as beans were gliding down with the current in a series of easy, weightless push-offs, as men bound on the moon. I didn't know whether to trace the progress of one turtle I was sure of, risking sticking my face in one of the bridge's spider webs made invisible by the gathering dark, or take a chance on seeing the carp, or scan the mudbank in hope of seeing a muskrat, or follow the last of the swallows who caught at my heart and trailed it after them like streamers as they appeared from directly below, under the log, flying upstream with the tails forked, so fast.

But shadows spread, and deepened, and stayed. After thousands of years we're still strangers to darkness, fearful aliens in an enemy camp with our arms crossed over our chests. I stirred. A land turtle on the bank, startled, hissed the air from its lungs and withdrew into its shell. An uneasy pink here, an unfathomable blue there, gave great suggestion of lurking beings. Things were going on. I couldn't see whether that sere rustle I heard was a distant rattlesnake, slit-eyed, or a nearby sparrow kicking in the dry flood debris slung at the foot of a willow. Tremendous action roiled the water everywhere I looked, big action, inexplicable. A tremor welled up beside a gaping muskrat burrow in the bank and I caught my breath, but no muskrat appeared. The ripples continued to fan upstream with a steady, powerful thrust. Night was knitting over my face an eyeless mask, and I still sat transfixed. A distant airplane, a delta wing out of nightmare, made a gliding shadow on the creek's bottom that looked like a stingray cruising upstream. At once a black fin slit the pink cloud on the water, shearing it in two. The two halves merged together and seemed to dissolve before my eyes. Darkness pooled in the cleft of the creek and rose, as water collects in a well. Untamed, dreaming lights flickered over the sky. I saw hints of hulking underwater shadows, two pale splashes out of the water, and round ripples rolling close together from a blackened center.

At last I stared upstream where only the deepest violet remained of the cloud, a cloud so high its underbelly still glowed feeble color reflected from a hidden sky lighted in turn by a sun halfway to China. And out of that violet, a sudden enormous black body arced over the water. I saw only a cylindrical sleekness. Head and tail, if there was a head and tail, were both submerged in cloud. I saw only one ebony fling, a headlong dive to darkness; then the waters closed, and the lights went out.

I walked home in a shivering daze, up hill and down. Later I lay open-mouthed in bed, my arms flung wide at my sides to steady the whirling darkness. At this latitude I'm spinning 836 miles an hour round the earth's axis; I often fancy I feel my sweeping fall as a break-neck arc like the dive of dolphins, and the hollow rushing of wind raises hair on my neck and the side of my face. In orbit around the sun I'm moving 64,800 miles an hour. The solar system as a whole, like a merry-go-round unhinged, spins, bobs, and blinks at the speed of 43,200 miles an hour along a course set east of Hercules. Someone has piped, and we are dancing a tarantella until the sweat pours. I open my eyes and I see dark, muscled forms curl out of water, with flapping gills and flattened eyes. I close my eyes and I see stars, deep stars giving way to deeper stars, deeper stars bowing to deepest stars at the crown of an infinite cone.

"Still," wrote van Gogh in a letter, "a great deal of light falls on everything." If we are blinded by darkness, we are also blinded by light. When too much light falls on everything, a special terror results. Peter Freuchen describes the notorious kayak sickness to which Greenland Eskimos are prone. "The Greenland fjords are peculiar for the spells of completely quiet weather, when there is not enough wind to blow out a match and the water is like a sheet of glass. The kayak hunter must sit in his boat without stirring a finger so as not to scare the shy seals away. . . . The sun, low in the sky, sends a glare into his eyes, and the landscape around moves into the realm of the unreal. The reflex from the mirrorlike water hypnotizes him, he seems to be unable to move, and all of a sudden it is as if he were floating in a bottomless void, sinking, sinking, and sinking. . . . Horror-stricken, he tries to stir, to cry out, but he cannot, he is completely paralyzed, he just falls and falls." Some hunters are especially cursed with this panic, and bring ruin and sometimes starvation to their families.

Sometimes here in Virginia at sunset low clouds on the southern or northern horizon are completely invisible in the lighted sky. I only know one is there because I can see its reflection in still water. The first time I discovered this mystery I looked from cloud to no-cloud in bewilderment, checking my bearings over and over, thinking maybe the ark of the covenant was just passing by south of Dead Man Mountain. Only much later did I read the explanation: Polarized light from the sky is very much weakened by reflection, but the light in clouds isn't polarized. So invisible clouds pass among visible clouds, till all slide over the mountains; so a greater light extinguishes a lesser as though it didn't exist.

In the great meteor shower of August, the Perseid, I wail all day for the shooting stars I miss. They're out there showering down, committing hara-kiri in a flame of fatal attraction, and hissing perhaps at last into the ocean. But at dawn what looks like a blue dome clamps down over me like a lid on a pot. The stars and planets could smash and I'd never know. Only a piece of ashen moon occasionally climbs up or down the inside of the dome, and our local star without surcease explodes on our heads. We have really only that one light, one source for all power, and yet we must turn away from it by universal decree. Nobody here on the planet seems aware of this strange, powerful taboo, that we all walk about carefully averting our faces, this way and that, lest our eyes be blasted forever.

Darkness appalls and light dazzles; the scrap of visible light that doesn't hurt my eyes hurts my brain. What I see sets me swaying. Size and distance and the sudden swelling of meanings confuse me, bowl me over. I straddle the sycamore log bridge over Tinker Creek in the summer. I look at the lighted creek bottom: Snail tracks tunnel the mud in quavering curves. A crayfish jerks, but by the time I absorb what has happened, he's gone in a billowing smokescreen of silt. I look at the water: minnows and shiners. If I'm thinking minnows, a carp will fill my brain till I scream. I look at the water's surface: skaters, bubbles, and leaves sliding down. Suddenly, my own face, reflected, startles me witless. Those snails have been tracking my face! Finally, with a shuddering wrench of the will, I see clouds, cirrus clouds. I'm dizzy, I fall in. This looking business is risky.

Once I stood on a humped rock on nearby Purgatory Mountain, watching through binoculars the great autumn hawk migration below, until I discovered that I was in danger of joining the hawks on a vertical migration of my own. I was used to binoculars, but not, apparently, to balancing on humped rocks while looking through them. I staggered. Everything advanced and receded by turns; the world was full of unexplained foreshortenings and depths. A distant huge tan object, a hawk the size of an elephant, turned out to be the browned bough of a nearby loblolly pine. I followed a sharp-shinned hawk against a featureless sky, rotating my head unawares as it flew, and when I lowered the glass a glimpse of my own looming shoulder sent me staggering. What prevents the men on Palomar from falling, voiceless and blinded, from their tiny, vaulted chairs?

I reel in confusion; I don't understand what I see. With the naked eye I can see two million light-years to the Andromeda galaxy. Often I slop some creek water in a jar and when I get home I dump it in a white china bowl. After the silt settles I return and see tracings of minute snails on the bottom, a planarian or two winding round the rim of water, roundworms shimmying frantically, and finally, when my eyes have adjusted to these dimensions, amoebae. At first the amoebae look like muscae volitantes, those curled moving spots you seem to see in your eyes when you stare at a distant wall. Then I see the amoebae as drops of water congealed, bluish, translucent, like chips of sky in the bowl. At length I choose one individual and give myself over to its idea of an evening. I see it dribble a grainy foot before it on its wet, unfathomable way. Do its unedited sense impressions include the fierce focus of my eyes? Shall I take it outside and show it Andromeda, and blow its little endoplasm? I stir the water with a finger, in case it's running out of oxygen. Maybe I should get a tropical aquarium with motorized bubblers and lights, and keep this one for a pet. Yes, it would tell its fissioned descendants, the universe is two feet by five, and if you listen closely you can hear the buzzing music of the spheres.

Oh, it's mysterious lamplit evenings, here in the galaxy, one after the other. It's one of those nights when I wander from window to window, looking for a sign. But I can't see. Terror and a beauty insoluble are a ribband of blue woven into the fringes of garments of things both great and small. No culture explains, no bivouac offers real haven or rest. But it could be that we are not seeing something. Galileo thought comets were an optical illusion. This is fertile ground: Since we are certain that they're not, we can look at what our scientists have been saying with fresh hope. What if there are *really* gleaming, castellated cities hung upside-down over the desert sand? What limpid lakes and cool date palms have our caravans always passed untried? Until, one by one, by the blindest of leaps, we light on the road to these places, we must stumble in darkness and hunger. I turn from the window. I'm blind as a bat, sensing only from every direction the echo of my own thin cries.

I chanced on a wonderful book by Marius von Senden, called *Space and Light.* When Western surgeons discovered how to perform safe cataract operations, they ranged across Europe and America operating on dozens of men and women of all ages who had been blinded by cataracts since birth. Von Senden collected accounts of such cases; the histories are fascinating. Many doctors had tested their patients' sense perceptions and ideas of space both before and after the operations. The vast majority of patients, of both sexes and all ages, had, in von Senden's opinion, no idea of space whatsoever. Form, distance, and size were so many meaningless syllables. A patient "had no idea of depth, confusing it with roundness." Before the operation a doctor would give a blind patient a cube and a sphere; the patient would tongue it or feel it with his hands, and name it correctly. After the operation the doctor would show the same objects to the patient without letting him touch them; now he had no clue whatsoever what he was seeing. One patient called lemonade "square" because it pricked on his tongue as a square shape pricked on the touch of his hands. Of another postoperative patient, the doctor writes, "I have found in her no notion of size, for example, not even within the narrow limits which she might have encompassed with the aid of touch. Thus when I asked her to show me how big her mother was, she did not stretch out her hands, but set her two index-fingers a few inches apart." Other doctors reported their patients' own statements to similar effect. "The room he was in . . . he knew to be but part of the house, yet he could not conceive that the whole house could look bigger"; "Those who are blind from birth . . . have no real conception of height or distance. A house that is a mile away is thought of as nearby, but requiring the taking of a lot of steps. . . . The elevator that whizzes him up and down gives no more sense of vertical distance than does the train of horizontal."

For the newly sighted, vision is pure sensation unencumbered by meaning: "The girl went through the experience that we all go through and forget, the moment we are born. She saw, but it did not mean anything but a lot of different kinds of brightness." Again, "I asked the patient what he could see; he answered that he saw an extensive field of light, in which everything appeared dull, confused, and in motion. He could not distinguish objects." Another patient saw "nothing but a confusion of forms and colours." When a newly sighted girl saw photographs and paintings, she asked, " 'Why do they put those dark marks all over them?' 'Those aren't dark marks,' her mother explained, 'those are shadows. That is one of the ways the eye knows that things have shape. If it were not for shadows many things would look flat.' 'Well, that's how things do look,' Joan answered. 'Everything looks flat with dark patches.'"

But it is the patients' concepts of space that are most revealing. One patient, according to his doctor, "practiced his vision in a strange fashion; thus he takes off one of his boots, throws it some way off in front of him, and then attempts to gauge the distance at which it lies; he takes a few steps toward the boot and tries to grasp it; on failing to reach it, he moves on a step or two and gropes for the boot until he finally gets hold of it." "But even at this stage, after three weeks' experience of seeing," von Senden goes on, " 'space,' as he conceives it, ends with visual space, i.e., with color-patches that happen to bound his view. He does not yet have the notion that a larger object (a chair) can mask a smaller one (a dog), or that the latter can still be present even though it is not directly seen."

In general the newly sighted see the world as a dazzle of color-patches. They are pleased by the sensation of color, and learn quickly to name the colors, but the rest of seeing is tormentingly difficult. Soon after his operation a patient "generally bumps into one of these color-patches and observes them to be substantial, since they resist him as tactual objects do. In walking about it also strikes him—or can if he pays attention—that he is continually passing in between the colors he sees, that he can go past a visual object, that a part of it then steadily disappears from view; and that in spite of this, however he twists and turns—whether entering the room from the door, for example, or returning back to it—he always has a visual space in front of him. Thus he gradually comes to realize that there is also a space behind him, which he does not see."

The mental effort involved in these reasonings proves overwhelming for many patients. It oppresses them to realize, if they ever do at all, the tremendous size of the world, which they had previously conceived of as something touchingly manageable. It oppresses them to realize that they have been visible to people all along, perhaps unattractively so, without their knowledge or consent. A disheartening number of them refuse to use their new vision, continuing to go over objects with their tongues, and lapsing into apathy and despair. "The child can see, but will not make use of his sight. Only when pressed can he with difficulty be brought to look at objects in his neighborhood; but more than a foot away it is impossible to bestir him to the necessary effort." Of a twenty-one-year-old girl, the doctor relates, "Her unfortunate father, who had hoped for so much from this operation, wrote that his daughter carefully shuts her eyes whenever she wishes to go about the house, especially when she comes to a staircase, and that she is never happier or more at ease than when, by closing her eyelids, she relapses into her former state of total blindness." A fifteen-year-old boy, who was also in love with a girl at the asylum for the blind, finally blurted out, "No, really, I can't stand it any more; I want to be sent back to the asylum again. If things aren't altered, I'll tear my eyes out."

Some do learn to see, especially the young ones. But it changes their lives. One doctor comments on "the rapid and complete loss of that striking and wonderful serenity which is characteristic only of those who have never yet seen." A blind man who learns to see is ashamed of his old habits. He dresses up, grooms himself, and tries to make a good impression. While he was blind he was indifferent to objects unless they were edible; now, "a sifting of values sets in . . . his thoughts and wishes are mightily stirred and some few of the patients are thereby led into dissimulation, envy, theft and fraud."

On the other hand, many newly sighted people speak well of the world, and teach us how dull is our own vision. To one patient, a human hand, unrecognized, is "something bright and then holes." Shown a bunch of grapes, a boy calls out, "It is dark, blue and shiny. . . . It isn't smooth, it has bumps and hollows." A little girl visits a garden. "She is greatly astonished, and can scarcely be persuaded to answer, stands speechless in front of the tree, which she only names on taking hold of it, and then as 'the tree with the lights in it.'" Some delight in their sight and give themselves over to the visual world. Of a patient just after her bandages were removed, her doctor writes, "The first things to attract her attention were her own hands; she looked at them very closely, moved them repeatedly to and fro, bent and stretched the fingers, and seemed greatly astonished at the sight." One girl was eager to tell her blind friend that "men do not really look like trees at all," and astounded to discover that her every visitor had an utterly different face. Finally, a twenty-two-year-old girl was dazzled by the world's brightness and kept her eyes shut for two weeks. When at the end of that time she opened her eyes again, she did not recognize any objects, but, "the more she now directed her gaze upon everything about her, the more it could be seen how an expression of gratification and astonishment overspread her features; she repeatedly exclaimed: 'Oh God! How beautiful!'"

I saw color-patches for weeks after I read this wonderful book. It was summer; the peaches were ripe in the valley orchards. When I woke in the morning, color-patches wrapped round my eyes, intricately, leaving not one unfilled spot. All day long I walked among shifting color-patches that parted before me like the Red Sea and closed again in silence, transfigured, wherever I looked back. Some patches swelled and loomed, while others vanished utterly, and dark marks flitted at random over the whole dazzling sweep. But I couldn't sustain the illusion of flatness. I've been around for too long. Form is condemned to an eternal danse macabre with meaning: I couldn't unpeach the peaches. Nor can I remember ever having seen without understanding; the color-patches of infancy are lost. My brain then must have been smooth as any balloon. I'm told I reached for the moon; many babies do. But the color-patches of infancy swelled as meaning filled them; they arrayed themselves in solemn ranks down distance which unrolled and stretched before me like a plain. The moon rocketed away. I live now in a world of shadows that shape and distance color, a world where space makes a kind of terrible sense. What gnosticism is this, and what physics? The fluttering patch I saw in my nursery window—silver and green and shape-shifting blue—is gone; a row of Lombardy poplars takes its place, mute, across the distant lawn. That humming oblong creature pale as light that stole along the walls of my room at night, stretching exhilaratingly around the corners, is gone, too, gone the night I ate of the bittersweet fruit, put two and two together and puckered forever my brain. Martin Buber tells this tale: "Rabbi Mendel once boasted to his teacher Rabbi Elimelekh that evenings he saw the angel who rolls away the light before the darkness, and mornings the angel who rolls away the darkness before the light. 'Yes,' said Rabbi Elimelekh, 'in my youth I saw that too. Later on you don't see these things any more.'"

Why didn't someone hand those newly sighted people paints and brushes from the start, when they still didn't know what anything was? Then maybe we all could see color-patches too, the world unraveled from reason, Eden before Adam gave names. The scales would drop from my eyes; I'd see trees like men walking; I'd run down the road against all orders, hallooing and leaping.

Seeing is of course very much a matter of verbalization. Unless I call my attention to what passes before my eyes, I simply won't see it. It is, as Ruskin says, "not merely unnoticed, but in the full, clear sense of the word, unseen." My eyes alone can't solve analogy tests using figures, the ones which show, with increasing elaborations, a big square, then a small square in a big square, then a big triangle, and expect me to find a small triangle in a big triangle. I have to say the words, describe what I'm seeing. If Tinker Mountain erupted, I'd be likely to notice. But if I want to notice the lesser cataclysms of valley life, I have to maintain in my head a running description of the present. It's not that I'm observant; it's just that I talk too much. Otherwise, especially in a strange place, I'll never know what's happening. Like a blind man at the ball game, I need a radio.

When I see this way I analyze and pry. I hurl over logs and roll away stones; I study the bank a square foot at a time, probing and tilting my head. Some days when a mist covers the mountains, when the muskrats won't show and the microscope's mirror shatters, I want to climb up the blank blue dome as a man would storm the inside of a circus tent, wildly, dangling, and with a steel knife claw a rent in the top, peep, and, if I must, fall.

But there is another kind of seeing that involves a letting go. When I see this way I sway transfixed and emptied. The difference between the two ways of seeing is the difference between walking with and without a camera. When I walk with a camera I walk from shot to shot, reading the light on a calibrated meter. When I walk without a camera, my own shutter opens, and the moment's light prints on my own silver gut. When I see this second way I am above all an unscrupulous observer.

It was sunny one evening last summer at Tinker Creek; the sun was low in the sky, upstream. I was sitting on the sycamore log bridge with the sunset at my back, watching the shiners the size of minnows who were feeding over the muddy sand in skittery schools. Again and again, one fish, then another, turned for a split second across the current and flash! the sun shot out from its silver side. I couldn't watch for it. It was always just happening somewhere else, and it drew my vision just as it disappeared: flash, like a sudden dazzle of the thinnest blade, a sparking over a dun and olive ground at chance intervals from every direction. Then I noticed white specks, some sort of pale petals, small, floating from under my feet on the creek's surface, very slow and steady. So I blurred my eyes and gazed toward the brim of my hat and saw a new world. I saw the pale white circles roll up, roll up, like the world's turning, mute and perfect, and I saw the linear flashes, gleaming silver, like stars being born at random down a rolling scroll of time. Something broke and something opened. I filled up like a new wineskin. I breathed an air like light; I saw a light like water. I was the lip of a fountain the creek filled forever; I was ether, the leaf in the zephyr; I was flesh-flake, feather, bone.

When I see this way I see truly. As Thoreau says, I return to my senses. I am the man who watches the baseball game in silence in an empty stadium. I see the game purely; I'm abstracted and dazed. When it's all over and the white-suited players lope off the green field to their shadowed dugouts, I leap to my feet; I cheer and cheer.

But I can't go out and try to see this way. I'll fail, I'll go mad. All I can do is try to gag the commentator, to hush the noise of useless interior babble that keeps me from seeing just as surely as a newspaper dangled before my eyes. The effort is really a discipline requiring a lifetime of dedicated struggle; it marks the literature of saints and monks of every order East and West, under every rule and no rule, discalced and shod. The world's spiritual geniuses seem to discover universally that the mind's muddy river, this ceaseless flow of trivia and trash, cannot be dammed, and that trying to dam it is a waste of effort that might lead to madness. Instead you must allow the muddy river to flow unheeded in the dim channels of consciousness; you raise your sights; you look along it, mildly, acknowledging its presence without interest and gazing beyond it into the realm of the real where subjects and objects act and rest purely, without utterance. "Launch into the deep," says Jacques Ellul, "and you shall see."

The secret of seeing is, then, the pearl of great price. If I thought he could teach me to find it and keep it forever I would stagger barefoot across a hundred deserts after any lunatic at all. But although the pearl may be found, it may not be sought. The literature of illumination reveals this above all: Although it comes to those who wait for it, it is always, even to the most practiced and adept, a gift and a total surprise. I return from one walk knowing where the killdeer nests in the field by the creek and the hour the laurel blooms. I return from the same walk a day later scarcely knowing my own name. Litanies hum in my ears; my tongue flaps in my mouth Ailinon, alleluia! I cannot cause light; the most I can do is try to put myself in the path of its beam. It is possible, in deep space, to sail on solar wind. Light, be it particle or wave, has force: you rig a giant sail and go. The secret of seeing is to sail on solar wind. Hone and spread your spirit till you yourself are a sail, whetted, translucent, broadside to the merest puff.

When her doctor took her bandages off and led her into the garden, the girl who was no longer blind saw "the tree with the lights in it." It was for this tree I searched through the peach orchards of summer, in the forests of fall and down winter and spring for years. Then one day I was walking along Tinker Creek thinking of nothing at all and I saw the tree with the lights in it. I saw the backyard cedar where the mourning doves roost charged and transfigured, each cell buzzing with flame. I stood on the grass with the lights in it, grass that was wholly fire, utterly focused and utterly dreamed. It was less like seeing than like being for the first time seen, knocked breathless by a powerful glance. The flood of fire abated, but I'm still spending the power. Gradually the lights went out in the cedar, the colors died, the cells unflamed and disappeared. I was still ringing. I had been my whole life a bell, and never knew it until at that moment I was lifted and struck. I have since only very rarely seen the tree with the lights in it. The vision comes and goes, mostly goes, but I live for it, for the moment when the mountains open and a new light roars in spate through the crack, and the mountains slam. ○

SEEING

1. Near the end of her essay Annie Dillard observes, "Seeing is of course very much a matter of verbalization" (para. 31). Reread "Seeing" and make a list of every idiom she uses to talk about seeing "truly." Consider, for example, the last line of paragraph 2: "What you see is what you get." Identify other, similar idiomatic expressions. Explain how Dillard plays with the literal and figurative dimensions of each one. With what effects? What does she mean when she says, "This looking business is risky" (para. 18)? One of the strongest elements of Dillard's style is her effective use of metaphor. Identify two or three especially striking examples of her command of metaphor, and explain the effects of each.

2. Near the end of paragraph 6, Dillard quotes the naturalist Stewart Edward White on seeing deer: "As soon as you can forget the naturally obvious and construct an artificial obvious, then you too will see deer." Dillard immediately observes, "But the artificial obvious is hard to see" (para. 7). What does "the artificial obvious" mean here, how do people construct it, and why is it "hard to see"? Later, Dillard describes another kind of seeing, "a letting go" (para. 33). What does she mean when she says, "when I see this . . . way I am above all an unscrupulous observer"?

WRITING

1. Most of us at one time or another have succumbed to the impulse to hide something and then either to lead people to it or to make it as difficult as possible for others to locate. Recall one such impulse that you had, and develop detailed notes about not only the circumstances but also the consequences of your yielding to the impulse. Draft an essay in which you recount this story and then use it as a harbinger of other, more important events or behavior in your life.

2. Reread Larry Woiwode's "Ode to an Orange" (p. 48). What do you think he would say about the nature of seeing? Using Woiwode's or any other work in this chapter, write a comparative essay in which you compare the author's philosophy about seeing with Dillard's—and argue that one is more compelling than the other.

Seeing
Annie Dillard

Looking Closer
Seeing Is Believing

Size matters—or so advertisers claim when they promote certain products or services. Scientists make much the same point: A photograph of a single living cell or of a distant star would be so small that it would be difficult to identify the subject without some indication of its size and scale.

Each of the essays and images on the following pages invites us to magnify our attention to discover the richness and complexity of familiar objects. Several images—from David Scharf's ***Kitchen Scouring Pad*** to Harold Edgerton's ***Milk Drop Coronet*** to Tom Friedman's ***Aspirin Self-Portrait***—reveal how a changed scale of vision can transform the nondescript. K. C. Cole's essay **"A Matter of Scale"** provides a vocabulary and frame of reference

with which to appreciate what is extraordinary about the ordinary; Felice Frankel and George M. Whitesides's ***Compact Disc*** shows us the face of music technology close up; and two perspectives of Chuck Close's ***Self-Portrait*** graphically prove that what we see depends on how closely we're looking.

THE FASCINATION OF THE MINIATURE

Steven Millhauser

Wherein lies the fascination of the miniature? Smallness alone compels no wonder. A grain of sand, an ant, a raindrop, a bottle cap, may interest or amaze the eye, but they do not arrest the attention with that peculiar intensity elicited by the miniature. They do not cast a spell. The miniature, then, must not be confused with the merely minute. For the miniature does not exist in isolation: it is by nature a smaller version of something else. The miniature, that is to say, implies a relation, a discrepancy. An object as large as a doll-house can exert the fascination of the miniature as fully as the minutest teacup in the doll's smallest cupboard.

But why should discrepancy possess an interest? I believe the answer is this, that discrepancy of size is a form of distortion, and all forms of distortion shock us into attention: the inattentive and jaded eye, passing through a world without interest, helplessly perceives that something in the bland panorama is not as it should be. The eye is irritated into attention. It is compelled to perform an act of recognition. Perhaps for the first time since childhood, it sees. But what I have said is true of all forms of discrepancy, and not only the particular discrepancy that is the miniature. Some understanding of the spell cast by this particular discrepancy may be gained by first considering the nature of the particular discrepancy that is the gigantic. ○

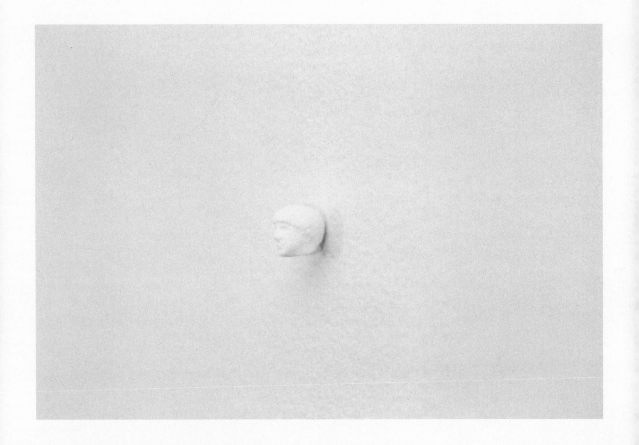

REFLECTIONS ON A MOTE OF DUST, MAY 11, 1996

Carl Sagan

WE SUCCEEDED IN TAKING THAT PICTURE (FROM deep space), and, if you look at it, you see a dot.

That's here. That's home. That's us.

On it, everyone you ever heard of, every human being who ever lived, lived out their lives. The aggregate of all our joys and sufferings, thousands of confident religions, ideologies and economic doctrines, every hunter and forager, every hero and coward, every creator and destroyer of civilizations, every king and peasant, every young couple in love, every hopeful child, every mother and father, every inventor and explorer, every teacher of morals, every corrupt politician, every superstar, every supreme leader, every saint and sinner in the history of our species, lived there on a mote of dust, suspended in a sunbeam.

The earth is a very small stage in a vast cosmic arena. Think of the rivers of blood spilled by all those generals and emperors so that in glory and in triumph they could become the momentary masters of a fraction of a dot. Think of the endless cruelties visited by the inhabitants of one corner of the dot on scarcely distinguishable inhabitants of some other corner of the dot. How frequent their misunderstandings, how eager they are to kill one another, how fervent their hatreds. Our posturings, our imagined self-importance, the delusion that we have some privileged position in the universe, are challenged by this point of pale light.

Our planet is a lonely speck in the great enveloping cosmic dark. In our obscurity—in all this vastness—there is no hint that help will come from elsewhere to save us from ourselves. It is up to us. It's been said that astronomy is a humbling, and I might add, a character-building experience. To my mind, there is perhaps no better demonstration of the folly of human conceits than this distant image of our tiny world.

To me, it underscores our responsibility to deal more kindly and compassionately with one another and to preserve and cherish that pale blue dot, the only home we've ever known. ○

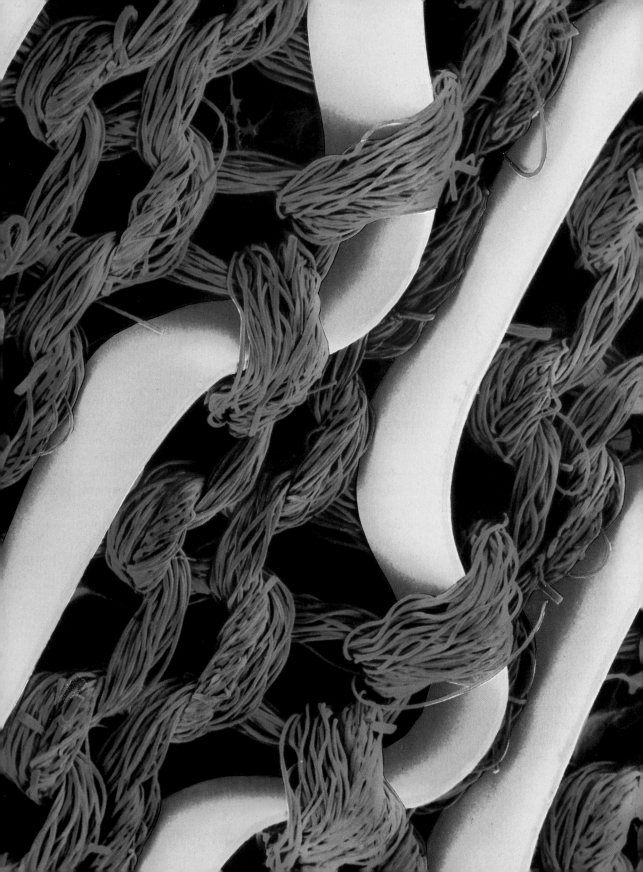

A Matter of Scale

K. C. Cole

How would you suspend 500,000 pounds of water in the
air with no visible means of support? (Answer: build a cloud.)
—artist Bob Miller

THERE IS SOMETHING MAGICALLY SEDUCTIVE about an invitation to a world where everything measures much bigger or smaller than ourselves. To contemplate the vast expanse of ocean or sky, to look at pond scum under a microscope, to imagine the intimate inner life of atoms, all cast spells that take us far beyond the realm of everyday living into exotic landscapes accessible only through the imagination. What would it be like to grow as big as a giant? As small as a bug? Alice ate a mushroom and puffed up like a Macy's Thanksgiving Day balloon, bursting out of her house; she ate some more and shrank like the Incredible Shrinking Woman, forever in fear of falling down the drain. From Stuart Little to King Kong, from *Honey, I Shrunk the Kids* to Thumbelina, the notion of changing size seems to have a powerful pull on our psyches.

There are good reasons to think a world that's different in scale will also be different in kind. More or less of something very often adds up to more than simply more or less; quantitative changes can make huge qualitative differences.

When the size of things changes radically, different laws of nature rule, time ticks according to different clocks, new worlds appear out of nowhere while old ones dissolve into invisibility. Consider the strange sit-

uation of a giant, for example. Big and strong to be sure, but size comes with distinct disadvantages. According to J. B. S. Haldane in his classic essay, "On Being the Right Size," a sixty-foot giant would break his thighbones at every step. The reason is simple geometry. Height increases only in one dimension, area in two, volume in three. If you doubled the height of a man, the cross section, or thickness, of muscle that supports him against gravity would quadruple (two times two) and his volume—and therefore weight—would increase by a factor of eight. If you made him ten times taller, his weight would be a thousand times greater, but the cross section of bones and muscles to support him would only increase by a factor of one hundred. Result: shattered bones.

To bear such weight would require stout, thick legs—think elephant or rhino. Leaping would be out of the question. Superman must have been a flea.

Fleas, of course, perform superhuman feats routinely (which is part of the science behind the now nearly extinct art of the flea circus). These puny critters can pull 160,000 times their own weight, and jump a hundred times their own height. Small creatures have so little mass compared to the area of their muscles that they seem enormously strong. While their muscles are many orders of magnitude weaker

5

than ours, the mass they have to push around is so much smaller that it makes each ant and flea into a superbeing. Leaping over tall buildings does not pose a problem.[1]

Neither does falling. The old saying is true: The bigger they come, the harder they fall. And the smaller they come, the softer their landings. Again, the reason is geometry. If an elephant falls from a building, gravity pulls strongly on its huge mass while its comparatively small surface area offers little resistance. A mouse, on the other hand, is so small in volume (and therefore mass) that gravity has little to attract; at the same time, its relative surface area is so huge that it serves as a built-in parachute.

A mouse, writes Haldane, could be dropped from a thousand-yard-high cliff and walk away unharmed. A rat would probably suffer enough damage to be killed. A person would certainly be killed. And a horse, he tells us, "splashes."

The same relationships apply to inanimate falling objects—say, drops of water. The atmosphere is drenched with water vapor, even when we can't see it in the form of clouds. However, once a tiny particle begins to attract water molecules to its sides, things change rapidly. As the diameter of the growing droplet increases by a hundred, the surface area increases by ten thousand, and its volume a millionfold. The larger surface area reflects far more light—making the cloud visible. The enormously increased volume gives the drops the gravitational pull they need to splash down to the ground as rain.

According to cloud experts, water droplets in the air are simultaneously pulled on by electrical forces of attraction—which keep them herded together in the cloud—and gravity, which pulls them down. When the drops are small, their surface area is huge compared to volume; electrical (molecular) forces rule and the drops stay suspended in midair. Once the drops get big enough, however, gravity always wins.

Pint-size objects barely feel gravity—a force that [10] only makes itself felt on large scales. The electrical forces that hold molecules together are trillions of times stronger. That's why even the slightest bit of electrical static in the air can make your hair stand on end.

These electrical forces would present major problems to flea-size Superman. For one thing, he'd have a hard time flying faster than a speeding bullet, because the air would be a thick soup of sticky molecules grasping him from all directions; it would be like swimming through molasses.

Flies have no problem walking on the ceiling because the molecular glue that holds their feet to the moldings is stronger than the puny weight pulling them down. The electrical pull of water, however, attracts the insects like magnets. As Haldane points out, the electrical attraction of water molecules makes going for a drink a dangerous endeavor for an insect. A bug leaning over a puddle to take a sip of water would be in the same position as a person leaning out over a cliff to pluck a berry off a bush.

Water is one of the stickiest substances around. A person coming out of the shower carries about a pound of extra weight, scarcely a burden. But a mouse coming out of the shower would have to lift its weight in water, according to Haldane. For a fly, water is as powerful as flypaper; once it gets wet, it's stuck for life. That's one reason, writes Haldane, that most insects have a long proboscis.

In fact, once you get down to bug size, almost everything is different. An ant-size person could never write a book: the keys to an ant-size typewriter would stick together; so would the pages of a manuscript. An ant couldn't build a fire because the smallest possible flame is larger than its body.

1. According to Exploratorium physicist Tom Humphrey, all animals jump to the same height, roughly speaking. Both fleas and humans can jump about a meter off the ground—an interesting invariant.

Shrinking down to atom size alters reality beyond recognition, opening doors into new and wholly unexpected vistas. Atom-size things do not behave like molecule-size things or human-size things. Atomic particles are ruled by the probabilistic laws of quantum mechanics. Physicists have to be very clever to lure these quantum mechanical attributes out in the open, because they simply don't exist on the scales of human instrumentation. We do not perceive that energy comes in precisely defined clumps or that clouds of electrons buzz around atoms in a permanent state of probabilistic uncertainty. These behaviors become perceptible macroscopically only in exotic situations—for example, superconductivity—a superordered state where pairs of loose electrons in a material line up like a row of Rockettes. With electrons moving in lockstep, electricity can flow through superconductors without resistance.

Scale up to molecule-size matter, and electrical forces take over; scale up further and gravity rules. As Philip and Phylis Morrison point out in the classic *Powers of Ten,* if you stick your hand in a sugar bowl, your fingers will emerge covered with tiny grains that stick to them due to electrical forces. However, if you stick your hand into a bowl of sugar cubes, you would be very surprised if a cube stuck to your fingers—unless you purposely set out to grasp one.

We know that gravity takes over in large-scale matters because everything in the universe larger than an asteroid is round or roundish—the result of gravity pulling matter in toward a common center. Everyday objects like houses and mountains come in every old shape, but mountains can only get so high before gravity pulls them down. They can get larger on Mars because gravity is less. Large things lose their rough edges in the fight against gravity. "No such thing as a teacup the diameter of Jupiter is possible in our world," say the Morrisons. As a teacup grew to Jupiter size, its handle and sides would be pulled into the center by the planet's huge gravity until it resembled a sphere.

Add more matter still, and the squeeze of gravity ignites nuclear fires; stars exist in a continual tug-of-war between gravitational collapse and the outward pressure of nuclear fire. Over time, gravity wins again. A giant star eventually collapses into a black hole. It doesn't matter whether the star had planets orbiting its periphery or what globs of gas and dust went into making the star in the first place. Gravity is very democratic. Anything can grow up to be a black hole.

Even time ticks faster in the universe of the small. Small animals move faster, metabolize food faster (and eat more); their hearts beat faster; their life spans are short. In his book *About Time,* Paul Davis raises the interesting question: Does the life of a mouse feel shorter to a mouse than our life feels to us?

Biologist Stephen Jay Gould has answered this question in the negative. "Small mammals tick fast, burn rapidly, and live for a short time; large mammals live long at a stately pace. Measured by their own internal clocks, mammals of different sizes tend to live for the same amount of time."

We all march to our own metronomes. Yet Davis suggests that all life shares the same beat because all life on Earth relies on chemical reactions—and chemical reactions take place in a sharply limited frame of time. In physicist Robert Forward's science fiction saga *Dragon's Egg,* creatures living on a neutron star are fueled by nuclear reactions; on their world, everything takes place millions of times faster. Many generations could be born and die before a minute passes on Earth.

And think how Earth would seem if we could slow our metabolism down. If our time ticked slowly enough, we could watch mountains grow and continental plates shift and come crashing together. The heavens would be bursting with supernovas, and comets would come smashing onto our shores with the regularity of shooting stars. Every day would be the Fourth of July.

An artist friend likes to imagine that if we could stand back far enough from Earth, but still see people, we would see enormous waves sweeping the globe every morning as people stood up from bed, and another huge wave of toothbrushing as people got ready to bed down for the night—one time zone after another, a tide of toothbrushing waxing and waning, following the shadow of the Sun across the land.

We miss a great deal because we perceive only things on our own scale. Exploring the invisible worlds beneath our skin can be a terrifying experience. I know because I tried it with a flexible microscope attached to a video camera on display at the Exploratorium in San Francisco. The skin on your arm reveals a dizzy landscape of nicks, creases, folds, and dewy transparent hairs the size of redwood trees—all embedded with giant boulders of dirt. Whiskers and eyelashes are disgusting—mascara dripping off like mud on a dog's tail. It is rather overwhelming to look through your own skin at blood cells coursing through capillaries. It's like looking at yourself without clothes. We forget the extent to which our view of the world is airbrushed, that we see things through a shroud of size, a blissfully out-of-focus blur.

An even more powerful microscope would reveal all the creatures that live on your face, dangling from tiny hairs or hiding out in your eyelashes. Not to mention the billions that share your bed every night and nest in your dish towels. How many bacteria can stand on the pointy end of a pin? You don't want to know.[2]

We're so hung up on our own scale of life that we miss most of life's diversity, says Berkeley microbiologist Norman Pace. "Who's in the ocean? People think of whales and seals, but 90 percent of organisms in the ocean are less than two micrometers."

In their enchanting journey *Microcosmos,* microbiologist Lynn Margulis and Dorion Sagan point out the fallacy of thinking that large beings are somehow supreme. Billions of years before creatures composed of cells with nuclei (like ourselves) appeared on Earth, simple bacteria transformed the surface of the planet and invented many high-tech processes that humans are still trying to understand—including the transformation of sunlight into energy with close to a 100 percent efficiency (green plants do it all the time). Indeed, they point out that fully 10 percent of our body weight (minus the water) consists of bacteria—most of which we couldn't live without.

Zoom in smaller than life-size, and solid tables become airy expanses of space, with an occasional nut of an atomic nucleus lost in the center, surrounded by furious clouds of electrons. As you zoom in, or out, the world looks simple, then complex, then simple again. Earth from far enough away would be a small blue dot; come in closer and you see weather patterns and ocean; closer still and humanity comes into view; closer still and it all fades away, and you're back inside the landscape of matter—mostly empty space.

So complexity, too, changes with scale. Is an egg complex? On the outside, it's a plain enough oval, like Jupiter's giant red spot. On the inside, it's white and yolk and blood vessels and DNA and squawking and pecking order and potential chocolate mousse or crème caramel.

The universe of the extremely small is so strange and rich that we can't begin to grasp it. No one said it better than Erwin Schrödinger himself:

> As our mental eye penetrates into smaller and smaller distances and shorter and shorter times, we find nature behaving so entirely differently from what we observe in visible and palpable bodies of our surroundings that no model shaped after our large-scale experiences can ever be "true." A complete satisfactory model of this type is not only practically inaccessible, but not even thinkable. Or, to be precise, we can, of course, think of it, but however we think it, it is wrong; not perhaps quite as meaningless as a "triangular circle," but more so than a "winged lion." ○

2. For an eye-opening view, read *The Secret House,* by David Bodanis.

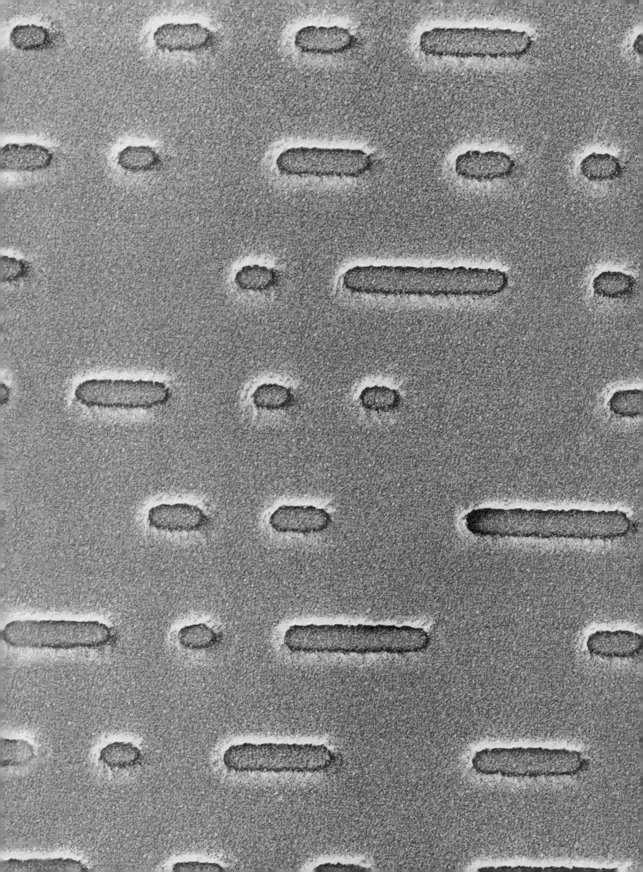

COMPACT DISC

George M. Whitesides

THESE PITS ARE BRAILLE FOR LIGHT.

The simplest alphabet is "binary code"—dots and spaces (the absence of dots), which can serve for all the letters and numbers—1 or 0, "yes" or "no." The binary code's combinations of 1 and 0 can spell out thought as clearly as the most elegant calligraphy.

The combination of eye and brain with which we read our world is a most remarkable system, capable of astonishing feats of recognition. Faces, moods, coming changes in the weather: a glimpse recognizes all. By comparison, a CD player is a one-eyed robot working in the dark with a head lamp: a simple red light illuminates the spinning disc; a simple, unblinking eye looks for reflected red light. If there is no pit, the light reflects; if there is one, it does not. Any information that can be coded by letters or numbers can be translated into the 1 and 0 of the binary code. Each letter and number is represented by a sequence of bits: the number "5" is "101" in binary. *The Well-Tempered Clavier* becomes a numerical record of the amplitude of the pressure exerted by the sound waves during performance on the recording microphone.

The challenge in a simple job is to do it fast, without making mistakes. CD players succeed. A beam illuminates the disc, and a photoreceptor registers the information faster than any human eye can appreciate, but there is no appreciation of style: just 1001011011001. *The Well-Tempered Clavier* and Led Zeppelin are both ruby glitters from a spinning disc. The light brushes the pits with the gentlest of fingers, and with no physical contact there is no wear.

Our appetite for stored information is voracious and largely unconscious. Learning how to make the pits smaller, and how to generate blue light rather than red (blue light has a shorter wavelength than red and needs a smaller pit as a mirror) are presently problems in the technology of storing information so that it can be read optically. By simply changing from red to blue light to read the disc, and by decreasing the spacing between the pits accordingly, it will be possible to store four times as much information per disc. ○

STEVEN MILLHAUSER

Steven Millhauser (b. 1943) is the author of three volumes of short stories, one collection of novellas, and four novels, including *Martin Dressler* (1996), which won the Pulitzer Prize for fiction in 1997. A graduate of Columbia College and Brown University, Millhauser lives in Saratoga Springs, New York, and is a professor of English at Skidmore College. "The Fascination of the Miniature" first appeared in the Summer 1983 issue of the quarterly magazine *Grand Street*.

TOM FRIEDMAN

Tom Friedman (b. 1965) carved his image into an aspirin tablet in this unusual twist on the self-portrait. In his sculptures and site-specific pieces, Friedman often plays with viewers' assumptions about scale. He might juxtapose his miniature self-portrait, for example, against *Total,* a three-foot box of Total cereal constructed out of tiny squares of regular-sized cereal boxes, or *Everything (1992–95),* a three-year-long project in which he copied onto a single piece of paper, a square yard in size, every entry in the *American Heritage Dictionary*. In all cases, Friedman's use of ordinary materials (e.g., sugar cubes, construction paper, spaghetti, and foam core) inspires a sense of fascination with the mundane. Friedman lives and works in Massachusetts.

VOYAGER 1

NASA's *Voyager 1* spacecraft was approximately 6.4 billion kilometers (4 billion miles) away when it took this photograph of the Earth on February 14, 1990. The Earth appears as only a small speck centered in a strip of light. In the original caption NASA wrote, "in this image the Earth is a mere point of light, a crescent only 0.12 pixel in size. Our planet was caught in the center of one of the scattered light rays resulting from taking the image so close to the sun." To view other images taken by NASA expeditions, visit NASA's Planetary Photojournal web site at photojournal.jpl.nasa.gov.

CARL SAGAN

American astronomer, educator, and author Carl Sagan (1934–1996) is perhaps best known for his award-winning PBS series *Cosmos*, in which he inspired a sense of wonder and excitement about his favorite subjects: the origins of life and the search for intelligent life in the universe.

In addition to holding a 25-year professorship at Cornell University, Sagan was the author of numerous scientific papers, popular articles, and books, including *Pale Blue Dot: A Vision of the Human Future in Space* (1994) and *The Dragons of Eden* (1977), for which he won the Pulitzer Prize in 1978. In the 1950s Sagan began serving as a consultant and adviser to NASA. He contributed to the Mariner, Viking, Voyager, and Galileo expeditions. "Reflections on a Mote of Dust" is an excerpt from a commencement address that Sagan delivered on May 11, 1996; it was inspired by *Pale Blue Dot*, an image of the earth taken by the *Voyager 1* spacecraft.

DAVID SCHARF

David Scharf's remarkable photographs of a kitchen scouring pad can be found among the more than 124,000 images available through the Science Photo Library, one of the world's largest photo agencies specializing in science. With contributors worldwide, the Science Photo Library aims "to make science imagery more accessible to the media and to increase public awareness of the wonders of science and nature."

K. C. COLE

K. C. Cole has commented that her "writing career has changed gear many times." After graduating from Columbia University, she was pursuing an interest in Eastern European affairs when she "stumbled upon the Exploratorium"—a hands-on science museum in San Francisco—and soon thereafter began a career as a science and health writer. "A Matter of Scale" is one of a series of essays in *The Universe and the Teacup: The Mathematics of Truth and Beauty* (1998), Cole's book on the relevance of mathematics to everyday life and on the ways in which math provides insight into social, political, and natural phenomena as diverse as calculating the risks of smoking to understanding election outcomes. Awarded the American Institute of Physics Award for Best Science Writer in 1995, Cole writes regularly on science for the *Los Angeles Times*.

HAROLD EDGERTON

Harold Edgerton (1903–1990) developed and popularized the use of the stroboscope, a controlled pulsating light that enables a camera to "freeze" precise moments on film. The technology he developed while teaching at the Massachusetts Institute of Technology found applications in countless fields of science and industry, but he may be most famous for creating artistic images such as this milk drop (1938).

**FELICE FRANKEL AND
GEORGE M. WHITESIDES**

A Guggenheim fellow, Felice
Frankel is an artist-in-residence
and research scientist at the
Massachusetts Institute of Technology. Her work in scientific
imaging and visual expression
has earned funding from the
National Science Foundation as
well as awards from the National
Endowment for the Arts and
several foundations. She is author of the award-winning book
*Modern Landscape Architecture:
Redefining the Garden* (1991).

George M. Whitesides is
Mallinckrodt Professor of Chemistry at Harvard University as
well as a member of the National
Academy of Sciences and the
American Academy of Arts and
Sciences. Author of more than
500 research and technical
articles and numerous scholarly
books, Whitesides continues to
teach—and take great pleasure
in—introductory courses in molecular biology and chemistry.

CHUCK CLOSE

Since the 1970s, Chuck Close
has worked with a painting style
known as photorealism or super-
realism, which attempts to re-
create in paint the aesthetic and
representational experience of
photography. Close paints enormous canvases of people's faces
that duplicate photographic
images in precise detail, such
as *Self-Portrait*.

Born in Monroe, Washington,
in 1940, Close has lived in New
York since 1967. In December
1988 he became paralyzed below
his shoulders after a spinal artery
suddenly collapsed, but he continues to paint colossal and powerful portraits using a brush held
in his mouth.

SEEING

1. A masterful exercise in observation and inference about aspects of the natural world we normally cannot see, K. C. Cole's essay stimulates and sustains our interest in the most common creatures and daily events. Reread Cole's essay and identify one or two paragraphs that you think are especially effective. What techniques does she use to capture your attention in these paragraphs? What is memorable and convincing about them? What does Cole identify that is so "magically seductive" about observing "a world where everything measures much bigger or smaller than ourselves" (para. 1)?

2. Examine the visual images included in this section: Felice Frankel's photograph of a compact disc; Harold Edgerton's photograph *Milk Drop Coronet*; David Scharf's image of a kitchen scouring pad; and Chuck Close's *Self-Portrait*. Where does your eye linger as you view each image? Comment on the role(s) that color, light, and shadow play in enhancing the effects of the image. Describe your overall impression of each image. How would you describe each one to someone who has never seen these images before? Try writing a paragraph or two about two images. Swap drafts with one or more students. How are your drafts different?

WRITING

1. Early in Cole's essay "A Matter of Scale," when she speaks of the difference scale can make in the natural world, she declares that "quantitative changes can make huge qualitative differences" (para. 2). Cole then offers compelling and convincing examples to demonstrate this assertion. As you reflect on your own experience and that of people you know, to what extent do you think that the same, or a similar, assertion can be made about aspects of the ordinary world? Draft an essay that seeks to validate or challenge the reasonableness of Cole's assertion—if it were applied to the scale of our everyday lives. Following her lead, reinforce each assertion you make with a detailed analysis of examples that your readers will find compelling and convincing.

2. Review the images gathered in "Seeing Is Believing." Which one interests you most? Why? What range of associations and metaphors does this image elicit from you? Using George Whitesides's *Compact Disc* as a model, draft an essay in which you use metaphor(s) to describe what you imagine to be the process involved in creating the image. What metaphors and other figurative language can you summon to describe this process?

Coming to Terms with Place

Chapter 2
Coming to Terms with Place

"Place" is a fundamental component of everyday life, the "where" that locates each event and experience in our lives. Place in this sense evokes public identity, the often easily recognized characteristics of behavior that inform our accents, our clothes, and our behavior.

"Where are you from?" This question invariably arises when two Americans meet for the first time—especially when traveling. "I'm from the South," "I'm from L.A.," "I'm from Cody, Wyoming"—each response conjures different cultural assumptions and associations. In fact, the meaning we invest in the responses we hear suggests that growing up in a particular place leaves a deep, if not indelible, mark on a person's character. As the popular saying goes, "You

Coca-Cola Company, **Advertisement**

can take the kid out of Brooklyn, but you can't take Brooklyn out of the kid."
Think of a place—a town, a city, or America itself, for example. If asked to
describe that place, what comes immediately to mind: people? buildings?
landscapes? landmarks? a "feeling"? What impact have the events of
September 11, 2001, had on people's awareness of "America" as a place?
Americans often classify people by where they are from, and in this we
are encouraged by film and television; just think of *Nashville, Chinatown,
L.A. Confidential, Beverly Hills 90210, Cheers, Seinfeld.*

Even as Americans invest meaning in geographical roots, fewer of us
remain in the same place for long. According to the U.S. Census Bureau,
16 percent of the American public moved between March 1996 and March

*It's a nice place to
visit, but I wouldn't
want to live there.*
*– Anonymous
American saying*

1997. Indeed, answering the question "Where are you from?" has become increasingly difficult for many Americans, given the range of places where they have lived. Airplane travel, mass transit, and freeways reduce the distances between places. And when we arrive at our destinations, we realize that American places look increasingly alike. Few communities across the nation are without familiar fast-food chains and shopping malls. Likewise, the borders between regions continue to dissolve. Consider the number of restaurants in different parts of the country, each boasting "authentic" regional cuisine. No matter where you find yourself, you can probably enjoy "down-home" Cajun cooking, Chicago pizza, New York bagels, or New England clam chowder.

Our sense of place is no longer limited to the physical realm. The Internet now offers its own electronic landscape, a virtual world in which we can frequent certain "spots" and form communities on particular "sites." Advertisers try to convince us that we can reach any place in the real or virtual world within seconds, without leaving "the privacy of your own home."

In contemporary American culture, the centuries-old distinctions between "place" and "space" seem to be disappearing. Jerry Brown, a former governor of California, candidate for president, and now mayor of Oakland, California, recently drew the following distinction between "place" and "space":

> People don't live in place, they live in space. The media used to accuse me of that—living in space. But it wasn't true. Now too many people just live in their minds, not in communities. They garage themselves in their homes and live in market space. It's an alienated way for human beings to live. It's the difference between a native and an immigrant. A native lives in place, not space.

For most people, coming to terms with place is ultimately a personal matter: It can mean the smell of chicken roasting in the oven, the sound of traffic or a certain song, the sight of a familiar stretch of land. In many respects, place is also about relationships, both (1) among people, and (2) between us and our experiences and associations with a particular time and space.

There are things you just can't do in life. You can't beat the phone company . . . and you can't go home again.
– Bill Bryson, 1999

The essays and images in this chapter represent an attempt to map out the ways we connect socially and culturally with others—and to understand how geographical location, or a sense of place, shapes our outlook on the world and who we are.

COCA-COLA

When Dr. John Stith Pemberton of Atlanta, Georgia, brewed a batch of fountain syrup in his backyard in 1886, he sold the drink, which he called Coca-Cola, at the drugstore soda fountain. An immediate success, it began to sell at the rate of nine drinks per day. Today, Coca-Cola sells one billion soft drinks daily in over two hundred countries. Defining the presence of American commerce wherever it is seen, the Coca-Cola trademark is the most recognized corporate logo in the world.

Nearly all sub-Saharan African nations sell Coca-Cola. France and Belgium boast the largest European consumption, and the Japanese market grows annually, fueled in part by the presence of 930,000 vending machines dispensing the soft drink. With headquarters in Atlanta, the Coca-Cola Company now owns a wide range of other industries. Because the soft drink is made and bottled in the countries where it is consumed, the recipe for Coca-Cola varies slightly by region. The exact flavorings used are a closely guarded secret.

The logo's distinctive white script was custom designed in 1894 for one of the company's early owners. The letter forms were created with the designer's conviction that "the large C's would look well in advertising." From electric billboards in San Francisco to the tiniest storefronts of Katmandu, the symbol of Coca-Cola remains potent.

SEEING

1. What are the effects of the advertiser's emphasis on the virtues of America as a place rather than the virtues of the soft drink? What associations is the ad encouraging between place and product? Comment on the effectiveness of this promotional strategy. What details in the language of the text enable you to determine the audience for this advertisement? What kind of person is addressed in this way? What words and phrases can you identify in the ad that indicate the probable age group, level of education, socioeconomic background, and political beliefs of the audience?

2. Reread the paragraph beginning "In fact, all of the good things in this country are real." What point(s) is the copywriter making here? What response does he or she elicit by referring to other Coca-Cola advertisements? What is meant by "looking up" in the last line? How is this phrase literally and figuratively related to Coca-Cola?

WRITING

1. Imagine that you have been asked to rewrite this advertisement for an audience of senior citizens. Please keep in mind that the ad should seek to capitalize on the traditional American values and ideals associated with place. What changes would you make in the language of the ad? in its use and placement of visual material and in its overall layout? Prepare a new draft of the language of the ad, along with a rough sketch of its layout.

2. Consider the ways in which a sense of place is used in television advertising to sell certain products. Choose one such advertisement, and write an analytical essay in which you evaluate the strategies the advertiser uses to promote the product by evoking a sense of place. Because you will be analyzing a television commercial (which may prove difficult to record for the purpose of studying it), you might want to examine the award-winning commercials that are gathered into video collections—such as the Clio Awards.

The process of arranging printed or graphic material on a page; the overall design of a page, including such elements as type size, typeface, titles, and page numbers.

Edward Hopper, **House by the Railroad**, 1925

EDWARD HOPPER AND THE
HOUSE BY THE RAILROAD (1925)
Edward Hirsch

Out here in the exact middle of the day,
This strange, gawky house has the expression
Of someone being stared at, someone holding
His breath underwater, hushed and expectant;

This house is ashamed of itself, ashamed   5
Of its fantastic mansard rooftop
And its pseudo-Gothic porch, ashamed
Of its shoulders and large, awkward hands.

But the man behind the easel is relentless;
He is as brutal as sunlight, and believes   10
The house must have done something horrible
To the people who once lived here

Because now it is so desperately empty,
It must have done something to the sky
Because the sky, too, is utterly vacant   15
And devoid of meaning. There are no

Trees or shrubs anywhere—the house
Must have done something against the earth.
All that is present is a single pair of tracks
Straightening into the distance. No trains pass.   20

Now the stranger returns to this place daily
Until the house begins to suspect
That the man, too, is desolate, desolate
And even ashamed. Soon the house starts

To stare frankly at the man. And somehow   25
The empty white canvas slowly takes on
The expression of someone who is unnerved,
Someone holding his breath underwater.

And then one day the man simply disappears.
He is a last afternoon shadow moving   30
Across the tracks, making its way
Through the vast, darkening fields.

This man will paint other abandoned mansions,
And faded cafeteria windows, and poorly lettered
Storefronts on the edges of small towns.   35
Always they will have this same expression.

The utterly naked look of someone
Being stared at, someone American and gawky,
Someone who is about to be left alone
Again, and can no longer stand it.   40

EDWARD HOPPER

Edward Hopper's signature vision is expressed in virtually all his paintings, which capture a wide array of American scenes ranging from rural landscapes and seascapes to street scenes, isolated buildings, and domestic interiors. Hopper masterfully expressed the isolation, boredom, and vacuity of modern life. Even his most colorful, luminous scenes are stripped of joy through an extreme spareness of composition and detail. His Depression-era work in particular evokes the mood of that time. However, Hopper claimed that his work expressed personal rather than national truths: "I don't think I ever tried to paint the American scene," he once said; "I'm trying to paint myself."

Born in 1882, Hopper grew up in Nyack, New York, and received his training in New York City and in Europe. He was still a young man when his work was included in the Armory Show of 1913, a New York City exhibition that featured what would become known as modernist paintings. But in spite of success among critics he had to work as a commercial illustrator in order to support himself. His career turned around when, in his forties, he married the artist Josephine Nivison (1883–1968). Through several decades of an emotionally turbulent but artistically productive marriage, Hopper created his most memorable paintings. He died in 1967.

EDWARD HIRSCH

The poet, critic, and teacher Edward Hirsch was born in 1950 in Chicago and attended Grinnell College and the University of Pennsylvania. Currently a professor of creative writing at the University of Houston, Hirsch has published poems and reviews in *The New Yorker, The Nation,* and the *New York Times Book Review,* among other leading journals. He has also published five volumes of poetry, including *Wild Gratitude* (1986), which won the National Book Critics Award, and *On Love* (1998). His most recent publication, *The Demon and the Angel* (2002), is a guide to the sources of inspiration for writers, poets, painters, and musicians. He has received numerous awards, including a MacArthur Foundation "genius" award and fellowships from the Guggenheim Foundation.

Hirsch also edited *Transforming Vision: Writers on Art* (1994), a book in which a number of prominent writers visit the Art Institute of Chicago and respond to a painting, sculpture, or photograph they saw there. Hirsch argues that "the proper response to a work of visual art may well be an ode or an elegy, a meditative lyric, a lyrical meditation" because poetic descriptions of art "teach us to look and look again more closely" and "dramatize with great intensity the actual experience of encounter." The poem "Edward Hopper and the House by the Railroad (1925)" dramatizes his own encounter with Hopper's famous painting.

SEEING

1. As you examine Edward Hopper's *House by the Railroad*, where does he direct your attention? What details do you notice about the house, its structure, and its relation to the railroad track and the sky? Where does your eye linger as you study the painting more carefully? How does each aspect of its presentation reinforce the overall effect of the painting?

2. What features of Hopper's painting does Edward Hirsch focus on in his poem? What effects does Hirsch create through *personification* of the house? Explain how his use of repetition (of words, phrases, and structural elements) reinforces—or detracts from—the overall impression or mood created in the poem. In what ways does Hirsch's poem change or enhance your initial reactions to Hopper's painting?

Often used as a poetic device, personifying means giving human qualities to an object or an idea.

WRITING

1. Write a page—in any form you prefer—in which you dramatize *your* encounter with Hopper's *House by the Railroad*. Do you agree with Hirsch that the house has the look of "someone American and gawky" (l. 38)?

2. Reread "Edward Hopper and the House by the Railroad (1925)" several times, until you feel comfortable describing and characterizing Hirsch's shifts in subject and tone. Based on your rereading of the poem, would you agree —or disagree—with the assertion that Hirsch seems more interested in Hopper the artist than in the scene he paints? How is the artist characterized in the poem? With what effects? At what point do the terms used to characterize house and artist seem to merge? What characteristics do the house and the artist share? What overall impression does Hirsch create in this comparison? Write the first draft of a comparative essay in which you use evidence from the poem and the painting to validate your own response to the assertion that Hirsch is far more interested in Hopper as artist than in the scene he paints.

In short stories and novels, Eudora Welty explored the frailty and strength of human character in her native Mississippi. A keen observer of behavior and social relations, she crafted fictional worlds that evoke compelling portraits of people and places. Born in Jackson in 1909, Welty published her first story in 1936. Since that time she received many awards, including a Pulitzer Prize for the novel *The Optimist's Daughter* (1972), the American Book Award for *The Collected Stories of Eudora Welty* (1980), and the National Book Critics Circle Award for her autobiographical essays in *One Writer's Beginnings* (1984). Welty died in 2001.

Like much of Welty's fiction, "The Little Store" (1975) draws on personal experience. Remembering experience, she said, helped her craft fiction out of "the *whole* fund of my feelings, my responses to the real experiences of my own life, to the relationships that formed and changed it, that I have given most of myself to."

The Little Store

Eudora Welty

TWO BLOCKS AWAY FROM THE MISSISSIPPI STATE Capitol, and on the same street with it, where our house was when I was a child growing up in Jackson, it was possible to have a little pasture behind your backyard where you could keep a Jersey cow, which we did. My mother herself milked her. A thrifty homemaker, wife, mother of three, she also did all her own cooking. And as far as I can recall, she never set foot inside a grocery store. It wasn't necessary.

For her regular needs, she stood at the telephone in our front hall and consulted with Mr. Lemly, of Lemly's Market and Grocery downtown, who took her order and sent it out on his next delivery. And since Jackson at the heart of it was still within very near reach of the open country, the blackberry lady clanged on her bucket with a quart measure at your front door in June without fail, the watermelon man rolled up to your house exactly on time for the Fourth of July, and down through the summer, the quiet of the early-morning streets was pierced by the calls of farmers driving in with their plenty. One brought his with a song, so plaintive we would sing it with him:

> "Milk, milk,
> Buttermilk,
> Snap beans—butterbeans—
> Tender okra—fresh greens . . .
> And buttermilk."

My mother considered herself pretty well prepared in her kitchen and pantry for any emergency that, in her words, might choose to present itself. But if she should, all of a sudden, need another lemon or find she was out of bread, all she had to do was call out, "Quick! Who'd like to run to the Little Store for me?"

I would.

She'd count out the change into my hand, and I was away. I'll bet the nickel that would be left over that all over the country, for those of my day, the neighborhood grocery played a similar part in our growing up.

Our store had its name—it was that of the grocer who owned it, whom I'll call Mr. Sessions—but "the Little Store" is what we called it at home. It was a block down our street toward the capitol and half a block further, around the corner, toward the cemetery. I knew even the sidewalk to it as well as I knew my own skin. I'd skipped my jumping-rope up and down it, hopped its length through mazes of hopscotch, played jacks in its islands of shade, serpentined along it on my Princess bicycle, skated it backward and forward. In the twilight I had dragged my steamboat by its string (this was homemade out of every new shoebox, with candle in the bottom lighted and shining through colored tissue paper pasted over windows scissored out in the shapes of the sun, moon and stars) across every crack of the walk without letting it bump or catch fire. I'd "played out" on that street after supper with my brothers and friends as long as "first-dark" lasted; I'd caught its lightning bugs. On the first Armistice Day (and this will set the time I'm speaking of) we made our own parade down that walk on a single velocipede—my brother pedaling, our little brother riding the handlebars, and myself standing on the back, all with arms wide, flying flags in each hand. (My father snapped that picture as we raced by. It came out blurred.)

As I set forth for the Little Store, a tune would float toward me from the house where there lived three sisters, girls in their teens, who ratted their hair over their ears, wore headbands like gladiators, and were considered to be very popular. They practiced for this in the daytime; they'd wind up the Victrola, leave the same record on they'd played before, and you'd see them bobbing past their dining-room windows while they danced with each other. Being three, they could go all day, cutting in:

> "Everybody ought to know-oh
> How to do the Tickle-Toe
>   (how to do the Tickle-Toe)"—

They sang it and danced to it, and as I went by to the same song, I believed it.

A little further on, across the street, was the house where the principal of our grade school lived—lived on, even while we were having vacation. What if she would come out? She would halt me in my tracks—she had a very carrying and well-known voice in Jackson, where she'd taught almost everybody—saying, "Eudora Alice Welty, spell OBLIGE." OBLIGE was the word that she of course knew had kept me from making 100 on my spelling exam. She'd make me miss it again now, by boring her eyes through me from across the street. This was my vacation fantasy, one good way to scare myself on the way to the store.

Down near the corner waited the house of a little boy named Lindsey. The sidewalk here was old brick, which the roots of a giant chinaberry had humped up and tilted this way and that. On skates, you took it fast, in a series of skittering hops, trying not to touch ground anywhere. If the chinaberries had fallen and rolled in the cracks, it was like skating through a whole shooting match of marbles. I crossed my fingers that Lindsey wouldn't be looking.

During the big flu epidemic he and I, as it happened, were being nursed through our sieges at the same time. I'd hear my father and mother murmuring to each other, at the end of a long day, "And I wonder how poor little *Lindsey* got along today?" Just as, down the street, he no doubt would have to hear his family saying, "And I wonder how is poor *Eudora* by now?" I got the idea that a choice was going to be made soon between poor little Lindsey and poor Eudora, and I came up with a funny poem. I wasn't prepared for it when my father told me it wasn't funny and my mother cried that if I couldn't be ashamed for myself, she'd have to be ashamed for me:

> There was a little boy and his name was Lindsey.
> He went to heaven with the influinzy.

He didn't, he survived it, poem and all, the same as I did. But his chinaberries could have brought me down in my skates in a flying act of contrition before his eyes, looking pretty funny myself, right in front of his house. *(caption) unforgetable*

Setting out in this world, a child feels so indelible. He only comes to find out later that it's all the others along his way who are making themselves indelible to him.

Our Little Store rose right up from the sidewalk; standing in a street of family houses, it alone hadn't any yard in front, any tree or flowerbed. It was a plain frame building covered over with brick. Above the door, a little railed porch ran across on an upstairs level and four windows with shades were looking out. But I didn't catch on to those.

Running in out of the sun, you met what seemed total obscurity inside. There were almost tangible smells—licorice recently sucked in a child's cheek, dill-pickle brine that had leaked through a paper sack in a fresh trail across the wooden floor, ammonia-loaded ice that had been hoisted from wet croker sacks and slammed into the icebox with its sweet butter at the door, and perhaps the smell of still-untrapped mice.

Then through the motes of cracker dust, cornmeal dust, the Gold Dust of the Gold Dust Twins that the floor had been swept out with, the realities emerged. Shelves climbed to high reach all the way around, set out with not too much of any one thing but a lot of things—lard, molasses, vinegar, starch, matches, kerosene, Octagon soap (about a year's worth of octagon-shaped coupons cut out and saved brought a signet ring addressed to you in the mail. Furthermore, when the postman arrived at your door, he blew a whistle). It was up to you to remember what you came for, while your eye traveled from cans of sardines to ice cream salt to harmonicas to flypaper (over your head, batting around on a thread beneath the blades of the ceiling fan, stuck with its testimonial catch).

Its confusion may have been in the eye of its beholder. Enchantment is cast upon you by all those things you weren't supposed to have need for, it lures you close to wooden tops you'd outgrown, boy's marbles and agates in little net pouches, small rubber balls that wouldn't bounce straight, frazzly kitestring, clay bubble-pipes that would snap off in your teeth, the stiffest scissors. *(with a caption to view, considered)* You could contemplate those long narrow boxes of sparklers gathering dust while you waited for it to be the Fourth of July or Christmas, and noisemakers in the shape of tin frogs for somebody's birthday party you hadn't been invited to yet, and see that they were all marvelous.

You might not have even looked for Mr. Sessions when he came around his store cheese (as big as a doll's house) and in front of the counter looking for you. When you'd finally asked him for, and received from him in its paper bag, whatever single thing it was that you had been sent for, the nickel that was left over was yours to spend.

Down at a child's eye level, inside those glass jars with mouths in their sides through which the grocer could run his scoop or a child's hand might be invited to reach for a choice, were wineballs, all-day suckers, gumdrops, peppermints. Making a row under the glass of a counter were the Tootsie Rolls, Hershey Bars, Goo-Goo Clusters, Baby Ruths. And whatever was the name of those pastilles that came stacked in a cardboard cylinder with a cardboard lid? They were thin and dry, about the size of tiddly-winks, and in the shape of twisted rosettes. A kind of chocolate dust came out with them when you shook them out in your hand. Were they chocolate? I'd say rather they were brown. They didn't taste of anything at all, unless it was wood. Their attraction was the number you got for a nickel.

Making up your mind, you circled the store around and around, around the pickle barrel, around the tower of Cracker Jack boxes; Mr. Sessions had built it for us himself on top of a packing case, like a house of cards.

If it seemed too hot for Cracker Jacks, I might get a cold drink. Mr. Sessions might have already stationed himself by the cold-drinks barrel, like a mind reader. Deep in ice water that looked black as ink, murky shapes that would come up as Coca-Colas, Orange Crushes, and various flavors of pop, were all swimming around together. When you gave the word, Mr. Sessions plunged his bare arm in to the elbow and fished out your choice, first try. I favored a locally bottled concoction called Lake's Celery. (What else could it be called? It was made by a Mr. Lake out of celery. It was a popular drink here for years but was not known universally, as I found out when I arrived in New York and ordered one in the Astor bar.) You drank on the premises, with feet set wide apart to miss the drip, and gave him back his bottle.

But he didn't hurry you off. A standing scales was by the door, with a stack of iron weights and a brass slide on the balance arm, that would weigh you up to three hundred pounds. Mr. Sessions, whose hands were gentle and smelled of carbolic, would lift you up and set your feet on the platform, hold your loaf of bread for you, and taking his time while you stood still for him, he would make certain of what you weighed today. He could even remember what you weighed the last time, so you could subtract and announce how much you'd gained. That was goodbye.

Is there always a hard way to go home? From the Little Store, you could go partway through the sewer. If your brothers had called you a scarecat, then across the next street beyond the Little Store, it was possible to enter this sewer by passing through a privet hedge, climbing down into the bed of a creek, and going into its mouth on your knees. The sewer—it might have been no more than a "storm sewer"—came out and emptied here, where Town Creek, a sandy, most often shallow little stream that ambled through Jackson on its way to the Pearl River, ran along the edge of the cemetery. You could go in darkness through this tunnel to where you next saw light (if you ever did) and climb out through the culvert at your own street corner.

I was a scarecat, all right, but I was a reader with my own refuge in storybooks. Making my way under

the sidewalk, under the street and the streetcar track, under the Little Store, down there in the wet dark by myself, I could be Persephone entering into my six-month sojourn underground—though I didn't suppose Persephone had to crawl, hanging onto a loaf of bread, and come out through the teeth of an iron grating. Mother Ceres would indeed be wondering where she could find me, and mad when she knew. "Now am I going to have to start marching to the Little Store for myself?"

I couldn't picture it. Indeed, I'm unable today to picture the Little Store with a grown person in it, except for Mr. Sessions and the lady who helped him, who belonged there. We children thought it was ours. The happiness of errands was in part that of running for the moment away from home, a free spirit. I believed the Little Store to be a center of the outside world, and hence of happiness—as I believed what I found in the Cracker Jack box to be a genuine prize, which was as simply as I believed in the Golden Fleece.

But a day came when I ran to the store to discover, sitting on the front step, a grown person, after all— more than a grown person. It was the Monkey Man, together with his monkey. His grinding-organ was lowered to the step beside him. In my whole life so far, I must have laid eyes on the Monkey Man no more than five or six times. An itinerant of rare and wayward appearances, he was not punctual like the Gipsies, who every year with the first cool days of fall showed up in the aisles of Woolworth's. You never knew when the Monkey Man might decide to favor Jackson, or which way he'd go. Sometimes you heard him as close as the next street, and then he didn't come up yours.

But now I saw the Monkey Man at the Little Store, where I'd never seen him before. I'd never seen him sitting down. Low on that familiar doorstep, he was not the same any longer, and neither was his monkey. They looked just like an old man and an old friend of his that wore a fez, meeting quietly together, tired, and resting with their eyes fixed on some place far away, and not the same place. Yet their romance for me didn't have it in its power to waver. I wavered. I simply didn't know how to step around them, to proceed on into the Little Store for my mother's emergency as if nothing had happened. If I could have gone in there after it, whatever it was, I would have given it to them—putting it into the monkey's cool little fingers. I would have given them the Little Store itself.

In my memory they are still attached to the store—so are all the others. Everyone I saw on my way seemed to me then part of my errand, and in a way they were. As I myself, the free spirit, was part of it too.

All the years we lived in that house where we children were born, the same people lived in the other houses on our street too. People changed through the arithmetic of birth, marriage and death, but not by going away. So families just accrued stories, which through the fullness of time, in those times, their own lives made. And I grew up in those.

But I didn't know there'd ever been a story at the Little Store, one that was going on while I was there. Of course, all the time the Sessions family had been living right overhead there, in the upstairs rooms behind the little railed porch and the shaded windows; but I think we children never thought of that. Did I fail to see them as a family because they weren't living in an ordinary house? Because I so seldom saw them close together, or having anything to say to each other? She sat in the back of the store, her pencil over a ledger, while he stood and waited on children to make up their minds. They worked in twin black eyeshades, held on their gray heads by elastic bands. It may be harder to recognize kindness—or unkindness, either—in a face whose eyes are in shadow. His face underneath his shade was as round as the little wooden wheels in the Tinker Toy box. So

was her face. I didn't know, perhaps didn't even wonder: were they husband and wife or brother and sister? Were they father and mother? There were a few other persons, of various ages, wandering singly in by the back door and out. But none of their relationships could I imagine, when I'd never seen them sitting down together around their own table.

The possibility that they had any other life at all, anything beyond what we could see within the four walls of the Little Store, occurred to me only when tragedy struck their family. There was some act of violence. The shock to the neighborhood traveled to the children, of course; but I couldn't find out from my parents what had happened. They held it back from me, as they'd already held back many things, "until the time comes for you to know."

You could find out some of these things by looking in the unabridged dictionary and the encyclopedia—kept to hand in our dining room—but you couldn't find out there what had happened to the family who for all the years of your life had lived upstairs over the Little Store, who had never been anything but patient and kind to you, who never once had sent you away. All I ever knew was its aftermath: they were the only people ever known to me who simply vanished. At the point where their life overlapped into ours, the story broke off.

We weren't being sent to the neighborhood grocery for facts of life, or death. But of course those are what we were on the track of, anyway. With the loaf of bread and the Cracker Jack prize, I was bringing home the intimations of pride and disgrace, and rumors and early news of people coming to hurt one another, while others practiced for joy—storing up a portion for myself of the human mystery. ○

Eudora Welty, **Storekeeper, 1935**

SEEING

1. What principles of selection and order does Eudora Welty use to organize her reminiscences of running errands to the local grocery store? Reread the opening paragraphs in which she affectionately recounts some of the games she played as a child. How do these moments express her feelings toward the store? What are the effects of presenting these paragraphs before she describes the store? To which senses does she appeal in describing "the Little Store"? What techniques does she use to reinforce the childlike perspective recaptured in the essay? In each instance, point to specific evidence to verify your points.

2. Eudora Welty is an accomplished photographer as well as a renowned writer. (Her photographs of people and places in the South are collected in *Eudora Welty Photographs*.) She seeks to capture "the moment in which people reveal themselves." After examining the photograph of the storekeeper, what do you think he reveals about himself? Take notes on as many details of the photograph as you can. What, for example, do you notice about this man's stance, body language, and facial expression? How does lighting affect your impression of him? How has Welty chosen to frame her subject? What has she included in the photograph? What has she omitted?

WRITING

1. In an interview about her photography, Welty suggested that both the writer and the photographer must learn about "accuracy of the eye, about observation, and about sympathy towards what is in front of you." Consider the meaning of each of the three components of her statement, and make a list of the ways in which you can apply them to writing and taking photographs. To what extent do writing and photography capture "accuracy of the eye," "observation," and "sympathy towards what is in front of you"? Write an analytical essay in which you explore Welty's statement about the similarities between writing and taking pictures, using her own visual and verbal takes on similar subjects to support your points.

2. Examine Welty's observation that she strives to capture in her photographs "the moment in which people reveal themselves." What assumptions about the relationship between photographs and spontaneity are embedded in the point she makes? Draft an analytical essay in which you defend or challenge the assertion that the recognized presence of a photographer precludes the possibility of capturing a spontaneous, non-posed moment. Whichever side you argue, please be sure to support your claims with evidence as well as to anticipate—and rebut—the point(s) of view of those arguing the other side.

The Little Store

Eudora Welty

I'm not very eloquent about things like this, but
I think that writing and photography go together.
I don't mean that they are related arts, because
they're not. But the person doing it, I think, learns
from both things about accuracy of the eye, about
observation and about sympathy toward what is in
front of you. It's about trying to see into the essence
of reality. It's about honesty, or truth telling, and a
way to find it in yourself, how to need it and learn
from it.

I still go back to a paragraph of mine from *One
Time, One Place* as the best expression I was ever
able to manage about what I did or was trying to
do in both fields. It's still the truth:

> I learned quickly enough when to click the shutter,
> but what I was becoming aware of more slowly was a
> story-writer's truth: The thing to wait on, to reach for,
> is the moment in which people reveal themselves. . . .
> I learned from my own pictures, one by one, and had
> to; for I think we are the breakers of our own hearts.

– Eudora Welty, from "Storekeeper, 1935"

ALBERT BIERSTADT

Albert Bierstadt (1830–1902) was a preeminent painter of nineteenth-century American landscapes. At age 2 he immigrated to the United States with his family and settled in Massachusetts. His parents tried to dissuade him from pursuing a career in art, but Bierstadt persisted and by 1853, had sold enough of his work to pay for four years of travel and education in Europe.

After returning to the United States in 1857, Bierstadt joined the expedition of General F. W. Lander that was sent to explore the Rocky Mountains. Bierstadt is best remembered for his paintings that resulted from this and other travels through the American West. Throughout his long career he celebrated the sublime beauty and power of romanticized landscapes. During the nineteenth century he was one of the leading interpreters of the West for sedentary easterners, who often built their aspirations for national expansion on romantic visions of pristine nature.

Albert Bierstadt, **Among the Sierra Nevada Mountains, California, 1868**

John Pfahl, **Rancho Seco Nuclear Plant, Sacramento, California, 1983**

Pfahl's collection of photographs, *A Distanced Land* (1990), presents industrial power plants in the context of natural scenic wonders. "By making the landscape appear so romantic," he asks, "would it promote the naive impression that these power plants were living in blissful harmony with nature? Would my work be co-opted by industry?"

SEEING

1. Albert Bierstadt traveled extensively through the Rocky Mountains and Sierra Nevada making drawings and oil sketches, from which he later painted large canvases. What is the dominant impression created by Bierstadt in this famous painting of a scene in the Sierra Nevada Mountains? What artistic choices—such as the use of color, light, perspective, and scale—does he make that account for this effect and for the popularity of this painting as an artistic rendition of the American West?

2. What is the dominant impression created by John Pfahl's photograph of the nuclear power plant at Rancho Seco in California? How do the elements of light and darkness reinforce this impression? In what ways might we say (and admiringly so) that Pfahl's photograph is "composed"? Consider, for example, his use of perspective. This photograph appeared as the cover illustration for an issue of *Aperture*, a prominent photography magazine, entitled "Beyond Wilderness." In what ways does the title of that issue serve as an apt—or ironic—gloss on Pfahl's photograph? Compare Bierstadt's painting with Pfahl's photograph. In what ways is the overall effect of each image similar? different?

WRITING

1. In an essay entitled "The Loss of the Creature," the renowned physician and writer Walker Percy talks about the difficulties of seeing the natural world around us. He asks: "Why is it almost impossible to gaze directly at the Grand Canyon . . . and see it for what it is? . . . The Grand Canyon has been appropriated by the symbolic complex which has already been formed in the sightseer's mind." Write the first draft of an expository essay in which you account for the ways in which Albert Bierstadt's painting *Among the Sierra Nevada Mountains* has contributed to the "symbolic complex which has already been formed in the sightseer's mind" when he or she travels to the American West for the first time. In what ways has Bierstadt's painting helped determine the American public's vision of the West?

2. What would you say and do if you were asked to state your position—and to vote—on the uses of nuclear energy in the twenty-first century? Enumerate, and then consider carefully, the advantages and disadvantages of nuclear energy in the coming decades. Draft an argumentative essay in which you articulate and defend your position that the federal and state governments ought to promote (increased or decreased) reliance on nuclear energy.

THE FAR SIDE® BY GARY LARSON

"Well, this is just going from bad to worse."

SCOTT RUSSELL SANDERS

The value of staying put is a re-curring theme in Scott Russell Sanders's essays, which are collected in *Secrets of the Universe* (1991), *Staying Put: Making a Home in a Restless World* (1993), *Writing from the Center* (1995), and *Hunting for Hope: A Father's Journeys* (1999). Sanders interweaves explorations of place with reflections on nature and the importance of the natural environment for healthful living.

Born in Memphis in 1945, Sanders has lived since 1971 in Bloomington, where he is a professor of English at Indiana University. Frequently compared to Henry David Thoreau and Wendell Berry, Sanders is devoted to exploring the unique aspects of nature and social life in the Midwest. "Because there is no true human existence apart from family and community," says Sanders, "I feel a deep commitment to my region, to the land, to the people and all other living things with which I share this place." This commitment, he adds, is strengthened by "a regard compounded of grief and curiosity and love." The essay "Homeplace" appeared in *Orion* magazine in 1992.

Homeplace

Scott Russell Sanders

AS A BOY IN OHIO, I KNEW A FARM FAMILY, THE Millers, who suffered from three tornadoes. The father, mother, and two sons were pulling into their driveway after church when the first tornado hoisted up their mobile home, spun it around, and carried it off. With the insurance money, they built a small frame house on the same spot.

Several years later, a second tornado peeled off the roof, splintered the garage, and rustled two cows. The Millers rebuilt again, raising a new garage on the old foundation and adding another story to the house. That upper floor was reduced to kindling by a third tornado, which also pulled out half the apple trees and slurped water from the stock pond. Soon after that I left Ohio, snatched away by college as forcefully as by any cyclone. Last thing I heard, the family was preparing to rebuild yet again.

Why did the Millers refuse to move? I knew them well enough to say they were neither stupid nor crazy. Plain stubbornness was a factor. These were people who, once settled, might have remained at the foot of a volcano or on the bank of a flood-prone river or beside an earthquake fault. They had relatives nearby, helpful neighbors, jobs and stores and schools within a short drive, and those were all good reasons to stay. But the main reason, I believe, was that the Millers had invested so much of their lives in the land, planting orchards and gardens, spreading manure on the fields, digging ponds, building sheds, seeding pastures. Out back of the house were groves of walnuts, hickories, and oaks, all started by hand from acorns and nuts. April through October, perennial flowers in the yard pumped out a fountain of blossoms. This farm was not just so many acres of dirt, easily exchanged for an equal amount elsewhere; it was a particular place, intimately known, worked on, dreamed over, cherished.

Psychologists tell us that we answer trouble with one of two impulses, either fight or flight. I believe that the Millers exhibited a third instinct, that of staying put. They knew better than to fight a tornado, and they chose not to flee. Their commitment to the place may have been foolhardy, but it was also grand. I suspect that most human achievements worth admiring are the result of such devotion.

The Millers dramatize a choice we are faced with 5 constantly: whether to go or stay, whether to move to a situation that is safer, richer, easier, more attractive, or to stick where we are and make what we can of it. If the shine goes off our marriage, our house, our car, do we trade it for a new one? If the fertility leaches out of our soil, the creativity out of our job, the money out of our pocket, do we start over somewhere else? There are voices enough, both inner and outer, urging us to deal with difficulties by pulling up stakes and heading for new territory. I know them well, for they have been calling to me all my days. I wish to raise here a contrary voice, to say a few words on behalf of staying put, learning the ground, going deeper.

Claims for the virtues of moving on are familiar and seductive to Americans, this nation founded by immigrants and shaped by restless seekers. From the beginning, our heroes have been sailors, explorers, cowboys, prospectors, speculators, backwoods ramblers, rainbow chasers, vagabonds of every stripe. Our Promised Land has always been over the next ridge or at the end of the trail, never under our feet. In our national mythology, the worst fate is to be trapped on a farm, in a village, in the sticks, in some dead-end job or unglamorous marriage or played-out game.

Stand still, we are warned, and you die. Americans have dug the most canals, laid the most rails, built the most roads and airports of any nation. In a newspaper I read that, even though our sprawling system of interstate highways is crumbling, politicians think we should triple its size. Only a populace drunk on driving, a populace infatuated with the myth of the open road, could hear such a proposal without hooting.

Novelist Salman Rushdie chose to leave his native India for England, where he has written a series of brilliant books from the perspective of a cultural immigrant. In his book of essays *Imaginary Homelands* he celebrates the migrant sensibility: "The effect of mass migrations has been the creation of radically new types of human being: people who root themselves in ideas rather than places, in memories as much as in material things." He goes on to say that "to be a migrant is, perhaps, to be the only species of human being free of the shackles of nationalism (to say nothing of its ugly sister, patriotism)." Lord knows we could do with less nationalism (to say nothing of its ugly siblings, racism, religious sectarianism, and class snobbery). But who would pretend that a history of migration has immunized the United States against bigotry? And even if, by uprooting ourselves, we shed our chauvinism, is that all we lose?

In this hemisphere, many of the worst abuses—of land, forests, animals, and communities—have been carried out by "people who root themselves in ideas rather than places." Migrants often pack up their visions and values with the rest of their baggage and carry them along. The Spaniards devastated Central and South America by imposing on this New World the religion, economics, and politics of the Old. Colonists brought slavery with them to North America, along with smallpox and Norway rats. The Dust Bowl of the 1930s was caused not by drought but by the transfer onto the Great Plains of farming methods that were suitable to wetter regions. The habit of our industry and commerce has been to force identical schemes onto differing locales, as though the mind were a cookie cutter and the land were dough.

I quarrel with Rushdie because he articulates as eloquently as anyone the orthodoxy that I wish to counter: the belief that movement is inherently good, staying put is bad; that uprooting brings tolerance, while rootedness breeds intolerance; that to be modern, enlightened, fully of our time is to be displaced. Wholesale displacement may be inevitable in today's world; but we should not suppose that it occurs without disastrous consequences for the earth and for ourselves. People who root themselves in places are likelier to know and care for those places than are people who root themselves in ideas. When we cease to be migrants and become inhabitants, we might begin to pay enough heed and respect to where we are. By settling in, we have a chance of making a durable home for ourselves, our fellow creatures, and our descendants.

The poet Gary Snyder writes frequently about our need to "inhabit" a place. One of the key problems in American society now, he points out, is people's lack of commitment to any given place:

Neighborhoods are allowed to deteriorate, landscapes are allowed to be strip-mined, because there is nobody who will live there and take responsibility; they'll just move on. The reconstruction of a people and of a life in the United States depends in part on people, neighborhood by neighborhood, county by county, deciding to stick it out and make it work where they are, rather than flee.

But if you stick in one place, won't you become a stick-in-the-mud? If you stay put, won't you be narrow, backward, dull? You might. I have met ignorant people who never moved; and I have also met ignorant people who never stood still. Committing yourself to a place does not guarantee that you will become wise, but neither does it guarantee that you will become parochial.

To become intimate with your home region, to know the territory as well as you can, to understand your life as woven into the local life does not prevent you from recognizing and honoring the diversity of other places, cultures, ways. On the contrary, how can you value other places if you do not have one of your own? If you are not yourself *placed*, then you wander the world like a sightseer, a collector of sensations, with no gauge for measuring what you see. Local knowledge is the grounding for global knowledge. Those who care about nothing beyond the confines of their parish are in truth parochial, and are at least mildly dangerous to their parish; on the other hand, those who *have* no parish, those who navigate ceaselessly among postal zones and area codes, those for whom the world is only a smear of highways and bank accounts and stores, are a danger not just to their parish but to the planet.

Since birth, my children have regularly seen images of the earth as viewed from space, images that I first encountered when I was in my 20s. Those photographs show vividly what in our sanest moments we have always known—that the earth is a closed circle, lovely and rare. On the wall beside me as I write there is a poster of the big blue marble encased in its white swirl of clouds. That is one pole of my awareness; but the other pole is what I see through my window. I try to keep both in sight at once.

For all my convictions, I still have to wrestle with the fear—in myself, in my children, and even in some of my neighbors—that our place is too remote from the action. This fear drives many people to pack their bags and move to some resort or burg they have seen on television, leaving behind what they learn to think of as the boondocks. I deal with my own unease by asking just what action I am remote *from*—a stock market? a debating chamber? a drive-in mortuary? The action that matters, the work of nature and community, goes on everywhere.

Since Copernicus, we have known better than to see the earth as the center of the universe. Since Einstein, we have learned that there is no center; or alternatively, that any point is as good as any other for observing the world. I find a kindred lesson in the words of the Zen master Thich Nhat Hanh: "This spot where you sit is your own spot. It is on this very spot and in this very moment that you can become enlightened. You don't have to sit beneath a special tree in a distant land." If you stay put, your place may become a holy center, not because it gives you special access to the divine, but because in your stillness you hear what might be heard anywhere.

I think of my home ground as a series of nested rings, with house and family and marriage at the center, surrounded by the wider and wider hoops of neighborhood and community, the bioregion within walking distance of my door, the wooded and rocky hills of southern Indiana, the watershed of the Ohio Valley, and so on outward—and inward—to the ultimate source.

The longing to become an inhabitant rather than a drifter sets me against the current of my culture, which nudges everyone into motion. Newton taught us that a body at rest tends to stay at rest, unless it is acted on by an outside force. We are acted on ceaselessly by outside forces—advertising, movies, magazines, speeches—and also by the inner force of biology. I am not immune to their pressure. Before settling in my present home, I lived in seven states and two countries, tugged from place to place in childhood by my father's work and in early adulthood by my own. This itinerant life is so common among the people I know that I have been slow to conceive of an alternative. Only by knocking against the golden calf of mobility, which looms so large and shines so brightly, have I come to realize that it is hollow. Like all idols, it distracts us from what is truly divine.

I am encouraged by the words of a Crow elder, quoted by Gary Snyder in *The Practice of the Wild:* "You know, I think if people stay somewhere long enough—even white people—the spirits will begin to speak to them. It's the power of the spirits coming up from the land. The spirits and the old powers aren't lost, they just need people to be around long enough and the spirits will begin to influence them."

As I write this, I hear the snarl of earth movers and chain saws a mile away destroying a farm to make way for another shopping strip. I would rather hear a tornado, whose damage can be undone. The elderly woman who owned the farm had it listed in the National Register, then willed it to her daughters on condition they preserve it. After her death, the daughters, who live out of state, had the will broken, so the land could be turned over to the chain saws and earth movers. The machines work around the clock. Their noise wakes me at midnight, at three in the morning, at dawn. The roaring abrades my dreams. The sound is a reminder that we are living in the midst of a holocaust. I do not use the word lightly. The earth is being pillaged, and every one of us, willingly or grudgingly, is taking part. We ask how sensible, educated, supposedly moral people could have tolerated slavery or the slaughter of Jews. Similar questions will be asked about us by our descendants, to whom we bequeath an impoverished planet. They will demand to know how we could have been party to such waste and ruin.

What does it mean to be alive in an era when the earth is being devoured, and in a country that has set the pattern for that devouring? What are we called to do? I think we are called to the work of healing, both inner and outer: healing of the mind through a change in consciousness, healing of the earth through a change in our lives. We can begin that work by learning how to inhabit a place.

"The man who is often thinking that it is better to be somewhere else than where he is excommunicates himself," we are cautioned by Thoreau, that notorious stay-at-home. The metaphor is religious: To withhold yourself from where you are is to be cut off from communion with the source. It has taken me half a lifetime of searching to realize that the likeliest path to the ultimate ground leads through my local ground. I mean the land itself, with its creeks and rivers, its weather, seasons, stone outcroppings, and all the plants and animals that share it. I cannot have a spiritual center without having a geographical one; I cannot live a grounded life without being grounded in a *place*.

In belonging to a landscape, one feels a rightness, an at-homeness, a knitting of self and world. This condition of clarity and focus, this being fully present, is akin to what the Buddhists call mindfulness, what Christian contemplatives refer to as recollection, what Quakers call centering down. I am suspicious of any philosophy that would separate this-worldly from other-worldly commitment. There is only one world, and we participate in it here and now, in our flesh and our place. ○

SEEING

1. Arguing against the "belief that movement is inherently good," Scott Russell Sanders asserts, "people who root themselves in places are likelier to know and care for those places than are people who root themselves in ideas" (para. 10). What strategies does Sanders use to build his argument on behalf of "staying put"? How, for example, does he define being "settled," being "placed," and being "an inhabitant rather than a drifter"? What factors does Sanders identify that prompt people to refuse to move? Comment on the nature and effectiveness of the examples he uses to illustrate each point. What additional sources and examples would strengthen his argument?

2. How does Gary Larson's cartoon "Entering the Middle of Nowhere" relate to Sanders's essay? What aspects of Sanders's discussion of the range of American notions of place does Larson address in this cartoon? To what extent, for example, does Larson's cartoon invoke the American fear of being "remote from the action" that Sanders describes?

WRITING

1. Sanders recounts the story of the Miller family, who refused to yield to the ravages of several tornadoes. He notes, "The Millers dramatize a choice we are faced with constantly: whether to go or stay, whether to move to a situation that is safer, richer, easier, more attractive, or to stick where we are and make what we can of it" (para. 5). Consider a difficult set of circumstances or a conflict that you, your family, or someone you know faced. Draft a personal essay in which you recount both the nature of the problem and whether you or someone else yielded, as Sanders notes, to voices "both inner and outer, urging us to deal with difficulties by pulling up stakes and heading for new territory" (para. 5).

2. Sanders claims that some of the "worst abuses" in this hemisphere have come about through "the habit of our industry and commerce . . . to force identical schemes onto differing locales" (para. 9). Select an example of this "habit" in contemporary American experience, and write an argumentative essay in which you consider equally whether it's better to move, as Salman Rushdie argues, or to stay, as Sanders contends (paras. 8–10). Please be sure to provide sufficient evidence to validate each point in your argument as well as to account for opposing points of view.

Retrospect
Camilo José Vergara's Photographs of 65 East 125th St., Harlem

December 1977

January 1980

March 1990

September 1992

June 1997

May 1998

December 1983

November 1988

March 1994

February 1996

August 2001

April 2002

MY PLACE

David Ignatow

I have a place to come to.
It's my place. I come to it
morning, noon and night
and it is there. I expect it
to be there whether or not   5
it expects me—my place
where I start from and go
towards so that I know
where I am going and what
I am going from, making me   10
firm in my direction.

I am good to talk to,
you feel in my speech
a location, an expectation
and all said to me in reply   15
is to reinforce this feeling
because all said is towards
my place and the speaker
too grows his
from which he speaks to mine   20
having located himself
through my place.

DAVID IGNATOW

David Ignatow writes with extraordinary discretion about such broad themes as love and death. He shares recollections delicately and personally to reveal a life that does not hide from rediscovery, on subjects as varied as Hebrew lessons, war, first love, friendships, and his wife's death. Ignatow was born in Brooklyn, New York, in 1914 and has spent most of his life in New York City. His mother, from Austria-Hungary, was the illiterate daughter of a forest warden; his father was born a Jew in the Czarist Ukraine. Ignatow's early life was full of hardship, and years later his son was overcome with a mental illness from which neither father nor son would ever recover. His family's strife spilled over into his writing, and for a while he wrote of little else.

Ignatow's many honors include a Bollingen Prize, two Guggenheim Fellowships, and a National Institute of Arts and Letters award "for a lifetime of creative effort." *Earth Hard* (1968), *Sunlight* (1979), *Conversations* (1980), and *Whisper to the Earth* (1981) are some of his books of poetry. Other publications include three collections of poetry, *The Notebooks of David Ignatow* (1973), and a series of essays, introductions, reviews, and interviews entitled *Open between Us* (1980). Wesleyan University Press has published several of his books of poetry, including *Against the Evidence* (1993), in which "My Place" was originally published.

SEEING

1. How would you describe the place that David Ignatow talks of in his poem? Reread the first stanza carefully. Is the speaker describing a real physical space, or is it purely psychological? How would you paraphrase this first stanza?

2. Read stanza two carefully, several times—until you are comfortable talking about it in some detail. What is the effect of the declaration in the first few lines that "I am good to talk to, / you feel in my speech / a location"? In what ways does the rest of the stanza support—or create a contrast to—these first few lines? Point to specific words and phrases to support your reading. In more general terms, how would you characterize the tone of voice in this poem? To what extent, and with what effects, does the voice we hear in the poem convey—through word choice, structure, and rhythm—a sense of "place" and "location"?

WRITING

1. Reread the last five lines of the poem carefully, several times. What point does the speaker make in these lines? What does Ignatow mean when he says that "the speaker . . . [has] located himself / through my place"? Write the first draft of an expository essay in which you explain how it is possible to establish a sense of place for others through the spaces we inhabit.

2. After rereading "My Place," take a few moments and read another poem, "Horizon," by the U.S. poet laureate Billy Collins (p. 44). As you reread each poem, what similarities do you see? What differences? Which poem do you find more engaging? Why? Which one has a lingering effect on you? Why? In what ways does each poem linger in your mind? If neither does, explain why. In an essay, compare and contrast the overall effects—and success—of each poem on sustaining your interest in either or both of them. Which poem do you think is more successful? Why? What implicit definition of "successful" are you applying to each poem?

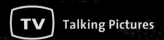
TV Talking Pictures

Early in his essay "Homeplace" (p. 145) Scott Russell Sanders explains that "claims for the virtues of moving on are familiar and seductive to Americans, this nation founded by immigrants and shaped by restless seekers. . . . Our Promised Land has always been over the next ridge or at the end of the trail, never under our feet. In our national mythology, the worst fate is to be trapped on a farm, in a village, in the sticks, in some dead-end job or unglamorous marriage or played-out game" (para. 6). Consider the ways in which our "national mythology" continues to be enacted on contemporary American television. Choose one example of a recent television program or an advertisement, and show how—in specific terms—it promotes the virtues of moving on.

MARK PETERSON
Born and raised in Minneapolis, Mark Peterson began his career as a photographer while doing odd jobs for a photojournalist. "I was failing miserably as a writer," he said in a recent interview, "and thought photography would be easy. That was my first mistake in photography." After working in both Minneapolis and New York, Peterson moved to New Jersey to pursue freelance photography. His photographs, which he describes as "day in the life" reportage, have appeared in *Life, Newsweek, Fortune,* and the *New York Times Magazine.* In 1992 Peterson was awarded the W. Eugene Smith support grant for his work with revolving-door alcoholics, during which he photographed a group of patients in Minneapolis over twelve years. Peterson's most recent projects include photographing teenagers in recovery from drug and alcohol addiction and capturing the lives of upper-class New Yorkers in a series entitled *The Highlife.* This photograph is from his series *Across the Street,* in which Peterson aimed to capture the divide between rich and poor living on and along Fifth Avenue in New York City.

Mark Peterson, **Image of Homelessness**

SEEING

1. What exactly is the place captured by this photograph—the box? the park? the urban scene? How does the person sleeping inside the box create a sense of place? What features of the arrangement of the box mark it as a "place"? How can you tell whether there is—or was—someone inside?

2. What does the photographer gain—and lose—by positioning the "place" of the homeless person clearly in the foreground? Given what is visible in the picture, what changes— say, in perspective or focus— might you suggest to highlight the dramatic impact of this redefinition of place? What effect(s) does the photographer accentuate in the image by including the phrase "HANDLE WITH CARE"? by including the out-of-focus background of Burger King?

WRITING

1. Imagine the following scenario. Shortly before the Opening Ceremony at the Olympic Games in 2012, which will take place in your state, the city council is debating the following resolution: that all homeless people in the city shall be removed to shelters for the duration of the Games. Now imagine yourself as the person charged with either advocating or challenging passage of the resolution. Write a draft of the speech you would make to the city council when this resolution is to be decided.

2. In an essay entitled "Distancing the Homeless," the writer and social critic Jonathan Kozol argues that the homeless are subject to many misconceptions. "A misconception . . . is not easy to uproot, particularly when it serves a useful social role. The notion that the homeless are largely psychotics who belong in institutions, rather than victims of displacements at the hands of enterprising realtors, spares us from the need to offer realistic solutions to the . . . extremes of wealth and poverty in the United States." Review the professional literature on the causes of homelessness published during the past eighteen months. Choose a still-popular misconception about homelessness—one that involves coming to terms with a sense of place—and write an argumentative essay in which you correct the mistaken or unexamined assumptions evident in this misconception.

DAVID GUTERSON

In both his fiction and essays, David Guterson's craft reminds one of an ornate tapestry: Intense focus on detail builds toward a complex and compelling portrait. He engages his readers on multiple levels—philosophical, psychological, and ethical—because, in his words, "I feel responsible to tell stories that inspire readers to consider more deeply who they are." In "No Place Like Home," which appeared in *Harper's* in November 1991, Guterson invites us to consider the kind of society we are producing as planned and gated communities proliferate. No matter where we live or aspire to live, Guterson asks us to reflect on our dreams of utopia and our apparently contradictory needs for freedom and security.

Guterson (b. 1956) lives near Seattle on Bainbridge Island, where he works as a high school English teacher. His publications include a collection of short stories, *The Country Ahead of Us, the Country Behind Us* (1989); an argument in favor of home schooling, *Family Matters* (1993); the celebrated novel *Snow Falling on Cedars* (1994); and *East of the Mountains* (1999).

NO PLACE LIKE HOME

On the Manicured Streets of a Master-Planned Community

David Guterson

TO THE CASUAL EYE, GREEN VALLEY, NEVADA, A corporate master-planned community just south of Las Vegas, would appear to be a pleasant place to live. On a Sunday last April—a week before the riots in Los Angeles and related disturbances in Las Vegas—the golf carts were lined up three abreast at the up-scale "Legacy" course; people in golf outfits on the clubhouse veranda were eating three-cheese omelets and strawberry waffles and looking out over the palm trees and fairways, talking business and reading Sunday newspapers. In nearby Parkside Village, one of Green Valley's thirty-five developments, a few home-owners washed cars or boats or pulled up weeds in the sun. Cars wound slowly over clean broad streets, ferrying children to swimming pools and backyard barbecues and Cineplex matinees. At the Silver Springs tennis courts, a well-tanned teenage boy in tennis togs pummeled his sweating father. Two twelve-year-old daredevils on expensive mountain bikes, decked out in Chicago Bulls caps and matching tank tops, watched and ate chocolate candies.

Green Valley is as much a verb as a noun, a place in the process of becoming what it purports to be. Everywhere on the fringes of its 8,400 acres one finds homes going up, developments going in (another twenty-one developments are under way), the desert in the throes of being transformed in accordance with the master plan of Green Valley's designer and builder, the American Nevada Corporation. The colors of its homes are muted in the Southwest manner: beiges, tans, dun browns, burnt reds, olive grays, rusts, and cinnamons. Its graceful, palm-lined boulevards and parkways are conspicuously devoid of gas stations, convenience stores, and fast-food restaurants, presenting instead a seamless facade of interminable, well-manicured developments punctuated only by golf courses and an occasional shopping plaza done in stucco. Within the high walls lining Green Valley's expansive parkways lie homes so similar they appear as uncanny mirror reflections of one another—and, as it turns out, they are. In most neighborhoods a prospective homeowner must choose from among a limited set of models with names like "Greenbriar," "Innisbrook," and "Tammaron" (or, absurdly, in a development called Heartland, "Beginnings," "Memories," and "Reflections"), each of which is merely a variation on a theme: Spanish, Moorish, Mexican, Territorial, Mediterranean, Italian Country, Mission. Each development inhabits a planned socioeconomic niche—$99,000, $113,900, $260,000 homes, and on into the stratosphere for custom models if a wealthy buyer desires. Neighborhoods are labyrinthine, confusing in their sameness; each block looks eerily like the next. On a spring evening after eight o'clock it is possible to drive through miles of them without seeing a single human being. Corners are marked with signs a visitor finds more than a little disconcerting: WARNING, they read, NEIGHBORHOOD WATCH PROGRAM IN FORCE. WE IMMEDIATELY REPORT ALL SUSPICIOUS PERSONS AND ACTIVITIES TO OUR POLICE DEPARTMENT. The signs on garages don't make me feel any better. WARNING, they read, YOUR NEIGHBORS ARE WATCHING.

I'd come to Green Valley because I was curious to meet the citizens of a community in which everything is designed, orchestrated, and executed by a corporation. More and more Americans, millions of them—singles, families, retirees—are living in such places. Often proximate to beltway interchanges and self-contained office parks of boxy glass buildings, these communities are everywhere now, although far more common in the West than elsewhere: its vast terrain, apparently, still lends itself to dreamers with grand designs. Irvine, California—the master-planned product of the Irvine Company, populated by 110,000 people and one of the fastest-growing *cities* in America—is widely considered a prototype, as are Reston, Virginia, and Columbia, Maryland, two early East Coast versions. Fairfield Communities, Inc., owns fourteen "Fairfield Communities": Fairfield in the Foothills, Fairfield's La Cholla, Fairfield's River Farm, and so forth. The Walt Disney Co. has its entry—Celebration—under way not far from Florida's Disney World. Las Colinas, Inc., invented Las Colinas, Texas, "America's Premier Master Planned Community," "America's Premier Development," and "America's Corporate Headquarters." The proliferation of planned communities is most visible in areas of rapid growth, which would certainly include the Las Vegas valley, the population of which has nearly doubled, to 799,381, since 1982.

That Sunday afternoon I made my way along peaceful boulevards to Green Valley's civic center, presumably a place where people congregate. A promotional brochure describes its plaza as "the perfect size for public gatherings and all types of social events," but on that balmy day, the desert in bloom just a few miles off, no one had, in fact, gathered here. The plaza had

the desultory ambience of an architectural mistake—deserted, useless, and irrelevant to Green Valley's citizens, who had, however, gathered in large numbers at stucco shopping centers not far off—at Spotlight Video, Wallpaper World, Record City, and Bicycle Depot, Rapunzel's Den Hair Salon, Enzo's Pizza and Ristorante, A Basket of Joy, and K-Mart.

Above the civic center, one after another, flew airplanes only seconds from touching down at nearby McCarran International Airport, which services Las Vegas casinogoers. Low enough that the rivets in their wings could be discerned, the planes descended at sixty-second intervals, ferrying fresh loads of gamblers into port. To the northeast, beyond a billboard put up by a developer—WATCH US BUILD THE NEW LAS VEGAS—lay a rectangle of desert as yet not built upon but useful as a dumping ground: scraps of plastic, bits of stucco, heaps of wire mesh and lumber ends were all scattered in among low creosote bush. The corporate master plan, I later learned, calls for hauling these things away and replacing them with, among other things, cinemas, a complex of swimming pools, restaurants, and substantially more places to shop.

Inside the civic center were plenty of potted palms, walls of black glass, and red marble floors, but again, no congregating citizens. Instead, I found the offices of the Americana Group Realtors; Lawyer's Title of Nevada, Inc.; RANPAC Engineering Corporation; and Coleman Homes, a developer. A few real estate agents were gearing up for Sunday home tours, dressed to kill and shuffling manila folders, their BMWs parked outside. Kirk Warren, a marketing specialist with the Americana Group, listened patiently to my explanation: I came to the civic center to talk to people; I wanted to know what brought them to a corporate-planned community and why they decided to stay.

"It's safe here," Warren explained, handing me a business card with his photograph on it. "And clean. And nice. The schools are good and the crime rate low. It's what buyers are looking for."

Outside the building, in the forlorn-looking plaza, six concrete benches had been fixed astride lawns, offering citizens twenty-four seats. Teenagers had scrawled their graffiti on the pavement (DARREN WAS HERE, JASON IS AWESOME), and a footlight beneath a miniature obelisk had been smashed by someone devoted to its destruction. Someone had recently driven past on a motorcycle, leaving telltale skid marks.

The history of suburbia is a history of gradual dysfunction, says Brian Greenspun, whose family owns the American Nevada Corporation (ANC), the entity that created Green Valley. Americans, he explains, moved to the suburbs in search of escape from the more undesirable aspects of the city and from undesirable people in particular. Time passed and undesirables showed up anyway; suburbia had no means to prevent this. But in the end, that was all right, Greenspun points out, because master planners recognized the problem as an enormously lucrative market opportunity and began building places like Green Valley.

Rutgers history professor Robert Fishman, author of *Bourgeois Utopias: The Rise and Fall of Suburbia,* would agree that suburbia hasn't worked. Suburbia, he argues, appeared in America in the middle of the nineteenth century, offering escape from the squalor and stench of the new industrial cities. The history of suburbia reached a climax, he says, with the rise of Los Angeles as a city that is in fact one enormous suburb. Today, writes Fishman, "the original concept of suburbia as an unspoiled synthesis of city and countryside has lost its meaning." Suburbia "has become what even the greatest advocates of suburban growth never desired—a new form of city." These new suburb-cities have, of course, inevitably developed the kinds of problems—congestion, crime, pollution, tawdriness—that the middle class left cities to avoid. Now, in the Nineties, developers and corporate master planners, recognizing an opportunity, have stepped in to supply the middle class, once again, with the promise of a bourgeois utopia.

As a product of the American Nevada Corporation, Green Valley is a community with its own marketing logo: the letters G and V intertwined quite cleverly to create a fanciful optical illusion—two leaves and a truncated plant stem. It is also a community with an advertising slogan: ALL THAT A COMMUNITY CAN BE. Like other master-planned communities in America, it is designed to embody a corporate ideal not only of streets and houses but of image and feeling. Green Valley's crisp lawns, culs-de-sac, and stucco walls suggest an amiable suburban existence where, as an advertising brochure tells us, people can enjoy life *more than they ever did before.* And, apparently, they do enjoy it. Thirty-four thousand people have filled Green Valley's homes in a mere fourteen years—the place is literally a boomtown. . . .

On weekday mornings, familiar yellow buses amble through Green Valley toward public schools built on acreage set aside in a 1971 land-sale agreement between ANC and Henderson, a blue-collar town just south of Vegas that was initially hostile to its new upscale neighbor but that now willingly participates in Green Valley's prosperity. Many parents prefer to drive their children to these schools before moving on to jobs, shopping, tennis, or aerobics classes. (Most Green Valley residents work in Las Vegas, commuting downtown in under twenty minutes.) The characteristic Green Valley family—a married couple with two children under twelve—has an average annual income of $55,000; about one in five are members of the Green Valley Athletic Club, described by master planners as "the focal point of the community" (family initiation fee: $1,000). The club's lavish swimming pools and air-conditioned tennis courts are, I was told, especially popular in summer, when Green Valley temperatures can reach 115 degrees and when whole caravans of Porsches and BMWs make their way toward its shimmering parking lots.

Inside is a state-of-the-art body-sculpting palace with Gravitron Upper Body Systems in its weight room, $3.99 protein drinks at its Health Bar, complimentary mouthwash in its locker rooms (swilled liberally by well-preserved tennis aficionados primping their thinning hair at mirrors before heading upstairs to Café Brigette Deux), and employees trained "to create an experience that brings a smile to every Member at every opportunity." I was given a tour by Jill Johnson, a Membership Service Representative, who showed me the Cybex systems in the weight room, the Life-Circuit computerized resistance equipment, the aerobics studio, and the day-care center.

Upstairs, the bartender mixed an "Arnold Schwarzenegger" for an adolescent boy with a crisp haircut and a tennis racket: yogurt, banana, and weight-gain powder. Later, in the weight room, I met a man I'll call Phil Anderson, an accountant, who introduced me to his wife, Marie, and to his children, Jason and Sarah. Phil was ruddy, overweight, and sweat-soaked, and had a towel draped over his shoulders. Marie was trim, dressed for tennis; the kids looked bored. Phil had been playing racquetball that evening while Marie took lessons to improve her serve and the children watched television in the kids' lounge. Like most of the people I met in Green Valley, the Andersons were reluctant to have their real names used ("We don't want the reaction," was how some residents explained it, including Marie and Phil). I coaxed them by promising to protect their true identities, and the Andersons began to chat.

"We moved here because Jase was getting on toward junior high age," Marie explained between sets on a machine designed to strengthen her triceps. "And in San Diego, where we lived before, there were these . . . *forces,* if you know what I mean. There were too many things we couldn't control. Drugs and stuff. It wasn't healthy for our kids."

"I had a job offer," Phil said. "We looked for a house. Green Valley was . . . the obvious place—just sort of obvious, really. Our real estate agent sized us up and brought us out here right away."

"We found a house in Silver Springs," Marie said. "You can go ahead and put that in your notes. It's a big development. No one will figure it out."

"But just don't use our names, okay?" Phil pleaded. "I would really appreciate that."

"We don't need problems," Marie added.

Master planners have a penchant not just for slogans but for predictable advertising strategies. Their pamphlets, packets, and brochures wax reverent about venerable founding fathers of passionate vision, men of foresight who long ago—usually in the Fifties—dreamed of building cities in their own image. Next comes a text promising an upscale pastoral: golf courses, blissful shoppers, kindly security guards, pleasant walkways, goodly physicians, yeomanly fire fighters, proficient teachers. Finally—invariably—there is culture in paradise: an annual arts and crafts festival, a sculpture, a gallery, Shakespeare in the park. In Las Colinas's Williams Square, for example, a herd of bronze mustangs runs pell-mell across a plaza, symbolizing, a brochure explains, a "heritage of freedom in a free land." Perhaps in the interstices of some sophisticated market analysis, these unfettered mustangs make perfectly good sense; in the context of a community whose dominant feature is walls, however, they make no sense whatsoever.

Walls are everywhere in Green Valley too; they're the first thing a visitor notices. Their message is subliminal and at the same time explicit; controlled access is as much metaphor as reality. Controlled access is also a two-way affair—both "ingress" and "egress" are influenced by it; both coming and going are made difficult. The gates at the thresholds of Green Valley's posher neighborhoods open with a macabre, mechanical slowness; their guards speak firmly and authoritatively to strangers and never smile in the manner of official greeters. One of them told me to take no pictures and to go directly to my destination "without stopping to look at anything." Another said that in an eight-hour shift he felt constantly nervous about going to the bathroom and feared that in abandoning his post to relieve himself he risked losing his job. A girl at the Taco Bell on nearby Sunset Road complained about Clark County's ten o'clock teen curfew—and about the guard at her neighborhood's gate who felt it was his duty to remind her of it. A ten-year-old pointed out that his friends beyond the wall couldn't join him inside without a telephone call to "security," which meant "the policeman in the guardhouse." Security, of course, can be achieved in many ways, but one implication of it, every time, is that security has insidious psychological consequences for those who contrive to feel secure.

"Before I built a wall," wrote Robert Frost, "I'd ask to know what I was walling in or walling out, and to whom I was like to give offense." The master planners have answers that are unassailably prosaic: "lot owners shall not change said walls in any manner"; "perimeter walls are required around all single family residential projects"; "side yard walls shall conform to the Guidelines for intersecting rear property walls." Their master plan weighs in with ponderous wall specifics, none of them in any way actionable: location, size, material, color, piers, pillars, openings. "Perimeter Project Walls," for example, "shall be made of gray colored, split face concrete masonry units, 8" by 16" by 6" in size, with a 4" high gray, split face, concrete block. . . . The block will be laid in a running bond pattern. . . . No openings are allowed from individual back yard lots into adjoining areas."

All of Green Valley is defined in this manner, by CC&Rs, as the planners call them—covenants, conditions, and restrictions embedded in deeds. Every community has some restrictions on matters such as the proper placement of septic tanks and the minimum distance allowed between homes, but in Green Valley the restrictions are detailed and pervasive, insuring the absence of individuality and suppressing the natural mess of humanity. Clotheslines and Winnebagos are not permitted, for example; no fowl, reptile, fish, or insect may be raised; there are to be no exterior speakers, horns, whistles, or bells. No debris of any kind, no open fires, no noise. Entries, signs, lights, mailboxes, sidewalks, driveways, rear yards, side yards, carports, sheds—the planners have had their say about each. All CC&Rs are inscribed into books of law that vary only slightly from development to development: the number of dogs and cats you can own (until recently, one master-planned community in Newport Beach, California, even limited the *weight* of dogs) as well as the placement of garbage cans, barbecue pits, satellite dishes, and utility boxes. The color of your home, the number of stories, the materials used, its accents and trim. The interior of your garage, the way to park your truck, the plants in your yard, the angle of your flagpole, the size of your address numbers, the placement of mirrored glass balls and birdbaths, the grade of your lawn's slope, and the size of your FOR SALE sign should you decide you want to leave.

"These things," explained Brad Nelson, an ANC vice president, "are set up to protect property values." ANC owner Greenspun put it another way: "The public interest and ANC's interest are one." . . .

As a journalist, I may have preferred a telling answer to my most frequent question—Why do you live here?—but the people of Green Valley, with disconcerting uniformity, were almost never entirely forthcoming. ("I moved here because of my job," they would say, or "I moved here because we found a nice house in Heartland.") Many had never heard of the American Nevada Corporation; one man took me for a representative of it and asked me what I was selling. Most had only a vague awareness of the existence of a corporate master plan for every detail of their community. The covenants, conditions, and restrictions of their lives were background matters of which they were cognizant but about which they were yawningly unconcerned. It did not seem strange to anyone I spoke with that a corporation should have final say about their mailboxes. When I explained that there were CC&Rs for nearly everything, most people merely shrugged and pointed out in return that it seemed a great way to protect property values. A woman in a grocery store checkout line explained that she'd come here from southern California because "even the good neighborhoods there aren't good anymore. You don't feel safe in L.A."

What the people of Green Valley want, explained a planner, is safety from threats both real and imagined and control over who moves in beside them. In this they are no different from the generation that preceded them in search of the suburban dream. The difference this time is that nothing has been left to chance and that everything has been left to the American Nevada Corporation, which gives Green Valley its contemporary twist: to achieve at least the illusion of safety, residents must buy in to an enor-

25

mous measure of corporate domination. Suburbia in the Nineties has a logo.

But even Eden—planned by God—had serpents, and so, apparently, does Green Valley. Last year a rapist ran loose in its neighborhoods; police suspected the man was a resident and responsible for three rapes and five robberies. George Hennard, killer of twenty-three people in a Killeen, Texas, cafeteria in October 1991, was a resident of Green Valley only months before his rampage and bought two of his murder weapons here in a private transaction. Joseph Weldon Smith, featured on the television series *Unsolved Mysteries,* strangled to death his wife and two stepdaughters in a posh Green Valley development called The Fountains.

The list of utopia's outrages also includes a November 1991 heist in which two armed robbers took a handcuffed hostage and more than $100,000 from a Green Valley bank, then fled and fired military-assault-rifle rounds at officers in hot pursuit. The same week police arrested a suspected child molester who had been playing football with Green Valley children and allegedly touching their genitals.

"You can run but you can't hide," one Green Valley resident told me when I mentioned a few of these incidents. "People are coming here from all over the place and bringing their problems with them." Perhaps she was referring to the gangs frequenting a Sunset Road fast-food restaurant—Sunset Road forms one fringe of Green Valley—where in the summer of 1991, according to the restaurant's manager, "the dining room was set on fire and there were fights every weekend." Perhaps she had talked to the teenagers who told me that LSD and crystal meth are the narcotics of choice at Green Valley High School, or to the doctor who simply rolled his eyes when I asked if he thought AIDS had arrived here.

Walls might separate paradise from heavy industry, but the protection they provide is an illusion. In May 1991 a leak at the nearby Pioneer Chlor Alkali plant spread a blanket of chlorine gas over Green Valley; nearly a hundred area residents were treated at hospitals for respiratory problems. The leak came three years after another nearby plant—this one producing rocket-fuel oxidizer for the space shuttle and nuclear missiles—exploded powerfully enough to register on earthquake seismographs 200 miles away. Two people were killed, 210 injured. Schools were closed and extra police officers called in to discourage the looting of area homes with doors and windows blown out.

And, finally, there is black comedy in utopia: a few days after Christmas last year, police arrested the Green Valley Community Association president for allegedly burglarizing a model home. Stolen items included pictures, cushions, bedspreads, and a gaudy brass figurine—a collection with no internal logic. A local newspaper described the civic leader running from the scene, dropping his loot piece by piece in his wake as he was chased by police to his residence. At home he hid temporarily in his attic but ultimately to no avail. The plaster cracked and he fell through a panel into the midst of the arresting officers.

Is it a coincidence that the one truly anomalous soul I met roams furtively the last unpaved place in Green Valley, a short stretch of desert called Pittman Wash?

Pittman Wash winds through quiet subdivisions, undeveloped chiefly because it is useful for drainage and unbuildable anyway. Lesser washes have been filled in, built on, and forgotten, but Pittman remains full of sand and desert hollyhock, a few tamarisks, some clumps of creosote bush. Children prefer it to the manicured squares of park grass provided for them by the master planners; teenagers drink beer here and write graffiti on the storm-drain access pillars buried in the wash's channel: FUCK HENDERSON PK. DSTC., and the like. Used condoms, rusting oil filters, a wind-whipped old sleeping bag, a rock wren, a yellow swallowtail butterfly.

Here I met nine-year-old Jim Collins, whose name has been changed—at his fervent request—on the off chance his mother reads these words and punishes him for playing in Pittman Wash again. Jim struck me as a lonesome, Huck Finn sort, brown-skinned and soft-spoken, with grit beneath his nails and sun-bleached hair. I found him down on his dirty knees, lazily poking a stick into a hole.

"Lizards," he explained. "I'm looking for lizards. [35] There's rattlers, chipmunks, coyote, mountain lion, black widows, and scorpions too." He regaled me with stories of parents in high dudgeon over creatures of the wash brought home. Then, unsolicited, he suddenly declared that "most of the time I'm bored out of my guts . . . the desert's all covered up with houses—that sucks."

He insisted, inexplicably, on showing me his backyard, which he described as "just like the desert." So we trudged out of the wash and walked the concrete trail the master planners have placed here. Jim climbed the border wall and ran along its four-inch top with the unconscious facility of a mountain goat. We looked at his yard, which had not yet been landscaped, a rectangle of cracked desert caliche. Next door three children dressed fashionably in sporting attire shot baskets on a Michael Jordan Air Attack hoop. "We don't get along," Jim said. He didn't want me to go away in the end, and as I left he was still chattering hopefully. "My favorite store is Wild Kingdom of Pets," he called. "If you go there you can see Tasha the wildcat."

Some might call Green Valley a simulacrum[1] of a real place, Disneyland's Main Street done in Mediterranean hues, a city of haciendas with cardboard souls, a valley of the polished, packaged, and perfected, an empyrean of emptiness, a sanitized wasteland. They will note the Southwest's pastel palette coloring a community devoid of improvisation, of caprice, spontaneity, effusiveness, or the charm of error—a place where the process of commodification has at last leached life of the accidental and ecstatic, the divine, reckless, and enraged.

Still, many now reside in this corporate domain, driven here by insatiable fears. No class warfare here, no burning city. Green Valley beckons the American middle class like a fabulous and eternal dream. In the wake of our contemporary trembling and discontent, its pilgrims have sought out a corporate castle where in exchange for false security they pay with personal freedoms; where the corporation that does the job of walling others out also walls residents in. The principle, once political, is now economic. Just call your real estate agent. ○

wall every other out
& resident in

---

1. *Simulacrum:* an insubstantial image of something real.

SEEING

1. "To the casual eye," writes David Guterson, "Green Valley, Nevada, . . . would appear to be a pleasant place to live" (para. 1). How does Guterson suggest the *critical eye* would see Green Valley? Find specific examples of the language Guterson uses and the details he focuses on to support your answer. What does he mean when he says that "Green Valley is as much a verb as a noun" (para. 2) or that Green Valley "is designed to embody a corporate ideal not only of streets and houses but of image and feeling" (para. 11)?

2. What principle of organization does Guterson employ in developing his analysis of planned communities? Do you think the organization is effective? What specific examples does he provide to illustrate his point that Green Valley is "a place where the process of commodification has at last leached life of the accidental and ecstatic, the divine, reckless, and enraged" (para. 37)? What sources and perspectives does he draw on to help paint a picture of suburban life in general? What opinions and perspectives does he omit? How would you characterize the tone of this piece? What passages, words, or phrases lead you to this characterization?

WRITING

1. "Walls are everywhere in Green Valley too," Guterson writes; "they're the first thing a visitor notices. Their message is subliminal and at the same time explicit; controlled access is as much metaphor as reality" (para. 21). Choose a wall, fence, or some other physical divider in your neighborhood or on campus. What purpose(s) does it serve? What does it keep in or out? Write the first draft of a descriptive essay in which you characterize the literal and metaphorical functions of the wall you have chosen.

A word or phrase that means one thing but is used to describe something else in order to suggest a relationship between the two.

2. "In the middle of the nineteenth century," according to Guterson, suburbia offered an "escape from the squalor and stench of the new industrial cities" (para. 10). Write an analytical essay in which you identify and discuss the middle-class ideal of the suburban or planned community. Why has the ideal of living in such communities remained attractive to middle-class Americans for so long, and why do the sales of these houses continue to rise? Do you think the suburban "dream" is a myth or reality? (You might also refer to the Visualizing Context feature in this chapter on p. 169.)

I've had the pleasure of thinking about what a sense of place means, and it occurs to me that it is as large as one's birthplace or the country one adopts. And it can be as small as a mood that has a ground, or as small as a thought that takes place in a room. In fact when thoughts do take place in a room they have a wonderful sense of place. At any rate, what I love about it is that, when you're writing, there's nothing more difficult than to come up with a good description of place. Writers often feel that sometimes they do what they do through their work, and once in a while they get a gift from the various powers either up there or coming up from below, and we've never asked where the gift comes from, whether on high or below; we're just happy enough to get the gift, 'cause writing can be a dreary activity. Anyway, when we get that good sense of place we're happy with it. And it doesn't happen that often.

—Norman Mailer, from *Three Minutes or Less*

MIRANDA LICHTENSTEIN >
Miranda Lichtenstein is a photographer living and working in New York City. Since receiving her M.F.A. degree from the California Institute of Arts in 1993, her work has been shown in galleries and museums around the United States. *Untitled #9* is from a series entitled *Danbury Road*, in which Lichtenstein photographed the outsides of middle-class homes in Connecticut at night. She used only ambient light from street lamps, the insides of houses, and her car to capture the images. "The photographs," she explains, "are made with a 2- to 4-minute exposure. The camera picks up details that are invisible to the human eye. As my car's headlights illuminate the landscape before me, I begin to predict the nuance and depth of the image that the light passing through the lens will produce. This is the effect that cinema can have on a recorded image as well. What you see is not necessarily what you get."

Suburban Connecticut was the focus of another recent series of Lichtenstein's photos entitled *Lover's Lane*, in which she explored "the woods as a space for teenagers to create their own domestic habitat." In 2001 she held her first solo museum exhibition at the Whitney Museum of American Art at Philip Morris. Entitled *Miranda Lichtenstein: Sanctuary for a Wild Child*, the show was inspired by cross-cultural legends about children brought up in the wild.

Miranda Lichtenstein, **Untitled #9**

SEEING

1. What did you first notice as you observed this photograph? To what extent does what you notice change with a second, more careful, examination of the image? Be as specific as possible. Comment on Lichtenstein's use of lighting in this photograph. What other images does her use of lighting recall? What aspects of popular culture does this photograph prompt you to recall? With what effect(s)? To what extent is this image "constructed"? Point to specific evidence to support your response. Imagine that you are one of the editors of this book and that you decide to re-position this image in another chapter in this book. Which chapter would you choose? Explain why.

2. Discuss the composition of this image. Comment on the effect(s) of the choices Lichtenstein has made in the use of light, the position of the house in relation to the landscape around it, and the like. What can you actually see in this photograph? What is concealed? Which aspect of the photograph evokes the strongest response in you? Explain why.

WRITING

1. You have most likely seen countless images of suburban homes on TV, on film, and in magazines. What do you notice as unusual or different about Lichtenstein's portrayal of suburbia in *Untitled #9*? What feelings toward and qualities of suburbia does it convey to you? How does the photo seem different from or similar to other images of suburbia you are familiar with? Choose one other portrayal of suburbia (a photograph, essay, or poem) from this book or an outside source. Write an essay in which you compare and contrast the ways in which each text captures such a common American landscape.

2. Spend some time comparing and contrasting Miranda Lichtenstein's photograph to the still shots from different American films (p. 169). What similarities and differences do you notice between the scene Lichtenstein depicts and those presented in the movie stills? Which image do you prefer? Explain why. What is so memorable about the movie stills? Choose one of the stills and write an expository essay in which you explain the specific ways in which it captures the spirit and substance of the theme, mood, or environment of this particular film.

Visualizing Context
Defining One Place in Terms of Another

E.T., 1978

Pleasantville, 1998

Ice Storm, 1999

American Beauty, 1999

One of the most useful ways to think about context is to consider the relationship between one text and another. Context refers to the setting that surrounds a particular word, passage, image, or text. Miranda Lichtenstein's *Untitled #9* is part of a series of photographs of suburban homes at night—and as such, it has a host of contexts, one of which is our shared cultural familiarity with the suburbs.

The movie stills at left—from *E.T.*, *American Beauty*, *Pleasantville*, and *Ice Storm*—are taken from four films that feature a suburban setting as a crucial part of their context. Can you apply the statements these movies make to Lichtenstein's photograph? If so, how?

Most dictionaries define *suburb* as "a residential area outside a city." Yet conceptually, suburban space represents much more: safety, isolation, conformity, and a way of life that is seductive for some and repellent to others. Miranda Lichtenstein's photograph plays with the suburban house as a discrete space and as a cultural concept. Her image evokes cinematic suburbs like the ones shown at left as well as in such horror movies as *Friday the 13th* and *Scream*, which often take place in quiet, safe spaces and feature many distant shots of a house at night, lit up from the inside, seen (we reasonably assume) from the killer's perspective.

Using your knowledge of the cultural relation between the movie stills shown at left or other movies that feature the suburbs, write the first draft of an essay that explores Miranda Lichtenstein's photograph in the context of film. How does her use of recognizable cinematic conventions prompt questions about what is real and what is not, what is natural and what is artificial?

www   **Re: Searching the Web**

The language of the Internet is full of spatial metaphors. Individuals and organizations spend time in "cyberspace," create "web sites," and frequent "chat rooms" and "multi-user domains" (MUDs). If we view the web as a landscape to be explored, what similarities do cyber spaces have to physical spaces? In what ways is this comparison useful? Where does the analogy break down? If we treat the Internet as a global village, what evidence of national or regional communities can be found? How does the Internet affect our notions of place?

Choose a web site, a chat room, a newsgroup, or a MUD as a focus for your exploration of the use of spatial or place-related metaphors to describe the Internet experience. What, if anything, about this site reminds you of a physical place? How is the space defined visually and verbally? How does the movement from page to page through links compare to physical travel?

After you have reviewed the notes you've developed in response to these questions, prepare the first draft of an expository essay in which you analyze the aptness of spatial metaphors in describing the nature and workings of the Internet.

RON HANSEN

A man of faith and clear vision, Ron Hansen (b. 1947) develops characters in spiritual or moral crisis, and his story lines often resonate with those found in murder mysteries and Westerns as well as more classic literary fiction. He names John Irving and John Gardner as two of his influences. According to *Contemporary Novelists,* Hansen's books "occupy a curious half-way house between popular and high culture; between the worlds of art and entertainment." His many books include *The Assassination of Jesse James by the Coward Robert Ford* (1984); *Mariette in Ecstasy* (1992); and a children's book, *The Shadowmaker* (1989). His novel *Atticus* (1996) was a finalist for the National Book Award. He is the author, most recently, of a collection of essays, *A Stay against Confusion: Essays on Faith and Fiction* (2002), and the novel *Hitler's Niece* (2000), a Literary Guild alternate. A native of Omaha, Hansen received the Award in Literature from the American Academy and Institute of Arts and Letters for *Nebraska* (1989), a collection of short fiction.

Hansen is also a screenplay writer. "I was as influenced by films as I was by fiction, and I think that has permeated my consciousness. Also, I began as a painter, so I think visually." Hansen is Gerard Manley Hopkins S.J. Professor of the Arts and Humanities at Santa Clara University. "Nebraska" is included in Hansen's book of short stories of the same name. The story originally appeared in *Prairie Schooner* and *Harper's.*

Nebraska

Ron Hansen

THE TOWN IS AMERICUS, COVENANT, DENMARK, Grange, Hooray, Jerusalem, Sweetwater—one of the lesser-known moons of the Platte, conceived in sickness and misery by European pioneers who took the path of least resistance and put down roots in an emptiness like the one they kept secret in their youth. In Swedish and Danish and German and Polish, in anxiety and fury and God's providence, they chopped at the Great Plains with spades, creating green sod houses that crumbled and collapsed in the rain and disappeared in the first persuasive snow and were so low the grown-ups stooped to go inside; and yet were places of ownership and a hard kind of happiness, the places their occupants gravely stood before on those plenary occasions when photographs were taken.

And then the Union Pacific stopped by, just a camp of white campaign tents and a boy playing his Harpoon at night, and then a supply store, a depot, a pine water tank, stockyards, and the mean prosperity of the twentieth century. The trains strolling into town to shed a boxcar in the depot sideyard, or crying past at sixty miles per hour, possibly interrupting a girl in her high-wire act, her arms looping up when she tips to one side, the railtop as slippery as a silver spoon. And then the yellow and red locomotive rises up from the heat shimmer over a mile away, the August noonday warping the sight of it, but cinders tapping away from the spikes and the iron rails already vibrating up inside the girl's shoes. She steps down to the roadbed and then into high weeds as the Union Pacific pulls Wyoming coal and Georgia-Pacific lumber and snowplow blades and aslant Japanese pickup trucks through the open countryside and on to Omaha. And when it passes by, a worker she knows is opposite her, like a pedestrian at a stoplight, the sun not letting up, the plainsong of grasshoppers going on and on between them until the worker says, "Hot."

Twice the Union Pacific tracks cross over the sidewinding Democrat, the water slow as an oxcart, green as silage, croplands to the east, yards and houses to the west, a green ceiling of leaves in some places, whirlpools showing up in it like spinning plates that lose speed and disappear. In winter and a week or more of just above zero, high-school couples walk the gray ice, kicking up snow as quiet words are passed between them, opinions are mildly compromised, sorrows are apportioned. And Emil Jedlicka unslings his blue-stocked .22 and slogs through high brown weeds and snow, hunting ring-necked pheasant, sidelong rabbits, and—always suddenly—quail, as his little brother Orin sprints across the Democrat in order to slide like an otter.

July in town is a gray highway and a Ford hay truck spraying by, the hay sailing like a yellow ribbon caught in the mouth of a prancing dog, and Billy Awalt up there on the camel's hump, eighteen years old and sweaty and dirty, peppered and dappled with hay dust, a lump of chew like an extra thumb under his lower lip, his blue eyes happening on a Dairy Queen and a pretty girl licking a pale trickle of ice cream from the cone. And Billy slaps his heart and cries, "Oh! I am pierced!"

And late October is orange on the ground and blue overhead and grain silos stacked up like white poker chips, and a high silver water tower belittled one night by the sloppy tattoo of one year's class at George W. Norris High. And below the silos and water tower are stripped treetops, their gray limbs still lifted up in alleluia, their yellow leaves crowding along yard fences and sheeping along the sidewalks and alleys under the shepherding wind.

Or January and a heavy snow partitioning the landscape, whiting out the highways and woods and cattle lots until there are only open spaces and steamed-up windowpanes, and a Nordstrom boy limping pitifully in the hard plaster of his clothes, the snow as deep as his hips when the boy tips over and cannot get up until a little Schumacher girl sitting by the stoop window, a spoon in her mouth, a bowl of Cheerios in her lap, says in plain voice, "There's a boy," and her mother looks out to the sidewalk.

Houses are big and white and two stories high, each a cousin to the next, with pigeon roosts in the attic gables, green storm windows on the upper floor, and a green screened porch, some as pillowed and couched as parlors or made into sleeping rooms for the boy whose next step will be the Navy and days spent on a ship with his hometown's own population, on gray water that rises up and is allayed like a geography of cornfields, sugar beets, soybeans, wheat, that stays there and says, in its own way, "Stay." Houses are turned away from the land and toward whatever is not always, sitting across from each other like dressed-up children at a party in daylight, their parents looking on with hopes and fond expectations. Overgrown elm and sycamore trees poach the sunlight from the lawns and keep petticoats of snow around them into April. In the deep lots out back are wire clotheslines with flapping white sheets pinned to them, property lines are hedged with sour green and purple grapes, or with rabbit wire and gardens of peonies, roses, gladiola, irises, marigolds, pansies. Fruit trees are so closely planted that they cannot sway without knitting. The apples and cherries drop and sweetly decompose until they're only slight brown bumps in the yards, but the pears stay up in the wind, drooping under the pecks of birds, withering down like peppers until their sorrow is justly noticed and they one day disappear.

Aligned against an alley of blue shale rock is a garage whose doors slash weeds and scrape up pebbles as an old man pokily swings them open, teetering with his last weak push. And then Victor Johnson rummages inside, being cautious about his gray sweater and high-topped shoes, looking over paint cans, junked electric motors, grass rakes and garden rakes and a pitchfork and sickles, gray doors and ladders piled overhead in the rafters, and an old windup Victrola and heavy platter records from the twenties, on one of them a soprano singing "I'm a Lonesome Melody." Under a green tarpaulin is a wooden movie projector he painted silver and big cans of tan celluloid, much of it orange and green with age, but one strip of it preserved: of an Army pilot in jodhpurs hopping from one biplane onto another's upper wing. Country people who'd paid to see the movie had been spellbound by the slight dip of the wings at the pilot's jump, the slap of his leather jacket, and how his hair strayed wild and was promptly sleeked back by the wind. But looking at the strip now, pulling a ribbon of it up to a windowpane and letting it unspool to the ground, Victor can make out only twenty frames of the leap, and then snapshot after snapshot of an Army pilot clinging to the biplane's wing. And yet Victor stays with it, as though that scene of one man staying alive were what he'd paid his nickel for.

Main Street is just a block away. Pickup trucks stop in it so their drivers can angle out over their brown left arms and speak about crops or praise the weather or make up sentences whose only real point is their lack of complication. And then a cattle truck comes up and they mosey along with a touch of their cap bills or a slap of the door metal. High-school girls in skin-tight jeans stay in one place on weekends, and jacked-up cars cruise past, rowdy farmboys overlapping inside, pulling over now and then in order to give the girls cigarettes and sips of pop and grief about their lipstick. And when the cars peel out, the girls say how a particular boy measured up or they swap gossip about Donna Moriarity and the scope she permitted Randy when he came back from boot camp.

Everyone is famous in this town. And everyone is necessary. Townspeople go to the Vaughn Grocery Store for the daily news, and to the Home Restaurant for history class, especially at evensong when the old people eat graveled pot roast and lemon meringue pie and calmly sip coffee from cups they tip to their mouths with both hands. The Kiwanis Club meets here on Tuesday nights, and hopes are made public, petty sins are tidily dispatched, the proceeds from the gumball machines are tallied up and poured into the upkeep of a playground. Yutesler's Hardware has picnic items and kitchen appliances in its one window, in the manner of those prosperous men who would prefer to be known for their hobbies. And there is one crisp, white, Protestant church with a steeple, of the sort pictured on calendars; and the Immaculate Conception Catholic Church, grayly holding the town at bay like a Gothic wolfhound. And there is an insurance agency, a county coroner and justice of the peace, a secondhand shop, a handsome chiropractor named Koch who coaches the Pony League baseball team, a post office approached on unpainted wood steps outside of a cheap mobile home, the Nighthawk tavern where there's Falstaff tap beer, a green pool table, a poster recording the Cornhuskers scores, a crazy man patiently tolerated, a gray-haired woman with an unmoored eye, a boy in spectacles thick as paperweights, a carpenter missing one index finger, a plump waitress whose day job is in a basement beauty shop, an old woman who creeps up to the side door at eight in order to purchase one shot glass of whiskey.

And yet passing by, and paying attention, an outsider is only aware of what isn't, that there's no bookshop, no picture show, no pharmacy or dry cleaners, no cocktail parties, extreme opinions, jewelry or piano stores, motels, hotels, hospital, political headquarters, philosophical theories about Being and the soul.

High importance is only attached to practicalities, and so there is the Batchelor Funeral Home, where a proud old gentleman is on display in a dark brown suit, his yellow fingernails finally clean, his smeared eyeglasses in his coat pocket, a grandchild on tiptoes by the casket, peering at the lips that will not move, the sparrow chest that will not rise. And there's Tommy Seymour's for Sinclair gasoline and mechanical repairs, a green balloon dinosaur bobbing from a string over the cash register, old tires piled beneath the cottonwood, For Sale in the sideyard a Case tractor, a John Deere reaper, a hay mower, a red manure spreader, and a rusty grain conveyor, green weeds overcoming them, standing up inside them, trying slyly and little by little to inherit machinery for the earth.

And beyond that are woods, a slope of pasture, six empty cattle pens, a driveway made of limestone pebbles, and the house where Alice Sorensen pages through a child's World Book Encyclopedia, stopping at the descriptions of California, Capetown, Ceylon, Colorado, Copenhagen, Corpus Christi, Costa Rica, Cyprus.

Widow Dworak has been watering the lawn in an open raincoat and apron, but at nine she walks the green hose around to the spigot and screws down the nozzle so that the spray is a misty crystal bowl softly baptizing the ivy. She says, "How about some camomile tea?" And she says, "Yum. Oh, boy. That hits the spot." And bends to shut the water off.

The Union Pacific night train rolls through town just after ten o'clock when a sixty-year-old man named Adolf Schooley is a boy again in bed, and when the huge weight of forty or fifty cars jostles his upstairs room like a motor he'd put a quarter in. And over the sighing industry of the train, he can hear the train saying *Nebraska, Nebraska, Nebraska, Nebraska.* And he cannot sleep.

Mrs. Antoinette Heft is at the Home Restaurant, placing frozen meat patties on waxed paper, pausing at times to clamp her fingers under her arms and press the sting from them. She stops when the Union Pacific passes, then picks a cigarette out of a pack of Kools and smokes it on the back porch, smelling air as crisp as Oxydol, looking up at stars the Pawnee Indians looked at, hearing the low harmonica of big rigs on the highway, in the town she knows like the palm of her hand, in the country she knows by heart. ○

15

SEEING

1. What is your overall impression of Ron Hansen's story? Which aspects—and sections—did you find most engaging? most challenging? most rewarding to read? Explain why. What seems fictional about this selection? Which aspects ring most true of *your* experience of rural America? Turn your attention now to the terms Hansen uses, *Americus* and *Democrat*, to describe the fictional town and its neighboring river. How would you characterize these terms? In what ways do they—and others like them—contribute to the story's overall impact? How would you characterize the rhythm of Hansen's writing? What compositional tools does he use to create this sense of movement? How does he convey a sense of time in the story? With what effect(s)?

2. Characterize the tone of Hansen's story, citing specific words and phrases (especially in the first paragraph) as examples. Does the narrator sound more like a native of this town or like an outsider? Imagine yourself directing someone to read this essay aloud. What tone of voice would you instruct the reader to use? Compare and contrast Hansen's tone of voice with that of Norman Mailer (p. 165). Which voice do you find more engaging? more convincing? Explain why.

WRITING

1. Comment on the effectiveness of Hansen's description of Nebraska. Which aspects of his story do you find most satisfying to read? Which are the most difficult to comprehend? How you can account for such a range of responses to Hansen's story? Write the first draft of an expository essay in which you enumerate the differences between those moments in his story when you thought it was a bit too fictional and those during which you felt the story was consistent with your own experiences of a rural American town. Which did you prefer—the fictional or nonfictional dimensions of the story?

2. Geography is an important and traditional source of encouraging respect for and understanding of cultural difference. Reread Hansen's essay carefully, and keep his story in mind as you read Eudora Welty's "The Little Store" (p. 134). Which story do you find more compelling? Why? What local and regional cultural assumptions does each writer draw on? Cite examples to support each of your assertions. Once you have finished responding to these questions, write an essay in which you compare and contrast the relative strengths and weaknesses of each story.

RICHARD MISRACH >

Four of the five photographs on the pages that follow are each drawn from a different Canto of Richard Misrach's portrait of the desert. Misrach's *Desert Cantos* is a book-length photographic essay modeled on the traditional literary form of the canto—a section of a long song or poem. In the "Afterword" to his volume, Misrach explains that "my focus has been the desert, or more accurately, 'desertness,' as I have tried to determine what makes the desert the desert."

The fifth image is Misrach's photograph of a diorama entitled *Palm Oasis,* which is on display at the Palm Springs Desert Museum.

"As interesting and provocative as the cultural geography might be," Misrach explains, "the desert may serve better as the backdrop for the problematic relationship between man and the environment. The human struggle, the successes and failures, the use and abuse, both noble and foolish, are readily apparent in the desert."

Born in Los Angeles in 1949, Richard Misrach graduated from the University of California, Berkeley, with a degree in psychology. He is the recipient of numerous fellowships and awards, including a Guggenheim fellowship and several from the National Endowment for the Arts. His most recent book-length cantos include *Golden Gate* (2001), sixty photographs of San Francisco's Golden Gate Bridge, and *The Sky Book* (2000), a photographic meditation on the desert sky.

Wind Mill Farm, San Gorgonio Pass

Waiting, Edwards Air Force Base

Diving Board, Salton Sea

Desert Fire #236

Palm Oasis

SEEING

1. The word desert usually means any area seemingly incapable of supporting life. What does the word mean to you? After studying the photographs by Richard Misrach, what do you think the word means to him? Use examples from his photos to support your answer.

2. What images of the desert come to mind when you think of such well-known areas as, say, Death Valley or Monument Valley? What's present in—or absent from—Misrach's photographs that you associate with the desert? What details in his photographs reinforce or challenge your sense of what the desert should look like? What evidence do you find in these photographs that illustrates Misrach's stance on larger issues such as the relationship between people and the environment?

WRITING

1. In the "Afterword" to *Desert Cantos*, Misrach suggests that the desert represents the "'civilized' cultural landscape of America—the result of man's conquest of the last great physical and psychological barrier to Manifest Destiny. The Great American Wasteland is now [1984] the home of more than a million people, with all their usual accoutrements—swimming pools, golf courses, condominiums, air-conditioned motels, shopping centers, 7-11s, and Dairy Queens." Despite Misrach's account of the literal transformation of the desert, clichés and stereotypes about this "wasteland" still abound. Develop a list of such stereotypes and clichés, and then draft an expository essay in which you assess the nature and extent to which this long-standing identity of the desert persists in American culture. What reasonable inferences about the desert's "place" in contemporary culture can you draw from the research you conduct?

2. Use one of Misrach's images as the basis for an argumentative essay in which you support or challenge his claim that "The human struggle, the successes and failures, the use and abuse, both noble and foolish, are readily apparent in the desert." Please be sure to validate each of your assertions with a detailed analysis of the photograph.

TONY HISS

The subtitle of Tony Hiss's book *The Experience of Place, A Completely New Way of Looking at and Dealing with Our Radically Changing Cities and Countryside,* introduces his ideas about how people can gain a more acute sense of the places that surround them. "Places have a real impact on us," Hiss says. "They can help us reconnect with the rest of creation and find fellowship with other human beings." The *New York Times Book Review* recommends that "The Experience of Place," published in 1990, "should be required reading for all planners, developers, and city administrators"; other fans are equally laudatory.

Hiss, a visiting scholar at the Taub Urban Research Center at New York University and a fellow of the New York Institute of the Humanities at NYU, spent over thirty years as a staff writer for *The New Yorker* and is the author of eleven books. One particularly notable book is a pastiche of letters his infamous father, Alger Hiss—a former State Department official accused of spying for the Soviets in the 1930s—sent to his family from his prison cell; the book is entitled *The View from Alger's Window: A Son's Memoir* (1999). Tony Hiss lives in New York City, in the same Greenwich Village apartment where he spent much of his early life. He shares his home with his wife, the young-adult novelist Lois Metzger, and their son, Jacob.

THE EXPERIENCE OF PLACE
Tony Hiss

WE ALL REACT, CONSCIOUSLY AND UNCONSCIOUSLY, to the places where we live and work, in ways we scarcely notice or that are only now becoming known to us. Ever-accelerating changes in most people's day-to-day circumstances are helping us and prodding us, sometimes forcing us, to learn that our ordinary surroundings, built and natural alike, have an immediate and a continuing effect on the way we feel and act, and on our health and intelligence. These places have an impact on our sense of self, our sense of safety, the kind of work we get done, the ways we interact with other people, even our ability to function as citizens in a democracy. In short, the places where we spend our time affect the people we are and can become.

As places around us change—both the communities that shelter us and the larger regions that support them—we all undergo changes inside. This means that whatever we experience in a place is both a serious environmental issue and a deeply personal one. Our relationship with the places we know and meet up with—where you are right now; and where you've been earlier today; and wherever you'll be in another few hours—is a close bond, intricate in nature, and not abstract, not remote at all: It's enveloping, almost a continuum with all we are and think. And the danger, as we are now beginning to see, is that whenever we make changes in our surroundings, we can all too easily shortchange ourselves, by cutting ourselves off from some of the sights or sounds, the shapes or textures, or other information from a place that have helped mold our understanding and are now necessary for us to thrive. Overdevelopment and urban sprawl can damage our own lives as much as they damage our cities and countryside.

The way to avoid the danger is to start doing three things at once: Make sure that when we change a place, the change agreed upon nurtures our growth as capable and responsible people, protects the natural environment, and develops jobs and homes enough for all.

Luckily, we have a hidden ally—or, if not hidden, at least a long-neglected, overlooked, undervalued one. This ally is our built-in ability to experience places directly, an ability that makes it possible for people to know personally, through their own senses, about many of the ways our surroundings work within us. Paying careful attention to our experiences of places, we can use our own responses, thoughts, and feelings to help us replenish the places we love.

We can experience any place because we've all re- 5 ceived, as part of the structure of our attention, a mechanism that drinks in whatever it can from our surroundings. This underlying awareness—I call it simultaneous perception—seems to operate continuously, at least during waking hours. While normal waking consciousness works to simplify perception, allowing us to act quickly and flexibly by helping us remain seemingly oblivious to almost everything except the task in front of us, simultaneous perception is more like an extra, or a sixth, sense: It broadens and diffuses the beam of attention evenhandedly across all the senses so we can take in whatever is around us— which means sensations of touch and balance, for instance, in addition to all sights, sounds, and smells.

Anytime we make conscious use of simultaneous perception, we can add on to our thinking. . . . It's simultaneous perception that allows any of us a direct sense of continuing membership in our communities, and our regions, and the fellowship of all living creatures.

Until recently, when people spoke about a vivid experience of a place, it would usually be a wonderful memory, a magic moment at one of the sweet spots of the world. These days people often tell me that some of their most unforgettable experiences of places are disturbingly painful and have to do with unanticipated loss. Sometimes there's less to see or hear or do in a place: A curving road in front of an old suburban house, for instance, gets straightened and widened, and suddenly a favorite grove of oaks or pines that the winds whistled through is chopped and paved over. A damaged experience is not only numbing; over time we can begin to mistake it for the original. A brand-new science of place, growing up out of a body of formal research, is examining housing projects, train stations, hospitals, and sealed and sometimes "sick" office buildings, parks, lawns, and traffic-clogged streets, entrances, steps, and views from windows, meadows, fields, and forests, light, colors, noises, and scents, the horizon, small-air ions, and wind speed, and privacy. Although most of the students of place are still working separately, they have a common interest—safeguarding, repairing, and enriching our experience of place.

Although we have always prided ourselves on our willingness to adapt to all habitats, and on our skill at prospering and making ourselves comfortable wherever we are—in a meadow, in a desert, on the tundra, or out on the ocean—we don't just adapt to places, or modify them in order to ease our burdens. We're the only species that over and over has deliberately transformed our surroundings in order to stretch our capacity for understanding and provoke new accomplishments. And our growing and enhanced understanding is our most valuable, and our most vulnerable, inheritance.

Now, late in the second half of the twentieth century, America's experiences are under seige. And all around the planet, the "typical" surroundings of vast numbers of people are radically changing character: Until recently, a large majority of the world's population lived in villages. Less than a decade from now, a small majority of the world's population (52 percent) will live in cities. And a hundred years from now, as many as 90 percent of all people may live in cities, and even today many city residents have little or no access to either wilderness areas or farming regions.

In our planetary environmental crisis, we face an epidemic of extinctions—so many plant and animal species could be lost by continued destruction of the tropical rain forests that it might take twenty million years before basic evolutionary processes could regenerate as much abundance as exists today. Humanity, in its slow rise, has been nurtured both by abundant places and by its fruitful experiences of those places—and in some cases the experiences themselves are now millions of years old. By keeping part of our attention on our experiencing, we can work to retain surroundings that offer richly nourishing experiences, making sure that we maintain for ourselves a planet capable of helping us toward the next boost in our understanding.

Conscious noticing of what we're experiencing, once we get back the hang of it, can be a common denominator, a language of connectedness between social, environmental, and economic concerns—just as Central Park in New York pulls people together for an outdoor concert on a summer night, and gives songbirds a stopover point every year on their spring migration north, and increases property values on Fifth Avenue. Using the things we know or sense about places but seldom put into words, we can bring all of our minds to bear on the problems of how our communities, regions, and landscapes should change. We each have a contribution to make.

We need to get started now . . . and this means seeking out some experiential goals that we can use to guide the development process. And we can also develop habits of experiential watchfulness. For a start, here are several sample experiential checklists:

1. *America the Beautiful.* Other than parks, what landscapes do you know and care about that you would nominate to a list of Outstanding National Landscapes? How secure are these places at this point? Who's in charge of them? What kind of changes to what you see, hear, smell, or touch would damage your sense of connectedness to these landscapes?

2. *Sweet Spots.* What are your favorite nearby places—rural or urban, public or private—within walking or driving distance to where you live or work? What's the nature of the experience there, and is it different during the daytime, at night, on a weekday, a weekend, a holiday? Is anything missing, or neglected, or not regularly maintained? Have any recent changes to such places changed what you can experience? Do you go less often? How vulnerable are those places?

3. *Reaching Out to a Region.* How closely connected do you feel to the people in neighboring communities, to other living creatures around you, to the land nearby? How many towns, counties, or states are part of your region? What are the region makers in your area—rivers, mountains, valleys, forests, lakes, trails, railroad tracks? How far do you have to travel to get a feeling not available in your own neighborhood—for instance, if you live in a city where's the nearest place that feels like countryside? Where's the nearest wilderness?

The experiences that places make available to people, as we're learning, are an inheritance that has been entrusted to our care. Guarding these experiences and championing them, as we're also learning, are skills that are natural to people—because each one of us has direct access to the experiences that pour into us at any moment. So getting good at replenishing the places around us will just need a small stretch in our understanding. ○

1. What does Tony Hiss mean when he talks about "simultaneous perception" (para. 5)? On what grounds (based on what evidence) does he build an argument that simultaneous perception is a useful tool for social change? According to Hiss, what are the essential problems involved in our relationships to place? What remedy does he suggest?

2. Look carefully at the overall structure of Hiss's essay. How does he construct—and formulate—his argument? If you had to draw a representation of Hiss's argument, what would it look like? How many parts is his argument divided into? With what effect(s)? What do you find useful in his "experiential checklists"? In what ways do you agree with—or disagree with—the proposition that they are effective tools for developing what Hiss calls "habits of experiential watchfulness" (para. 12)?

3. Joel Sternfeld's book *On This Site* deals with another kind of experience of place; he photographs sites where violence has occurred, such as the site of the 1970 Kent State shootings, shown on the next page. What do you think Sternfeld is saying by juxtaposing this photograph with the brief verbal description of what happened there?

1. Hiss argues that developing our perception is an important step in understanding and changing our relationship to a sense of place—as well as in helping tackle such social problems as overdevelopment and urban sprawl. Prepare an outline of the major points Hiss makes as he argues his case. On which points is he most vulnerable to a counterargument? Why? On which is he least vulnerable? Why? As soon as you have established the basis for your critique (or endorsement) of his argument, write the first draft of an argumentative essay in which you convince your audience to support—or challenge—Hiss's reasoning and his conclusion.

2. Tony Hiss and Bill McKibben are two of America's most eloquent writers on the subject of place. Whereas Hiss argues that we ought to reconnect to our sense of place by sharpening our perception, McKibben claims that in many respects it is too late to do so: We can no longer see nature clearly because we have altered it irrevocably. (The title of McKibben's most recent book is *The End of Nature*.) Consider each point of view carefully, and then decide which one comes closest to your own thinking about our relationship to nature. Write an argumentative essay in which you offer a detailed and carefully reasoned account of the grounds on which you support either McKibben's or Hiss's point of view on this subject.

President Nixon's decision on April 30, 1970, to expand the Vietnam War into Cambodia incited protests throughout the nation. At Kent State University, demonstrators took over the campus and burned the ROTC building. On May 4, at 12:24 p.m., twenty-eight Ohio National Guardsmen opened fire on students for thirteen seconds, killing Allison Krause, Jeffrey Miller, William Schroeder, and Sandra Scheuer in this parking lot.

Nine years later, without acknowledging wrongdoing, the state of Ohio paid the parents of each dead student $15,000.

– Joel Sternfeld

Joel Sternfeld, **Taylor Hall Parking Lot,
Kent State University, Kent, OH, May 1994**

PICO IYER

"Travel is the best way we have of rescuing the humanity of places and saving them from abstraction and ideology," Pico Iyer writes. He views travel as a chance to witness the crisscrossing of many distinct cultures and explains that "a foreigner tends to see paradise where a native sees purgatory, insofar as a foreigner ... has more appreciative eyes, undimmed by familiarity." At the same time, Iyer worries that we are losing touch with each other and reality because most of us learn about the world not by traveling but through technological devices and media images.

Iyer was born in 1957 to Indian parents while they were living in Oxford, England. He was educated at Eton, Oxford, and Harvard before he started globetrotting. Most famous as a travel writer, he has written numerous books, including travel narratives: *Video Night in Kathmandu: And Other Reports from the Not-So-Far East* (1988), *The Lady and the Monk: Four Seasons in Kyoto* (1991) and *The Global Soul* (2000). His essays appear in magazines and journals worldwide, and he writes regularly for *Time*, *Harper's*, *The New York Review of Books*, the *New York Times*, *Sports Illustrated*, and other publications. "Why We Travel" first appeared in *Salon Travel* (2000).

Why We Travel

Pico Iyer

WE TRAVEL, INITIALLY, TO LOSE OURSELVES; AND WE travel, next, to find ourselves. We travel to open our hearts and eyes and learn more about the world than our newspapers will accommodate. We travel to bring what little we can, in our ignorance and knowledge, to those parts of the globe whose riches are differently dispersed. And we travel, in essence, to become young fools again—to slow time down and get taken in, and fall in love once more. The beauty of this whole process was best described, perhaps, before people even took to frequent flying, by George Santayana in his lapidary essay "The Philosophy of Travel." We "need sometimes," the Harvard philosopher wrote, "to escape into open solitudes, into aimlessness, into the moral holiday of running some pure hazard, in order to sharpen the edge of life, to taste hardship, and to be compelled to work desperately for a moment at no matter what."

I like that stress on work, since never more than on the road are we shown how proportional our blessings are to the difficulty that precedes them; and I like the stress on a holiday that's "moral" since we fall into our ethical habits as easily as into our beds at night. Few of us ever forget the connection between "travel" and "travail," and I know that I travel in large part in search of hardship—both my own, which I want to feel, and others', which I need to see. Travel in that sense guides us toward a better balance of wisdom and compassion—of seeing the world clearly, and yet feeling it truly. For seeing without feeling can obviously be uncaring; while feeling without seeing can be blind.

Yet for me the first great joy of traveling is simply the luxury of leaving all my beliefs and certainties at home, and seeing everything I thought I knew in a different light, and from a crooked angle. In that regard, even a Kentucky Fried Chicken outlet (in Beijing) or a scratchy revival showing of *Wild Orchids* (on the Champs-Elysées) can be both novelty and revelation: In China, after all, people will pay a whole week's wages to eat with Colonel Sanders, and in Paris, Mickey Rourke is regarded as the greatest actor since Jerry Lewis.

If a Mongolian restaurant seems exotic to us in Evanston, Illinois, it only follows that a McDonald's would seem equally exotic in Ulan Bator—or, at least, equally far from everything expected. Though it's fashionable nowadays to draw a distinction between the "tourist" and the "traveler," perhaps the real distinction lies between those who leave their assumptions at home and those who don't: Among those who don't, a tourist is just someone who complains, "Nothing here is the way it is at home," while a traveler is one who grumbles, "Everything here is the same as it is in Cairo—or Cuzco or Kathmandu." It's all very much the same.

But for the rest of us, the sovereign freedom of traveling comes from the fact that it whirls you around and turns you upside down, and stands everything you took for granted on its head. If a diploma can famously be a passport (to a journey through hard realism), a passport can be a diploma (for a crash course in cultural relativism). And the first lesson we learn on the road, whether we like it or not, is how provisional and provincial are the things we imagine to be universal. When you go to North Korea, for example, you really do feel as if you've landed on a different planet—and the North Koreans doubtless feel that they're being visited by an extra-terrestrial too (or else they simply assume that you, as they do, receive orders every morning from the Central Committee on what clothes to wear and what route to use when walking to work, and you, as they do, have loudspeakers in your bedroom broadcasting propaganda every morning at dawn, and you, as they do, have your radios fixed so as to receive only a single channel).

We travel, then, in part just to shake up our complacencies by seeing all the moral and political urgencies, the life-and-death dilemmas, that we seldom have to face at home. And we travel to fill in the gaps left by tomorrow's headlines: When you drive down the streets of Port-au-Prince, for example, where there is almost no paving and women relieve themselves next to mountains of trash, your notions of the Internet and a "one world order" grow usefully revised. Travel is the best way we have of rescuing the humanity of places, and saving them from abstraction and ideology.

And in the process, we also get saved from abstraction ourselves, and come to see how much we can bring to the places we visit, and how much we can become a kind of carrier pigeon—an anti-Federal Express, if you like—in transporting back and forth what every culture needs. I find that I always take Michael Jordan posters to Kyoto and bring woven ikebana baskets back to California; I invariably travel to Cuba with a suitcase piled high with bottles of Tylenol and bars of soap and come back with one piled high with salsa tapes, and hopes, and letters to long-lost brothers.

But more significantly, we carry values and beliefs and news to the places we go, and in many parts of the world, we become walking video screens and living newspapers, the only channels that can take people out of the censored limits of their homelands. In closed or impoverished places, like Pagan or Lhasa or Havana, we are the eyes and ears of the people we meet, their only contact with the world outside and, very often, the closest, quite literally, they will ever come to Michael Jackson or Bill Clinton. Not the least of the challenges of travel, therefore, is learning how to import—and export—dreams with tenderness.

By now all of us have heard (too often) the old Proust line about how the real voyage of discovery consists not in seeing new places but in seeing with new eyes. Yet one of the subtler beauties of travel is that it enables you to bring new eyes to the people you encounter. Thus even as holidays help you appreciate your own home more—not least by seeing it through a distant admirer's eye—they help you bring newly appreciative—distant—eyes to the places you visit. You can teach them what they have to celebrate as much as you celebrate what they have to teach. This, I think, is how tourism, which so obviously destroys cultures, can also resuscitate or revive them, how it has created new "traditional" dances in Bali, and caused craftsmen in India to pay new attention to their works. If the first thing we can bring the Cubans is a real and balanced sense of what contemporary America is like, the second—and perhaps more important—thing we can bring them is a fresh and renewed sense of how special are the warmth and beauty of their country, for those who can compare it with other places around the globe.

Thus travel spins us round in two ways at once: It shows us the sights and values and issues that we might ordinarily ignore; but it also, and more deeply, shows us all the parts of ourselves that might otherwise grow rusty. For in traveling to a truly foreign place, we inevitably travel to moods and states of mind and hidden inward passages that we'd otherwise seldom have cause to visit.

On the most basic level, when I'm in Thailand, though a teetotaler who usually goes to bed at 9:00 P.M., I stay up till dawn in the local bars; and in Tibet, though not a real Buddhist, I spend days on end in temples, listening to the chants of sutras. I go to Iceland to visit the lunar spaces within me, and, in the uncanny quietude and emptiness of that vast and treeless world, to tap parts of myself generally obscured by chatter and routine.

We travel, then, in search of both self and anonymity—and, of course, in finding the one we apprehend the other. Abroad, we are wonderfully free of caste and job and standing; we are, as Hazlitt puts it, just the "gentlemen in the parlour," and people cannot put a name or tag to us. And precisely because we are clarified in this way, and freed of inessential labels, we have the opportunity to come into contact with more essential parts of ourselves (which may begin to explain why we may feel most alive when far from home).

Abroad is the place where we stay up late, follow impulse, and find ourselves as wide open as when we are in love. We live without a past or future, for a moment at least, and are ourselves up for grabs and open to interpretation. We even may become mysterious—to others, at first, and sometimes to ourselves—and, as no less a dignitary than Oliver Cromwell once noted, "A man never goes so far as when he doesn't know where he is going."

There are, of course, great dangers to this, as to every kind of freedom, but the great promise of it is that, traveling, we are born again, and able to return at moments to a younger and a more open kind of self. Traveling is a way to reverse time, to a small extent, and make a day last a year—or at least forty-five hours—and traveling is an easy way of surrounding ourselves, as in childhood, with what we cannot understand. Language facilitates this cracking open, for when we go to France, we often migrate to French and the more childlike self, simple and polite, that speaking a foreign language educes. Even when I'm not speaking pidgin English in Hanoi, I'm simplified in a positive way, and concerned not with expressing myself but simply with making sense.

So travel, for many of us, is a quest for not just the unknown but the unknowing; I, at least, travel in search of an innocent eye that can return me to a more innocent self. I tend to believe more abroad than I do at home (which, though treacherous again, can at least help me to extend my vision), and I tend to be more easily excited abroad, and even kinder. And since no one I meet can "place" me—no one can fix me in my résumé—I can remake myself for better, as well as, of course, for worse (if travel is notoriously a cradle for false identities, it can also, at its best, be a crucible for truer ones). In this way, travel can be a kind of monasticism on the move: On the road, we often live more simply (even when staying in a luxury hotel), with no more possessions than we can carry, and surrendering ourselves to chance.

And that is why many of us travel in search not of answers but of better questions. I, like many people, tend to ask questions of the places I visit, and relish most the ones that ask the most searching questions back of me. In Paraguay, for example, where one car in every two is stolen, and two-thirds of the goods on sale are smuggled, I have to rethink my every Californian assumption. And in Thailand, where many young women give up their bodies in order to protect their families—to become better Buddhists—I have to question my own too-ready judgments.

"The ideal travel book," Christopher Isherwood once said, "should be perhaps a little like a crime story in which you're in search of something." And it's the best kind of something, I would add, if it's one that you can never quite find.

I remember, in fact, after my first trips to Southeast Asia, more than a decade ago, how I would come back to my apartment in New York and lie in my bed, kept up by something more than jet lag, playing back in my memory, over and over, all that I had experienced, and paging wistfully through my photographs and reading and rereading my diaries, as if to extract some mystery from them. Anyone witnessing this strange scene would have drawn the right conclusion: I was in love.

For if every true love affair can feel like a journey to a foreign country, where you can't quite speak the language and you don't know where you're going and you're pulled ever deeper into the inviting darkness, every trip to a foreign country can be a love affair, where you're left puzzling over who you are and whom you've fallen in love with. All the great travel books are love stories, by some reckoning—from the *Odyssey* and the *Aeneid* to the *Divine Comedy* and the New Testament—and all good trips are, like love, about being carried out of yourself and deposited in the midst of terror and wonder.

And what this metaphor also brings home to us is 20 that all travel is a two-way transaction, as we too easily forget, and if warfare is one model of the meeting of nations, romance is another. For what we all too often ignore when we go abroad is that we are objects of scrutiny as much as the people we scrutinize, and we are being consumed by the cultures we consume, as much on the road as when we are at home. At the very least, we are objects of speculation (and even desire) who can seem as exotic to the people around us as they do to us.

We are the comic props in Japanese home movies, the oddities in Malian anecdotes, and the fall guys in Chinese jokes; we are the moving postcards or bizarre *objets trouvés* that villagers in Peru will later tell their friends about. If travel is about the meeting of realities, it is no less about the mating of illusions: You give me my dreamed-of vision of Tibet, and I'll give you your wished-for California. And in truth, many of us, even (or especially) the ones who are fleeing America abroad, will get taken, willy-nilly, as symbols of the American Dream.

That, in fact, is perhaps the most central and most wrenching of the questions travel proposes to us: how to respond to the dream that people tender to you? Do you encourage their notions of a Land of Milk and Honey across the horizon, even if it is the same land you've abandoned? Or do you try to

dampen their enthusiasm for a place that exists only in the mind? To quicken their dreams may, after all, be to matchmake them with an illusion; yet to dash them may be to strip them of the one possession that sustains them in adversity.

That whole complex interaction—not unlike the dilemmas we face with those we love (how do we balance truthfulness and tact?)—is partly the reason why so many of the great travel writers, by nature, are enthusiasts: not just Pierre Loti, who famously, infamously, fell in love wherever he alighted (an archetypal sailor leaving offspring in the form of *Madame Butterfly* myths), but also Henry Miller, D. H. Lawrence, and Graham Greene, all of whom bore out the hidden truth that we are optimists abroad as readily as pessimists at home. None of them was by any means blind to the deficiencies of the places around them, but all, having chosen to go there, chose to find something to admire.

All, in that sense, believed in "being moved" as one of the points of taking trips, and "being transported" by private as well as public means; all saw that "ecstasy" ("ex-stasis") tells us that our highest moments come when we're not stationary, and that epiphany can follow movement as much as it precipitates it. I remember once asking the great travel writer Norman Lewis if he'd ever be interested in writing on apartheid South Africa. He looked at me, astonished. "To write well about a thing," he said, "I've got to like it!"

At the same time, as all this is intrinsic to travel, 25 from Ovid to O'Rourke, travel itself is changing as the world does, and with it, the mandate of the travel writer. It's not enough to go to the ends of the earth these days (not least because the ends of the earth are often coming to you); and where a writer like Jan Morris could, a few years ago, achieve something miraculous simply by voyaging to all the great cities of the globe, now anyone with a Visa card can do that. So where Morris, in effect, was chronicling the last days of the empire, a younger travel writer is in a better position to chart the first days of a new empire, postnational, global, mobile, and yet as diligent as the Raj in transporting its props and its values around the world.

In the mid-nineteenth century, the British famously sent the Bible and Shakespeare and cricket round the world; now a more international kind of empire is sending Madonna and the Simpsons and Brad Pitt. And the way in which each culture takes in this common pool of references tells you as much about them as their indigenous products might. Madonna in an Islamic country, after all, sounds radically different from Madonna in a Confucian one, and neither begins to mean the same as Madonna on East 14th Street. When you go to a McDonald's outlet in Kyoto, you will find Teriyaki McBurgers and Bacon Potato Pies. The place mats offer maps of the great temples of the city, and the posters all around broadcast the wonders of San Francisco. And—most crucial of all—the young people eating their Big Macs, with baseball caps worn backward and tight 501 jeans, are still utterly and inalienably Japanese in the way they move, they nod, they sip their oolong teas—and never to be mistaken for the patrons of a McDonald's outlet in Rio, Morocco, or Managua. These days a whole new realm of exotica arises out of the way one culture colors and appropriates the products of another.

The other factor complicating and exciting all of this is people, who are, more and more, themselves as many-tongued and mongrel as cities like Sydney or Toronto or Hong Kong. I am in many ways an increasingly typical specimen, if only because I was born, as the son of Indian parents, in England, moved to America at seven, and cannot really call myself an Indian, an American, or an Englishman. I was, in short, a traveler at birth, for whom even a visit to the candy store was a trip through a foreign world where no one I saw quite matched my parents' inheritance, or my own. And though some of this is involuntary and tragic—the number of refugees in the world, which came to just 2.5 million in 1970, is now at least 27.4 million—it does involve, for some

of us, the chance to be transnational in a happier sense, able to adapt anywhere, used to being outsiders everywhere, and forced to fashion our own rigorous sense of home. (And if nowhere is quite home, we can be optimists everywhere.)

Besides, even those who don't move around the world find the world moving more and more around them. Walk just six blocks in Queens or Berkeley, and you're traveling through several cultures in as many minutes; get into a cab outside the White House, and you're often in a piece of Addis Ababa. And technology too compounds this (sometimes deceptive) sense of availability, so that many people feel they can travel around the world without leaving the room—through cyberspace or CD-ROMs, videos and virtual travel. There are many challenges in this, of course, in what it says about essential notions of family and community and loyalty, and in the worry that air-conditioned, purely synthetic versions of places may replace the real thing—not to mention the fact that the world seems increasingly in flux, a moving target quicker than our notions of it. But there is, for the traveler at least, the sense that learning about home and learning about a foreign world can be one and the same thing.

All of us feel this from the cradle, and know, in some sense, that all the significant movement we ever take is internal. We travel when we see a movie, strike up a new friendship, get held up. Novels are often journeys as much as travel books are fictions; and though this has been true since at least as long ago as Sir John Mandeville's colorful fourteenth-century accounts of a Far East he'd never visited, it's an even more shadowy distinction now, as genre distinctions join other borders in collapsing.

In Mary Morris's *House Arrest,* a thinly disguised 30 account of Castro's Cuba, the novelist reiterates, on the copyright page, "All dialogue is invented. Isabella, her family, the inhabitants, and even *la isla* itself are creations of the author's imagination." On page 172, however, we read, "*La isla,* of course, does exist. Don't let anyone fool you about that. It just feels as if it doesn't. But it does." No wonder the travel-writer narrator—a fictional construct (or not)?—confesses to devoting her travel magazine column to places that never existed. "Erewhon," after all, the undiscovered land in Samuel Butler's great travel novel, is just "nowhere" rearranged.

Travel, then, is a voyage into that famously subjective zone, the imagination, and what the traveler brings back is—and has to be—an ineffable compound of himself and the place, what's really there and what's only in him. Thus Bruce Chatwin's books seem to dance around the distinction between fact and fancy. V.S. Naipaul's recent book *A Way in the World* was published as a non-fictional "series" in England and a "novel" in the United States. And when some of the stories in Paul Theroux's half-invented memoir, *My Other Life*, were published in *The New Yorker*, they were slyly categorized as "Fact and Fiction."

And since travel is, in a sense, about the conspiracy of perception and imagination, the two great travel writers, for me, to whom I constantly return are Emerson and Thoreau (the one who famously advised that "traveling is a fool's paradise," and the other who "traveled a good deal in Concord"). Both of them insist on the fact that reality is our creation, and that we invent the places we see as much as we do the books that we read. What we find outside ourselves has to be inside ourselves for us to find it. Or, as Sir Thomas Browne sagely put it, "We carry within us the wonders we seek without us. There is Africa and her prodigies in us."

So, if more and more of us have to carry our sense of home inside us, we also—Emerson and Thoreau remind us—have to carry with us our sense of desti-

nation. The most valuable Pacifics we explore will always be the vast expanses with us, and the most important Northwest Crossings the thresholds we cross in the heart. The virtue of finding a gilded pavilion in Kyoto is that it allows you to take back a more lasting, private Golden Temple to your office in Rockefeller Center.

And even as the world seems to grow more exhausted, our travels do not, and some of the finest travel books in recent years have been those that undertake a parallel journey, matching the physical steps of a pilgrimage with the metaphysical steps of a questioning (as in Peter Matthiessen's great *The Snow Leopard*), or chronicling a trip to the farthest reaches of human strangeness (as in Oliver Sacks's *Island of the Colorblind*, which features a journey not just to a remote atoll in the Pacific but to a realm where people actually see light differently). The most distant shores, we are constantly reminded, lie within the person asleep at our side.

So travel, at heart, is just a quick way of keeping our minds mobile and awake. As Santayana, the heir to Emerson and Thoreau with whom I began, wrote, "There is a wisdom in turning as often as possible from the familiar to the unfamiliar; it keeps the mind nimble; it kills prejudice, and it fosters humor." Romantic poets inaugurated an era of travel because they were the great apostles of open eyes. Buddhist monks are often vagabonds, in part because they believe in wakefulness. And if travel is like love, it is, in the end, mostly because it's a heightened state of awareness, in which we are mindful, receptive, undimmed by familiarity and ready to be transformed. That is why the best trips, like the best love affairs, never really end. ○

SEEING

1. Pico Iyer enumerates a series of reasons why we travel. Reread his essay carefully, and generate a list of these reasons. Which do you find most appealing? Which do you find least engaging? Why? In what ways do these reasons constitute an argument about why we travel? How does Iyer strengthen or weaken his case for travel when he quotes the philosopher George Santayana (para. 1)? At the end of paragraph 2, Iyer says: "For seeing without feeling can obviously be uncaring: while feeling without seeing can be blind." Make a list of the instances when Iyer refers to seeing in this essay. In what ways do these references to seeing clarify his purpose in writing this essay?

2. How does Iyer distinguish between a "traveler" and a "tourist"? Consider carefully Duane Hanson's "portrait" of two tourists (p. 295). To what extent might you read Hanson's sculpture as an illustration of Iyer's definition of a tourist? What does Iyer account for in his definition that Hanson seems to omit? What does Hanson address that Iyer omits? With what effect(s) in each case? Who do you imagine to be the "we" in Iyer's essay? How would you explain the significance of his assertion that travel is a "two-way transaction"? Iyer compares travel to a broad range of concepts: work, love, discovery, and the like. Which of these metaphors do you find most engaging? Why?

WRITING

1. Iyer begins his final paragraph by noting, "So travel, at heart, is just a quick way of keeping our minds mobile and awake." As you reflect about the point Iyer makes here, consider the ways in which travel has helped you to remain mobile and awake. Write the first draft of a personal essay in which you recount—with as much specificity as you can command—exactly how the experience of traveling has kept your mind mobile and awake.

2. Examine carefully the point Iyer underscores in paragraph 12: "We travel, then, in search of both self and anonymity—and, of course, in finding the one we apprehend the other. Abroad, we are wonderfully free of caste and job and standing; we are, as Hazlitt puts it, just the 'gentlemen in the parlour,' and people cannot put a name or tag to us." To what extent do you agree with Iyer's assertions here? To what extent does Duane Hanson's *Tourists* (p. 295) illustrate or challenge Iyer's claim? Write an argumentative essay in which you support (or refute) Iyer's declaration.

More than the stated goal—to write an argument, for example—*purpose* refers to the effect you want to have on your audience. A writer's purpose is the *why* behind a text.

Visualizing Composition
Tone

In Chapter 1's Visualizing Composition (p. 54) the focus is on details—you practiced looking closely at specific aspects of technique, content, or style. Reading for and articulating a distinctive tone of voice builds on the skills of close reading.

In its simplest sense, tone refers to the quality or character of communication. We talk about the tone of someone's voice: *She sounds mad* or *He had a resigned tone when he said he couldn't go.* The poet Robert Frost calls our ability to read tone "the hearing imagination"—we can read tone of voice even when we can't make out the exact words someone is saying. In a musical composition, tone refers to a distinct note, pitch, or the character of sound from a particular instrument (*the plaintive tone of a bassoon*). In art, tone indicates the quality of color or the general effect of light in a painting or photograph. When we're talking about our bodies, tone refers to how visible our muscles are to the people who see us.

In writing, tone indicates the character of a text, reflecting the feelings of the writer. A letter, an essay, or a poem might be described as angry or skeptical in tone, formal or informal. When you are writing, no matter what the subject is, remember that it is important to maintain a consistent tone and that the words you choose determine the tone your readers will hear.

Following are the opening paragraphs of two newspaper editorials on the same subject: the murder of a young woman in New York City. We've highlighted several (but not all) of the words and phrases that characterize the writers' different tones of voice. As you read the texts in this book—and compose your own—practice your own ability to hear and strike a distinctive tone.

What Kind of People Are We?

Seldom has the Times published a more horrifying story than its account of how 38 respectable, law-abiding, middle-class Queens citizens watched a killer stalk his young woman victim in a parking lot in Kew Gardens over a half-hour period without one of them making a call to the Police Department that might have saved her life. They would not have been exposed to any danger themselves; a simple telephone call in the privacy of their own homes was all that was needed. How incredible is it that such motivations as "I don't want to get involved" deterred them from this act of simple humanity? Does residence in a great city destroy all sense of personal responsibility for one's neighbors? Who can explain such shocking indifference on the part of a cross-section of our fellow New Yorkers? We regretfully admit that we do not know the answers.

- NEW YORK TIMES, MARCH 28, 1964

The titles reveal a lot about the tone of the writing to come—personal outrage versus a measured call for responsibility.

Using "we" instead of "citizens" implicates the writer as sharing in the guilt.

RAGHUBIR SINGH >
Born in 1942, photographer
Raghubir Singh was raised in
Jaipur, India. Unable to find work
as a tea planter, he studied at
Hindu College at Delhi University
and took photo assignments for
Indian and foreign publications
such as the *New York Times* and
Life magazine.

In his thirty-year career he
published thirteen collections
of photographs depicting a wide
range of Indian places and people. His books include *Kerala: The
Spice Coast of India* (1986); *Kash-
mir* (1987); *Rajasthan: India's En-
chanted Land* (1990); *The Grand
Trunk Road: A Passage through
India* (1995). A retrospective of
over thirty years of his work, *River
of Colour: The India of Raghubir
Singh*, was in progress at the Art
Institute of Chicago and the
National Gallery of Modern Art in
New Delhi and in Mumbai at the
time of his death in 1999. An accompanying book of the same
title, in which these two photographs are included, was published in 1998.

It is no coincidence that the
photographs in these collections
are exclusively in color. Seeing
the world in color, Singh explains,
is a distinctly Indian way of seeing. "Colour has never been an
unknown force in India," he
wrote in the introduction to *River
of Colour;* "it is the fountain not
of new styles and ideas, but of
the continuum of life itself. . . .
Indians know colour through
intuition, while the West tries to
know it through the mind."

Civic Duty

Fighting crime is essentially a police job.
But it is the responsibility of decent
citizens not only to obey the law but also
to help the authorities enforce it.

A shocking demonstration of public
default occurred recently in a Long
Island community. A thug, in three
separate attacks within a half hour,
stabbed a woman to death. A number
of neighbors watched the ghastly street
scene from their windows. None called
police. Finally, after the attacker had
fled, the police were notified. The
neighbors' excuse? They didn't want to
"get involved"!

The police do not suggest that any
witness should have engaged the armed
thug. But it is cowardly and callous when
anyone in a position to summon help fails
to do so. In a moral sense, that is abetting
the crime and aiding the criminal.
Citizens have an obligation to the law as
well as a right to its protection.

- NEWARK EVENING NEWS, MARCH 30, 1964

Raghubir Singh, **Durga Puja Immersion, Where the Ganges and the GT Meet, West Bengal**

Raghubir Singh, **Diwali Day Pilgrims at the Golden Temple**

SEEING

1. Raghubir Singh's photographs of scenes along a river offer what one critic has called "the rich palette of India's landscape and peoples." What do these photographs reveal about the public spaces they present? Be as specific as possible in your observations, pointing to details in each photo to validate your assertions. In what ways are these public spaces different from—and similar to—the public spaces that you visit frequently?

2. Observe carefully both photographs once again, this time with an eye on the similarities and differences you notice about each. Consider, for example, the nature of the "built environment" in each. How does Singh present people in each photograph? How does he frame each scene? What angle of vision, or perspective, does he use? Comment on the accuracy of the following observation about Singh's photographs: "Many of his pictures reveal an Indian way of seeing, in that they simultaneously capture several equally important knots of activity in the manner of old miniatures, rather than leading the viewer's eye to some primary focal point." What would you offer as a definition, however provisional, or an "American way of seeing"?

WRITING

1. In an essay written shortly before his death in 1999, Singh talked about the importance of color in daily Indian life: "Indians know colour through intuition, while the West tries to know it through the mind. . . . If photography had been an Indian invention, I believe that seeing in colour would never have posed the theoretical or artistic problems perceived by Western photographers." Write the first draft of an essay in which you compare and contrast the use of color in these two photographs. Which photograph highlights more effectively the notion of an "Indian way of seeing"?

2. As soon as you are reasonably in command of the distinctive features of Singh's use of color in these two photographs, turn your attention to the other photographs in this chapter. (See, for example, the portfolio of photographs by Richard Misrach, pp. 176–81, or the photograph by Miranda Lichtenstein, p. 166.) What differences—and similarities—do you notice in the use of color in the work of *two* of these photographers? Write a comparative essay in which you extrapolate a larger statement about an Indian way of seeing versus an American way of seeing from the photographs you choose.

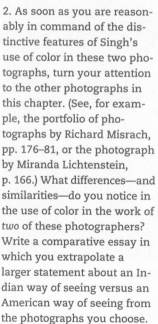

Looking Closer
Going Home

In a nation founded by people who left their *homelands*, the word *home* soon became an obsession. Indeed, this parent word has generated more offspring than virtually any other in the lexicon. We speak of *homefries, homemakers,* the *homeless, homesteads, hometowns,* even being *homesick*. In fact, recent estimates suggest that one in eight Americans spends most of her Thanksgiving weekend traveling substantial distances to *home*.

"Writers are always headed or looking for home" writes Marita Golden in **"A Sense of Place,"** an observation proved true by the visual and verbal selections that follow. For Chang-rae Lee, cooking for his dying mother made it possible to endure the anguish of **"Coming Home Again";** Lucille Clifton hears and smells "the tremors of that house" in **"When I Go Home";** the kitchen table serves as the emotional hearth for Carmen Lomas Garza's painting **Tamalada** and Tina Barney's photograph **Family in Kitchen.** And the telecommunications company Ericsson promises that if you buy its phone, you are always home: **"You Are Everywhere."** Going home is never a one-sided matter. It is a ritual rooted in a search for the comforts of the familiar—experiences of a specific place and of the individuals who remain there, waiting for us to return.

A SENSE OF PLACE
Marita Golden

Coming Home Again
Chang-rae Lee

WHEN I GO HOME
Lucille Clifton

i go to where my mother is,
alive again and humming,
in a room
warm with the scent of dough
rising under damp towels,
and i walk
limbless again, hard against
the splintered floorboards
that she held
together with her song,
i hear and smell and almost taste
the tremors of that house
and i am home, i have gone home
wherever i might find myself,
home
where the memory is.

A SENSE OF PLACE
Marita Golden

WRITERS ARE ALWAYS HEADED OR LOOKING FOR home. Home is the first sentence, questing into the craggy terrain of imagination. Home is the final sentence, polished, perfected, nailed down. I am an American writer, and so my sense of place is fluid, ever shifting, ever salt. The spaciousness of this land reigns and pushes against the borders of self-censorship and hesitation. I have claimed at one point or other everyplace as my home.

My people were brought to this country in an act of grand theft, actually. With no return ticket. Part of a perverse, stunning, triangular trade-off of culture and identity. Launched in the middle passage we have sojourned from Accra in Ghana, Ondo in Nigeria, to Tougaloo in Mississippi and Oakland in California. Our sojourns have required few passports, and we have indelibly stamped, reshaped, and claimed each place we have called ours.

Like their creator, my fictional characters reject the notion of life lived on automatic pilot. The most important people in my books see life as a flame, something that when lived properly bristles and squirms, even as it glows. In the autobiography *Migrations of the Heart*, the heroine, who just happened to be me, came of age in Washington and began the process of becoming an adult person everywhere else. If you sell your first piece of writing in Manhattan, give birth to your only child in Lagos, experience Paris in the spring—yes—with someone you love, and return to Washington after thirteen years of self-imposed exile to write the Washington novel nobody else had (and you thought you never would), tickets, visas, *lingua franca* will all become irrelevant. When all places fingerprint the soul, which grasp is judged to be the strongest? In my novel *A Woman's Place*, one woman leaves America to join a liberation struggle in Africa. In *Long Distance Life*, Naomi Johnson flees 1930s North Carolina and comes up north to Washington, D.C., to find and make her way. Thirty years later her daughter returns to that complex, unpredictable geography and is sculpted like some unexpected work of art by the civil-rights movement.

I am a Washington writer, who keeps one bag in the closet packed, just in case. I am an American, who knows the true color of the nation's culture and its heart, a stubborn, wrenching, rainbow. I am Africa's yearning stepchild, unforgotten, misunderstood, necessary. Writers are always headed or looking for home. The best of us embrace and rename it when we get there. ○

You are everywhere. Now there's a phone that works everywhere too. The Ericsson 788 is the smallest Go-Everywhere™ tri-mode phone around. Which means you get unsurpassed coverage in all 50 states and a phone that fits in your shirt pocket. And as small as the 788 is, it has the ability to store up to 200 numbers, plus voice mail, paging and the ability to vibrate when you get a call. So you can be reached discreetly and still **make yourself heard.**

ERICSSON ⋛

Digital TDMA

Coming Home Again

Chang-rae Lee

WHEN MY MOTHER BEGAN USING THE ELECTRONIC pump that fed her liquids and medication, we moved her to the family room. The bedroom she shared with my father was upstairs, and it was impossible to carry the machine up and down all day and night. The pump itself was attached to a metal stand on casters, and she pulled it along wherever she went. From anywhere in the house, you could hear the sound of the wheels clicking out a steady time over the grout lines of the slate-tiled foyer, her main thoroughfare to the bathroom and the kitchen. Sometimes you would hear her halt after only a few steps, to catch her breath or steady her balance, and whatever you were doing was instantly suspended by a pall of silence.

I was usually in the kitchen, preparing lunch or dinner, poised over the butcher block with her favorite chef's knife in my hand and her old yellow apron slung around my neck. I'd be breathless in the sudden quiet, and, having ceased my mincing and chopping, would stare blankly at the brushed sheen of the blade. Eventually, she would clear her throat or call out to say she was fine, then begin to move again, starting her rhythmic *ka-jug;* and only then could I go on with my cooking, the world of our house turning once more, wheeling through the black.

I wasn't cooking for my mother but for the rest of us. When she first moved downstairs she was still eating, though scantily, more just to taste what we were having than from any genuine desire for food. The point was simply to sit together at the kitchen table and array ourselves like a family again. My mother would gently set herself down in her customary chair near the stove. I sat across from her, my father and sister to my left and right, and crammed in the center was all the food I had made—a spicy codfish stew, say, or a casserole of gingery beef, dishes that in my youth she had prepared for us a hundred times.

It had been ten years since we'd all lived together in the house, which at fifteen I had left to attend boarding school in New Hampshire. My mother would sometimes point this out, by speaking of our present time as being "just like before Exeter," which surprised me, given how proud she always was that I was a graduate of the school.

My going to such a place was part of my mother's 5 not so secret plan to change my character, which she worried was becoming too much like hers. I was clever and able enough, but without outside pressure I was readily given to sloth and vanity. The famous school—which none of us knew the first thing about—would prove my mettle. She was right, of course, and while I was there I would falter more than a few times, academically and otherwise. But I never thought that my leaving home then would ever be a problem for her, a private quarrel she would have even as her life waned.

Now her house was full again. My sister had just resigned from her job in New York City, and my father, who typically saw his psychiatric patients until eight or nine in the evening, was appearing in the driveway at four-thirty. I had been living at home for nearly a year and was in the final push of work on what would prove a dismal failure of a novel. When I wasn't struggling over my prose, I kept occupied with the things she usually did—the daily errands, the grocery shopping, the vacuuming and the cleaning, and, of course, all the cooking.

When I was six or seven years old, I used to watch my mother as she prepared our favorite meals. It was one of my daily pleasures. She shooed me away in the beginning, telling me that the kitchen wasn't my place, and adding, in her half-proud, half-deprecating way, that her kind of work would only serve to weaken me. "Go out and play with your friends," she'd snap in Korean, "or better yet, do your reading and homework." She knew that I had already done both, and that as the evening approached there was no place to go save her small and tidy kitchen, from which the clatter of her mixing bowls and pans would ring through the house.

I would enter the kitchen quietly and stand beside her, my chin lodging upon the point of her hip. Peering through the crook of her arm, I beheld the movements of her hands. For *kalbi*, she would take up a butchered short rib in her narrow hand, the flinty bone shaped like a section of an airplane wing and deeply embedded in gristle and flesh, and with the point of her knife cut so that the bone fell away, though not completely, leaving it connected to the meat by the barest opaque layer of tendon. Then she methodically butterflied the flesh, cutting and unfolding, repeating the action until the meat lay out on her board, glistening and ready for seasoning. She scored it diagonally, then sifted sugar into the crevices with her pinched fingers, gently rubbing in the crystals. The sugar would tenderize as well as sweeten the meat. She did this with each rib, and then set them all aside in a large shallow bowl. She minced a half-dozen cloves of garlic, a stub of gingerroot, sliced up a few scallions, and spread it all over the meat. She wiped her hands and took out a bottle of sesame oil, and, after pausing for a moment, streamed the dark oil in two swift circles around the bowl. After adding a few splashes of soy sauce, she thrust her hands in and kneaded the flesh, careful not to dislodge the bones. I asked her why it mattered that they remain connected. "The meat needs the bone nearby," she said, "to borrow its richness." She wiped her hands clean of the marinade, except for her little finger, which she would flick with her tongue from time to time, because she knew that the flavor of a good dish developed not at once but in stages.

Whenever I cook, I find myself working just as she would, readying the ingredients—a mash of garlic, a julienne of red peppers, fantails of shrimp—and piling them in little mounds about the cutting surface. My mother never left me any recipes, but this is how I learned to make her food, each dish coming not from a list or a card but from the aromatic spread of a board.

I've always thought it was particularly cruel that 10 the cancer was in her stomach, and that for a long time at the end she couldn't eat. The last meal I made for her was on New Year's Eve, 1990. My sister suggested that instead of a rib roast or a bird, or the usual overflow of Korean food, we make all sorts of finger dishes that our mother might fancy and pick at.

We set the meal out on the glass coffee table in the family room. I prepared a tray of smoked-salmon canapés, fried some Korean bean cakes, and made a few other dishes I thought she might enjoy. My sister supervised me, arranging the platters, and then with some pomp carried each dish in to our parents. Finally, I brought out a bottle of champagne in a bucket of ice. My mother had moved to the sofa and was sitting up, surveying the low table. "It looks pretty nice," she said. "I think I'm feeling hungry."

This made us all feel good, especially me, for I couldn't remember the last time she had felt any hunger or had eaten something I cooked. We began to eat. My mother picked up a piece of salmon toast and took a tiny corner in her mouth. She rolled it around for a moment and then pushed it out with the tip of her tongue, letting it fall back onto her plate. She swallowed hard, as if to quell a gag, then glanced up to see if we had noticed. Of course we all had. She attempted a bean cake, some cheese, and then a slice of fruit, but nothing was any use.

She nodded at me anyway, and said, "Oh, it's very good." But I was already feeling lost and I put down my plate abruptly, nearly shattering it on the thick glass. There was an ugly pause before my father asked me in a weary, gentle voice if anything was wrong, and I answered that it was nothing, it was the last night of a long year, and we were together, and I was simply relieved. At midnight, I poured out glasses of champagne, even one for my mother, who took a deep sip. Her manner grew playful and light, and I helped her shuffle to her mattress, and she lay down in the place where in a brief week she was dead.

My mother could whip up most anything, but during our first years of living in this country we ate only Korean foods. At my harangue-like behest, my mother set herself to learning how to cook exotic American dishes. Luckily, a kind neighbor, Mrs. Churchill, a tall florid young woman with flaxen hair, taught my mother her most trusted recipes.

Mrs. Churchill's two young sons, palish, weepy boys with identical crew cuts, always accompanied her, and though I liked them well enough, I would slip away from them after a few minutes, for I knew that the real action would be in the kitchen, where their mother was playing guide. Mrs. Churchill hailed from the state of Maine, where the finest Swedish meatballs and tuna casserole and angel food cake in America are made. She readily demonstrated certain techniques—how to layer wet sheets of pasta for a lasagna or whisk up a simple roux, for example. She often brought gift shoeboxes containing curious ingredients like dried oregano, instant yeast, and cream of mushroom soup. The two women, though at ease and jolly with each other, had difficulty communicating, and this was made worse by the often confusing terminology of Western cuisine ("corned beef," "deviled eggs"). Although I was just learning the language myself, I'd gladly play the interlocutor, jumping back and forth between their places at the counter, dipping my fingers into whatever sauce lay about.

I was an insistent child, and, being my mother's firstborn, much too prized. My mother could say no to me, and did often enough, but anyone who knew us—particularly my father and sister—could tell how much the denying pained her. And if I was overconscious of her indulgence even then, and suffered the rushing pangs of guilt that she could inflict upon me with the slightest wounded turn of her lip, I was too happily obtuse and venal to let her cease. She reminded me daily that I was her sole son, her reason for living, and that if she were to lose me, in either body or spirit, she wished that God would mercifully smite her, strike her down like a weak branch.

In the traditional fashion, she was the house accountant, the maid, the launderer, the disciplinarian, the driver, the secretary, and, of course, the cook. She was also my first basketball coach. In South Korea, where girls' high school basketball is a popular spectator sport, she had been a star, the point guard for the national high school team that once won the all-Asia championships. I learned this one Saturday during the summer, when I asked my father if he would go down to the schoolyard and shoot some baskets with me. I had just finished the fifth grade, and wanted desperately to make the middle school team the coming fall. He called for my mother and sister to come along. When we arrived, my sister immediately ran off to the swings, and I recall being annoyed that my mother wasn't following her. I dribbled clumsily around the key, on the verge of losing control of the ball, and flung a flat shot that caromed wildly off the rim. The ball bounced to my father, who took a few not so graceful dribbles and made an easy layup. He dribbled out and then drove to the hoop for a layup on the other side. He rebounded his shot and passed the ball to my mother, who had been watching us from the foul line. She turned from the basket and began heading the other way.

"*Um-mah,*" I cried at her, my exasperation already bubbling over, "the basket's over *here!*"

After a few steps she turned around, and from where the professional three-point line must be now, she effortlessly flipped the ball up in a two-handed set shot, its flight truer and higher than I'd witnessed from any boy or man. The ball arced cleanly into the hoop, stiffly popping the chain-link net. All afternoon, she rained in shot after shot, as my father and I scrambled after her.

When we got home from the playground, my mother showed me the photograph album of her team's championship run. For years I kept it in my room, on the same shelf that housed the scrapbooks I made of basketball stars, with magazine clippings of slick players like Bubbles Hawkins and Pistol Pete and George (the Iceman) Gervin.

It puzzled me how much she considered her own 20 history to be immaterial, and if she never patently diminished herself, she was able to finesse a kind of self-removal by speaking of my father whenever she could. She zealously recounted his excellence as a student in medical school and reminded me, each night before I started my homework, of how hard he

drove himself in his work to make a life for us. She said that because of his Asian face and imperfect English, he was "working two times the American doctors." I knew that she was building him up, buttressing him with both genuine admiration and her own brand of anxious braggadocio, and that her overarching concern was that I might fail to see him as she wished me to—in the most dawning light, his pose steadfast and solitary.

In the year before I left for Exeter, I became weary of her oft-repeated accounts of my father's success. I was a teenager, and so ever inclined to be dismissive and bitter toward anything that had to do with family and home. Often enough, my mother was the object of my derision. Suddenly, her life seemed so small to me. She was there, and sometimes, I thought, *always* there, as if she were confined to the four walls of our house. I would even complain about her cooking. Mostly, though, I was getting more and more impatient with the difficulty she encountered in doing everyday things. I was afraid for her. One day, we got into a terrible argument when she asked me to call the bank, to question a discrepancy she had discovered in the monthly statement. I asked her why she couldn't call herself. I was stupid and brutal, and I knew exactly how to wound her.

"Whom do I talk to?" she said. She would mostly speak to me in Korean, and I would answer in English.

"The bank manager, who else?"

"What do I say?"

"Whatever you want to say."

"Don't speak to me like that!" she cried.   25

"It's just that you should be able to do it yourself," I said.

"You know how I feel about this!"

"Well, maybe then you should consider it *practice,*" I answered lightly, using the Korean word to make sure she understood.

Her face blanched, and her neck suddenly became 30 rigid, as if I were throttling her. She nearly struck me right then, but instead she bit her lip and ran upstairs. I followed her, pleading for forgiveness at her door. But it was the one time in our life that I couldn't convince her, melt her resolve with the blandishments of a spoiled son.

When my mother was feeling strong enough, or was in particularly good spirits, she would roll her machine into the kitchen and sit at the table and watch me work. She wore pajamas day and night, mostly old pairs of mine.

She said, "I can't tell, what are you making?"

"*Mahn-doo* filling."

"You didn't salt the cabbage and squash."

"Was I supposed to?"

"Of course. Look, it's too wet. Now the skins will get soggy before you can fry them."

"What should I do?"

"It's too late. Maybe it'll be OK if you work quickly. Why didn't you ask me?"

"You were finally sleeping."

"You should have woken me."

"No way."

She sighed, as deeply as her weary lungs would allow.

"I don't know how you were going to make it without me."

"I don't know, either. I'll remember the salt next time."

"You better. And not too much."

We often talked like this, our tone decidedly matter-of-fact, chin up, just this side of being able to bear it. Once, while inspecting a potato fritter batter I was making, she asked me if she had ever done anything that I wished she hadn't done. I thought for a moment, and told her no. In the next breath, she wondered aloud if it was right of her to have let me go to Exeter, to live away from the house while I was so young. She tested the batter's thickness with her finger and called for more flour. Then she asked if, given a choice, I would go to Exeter again.

I wasn't sure what she was getting at, and I told her that I couldn't be certain, but probably yes, I would. She snorted at this and said it was my leaving home that had once so troubled our relationship.

"Remember how I had so much difficulty talking to you? Remember?"

She believed back then that I had found her more and more ignorant each time I came home. She said she never blamed me, for this was the way she knew it would be with my wonderful new education. Nothing I could say seemed to quell the notion. But I knew that the problem wasn't simply the *education;* the first time I saw her again after starting school, barely six weeks later, when she and my father visited me on Parents Day, she had already grown nervous and distant. After the usual campus events, we had gone to the motel where they were staying in a nearby town and sat on the beds in our room. She seemed to sneak looks at me, as though I might discover a horrible new truth if our eyes should meet.

My own secret feeling was that I had missed my parents greatly, my mother especially, and much more than I had anticipated. I couldn't tell them that these first weeks were a mere blur to me, that I felt completely overwhelmed by all the studies and my much brighter friends and the thousand irritating details of living alone, and that I had really learned nothing, save perhaps how to put on a necktie while sprinting to class. I felt as if I had plunged too deep into the world, which, to my great horror, was much larger than I had ever imagined.

I welcomed the lull of the motel room. My father and I had nearly dozed off when my mother jumped up excitedly, murmured how stupid she was, and hurried to the closet by the door. She pulled out our old metal cooler and dragged it between the beds. She lifted the top and began unpacking plastic containers, and I thought she would never stop. One after the other they came out, each with a dish that traveled well—a salted stewed meat, rolls of Korean-style sushi. I opened a container of radish kimchi and suddenly the room bloomed with its odor, and I reveled in the very peculiar sensation (which perhaps only true kimchi lovers know) of simultaneously drooling and gagging as I breathed it all in. For the next few minutes, they watched me eat. I'm not certain that I was even hungry. But after weeks of pork parmigiana and chicken patties and wax beans, I suddenly realized that I had lost all the savor in my life. And it seemed I couldn't get enough of it back. I ate and I ate, so much and so fast that I actually went to the bathroom and vomited. I came out dizzy and sated with the phantom warmth of my binge.

And beneath the face of her worry, I thought, my mother was smiling.

From that day, my mother prepared a certain meal to welcome me home. It was always the same. Even as I rode the school's shuttle bus from Exeter to Logan airport, I could already see the exact arrangement of my mother's table.

I knew that we would eat in the kitchen, the table brimming with plates. There was the *kalbi*, of course, broiled or grilled depending on the season. Leaf lettuce, to wrap the meat with. Bowls of garlicky clam broth with miso and tofu and fresh spinach. Shavings of cod dusted in flour and then dipped in egg wash and fried. Glass noodles with onions and shiitake. Scallion-and-hot-pepper pancakes. Chilled steamed shrimp. Seasoned salads of bean sprouts, spinach, and white radish. Crispy squares of seaweed. Steamed rice with barley and red beans. Homemade kimchi. It was all there—the old flavors I knew, the beautiful salt, the sweet, the excellent taste.

After the meal, my father and I talked about school, but I could never say enough for it to make any sense. My father would often recall his high school principal, who had gone to England to study the methods and traditions of the public schools, and regaled students with stories of the great Eton man. My mother sat with us, paring fruit, not saying a word but taking everything in. When it was time to go to bed, my father said good night first. I usually watched television until the early morning. My mother would sit with me for an hour or two, perhaps until she was accustomed to me again, and only then would she kiss me and head upstairs to sleep.

During the following days, it was always the cook- ing that started our conversations. She'd hold an inquest over the cold leftovers we ate at lunch, discussing each dish in terms of its balance of flavors or what might have been prepared differently. But mostly I begged her to leave the dishes alone. I wish I had paid more attention. After her death, when my father and I were the only ones left in the house, drifting through the rooms like ghosts, I sometimes tried to make that meal for him. Though it was too much for two, I made each dish anyway, taking as much care as I could. But nothing turned out quite right—not the color, not the smell. At the table, neither of us said much of anything. And we had to eat the food for days.

I remember washing rice in the kitchen one day and my mother's saying in English, from her usual seat, "I made a big mistake."

"About Exeter?"

"Yes. I made a big mistake. You should be with us for that time. I should never let you go there."

"So why did you?" I said.

"Because I didn't know I was going to die."

I let her words pass. For the first time in her life, she was letting herself speak her full mind, so what else could I do?

"But you know what?" she spoke up. "It was better for you. If you stayed home, you would not like me so much now."

I suggested that maybe I would like her even more.

She shook her head. "Impossible."

Sometimes I still think about what she said, about having made a mistake. I would have left home for college, that was never in doubt, but those years I was away at boarding school grew more precious to her as her illness progressed. After many months of exhaustion and pain and the haze of the drugs, I thought that her mind was beginning to fade, for more and more it seemed that she was seeing me again as her fifteen-year-old boy, the one she had dropped off in New Hampshire on a cloudy September afternoon.

I remember the first person I met, another new student, named Zack, who walked to the welcome picnic with me. I had planned to eat with my parents—my mother had brought a coolerful of food even that first day—but I learned of the cookout and told her that I should probably go. I wanted to go, of course. I was excited, and no doubt fearful and nervous, and I must have thought I was only thinking ahead. She agreed wholeheartedly, saying I certainly should. I walked them to the car, and perhaps I hugged them, before saying goodbye. One day, after she died, my father told me what happened on the long drive home to Syracuse.

He was driving the car, looking straight ahead. Traffic was light on the Massachusetts Turnpike, and the sky was nearly dark. They had driven for more than two hours and had not yet spoken a word. He then heard a strange sound from her, a kind of muffled chewing noise, as if something inside her were grinding its way out.

"So, what's the matter?" he said, trying to keep an edge to his voice.

She looked at him with her ashen face and she burst into tears. He began to cry himself, and pulled the car over onto the narrow shoulder of the turnpike, where they stayed for the next half hour or so, the blank-faced cars droning by them in the cold, on-rushing night.

Every once in a while, when I think of her, I'm 70 driving alone somewhere on the highway. In the twilight, I see their car off to the side, a blue Olds coupe with a landau top, and as I pass them by I look back in the mirror and I see them again, the two figures huddling together in the front seat. Are they sleeping? Or kissing? Are they all right? ○

WHEN I GO HOME
Lucille Clifton

i go to where my mother is,
alive again and humming,
in a room
warm with the scent of dough
rising under damp towels,   5
and i walk
linoleum again, hard against
the splintered floorboards
that she held
together with her song.   10
i hear and smell and almost taste
the tremors of that house
and i am home, i have gone home
wherever i might find myself,
home   15
where the memory is.

Home is the place where you feel safe, where despite disquieting news that arrives by cable or optical fibre, you can leave the door on the latch and wander outside in your old terrycloth bathrobe and a pair of muddy clogs to check on whether or not the brave arrows of the crocuses are poking through the snow.

As a child, not knowing there is an alternative, you never really appreciate home. As a young adult, home is where you want to leave as soon as possible, brandishing a new driver's license and a boyfriend.

Only in midlife—our sexy new euphemism for dread old middle age—does home beckon seductively again, inviting you to pleasures running away can never supply. Home is where your books are. . . . Home is where you know all the quirks of the plumbing but they comfort rather than irritate you. Home is where you get out of bed at 3 A.M., wink at the full moon through the bathroom skylight, and go back to sleep perfectly contented, knowing no demons can follow you here.

–Erica Jong, from "Coming Home to Connecticut"

MARITA GOLDEN

Marita Golden (b. 1950) grew up in Washington, D.C. Her father shared with her his vast knowledge of African and African American history, and when Golden was 14 years old, her mother predicted she would write a book someday. In fact, Golden has written seven, including a memoir about her experience marrying a Nigerian, four novels on contemporary African American life, and a book called *Saving Our Sons* (1995) about the trials black parents face trying to raise male children in modern America. Golden has also edited two anthologies and has recently finished writing a book about single mothers. She founded and served as the first president of the African American Writers Guild, and since 1990 she has headed the Zora Neale Hurston / Richard Wright Foundation.

CHANG-RAE LEE

At age 3 Chang-rae Lee came to the United States with his family from South Korea. He graduated from Yale University and earned a Master of Fine Arts degree at the University of Oregon, where he taught creative writing. He currently teaches at Princeton University. In 1996, Lee's novel *Native Speaker* won the Ernest Hemingway Foundation/Pen Award for first fiction. The novel tells the story of Henry Park, a native Korean who tries to become a "real" American but whose efforts only increase his cultural alienation. His most recent work is *A Gesture Life* (1999).

ERICCSON

Since 1876, the telecommunications company Ericsson has been active worldwide and today operates in more than 140 countries. Four out of every ten mobile calls are handled by Ericsson equipment. It is the world's leading supplier in telecommunications, and its products cover everything from systems and applications to mobile phones and other communications tools. The company's vision: "We believe in an 'all communicating' world. Voice, data, images, and video are conveniently communicated anywhere and anytime in the world, increasing both quality-of-life, and productivity and enabling a more resource-efficient world. We are one of the major progressive forces, active around the globe, driving for this advanced communication to happen."

CARMEN LOMAS GARZA

Carmen Lomas Garza (b. 1948) grew up in Texas with the pain and confusion of discrimination. In *A Piece of My Heart / Pedacito de mi Corazon* (1991), from which the painting *Tamalada (Making Tamales)* (1987) is reprinted, Lomas Garza explains that her paintings "helped heal the wounds inflicted by discrimination and racism. . . . I felt I had to start with my earliest recollections of my life and validate each event or incident by depicting it in a visual format." In *Tamalada* Lomas Garza takes us into the heart of the *familia* as several generations nurture a delectable tradition.

Coming Home Again
Chang-rae Lee

LUCILLE CLIFTON

Lucille Clifton is the author of several volumes of poetry, more than a dozen children's books, and a memoir, *Generations* (1976), that traces five generations of her family history. Among the themes that recur throughout her work, Clifton places special emphasis on the resilience and dignity of African American families and the importance of finding one's center "at home." Born in 1936 in Depew, New York, Clifton has taught poetry at colleges and universities in New York, California, and Maryland, where she was named state poet laureate in 1979.

WHEN I GO HOME
Lucille Clifton

i go to where my mother is,
alive again and humming,
in a room
warm with the scent of dough
rising under damp towels,
and i walk
linoleum again, hard against
the splintered floorboards
that she held
together with her song
i hear and smell and almost taste
the tremors of that house
and i am home, i have gone home
whenever i might find myself,
home
where the memory is.

MARGARET MORTON

Margaret Morton has spent over a decade photographing homeless people and their shelters in New York City. "These improvised habitats," wrote Morton, "are as diverse as the people who build them and they bear witness to the profound human need to create a sense of place, no matter how extreme one's circumstances." *Mr. Lee's house, the Hill, 1991* is included in *Fragile Dwelling*, Morton's fourth collection of photographs, published in 2000. According to Morton, the photo captures "the curious home of Mr. Lee, an immigrant from Guangdong Province in China," who "brought few possessions but soon astonished his neighbors by constructing a house without pounding a nail or sawing a board. Morton received an undergraduate degree in art from Kent State University and completed graduate studies at Yale University. She is a professor of art at The Cooper Union for the Advancement of Science and Art.

TINA BARNEY

Photographer Tina Barney's book, *Theater of Manners* (1997), presents views of her extended family in intimate and candid scenes of daily life. Whether her subjects are getting dressed in the bathroom or reading the paper at the kitchen table, Barney presents them in what she calls "a very personal way." Reflecting the tradition of narrative storytelling, her photos often feature the telling details that surround a certain upper-class segment of East Coast society. Born in New York in 1946, Barney began taking photographs when she moved to Sun Valley, Idaho, in 1974. There have been several solo exhibits of her work in New York galleries.

SEEING

1. Chang-rae Lee presents a poignant account of the personal pleasures and painful ironies associated with going home. As you reread his essay, pay special attention to the narrative and descriptive devices that he uses to both structure the story and build unity and coherence in it. What, for example, does Lee gain and lose by opening the narrative with his mother on the verge of death? Much of his story is organized around literal senses of place—a kitchen, a motel room, a boarding school. What descriptive details does Lee associate with each of these places, and how is each one related to his expectations of going home?

2. "I have claimed at one point or another everyplace as my home," asserts Marita Golden in "Going Home." "Writers are always headed or looking for home. The best of us embrace and rename it when we get there." Identify the techniques Golden uses to articulate her experience as you examine the verbal and visual accounts of going home included in this section. How does each scene suggest a notion of home? How does that compare to the notion of going home that Golden describes? Write a set of detailed notes for class discussion that focus on the features in each text that establish this sense of place and convey the meanings of going home.

WRITING

1. Chang-rae Lee explains that the idea of coming home involves a specific sense of place—in this case, the kitchen table: "The point was simply to sit together at the kitchen table and array ourselves like a family again" (para. 3). What sense of place do you most associate with "coming home"? Draft an essay in which you describe this place in detail. Consider how you can incorporate events that normally occur in that space to evoke a range of emotions associated with going home. Because this exercise involves description and narration, choose details that evoke the widest and deepest array of emotions in the reader.

2. Cooking is a theme that unifies Chang-rae Lee's account of his relations with his parents, and especially with his mother. Preparing food not only links mother and son emotionally but also provides an opportunity for her to "Americanize" herself. Yet when his parents visit him at boarding school, his mother brings special Korean delicacies. "From that day," Lee notes, "my mother prepared a certain meal to welcome me home" (para. 52). Consider what that meal would be when you want to be welcomed home. Draft an essay in which you not only describe this meal in sensuous detail but also explain why it reinforces your sense of personal, familial, and ethnic identity.

Capturing Memorable Moments

Chapter 3
Capturing Memorable Moments

Each generation of Americans shares memorable moments. Most Americans over age 50, for example, remember precisely where they were and what they were doing when they heard the news that President John F. Kennedy had been assassinated. No matter what our age, we have all seen the film footage of JFK and Jackie waving from their car in Dallas the second before the fatal shots were fired.

Identifying a single memorable moment for younger generations of Americans may have been more difficult—until September 11, 2001, when suicide terrorists attacked the World Trade Center and the Pentagon. Whatever generation we represent, each of us will never forget being glued to the television, watching in horror as the second plane hit the World

Patrick Witty, **Witnessing a Dreadful Moment in History**
Jeff Mermelstein, **Here Is New York**

Trade Center, and then seeing innumerable replays as television commentators, like the rest of us, tried to make sense of what we had witnessed.

Prior to September 11, the most widely viewed media images were of the beating of Rodney King, "live" helicopter shots of O. J. Simpson slumped across the back seat of a white Bronco; the shooting of rap artist Tupac Shakur; the image of wreckage in a Paris tunnel after the death of Princess Di; or the footage of Monica Lewinsky hugging President Clinton. But none of these moments defined today's generation.

Before September 11, according to Brian A. Gnatt, the student editor of the University of Michigan *Daily Arts*, the defining moments of his generation could be found in Hollywood rather than in the political realm. "While my parents' generation vividly remembers where they were when JFK was shot," Gnatt explains, "my generation [had] no single event of the same caliber."

> I do remember when, where and who I was with when I saw the *Star Wars* films. To my generation, nothing we have experienced together has been as huge a phenomenon as *Star Wars*. Luke Skywalker and Han Solo are more than household names—they will be ingrained in all of our memories until the day we die.

Of course, the events of September 11 have changed the American political and cultural landscape in profound ways. The images of that day will be ingrained in our consciousness until the moment we die. So, too, our perspectives on who we are—as individuals and as a nation—have been seared by our awareness of what took place on that morning on board four flights that were deliberately crashed by murderers in New York City and Washington, D.C., and by heroes (innocent passengers) in a field in Pennsylvania. Contemporary American political and cultural life will be replete for years to come with striking and powerful images that remind us of the horrific events of September 11.

Capturing memorable moments is also often a matter not only of national consciousness but also of personal interest. In this sense, it is far more difficult to sift through diverse and idiosyncratic personal experience to find a single image or event that unites the more private lives of college students. After all, each of us has different personal rites of passage and customs: confirmations or bat mitzvah ceremonies, Eagle Scout or sports rituals, a first date, a first day at a first job, winning a championship game, or graduating from high school. The moments we expect—or are expected—to remember, the events and ceremonies we feel obliged to record in our photo albums and scrapbooks, are not always those that affect the largest number of people. Often the most memorable experiences occur when we least expect them or are difficult to capture in a picture frame on a mantel: becoming blood sisters with a childhood friend; nervously finding a seat in your first college lecture class, only to find that you're in the wrong room; struggling through a complex mathematical equation and finally "getting" it; or receiving the news that a loved one has died.

In America, the photographer is not simply the person who records the past, but the one who invents it.
— Susan Sontag, 1977

Telling stories about the most memorable moments in our lives often includes explaining *how* they have become etched into our minds. In fact, private moments, like public ones, are inextricably linked to the technologies with which we record them. Most of our special occasions involve cameras; for example, the video camera at a wedding, rather than the bride and groom, often commands everyone's attention and cooperation. It almost seems as though an event has not taken place if it hasn't been photographed or videotaped. Instant replay and stop-action photography allow us to relive, slow down, and freeze our most cherished or embarrassing moments. The success of shows like *TV's Funniest Home Videos,* as well as the popularity of web sites featuring 24-hour live feeds to "real life" living rooms, testify to the increasing importance of the video camera in Americans' private lives.

Whether we take photographs, create scrapbooks, use home-video cameras, keep journals, describe our experiences in letters or e-mails to friends, share family stories during the holidays, or simply replay memories in our minds, we are framing our experiences—for ourselves and often for others. As those memorable events drift into the past, we often revise and embellish our stories about them. Indeed, we continually reshape the nature and tone of our stories each time we recall them.

The selections that follow provide an opportunity for you to practice and develop your skills of narration and revision by noticing how other writers and artists capture memorable moments. From Joe Rosenthal's dramatic photograph of Marines raising the American flag at Iwo Jima to Don DeLillo's insightful reflections on terror and loss in the wake of September 11, each selection in this chapter conveys a public or personal moment of revelation. Pay attention to the techniques and methods each artist and writer employs to tell his or her story. As you read, observe, and write about these selections, consider the range of ways in which you capture the memorable moments in your own life. How does the process of transcribing (writing, photographing, painting, videotaping, etc.) shape or change your understanding of those moments? How can you as a writer enable readers to "get inside" your own experience—to understand the details and nuances that make each particular experience memorable?

PATRICK WITTY

"New York City was left in shock," in the wake of September 11, writes photographer Patrick Witty. "Below Fourteenth Street, there was no traffic. The streets were silent. There were no planes in the air, no rumble of trucks, no cars in the street. Only people walking, dazed. For three days it could have been Sunday morning." Witty took this photograph of onlookers staring up in shock as the attacks began on the twin towers.

In addition to his work as a freelance photographer in New York City, Witty is the editor of *Untitled Magazine*, <www. untitledmagazine.com>, an on-line documentary photography site created in January 1998. This photograph is posted on *Untitled Magazine* and was reprinted in the December 2001 issue of *Newsweek*, a special double issue devoted to the events of September 11.

JEFF MERMELSTEIN

"I do not have a conscious memory of taking most of these pictures," said Jeff Mermelstein about his experience photographing ground zero. "I was on total autopilot the day of the attack. I don't really remember finding that statue covered in debris." A freelance photographer living and working in New York for over twenty years, Mermelstein is accustomed to capturing the city's sidewalk spaces. This photo of Nassau Street appeared in the *New York Times Magazine* and is part of the ongoing exhibit of September 11 photographs entitled *Here Is New York.* "I shot fourteen rolls of film the afternoon of the attack," he explains. "I'm not a war photographer, so this wasn't an easy experience for me. The constantly shattering glass was terrifying and distracting, and my camera kept getting completely covered in ash. But because for years I have been taking documentary pictures of New Yorkers out on the sidewalks, there is a way in which I was prepared. It sounds crazy to say it, but these images are a direct extension of what I've been doing all along: capturing life on the streets of this city."

Mermelstein's work has appeared in *Life,* the *New York Times Magazine, Doubletake,* and *The New Yorker* as well as in galleries and museums around the country. *Sidewalk* (2000) is a collection of his photographs of New York City taken between 1987 and 1999. Mermelstein teaches at the International Center for Photography in New York.

SEEING

1. The horrific events of September 11, 2001, have been recounted in innumerable ways and from innumerable points of view—through eyewitness accounts; through political, economic, social, and religious analyses; as well as through television and videotape footage, to name but a few. Each account contributes a new angle on one of the most terrifying events in recent American history. What reactions does Jeff Mermelstein's photograph—taken moments after the collapse of the World Trade Center's twin towers—evoke in you? As you examine the image again, more carefully, what details in the scene and the person depicted attract your attention? Explain why. On what specific aspects of the image does your eye linger? With what effect(s)? What overall point(s) does this photograph convey about the terrorist attack on the World Trade Center as well as about the indirect effects of the event on the nation's sense of security?

2. Compare and contrast Jeff Mermelstein's photograph with Patrick Witty's picture of witnesses as they stare up in shock as the destruction of the World Trade Center begins. Comment on the position of the photographer in relation to his subject in each photograph. How do the different camera angles produce different "takes" on the events of September 11? To what extent—and how—do these two very different images change what you already knew about the event?

WRITING

1. Consider for a few moments what you would propose as the most memorable events in your own experience. What would your personal timeline of memorable moments include? Which moments have made an indelible impression on you? Why? Write down your most memorable moments, explaining the nature and significance of each event. What details do you remember about each event? What makes each one significant? Choose one event, and write a narrative essay in which you recount what happened and why the event is significant to you.

2. Many young Americans have called the events of September 11 the "defining moment" of their generation. Write an argumentative essay in which you support or challenge this assertion. In developing your essay, you might find it helpful to address the following questions: What makes an event significant to an entire generation? to an entire nation? What constitutes a generation to you as an individual? To what extent are your notions of memorable moments mediated by the filters of print and visual media?

Joe Rosenthal, **Marines Raising the Flag on Mount Suribachi, Iwo Jima,** 1945

FLAG RAISING ON IWO JIMA, FEBRUARY 23, 1945
Joe Rosenthal

ON THE FOURTH DAY OF THE BATTLE I HAD gone out to the command ship to send a package of film back to Guam to be processed at headquarters. The next morning, I was informed that General Holland Smith and the secretary of the navy were on a smaller ship and were going in one mile offshore with binoculars to scan the battlefield. So I transferred to this boat. I took a photo of General Smith and Secretary of the Navy Forrestal at the railing with Mount Suribachi in the background. This was still in the morning, so I transferred to another boat so I could get closer to shore and then on to another that could take me in. I heard from a radioman that there was a patrol going up the mountain to plant our flag. I was surprised, you know, that by the morning of the fifth day they could do this. I said, "I gotta get a picture of that." About halfway up we ran into four marines, including Staff Sergeant Louis Lowery, who was a photographer for the marines' magazine, *Leatherneck.* Lowery and the others said that the patrol had raised a flag at the summit and that he had photographed the flag raising, but I made up my mind that I wanted to get a shot of the flag anyway. There continued isolated fire, but mortar was not reaching us. At the northern end of the island a mile and a half away there was still heavy fighting. When I came to an area where I could see over a rise, I could see our flag fluttering. I clutched my throat. It was our flag. As I got closer I observed there were three marines kneeling beside a long pole, and one of them had a flag folded in the triangled, traditional manner. "What's doing, fellas?" "We're going to raise this larger flag so it can be seen by the troops all over the island," and they added they were going to keep the first one as a souvenir. I moved around to where I could await what these fellas had told me they were going to do. I selected a position, and then I had to estimate how far back to get in order to get the full length of this pole swinging up. Because there were some chewed-up bushes in the foreground that might cut off the bottom half of these marines that were going to raise the flag, I grabbed a couple of rocks and a couple of old sandbags left from a Japanese outpost that had been blasted there, to stand on. This got me up a foot or two. Just about the time that I stood on top, Bill Genaust, a marine movie cameraman, came across and went to my right at arm's length and asked, "I'm not in your way, am I, Joe?" And I turned and said, "No, Bill, that's fine—oh, there it goes, Bill!" Bill had just time to swing his camera around to capture that wonderful, beautiful, extraordinary movie that shows the flag raising from the ground up. You notice it doesn't start with any preliminary footage. We had no signal beforehand. [Genaust was killed in action nine days after the flag raising.] The pole was a heavy iron or lead pipe probably twenty feet long. It came from either a heating system or water system for the Japanese outpost that was up there. It was originally the three marines I had met, but a couple of others saw what they were doing and could observe that it required more heft to lift it. One man kneeled down to hold it in position. When they got it into a little indentation in the ground—not very deep—three of the men held it there while one got a rope and tied it down three ways. Then they shoved a lot of rocks to keep it in position. Later, down below, I was told that it had raised a great cheer. I was more or less reporting an incident in the turn of the battle. Up until this point the news going back home from Iwo Jima was very sad. On Iwo Jima it was touch and go. Some of the advances were measured in a couple of feet. So this was a great boost to the people back home. ○

JOE ROSENTHAL

Born in Washington state in 1911, Joe Rosenthal became a staff photographer with the *San Francisco Examiner* soon after graduating from college. His poor eyesight made him ineligible as a U.S. military photographer at the outbreak of World War II, but he was later sent to cover the Pacific War by the Associated Press. On February 23, 1945, he took what would become the most celebrated photograph of his career: Joe Rosenthal's *Flag Raising on Iwo Jima, February 23, 1945* has been characterized as one of the most famous images of war in the twentieth century. The photograph won him the Pulitzer Prize; inspired the U.S. Marine Corps Memorial in Washington, D.C.; served as the image for the Iwo Jima U.S. Commemorative Stamp (1945); and has been reproduced in countless personal and public monuments, events, and art pieces.

After the war, Rosenthal became chief photographer and manager of Times Wide World Photos and a photographer for the *San Francisco Chronicle,* though he modestly downplayed his own role as photographer: "I can best sum up what I feel by saying that of all the elements that went into the making of this picture, the part I played was the least important. To get that flag up there, America's fighting men had to die on that island and on other islands and off the shores and in the air. What difference does it make who took the picture? I took it, but the Marines took Iwo Jima."

SEEING

1. Joe Rosenthal's photograph of the raising of the flag on Iwo Jima is one of the most celebrated in American history. Examine this image carefully. What observations can you make about the photograph? Where, for example, is your eye first drawn in the photograph? Where does your attention linger? Explain why. How does the fact that we cannot see the faces of the Marines impact what you see and remember from the image? What observations can you make about the ground in which the flag is being positioned? What reasonable inferences can you draw from what you notice there?

2. Look at the way in which Rosenthal frames this photograph. What does he emphasize? What does he leave out? What new information does Rosenthal's essay give? Does this information strengthen or weaken your sense of the importance of this photograph? What details do you notice that Rosenthal *doesn't* comment on in his essay?

FLAG RAISING ON IWO JIMA, FEBRUARY 23, 1945
Joe Rosenthal

WRITING

1. After Rosenthal shot this picture, it may well have taken days or weeks before the image could reach the United States and be distributed to the American public through newspapers. Technological advances later in the twentieth century have made it possible to broadcast such moments to global audiences almost instantly. So, too, television, magazines, and the Internet enable us to visit scenes of great historical significance or moments of incalculable personal joy or sorrow, without ever leaving the comfort of our homes. Choose one publicly printed photograph or image of such a "memorable moment" that made a profound impression on you. Write an essay that both describes your first impression and accounts for the historical or cultural significance of the image.

2. The celebrated novelist Isabel Allende has noted that "the wonder of photography is that it does what no words can." In what ways does Joe Rosenthal's photograph "speak" to Americans? To what values does the image speak most successfully? To what extent can these values be identified as specifically American? What values are not addressed either in the image of Marines raising the American flag on Iwo Jima or in Rosenthal's account of taking the photograph? Write an expository essay in which you explain why this image has been so popular in American history and popular culture.

Visualizing Context
Raising the Flag

It has been, it is said, the most widely reproduced photograph of all time. An engraving from it appeared on an issue of three-cent postage stamps. A painting of it was used as a symbol of the Seventh War Loan Drive, and appeared on 3,500,000 postcards, 15,000 outdoor panels, and 175,000 car cards. It has been done in oils, watercolors, pastels, chalk, and matchsticks. A float based on it won a prize in a Rose Bowl parade…. It has been sculptured in ice and in hamburger and, by the Seabees, in sandstone on Iwo Jima." –Joe Rosenthal, from *Collier's*, 1955

The word *context* is used to refer to the historical circumstances within which a text emerges. Contemporary visual and verbal texts often refer directly or indirectly to the work of writers, artists, or cultural artifacts from the past—whether the references come in the form of recognizable quotations, ideas, images, or shared cultural assumptions. Recognizing such echoes can vastly enrich our reading of what we see in today's world.

One very good example of such historical sampling can be seen in the images on this page, all reminiscent or derivative of the photograph of marines raising the flag on Mount Suribachi on Iwo Jima in 1945 (p. 228). Thomas E. Franklin snapped the shot of three firemen raising a flag in the wreckage of the World Trade Center in the week after September 11; his photograph was featured on the cover of a special issue of *Newsweek* on September 24, 2001. This image has since appeared in many places, in many forms, and may become the basis for a statue in New York City memorializing the firemen who were killed.

The image has obviously resonated with many Americans. How important do you think the context is—the fact that a similar image became a symbol for American victory in World War II? (Anecdotal evidence claims that on the day the three-cent stamp was released in July 1945 featuring an engraving of the photograph, people stood in long lines waiting to buy them.) Did you know the when, where, and why of the Iwo Jima image before this textbook gave you the information? Did you recognize the 1945 photograph? When you saw the 2001 image from the World Trade Center, did you connect it with the earlier one?

Using your own impressions of Franklin's photograph, write the first draft of an essay that discusses the importance of knowing the historical context of a text when responding to it. How do reflections from the past superimpose themselves on the present? Why might those reflections strengthen the response that a group of people with shared assumptions—in this case, Americans—have to this particular image? In your opinion, which image is more powerful: the one from 1945 or the one from 2001? Why?

left to right: David J. Phillip, **Superbowl XXXVI,** 2002 ; Thomas E. Franklin, **Flag Raising, World Trade Center,** 2001;
U.S. Postal Service, **Three-Cent Stamp**, 1945

SARAH VOWELL

Author and social observer Sarah Vowell (b. 1969) is best known for the "funny, querulous voice and shrewd comic delivery" of the monologues and documentaries she delivers for National Public Radio's *This American Life*. A contributing editor for the program since 1996, she has written about everything from her father's homemade cannon and her obsession with the *Godfather* films to the New Hampshire primary and her Cherokee ancestors' forced march on the Trail of Tears. *Newsweek* magazine named her Rookie of the Year for nonfiction in 1997 for her first book, *Radio On: A Listener's Diary* (1998). *People* magazine called her second book—an essay collection entitled *Take the Cannoli: Stories from the New World* (2001)—"wise, witty and refreshingly warm-hearted." The essays in *Cannoli*, which include "Shooting Dad," look at American history, pop culture, and Vowell's own family and "reveal the bonds holding together a great, if occasionally weird, nation."

Vowell's writing has appeared in numerous newspapers and magazines, including *Esquire, GQ, Artforum, The Los Angeles Times, The Village Voice, Spin,* and *McSweeney's*. She has covered education for *Time*; American culture for *Salon.com;* and pop music for the *San Francisco Weekly,* for which she won a 1996 Music Journalism Award. She is at work on her third book, *Partly Cloudy Patriot* (2002). A native of Oklahoma and Montana, and a long-time resident of Chicago, Vowell currently lives in New York City.

Shooting Dad

Sarah Vowell

IF YOU WERE PASSING BY THE HOUSE WHERE I grew up during my teenage years and it happened to be before Election Day, you wouldn't have needed to come inside to see that it was a house divided. You could have looked at the Democratic campaign poster in the upstairs window and the Republican one in the downstairs window and seen our home for the Civil War battleground it was. I'm not saying who was the Democrat or who was the Republican—my father or I—but I will tell you that I have never subscribed to *Guns & Ammo*, that I did not plaster the family vehicle with National Rifle Association stickers, and that hunter's orange was never my color.

About the only thing my father and I agree on is the Constitution, though I'm partial to the First Amendment, while he's always favored the Second.

I am a gunsmith's daughter. I like to call my parents' house, located on a quiet residential street in Bozeman, Montana, the United States of Firearms. Guns were everywhere: the so-called pretty ones like the circa 1850 walnut muzzleloader hanging on the wall, Dad's clients' fixer-uppers leaning into corners, an entire rack right next to the TV. I had to move revolvers out of my way to make room for a bowl of Rice Krispies on the kitchen table.

I was eleven when we moved into that Bozeman house. We had never lived in town before, and this was a college town at that. We came from Oklahoma—a dusty little Muskogee County nowhere called Braggs. My parents' property there included an orchard, a horse pasture, and a couple of acres of woods. I knew our lives had changed one morning not long after we moved to Montana when, during breakfast, my father heard a noise and jumped out of his chair. Grabbing a BB gun, he rushed out the front door. Standing in the yard, he started shooting at crows. My mother sprinted after him screaming, "Pat, you might ought to check, but I don't think they do that up here!" From the look on his face, she might as well have told him that his American citizenship had been revoked. He shook his head, mumbling, "Why, shooting crows is a national pastime, like baseball and apple pie." Personally, I preferred baseball and apple pie. I looked up at those crows flying away and thought, I'm going to like it here.

Dad and I started bickering in earnest when I was 5 fourteen, after the 1984 Democratic National Convention. I was so excited when Walter Mondale chose Geraldine Ferraro as his running mate that I taped the front page of the newspaper with her picture on it to the refrigerator door. But there was some sort of mysterious gravity surge in the kitchen. Somehow, that picture ended up in the trash all the way across the room.

Nowadays, I giggle when Dad calls me on Election Day to cheerfully inform me that he has once again canceled out my vote, but I was not always so mature. There were times when I found the fact that he was a gunsmith horrifying. And just *weird*. All he ever cared about were guns. All I ever cared about was art. There were years and years when he hid out by himself in the garage making rifle barrels and I holed up in my room reading Allen Ginsberg poems, and we were incapable of having a conversation that didn't end in an argument.

Our house was partitioned off into territories. While the kitchen and the living room were well within the DMZ, the respective work spaces governed by my father and me were jealously guarded totalitarian states in which each of us declared ourselves dictator. Dad's shop was a messy disaster area, a labyrinth of lathes. Its walls were hung with the mounted antlers of deer he'd bagged, forming a makeshift museum of death. The available flat sur-

faces were buried under a million scraps of paper on which he sketched his mechanical inventions in blue ball-point pen. And the floor, carpeted with spiky metal shavings, was a tetanus shot waiting to happen. My domain was the cramped, cold space known as the music room. It was also a messy disaster area, an obstacle course of musical instruments—piano, trumpet, baritone horn, valve trombone, various percussion doodads (bells!), and recorders. A framed portrait of the French composer Claude Debussy was nailed to the wall. The available flat surfaces were buried under piles of staff paper, on which I penciled in the pompous orchestra music given titles like "Prelude to the Green Door" (named after an O. Henry short story by the way, not the watershed porn flick *Behind the Green Door*) I starting writing in junior high.

It has been my experience that in order to impress potential suitors, skip the teen Debussy anecdotes and stick with the always attention-getting line "My dad makes guns." Though it won't cause the guy to like me any better, it will make him handle the inevitable breakup with diplomacy—just in case I happen to have any loaded family heirlooms lying around the house.

But the fact is, I have only shot a gun once and once was plenty. My twin sister, Amy, and I were six years old—six—when Dad decided that it was high time we learned how to shoot. Amy remembers the day he handed us the gun for the first time differently. She liked it.

Amy shared our father's enthusiasm for firearms 10 and the quick-draw cowboy mythology surrounding them. I tended to daydream through Dad's activities—the car trip to Dodge City's Boot Hill, his beloved John Wayne Westerns on TV. My sister, on the other hand, turned into Rooster Cogburn Jr., devouring Duke movies with Dad. In fact, she named her teddy bear Duke, hung a colossal John Wayne portrait next to her bed, and took to wearing one of those John Wayne shirts that button on the side. So when Dad led us out to the backyard when we were six and, to Amy's delight, put the gun in her hand, she says she felt it meant that Daddy trusted us and that he thought of us as "big girls."

But I remember holding the pistol only made me feel small. It was so heavy in my hand. I stretched out my arm and pointed it away and winced. It was a very long time before I had the nerve to pull the trigger and I was so scared I had to close my eyes. It felt like it just went off by itself, as if I had no say in the matter, as if the gun just had this *need.* The sound it made was as big as God. It kicked little me back to the ground like a bully, like a foe. It hurt. I don't know if I dropped it or just handed it back over to my dad, but I do know that I never wanted to touch another one again. And, because I believed in the devil, I did what my mother told me to do every time I felt an evil presence. I looked at the smoke and whispered under my breath, "Satan, I rebuke thee."

It's not like I'm saying I was traumatized. It's more like I was decided. Guns: Not For Me. Luckily, both my parents grew up in exasperating households where children were considered puppets and/or slaves. My mom and dad were hell-bent on letting my sister and me make our own choices. So if I decided that I didn't want my father's little death sticks to kick me to the ground again, that was fine with him. He would go hunting with my sister, who started calling herself "the loneliest twin in history" because of my reluctance to engage in family activities.

Of course, the fact that I was allowed to voice my opinions did not mean that my father would silence his own. Some things were said during the Reagan administration that cannot be taken back. Let's just say that I blamed Dad for nuclear proliferation and Contra aid. He believed that if I had my way, all the guns would be confiscated and it would take the commies about fifteen minutes to parachute in and assume control.

We're older now, my dad and I. The older I get, the more I'm interested in becoming a better daughter. First on my list: Figure out the whole gun thing.

Not long ago, my dad finished his most elaborate tool of death yet. A cannon. He built a nineteenth-century cannon. From scratch. It took two years.

My father's cannon is a smaller replica of a cannon called the Big Horn Gun in front of Bozeman's Pioneer Museum. The barrel of the original has been filled with concrete ever since some high school kids in the '50s pointed it at the school across the street and shot out its windows one night as a prank. According to Dad's historical source, a man known to scholars as A Guy at the Museum, the cannon was brought to Bozeman around 1870, and was used by local white merchants to fire at the Sioux and Cheyenne Indians who blocked their trade access to the East in 1874.

"Bozeman was founded on greed," Dad says. The courthouse cannon, he continues, "definitely killed Indians. The merchants filled it full of nuts, bolts, and chopped-up horseshoes. Sitting Bull could have been part of these engagements. They definitely ticked off the Indians, because a couple of years later, Custer wanders into them at Little Bighorn. The Bozeman merchants were out to cause trouble. They left fresh baked bread with cyanide in it on the trail to poison a few Indians."

Because my father's sarcastic American history yarns rarely go on for long before he trots out some nefarious ancestor of ours—I come from a long line of moonshiners, Confederate soldiers, murderers, even Democrats—he cracks that the merchants hired some "community-minded Southern soldiers from North Texas." These soldiers had, like my great-great-grandfather John Vowell, fought under pro-slavery guerrilla William C. Quantrill. Quantrill is most famous for riding into Lawrence, Kansas, in 1863 flying a black flag and commanding his men pharaohlike to "kill every male and burn down every house."

"John Vowell," Dad says, "had a little rep for killing people." And since he abandoned my great-grandfather Charles, whose mother died giving birth to him in 1870, and wasn't seen again until 1912,

Dad doesn't rule out the possibility that John Vowell could have been one of the hired guns on the Bozeman Trail. So the cannon isn't just another gun to my dad. It's a map of all his obsessions—firearms, certainly, but also American history and family history, subjects he's never bothered separating from each other.

After tooling a million guns, after inventing and [20] building a rifle barrel boring machine, after setting up that complicated shop filled with lathes and blueing tanks and outmoded blacksmithing tools, the cannon is his most ambitious project ever. I thought that if I was ever going to understand the ballistic bee in his bonnet, this was my chance. It was the biggest gun he ever made and I could experience it and spend time with it with the added bonus of not having to actually pull a trigger myself.

I called Dad and said that I wanted to come to Montana and watch him shoot off the cannon. He was immediately suspicious. But I had never taken much interest in his work before and he would take what he could get. He loaded the cannon into the back of his truck and we drove up into the Bridger Mountains. I was a little worried that the National Forest Service would object to us lobbing fiery balls of metal onto its property. Dad laughed, assuring me that "you cannot shoot fireworks, but this is considered a fire*arm*."

It is a small cannon, about as long as a baseball bat and as wide as a coffee can. But it's heavy—110 pounds. We park near the side of the hill. Dad takes his gunpowder and other tools out of this adorable wooden box on which he has stenciled "PAT G. VOWELL CANNONWORKS." Cannonworks: So that's what NRA members call a metal-strewn garage.

Dad plunges his homemade bullets into the barrel, points it at an embankment just to be safe, and lights the fuse. When the fuse is lit, it resembles a cartoon. So does the sound, which warrants Ben Day[1] dot words along the lines of *ker-pow!* There's so much Fourth of July smoke everywhere I feel compelled to sing the national anthem.

I've given this a lot of thought—how to convey the giddiness I felt when the cannon shot off. But there isn't a sophisticated way to say this. It's just really, really cool. My dad thought so, too.

Sometimes, I put together stories about the more [25] eccentric corners of the American experience for public radio. So I happen to have my tape recorder with me, and I've never seen levels like these. Every time the cannon goes off, the delicate needles which keep track of the sound quality lurch into the bad, red zone so fast and so hard I'm surprised they don't break.

The cannon was so loud and so painful, I had to touch my head to make sure my skull hadn't cracked open. One thing that my dad and I share is that we're both a little hard of hearing—me from Aerosmith, him from gunsmith.

He lights the fuse again. The bullet knocks over the log he was aiming at. I instantly utter a sentence I never in my entire life thought I would say. I tell him, "Good shot, Dad."

Just as I'm wondering what's coming over me, two hikers walk by. Apparently, they have never seen a man set off a homemade cannon in the middle of the wilderness while his daughter holds a foot-long microphone up into the air recording its terrorist boom. One hiker gives me a puzzled look and asks, "So you work for the radio and that's your dad?"

Dad shoots the cannon again so that they can see how it works. The other hiker says, "That's quite the machine you got there." But he isn't talking about the cannon. He's talking about my tape recorder and my microphone—which is called a *shotgun* mike. I stare back at him, then I look over at my father's cannon, then down at my microphone, and I think, Oh. My. God. My dad and I are the same person. We're both smart-alecky loners with goofy projects and weird equipment. And since this whole target practice outing was my idea, I was no longer his adversary. I was his accomplice. What's worse, I was liking it.

I haven't changed my mind about guns. I can get be- [30] hind the cannon because it is a completely ceremonial object. It's unwieldy and impractical, just like everything else I care about. Try to rob a convenience store with this 110-pound Saturday night special, you'd still be dragging it in the door Sunday afternoon.

I love noise. As a music fan, I'm always waiting for that moment in a song when something just flies out of it and explodes in the air. My dad is a one-man garage band, the kind of rock 'n' roller who slaves away at his art for no reason other than to make his own sound. My dad is an artist—a pretty driven, idiosyncratic one, too. He's got his last *Gesamtkunstwerk*[2] all planned out. It's a performance piece. We're all in it—my mom, the loneliest twin in history, and me.

When my father dies, take a wild guess what he wants done with his ashes. Here's a hint: It requires a cannon.

"You guys are going to love this," he smirks, eyeballing the cannon. "You get to drag this thing up on top of the Gravellies on opening day of hunting season. And looking off at Sphinx Mountain, you get to put me in little paper bags. I can take my last hunting trip on opening morning."

I'll do it, too. I will have my father's body burned into ashes. I will pack these ashes into paper bags. I will go to the mountains with my mother, my sister, and the cannon. I will plunge his remains into the barrel and point it into a hill so that he doesn't take anyone with him. I will light the fuse. But I will not cover my ears. Because when I blow what used to be my dad into the earth, I want it to hurt. ○

---

1. *Ben Day:* In 1879, New York printer Benjamin Day (1838–1916) invented a method of color printing that uses a celluloid sheet of dots or other patterns to achieve correct shading and color for illustrations and maps.

2. *Gesamtkunstwerk:* German, "total work of art," meaning someone trying to bring together all kinds of art.

SEEING

1. A wickedly intelligent writer, Sarah Vowell treats the most controversial subjects in American political and social life with devastating humor and an ironic edge. What does Vowell make the ostensible subject of her essay? In what larger sense can her essay be said to be about a memorable moment in her life? In what specific ways might this essay be read as a portrait of her father? as a self-portrait? as a portrait of a father-daughter relationship? Which characterization do you find most accurate and appropriate? Explain why.

2. Reread the opening line of Vowell's essay. What response does this sentence elicit from you? How is this opening line similar to—and different from—other moments in her essay? Be as specific as possible. How, for example, does she create a sense of time in this sentence? a tone of voice for herself? an overall mood for the essay? Identify other sentences that recall this one. How are they similar in tone and style? Comment on the effectiveness of Vowell's use of irony throughout her essay. Point to specific examples to validate the point(s) you make. What observations can you make about the overall structure of this essay? Show how Vowell maintains—or changes—her point of view during the essay.

WRITING

1. Vowell often can be heard on the radio, especially on National Public Radio. Many of the essays that appear in *Take the Cannoli* (including "Shooting Dad") were originally written for broadcasting. Go to the web site for the *This American Life* radio show <www.thislife.org> and listen to episode #81 in the archives. As you listen, compare and contrast her spoken voice to her authorial voice. In what ways does her spoken voice change your understanding—and appreciation—of her essay? Write an essay in which you compare and contrast Vowell's voice in these two media. Which do you prefer? Why?

2. In a recent interview Vowell said, "I feel really almost religious about being an American, but I think that fervor comes from difference rather than sameness. . . . The thing that I always loved about this country wasn't the way we pulled together, but the way we sort of bickered. I've always been very proud of that." One of the issues in the United States that has caused a great deal of "bickering" is gun control. Vowell and her father represent different ends of the political spectrum on this subject. Reread Vowell's essay and use it as the launching point for an argumentative essay in which you support or reject stricter federal gun control laws. What are the current federal laws on this subject? How would you propose to tighten or loosen federal control of purchasing guns?

Shooting Dad
Sarah Vowell

A technique in which words express something different from and often opposite to their literal meaning. In effect, irony highlights a deliberate contrast between a writer's apparent and intended meaning.

Britta Jaschinski, **Malayan Tapir, London 1992**

BARRY LOPEZ

Barry Lopez (b. 1945) is an essayist, author, and short story writer
who has traveled extensively in
remote parts of the world. Recent
trips have taken him to the
Tanami Desert in Australia's
Northern Territory, into the
Transantarctic Mountains, to
northern Kenya, and to the Wed-
dell Sea in the Southern Ocean.
His writing crosses into the territory where mind and physical
landscape become one. He is also
the rare Western writer who is
appreciated in New York literary
circles and loved at home.

Lopez contributes regularly
to *Harper's*, *The Georgia Review*,
American Short Fiction, *Story*, the
Paris Review, *DoubleTake*, *Orion*,
Outside, *Manoa*, and other publications in the United States and
abroad. His work appears in
dozens of anthologies and has
been widely translated. Recent
publications include his nonfictional *Arctic Dreams: Imagination
and Desire in a Northern Landscape* (2001), a naturalist's medi-
tations on landscape and sight,
and his fictional *Crow and Weasel*
(1998). Lopez has received many
awards, including the Award in
Literature from the American
Academy of Arts and Letters, a
Guggenheim Fellowship, the Lan-
nan Foundation Award, Pushcart
Prizes in fiction and nonfiction, a
Governor's Award, and other honors. Although he has been a full-
time writer since leaving graduate
school in 1970, Lopez also worked
as a landscape photographer and
continues to maintain ties with
a diverse community of artists.
"Learning to See" was first published in *DoubleTake* (Spring 1998).

Learning to See

Barry Lopez

IN JUNE 1989, I RECEIVED A PUZZLING LETTER from the Amon Carter Museum in Fort Worth, Texas, an invitation to speak at the opening of a retrospective of the work of Robert Adams. The show, "To Make It Home: Photographs of the American West, 1965–1985," had been organized by the Philadelphia Museum of Art and would travel to the Los Angeles County Museum and the Corcoran Gallery of Art in Washington, D.C., before being installed at the Amon Carter, an institution renowned for its photographic collections, in the spring of 1990.

Robert Adams, an un-self-promoting man who has published no commercially prominent book of photographs, is routinely referred to as one of the most important landscape photographers in America, by both art critics and his colleagues. His black-and-white images are intelligently composed and morally engaged. They're also hopeful, despite their sometimes depressing subject matter—brutalized landscapes and the venality of the American Dream as revealed in suburban life. Adams doesn't hold himself apart from what he indicts. He photographs with compassion and he doesn't scold. His pictures are also accessible, to such a degree that many of them seem casual. In 1981 he published *Beauty in Photography: Essays in Defense of Traditional Values,* one of the clearest statements of artistic responsibility ever written by a photographer.

If there is such a thing as an ideal of stance, technique, vision, and social contribution toward which young photographers might aspire, it's embodied in this man.

I suspected the Amon Carter had inadvertently invited the wrong person to speak. I'd no knowledge of the history of American photography sufficient to situate Robert Adams in it. I couldn't speak to the technical perfection of his prints. I'd no credentials as an art critic. As an admirer of the work, of course, I'd have something to say, but it could only be that, the words of an amateur who admired Adams's accomplishment.

I wondered for days what prompted the invitation. For about fifteen years, before putting my cameras down on September 13, 1981, never to pick them up again, I'd worked as a landscape photographer, but it was unlikely anyone at the Amon Carter knew this. I'd visited the museum in the fall of 1986 to see some of their luminist paintings and had met several of the curators, but our conversations could not have left anyone with the impression that I had the background to speak about Adams's work.

I finally decided to say yes. I wrote and told the person coordinating the program, Mary Lampe, that though I didn't feel qualified to speak I admired Mr. Adams's work, and further, I presumed an affinity with his pursuits and ideals as set forth in *Beauty in Photography*. And I told her I intended to go back and study the work of Paul Strand, Wynn Bullock, Minor White, Harry Callahan, and others who'd been an influence on my own work and thought, in order to prepare my lecture.

Months later, when I arrived at the museum, I asked Ms. Lampe how they had come to invite me and not someone more qualified. She said Mr. Adams had asked them to do so. I sensed she believed Robert Adams and I were good friends and I had to tell her I didn't know him at all. We'd never met, never corresponded, had not spoken on the phone. I was unaware, even, that it was "Bob" Adams, as Ms. Lampe called him.

"But why did you agree to come?" she asked.

"Out of respect for the work," I said. "Out of enthusiasm for the work." I also explained that I was intimidated by the prospect, and that sometimes I felt it was good to act on things like that.

Ms. Lampe subsequently sent Robert Adams a tape of my talk. He and I later met and we now correspond and speak on the phone regularly. He set the course of our friendship in the first sentence of a letter he wrote me after hearing my presentation. "Your willingness to speak in my behalf," he wrote, "confirms my belief in the community of artists."

He believed from work of mine that he'd read that we shared a sensibility, that we asked similar questions about the relationship between culture and landscape, and that our ethical leanings and our sense of an artist's social responsibility were similar. He later told me that for these reasons he'd given my name, hopefully but somewhat facetiously, to Ms. Lampe, not knowing the curators and I were acquainted and that they would write me.

I've long been attracted to the way visual artists like Robert Adams imagine the world. The emotional impact of their composition of space and light is as clarifying for me as immersion in a beautifully made story. As with the work of a small group of poets I read regularly—Robert Hass, Pattiann Rogers, Garrett Hongo—I find healing in their expressions. I find reasons not to give up.

Though I no longer photograph, I have maintained since 1981 a connection with photographers and I keep up a sort of running conversation with several of them. We talk about the fate of photography in the United States, where of course art is increasingly more commodified and where, with the advent of computer manipulation, photography is the art most likely to mislead. Its history as a purveyor of objective reality, the idea that "the camera never lies," is specious, certainly; but with some artistic endeavors, say those of Cartier-Bresson, Aaron Siskind, or W. Eugene Smith, and in the fields of documentary photography, which would include some news photography, and nature photography, one can assert that the authority of the image lies with the subject. With the modern emphasis on the genius of the individual artist, however, and with the arrival of computer imaging, authority in these areas now more often lies with the photographer. This has become true to such an extent that the reversal that's occurred—the photographer, not the subject, is in charge—has caused the rules of evidence to be changed in courts of law; and it has foisted upon an unwitting public a steady stream, for example, of fabricated images of wildlife.

As a beginning photographer I was most attracted to color and form, to the emotional consequence of line. It is no wonder, looking back now, that I pored over the images of someone like Edward Weston, or that I felt isolated in some of my pursuits because at the time few serious photographers outside Ernst Haas and Eliot Porter worked as I did in color. I wanted to photograph the streaming of light. For a long while it made no difference whether that light was falling down the stone walls of a building in New York or lambent on the corrugations of a wheat field. Ansel Adams was suggested to me early on as a model, but he seemed to my eye inclined to overstate. I wanted the sort of subtlety I would later come to admire in Bob Adams's work and in the aerial photographs of Emmet Gowin.

The more I gravitated as a writer toward landscape as a context in which to work out what I was thinking as a young man about issues like justice, tolerance, ambiguity, and compassion, the more I came to concentrate on landforms as a photographer. I valued in particular the work of one or two wildlife photographers shooting *in situ,* in the bush. (I remember enthusiastically contacting friends about John Dominis's groundbreaking portfolio of African cat photographs, which appeared in three successive issues of *Life* in January 1967.) But I was not inclined toward mastering the kind of technical skill it took to make such photographs. More fundamentally, I had misgivings about what I regarded as invasions of the privacy of wild animals. The latter notion I thought so personal an idea I kept it mostly to myself; today, of course, it's a central concern of wildlife photographers, especially for a contingent that includes Frans Lanting, the late Michio Hoshino, Gary Braasch, Tui De Roy, and the team of Susan Middleton and David Liittschwager.

I began photographing in a conscientious way in the summer of 1965. I was soon concentrating on landscapes, and in the mid-1970s, with a small list of publication credits behind me, I made an appointment to see Joe Scherschel, an assistant director of the photographic staff at *National Geographic.* He told me frankly that though my landscape portfolio was up to the standards of the magazine, the paucity of wildlife images and human subjects made it unlikely that he could offer me any assignments. In response I remember thinking this was unlikely to change, for either of us. Discouraged, I started to scale back the effort to market my photographs and to make part of my living that way. I continued to make pictures, and I was glad that much of this work was still effectively represented by a stock agency in New York; but by 1978 I knew photography for me was becoming more a conscious exercise in awareness, a technique for paying attention. It would finally turn into a sequestered exploration of light and spatial volume.

Three events in the late 1970s changed the way I understood myself as a photographer. One summer afternoon I left the house for an appointment with an art director in a nearby city. Strapped to the seat of my motorcycle was a box of photographs, perhaps three hundred images representative of the best work I had done. The two-lane road I traveled winds gently through steep mountainous country. When I got to town the photographs were gone. I never found a trace of them, though I searched every foot of the road for two days. The loss dismantled my enthusiasm for photography so thoroughly that I took it for a message to do something else.

In the summer of 1976 my mother was dying of cancer. To ease her burden, and to brighten the sterile room in Lenox Hill Hospital in New York where she lay dying, I made a set of large Cibachrome prints from some of my 35-mm Kodachrome images—a white horse standing in a field of tall wild grasses bounded by a white post-and-plank fence; a faded pink boat trailer from the 1940s, abandoned in the woods; a small copse of quaking aspen, their leaves turning bright yellow on the far side of a remote mountain swamp. It was the only set of prints I would ever make. As good as they were, the change in color balance and the loss of transparency and contrast when compared with the originals, the reduction in sharpness, created a deep doubt about ever wanting to do such a thing again. I hung the images in a few shows, then put them away. I knew if I didn't start developing and printing my own images, I wouldn't be entering any more shows.

I winced whenever I saw my photographs reproduced in magazines and books, but I made my peace with that. Time-Life Books was publishing a series then called *American Wilderness,* each volume of which was devoted to a different landscape—the Maine woods, the Cascade Mountains, the Grand Canyon. I was pleased to see my work included in these volumes, but I realized that just as the distance between what I saw and what I was able to record was huge, so was that between what I recorded and what people saw. Seeing the printed images on the page was like finding one's haiku published as nineteen-syllable poems.

The third event occurred around the first serious [20] choice I made as a photographer to concentrate on a limited subject. The subject was always light, but I wanted to explore a single form, which turned out to be the flow of water in creeks and rivers near my home. I photographed in every season, when the water was high in February and March, when it was low in August, when it was transparent in July, when it was an opaque jade in December. In 1980 I began to photograph moving water in moonlight, exposures of twenty-five or thirty minutes. These images suffered from reciprocity failure—the color balance in them collapsed—but they also recorded something extraordinary, a pattern of flow we cannot actually see. They revealed the organizing principle logicians would one day call a strange attractor.

The streaming of water around a rock is one of the most complex motions of which human beings are aware. The change from a laminar, more or less uniform flow to turbulent flow around a single rock is so abstruse a transition mathematically that even the most sophisticated Cray computer cannot make it through to a satisfactory description.

Aesthetically, of course, no such difficulty exists. The eye dotes on the shift, delights in the scintillating sheeting, the roll-off of light around a rock, like hair responding to the stroke of a brush. Sometimes I photographed the flow of water in sunshine at 1/2000 of a second and then later I'd photograph the same rock in moonlight. Putting the photos side by side, I could see something hidden beneath the dazzle of the high-speed image that compared with our renderings of the Milky Way from space: the random pin-dot infernos of our own and every other sun form a spiraling, geometrical shape motionless to our eyes. In the moonlit photographs, the stray streaks from errant water splashes were eliminated (in light that weak, they occur too quickly to be recorded); what was etched on the film instead were orderly, fundamental lines of flow, created by particle after illuminated particle of gleaming water, as if each were a tracer bullet. (Years later, reading *Chaos,* James Gleick's lucid report on chaos theory, I would sit bolt upright in my chair. What I'd photographed was the deep pattern in turbulence, the clothing, as it were, of the strange attractor.)

In the months I worked at making these photographs, I came to realize I actually had two subjects as a photographer. First, these still images of a moving thing, a living thing—as close as I would probably ever come to fully photographing an animal. Second, natural light falling on orchards, images of a subject routinely understood as a still life. The orchards near me were mostly filbert orchards. In their change of color and form through the seasons, in the rain and snow that fell through them, in crows that sat on their winter branches, in leaves accumulated under them on bare dark ground, in the wind that coursed them, in the labyrinths of their limbs, ramulose within the imposed order of the orchard plot, I saw the same profundity of life I found in literature.

This was all work I was eager to do, but I would never get to it.

In September 1981 I was working in the Beaufort Sea off the north coast of Alaska with several marine biologists. We were conducting a food-chain survey intended to provide baseline data to guide offshore oil drilling, an impulsive and politically motivated development program funded by the Bureau of Land Management and pushed hard at the time by the Reagan government. On September 12, three of us rendezvoused at Point Barrow with a National Oceanic and Atmospheric Administration research vessel, the *Oceanographer.* They hoisted us, our gear, and our twenty-foot Boston Whaler aboard and we sailed west into pack ice in the northern Chukchi Sea.

Scientific field research is sometimes a literally bloody business. In our study we were trying to determine the flow of energy through various "levels" (artificially determined) of the marine food web. To gather data we retrieved plankton and caught fish with different sorts of traps and trawls, and we examined the contents of bearded seal, ringed seal, and spotted seal stomachs. To accomplish the latter, we shot and killed the animals. Shooting seals located us squarely in the moral dilemma of our work, and it occasioned talk aboard the *Oceanographer* about the barbarousness of science. The irony here was that without these data creatures like the ringed seal could not be afforded legal protection against oil development. The killings were a manifestation of the perversions in our age, our Kafkaesque predicaments.

I was disturbed by the fatal aspects of our work, as were my companions, but I willingly participated. I would later write an essay about the killing, but something else happened during that trip, less dramatic and more profound in its consequences for me.

Late one afternoon, working our way back to the *Oceanographer* through a snow squall, the three of us came upon a polar bear. We decided to follow him for a few minutes and I got out my cameras. The bear, swimming through loose pack ice, was clearly annoyed by our presence, though in our view we were maintaining a reasonable distance. He very soon climbed out on an ice floe, crossed it, and dropped into open water on the far side. We had to go the long way around in the workboat, but we caught up. He hissed at us and otherwise conveyed his irritation, but we continued idling along beside him.

Eventually we backed off. The bear disappeared in gauze curtains of blowing snow. We returned to the *Oceanographer,* to a warm meal and dry clothes.

Once the boat was secure and our scientific samples squared away in the lab, I went to my cabin. I dropped my pack on the floor, stripped off my heavy clothes, showered, and lay down in my bunk. I tried to recall every detail of the encounter with the bear. What had he been doing when we first saw him? Did he change direction then? How had he proceeded? Exactly how did he climb out of the water onto the ice floe? What were the mechanics of it? When he shook off seawater, how was it different from a dog shucking water? When he hissed, what color was the inside of his mouth?

I don't know how long I lay there, a half hour perhaps, but when I was through, when I'd answered these questions and was satisfied that I'd recalled the sequence of events precisely and in sufficient detail, I got up, dressed, and went to dinner. Remembering what happened in an encounter was crucial to my work as a writer, and attending to my cameras during our time with the bear had altered and shrunk my memory of it. While the polar bear was doing something, I was checking f-stops and attempting to frame and focus from a moving boat.

I regarded the meeting as a warning to me as a writer. Having successfully recovered details from each minute, I believed, of that encounter, having disciplined myself to do that, I sensed I wouldn't pick up a camera ever again.

It was not solely contact with this lone bear a hundred miles off the northwest coast of Alaska, of course, that ended my active involvement with photography. The change had been coming for a while. The power of the polar bear's presence, his emergence from the snow squall and his subsequent disappearance, had created an atmosphere in which I could grasp more easily a complex misgiving that had been building in me. I view any encounter with a wild animal in its own territory as a gift, an opportunity to sense the real animal, not the zoo creature, the TV creature, the advertising creature. But this gift had been more overwhelming. In some way the bear had grabbed me by the shirtfront and said, Think

about this. Think about what these cameras in your hands are doing.

Years later, I'm still thinking about it. Some of what culminated for me that day is easy to understand. As a writer, I had begun to feel I was missing critical details in situations such as this one because I was distracted. I was also starting to feel uncomfortable about the way photographs tend to collapse events into a single moment, about how much they leave out. (Archeologists face a similar problem when they save only what they recognize from a dig. Years afterward, the context long having been destroyed, the archeologist might wonder what was present that he or she didn't recognize at the time. So begins a reevaluation of the meaning of the entire site.)

I was also disturbed about how nature and landscape photographs, my own and others', were coming to be used, not in advertising where you took your chances (some photographers at that time began labeling their images explicitly: NO TOBACCO, NO ALCOHOL), but in the editorial pages of national magazines. It is a polite fiction of our era that the average person, including the average art director, is more informed about natural history than an educated person was in Columbus's age. Because this is not true, the majority of nature photographers who work out in the field have felt a peculiar burden to record accurately the great range of habitat and animal behavior they see, including nature's "dark" side. (Photographers accepted the fact back then that magazines in the United States, generally speaking, were not interested in photographs of mating animals—unless they were chaste or cute—or in predatory encounters if they were bloody or harrowing, as many were.)

What happened as a result of this convention was that people looking at magazines in the 1970s increasingly came to think of wild animals as vivacious and decorative in the natural world. Promoted as elegant, brave, graceful, sinister, wise, etc., according to their species, animals were deprived of personality and the capacity to be innovative. Every wildlife photographer I know can recount a story of confrontation with an art director in which he or she argued unsuccessfully for an image that told a fuller or a truer story about a particular species of animal in a layout. It was the noble lion, the thieving hyena, and the mischievous monkey, however, who routinely triumphed. A female wolf killing one of her pups, or a male bonobo approaching a female with a prominent erection, was not anything magazine editors were comfortable with.

In the late seventies, I asked around among several publishers to see whether they might have any interest in a series of disturbing photographs made in a zoo by a woman named Ilya. She'd taken them on assignment for *Life*, but very few of them were ever published because she'd concentrated on depicting animals apparently driven insane by their incarceration. I remember as particularly unsettling the look of psychosis in the face of a male lion, its mane twisted into knots. I could develop no interest in publishing her work. An eccentric view, people felt. Too distressing.

So, along with a growing political awareness of endangered landscapes and their indigenous animals in the 1970s came, ironically, a more and more dazzling presentation of those creatures in incomplete and prejudicial ways. Photo editors made them look not like what they were but the way editors wanted them to appear—well-groomed, appropriate to stereotype, and living safely apart from the machinations of human enterprise. To my mind there was little difference then between a *Playboy* calendar and a wildlife calendar. Both celebrated the conventionally gorgeous, the overly endowed, the seductive. I and many other photographers at the time were apprehensive about the implications of this trend.

Another concern I had that September afternoon, a more complicated one, was what was happening to memory in my generation. The advertising injunction to preserve family memories by taking photographs had become so shrill a demand, and the practice had become so compulsive, that recording the event was more important for some than participating in it. The inculcated rationale which grew up around this practice was that to take and preserve family photos was to act in a socially responsible way. The assumption seemed specious to me. My generation was the first to have ready access to inexpensive tape recorders and cameras. Far from recording memories of these talks and events, what we seemed to be doing was storing memories that would never be retrieved, that would never form a coherent narrative. In the same way that our desk drawers and cabinet shelves slowly filled with these "personal" sounds and images, we were beginning, it seemed to me, to live our lives in dissociated bits and pieces. The narrative spine of an individual life was disappearing. The order of events was becoming increasingly meaningless.

This worry, together with the increasingly commercial use to which the work of photographers like myself was being put and the preference for an entertaining but not necessarily coherent landscape of wild animals (images that essentially lied to children), made me more and more reluctant to stay involved. Some of the contemporary photographers I most respect—Lanting, Hoshino, Braasch, De Roy, Jim Brandenburg, Flip Nicklin, Sam Abell, Nick Nichols, Galen Rowell—have managed through the strength of their work and their personal integrity to overcome some of these problems, which are part and parcel of working in a world dominated more and more by commercial interests pursuing business strategies. But I knew I had no gift here to persevere. That realization, and my reluctance to photograph animals in the first place, may have precipitated my decision that day in the Chukchi.

As a writer, I had yet other concerns, peculiar to that discipline. I had begun to wonder whether my searching for the telling photographic image in a situation was beginning to interfere with my writing about what happened. I was someone who took a long time to let a story settle. I'd begun to suspect that the photographs made while I was in a note-taking stage were starting to lock my words into a pattern, and that the pattern was being determined too early. Photographs, in some way, were introducing preconceptions into a process I wanted to keep fluid. I often have no clear idea of what I'm doing. I just act. I pitch in, I try to stay alert to everything around me. I don't want to stop and focus on a finished image, which I'm inclined to do as a photographer. I want, instead, to see a sentence fragment scrawled in my notebook, smeared by rain. I don't want the clean, fixed image right away.

An attentive mind, I'm sure, can see the flaws in my reasoning. Some photographers are doing no more than taking notes when they click the shutter. It's only after a shoot that they discover what the story is. But by trying to both photograph and write, I'd begun to feel I was attempting to create two parallel but independent stories. The effort had become confusing and draining. I let go of photography partly because its defining process, to my mind, was less congruent with the way I wanted to work.

On June 16, 1979, forty-one sperm whales beached themselves at the mouth of the Siuslaw River on the Oregon coast, about one hundred miles from my home. I wrote a long essay about the stranding but didn't start work on it until after I'd spent two days photographing the eclipse of these beasts' lives and the aftermath of their deaths. That was the last time I attempted to do both things.

Perhaps the most rarefied of my concerns about photography that day in the Chukchi was one that lay for me at the heart of photography: recording a fleeting pattern of light in a defined volume of space. Light always attracted me. Indeed, twenty-five years after the fact, I can still vividly recall the light falling at dusk on a windbreak of trees in Mitchell, Oregon. It rendered me speechless when I saw it, and by some magic I managed to get it down on film. The problem of rendering volume in photography, however, was one I never solved beyond employing the conventional solutions of perspective and depth of field. I could recognize spatial volume successfully addressed in the work of other photographers—in

Adams's work, for example, partly because so many of his photographs do not have an object as a subject. Finding some way myself to render volume successfully in a photograph would mean, I believed, walking too far away from my work as a writer. And, ultimately, it was as a writer that I felt more comfortable.

I miss making photographs. A short while ago I received a call from a curator at the Whitney Museum in New York named May Castleberry. She had just mounted a show called "Perpetual Mirage: Photographic Narratives of the Desert West" and I had been able to provide some minor assistance with it. She was calling now to pursue a conversation we'd begun at the time about Rockwell Kent, an illustrator, painter, and socialist widely known in the thirties, forties, and fifties. She wanted to hang a selection of his "nocturnes," prints and drawings Kent had made of people under starlit night skies. She was calling to see what I could suggest about his motivation.

Given Kent's leanings toward Nordic myth and legend and his espousal of Teddy Roosevelt's "strenuous life," it seemed obvious to me that he would want to portray his heroic (mostly male) figures against the vault of the heavens. But there were at least two other things at work here, I believed. First, Kent was strongly drawn to high latitudes, like Greenland, where in winter one can view the deep night sky for weeks on end. It was not really the "night" sky, however, he was drawing; it was the sunless sky of a winter day. Quotidian life assumes mythic proportions here not because it's heroic, but because it's carried out beneath the stars.

Secondly, I conjectured, because Kent was an artist working on flat surfaces, he sought, like every such artist, ways to suggest volume, to make the third dimension apparent. Beyond what clouds provide, the daytime sky has no depth; it's the night sky that gives an artist volume. While it takes an extraordinary person—the light and space artist James Turrell, say—to make the celestial vault visible in sunshine, many artists have successfully conveyed a sense of the sky's volume by painting it at night.

The conceit can easily grow up in a photographer that he or she has pretty much seen all the large things—the range of possible emotion to be evoked with light, the contrasts to be made by arranging objects in different scales, problems in the third and fourth dimension. But every serious photographer, I believe, has encountered at some point ideas unanticipated and dumbfounding. The shock causes you to reexamine all you've assumed about your own work and the work of others, especially the work of people you've never particularly understood. This happened most recently for me in seeing the photography of Linda Connor. While working on a story about international air freight, I became so disoriented, flying every day from one spot on the globe to another thousands of miles away, I did not know what time I was living in. Whatever time it was, it was out of phase with the sun, a time not to be dialed up on a watch, mine or anyone else's.

At a pause in this international hurtling, during a six-hour layover in Cape Town, I went for a ride with an acquaintance. He drove us out to Clifton Bay on the west side of Table Mountain. I was so dazed by my abuse of time that I was open to thoughts I might otherwise never have had. One of those thoughts was that I could recognize the physicality of time. We can discern the physical nature of space in a picture, grasp the way, for example, Robert Adams is able to photograph the air itself, making it visible like a plein air painter. In Cape Town that day I saw what I came to call indigenous time. It clung to the flanks of Table Mountain. It resisted being absorbed into my helter-skelter time. It seemed not yet to have been subjugated by Dutch and British colonial expansion, as the physical landscape so clearly had been. It was time apparent to the senses, palpable. What made me believe I was correct in this perception was that, only a month before, I'd examined a collection of Linda Connor's work, a book called *Luminance*. I realized there at Table Mountain that she'd photographed what I was looking at. She'd photographed indigenous time.

I'd grasped Ms. Connor's photographs in some fashion after an initial pass, but I hadn't sensed their depth, their power, what Gerard Manley Hopkins called "the achieve of the thing." With this new insight I wrote her an excited note, an attempt to thank her for work that opened the door to a room I'd never explored.

One of the great blessings of our modern age, a kind of redemption for its cruelties and unmitigated greed, is that one can walk down to a corner bookstore and find a copy of Ms. Connor's book. Or of Robert Adams's *What We Brought: The New World*, or Frans Lanting's *Bonobo: The Forgotten Ape*, or, say, Mary Peck's *Chaco Canyon: A Center and Its World*, and then be knocked across the room by a truth one had not, until that moment, clearly discerned.

It is more than illumination, though, more than a confirmation of one's intuition, aesthetics, or beliefs that comes out of the perusal of such a photographer's images. It's regaining the feeling that one is not cut off from the wellsprings of intelligence and goodwill, of sympathy for human plight.

I do not know, of course, why the photographers I admire, even the ones I know, photograph, but I am acutely aware that without the infusion of their images hope would wither in me. I feel an allegiance to their work more as a writer than as someone who once tried to see in this way, perhaps because I presume we share certain principles related to the effort to imagine or explain.

It is correct, I think, as Robert Adams wrote me that day, to believe in a community of artists stimulated by and respectful of one another's work. But it's also true that without an audience (of which we're all a part) the work remains unfinished, unfulfilled. A photographer seeks intimacy with the world and then endeavors to share it. Inherent in that desire to share is a love of humanity. In different media, and from time to time, we have succeeded, I believe, in helping one another understand what is going on. We have come to see that, in some way, this is our purpose with each other. ○

SEEING

1. In what ways does Barry Lopez's title, "Learning to See," reflect his overall purpose? How does he learn to see during the course of the essay? Explain your answer and support it by pointing to specific passages in the text. What does Lopez mean when he says that increasingly the authority of the image "lies with the photographer" (para. 13)? What factors contributed, according to Lopez, to his shift from being a photographer to a writer? Lopez describes his meeting with the bear as "a warning to me as a writer" (para. 32). What, exactly, was the nature of this warning? How was that experience poignant for him? What does he see as the disadvantages of being a photographer? What, more specifically, does he find disturbing about most nature photography?

2. Lopez notes that "I've long been attracted to the way visual artists like Robert Adams imagine the world." The emotional impact of their composition of space and light is as clarifying for me as immersion in a beautifully made story" (para. 12). In what sense is Lopez using the word *composition* here? How does the meaning of the word *composition* differ in the contexts of photography and writing? Consider the composition of this essay. What techniques does Lopez use to capture his readers' attention?

WRITING

1. Examine carefully the photograph by Britta Jaschinski, entitled *Malayan Tapir, London 1992* (p. 237). What details do you notice about this photograph? What reasonable inferences can you draw from these observations—about the overall effect of her photograph as well as her purpose in taking the picture? Write an expository essay in which you "read" Jaschinski's photograph within the context of Lopez's essay. To what extent might Jaschinski's photograph serve as an illustration of Lopez's assertions?

2. One of Lopez's principal concerns in this essay is his own ambivalence about killing animals in order to conduct scientific research: "Shooting seals located us squarely in the moral dilemma of our work," he says (para. 26). How does Lopez resolve this moral dilemma for himself? What are your views of using animals in scientific experiments? of killing them in such experiments? Write an argumentative essay in which you advocate for or criticize the use of animals in scientific research designed to benefit humans.

Learning to See
Barry Lopez

Retrospect
Some Enchanted Evening

SHERMAN ALEXIE

A Spokane/Coeur d'Alene Indian, Sherman J. Alexie (b. 1966) grew up on the Spokane Indian Reservation in Wellpinit, Washington. Alexie planned to be a doctor until he "fainted three times in human anatomy class and needed a career change." That change began when he stumbled into a poetry workshop at Washington State University, and it came to fruition when he received the Washington State Arts Commission Poetry Fellowship in 1991 and the National Endowment for the Arts Poetry Fellowship in 1992. Two of Alexie's poetry collections appeared during this time—*The Business of Fancydancing* (1992) and *I Would Steal Horses* (1993)—followed soon thereafter by his first collection of short stories, *The Lone Ranger and Tonto Fistfight in Heaven* (1994). His first novel, *Reservation Blues* (1996), won the Before Columbus Foundation's American Book Award and the Murray Morgan Prize. His second novel, *Indian Killer* (1998), was named one of *People's* Best of Pages and a *New York Times* Notable Book.

Alexie worked on the screenplay that was released as *Smoke Signals* at the Sundance Film Festival in January 1998. It was later distributed by Miramax and collected an impressive number of awards. Alexie has published fourteen books to date, including *One Stick Song* (2000), a collection of poetry, and *The Toughest Indian in the World* (2001), his most recent collection of short stories. "The Joy of Reading and Writing" first appeared in an anthology entitled *The Most Wonderful Books* (1997).

THE JOY OF READING AND WRITING:
SUPERMAN AND ME

Sherman Alexie

I LEARNED TO READ WITH A *SUPERMAN* COMIC book. Simple enough, I suppose. I cannot recall which particular Superman comic book I read, nor can I remember which villain he fought in that issue. I cannot remember the plot, nor the means by which I obtained the comic book. What I can remember is this: I was three years old, a Spokane Indian boy living with his family on the Spokane Indian Reservation in eastern Washington state. We were poor by most standards, but one of my parents usually managed to find some minimum-wage job or another, which made us middle-class by reservation standards. I had a brother and three sisters. We lived on a combination of irregular paychecks, hope, fear, and government surplus food.

My father, who is one of the few Indians who went to Catholic school on purpose, was an avid reader of westerns, spy thrillers, murder mysteries, gangster epics, basketball player biographies, and anything else he could find. He bought his books by the pound at Dutch's Pawn Shop, Goodwill, Salvation Army, and Value Village. When he had extra money, he bought new novels at supermarkets, convenience stores and hospital gift shops. Our house was filled with books. They were stacked in crazy piles in the bathroom, bedrooms, and living room. In a fit of unemployment-inspired creative energy, my father built a set of bookshelves and soon filled them with a random assortment of books about the Kennedy assassination, Watergate, the Vietnam War, and the entire twenty-three-book series of the Apache westerns. My father loved books, and since I loved my father with an aching devotion, I decided to love books as well.

I can remember picking up my father's books before I could read. The words themselves were mostly foreign, but I still remember the exact moment when I first understood, with a sudden clarity, the purpose of a paragraph. I didn't have the vocabulary to say "paragraph," but I realized that a paragraph was a fence that held words. The words inside a paragraph worked together for a common purpose. They had some specific reason for being inside the same fence. This knowledge delighted me. I began to think of everything in terms of paragraphs. Our reservation was a small paragraph within the United States. My family's house was a paragraph, distinct from the other paragraphs of the LeBrets to the north, the Fords to our south, and the Tribal School to the west. Inside our house, each family member existed as a separate paragraph but still had genetics and common experiences to link us. Now, using this logic, I can see my changed family as an essay of seven paragraphs: mother, father, older brother, the deceased sister, my younger twin sisters, and our adopted little brother.

At the same time I was seeing the world in paragraphs, I also picked up the *Superman* comic book. Each panel, complete with picture, dialogue, and narrative, was a three-dimensional paragraph. In one panel, Superman breaks through a door. His suit is red, blue, and yellow. The brown door shatters into many pieces. I look at the narrative above the picture. I cannot read the words, but I assume it tells me that "Superman is breaking down the door." Aloud, I pretend to read the words and say, "Superman is breaking down the door." Words, dialogue, also float out of Superman's mouth. Because he is breaking down the door, I assume he says, "I am breaking down the door." Once again, I pretend to read the words and say aloud, "I am breaking down the door." In this way, I learned to read.

This might be an interesting story all by itself. A little Indian boy teaches himself to read at an early age and advances quickly. He reads *Grapes of Wrath* in kindergarten when other children are struggling through Dick and Jane. If he'd been anything but an Indian boy living on the reservation, he might have been called a prodigy. But he is an Indian boy living on the reservation and is simply an oddity. He grows into a man who often speaks of his childhood in the third-person, as if it will somehow dull the pain and make him sound more modest about his talents.

A smart Indian is a dangerous person, widely feared and ridiculed by Indians and non-Indians alike. I fought with my classmates on a daily basis. They wanted me to stay quiet when the non-Indian teacher asked for answers, for volunteers, for help. We were Indian children who were expected to be stupid. Most lived up to those expectations inside the classroom but subverted them on the outside. They struggled with basic reading in school but could re-member how to sing a few dozen powwow songs. They were monosyllabic in front of their non-Indian teachers but could tell complicated stories and jokes at the dinner table. They submissively ducked their heads when confronted by a non-Indian adult but would slug it out with the Indian bully who was ten years older. As Indian children, we were expected to fail in the non-Indian world. Those who failed were ceremonially accepted by other Indians and appro-priately pitied by non-Indians.

I refused to fail. I was smart. I was arrogant. I was lucky. I read books late into the night, until I could barely keep my eyes open. I read books at recess, then during lunch, and in the few minutes left after I had finished my classroom assignments. I read books in the car when my family traveled to powwows or bas-ketball games. In shopping malls, I ran to the book-stores and read bits and pieces of as many books as I could. I read the books my father brought home from the pawnshops and secondhand. I read the books I borrowed from the library. I read the backs of cereal boxes. I read the newspaper. I read the bul-letins posted on the walls of the school, the clinic, the tribal offices, the post office. I read junk mail. I read auto-repair manuals. I read magazines. I read any-thing that had words and paragraphs. I read with equal parts joy and desperation. I loved those books, but I also knew that love had only one purpose. I was trying to save my life.

Despite all the books I read, I am still surprised I became a writer. I was going to be a pediatrician. These days, I write novels, short stories, and poems. I visit schools and teach creative writing to Indian kids. In all my years in the reservation school system, I was never taught how to write poetry, short stories, or novels. I was certainly never taught that Indians wrote poetry, short stories, and novels. Writing was something beyond Indians. I cannot recall a single time that a guest teacher visited the reservation. There must have been visiting teachers. Who were they? Where are they now? Do they exist? I visit the schools as often as possible. The Indian kids crowd the classroom. Many are writing their own poems, short stories, and novels. They have read my books. They have read many other books. They look at me with bright eyes and arrogant wonder. They are try-ing to save their lives. Then there are the sullen and already defeated Indian kids who sit in the back rows and ignore me with theatrical precision. The pages of their notebooks are empty. They carry neither pencil nor pen. They stare out the window. They refuse and resist. "Books," I say to them. "Books," I say. I throw my weight against their locked doors. The door holds. I am smart. I am arrogant. I am lucky. I am trying to save our lives. ○

SEEING

1. The overarching subject of Sherman Alexie's essay is what he calls "the joy of reading and writing." How many different stories does he tell to illustrate the joy of reading and writing? Which ones do you find most engaging? Explain why. What reasonable inferences can you draw from his statement that "a smart Indian is a dangerous person, widely feared and ridiculed by Indians and non-Indians alike" (para. 6)? Reread the final lines of this essay carefully: ". . . what you read is unfinished until completed in the self. The first text is the soul. And the last." What significance do you attach to this assertion?

2. Comment on the effectiveness of the opening four sentences of Alexie's essay. What does he gain and lose by choosing to open his essay on a series of negative assertions? What does Alexie mean when he defines a paragraph as "a fence that held words" (para. 3)? How does this metaphor help structure his essay? Be as specific as possible. Review each of the eight paragraphs in this essay. What idea does each paragraph "fence in"? What technique does Alexie use to build each paragraph into a cohesive whole?

WRITING

1. Alexie creates a vivid sense of his earliest recollections of reading and writing. Based on this essay, do you think he prefers reading or writing? Recall your own earliest recollections of reading and writing. Were they linked in your mind? in your experience? Write the first draft of a narrative essay in which you recount your earliest recollections of reading and writing. Build your narrative to lead to a conclusion, to a point that you want to make about the experience.

2. In a July 1998 "Dialogue on Race" with President Bill Clinton, Sherman Alexie said: "I think the primary thing that people need to know about Indians is that our identity is much less cultural now and much more political. That we really do exist as political entities and sovereign political nations. That's the most important thing for people to understand, that we are separate politically and economically." Spend some time on the web and in the library looking for primary and secondary research sources on the historical independence of Native American nations. Then use these sources to write a researched essay that validates—or challenges—the accuracy of Alexie's assertion. When did this shift in Indian identity—from cultural to political—occur? What cultural or political circumstances prompted the change? What other factors helped prompt the change?

LAUREN GREENFIELD

Freelance photographer Lauren Greenfield was born in Boston in 1966 and grew up in Venice, California. Greenfield attended Harvard University and returned to Los Angeles to launch a career with her photographic documentary *Fast Forward: Growing Up in the Shadow of Hollywood* (1997). In her colorful and disquieting photographs Greenfield captures a wide range of Los Angeles youth, from Beverly Hills debutantes to gang members. Reviewing Greenfield's photographs, Richard Rodriguez notes that "What L.A. sells America, what L.A. sells the entire world, is a dream of adolescence." Greenfield underscores the extent to which that dream can become nightmarish for those who live it. She considers this documentary series to be autobiographical insofar as the images convey a sense of her own experience growing up in L.A. She offers unremitting criticism of a culture that measures success by how closely individuals conform to stereotypical images of power, wealth, and beauty.

Fast Forward, the collection from which this photo of "Ashleigh" is reproduced, received the Community Awareness Award from the National Press Photographers' Pictures of the Year competition and the 1997 International Center of Photography Infinity Award for Young Photographers. Greenfield's photographs have appeared in *Time, Newsweek, Vanity Fair, Life,* and the *New York Times Magazine.*

Lauren Greenfield, **Ashleigh, 13, with Her Friend and Parents, Santa Monica**

1. How would you describe the moment that Lauren Greenfield has captured in this photograph? While Ashleigh is looking intently down at the scale, where are each of the other figures in the photograph looking? What do you imagine each of these figures is "saying" with his or her facial expression and body language?

2. If each of the figures in Greenfield's photograph is looking intently at something or someone, what photographic angle has Greenfield chosen from which to view and capture this scene? What aspects of this scene does the framing reveal about the subject or its author? What does it conceal? With what effects?

1. Write a one-paragraph character sketch on each of the figures in Greenfield's photograph—as if they were characters in a play or movie. What revealing details do you notice about their postures, facial expressions, and clothes, as well as the objects around them? Given your observations, what might you infer about each of their personalities, their reactions to this moment, and their relationships to each other? Now write a brief dialogue for the moments before, during, and after this photograph was taken.

2. Richard Rodriguez writes that Greenfield's photographs reveal "what L.A. sells the entire world is a dream of adolescence." Do you think "Ashleigh, 13, with Her Friend and Parents, Santa Monica" has this effect? Write an argumentative essay that starts with what you know about Hollywood, L.A., and movie culture and ends by arguing either that Rodriguez is right (based on this photograph) or that the photograph offers something else entirely.

Front page of the *New York Times*, Tuesday, Sept. 11, 2001

"Big stories change media," wrote writer and cultural critic Jon Katz on the webzine *Slashdot* after the events of September 11, 2001. "Radio's high-water mark was World War II, and TV news came of age after John F. Kennedy's assassination. Elvis and his death gave birth to modern mass-marketed tabloid media. Increasingly, it appears the attack on the World Trade Center and Pentagon and the shooting war that began last night [in Afghanistan] have made more distinct another evolutionary leap in information: The Net is emerging as our most serious communications medium and clearly the freest and most diverse. Conventional journalists are still obsessed with hackers and pornographers; still fuss about whether the Net is safe or factual. But increasingly, they steer readers to their web sites for more in-depth information and conversation."

To what extent do you agree with Katz's assertion? How does online news coverage differ from print, radio, and television news coverage? What, in your opinion, are the significant advantages and disadvantages of each? How have the events of September 11 altered the media? Choose a current news event, and consider its coverage in various media. Then write an essay in which you argue for or against Katz's point of view, using your news story as a case study.

DOROTHY ALLISON

"I know in my bones that to write well you must inhabit your creations: male, female, whatever," says Dorothy Allison, a self-described "lesbian, feminist, Southern femme partnered to a self-defined butch musician, incest survivor, 46-year-old mother of a 3-year-old son, peri-menopausal, working-class escapee."

Born in Greenville, South Carolina, Allison grew up in a poor, working-class family. She says that she knew from her earliest years that she was an outsider, that she didn't fit in, but that not fitting in is one of her strengths as a writer. "Some days I think I have a unique advantage, an outsider's perspective that lets me see what others ignore." Her writing gives voice to her experience of the working-poor South, where her stepfather raped her when she was 5 years old. Her first novel, *Bastard Out of Carolina* (1992), which was a finalist for the National Book Award, is about escaping from that world. Her second novel, *Cavedweller* (1998), is about getting back to it.

"As a teacher I invariably require that my students write across their own barriers," she says, "forcing young lesbians to write as middle-aged men (straight or gay) and the most fervently macho men to speak as tender girls. Climbing into a stranger's skin is the core of the writer's experience, stretching the imagination to incorporate the unimagined."

This Is Our World

Dorothy Allison

THE FIRST PAINTING I EVER SAW UP CLOSE WAS at a Baptist church when I was seven years old. It was a few weeks before my mama was to be baptized. From it, I took the notion that art should surprise and astonish, and hopefully make you think something you had not thought until you saw it. The painting was a mural of Jesus at the Jordan River done on the wall behind the baptismal font. The font itself was a remarkable creation—a swimming pool with one glass side set into the wall above and behind the pulpit so that ordinarily you could not tell the font was there, seeing only the painting of Jesus. When the tank was flooded with water, little lights along the bottom came on, and anyone who stepped down the steps seemed to be walking past Jesus himself and descending into the Jordan River. Watching baptisms in that tank was like watching movies at the drive-in, my cousins had told me. From the moment the deacon walked us around the church, I knew what my cousin had meant. I could not take my eyes off the painting or the glass-fronted tank. It looked every moment as if Jesus were about to come alive, as if he were about to step out onto the water of the river. I think the way I stared at the painting made the deacon nervous.

The deacon boasted to my mama that there was nothing like that baptismal font in the whole state of South Carolina. It had been designed, he told her, by a nephew of the minister—a boy who had gone on to build a shopping center out in New Mexico. My mama was not sure that someone who built shopping centers was the kind of person who should have been designing baptismal fonts, and she was even more uncertain about the steep steps by Jesus' left hip. She asked the man to let her practice going up and down, but he warned her it would be different once the water poured in.

"It's quite safe though," he told her. "The water will hold you up. You won't fall."

I kept my attention on the painting of Jesus. He was much larger than I was, a little bit more than life-size, but the thick layer of shellac applied to protect the image acted like a magnifying glass, making him seem larger still. It was Jesus himself that fascinated me, though. He was all rouged and pale and pouty as Elvis Presley. This was not my idea of the Son of God, but I liked it. I liked it a lot.

"Jesus looks like a girl," I told my mama.   5

She looked up at the painted face. A little blush appeared on her cheekbones, and she looked as if she would have smiled if the deacon were not frowning so determinedly. "It's just the eyelashes," she said. The deacon nodded. They climbed back up the stairs. I stepped over close to Jesus and put my hand on the painted robe. The painting was sweaty and cool, slightly oily under my fingers.

"I liked that Jesus," I told my mama as we walked out of the church. "I wish we had something like that." To her credit, Mama did not laugh.

"If you want a picture of Jesus," she said, "we'll get you one. They have them in nice frames at Sears." I sighed. That was not what I had in mind. What I wanted was a life-size, sweaty painting, one in which Jesus looked as hopeful as a young girl—something other-worldly and peculiar, but kind of wonderful at the same time. After that, every time we went to church I asked to go up to see the painting, but the baptismal font was locked tight when not in use.

The Sunday Mama was to be baptized, I watched the minister step down into that pool past the Son of God. The preacher's gown was tailored with little weights carefully sewn into the hem to keep it from rising up in the water. The water pushed up at the fabric while the weights tugged it down. Once the minister was all the way down into the tank, the robe floated up a bit so that it seemed to have a shirred ruffle all along the bottom. That was almost enough to pull my eyes away from the face of Jesus, but not quite. With the lights on in the bottom of the tank, the eyes of the painting seemed to move and shine. I tried to point it out to my sisters, but they were uninterested. All they wanted to see was Mama.

Mama was to be baptized last, after three little boys, and their gowns had not had any weights attached. The white robes floated up around their necks so that their skinny boy bodies and white cotton underwear were perfectly visible to the congregation. The water that came up above the hips of the minister lapped their shoulders, and the shortest of the boys seemed panicky at the prospect of gulping water, no matter how holy. He paddled furiously to keep above the water's surface. The water started to rock violently at his struggles, sweeping the other boys off their feet. All of them pumped their knees to stay upright and the minister, realizing how the scene must appear to the congregation below, speeded up the baptismal process, praying over and dunking the boys at high speed.

Around me the congregation shifted in their seats. My little sister slid forward off the pew, and I quickly grabbed her around the waist and barely stopped myself from laughing out loud. A titter from the back of the church indicated that other people were having the same difficulty keeping from laughing. Other people shifted irritably and glared at the noisemakers. It was clear that no matter the provocation, we were to pretend nothing funny was happening. The minister frowned more fiercely and prayed louder. My mama's friend Louise, sitting at our left, whispered a soft "Look at that" and we all looked up in awe. One of the hastily blessed boys had dog-paddled over to the glass and was staring out at us, eyes wide and his hands pressed flat to the glass. He looked as if he hoped someone would rescue him. It was too much for me. I began to giggle helplessly, and not a few of the people around me joined in. Impatiently the minister hooked the boy's robe, pulled him back, and pushed him toward the stairs.

My mama, just visible on the staircase, hesitated briefly as the sodden boy climbed up past her. Then she set her lips tightly together, and reached down and pressed her robe to her thighs. She came down the steps slowly, holding down the skirt as she did so, giving one stern glance to the two boys climbing past her up the steps, and then turning her face deliberately up to the painting of Jesus. Every move she made communicated resolution and faith, and the congregation stilled in respect. She was baptized looking up stubbornly, both hands holding down that cotton robe while below, I fought so hard not to giggle, tears spilled down my face.

Over the pool, the face of Jesus watched solemnly with his pink, painted cheeks and thick, dark lashes. For all the absurdity of the event, his face seemed to me startlingly compassionate and wise. That face understood fidgety boys and stubborn women. It made me want the painting even more, and to this day I remember it with longing. It had the weight of art, that face. It had what I am sure art is supposed to have—the power to provoke, the authority of a heartfelt vision.

I imagine the artist who painted the baptismal font in that Baptist church so long ago was a man who did not think himself much of an artist. I have seen paintings like his many times since, so perhaps he worked from a model. Maybe he traced that face off another he had seen in some other church. For a while, I tried to imagine him a character out of a Flannery O'Connor short story, a man who traveled around the South in the fifties painting Jesus wherever he was needed, giving the Son of God the long lashes and pink cheeks of a young girl. He would be the kind of man who would see nothing blasphemous in painting eyes that followed the congregation as they moved up to the pulpit to receive a blessing and back to the pews to sit chastened and still for the benediction. Perhaps he had no sense of humor, or perhaps he had one too refined for intimidation. In my version of the story, he would have a case of whiskey in his van, right behind the gallon containers of shellac and buried notebooks of his own sketches. Sometimes, he would read thick journals of art criticism while sitting up late in cheap hotel rooms and then get roaring drunk and curse his fate.

"What I do is wallpaper," he would complain. 15 "Just wallpaper." But the work he so despised would grow more and more famous as time passed. After his death, one of those journals would publish a careful consideration of his murals, calling him a gifted primitive. Dealers would offer little churches large sums to take down his walls and sell them as installations to collectors. Maybe some of the churches would refuse to sell, but grow uncomfortable with the secular popularity of the paintings. Still, somewhere there would be a little girl like the girl I had been, a girl who would dream of putting her hand on the cool, sweaty painting while the Son of God blinked down at her in genuine sympathy. Is it a sin, she would wonder, to put together the sacred and the absurd? I would not answer her question, of course. I would leave it, like the art, to make everyone a little nervous and unsure.

I love black-and-white photographs, and I always have. I have cut photographs out of magazines to paste in books of my own, bought albums at yard sales, and kept collections that had one or two images I wanted near me always. Those pictures tell me stories—my own and others, scary stories sometimes, but more often simply everyday stories, what happened in that place at that time to those people. The pictures I collect leave me to puzzle out what I think about it later. Sometimes, I imagine my own life as a series of snapshots taken by some omniscient artist who is just keeping track—not interfering or saying anything, just capturing the moment for me to look back at it again later. The eye of God, as expressed in a Dorothea Lange or Wright Morris. This is the way it is, the photograph says, and I nod my head in appreciation. The power of art is in that nod of appreciation, though sometimes I puzzle nothing out, and the nod is more a shrug. No, I do not understand this one, but I see it. I take it in. I will think about it. If I sit with this image long enough, this story, I have the hope of understanding something I did not understand before. And that, too, is art, the best art.

My friend Jackie used to call my photographs sentimental. I had pinned them up all over the walls of my apartment, and Jackie liked a few of them but thought on the whole they were better suited to being tucked away in a book. On her walls, she had half a dozen bright prints in bottle-cap metal frames, most of them bought from Puerto Rican artists at street sales when she was working as a taxi driver and always had cash in her pockets. I thought her prints garish and told her so when she made fun of my photographs.

"They remind me of my mama," she told me. I had only seen one photograph of Jackie's mother, a wide-faced Italian matron from Queens with thick, black eyebrows and a perpetual squint.

"She liked bright colors?" I asked.

Jackie nodded. "And stuff you could buy on the 20 street. She was always buying stuff off tables on the street, saying that was the best stuff. Best prices. Cheap skirts that lost their dye after a couple of washes, shoes with cardboard insoles, those funky little icons, weeping saints and long-faced Madonnas. She liked stuff to be really colorful. She painted all the ceilings in our apartment red and white. Red-red and white-white. Like blood on bone."

I looked up at my ceiling. The high tin ceiling was uniformly bloody when I moved in, with paint put on so thick, I could chip it off in lumps. I had climbed on stacks of boxes to paint it all cream white and pale blue.

"The Virgin's colors," Jackie told me. "You should put gold roses on the door posts."

"I'm no artist," I told her.

"I am," Jackie laughed. She took out a pencil and sketched a leafy vine above two of my framed photographs. She was good. It looked as if the frames were pinned to the vine. "I'll do it all," she said, looking at me to see if I was upset.

"Do it," I told her.

Jackie drew lilies and potato vines up the hall while I made tea and admired the details. Around the front door she put the Virgin's roses and curious little circles with crosses entwined in the middle. "It's beautiful," I told her.

"A blessing," she told me. "Like a bit of magic. My mama magic." Her face was so serious, I brought back a dish of salt and water, and we blessed the entrance. "Now the devil will pass you by," she promised me.

I laughed, but almost believed.

For a few months last spring I kept seeing an ad in all the magazines that showed a small child high in the air dropping toward the upraised arms of a waiting figure below. The image was grainy and distant. I could not tell if the child was laughing or crying. The copy at the bottom of the page read: "Your father always caught you."

"Look at this," I insisted the first time I saw the ad. "Will you look at this?"

A friend of mine took the magazine, looked at the ad, and then up into my shocked and horrified face.

"They don't mean it that way," she said.

I looked at the ad again. They didn't mean it that way? They meant it innocently? I shuddered. It was supposed to make you feel safe, maybe make you buy insurance or something. It did not make me feel safe. I dreamed about the picture, and it was not a good dream.

I wonder how many other people see that ad the way I do. I wonder how many other people look at the constant images of happy families and make wry faces at most of them. It's as if all the illustrators have television sitcom imaginations. I do not believe in those families. I believe in the exhausted mothers, frightened children, numb and stubborn men. I believe in hard-pressed families, the child huddled in fear with his face hidden, the father and mother confronting each other with their emotions hidden, dispassionate passionate faces, and the unsettling sense of risk in the baby held close to that man's chest. These images make sense to me. They are about the world I know, the stories I tell. When they are accompanied by wry titles or copy that is slightly absurd or unexpected, I grin and know that I will puzzle it out later, sometimes a lot later.

I think that using art to provoke uncertainty is what great writing and inspired images do most brilliantly. Art should provoke more questions than answers and, most of all, should make us think about what we rarely want to think about at all. Sitting down to write a novel, I refuse to consider if my work is seen as difficult or inappropriate or provocative. I choose my subjects to force the congregation to look at what they try so stubbornly to pretend is not happening at all, deliberately combining the horribly serious with the absurd or funny, because I know that if I am to reach my audience I must first seduce their attention and draw them into the world of my imagination. I know that I have to lay out my stories, my difficult people, each story layering on top of the one before it with care and craft, until my audience sees something they had not expected. Frailty—stubborn, human frailty—that is what I work to showcase. The wonder and astonishment of the despised and ignored, that is what I hope to find in art and in the books I write—my secret self, my vulnerable and embattled heart, the child I was and the woman I have become, not Jesus at the Jordan but a woman with only her stubborn memories and passionate convictions to redeem her.

"You write such mean stories," a friend once told me. "Raped girls, brutal fathers, faithless mothers, and untrustworthy lovers—meaner than the world really is, don't you think?"

I just looked at her. Meaner than the world really is? No. I thought about showing her the box under my desk where I keep my clippings. Newspaper stories and black-and-white images—the woman who drowned her children, the man who shot first the babies in her arms and then his wife, the teenage boys who led the three-year-old away along the train track, the homeless family recovering from frostbite with their eyes glazed and indifferent while the doctor scowled over their shoulders. The world is meaner than we admit, larger and more astonishing. Strength appears in the most desperate figures, tragedy when we have no reason to expect it. Yes, some of my stories are fearful, but not as cruel as what I see in the world. I believe in redemption, just as I believe in the nobility of the despised, the dignity of the outcast, the intrinsic honor among misfits, pariahs, and queers. Artists—those of us who stand outside the city gates and look back at a society that tries to ignore us—we have an angle of vision denied to whole sectors of the sheltered and indifferent population within. It is our curse and our prize, and for everyone who will tell us our work is mean or fearful or unreal, there is another who will embrace us and say with tears in their eyes how wonderful it is to finally feel as if someone else has seen their truth and shown it in some part as it should be known.

"My story," they say. "You told my story. That is me, mine, us." And it is.

We are not the same. We are a nation of nations. Regions, social classes, economic circumstances, ethical systems, and political convictions—all separate us even as we pretend they do not. Art makes that plain. Those of us who have read the same books, eaten the same kinds of food as children, watched the same television shows, and listened to the same music, we believe ourselves part of the same nation—and we are continually startled to discover that our versions of reality do not match. If we were more the same, would we not see the same thing when we look at a painting? But what is it we see when we look at a work of art? What is it we fear will be revealed? The artist waits for us to say. It does not matter that each of us sees something slightly different. Most of us, confronted with the artist's creation, hesitate, stammer, or politely deflect the question of what it means to us. Even those of us from the same background, same region, same general economic and social class, come to "art" uncertain, suspicious, not wanting to embarrass ourselves by revealing what the work provokes in us. In fact, sometimes we are not sure. If we were to reveal what we see in each painting, sculpture, installation, or little book, we would run the risk of exposing our secret selves, what we know and what we fear we do not know, and of course incidentally what it is we truly fear. Art is the Rorschach test for all of us, the projective hologram of our secret lives. Our emotional and intellectual lives are laid bare. Do you like hologram roses? Big, bold, brightly painted canvases? Representational art? Little boxes with tiny figures posed precisely? Do you dare say what it is you like?

For those of us born into poor and working-class [40] families, these are not simple questions. For those of us who grew up hiding what our home life was like, the fear is omnipresent—particularly when that home life was scarred by physical and emotional violence. We know if we say anything about what we see in a work of art we will reveal more about ourselves than the artist. What do you see in this painting, in that one? I see a little girl, terrified, holding together the torn remnants of her clothing. I see a child, looking back at the mother for help and finding none. I see a mother, bruised and exhausted, unable to look up for help, unable to believe anyone in the world will help her. I see a man with his fists raised, hating himself but making those fists tighter all the time. I see a little girl, uncertain and angry, looking down at her own body with hatred and contempt. I see that all the time, even when no one else sees what I see. I know I am not supposed to mention what it is I see. Perhaps no one else is seeing what I see. If they are, I am pretty sure there is some cryptic covenant that requires that we will not say what we see. Even when looking at an image of a terrified child, we know that to mention why that child might be so frightened would be a breach of social etiquette. The world requires that such children not be mentioned, even when so many of us are looking directly at her.

There seems to be a tacit agreement about what it is not polite to mention, what it is not appropriate to portray. For some of us, that polite behavior is set so deeply we truly do not see what seems outside that tacit agreement. We have lost the imagination for what our real lives have been or continue to be, what happens when we go home and close the door on the outside world. Since so many would like us to never mention anything unsettling anyway, the impulse to be quiet, the impulse to deny and pretend, becomes very strong. But the artist knows all about that impulse. The artist knows that it must be resisted. Art is not meant to be polite, secret, coded, or timid. Art is the sphere in which that impulse to hide and lie is the most dangerous. In art, transgression is holy, revelation a sacrament, and pursuing one's personal truth the only sure validation.

Does it matter if our art is canonized, if we become rich and successful, lauded and admired? Does it make any difference if our pictures become popular, our books made into movies, our creations win awards? What if we are the ones who wind up going from town to town with our notebooks, our dusty boxes of prints or Xeroxed sheets of music, never acknowledged, never paid for our work? As artists, we know how easily we could become a Flannery O'Connor character, reading those journals of criticism and burying our faces in our hands, staggering under the weight of what we see that the world does not. As artists, we also know that neither worldly praise nor critical disdain will ultimately prove the worth of our work.

Some nights I think of that sweating, girlish Jesus above my mother's determined features, those hands outspread to cast benediction on those giggling uncertain boys, me in the congregation struck full of wonder and love and helpless laughter. If no one else ever wept at that image, I did. I wished the artist who painted that image knew how powerfully it touched me, that after all these years his art still lives inside me. If I can wish for anything for my art, that is what I want—to live in some child forever—and if I can demand anything of other artists, it is that they attempt as much. ○

SEEING

1. At several points in "This Is Our World," Dorothy Allison invokes the image of a magazine ad "that showed a small child high in the air dropping toward the upraised arms of a waiting figure below" (para. 29). What varying "versions of reality" does Allison see in this image? How does her description of each version exemplify her point that "if we were to reveal what we see in each painting, sculpture, installation, or little book, we would run the risk of exposing our secret selves" (para. 39)?

2. Allison begins her essay with a childhood anecdote of her reactions to the first painting she "ever saw up close." At what points—and with what effects—does she refer to this anecdote later in the essay? When does Allison shift from personal anecdotes to more general commentary? To what extent do you think these moves are successful?

WRITING

1. "The world is meaner than we admit," Allison writes, referring to the stash of newspaper clippings she keeps under her desk (para. 37). Use a newspaper clipping of your choice—or the *New York Times* front page (p. 257) showing the news of the day on September 11, 2001—to agree or disagree with Allison's assertion. Use details from your text and your knowledge of political violence to support your points.

2. From the painting of Jesus she marveled at as a child, Allison writes, she "took the notion that art should surprise and astonish, and hopefully make you think something you had not thought until you saw it" (para. 1). Choose a piece of art—a visual image, an essay, or some other work—that surprised and astonished you, and use it to support or refute Allison's claim about what art should do. If you disagree with Allison, make sure you start with your own definition of the purpose of art.

Visualizing Composition
Structure

Left: **Aerial view of a train wreck,** April 1966; above: William Neill, **Meander Along the Green River**

Examine carefully the two photographs here. The first was taken in April 1966 when a Southern Railway freight train transporting 700-foot-long metal rails collided with a bulldozer and derailed. The force of the collision had a remarkable impact on the rails; it bent them into a series of smooth curves—much like the smooth and almost elegant curves of a meandering river, shown in the second photograph.

What do you notice in each photograph? How would you describe the patterns you notice in each? Looking for patterns in such scenes and circumstances is one of the most fundamental acts of intellectual analysis. We often instinctively look for such patterns in our everyday experiences.

What, exactly, is a *pattern*? Most dictionaries define the term as a plan or diagram to be followed in making something, such as a pattern for a jacket. The term is also used to refer to an artistic or decorative design, such as a herringbone pattern in a fabric as well as a path or course of action, such as a flight pattern for an airplane.

Structure is a similar term that arises in discussions of the arts and sciences. In biology, *structure* refers to the arrangement or formation of the tissues, organs, or other parts of an organism. In the social sciences, structure points to something that is made up of a number of parts, as in a hierarchical social structure. In writing in general, and literature in particular, structure can be defined as the planned framework of a story, poem, play, or essay. In an essay, structure can usually be mapped by following the organizing pattern of topics that the writer presents.

Choose a photograph or painting presented in any recently published magazine. Examine the image carefully, paying special attention to the way in which the scene or circumstances is presented and framed. Write an essay in which you use this painting or photograph to illustrate your working definition of structure.

ANDREW SAVULICH >

Andrew Savulich worked as a
landscape architect before turning to freelance photography
and, fifteen years later, becoming
a staff photographer for the *New
York Daily News* (which, according to its masthead, is "New
York's Picture Newspaper"). His
work has been exhibited in the
United States and abroad, and he
has received numerous awards,
including a National Endowment
for the Arts fellowship grant in
photography.

Savulich is a master of "spot
news"—spontaneous photo-
graphs of the violence and accidents, the humorous and odd
events of everyday life, especially
in urban areas. He explains
his motivation: "We're at a point
in our society where very weird
things are happening in the
streets, and I like taking pictures
because I feel I'm recording
something that's really *happening.*" He thrives on the spontaneity of "hunting" for memorable
pictures: "There's a kind of adren-
aline rush when you're doing this
work. . . . It's all spontaneous: you
have to figure things out, and
you never really know what you
have. That uncertainty is attractive, I think."

Savulich adds a handwritten
caption below each photograph
he takes. "I felt that the pictures
needed something to describe
what was happening. And I
thought the easiest way would
be just to write a little description on the prints themselves.
And I liked the way it looked."

PEOPLE WATCHING JUMPER ON HOTEL ROOF.

MAN complaining THAT HE WAS ATTACKED AFTER HE gave HIS money TO Robbers.

TAXI DRIVER EXPLAINING HOW AN ARGUEMENT WITH HIS PASSENGER CAUSED HIM
TO DRIVE INTO THE RESTAURANT.

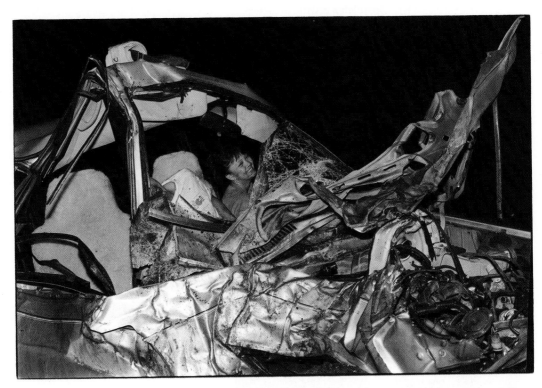

WOMAN laughing AFTER CAR WRECK.

1. What story does each of these photographs tell? What is especially striking and memorable about them? What similarities or differences do you see between and among the four photos?

2. Look carefully at each of the photographs for Andrew Savulich's artistic presence. Comment, for example, on the camera angle, the precise moment at which he chooses to take each photograph, as well as what he includes. What makes his style distinct from that of any of the other photographers whose work is presented in this chapter?

1. Much of the story in each of Savulich's photographs is conveyed by its caption. Think of alternate captions for each image. Would a different caption significantly change how you "read" the photograph? Why or why not?

2. Choose one of Savulich's photographs, and write a two-page journalistic account that you imagine would accompany the image in a newspaper. Include the sequence of events that led to the moment depicted in the photograph, conveying the emotional aspects of the event as you do so. Base as much of your report as possible on details you see in the image, and then embellish your report in any way you wish—with quotations, names, background information—to make your news story compelling.

PEOPLE WATCHING JUMPER ON HOTEL ROOF.

TAXI DRIVER EXPLAINING HOW AN ARGUMENT WITH HIS PASSENGER CAUSED HIM TO DRIVE INTO THE RESTAURANT.

MAN COMPLAINING THAT HE WAS ARRESTED AFTER HE GAVE HIS MONEY TO ROBBERS.

WOMAN LAUGHING AFTER CAR WRECK.

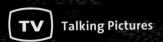

Talking Pictures

Many people would say that the events of September 11, 2001, reaffirmed Andrew Savulich's description of New York City as a place where "something is wrong," where daily life is a "no-mercy situation." "Anybody who's lived in New York for the last ten years, or even less, knows that." Many other people would say that the outpouring of concern and generosity in the wake of September 11 would challenge Savulich's view of New York City. In either case, his photographs record everyday events there from an angle that delicately balances horror and humor.

The ubiquitous reruns of such television news and tabloid shows as *America's Most Wanted, Rescue 911, Cops,* and *Hard Copy* serve as the mundane stage on which dramatic slow-motion replays of real-life violence and crime are played out. These programs project the image that no one is safe on the nation's urban streets. Write the first draft of an expository essay in which you explain why so many Americans seem frightened on the streets and yet can't seem to get enough violence on television when they arrive home.

JAMES NACHTWEY >

"The primary function of my photographs," explained James Nachtwey recently, "is to be in mass-circulation publications—during the time that the events are happening. I want them to become part of people's daily dialogue and create public awareness, public opinion, that can help bring pressure for change. That's the first and most important use of my work. A secondary use is to become an archive, entered into our collective memory, so that these events are never forgotten."

Born in Syracuse, New York, in 1948, Nachtwey has photographed violence around the world—most recently in Kosovo, Chechnya, and Afghanistan. Appearing in *Time, Life,* the *New York Times Magazine, Newsweek,* and *National Geographic,* he has also published three collections of photographs: *Deeds of War* (1989), *James Nachtwey: Civil Wars* (1999), and *Inferno* (2000), a retrospective of his work in the 1990s.

Despite an impressive list of photojournalism accolades, Nachtwey would prefer his viewers to focus on the subjects of his images rather than the photographer behind them. "I don't want people to be concerned about me," he recently explained, "I want them to be concerned about the people in the pictures. . . . I want the first impact, and by far the most powerful impact, to be about an emotional, intellectual, and moral reaction to what is happening to these people. I want my presence to be transparent."

Ground Zero
James Nachtwey

When the attack first started, I was in my own apartment near the South Street Seaport, directly across lower Manhattan. I heard a sound that was out of the ordinary. I was far enough away so that the sound wasn't alarming, but it was definitely out of the ordinary.

When I saw the towers burning, my first reaction was to take a camera, to load it with film, go up on my roof, where I had a clear view, and photograph the first tower burning. Then I wanted to go directly to the site. I went back down and loaded my gear and went over. It was a ten-minute walk.

When I got there, people were being evacuated from both towers. In the interim, the plane had hit the second tower. Medical treatment centers were being set up on the sidewalks. It wasn't as chaotic as you might think. On the street, the people coming out initially were not seriously wounded. They were frightened, some were hurt in a minor way. I think that the real chaos was happening up inside the towers with the people who were trapped.

When the first tower fell, people ran in panic. They ran from the falling debris, girders that were falling down in an avalanche in the thick smoke and dust. Documenting a crisis situation that's clearly out of control is always very instinctual. There's no road map. No ground rules. It's all improvisations. My instinct initially, in this case, was to photograph the human situation. But once the tower fell, the people really all disappeared. They either ran away or were trapped. So my instinct then was to go to where the tower had fallen. It seemed to me absolutely unbelievable that the World Trade Center could be lying in the

street, and I felt compelled to make an image of this. I made my way there through the smoke. The area was virtually deserted. It seemed like a movie set from a science-fiction film. Very apocalyptic—sunlight filtering through the dust and the destroyed wreckage of the buildings lying in the street.

As I was photographing the destruction of the first tower, the second tower fell, and I was standing right under it, literally right under it. Fortunately for me, and unfortunately for people on the west side of the building, it listed to the west. But I was still underneath this avalanche of falling debris—structural steel and aluminum siding, glass, just tons of material falling directly down onto me. I realized that I had a few seconds to find cover or else I'd be killed. I dashed into the lobby of the Millenium Hilton hotel, directly across the street from the North Tower, and I realized instantly that this hotel lobby was going to be taken out, that the debris would come flying through the plate glass and there would be no protection at all. There was no other place to turn, certainly no more time.

I saw an open elevator and dashed inside. I put my back against the wall, and about a second later the lobby was taken out. There was a construction worker who dashed inside there with me just as the debris swept through the lobby. It instantly became pitch black, just as if you were in a closet with the light out and a blindfold on. You could not see anything. It was very difficult to breathe. My nose, my mouth, my eyes were filled with ash. I had a hat on, so I put it over my face and began to breathe through it. And together, this other man and I crawled, groping,

5

JAMES NACHTWEY, *CRUSHED CAR*

trying to find our way out. I initially thought that the building had fallen on us and that we were in a pocket, because it was so dark. We just continued to crawl, and I began to see small blinking lights, and I realized that these were the turn signals of cars that had been destroyed and the signals were still on. At that point I realized that we were in the street, although it was just as black in the street as it was in the hotel lobby, and that we would be able to find our way out.

My experiences photographing combat and being in life-threatening situations played a very important part in my being able to survive this and continue to work. It was, as I said, all instinct. I was making fast decisions with very little time to spare. And I guess that I made the right decisions, because I'm still here. I was lucky, too. I don't fold up in these situations. I've been in them enough times to somehow have developed the capacity to continue to do my job. On my way out of the smoke and ash, I was actually photographing searchers coming in. Once I got clear, I tried to clear my eyes as best I could and catch my breath. I realized I had to make my way toward what has now become known as Ground Zero. It took a while to make my way there. I spent the day there, photographing the firemen searching for people who had been trapped.

If I had been needed to help someone, I certainly would have done it, as I have many times in the past. I would have put down my camera to lend a hand, as I think anyone would have. The place was filled with firemen and rescue workers and police, and I was not needed to play that role. I realized that very clearly and therefore went about doing my job.

When I'm photographing I don't censor myself, or second-guess myself. I try to be aware of my own inner voice, my own instincts, as much as I can, and I try to follow them.

The level of dust and ash in the air was so intense that it was impossible to protect myself or my camera or my film. I've never had negatives that were so scratched and filled with marks as these. It looks like there are railroad tracks across my negatives. Every time you opened your camera back, there was no time even to dust it off, because more ash would fall in.

I worked all day until night, at which point I felt that it was time to leave. I was exhausted; I felt rather sick from all the smoke and ash that I had inhaled—not only initially, but all day long. The scene was burning and filled with acrid smoke; my lungs had burned all day long. The next day I was quite sick, almost incapacitated. Feeling dizzy, exhausted. Quite out of it.

After the buildings fell, there wasn't really any more danger, as long as you watched your footing. It wasn't as if people were shooting at us or we were being shelled or there were land minds there.

The frontline troops in this particular battle were firemen, and they put themselves in jeopardy. A lot of them lost their lives. They were frontline troops [who] didn't kill anyone; they were there to save people. That made this story very different from the wars I've covered.

The rescue workers were generally too busy to pay us [photographers] much mind. And because we weren't in the way they didn't have to pay us much mind, unless they felt like it, for whatever personal reason they might have had. The police were another matter. They instinctively try to keep us away from anything. I think that it's just the nature of the relationship, unfortunately. But there was so much chaos at the beginning that it was easy to elude the police, and once you were with the rescue workers, they didn't seem to mind at all.

I didn't see the dead. They were underneath, and it wasn't clear how many were under there at that moment. I didn't witness people suffering, because they were invisible. I didn't feel it as strongly as when I witnessed people starving to death or when I've seen innocent people cut down by sniper fire. I haven't completely processed this event.

For me personally, the worst moment was when I was underneath the second tower as it fell and this tidal wave of deadly debris was about to fall on me. When I saw Ground Zero I was in a state of disbelief. It was disturbing to see this massive destruction in my own city, in my own country. I was in Grozny when it was being pulverized by Russian artillery and aircraft. I spent a couple of years in Beirut during various sieges and bombardments. But now it was literally in my own backyard, and I think one thing Americans are learning from this is that now we are a part of the world in a way we never have been before.

The first day that Time.com had my essay on their Web-site, at least 600,000 people had a look at it. To me, as a communicator, that's very gratifying. I hope publishers and editors are paying attention to this. There is power in the still image that doesn't exist in other forms. I think that there even is a necessity for it, because that many people wouldn't be looking at still pictures unless they needed to do that. I know that 600,000 people looking at a Web-site is small compared to a typical TV audience, but it is [nonetheless] a sizable number of people, and the fact that people are turning to the Internet instead of television is significant. This is sort of a test case of mass appeal.

To me it's quite obvious that a tremendous crime against humanity—a barbaric act—has been perpetrated on innocent civilians. There's nothing that can justify that act.

Many years ago, I felt that I had seen too much [violence], that I didn't want to see any more tragedies in this world. But unfortunately history continues to produce tragedies, and it is very important that they be documented with compassion and in a compelling way. I feel a responsibility to continue. But believe me when I say that I would much rather these things never happen [so that] I could either photograph something entirely different or not be a photographer at all. But that's not the way the world is. ○

SEEING

1. James Nachtwey is a veteran photographer who has documented wars in several parts of the world. In what ways does he draw on this breadth of experience to establish his point of view? Point to specific passages in your response. What similarities and differences does he establish between those wartime experiences and his photographing the collapse of the twin towers at the World Trade Center? In paragraph 8 Nachtwey explains that "the place was filled with firemen and rescue workers and police, and I was not needed to play that role. I realized that very clearly and therefore went about doing my job." What do you think the role of a photographer should be during a time of war or during a crisis situation?

2. In paragraph 17 Nachtwey tells us that "there is power in the still image that doesn't exist in other forms. I think that there even is a necessity for it, because that many people wouldn't be looking at still pictures unless they needed to do that." Compare and contrast the "power" of Nachtwey's prose narrative of the events of September 11 to *Crushed Car*, one of the photographs he took that day (p. 274). You can find this image as part of a larger photo essay at www.time.com /photoessays/shattered. Which one do you find more articulate—his prose or his visual essay? Please explain why. Explain the extent to which the "power" of each is a reflection of its medium.

WRITING

1. The National Press Photographers' Association career guide notes that "many publications and stations have conduct codes or ethics codes requiring photojournalists to report truthfully, honestly and objectively. Their codes might include statements such as 'photojournalists should at all times maintain the highest standards of ethical conduct in serving the public interest' or 'a member shall present himself, his work, his services and his premises in such a manner as will uphold and dignify his professional status and the reputation of the station.' " Using samples from Nachtwey's photojournalism, write an expository essay in which you apply these standards to combat photography.

2. In paragraph 17, Nachtwey announces that he found it "very gratifying" to know that there were 600,000 visits to his photo essay on the *Time* web site. "The fact that people are turning to the Internet instead of television is significant. This is sort of a test case of mass appeal." Write an argumentative essay in which you support—or challenge— the assertion that the events of September 11 caused a shift in the ways we receive information and the sources of that information.

DON DELILLO

Don DeLillo is one of the most acute observers of contemporary society who is writing fiction today. In more than ten novels and numerous short stories, he manages to capture the intangible essence of modern life in language that is at once direct, clear, and incisive. His novels focus on a range of subjects, including modern science in *Ratner's Star* (1976), terrorism in *Players* (1977), chemical accidents in *White Noise* (1985), religious fanaticism in *Mao II* (1991), and the cold war in *Underworld* (1997). Across this array of topics DeLillo explores the ways in which individuals cope with the pressures of technology, mass media, and depersonalizing institutions. His enduring fascination with the cultural function of film and video is apparent in "In the Ruins of the Future," which was published in the December 2001 issue of *Harper's* magazine.

Born in New York City in 1936, DeLillo is often linked with a group of contemporary writers whose focus is language, especially experimental language. His work is particularly celebrated for its crafted, hard edge. "What writing means to me," DeLillo explains, "is trying to make interesting, clear, beautiful language."

Ground Zero
James Nachtwey

IN THE RUINS OF THE FUTURE

Reflections on terror and loss in the shadow of September

Don DeLillo

1.

IN THE PAST DECADE THE SURGE OF CAPITAL markets has dominated discourse and shaped global consciousness. Multinational corporations have come to seem more vital and influential than governments. The dramatic climb of the Dow and the speed of the Internet summoned us all to live permanently in the future, in the utopian glow of cyber-capital, because there is no memory there and this is where markets are uncontrolled and investment potential has no limit.

All this changed on September 11. Today, again, the world narrative belongs to terrorists. But the primary target of the men who attacked the Pentagon and the World Trade Center was not the global economy. It is America that drew their fury. It is the high gloss of our modernity. It is the thrust of our technology. It is our perceived godlessness. It is the blunt force of our foreign policy. It is the power of American culture to penetrate every wall, home, life, and mind.

Terror's response is a narrative that has been developing over years, only now becoming inescapable. It is *our* lives and minds that are occupied now. This catastrophic event changes the way we think and act, moment to moment, week to week, for unknown weeks and months to come, and steely years. Our world, parts of our world, have crumbled into theirs, which means we are living in a place of danger and rage.

The protesters [opposed to the World Trade Organization] in Genoa, Prague, Seattle, and other cities want to decelerate the global momentum that seemed to be driving unmindfully toward a landscape of consumer-robots and social instability, with the chance of self-determination probably diminishing for most people in most countries. Whatever acts of violence marked the protests, most of the men and women involved tend to be a moderating influence, trying to slow things down, even things out, hold off the white-hot future.

The terrorists of September 11 want to bring back the past.

2.

Our tradition of free expression and our justice system's provisions for the rights of the accused can only seem an offense to men bent on suicidal terror.

We are rich, privileged, and strong, but they are willing to die. This is the edge they have, the fire of aggrieved belief. We live in a wide world, routinely filled with exchange of every sort, an open circuit of work, talk, family, and expressible feeling. The terrorist, planted in a Florida town, pushing his supermarket cart, nodding to his neighbor, lives in a far narrower format. This is his edge, his strength. Plots reduce the world. He builds a plot around his anger and our indifference. He lives a certain kind of apartness, hard and tight. This is not the self-watcher, the soft white dangling boy who shoots someone to keep from disappearing into himself. The terrorist shares a secret and a self. At a certain point he and his brothers may begin to feel less motivated by politics and personal hatred than by brotherhood itself. They share the codes and protocols of their mission here and something deeper as well, a vision of judgment and devastation.

Does the sight of a woman pushing a stroller soften the man to her humanity and vulnerability, and her child's as well, and all the people he is here to kill?

This is his edge, that he does not see her. Years here, waiting, taking flying lessons, making the routine gestures of community and home, the credit card, the bank account, the post-office box. All tactical, linked, layered. He knows who we are and what we mean in the world—an idea, a righteous fever in the brain. But there is no defenseless human at the end of his gaze.

The sense of disarticulation we hear in the term "Us and Them" has never been so striking, at either end.

We can tell ourselves that whatever we've done to inspire bitterness, distrust, and rancor, it was not so damnable as to bring this day down on our heads.

But there is no logic in apocalypse. They have gone beyond the bounds of passionate payback. This is heaven and hell, a sense of armed martyrdom as the surpassing drama of human experience.

He pledges his submission to God and meditates on the blood to come.

3.

The Bush Administration was feeling a nostalgia for the Cold War. This is over now. Many things are over. The narrative ends in the rubble, and it is left to us to create the counter-narrative.

There are a hundred thousand stories crisscrossing New York, Washington, and the world. Where we were, whom we know, what we've seen or heard. There are the doctors' appointments that saved lives, the cell phones that were used to report the hijackings. Stories generating others and people running north out of the rumbling smoke and ash. Men running in suits and ties, women who'd lost their shoes, cops running from the skydive of all that towering steel.

People running for their lives are part of the story that is left to us.

There are stories of heroism and encounters with dread. There are stories that carry around their edges the luminous ring of coincidence, fate, or premonition. They take us beyond the hard numbers of dead and missing and give us a glimpse of elevated being. For a hundred who are arbitrarily dead, we need to find one person saved by a flash of forewarning. There are configurations that chill and awe us both. Two women on two planes, best of friends, who die together and apart, Tower 1 and Tower 2. What desolate epic tragedy might bear the weight of such juxtaposition? But we can also ask what symmetry, bleak and touching both, takes one friend, spares the other's grief?

The brother of one of the women worked in one of the towers. He managed to escape.

In Union Square Park, about two miles north of the attack site, the improvised memorials are another part of our response. The flags, flower beds, and votive candles, the lamppost hung with paper airplanes, the passages from the Koran and the Bible, the letters and poems, the cardboard John Wayne, the children's drawings of the Twin Towers, the hand-painted signs for Free Hugs, Free Back Rubs, the graffiti of love and peace on the tall equestrian statue.

There are many photographs of missing persons, some accompanied by hopeful lists of identifying features. (Man with panther tattoo, upper right arm.) There is the saxophonist, playing softly. There is the sculptured flag of rippling copper and aluminum, six feet long, with two young people still attending to the finer details of the piece.

Then there are the visitors to the park. The arti-facts on display represent the confluence of a number of cultural tides, patriotic and multidevotional and retro hippie. The visitors move quietly in the floating aromas of candlewax, roses, and bus fumes. There are many people this mild evening, and in their voices, manner, clothing, and in the color of their skin they recapitulate the mix we see in the photocopied faces of the lost.

For the next fifty years, people who were not in the area when the attacks occurred will claim to have been there. In time, some of them will believe it. Others will claim to have lost friends or relatives, although they did not.

This is also the counter-narrative, a shadow history of false memories and imagined loss.

The Internet is a counter-narrative, shaped in part by rumor, fantasy, and mystical reverberation.

The cell phones, the lost shoes, the handkerchiefs mashed in the faces of running men and women. The box cutters and credit cards. The paper that came streaming out of the towers and drifted across the river to Brooklyn back yards: status reports, résumés, insurance forms. Sheets of paper driven into concrete, according to witnesses. Paper slicing into truck tires, fixed there.

These are among the smaller objects and more marginal stories in the sifted ruins of the day. We need them, even the common tools of the terrorists, to set against the massive spectacle that continues to seem unmanageable, too powerful a thing to set into our frame of practiced response.

4.

Ash was spattering the windows. Karen was half dressed, grabbing the kids and trying to put on some clothes and talking with her husband and scooping things to take out to the corridor, and they looked at her, twin girls, as if she had fourteen heads.

They stayed in the corridor for a while, thinking there might be secondary explosions. They waited, and began to feel safer, and went back to the apartment.

At the next impact, Marc knew in the sheerest second before the shock wave broadsided their building that it was a second plane, impossible, striking the second tower. Their building was two blocks away, and he'd thought the first crash was an accident.

They went back to the hallway, where others began to gather, fifteen or twenty people.

Karen ran back for a cell phone, a cordless phone, a charger, water, sweaters, snacks for the kids, and then made a quick dash to the bedroom for her wedding ring.

From the window she saw people running in the street, others locked shoulder to shoulder, immobilized, with debris coming down on them. People were trampled, struck by falling objects, and there was ash and paper everywhere, paper whipping through the air, no sign of light or sky.

Cell phones were down. They talked on the cordless, receiving information measured out in eyedrops. They were convinced that the situation outside was far more grave than it was here.

Smoke began to enter the corridor.

Then the first tower fell. She thought it was a bomb. When she talked to someone on the phone and found out what had happened, she felt a surreal relief. Bombs and missiles were not falling everywhere in the city. It was not all-out war, at least not yet.

Marc was in the apartment getting chairs for the older people, for the woman who'd had hip surgery.

When he heard the first low drumming rumble, he stood in a strange dead calm and said, "Something is happening." It sounded exactly like what it was, a tall tower collapsing.

The windows were surfaced with ash now, blacked out completely, and he wondered what was out there. What remained to be seen and did he want to see it?

They all moved into the stairwell, behind a fire door, but smoke kept coming in. It was gritty ash, and they were eating it.

He ran back inside, grabbing towels off the racks and washcloths out of drawers and drenching them in the sink, and filling his bicycle water bottles, and grabbing the kids' underwear.

He thought the crush of buildings was the thing to fear most. This is what would kill them.

Karen was on the phone, talking to a friend in the 40 district attorney's office, about half a mile to the north. She was pleading for help. She begged, pleaded, and hung up. For the next hour a detective kept calling with advice and encouragement.

Marc came back out to the corridor. I think we *might* die, he told himself, hedging his sense of what would happen next.

The detective told Karen to stay where they were.

When the second tower fell, my heart fell with it. I called Marc, who is my nephew, on his cordless. I couldn't stop thinking of the size of the towers and the meager distance between those buildings and his. He answered, we talked. I have no memory of the conversation except for his final remark, slightly urgent, concerning someone on the other line, who might be sending help.

Smoke was seeping out of the elevator shaft now. Karen was saying goodbye to her father in Oregon. Not hello-goodbye. But goodbye-I-think-we-are-going-to-die. She thought smoke would be the thing that did it.

People sat on chairs along the walls. They chatted 45 about practical matters. They sang songs with the kids. The kids in the group were cooperative because the adults were damn scared.

There was an improvised rescue in progress. Karen's friend and a colleague made their way down from Centre Street, turning up with two policemen they'd enlisted en route. They had dust masks and a destination, and they searched every floor for others who might be stranded in the building.

They came out into a world of ash and near night. There was no one else to be seen now on the street. Gray ash covering the cars and pavement, ash falling in large flakes, paper still drifting down, discarded shoes, strollers, briefcases. The members of the group were masked and toweled, children in adults' arms, moving east and then north on Nassau Street, trying not to look around, only what's immediate, one step and then another, all closely focused, a pregnant woman, a newborn, a dog.

They were covered in ash when they reached shelter at Pace University, where there was food and water, and kind and able staff members, and a gas-leak scare, and more running people.

Workers began pouring water on the group. *Stay wet, stay wet.* This was the theme of the first half hour.

Later a line began to form along the food counter. 50 Someone said, "I don't want cheese on that." Someone said, "I like it better not so cooked."

Not so incongruous really, just people alive and hungry, beginning to be themselves again.

5.

Technology is our fate, our truth. It is what we mean when we call ourselves the only superpower on the planet. The materials and methods we devise make it possible for us to claim our future. We don't have to depend on God or the prophets or other astonishments. We are the astonishment. The miracle is what we ourselves produce, the systems and networks that change the way we live and think.

But whatever great skeins of technology lie ahead, ever 55 more complex, connective, precise, micro-fractional, the future has yielded, for now, to medieval expedience, to the old slow furies of cutthroat religion.

Kill the enemy and pluck out his heart.

If others in less scientifically advanced cultures were able to share, wanted to share, some of the blessings of our technology, without a threat to their faith or traditions, would they need to rely on a God in whose name they kill the innocent? Would they need to invent a God who rewards violence against the innocent with a promise of "infinite paradise," in the words of a handwritten letter found in the luggage of one of the hijackers?

For all those who may want what we've got, there are all those who do not. These are the men who have fashioned a morality of destruction. They want what they used to have before the waves of Western influence. They surely see themselves as the elect of God whether or not they follow the central precepts of Islam. It is the presumptive right of those who choose violence and death to speak directly to God. They will kill and then die. Or they will die first, in the cockpit, in clean shoes, according to instructions in the letter.

Six days after the attacks, the territory below Canal Street is hedged with barricades. There are few civilians in the street. Police at some checkpoints, troops in camouflage gear at others, wearing gas masks, and a pair of state troopers in conversation, and ten burly men striding east in hard hats, work pants, and NYPD jackets. A shop owner tries to talk a cop into letting him enter his place of business. He is a small elderly man with a Jewish accent, but there is no relief today. Garbage bags are everywhere in high broad stacks. The area is bedraggled and third-worldish, with an air of permanent emergency, everything surfaced in ash.

It is possible to pass through some checkpoints, detour around others. At Chambers Street I look south through the links of the National Rent-A-Fence barrier. There stands the smoky remnant of filigree that marks the last tall thing, the last sign in the mire of wreckage that there were towers here that dominated the skyline for over a quarter of a century.

Ten days later and a lot closer, I stand at another barrier with a group of people, looking directly into the strands of openwork facade. It is almost too close. It is almost Roman, I-beams for stonework, but not nearly so salvageable. Many here describe the scene to others on cell phones.

"Oh my god I'm standing here," says the man next to me.

The World Trade towers were not only an emblem of advanced technology but a justification, in a sense, for technology's irresistible will to realize in solid form whatever becomes theoretically allowable. Once defined, every limit must be reached. The tactful sheathing of the towers was intended to reduce the direct threat of such straight-edge enormity, a gigantism that eased over the years into something a little more familiar and comfortable, even dependable in a way.

Now a small group of men have literally altered our skyline. We have fallen back in time and space. It is their technology that marks our moments, the small lethal devices, the remote-control detonators they fashion out of radios, or the larger technology they borrow from us, passenger jets that become manned missiles.

Maybe this is a grim subtext of their enterprise. They see something innately destructive in the nature of technology. It brings death to their customs and beliefs. Use it as what it is, a thing that kills.

6.

Nearly eleven years ago, during the engagement in the Persian Gulf, people had trouble separating the war from coverage of the war. After the first euphoric days, coverage became limited. The rush of watching all that eerie green night-vision footage, shot from fighter jets in combat, had been so intense that it became hard to honor the fact that the war was still going on, untelevised. A layer of consciousness had been stripped away. People shuffled around, muttering. They were lonely for their war.

The events of September 11 were covered unstintingly. There was no confusion of roles on TV. The raw event was one thing, the coverage another. The event dominated the medium. It was bright and totalizing, and some of us said it was unreal. When we say a thing is unreal, we mean it is too real, a phenomenon so unaccountable and yet so bound to the power of objective fact that we can't tilt it to the slant of our perceptions. First the planes struck the towers. After a time it became possible for us to absorb this, barely. But when the towers fell. When the rolling smoke began moving downward, floor to floor. This was so vast and terrible that it was outside imagining even as it happened. We could not catch up to it. But it was real, punishingly so, an expression of the physics of structural limits and a void in one's soul, and there was the huge antenna falling out of the sky, straight down, blunt end first, like an arrow moving backward in time.

The event itself has no purchase on the mercies of analogy or simile. We have to take the shock and horror as it is. But living language is not diminished. The writer wants to understand what this day has done to us. Is it too soon? We seem pressed for time, all of us. Time is scarcer now. There is a sense of compression, plans made hurriedly, time forced and distorted. But language is inseparable from the world that provokes it. The writer begins in the towers, trying to imagine the moment, desperately. Before politics, before history and religion, there is the primal terror. People falling from the towers hand in hand. This is part of the counter-narrative, hands and spirits joining, human beauty in the crush of meshed steel.

In its desertion of every basis for comparison, the event asserts its singularity. There is something empty in the sky. The writer tries to give memory, tenderness, and meaning to all that howling space.

7.

We like to think America invented the future. We are comfortable with the future, intimate with it. But there are disturbances now, in large and small ways, a chain of reconsiderations. Where we live, how we travel, what we think about when we look at our children. For many people, the event has changed the grain of the most routine moment.

We may find that the ruin of the towers is implicit in other things. The new PalmPilot at fingertip's reach, the stretch limousine parked outside the hotel, the midtown skyscraper under construction, carrying the name of a major investment bank—all haunted in a way by what has happened, less assured in their authority, in the prerogatives they offer.

There is fear of other kinds of terrorism, the prospect that biological and chemical weapons will contaminate the air we breathe and the water we drink. There wasn't much concern about this after earlier terrorist acts. This time we are trying to name the future, not in our normally hopeful way but guided by dread.

What has already happened is sufficient to affect the air around us, psychologically. We are all breathing the fumes of lower Manhattan, where traces of the dead are everywhere, in the soft breeze off the river, on rooftops and windows, in our hair and on our clothes.

Think of a future in which the components of a microchip are the size of atoms. The devices that pace our lives will operate from the smart quantum spaces of pure information. Now think of people in countless thousands massing in anger and vowing revenge. Enlarged photos of martyrs and holy men dangle from balconies, and the largest images are those of a terrorist leader.

Two forces in the world, past and future. With the end of Communism, the ideas and principles of modern democracy were seen clearly to prevail, whatever the inequalities of the system itself. This is still the case. But now there is a global theocratic state, unboundaried and floating and so obsolete it must depend on suicidal fervor to gain its aims.

Ideas evolve and de-evolve, and history is turned on end.

8.

On Friday of the first week a long series of vehicles moves slowly west on Canal Street. Dump trucks, flatbeds, sanitation sweepers. There are giant earth-movers making a tremendous revving sound. A scant number of pedestrians, some in dust masks, others just standing, watching, the indigenous people, clinging to walls and doorways, unaccustomed to traffic that doesn't bring buyers and sellers, goods and cash. The fire rescue car and state police cruiser, the staccato sirens of a line of police vans. Cops stand at the sawhorse barriers, trying to clear the way. Ambulances, cherry pickers, a fleet of Con Ed trucks, all this clamor moving south a few blocks ahead, into the cloud of sand and ash.

One month earlier I'd taken the same walk, early evening, among crowds of people, the panethnic swarm of shoppers, merchants, residents and passersby, with a few tourists as well, and the man at the curbstone doing acupoint massage, and the dreadlocked kid riding his bike on the sidewalk. This was the spirit of Canal Street, the old jostle and stir unchanged for many decades and bearing no sign of SoHo just above, with its restaurants and artists' lofts, or TriBeCa below, rich in architectural textures. Here were hardware bargains, car stereos, foam rubber and industrial plastics, the tattoo parlor and the pizza parlor.

Then I saw the woman on the prayer rug. I'd just turned the corner, heading south to meet some friends, and there she was, young and slender, in a silk headscarf. It was time for sunset prayer, and she was kneeling, upper body pitched toward the edge of the rug. She was partly concealed by a couple of vendors' carts, and no one seemed much to notice her. I think there was another woman seated on a folding chair near the curbstone. The figure on the rug faced east, which meant most immediately a storefront just a foot and a half from her tipped head but more distantly and pertinently toward Mecca, of course, the holiest city of Islam.

Some prayer rugs include a *mihrab* in their design, an arched element representing the prayer niche in a mosque that indicates the direction of Mecca. The only locational guide the young woman needed was the Manhattan grid.

I looked at her in prayer and it was clearer to me than ever, the daily sweeping taken-for-granted greatness of New York. The city will accommodate every language, ritual, belief, and opinion. In the rolls of the dead of September 11, all these vital differences were surrendered to the impact and flash. The bodies themselves are missing in large numbers. For the survivors, more grief. But the dead are their own nation and race, one identity, young or old, devout or unbelieving—a union of souls. During the *hadj*, the annual pilgrimage to Mecca, the faithful must eliminate every sign of status, income, and nationality, the men wearing identical strips of seamless white cloth, the women with covered heads, all recalling in prayer their fellowship with the dead.

Allahu akbar. God is great. ○

SEEING

1. DeLillo talks frequently about "narratives" and "counter-narratives." Make a list of the instances when and how he uses these terms, and with what effects. What stories does he tell? Whose stories are they? What overarching story do these narratives and counter-narratives tell? What point of view, what authorial stance, does DeLillo adopt in telling them? How does he expect his readers to respond? How would you describe the narrative voice in this essay? Point to specific evidence to verify each of your responses.

2. DeLillo creates an eight-part structure for his essay. How does this structure contribute to the overall impact of the essay? What relationships do you notice between and among the sections? What would DeLillo gain and lose if he also had created a title for each of the eight sections? If you were his editor, what would you suggest he entitle each section? Explain why. Notice how often DeLillo refers to time throughout the essay—past, present, and future. How does he use these occasions to comment on our relationship with time and the ways in which the events of September 11 altered that relationship?

WRITING

1. Early in the essay, DeLillo asserts, "This catastrophic event changes the way we think and act, moment to moment, week to week, for unknown weeks and months to come, and steely years" (para. 3). To what extent does your own experience since September 11, 2001, illustrate or undercut this statement? Write an expository essay in which you explain the impact the events of September 11 have had on the ways in which you conduct your life.

2. Near the end of section 6, DeLillo observes: "The writer wants to understand what this day has done to us. Is it too soon?" (para. 68). Consider the role of the writer in dealing with a catastrophic event such as the attacks on the World Trade Center and the Pentagon. Write an expository essay in which you explain what role(s) you perceive for writers in responding to such horrific events. For example, is the primary obligation for writers to describe, to narrate, to explain, to analyze, to argue, to persuade? Something else? You might want to compare and contrast the primary role of the writer to that of the photographer. In this respect, you will find the essay by the photographer James Nachtwey especially helpful (p. 274). In what specific ways are the primary roles of writer and photographer similar? different? How so? (You need not write about the events of September 11.)

Looking Closer
Taking Pictures

When George Eastman introduced the simple and inexpensive box camera in 1888, the medium of photography came within the reach of most Americans. Anyone could buy the pre-loaded "Kodak #1," take 100 exposures, and then send the camera back to Kodak to develop the film. "You press the button, we do the rest" was the slogan that enticed generations of Americans to take snapshots.

On Photography
Susan Sontag

The writers and photographers whose work is presented on the following pages explore the ways in which pictures and picture taking have become part of American culture. Susan Sontag speculates about the significance of photographs in an excerpt from her now-classic essay **"On Photography."** The ad **"Keep the story with a *KODAK*"** provides a glimpse into the language and imagery used to familiarize Americans with the "point and shoot" process. Ethan Canin uses a family snapshot called ***Vivian, Fort Barnwell*** to imagine the very short story in "Viewfinder," and N. Scott Momaday uses a snapshot as an occasion for a short essay in "The Photograph." Three snapshots from Shizuka Yokomizo's ***Dear Stranger*** show the uneasy face of the unknowing subject of photography, while Martin Parr's ***Kalkan, Turkey*** and Duane Hanson's ***Tourists*** offer ironic views of tourists in search of unique experience.

THE PHOTOGRAPH
N. Scott Momaday

WHEN I FIRST LIVED ON THE NAVAJO RESERVATION there were no cars, except those that were government property or that belonged to the Indian Service employees. The Navajos went about in wagons and on horseback, everywhere. My father worked for the Roads Department on the Navajo reservation. I lived for those trips, for he would often take me with him. I got a sense of the country then; it was wild and unending. In rainy weather the roads became channels of running water, and sometimes a flash flood would simply wash them away altogether, and we would have to dig ourselves out of the mud or wait for the ground to freeze. And then the wagons would pass us by or, if we were lucky, some old man would unhitch his team and pull us out to firm ground.

"*Ya'at'eeh,*" the old man would say.

"*Ya'at'eeh, shicheii,*" my father would reply.

"*Hagosha' diniya?*"

"Nowhere," my father would say, "we are going 5 nowhere."

"*Aoo', atiin ayoo hastlish.*" Yes, the road is very muddy, the old man would answer, laughing, and we knew then that we were at his mercy, held fast in the groove of his humor and goodwill. My father learned to speak the Navajo language in connection with his work, and I learned something of it, too—a little. Later, after I had been away from the Navajo country for many years, I returned and studied the language formally in order to understand not only the meaning but the formation of it as well. It is a beautiful language, intricate and full of subtlety, and very difficult to learn.

There were sheep camps in the remote canyons and mountains. When we ventured out into those areas, we saw a lot of people, but they were always off by themselves, it seemed, living a life of their own, each one having an individual existence in that huge landscape. Later, when I was learning to fly an airplane, I saw the land as a hawk or an eagle sees it, immense and wild and all of a piece. Once I flew with a friend to the trading post at Low Mountain where we landed on a dirt road in the very middle of the reservation. It was like going backward in time, for Low Mountain has remained virtually undiscovered in the course of years, and there you can still see the old people coming in their wagons to get water and to trade. It is like Kayenta was in my earliest time on the reservation, so remote as to be almost legendary in the mind.

My father had a little box camera with which he liked to take photographs now and then. One day an old Navajo crone came to our house and asked to have her picture taken. She was a gnarled old woman with gray hair and fine pronounced features. She made a wonderful subject, and I have always thought very well of the photograph that my father made of her. Every day thereafter she would come to the house and ask to see the print, and every day my father had to tell her that it had not yet come back in the mail. Having photographs processed was a slow business then in that part of the world. At last the day came when the print arrived. And when the old woman came, my father presented it to her proudly. But when she took a look at it, she was deeply disturbed, and she would have nothing to do with it. She set up such a jabber, indeed, that no one could understand her, and she left in a great huff. I have often wondered that she objected so to her likeness, for it was a true likeness, as far as I could tell. It is quite possible, I think, that she had never seen her likeness before, not even in a mirror, and that the photograph was a far cry from what she imagined herself to be. Or perhaps she saw, in a way that we could not, that the photograph misrepresented her in some crucial respect, that in its dim, mechanical eye it had failed to see into her real being. ○

On Photography

Susan Sontag

RECENTLY, PHOTOGRAPHY HAS BECOME ALMOST as widely practiced an amusement as sex and dancing—which means that, like every mass art form, photography is not practiced by most people as an art. It is mainly a social rite, a defense against anxiety, and a tool of power.

Memorializing the achievements of individuals considered as members of families (as well as of other groups) is the earliest popular use of photography. For at least a century, the wedding photograph has been as much a part of the ceremony as the prescribed verbal formulas. Cameras go with family life. According to a sociological study done in France, most households have a camera, but a household with children is twice as likely to have at least one camera as a household in which there are no children. Not to take pictures of one's children, particularly when they are small, is a sign of parental indifference, just as not turning up for one's graduation picture is a gesture of adolescent rebellion.

Through photographs, each family constructs a portrait-chronicle of itself—a portable kit of images that bears witness to its connectedness. It hardly matters what activities are photographed so long as photographs get taken and are cherished. Photography becomes a rite of family life just when, in the industrializing countries of Europe and America, the very institution of the family starts undergoing radical surgery. As that claustrophobic unit, the nuclear family, was being carved out of a much larger family aggregate, photography came along to memorialize, to restate symbolically, the imperiled continuity and vanishing extendedness of family life. Those ghostly traces, photographs, supply the token presence of the dispersed relatives. A family's photograph album is generally about the extended family—and, often, is all that remains of it.

As photographs give people an imaginary possession of a past that is unreal, they also help people to take possession of space in which they are insecure. Thus, photography develops in tandem with one of the most characteristic of modern activities: tourism. For the first time in history, large numbers of people regularly travel out of their habitual environments for short periods of time. It seems positively unnatural to travel for pleasure without taking a camera along. Photographs will offer indisputable evidence that the trip was made, that the program was carried out, that fun was had. Photographs document sequences of consumption carried on outside the view of family, friends, neighbors. But dependence on the camera, as the device that makes real what one is experiencing, doesn't fade when people travel more. Taking photographs fills the same need for the cosmopolitans accumulating photograph-trophies of their boat trip up the Albert Nile or their fourteen days in China as it does for lower-middle-class vacationers taking snapshots of the Eiffel Tower or Niagara Falls.

A way of certifying experience, taking photographs 5 is also a way of refusing it—by limiting experience to a search for the photogenic, by converting experience into an image, a souvenir. Travel becomes a strategy for accumulating photographs. The very activity of taking pictures is soothing, and assuages general feelings of disorientation that are likely to be exacerbated by travel. Most tourists feel compelled to put the camera between themselves and whatever is remarkable that they encounter. Unsure of other responses, they take a picture. This gives shape to experience: stop, take a photograph, and move on. The method especially appeals to people handicapped by a ruthless work ethic—Germans, Japanese, and Americans. Using a camera appeases the anxiety which the work-driven feel about not working when they are on vacation and supposed to be having fun. They have something to do that is like a friendly imitation of work: they can take pictures.

People robbed of their past seem to make the most fervent picture takers, at home and abroad. Everyone who lives in an industrialized society is obliged gradually to give up the past, but in certain countries, such as the United States and Japan, the break with the past has been particularly traumatic. In the early 1970s, the fable of the brash American tourist of the 1950s and 1960s, rich with dollars and

Babbittry,[1] was replaced by the mystery of the group-minded Japanese tourist, newly released from his island prison by the miracle of overvalued yen, who is generally armed with two cameras, one on each hip.

Photography has become one of the principal devices for experiencing something, for giving an appearance of participation. One full-page ad shows a small group of people standing pressed together, peering out of the photograph, all but one looking stunned, excited, upset. The one who wears a different expression holds a camera to his eye; he seems self-possessed, is almost smiling. While the others are passive, clearly alarmed spectators, having a camera has transformed one person into something active, a voyeur: only he has mastered the situation. What do these people see? We don't know. And it doesn't matter. It is an Event: something worth seeing—and therefore worth photographing. The ad copy, white letters across the dark lower third of the photograph like news coming over a teletype machine, consists of just six words: ". . . Prague . . . Woodstock . . . Vietnam . . . Sapporo . . . Londonderry . . . LEICA." Crushed hopes, youth antics, colonial wars, and winter sports are alike—are equalized by the camera. Taking photographs has set up a chronic voyeuristic relation to the world which levels the meaning of all events.

A photograph is not just the result of an encounter between an event and a photographer; picture-taking is an event in itself, and one with ever more peremptory rights—to interfere with, to invade, or to ignore whatever is going on. Our very sense of situation is now articulated by the camera's interventions. The omnipresence of cameras persuasively suggests that time consists of interesting events, events worth photographing. This, in turn, makes it easy to feel that any event, once underway, and whatever its moral character, should be allowed to complete itself—so that something else can be brought into the world, the photograph. After the event has ended, the picture will still exist, conferring on the event a kind of immortality (and importance) it would never otherwise have enjoyed. While real people are out there killing themselves or other real people, the photographer stays behind his or her camera, creating a tiny element of another world: the image-world that bids to outlast us all.

Photographing is essentially an act of non-intervention. Part of the horror of such memorable coups of contemporary photojournalism as the pictures of a Vietnamese bonze[2] reaching for the gasoline can, of a Bengali guerrilla in the act of bayoneting a trussed-up collaborator, comes from the awareness of how plausible it has become, in situations where the photographer has the choice between a photograph and a life, to choose the photograph. The person who intervenes cannot record; the person who is recording cannot intervene. Dziga Vertov's great film, *Man with a Movie Camera* (1929), gives the ideal image of the photographer as someone in perpetual movement, someone moving through a panorama of disparate events with such agility and speed that any intervention is out of the question. Hitchcock's *Rear Window* (1954) gives the complementary image: the photographer played by James Stewart has an intensified relation to one event, through his camera, precisely because he has a broken leg and is confined to a wheelchair; being temporarily immobilized prevents him from acting on what he sees, and makes it even more important to take pictures. Even if incompatible with intervention in a physical sense, using a camera is still a form of participation. Although the camera is an observation station, the act of photographing is more than passive observing. Like sexual voyeurism, it is a way of at least tacitly, often explicitly, encouraging whatever is going on to keep on happening. To take a picture is to have an interest in things as they are, in the status quo remaining unchanged (at least for as long as it takes to get a "good" picture), to be in complicity with whatever makes a subject interesting, worth photographing—including, when that is the interest, another person's pain or misfortune. ○

---

1. *Babbittry* is a term, based on Sinclair Lewis's novel *Babbit* (1925), for Americans who define themselves by ready-made products and opinions.

2. A *bonze* is a Buddhist monk.

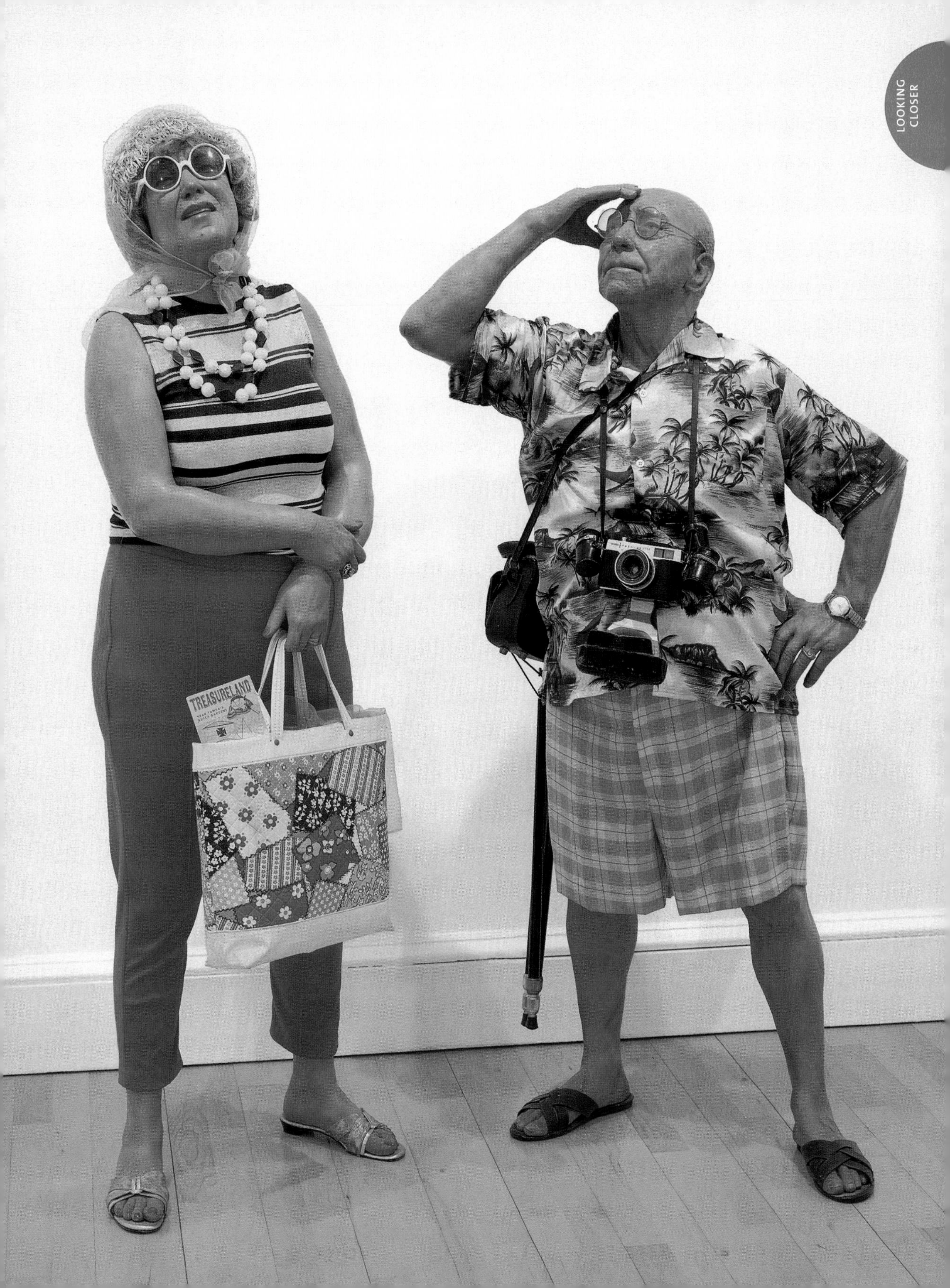
TREASURELAND

Viewfinder

Ethan Canin

I TELL MY WIFE, I'LL ALWAYS REMEMBER THIS photograph of my mother. She's out in back, hanging the blankets to dry on our backyard lines after one of our picnics, and she looks so young, the way I remember her before we moved to California. I was ten, I think. We used to have picnics out there under the water tower when my father got home from work, out in back on the grass on a set of big gray movers' blankets. My father and the man next door had built a pool from a truck tire set in concrete, and they filled it with water for my brother and me to splash in. I remember the day this picture was taken, because my mother had to hang the blankets to dry after we'd soaked them from the pool. My father was mad but she wasn't. She was never mad at us. I haven't seen that picture in years, I tell my wife. But I remember it.

And then one day, for no reason I can fathom, my wife is looking through the old cardboard-sided valise where my mother had kept her pictures, and she says, Here? Is this the one you're always talking about? And I say, Yes, I can't believe you found it. And she says, Those aren't movers' blankets, those are some kind of leaves up in the foreground. They look like something tropical, maybe rubber leaves. She's not hanging laundry at all. I say, Wait a minute—let me see. And I laugh and say, You're right. How can that be? My whole life I've remembered that picture of her hanging those blankets after we'd soaked them. I can even remember the picnic. She says, That's funny, isn't it? I say, My mother was so beautiful.

Our own children are out back in our own yard. It's too cool here for a pool, but I've built them a swingset from redwood, and I take a look out the window at them climbing it the way I've told them not to.

And then a few minutes later my wife says, Look at this, and she hands me the picture again, turned over. On the back it says, Vivian, Fort Barnwell, 1931. That's not your mother at all, she says. That's your grandmother. I say, Let me see that. I say, My God, you're right. How could that have happened? ○

Keep the story with a KODAK

Today it's a picture of Grandmother reading to the children. Tomorrow it may be Bobbie playing traffic policeman or Aunt Edna at the wheel of her new car or Brother Bill back from college for the week-end or— There's always another story waiting for your Kodak.

Free at your dealer's or from us—"At Home with the Kodak," a well illustrated little book that will help in picture-making at your house.

Autographic Kodaks *$6.50 up*

Eastman Kodak Company, Rochester, N. Y., *The Kodak City*

☑ Minutes to enlarge

☑ Minutes to enhance

☑ A moment shared forever

Use the **KODAK Picture Maker** to enlarge, restore or enhance your pictures. Make gifts without negatives all by yourself from a photo or digital camera in just 5 minutes. Call 1-800-939-1302 or visit kodak.com/go/picturemaker for a location near you.

 Share Moments. Share Life.™

SUSAN SONTAG

From the 1960s through the 1980s, Susan Sontag was one of America's foremost intellectuals, cultural commentators, and provocateurs. Her essays brilliantly explained the country and its culture, especially the avant garde. In *Notes on Camp* (1964) she accurately described the absurdity of attributes of taste; in *Against Interpretation* (1966) she limned Anglo-American fiction; in *Illness as Metaphor* (1978), which grew out of her own battle with breast cancer, she cast a fresh eye on disease, a subject that she revisited in *AIDS and Its Metaphors* (1988). Her novel *The Volcano Lover* (1992) was a bestseller: "No book I ever wrote came near to selling as many copies or reaching as many readers," she has said.

Sontag was born in New York City in 1933 but was raised in Tucson, Arizona, and Los Angeles.

On Photography
Susan Sontag

DUANE HANSON

Sculptor Duane Hanson (1926–1996) made his mark on the art world in the 1970s with true-to-life, cast fiberglass people. The unattractive, the elderly, the ordinary people whom we overlook every day are transformed by Hanson's sculpture into art objects worthy of our close inspection. Dressed in real clothing and equipped with accessories, Hanson's models are shocking in their "aliveness."

Born in Minnesota, Hanson spent much of his life in Miami. The Whitney Museum of American Art, in New York, held a retrospective of his work in 1999.

ETHAN CANIN

Ethan Canin was born in 1960 in Ann Arbor, Michigan, and grew up in California. He studied engineering at Stanford University and then earned a Master of Fine Arts degree from the University of Iowa in 1984. Never expecting that he could earn a living from writing, he attended medical school at Harvard University and earned his M.D. in 1991. Canin's career plans were changed permanently when his first collection of short stories, *Emperor of the Air* (1989), became a critically acclaimed bestseller. Since then he has published a second collection of short stories, *The Palace Thief* (1994), and three novels, *Blue River* (1991), *For Kings and Planets* (1998), and *Carry Me Across the Water* (2001).

SHIZUKA YOKOMIZO

In her series *Strangers,* photographer Shizuka Yokomizo sent letters to people she'd never met asking to photograph them anonymously. The strangers were invited to stand looking out of a window in their home at a particular time in the evening. Yokomizo captured the expressions of these individuals and their homes, illuminated only by house lights. Yokomizo was born in 1966 in Tokyo and currently lives and works in London.

MARTIN PARR

"The best way to describe my work," says Martin Parr, "is subjective documentary." Over the past twenty-five years the British-born photographer has established an international reputation for making photographs that document the social foibles, stereotypes, and iconography of various places and people. A member of the prestigious photographers' collective Magnum Photos since 1992, he is the recipient of numerous awards and has published numerous books and catalogues. In *A Small World* (1995), Parr captures with wit and irony the discovery made by many tourists—seeking unique experiences in unison, they invariably find each other.

KODAK

George Eastman's first "photographic outfit," which he purchased in 1875, weighed about 100 pounds and required the use of wet glass plates and a crate of chemicals. In 1878 Eastman founded the Kodak Company with the intention of "making photography as convenient as a pencil." The invention of roll film in 1889, portable hand-held cameras, home movie cameras, sound-sensitive movie film, color-slide film, automated film development, photo billboards, and digital cameras are just a few of Kodak's developments. One of the twenty-five largest companies in the United States, Kodak continues to pioneer new "image technologies" that affect the visual content of our daily lives.

N. SCOTT MOMADAY

N. Scott Momaday was born on a Kiowa reservation in Oklahoma in 1934. His father was Kiowa; his mother was Cherokee, French, and English. He has spent his life and his career reconstructing the story of the Kiowa tribe—its myths, its history, and, most important, its oral tradition. His first novel, *House Made of Dawn* (1968), focuses on the clash between the Native American world and the white world; it won a Pulitzer Prize. Momaday has since written essays, poetry, autobiography, and fiction, almost all of which draws on and explores the story of his people and their land.

SEEING

1. Susan Sontag observes that "photography is not practiced by most people as an art. It is mainly a social rite, a defense against anxiety, and a tool of power" (para. 1). Given your own experience taking pictures, would you agree or disagree with her assertion? Now examine each of the visual images and prose selections included in this section. To what extent do you think each writer and photographer represented here would agree or disagree with Sontag? Are photos like the ones shown by Shizuka Yokomizo or Martin Parr merely a "defense against anxiety"? If so, anxiety about what? Does Ethan Canin's short story treat the photograph as a "tool of power"? If so, what kind of power?

2. Sontag declares that "a photograph is not just the result of an encounter between an event and a photographer; picture-taking is an event in itself, and one with ever more peremptory rights— to interfere with, to invade, or to ignore whatever is going on. Our very sense of situation is now articulated by the camera's interventions" (para. 8). Sontag seems to be saying that the camera or act of taking pictures is more important than either the photographer or the event. Use any of the selections in this section as support for explaining why you do or do not agree with her.

WRITING

1. Sontag writes: "For at least a century, the wedding photograph has been as much a part of the ceremony as the prescribed verbal formulas" (para. 2). Write a comparative essay in which you compare the differences between (1) the function—and the visibility—of photography in your parents' wedding and (2) its presence and role in a wedding you attended in the past year or two. Draw inferences about the extent to which the role of photography in the more recent wedding has become analogous to what Sontag calls "prescribed verbal formulas."

2. Sontag observes that "A family's photograph album is generally about the extended family—and, often, is all that remains of it" (para. 3). How important are photographs to your sense of family? Write a descriptive essay in which you describe your extended family—grandparents, aunts, uncles, cousins—using the role of family photographs as a way to frame your argument.

Embodying Identity

Chapter 4
Embodying Identity

Images of the relationship between the body and self-identity are everywhere to be seen in American popular culture: on billboards along the side of the road, on computer and TV screens, on the pages of magazines and newspapers, in museums, galleries, and libraries. It's difficult to believe that a hundred years ago the American public was shocked by a glimpse of a woman's naked ankle. Today we're all accustomed to advertisers using bulging biceps and bare necks to sell everything from cigarettes and cars to cereal and cell phones.

Magazine headlines entice readers with the keys to achieving "The Perfect Body" and to fashioning an identity for ourselves through purchasing. The language surrounding the shaping of the body and the fashioning of an identity is common-place; *toning, nipping, tucking, shaping,* and *figuring* are all terms in everyday public discourse.

An entire industry of products promoting beauty and well-being reveals a health-obsessed culture, one that privileges images of the body in establishing self-identity. Gyms and fitness clubs are ubiquitous in cities and small towns across America. Infomercials, self-help manuals, talk shows, and dieting centers all cater to—and perpetuate—Americans' obsession with the role of weight and fat in determining self-definition and self-worth. Food packaging appeals to health-conscious consumers by highlighting such terms as *natural, low-fat, low-cholesterol,* and *healthy.* The athletic look has become such an important measure of self-definition that even if you've never shot a basket or lifted a dumbbell, you can look like you've just stepped out of the gym.

To judge from consumer culture, the body is the celebrated center of self-identity and public life. However, the private body is also often a source of shame and fear, something to be controlled and yet beyond control. Whether it's "heroin chic" or the healthy athletic and "natural" look, few Americans actually reflect the latest trend in body type represented in fashion and advertising. Nevertheless more and more Americans—and young Americans in particular—see their self-identity through the lenses of popular images of the body. It is no surprise that the incidence of anorexia and bulimia among teenage girls is on the rise.

Artists and writers are reimagining the body, and scientists and engineers are redesigning and rebuilding it. Body parts are now transferable, the genetic code alterable. Childbirth can be contracted to surrogate mothers, and life prolonged far beyond the brain's ceasing to function. The body can be transformed even after death; an endless supply of digital cadavers are now available "on line" and in "living color." By the end of the twentieth century, the historian Joan Jacobs Brumberg could note in her study *The Body Project* (1997) that "the body is regarded as something to be managed and maintained, usually through expenditures on clothes and personal grooming items, with special attention to exterior surfaces—skin, hair, and contours. In adolescent girls' private diaries and journals, the body is a consistent preoccupation, second only to peer relationships. 'I'm so fat, [hence]

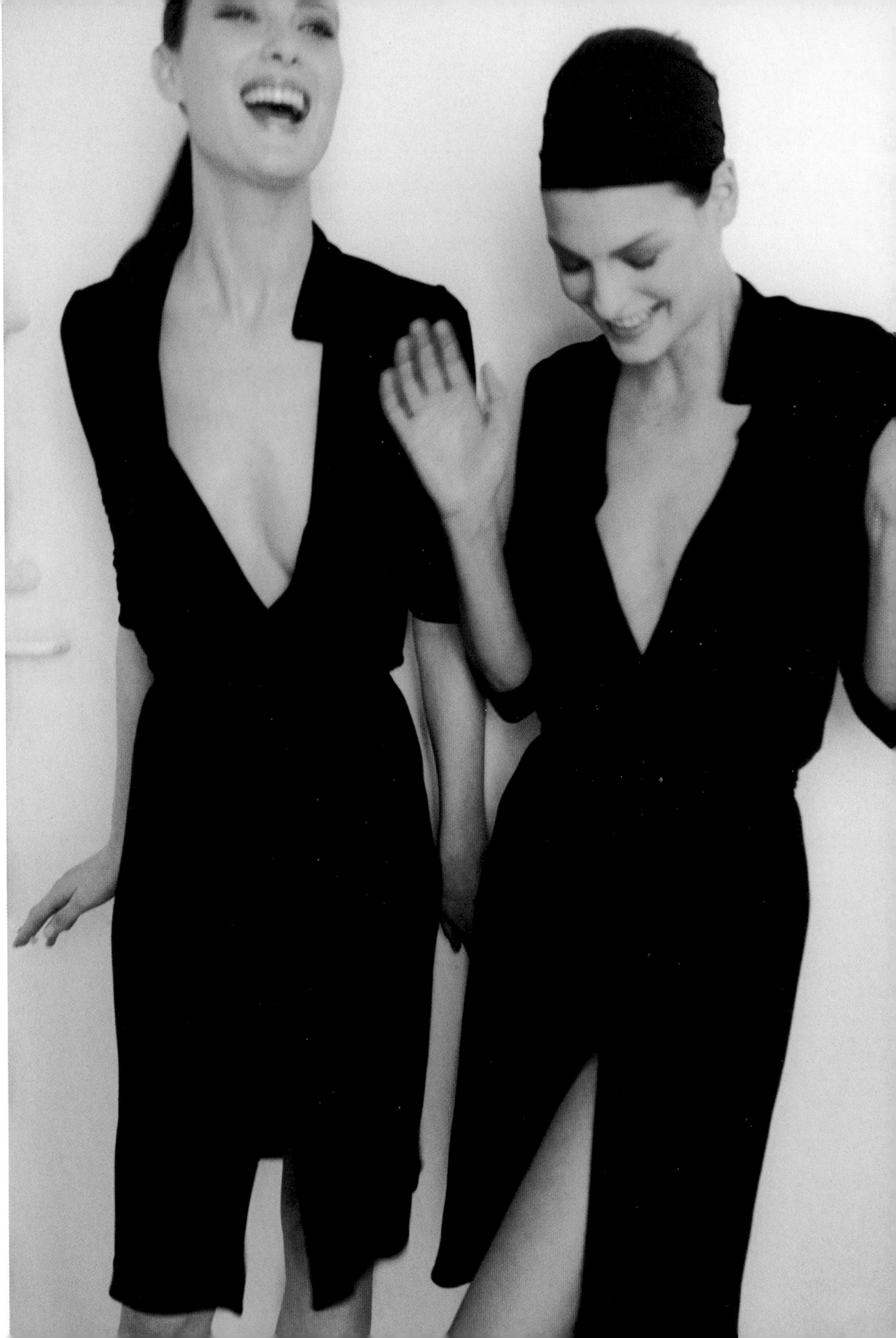

Mario Testino, **Shalom and Linda, Paris**

I'm so ugly,' is as common a comment today as are classic adolescent ruminations about whether Jennifer is a true friend or if Scott likes Amy."

Even as Americans regard the body as something to be mastered and shaped, it is also a site of identity—our bodies shape who we are, how we see ourselves, and how we are perceived. We inherit our mother's hands or our grandfather's eyes. We communicate through body language: posture, facial expression, gesture, speech, accent, height, skin color. If the body can be the site of torment and pain, it can also be the vehicle for achieving artistic and athletic excellence as well as personal identity. We stand in awe of the mastery of great athletes and the graceful power of skilled dancers. Indeed, dancers and athletes focus countless hours on making their bodies the sites of perfect motion, while politicians and actors study how to communicate compassion, strength, or determination through simple gesture and facial expression.

> The body says what words cannot.
> – Martha Graham, 1991

Although the terms and the images have changed over the decades, Americans continue to be obsessed with the body and its relationship to self-identity. A recent study revealed that by age 13, "53 percent of American girls are unhappy with their bodies; by age 17, 78 percent are dissatisfied." This sense of unease is long-standing in American culture. From turn-of-the-century hygiene manuals that proclaimed physical fitness as a "sign" of moral purity, to the latest trends in cosmetic surgery, piercing, and tattooing, the body continues to serve as a display board for what is *en vogue* and as a locus for expressing ourselves and fashioning an identity.

> Fashion is not something that exists in dresses only ... fashion has to do with ideas, the way we live, what is happening.
> –Gabrielle "Coco" Chanel, 1990

Now equally the province of anthropologists, historians, writers, psychologists, philosophers, sociologists, physicians, and artists, the body has been so analyzed and scrutinized that it is at once an anatomical object and a social construction. In the public eye, the body has been reconceived as both a playground and a battleground, a site for what the sociologist Carol Gilligan calls "a repository of experience and desire." The selections that follow illustrate the role it plays in embodying identity.

MARIO TESTINO

Born in Peru in 1954, Mario Testino is one of the world's premier fashion photographers and an integral part of the fashionable world he photographs. His dressing-room photos of "supermodels" reveal the private emotions behind the scenes of the fashion industry.

Testino's photographs of the late Princess Diana in the July 1997 Issue of *Vanity Fair* are among his most famous, exemplifying his glamorous vision of richly saturated colors and dramatic settings. In 1998 Testino published a book of photographs entitled *Any Objections,* from which these two images are drawn. In this compilation, writes Patrick Kinmouth, "he did not choose to assemble the kind of pictures that have made him famous.... Instead he has selected largely unseen pictures ... and made them into a documentary.... This process he describes as distinct from the business of taking fashion pictures. There his role is carefully to construct the image; here, his role is immediately to trap it as it flashes by."

Testino has also published *Front Row Back Stage* (1999), an on-the-runway and behind-the-scenes look at the world of haute couture, and most recently *Mario Testino: Portraits* (2002), a collection of his celebrity and fashion photography.

SEEING

1. What do you notice first about the photograph of the two men? of the two women? How would you characterize the depiction of their bodies in each photograph (the way the photos are cropped, the amount of body exposed, etc.)? In what ways do the people in each photograph acknowledge the presence of the photographer? What additional points of comparison and contrast do you notice in the two photographs?

2. Testino's photograph of the two women could easily be placed in any fashion magazine. Would you be surprised to find the photo of the two men in *Allure* or *Elle?* Why or why not? What would be the effect of reversing the order of these images? What is the overall effect of juxtaposing the two very different images? (Does it change the way you perceive one or the other?)

WRITING

1. Which of Testino's photographs do you like better? Write an informal essay in two parts: In the first part, carefully describe the figures in each photograph, what's in the background, and the mood evoked by each; in the second part, try to articulate why you respond more positively to one than the other.

2. In the Preface to his beautifully illustrated and insightful study *The Body,* author and photo curator William Ewing asks: "Why is it today that the human body is at the centre of so much attention? Why are magazines, newspapers, television, and advertisements saturated with images of naked, or virtually naked, bodies? Why are so many writers, artists and photographers so profoundly concerned with the subject?" Write the first draft of a cause-and-effect essay in which you answer Ewing's question and try to account for the preoccupation with the body in contemporary American culture.

BATO CON KHAKIS

Jacinto Jesús Cardona

Too bold for my mother's blood,
bato was not a household word.
Oh, but to be a bato con khakis
waiting to catch the city bus,

my thin belt exuding attitude,   5
looking limber in a blue vest,
laid-back in my dark shades.

Alas! I'm the bifocals kid;
cool bato I am not,
but I could spell gelato.   10
Could I be the bookish bato?

Oh, but to be a bato con khakis
deep in the Hub of South Texas,
blooming among bluebonnets.

César A. Martínez, **Bato Con Khakis, 1982**

JACINTO JESÚS CARDONA

Jacinto Jesús (Jesse) Cardona was born in the town of Palacios along the coast of Texas but grew up in Alice, a small town in the heartland of South Texas. His poetry reflects this upbringing, and the images in poems such as "Bato Con Khakis" are strongly reminiscent of life in a small South Texas town. He has taught English at John F. Kennedy High School and at Incarnate Word High School, both in San Antonio. He received his B.S. degree in English at Texas A & I College in Kingsville, and he often returns to college and high school campuses to read his poetry. Cardona received the Imagineer Award for teaching creative writing and has published his poetry in various literary journals. He is the author of a chapbook, "At the Wheel of a Blue Chevrolet," and *Pan Dulce*, a book of poems. He has read from this collection on National Public Radio and PBS stations in San Antonio and Austin. Cardona is also a faculty member of the Upward Bound Program, which is designed to assist low-income and "first-generation" college students in pursuing post-secondary education through enhancement of academic, cultural, interpersonal, and personal development. "Bato Con Khakis" was first published in *Heart to Heart, New Poems Inspired by Twentieth Century American Art* (2001).

CÉSAR A. MARTÍNEZ

César A. Martínez was born in Laredo, Texas, in 1944 and has become well known for his depictions of South Texans. His Mexican-influenced portraiture, which has spanned over a quarter of a century, presents images of Latinos that go a long way in defining Latin American culture. In 1999, Martínez was named the San Antonio Art League's Artist of the Year for "his significant contribution to the arts in South Texas as well as to the history of Chicano Art." Thirty-one pieces of his art were on exhibition following this honor. Martínez has also participated in the creation of many short films and books on Latin American art and has become a strong voice for Chicano art in San Antonio. He has participated in programs such as the Visual Arts Visiting Artist Program at the University of Texas, San Antonio, and a residency at ArtPace International.

BATO CON KHAKIS
Jacinto Jesús Cardona

Too bold for my mother's blood,
bato was not a household word.
Oh, but to be a bato con khakis
waiting to catch the city bus,

my thin belt exuding attitude,
looking limber in a blue seat,
laid-back in my dark shades.

Alas! I'm the bifocals kid,
cool bato I am not,
but I could spell *gelato*.
Could I be the bookish bato?

Oh, but to be a bato con khakis
deep in the Hub of South Texas,
blooming among bluebonnets.

SEEING

1. After first reading this poem, what did you think the word *bato* meant? What associations did the word summon? "Bato," reports the poet Jacinto Jesús Cardona, is "a Spanglish greeting equivalent to 'Hey, man!' but it's also associated with pachucos, the alienated youth associated with the zoot suiters." What does the term *Spanglish* mean? What other words can you identify as examples of Spanglish? To what extent does the term *bato* work effectively in this poem? Why? How successfully does César Martínez's painting represent your image of a zoot suiter? Point to specific features of the image to verify your response. How do these details embody the character's identity?

2. Why is *bato* "too bold" a word for the speaker's "mother's blood" (line 1)? How does the "thin belt" exude "attitude" in this piece of mixed media art? What other details in the painting can you identify that reinforce this image? What do you make of the third stanza of the poem (lines 8–11)? What does it add to the meaning and success of the poem? What do the lines "deep in the Hub of South Texas, / blooming among bluebonnets" contribute to the poem?

WRITING

1. Imagine that César Martínez is a friend who approaches you with the original of the mixed media work of art reproduced here, and that he invites you to write a poem or prose piece based on this illustration. Which would you prefer to write—a poem, a piece of fiction, or an autobiographical or expository essay? Why? Write the first draft of your own poem or prose work that is inspired by carefully observing this mixed media work. Which elements in the image would you emphasize? Why? What criteria ought to be applied to measuring your success in establishing connections between the mixed media work of art and your own writing?

2. Now that you have had the opportunity to examine both the visual work and the poem about "Bato Con Khakis," consider whether the effectiveness of the poem depends on César Martínez's mixed media rendition of it on paper. Write an argumentative essay in which you defend—or challenge—the claim that this poem would be ineffective were it not accompanied by Martínez's work.

A Southwestern Chicano subculture prevalent in the 1940s distinguished by clothing—oversized zoot suits—and versions of Spanish dialect. Because of their distrust of mainstream assimilation, *pachucos* were sometimes seen as gangsters.

JUDITH ORTIZ COFER

In an essay entitled "The Myth of the Latin Woman: I Just Met a Girl Named Maria," Judith Ortiz Cofer (b. 1952) talks of the prejudice she encountered as a youth: "As a Puerto Rican girl growing up in the United States and wanting like most children to 'belong,' I resented the stereotype that my Hispanic appearance called forth from many people I met."

Ortiz Cofer speaks with insight and eloquence about the costs of cultural transplantation and has established a reputation for writing finely crafted and deeply moving expressions of contemporary Puerto Rican experience. She first earned recognition for her literary talents through several collections of poetry. Her first novel, *The Line of the Sun* (1989), was nominated for a Pulitzer Prize and was followed by a compilation of poems and essays. More recently she has published prose and poetry in *The Latin Deli* (1993), *An Island Like You* (1995), and *The Year of Our Revolution* (1998).

Ortiz Cofer explains that "my personal goal in my public life is to replace the old pervasive stereotypes and myths about Latinas with a much more interesting set of realities.... I hope the stories I tell, the dreams and fears I examine in my work, can achieve some universal truth which will get my audience past the particulars of my skin color, my accent, or my clothes."

The Story of My Body

Judith Ortiz Cofer

Migration is the story of my body.
— Victor Hernández Cruz

SKIN

I WAS BORN A WHITE GIRL IN PUERTO RICO BUT became a brown girl when I came to live in the United States. My Puerto Rican relatives called me tall; at the American school, some of my rougher classmates called me Skinny Bones, and the Shrimp because I was the smallest member of my classes all through grammar school until high school, when the midget Gladys was given the honorary post of front row center for class pictures and scorekeeper, bench warmer, in P.E. I reached my full stature of five feet in sixth grade.

I started out life as a pretty baby and learned to be a pretty girl from a pretty mother. Then at ten years of age I suffered one of the worst cases of chicken pox I have ever heard of. My entire body, including the inside of my ears and in between my toes, was covered with pustules which in a fit of panic at my appearance I scratched off my face, leaving permanent scars. A cruel school nurse told me I would always have them—tiny cuts that looked as if a mad cat had plunged its claws deep into my skin. I grew my hair long and hid behind it for the first years of my adolescence. This was when I learned to be invisible.

COLOR

In the animal world it indicates danger: the most colorful creatures are often the most poisonous. Color is also a way to attract and seduce a mate. In the human world color triggers many more complex and often deadly reactions. As a Puerto Rican girl born of "white" parents, I spent the first years of my life hearing people refer to me as *blanca,* white. My mother insisted that I protect myself from the intense island sun because I was more prone to sunburn than some of my darker, *trigueño* playmates. People were always commenting within my hearing about how my black hair contrasted so nicely with my "pale" skin. I did not think of the color of my skin consciously except when I heard the adults talking about complexion. It seems to me that the subject is much more common in the conversation of mixed-race peoples than in mainstream United States society, where it is a touchy and sometimes even embarrassing topic to discuss, except in a political context. In Puerto Rico I heard many conversations about skin color. A pregnant woman could say, "I hope my baby doesn't turn out *prieto*" (slang for "dark" or "black") "like my husband's grandmother, although she was a good-looking *negra* in her time." I am a combination of both, being olive-skinned—lighter than my mother yet darker than my fair-skinned father. In America, I am a person of color, obviously a Latina. On the Island I have been called everything from a *paloma blanca,* after the song (by a black suitor), to *la gringa.*

My first experience of color prejudice occurred in a supermarket in Paterson, New Jersey. It was Christmastime, and I was eight or nine years old. There was a display of toys in the store where I went two or three times a day to buy things for my mother, who never made lists but sent for milk, cigarettes, a can of this or that, as she remembered from hour to hour. I enjoyed being trusted with money and walking half a city block to the new, modern grocery store. It was owned by three good-looking Italian brothers. I liked the younger one with the crew-cut blond hair. The two older ones watched me and the other Puerto Rican kids as if they thought we were going to steal something. The oldest one would sometimes even try to hurry me with my purchases, although part of my pleasure in these expeditions came from looking at everything in the well-stocked aisles. I was also teaching myself to read English by sounding out the labels on packages: L&M cigarettes, Borden's homogenized milk, Red Devil potted ham, Nestle's chocolate mix, Quaker oats, Bustelo coffee, Wonder bread, Colgate toothpaste, Ivory soap, and Goya (makers of products used in Puerto Rican dishes) everything—these are some of the brand names that taught me nouns. Several times this man had come up to me, wearing his blood-stained butcher's apron, and towering over me had asked in a harsh voice whether there was something he could help me find. On the way out I would glance at the younger brother who ran one of the registers and he would often smile and wink at me.

It was the mean brother who first referred to me as "colored." It was a few days before Christmas, and my parents had already told my brother and me that since we were in Los Estados now, we would get our presents on December 25 instead of Los Reyes, Three Kings Day, when gifts are exchanged in Puerto Rico. We were to give them a wish list that they would take to Santa Claus, who apparently lived in the Macy's store downtown—at least that's where we had caught a glimpse of him when we went shopping. Since my parents were timid about entering the fancy store, we did not approach the huge man in the red suit. I was not interested in sitting on a stranger's lap anyway. But I did covet Susie, the talking schoolteacher doll that was displayed in the center aisle of the Italian brothers' supermarket. She talked when you pulled a string on her back. Susie had a limited repertoire of three sentences: I think she could say: "Hello, I'm Susie Schoolteacher," "Two plus two is four," and one other thing I cannot remember. The day the older brother chased me away, I was reaching to touch Susie's blonde curls. I had been told many times, as most children have, not to touch anything in a store that I was not buying. But I had been looking at Susie for weeks. In my mind, she was my doll. After all, I had put her on my Christmas wish list. The moment is frozen in my mind as if there were a photograph of it on file. It was not a turning point, a disaster, or an earth-shaking revelation. It was simply the first time I considered—if naively—the meaning of skin color in human relations.

I reached to touch Susie's hair. It seems to me that I had to get on tiptoe, since the toys were stacked on a table and she sat like a princess on top of the fancy box she came in. Then I heard the booming "Hey, kid, what do you think you're doing!" spoken very loudly from the meat counter. I felt caught, although I knew I was not doing anything criminal. I remember not looking at the man, but standing there, feeling humiliated because I knew everyone in the store must have heard him yell at me. I felt him approach, and when I knew he was behind me, I turned around to face the bloody butcher's apron. His large chest was at my eye level. He blocked my way. I started to run out of the place, but even as I reached the door I heard him shout after me: "Don't come in here unless you gonna buy something. You PR kids put your dirty hands on stuff. You always look dirty. But maybe dirty brown is your natural color." I heard him laugh and someone else too in the back. Outside in the sunlight I looked at my hands. My nails needed a little cleaning as they always did, since I liked to paint with watercolors, but I took a bath every night. I thought the man was dirtier than I was in his stained apron. He was also always sweaty—it showed in big yellow circles under his shirt-sleeves. I sat on the front steps of the apartment building where we lived and looked closely at my hands, which showed the only skin I could see, since it was bitter cold and I was wearing my quilted play coat, dungarees, and a knitted navy cap of my father's. I was not pink like my friend Charlene and her sister Kathy, who had blue eyes and light brown hair. My skin is the color of the coffee my grandmother made, which was half milk, *leche con café* rather than *café con leche.* My mother is the opposite mix. She has a lot of *café* in her color. I could not understand how my skin looked like dirt to the supermarket man.

I went in and washed my hands thoroughly with soap and hot water, and borrowing my mother's nail file, I cleaned the crusted watercolors from underneath my nails. I was pleased with the results. My skin was the same color as before, but I knew I was clean. Clean enough to run my fingers through Susie's fine gold hair when she came home to me.

SIZE

My mother is barely four feet eleven inches in height, which is average for women in her family. When I grew to five feet by age twelve, she was amazed and began to use the word tall to describe me, as in "Since you are tall, this dress will look good on you." As with the color of my skin, I didn't consciously think about my height or size until other people made an issue of it. It is around the preadolescent years that in America the games children play for fun become fierce competitions where everyone is out to "prove" they are better than others. It was in the playground and sports fields that my size-related problems began. No matter how familiar the story is, every child who is the last chosen for a team knows the torment of waiting to be called up. At the Paterson, New Jersey, public schools that I attended, the volleyball or softball game was the metaphor for the battlefield of life to the inner city kids—the black kids versus the Puerto Rican kids, the whites versus the blacks versus the Puerto Rican kids; and I was 4F, skinny, short, bespectacled, and apparently impervious to the blood thirst that drove many of my classmates to play ball as if their lives depended on it. Perhaps they did. I would rather be reading a book than sweating, grunting, and running the risk of pain and injury. I simply did not see the point in competitive sports. My main form of exercise then was walking to the library, many city blocks away from my barrio.

Still, I wanted to be wanted. I wanted to be chosen for the teams. Physical education was compulsory, a class where you were actually given a grade. On my mainly all A report card, the C for compassion I always received from the P.E. teachers shamed me the same as a bad grade in a real class. Invariably, my father would say: "How can you make a low grade for *playing games?*" He did not understand. Even if I had managed to make a hit (it never happened) or get the ball over that ridiculously high net, I already had a reputation as a "shrimp," a hopeless nonathlete. It was an area where the girls who didn't like me for one reason or another—mainly because I did better than they in academic subjects—could lord it over me; the playing field was the place where even the smallest girl could make me feel powerless and inferior. I instinctively understood the politics even then; how the *not* choosing me until the teacher forced one of the team captains to call my name was a coup of sorts—there, you little show-off, tomorrow you can beat us in spelling and geography, but this afternoon you are the loser. Or perhaps those were only my own bitter thoughts as I sat or stood in the sidelines while the big girls were grabbed like fish and I, the little brown tadpole, was ignored until Teacher looked over in my general direction and shouted, "Call Ortiz," or, worse, "Somebody's *got* to take her."

No wonder I read Wonder Woman comics and 10 had Legion of Super Heroes daydreams. Although I wanted to think of myself as "intellectual," my body was demanding that I notice it. I saw the little swelling around my once-flat nipples, the fine hairs growing in secret places; but my knees were still bigger than my thighs, and I always wore long- or half-sleeve blouses to hide my bony upper arms. I wanted flesh on my bones—a thick layer of it. I saw a new product advertised on TV. Wate-On. They showed skinny men and women before and after taking the stuff, and it was a transformation like the ninety-seven-pound-weakling-turned-into-Charles-Atlas ads that I saw on the back covers of my comic books. The Wate-On was very expensive. I tried to explain my need for it in Spanish to my mother, but it didn't translate very well, even to my ears—and she said with a tone of finality, eat more of my good food and you'll get fat—anybody can get fat. Right. Except me. I was going to have to join a circus someday as Skinny Bones, the woman without flesh.

Wonder Woman was stacked. She had a cleavage framed by the spread wings of a golden eagle and a muscular body that has become fashionable with women only recently. But since I wanted a body that would serve me in P.E., hers was my ideal. The breasts were an indulgence I allowed myself. Perhaps the daydreams of bigger girls were more glamorous, since our ambitions are filtered through our needs, but I wanted first a powerful body. I daydreamed of leaping up above the gray landscape of the city to where the sky was clear and blue, and in anger and self-pity, I fantasized about scooping my enemies up by their hair from the playing fields and dumping them on a barren asteroid. I would put the P.E. teachers each on their own rock in space too, where they would be the loneliest people in the universe, since I knew they had no "inner resources," no imagination, and in outer space, there would be no air for them to fill their deflated volleyballs with. In my mind all P.E. teachers have blended into one large spiky-haired woman with a whistle on a string around her neck and a volleyball under one arm. My Wonder Woman fantasies of revenge were a source of comfort to me in my early career as a shrimp.

I was saved from more years of P.E. torment by the fact that in my sophomore year of high school I transferred to a school where the midget, Gladys, was the focal point of interest for the people who must rank according to size. Because her height was considered a handicap, there was an unspoken rule about mentioning size around Gladys, but of course, there was no need to say anything. Gladys knew her place: front row center in class photographs. I gladly moved to the left or to the right of her, as far as I could without leaving the picture completely.

LOOKS

Many photographs were taken of me as a baby by my mother to send to my father, who was stationed overseas during the first two years of my life. With the army in Panama when I was born, he later traveled often on tours of duty with the navy. I was a healthy, pretty baby. Recently, I read that people are drawn to big-eyed round-faced creatures, like puppies, kittens, and certain other mammals and marsupials, koalas, for example, and, of course, infants. I was all eyes, since my head and body, even as I grew older, remained thin and small-boned. As a young child I got a lot of attention from my relatives and many other people we met in our barrio. My mother's beauty may have had something to do with how much attention we got from strangers in stores and on the street. I can imagine it. In the pictures I have seen of us together, she is a stunning young woman by Latino standards: long, curly black hair, and round curves in a compact frame. From her I learned how to move, smile, and talk like an attractive woman. I remember going into a bodega for our groceries and being given candy by the proprietor as a reward for being *bonita*, pretty.

I can see in the photographs, and I also remember, that I was dressed in the pretty clothes, the stiff, frilly dresses, with layers of crinolines underneath, the glossy patent leather shoes, and, on special occasions, the skull-hugging little hats and the white gloves that were popular in the late fifties and early sixties. My mother was proud of my looks, although I was a bit too thin. She could dress me up like a doll and take me by the hand to visit relatives, or go to the Spanish mass at the Catholic church, and show me off. How was I to know that she and the others who called me "pretty" were representatives of an aesthetic that would not apply when I went out into the mainstream world of school?

In my Paterson, New Jersey, public schools there were still quite a few white children, although the demographics of the city were changing rapidly. The original waves of Italian and Irish immigrants, silk-mill workers, and laborers in the cloth industries had been "assimilated." Their children were now the middle-class parents of my peers. Many of them moved their children to the Catholic schools that proliferated enough to have leagues of basketball teams. The names I recall hearing still ring in my ears: Don Bosco High versus St. Mary's High, St. Joseph's versus St. John's. Later I too would be transferred to the safer environment of a Catholic school. But I started school at Public School Number 11. I came there from Puerto Rico, thinking myself a pretty girl, and found that the hierarchy for popularity was as follows: pretty white girl, pretty Jewish girl, pretty Puerto Rican girl, pretty black girl. Drop the last two categories; teachers were too busy to have more than one favorite per class, and it was simply understood that if there was a big part in the school play, or any competition where the main qualification was "presentability" (such as escorting a school visitor to or from the principal's office), the classroom's public address speaker would be requesting the pretty and/or nice-looking white boy or girl. By the time I was in the sixth grade, I was sometimes called by the principal to represent my class because I dressed neatly (I knew this from a progress report sent to my mother, which I translated for her) and because all the "presentable" white girls had moved

15

to the Catholic schools (I later surmised this part). But I was still not one of the popular girls with the boys. I remember one incident where I stepped out into the playground in my baggy gym shorts and one Puerto Rican boy said to the other: "What do you think?" The other one answered: "Her face is OK, but look at the toothpick legs." The next best thing to a compliment I got was when my favorite male teacher, while handing out the class pictures, commented that with my long neck and delicate features I resembled the movie star Audrey Hepburn. But the Puerto Rican boys had learned to respond to a fuller figure: long necks and a perfect little nose were not what they looked for in a girl. That is when I decided I was a "brain." I did not settle into the role easily. I was nearly devastated by what the chicken pox episode had done to my self-image. But I looked into the mirror less often after I was told that I would always have scars on my face, and I hid behind my long black hair and my books.

After the problems at the public school got to the point where even nonconfrontational little me got beaten up several times, my parents enrolled me at St. Joseph's High School. I was then a minority of one among the Italian and Irish kids. But I found several good friends there—other girls who took their studies seriously. We did our homework together and talked about the Jackies. The Jackies were two popular girls, one blonde and the other red-haired, who had women's bodies. Their curves showed even in the blue jumper uniforms with straps that we all wore. The blonde Jackie would often let one of the straps fall off her shoulder, and although she, like all of us, wore a white blouse underneath, all the boys stared at her arm. My friends and I talked about this and practiced letting our straps fall off our shoulders. But it wasn't the same without breasts or hips.

My final two and a half years of high school were spent in Augusta, Georgia, where my parents moved our family in search of a more peaceful environment. There we became part of a little community of our army-connected relatives and friends. School was yet another matter. I was enrolled in a huge school of nearly two thousand students that had just that year been forced to integrate. There were two black girls and there was me. I did extremely well academically. As to my social life, it was, for the most part, uneventful—yet it is in my memory blighted by one incident. In my junior year, I became wildly infatuated with a pretty white boy. I'll call him Ted. Oh, he was pretty: yellow hair that fell over his forehead, a smile to die for—and he was a great dancer. I watched him at Teen Town, the youth center at the base where all the military brats gathered on Saturday nights. My father had retired from the navy, and we had all our base privileges—one other reason we had moved to Augusta. Ted looked like an angel to me. I worked on him for a year before he asked me out. This meant maneuvering to be within the periphery of his vision at every possible occasion. I took the long way to my classes in school just to pass by his locker, I went to football games, which I detested, and I danced (I too was a good dancer) in front of him at Teen Town—this took some fancy footwork, since it involved subtly moving my partner toward the right spot on the dance floor. When Ted finally approached me, "A Million to One" was playing on the jukebox, and when he took me into his arms, the odds suddenly turned in my favor. He asked me to go to a school dance the following Saturday. I said yes, breathlessly. I said yes, but there were obstacles to surmount at home. My father did not allow me to date casually. I was allowed to go to major events like a prom or a concert with a boy who had been properly screened. There was such a boy in my life, a neighbor who wanted to be a Baptist missionary and was practicing his anthropological skills on my family. If I was desperate to go somewhere and needed a date, I'd resort to Gary. This is the type of religious nut that Gary was: when the school bus did not show up one day, he put his hands over his face and prayed to Christ to get us a way to get to school. Within ten minutes a mother in a station wagon, on her way to town, stopped to ask why we weren't in school. Gary informed her that the Lord had sent her just in time to find us a way to get there in time for roll call. He assumed that I was impressed. Gary was even good-looking in a bland sort of way, but he kissed me with his lips tightly pressed together. I think Gary probably ended up marrying a native woman from wherever he may have gone to preach the Gospel according to Paul. She probably believes that all white men pray to God for transportation and kiss with their mouths closed. But it was Ted's mouth, his whole beautiful self, that concerned me in those days. I knew my father would say no to our date, but I planned to run away from home if necessary. I told my mother how important this date was. I cajoled and pleaded with her from Sunday to Wednesday. She listened to my arguments and must have heard the note of desperation in my voice. She said very gently to me: "You better be ready for disappointment." I did not ask what she meant. I did not want her fears for me to taint my happiness. I asked her to tell my father about my date. Thursday at breakfast my father looked at me across the table with his eyebrows together. My mother looked at him with her mouth set in a straight line. I looked down at my bowl of cereal. Nobody said anything. Friday I tried on every dress in my closet. Ted would be picking me up at six on Saturday: dinner and then the sock hop at school. Friday night I was in my room doing my nails or something else in preparation for Saturday (I know I groomed myself nonstop all week) when the telephone rang. I ran to get it. It was Ted. His voice sounded funny when he said my name, so funny that I felt compelled to ask: "Is something wrong?" Ted blurted it all out without a preamble. His father had asked who he was going out with. Ted had told him my name. "Ortiz? That's

Spanish, isn't it?" the father had asked. Ted had told him yes, then shown him my picture in the yearbook. Ted's father had shaken his head. No. Ted would not be taking me out. Ted's father had known Puerto Ricans in the army. He had lived in New York City while studying architecture and had seen how the spics lived. Like rats. Ted repeated his father's words to me as if I should understand *his* predicament when I heard why he was breaking our date. I don't remember what I said before hanging up. I do recall the darkness of my room that sleepless night and the heaviness of my blanket in which I wrapped myself like a shroud. And I remember my parents' respect for my pain and their gentleness toward me that weekend. My mother did not say "I warned you," and I was grateful for her understanding silence.

In college, I suddenly became an "exotic" woman to the men who had survived the popularity wars in high school, who were now practicing to be worldly: they had to act liberal in their politics, in their lifestyles, and in the women they went out with. I dated heavily for a while, then married young. I had discovered that I needed stability more than social life. I had brains for sure and some talent in writing. These facts were a constant in my life. My skin color, my size, and my appearance were variables—things that were judged according to my current self-image, the aesthetic values of the times, the places I was in, and the people I met. My studies, later my writing, the respect of people who saw me as an individual person they cared about, these were the criteria for my sense of self-worth that I would concentrate on in my adult life. ○

1. What are the features of the ideal body that Judith Ortiz Cofer imagines for herself? What kind of language does she use to describe her own, real body? Who are the figures she looks up to during her childhood? Why? From what aspects of the culture were these figures drawn? In what specific ways does Ortiz Cofer's memory of going to the local grocery store remind you of Eudora Welty's account of a similar experience? (See "The Little Store," p. 134.) In what ways is Ortiz Cofer's "portrait" of her body similar to—and different from—the concept of "double consciousness" defined by W. E. B. DuBois (p. 563)?

2. What principle of organization governs Ortiz Cofer's essay? What logical thread links one paragraph to another? Comment on the effectiveness of her use of metaphor and irony, and please support your response with specific examples. What does Cofer identify as the constant and the variables in her life? What conclusions do you draw from the "ending" of this essay? To what extent, for example, does our identity vary according to the context in which we find ourselves? Having reread the essay and thought about it carefully, what cultural implications can you identify in the title "The Story of My Body"?

1. Ortiz Cofer's account of her childhood is punctuated by an oft-repeated admonition: "I had been told many times, as most children have, not to touch anything in a store that I was not buying" (para. 5). What repeated admonitions can you recall hearing as a child? Which ones do you associate with an especially memorable experience? Write the first draft of a narrative essay in which you recount how this maxim was invoked as a means of regulating your behavior.

2. At several points in her essay, Ortiz Cofer speaks of herself as "the Shrimp" and as "Skinny Bones." What nicknames have your peers applied to you, or what self-deprecating identity have you created for yourself? Write the first draft of an expository essay in which you account for the origins—and the personal consequences—of having taken on this nickname, willingly or not.

An often humorous aspect of writing that calls attention to the difference between the actual result of a sequence of events and the expected result.

The Story of My Body
Judith Ortiz Cofer

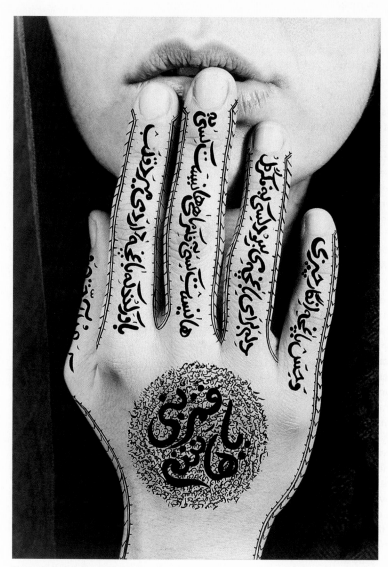

Shirin Neshat, **Grace Under Duty, 1994**

SHIRIN NESHAT

Shirin Neshat was born in Qazvin, Iran, in 1957 and today lives in New York while her family still lives in Iran. In 1979, during the Islamic Revolution, Neshat was exiled from Iran. Her artwork explores issues of Islamic society, especially the position of women, although she takes care not to bring a political message to her audience. Rather, her message is a personal one that is often draped in the political dressings that women in Iran cannot escape. "Grace Under Duty, 1994" is from an early photographic series, *Women of Allah* (1993–1997), that explores images of radical female Islamic identity. Neshat's most recent work has consisted of a video play; her film *Soliloquy*, which she directed and acted in, tells the story of a Muslim woman who is caught up by the attraction and repulsion of the East and West, and between traditional and modern pressures.

Neshat's photographs and videos have been included in many international exhibitions. In 1996 she was awarded a grant from the Louis Comfort Tiffany Foundation. Neshat's solo exhibitions have been presented at Franklin Furnace, New York (1993); the Centre d'art contemporain, Fribourg (1996); the Museum of Modern Art, Ljubljana (1997); the Whitney Museum of American Art, New York, and the Tate Gallery of Modern Art at St. Mary-le-Bow Church, Cheapside, London (1998); and the Art Institute of Chicago (1999).

SEEING

1. In an interview about *Women of Allah*, the series of photographs that includes the one reproduced here, Shirin Neshat explains: "I'm an artist so I'm not an activist. I don't have an agenda. I'm creating work simply to entice a dialogue and that's all. I do tend to show the stereotype head on and then break it down. There's the stereotype about the women—they're all victims and submissive—and they're not. Slowly I subvert that image by showing in the most subtle and candid way how strong these women are." In what ways does Neshat's image presented here "subvert" stereotypes about Muslim women?

2. What is emphasized in this image? What is omitted? Comment on the effectiveness of the ways in which the photographer frames this image. What, more specifically, do you notice about the positioning of the hand? the writing on the hand? How do you "read" the writing on the hand?

WRITING

1. "I like works that take my breath away or make me want to cry . . . almost a religious experience," remarked Neshat in a recent interview with *Time* magazine. "I'm creating a very brief experience for people so they can take away with them not some heavy political statement but something that really touches them on the most emotional level." Read the essay about Shirin Neshat on the Time.com web site, or do some other research on the web about Neshat's work. Then write an argumentative essay in which you defend or challenge the proposition that having more biographical information about an artist enhances our understanding and appreciation of his or her work.

2. Neshat's photographs in the *Women of Allah* series challenge the stereotypes of Muslim women in the popular media. Choose one such medium (say, television or newspapers, or magazines), and write an expository essay in which you document the nature and extent of stereotyping of Muslim women—and offer one or more solutions to this problem of public perception.

www   Re: Searching the Web

"In the age of the Internet, people are able to construct themselves," said Sherry Turkle, sociologist and author of *Life on the Screen: Identity in the Age of the Internet* (1997). "Virtual communities can be seen as a new genre of artistic endeavor, a new form of performance art or improvisational theater. What distinguishes the virtual are the new genres developed through computer-aided design." In chat rooms, MUDs (multi-user domains), message boards, and Instant Messaging, computer users are free to assume screen names, personalities, and even virtual appearances that may bear little resemblance to their off-line identities.

At the same time, the issue of maintaining online privacy and protecting personal information is under increasing scrutiny. Although it is now easier than ever to become someone else in virtual space, it's less difficult for others to find critical personal information (e-mail address, credit card information) and track online habits. Draft an essay in which you explore how identity is constructed and contested in virtual space. How do online environments help shape our sense of self? As an alternative writing exercise, you might draft an argumentative essay in which you support or refute the assertion that technology, and especially the Internet, has made anonymity increasingly difficult to maintain.

PETER ROSTOVSKY

Peter Rostovsky was born in St. Petersburg, Russia, in 1970. He was educated at Cornell University and attended the Cooper Union School of Art and the Parson School of Design; he also was a Whitney Museum Independent Study program scholar and studio resident in 1995–1996. His sculptures and paintings re-examine the overused symbols produced throughout history by putting them into modern contexts to explore personal nostalgia and hope for human society. His group exhibitions in New York include *The Project*; *Untold Stories*; *Local Color*; and *Summer Carnival*. Rostovsky has had solo exhibitions at The Project, New York (1999), at the Olive Tjaden Gallery, Ithaca, New York (1995), and at the Rockville Center Public Library, Rockville Center, New York (1994).

A recent recipient of a Public Art Fund commission and a participant in the annual show at the MetroTech Commons in Brooklyn, Rostovsky is also a participant in the first quadrennial of contemporary art held in Ghent, Belgium. He is an artist-in-residence in the graduate program at the Mount Royal School of Art, part of the Maryland Institute College of Art.

The three paintings from the *Portrait Connection* were first published in the Winter 2001 issue of *Cabinet* magazine. The editors solicited personal descriptions from *Cabinet* readers, which Rostovsky then used to image this portrait series.

HAIR: fire and cognition / HEAD: torpor and oblivion / EYES: congestion, edges, fog / EARS: echolocation / NOSE: oysters, marshes, poison / LIPS: suction, whistles, blood / A NECK to melt the ice cap / A CHEST to chasten all critics / ARMS that embrace shadows / FINGERS that itch every scratch / CLOTHES that make the man in BLACKS, BLUES, and RED. No HAT.

Peter Rostovsky, **"HAIR: fire and cognition"**

I work for a government agency. I work hard; can't tell you much. I'm slim and muscular. I run. I read lots. Sandy hair, freckles. Team player. Tennis champ. Blue eyes. I pack a small .38. It's personal. I write long reports into the night, and now must wear glasses.

Peter Rostovsky, **"I work for a government agency."**

slim as a beanpole / clear perfect complexion / art history major, with a background in sociology / very very ambitious / black long hair, like a Modigliani / nose too big but I can live with it / good hygiene / like to talk a lot, big mouth / nice lips / well-dressed / love Europe / love Kate Spade

Peter Rostovsky, **"slim as a beanpole"**

SEEING

1. Which aspects of each personal description stand out to you the most? How and where do you see these words reflected in Rostovsky's paintings? If you were the artist, which words would you have chosen to emphasize more and less?

2. Comment on the extent to which you think Rostovsky's portraits illustrate the qualities and details included in the personal descriptions. Which portrait do you think is most "true" to the written description? Explain why. Consider the written personal descriptions as a group. What similarities and differences do you notice? What generalizations can you make about them? What aspects of identity do these individuals focus on most often: appearance? personality? religious or spiritual beliefs? cultural values or associations? hobbies? something else?

WRITING

1. Following the guidelines specified in the advertisement for the *Portrait Connection* (at right), write your own description to submit to the project. After you have drafted your personal statement, trade your description with one of your classmates. Then write a two-page character profile based on your classmate's description of herself or himself.

2. What would you characterize Rostovsky's style as a painter? Choose another painter and write an essay in which you compare and contrast the two artists, focusing on the similarities and differences in their styles. In your analysis, you might consider choice of materials, subjects, color palette, composition. Which painter's work do you appreciate more? Why?

WHO SAYS MASTERPIECES CAN'T BE MADE TO ORDER?

THIS ONE WAS.

NOW IS YOUR CHANCE TO HAVE AN ELEGANT PORTRAIT OF YOURSELF PAINTED
BY ONE OF THE CLASSICALLY-TRAINED ARTISTS AT THE PORTRAIT CONNECTION.
FOR THIS EXTREMELY LIMITED PROMOTIONAL CAMPAIGN,
THIS PREMIERE PORTRAIT AGENCY IS EXECUTING A SERIES OF ITS DISTINCTIVE PORTRAITS
BASED ENTIRELY ON YOUR DEMANDS AND ON THE INFORMATION THAT YOU WISH TO PROVIDE.

TO PARTICIPATE, JUST SEND US A BRIEF 50-WORD DESCRIPTION OF ALL THE FEATURES AND QUALITIES
THAT DESCRIBE THE PERSON YOU ARE, WERE, OR HOPE TO BE.
REST ASSURED THAT OUR SKILLED ARTISTS WILL WORK TIRELESSLY
TO CREATE YOUR PORTRAIT IN THE FINEST TRADITION OF EUROPEAN PORTRAITURE.
AS THIS IS STRICTLY A PROMOTIONAL CAMPAIGN,
YOU ARE UNDER NO OBLIGATION TO BUY UNLESS YOU CHOOSE TO DO SO.
IF SELECTED, YOUR PORTRAIT WILL BE DISPLAYED IN THE WINTER 2004 ISSUE OF CABINET.

WRITE US AT THE PORTRAIT CONNECTION
AND CONNECT TO THE EXCITING WORLD OF ART.

PLEASE SEND YOUR DESCRIPTIONS TO PORTRAITCONNECTION@IMMATERIAL.NET.

Cabinet, **Portrait Connection**

Visualizing Context
Advertising the Self

SILLY QUIET WRITER SJF, creative Democrat, seeks brilliant, funny, bookish, introspective, hard-working, dog-loving, clean-cut SWM with SAT scores over 1400 for immature adventures, no piercings. Under 5'11" a+.

CUTE, RUBENESQUE SWF Long dark hair, 27, 195 lbs, brown eyes, spiritual, adventurous, affectionate, jeans and platforms type into ethnic food, rock/folk, museums, travel, camping, ISO SW/H/A/M soulmate, fit with longish hair.

PROFOUND YET PLAYFUL Humanistic but realistic PhD candidate, Latina, 26, cute, petite, with a zest for life and passion for learning. Adventurous, resilient, affectionate, considerate, relaxed, optimistic. Love animals, camping, hiking, swimming, scuba diving, cultural activities. You: professional, mature, compassionate, expressive, dynamic, for solid friendship, maybe romance.

I PUT THE SEAT DOWN Suit by day, philosopher by night. SWM, 27, 5'10", 168 lbs. Athletic, sarcastic, committed, prurient, discriminating, droll. Half Ren, half Stimpy. Seeking one who can tell a malapropism from a non sequitur. Emotional availability more important than physical presence (but both don't hurt).

There is a long history in American culture of people attempting to distinguish themselves from the crowd and to advertise themselves in public. One of the most important traditions is the personal ad. Since the nineteenth century, people have been summing up their identities in compact phrases at the back of newspapers and magazines, and more recently on the web—all with the hope of finding romance or, failing that, simply prompting a response.

Traditional text-based personal ads require people to conjure an image of the person describing him- or herself. There's often a sense of mysteriousness about such ads; they rely on a command of language in order to develop an impression of the person being described.

Consider the personal ads printed here. What assumptions about self-identity are evident in these self-advertisements? What inferences can you draw from each about the state of contemporary American culture and social experience? How do abbreviations such as SWF and SJF shape one's sense of self-identity?

In the *Portrait Connection* (pp. 324–29), Peter Rostovsky uses high art to represent something as seemingly ordinary as personal ads, converting them into portraits. Rostovsky's paintings are his interpretations of personal verbal descriptions of complete strangers. Increasingly, online sites featuring personal ads enable people to post photographs and text descriptions of themselves. Examine carefully Rostovsky's portraits. Then write an essay in which you compare the advantages/disadvantages of including a photograph in a personal ad.

More historically minded readers might prefer to write an essay that documents the changes in individual and collective hopes, fears, and anxieties related to self-identity as they are revealed in personal ads from different periods in American history.

BRUCE BOWER >

Bruce Bower has been writing
about behavioral science and
other topics for *Science News*
magazine since 1984. He compares the arena of behavioral
sciences today to the Wild West,
where many ideas vie for territory like so many settlers. "The
problem with the field is that
there is just no accurate way to
measure many different human
reactions," he remarks. In viewing
scientific work, Bower urges that
we look beyond our own cultural
norms "not only at the evidence
presented, but at the assumptions that underlie the evidence.
Often scientists themselves are
not aware of their assumptions."

Regarding the state of popular
science research today, Bower
suggests that the developments
we read about may not always be
the most critical issues. "People
who can present simple 'sound
bite' answers are often given attention over those who are doing
work that is harder to summarize." The essay "Average Attractions" first appeared in *Science
News* in 1990; in it, Bower reports
on a study that attempts to
define standards of beauty.

Among other topics covered in
Bower's numerous articles are
the relationship between sex and
cigarettes, Western notions of
the mind, and the basis of decision making and intuition. He
attended Pepperdine University,
where he studied psychology,
as well as the University of
Missouri School of Journalism.

Bruce Bower

Average Attractions

Here she comes, Miss America. Her demeanor exudes poise, her figure curves gracefully, her face is incredibly average.

That's right, average. And no, the computer did not jumble the judges' votes, at least not according to Judith H. Langlois of the University of Texas at Austin and Lori A. Roggman of the University of Arkansas at Fayetteville. These two psychologists have provided a scientific answer to a question that has puzzled philosophers for centuries: What constitutes physical beauty? Their surprising answer: The most attractive people are not blessed with rare physical qualities others can only dream about. A knockout face possesses features that approximate the mathematical average of all faces in a particular population.

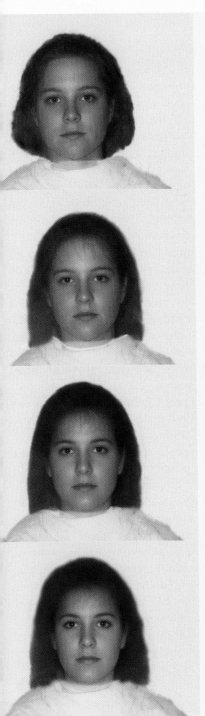

In other words, Miss America's face is an extremely typical example of all faces, constituting what psychologists call a facial "prototype." Strictly speaking, her beauty is average. And the same goes for handsome male faces.

"This is a very exciting principle," says psychologist Ellen S. Berscheid of the University of Minnesota in Minneapolis. "We can get an empirical handle on facial beauty now."

Until seeing Langlois and Roggman's data, Berscheid, like most other investigators of physical attraction, contended that physical beauty was unmeasurable. Good looks were assumed to be perceived as a unified whole, a kind of "gestalt face" that could not be broken down or averaged in the laboratory. "We thought it was impossible to determine whether, say, Cary Grant's ears or Elizabeth Taylor's nose are attractive in an absolute sense," Berscheid remarks.

If Berscheid's about-face foreshadows a widespread adoption of the notion that attractive faces are average, the implications will extend beyond rating the raw beauty of movie stars. For instance, an analysis of groups of children's faces at different ages might provide surgeons with reliable guideposts for reconstructing craniofacial deformities resulting from accidents or inborn defects, Langlois says. Craniofacial surgeons currently operate with no standardized, age-based criteria for reshaping a disfigured face, she adds.

For now, the theory of "average beauty" rests on an intriguing facial analysis of 96 male and 96 female college students. Mug shots of the students—predominantly Caucasian, but including some Hispanics and Asians—were scanned by a video lens hooked up to a computer that converted each picture into a matrix of tiny digital units with numerical values.

Langlois and Roggman divided each group into three sets of 32 faces. In each set, the computer randomly chose two faces and mathematically averaged their digitized values. It then transformed this information into a composite face of the two individuals. Composite faces

Although these look like photographs of real-life women, they are actually computer-generated composite faces. The top image consists of four faces; the second from the top consists of eight faces; the third from the top combines sixteen faces; the bottom comprises thirty-two faces. When asked to rank faces like these, college students rated the bottom two composites as most attractive, even compared with the individual faces that made up the composites.

were then generated for four, eight, 16 and 32 members of each set.

Each set of individual faces and its corresponding composites was then judged by at least 65 college students, including both males and females. The students rated composite faces as more attractive than virtually any of the individual faces, Langlois and Roggman report in the March *Psychological Science*.

Student judges attributed the most striking physical superiority to the 16- and 32-face composites. Composites made from eight or fewer faces did not receive attractiveness ratings significantly greater, in a statistical sense, than individual ratings.

Not only does the averaging of 16 or more faces produce a highly attractive composite image; it also seems to produce a prototypical face. The 16- and 32-face composites in each set looked very similar to each other, and also looked similar to the corresponding composites in the other two same-sex sets, the researchers note. It did not matter that some composites were randomly generated from individual faces rated more unattractive than attractive, while other composites consisted of a majority of faces judged as attractive.

Although a composite of a different racial group—say, 32 Asian faces— would surely look different from a predominantly Caucasian composite, Langlois predicts that both Asian and non-Asian judges would rate a composite Asian face as very attractive.

"We don't claim to have simulated what the human mind does," Langlois says. "Our digitized images only approximate the averaging process that is assumed to occur when humans form mental prototypes [of an attractive face]."

The finding helps explain numerous recent observations that both infants as young as 2 months old and adults perceive the same faces as attractive, regardless of the racial or cultural background of the person viewing a face. In the January *Developmental Psychology*, Langlois and her co-workers report that 1-year-olds are happier, less withdrawn and more likely to play with a female stranger judged as attractive by adults than with an equally unfamiliar female rated unattractive. The same infants play significantly longer with a doll possessing an attractive face as judged by adults than with a doll whose face is unattractive to adults.

Faces serve as a critical source of social information, especially for babies, who may prefer an attractive or prototypical face because it is easier to classify as a face, Langlois suggests. In fact, she says, evolutionary pressures over the past several million years may have endowed humans with a built-in "beauty-detecting" mechanism that averages facial features. According to this scenario— which is admittedly difficult to test— humans have evolved to respond most strongly to the most prototypical faces, which most readily yield social information through such facial expressions as happiness or disgust.

On the other hand, people may acquire preferences for attractive faces early in infancy, when the ability to sort diverse stimuli into meaningful categories organized around prototypes is apparently already in place. For example, 6-month-olds respond most strongly to basic vowel sounds—the long "e" in the word "peep," for example—that adults perceive as the best examples of particular vowels. This suggests that specific speech sounds serve as "perceptual anchors" from infancy onward.

Whatever the case, the principle that averageness is a critical element of attractiveness probably applies to as many as nine out of 10 people whose countenances are considered alluring, Berscheid says. Most exceptions may be individuals in the public eye, such as movie stars, whose appeal sometimes lies largely in perceptions indirectly linked to facial beauty, such as glamour and fame.

Langlois agrees, citing Cher as one such exception. Cher's facial features are clearly not average, but many people view her as attractive, Langlois says. Opinions about Cher's facial beauty are undoubtedly affected by her expressions in photographs, the youthfulness of her face, her glamorous image and numerous media reports describing her younger boyfriends, the Texas psychologist points out.

For similar reasons, raters might judge a sample of movie stars as more attractive than student composites, Langlois asserts. Further research is needed to investigate attractiveness factors that lie beyond the bounds of an absolute measure of beauty, she says.

In the meantime, those of us who [20] muddle by without Cary Grant's ears or Elizabeth Taylor's nose can find solace in the suggestion that attractive faces are, in fact, only average.

And even Cher can take comfort. Neither Langlois nor anyone else has the faintest idea how to quantify charisma. ○

SEEING

1. What features does Bruce Bower focus on in defining physical beauty? What assumptions about physical beauty seemed to prevail in the American popular imagination prior to the study conducted by Professors Langlois and Roggman? To what useful purposes does Bower suggest that Langlois and Roggman's findings might be put? How does Bower define "average" in this essay? What information does he provide about the ethnic and racial makeup of the participants in Langlois and Roggman's study? What impact does this factor have on their findings? What claim(s) do they make about the adaptability of their findings to different races?

2. According to Bower, Langlois and Roggman suggest that exceptions to the rule of "average attractions" might be "individuals in the public eye, such as movie stars, whose appeal sometimes lies largely in perceptions indirectly linked to facial beauty, such as glamour and fame" (para. 17). If there can be so many exceptions, what then constitutes the nature of "average" attractions? Compare the computer-generated composite photographs of the faces of real-life women (p. 333) to the photograph of the altered body of Cindy Jackson (p. 370). Which image of beauty do you find more attractive? Why?

WRITING

1. In paragraph 17, Bower asserts the principle that "averageness is a critical element of attractiveness." What assumptions are embedded in this claim? What does your own experience suggest about the accuracy of this assertion? Write an essay in which you support—or refute—Bower's claim. Please be sure to include a detailed analysis of examples to verify each of your contentions.

2. Stop at the campus bookstore or local magazine stand. Which magazines trade on selling images of physical beauty? Choose the magazine you judge to be most visibly committed to capitalizing on its readers' interest in physical beauty. Examine that magazine carefully, paying special attention to the images that focus on features of the body that project beauty. Draft an essay in which you examine those images carefully and extrapolate from them the magazine's definition of beauty. How "average" is the attractiveness projected in the magazine?

MARGE PIERCY

Marge Piercy is a novelist, essayist, and poet, and much of her
writing has a political dimension
that stems from her hardscrabble childhood in Detroit during
the Depression. She attended
the University of Michigan on a
scholarship, earned an M.A. at
Northwestern University, lived in
France for several years, and then
moved to Chicago, where she
supported herself with a variety
of low-paying, part-time jobs, including secretary, department
store clerk, and artists' model.

All the while, she wrote novels
but could not get them published.
She says she knew two things
about her fiction: She wanted it
to be political, and she wanted
to write about working-class
people. After moving to Cape Cod
in 1971, Piercy took up gardening,
became active in the women's
movement, and found renewed
creative energy for writing poetry.

"Piercy doesn't understand
writers who complain about writing," states the biography on her
World Wide Web homepage, "not
because it is easy for her but because it is so absorbing that she
can imagine nothing more consuming and exciting. . . . So long
as she can make her living
at writing, she will consider herself lucky."

IMAGING

Marge Piercy

I am my body.
This is not a dress, a coat;
not a house I live in;
not a suit of armor for close fighting;
not a lump of meat in which I nuzzle like a worm.   5

I issue orders from the command tower;
I look out the twin windows staring,
reading the buzz from ears, hands, nose,
weighing, interpreting, forecasting.
Downstairs faceless crowds labor.   10

I am those mute crowds rushing.
I must glide down the ladder of bone,
I must slide down the silken ropes
of the nerves burning in their darkness.
I must ease into the warm egg of the limbic brain.   15

Like learning the chemical language of ants,
we enter and join to the body lying
down as if to a lover. We ourselves,
caves we must explore in the dark,
eyes shut tight and hands unclenched.   20

Estranged from ourselves to the point
where we scarcely credit the body's mind,
in we go reclaiming what once we knew.
We wrestle the dark angel of our hidden
selves, fighting all night for our lives.   25

Who is this angel I meet on my back,
radiant as molten steel pouring from the ladle,
dark as the inside of the moon?
Whose is this strength I wrestle?
—the other, my lost holy self.   30

1. Marge Piercy opens *Imaging* with a simple declarative sentence: "I am my body." What do you understand this assertion to mean? How is this claim illustrated in the lines that follow? Comment on the effects of Piercy's use of negatives in the first stanza. Explain how lines 2–5 reinforce or subvert her opening statement. How would you summarize the final two stanzas of the poem? How does the poem end differently from where it began? With what effects?

2. What organizational principles lend coherence to this poem? What kinds of movement can you identify in it? Examine the metaphors used in the final stanza. How has Piercy prepared her readers for the use of these metaphors? What effects do they have?

1. The artist Barbara Kruger presents a provocative metaphor for the female body, calling it a "battleground." What examples can you point to in Piercy's poem that either support or challenge Kruger's assertion? Write an essay in which you argue for or against Kruger's claim that a woman's body is a battleground. Please be sure to define the terms you use and to validate each of your claims with examples drawn from Piercy's poem or other sources.

2. Philosophers have struggled for centuries to come to terms with the question of who we are. The Western philosophical tradition, for example, holds that who we are is determined by our consciousness and rationality—and that this consciousness is separate from and transcends the physical body, which functions according to physical laws, needs, and desires. This classical distinction between subject and object helps us to understand what it is to be human. Reread *Imaging* carefully, several times, until you feel comfortable with thinking and writing about the poem. Then draft an essay in which you explain whether Piercy's poem endorses this distinction between subject and object.

Barbara Kruger, **Your Body Is a Battleground**

TV Talking Pictures

Television and motion pictures are among the most powerful vehicles for establishing and distributing an ideal of physical beauty in American popular culture. Which television programs and recent films can you identify that capitalize on portraying such standards of beauty? Choose one television program or film. What visual and verbal strategies do the creators use to convey this standard of beauty? Which physical features do they focus on in order to promote it? What aspects of the body are given the most attention?

Review the research findings of Professors Langlois and Roggman as summarized in Bruce Bower's essay "Average Attractions" (see p. 332). What do you think their reaction would be to the standards promoted by the movie or television show you have chosen? Write an essay in which you analyze the features of physical beauty projected in the film or television show. Explain to what extent these features are the same as the standard "average" that Americans apply to themselves.

GISH JEN
Born in 1956, Gish Jen grew up in Scarsdale, New York, the second of five children of immigrant Chinese parents. "We were almost the only Asian American family in town," she remembers. "People threw things at us and called us names. We thought it was normal; it was only much later that I realized it had been hard." Jen draws on her experience growing up Asian American in her two critically acclaimed novels, *Typical American* (1991) and *Mona in the Promised Land* (1996), and in her most recent collection of short stories, *Who's Irish?* (2000).

"I have my own definition of American," says Jen. "It is not something that you come into [and] particularly does not involve abandoning where you came from. I think of Americanness as a preoccupation with identity. It is the hallmark of the New World because we live in a society where you are not only who your parents were, and you don't already know what your children will be. That is not to say that I am blond and eat apple pie, but any definition that finds me less American—well, all I can say is that something is wrong with the definition." Jen is a regular contributor to periodicals such as *The New Yorker, Atlantic Monthly, Yale Review, Fiction International,* and *Iowa Review.*

What Means Switch

Gish Jen

THERE WE ARE, NICE CHINESE FAMILY—FATHER, mother, two born-here girls. Where should we live next? My parents slide the question back and forth like a cup of ginseng neither one wants to drink. Until finally it comes to them, what they really want is a milkshake (chocolate) and to go with it a house in Scarsdale. What else? The broker tries to hint: the neighborhood, she says. Moneyed. Many delis. Meaning rich and Jewish. But someone has sent my parents a list of the top ten schools nation-wide (based on the opinion of selected educators and others) and so *many-deli* or not we nestle into a Dutch colonial on the Bronx River Parkway. The road's windy where we are, very charming; drivers miss their turns, plow up our flower beds, then want to use our telephone. "Of course," my mom tells them, like it's no big deal, we can replant. We're the type to adjust. You know—the lady drivers weep, my mom gets out the Kleenex for them. We're a bit down the hill from the private plane set, in other words. Only in our dreams do our jacket zippers jam, what with all the lift tickets we have stapled to them, Killington on top of Sugarbush on top of Stowe, and we don't even know where the Virgin Islands are—although certain of us do know that virgins are like priests and nuns, which there were a lot more of in Yonkers, where we just moved from, than there are here.

This is my first understanding of class. In our old neighborhood everybody knew everything about virgins and non-virgins, not to say the technicalities of staying in between. Or almost everybody, I should say; in Yonkers I was the laugh-along type. Here I'm an expert.

"You mean the man . . . ?" Pig-tailed Barbara Gugelstein spits a mouthful of Coke back into her can. "That is *so* gross!"

Pretty soon I'm getting popular for a new girl. The only problem is Danielle Meyers, who wears blue mascara and has gone steady with two boys. "How do *you* know," she starts to ask, proceeding to edify us all with how she French-kissed one boyfriend and just regular kissed another. ("Because, you know, he had braces.") We hear about his rubber bands, how once one popped right into her mouth. I begin to realize I need to find somebody to kiss too. But how?

Luckily, I just about then happen to tell Barbara 5 Gugelstein I know karate. I don't know why I tell her this. My sister Callie's the liar in the family; ask anybody. I'm the one who doesn't see why we should have to hold our heads up. But for some reason I tell Barbara Gugelstein I can make my hands like steel by thinking hard. "I'm not supposed to tell anyone," I say.

The way she backs away, blinking, I could be the burning bush.

"I can't do bricks," I say—a bit of expectation management. "But I can do your arm if you want." I set my hand in chop position.

"Uhh, it's okay," she says. "I know you can, I saw it on TV last night."

That's when I recall that I too saw it on TV last night—in fact, at her house. I rush on to tell her I know how to get pregnant with tea.

"With *tea*?"

"That's how they do it in China."

She agrees that China is an ancient and great civilization that ought to be known for more than spaghetti and gunpowder. I tell her I know Chinese. "*Be-yeh fa-foon,*" I say. "*Shee-veh. Ji nu.*" Meaning, "Stop acting crazy. Rice gruel. Soy sauce." She's impressed. At lunch the next day, Danielle Meyers and Amy Weinstein and Barbara's crush, Andy Kaplan, are all impressed too. Scarsdale is a liberal town, not like Yonkers, where the Whitman Road Gang used to throw crabapple mash at my sister Callie and me and tell us it would make our eyes stick shut. Here we're like permanent exchange students. In another ten years, there'll be so many Orientals we'll turn into Asians; a Japanese grocery will buy out that one deli too many. But for now, the mid-sixties, what with civil rights on TV, we're not so much accepted as embraced. Especially by the Jewish part of town—which, it turns out, is not all of town at all. That's just an idea people have, Callie says, and lots of them could take us or leave us same as the Christians, who are nice too; I shouldn't generalize. So let me not generalize except to say that pretty soon I've been to so many bar and bas mitzvahs, I can almost say myself whether the kid chants like an angel or like a train conductor, maybe they could use him on the commuter line. At seder I know to forget the bricks, get a good pile of that mortar. Also I know what is schmaltz. I know that I am a goy. This is not why people like me, though. People like me because I do not need to use deodorant, as I demonstrate in the locker room before and after gym. Also, I can explain to them, for example, what is tofu (*der-voo,* we say at home). Their mothers invite me to taste-test their Chinese cooking.

"Very authentic." I try to be reassuring. After all, they're nice people, I like them. "De-lish." I have seconds. On the question of what we eat, though, I have to admit, "Well, no, it's different than that." I have thirds. "What my mom makes is home style, it's not in the cookbooks."

Not in the cookbooks! Everyone's jealous. Meanwhile, the big deal at home is when we have turkey pot pie. My sister Callie's the one introduced them—Mrs. Wilder's, they come in this green-and-brown box—and when we have them, we both get suddenly interested in helping out in the kitchen. You know, we stand in front of the oven and help them bake. Twenty-five minutes. She and I have a deal, though, to keep it secret from school, as everybody else thinks they're gross. We think they're a big improvement over authentic Chinese home cooking. Oxtail soup—now that's gross. Stir-fried beef with tomatoes. One day I say, "You know Ma, I have never seen a stir-fried tomato in any Chinese restaurant we have ever been in, ever."

"In China," she says, real lofty, "we consider tomatoes are a delicacy."

"Ma," I say. "Tomatoes are *Italian.*"

"No respect for elders." She wags her finger at me, but I can tell it's just to try and shame me into believing her. "I'm tell you, tomatoes *invented* in China."

"*Ma.*"

"Is true. Like noodles. Invented in China."

"That's not what they said in *school.*"

"In *China,*" my mother counters, "we also eat tomatoes uncooked, like apple. And in summertime we slice them, and put some sugar on top."

"Are you sure?"

My mom says of course she's sure, and in the end I give in, even though she once told me that China was such a long time ago, a lot of things she can hardly remember. She said sometimes she has trouble remembering her characters, that sometimes she'll be writing a letter, just writing along, and all of a sudden she won't be sure if she should put four dots or three.

"So what do you do then?"

"Oh, I just make a little sloppy."

"You mean you *fudge*?"

She laughed then, but another time, when she was showing me how to write my name, and I said, just kidding, "Are you sure that's the right number of dots now?" she was hurt.

"I mean, of course you know," I said. "I mean, *oy*."

Meanwhile, what *I* know is that in the eighth grade, what people want to hear does not include how Chinese people eat sliced tomatoes with sugar on top. For a gross fact, it just isn't gross enough. On the other hand, the fact that somewhere in China somebody eats or has eaten or once ate living monkey brains—now that's conversation.

"They have these special tables," I say, "kind of like a giant collar. With a hole in the middle, for the monkey's neck. They put the monkey in the collar, and then they cut off the top of its head."

"Whadda they use for cutting?"

I think. "Scalpels."

"*Scalpels?*" says Andy Kaplan.

"Kaplan, don't be dense," Barbara Gugelstein says. "The Chinese *invented* scalpels."

Once a friend said to me, You know, everybody is valued for something. She explained how some people resented being valued for their looks; others resented being valued for their money. Wasn't it still better to be beautiful and rich than ugly and poor, though? You should be just glad, she said, that you have something people value. It's like having a special talent, like being good at ice-skating, or opera-singing. She said, You could probably make a career out of it.

Here's the irony: I am.

Anyway. I am ad-libbing my way through eighth grade, as I've described. Until one bloomy spring day, I come in late to homeroom, and to my chagrin discover there's a new kid in class.

Chinese.

So what should I do, pretend to have to go to the girls' room, like Barbara Gugelstein the day Andy Kaplan took his ID back? I sit down; I am so cool I remind myself of Paul Newman. First thing I realize,

though, is that no one looking at me is thinking of Paul Newman. The notes fly:

"*I* think he's cute."

"Who?" I write back. (I am still at an age, understand, when I believe a person can be saved by aplomb.)

"I don't think he talks English too good. Writes it either."

"Who?"

"They might have to put him behind a grade, so don't worry."

"He has a crush on you already, you could tell as soon as you walked in, he turned kind of orangeish."

I hope I'm not turning orangeish as I deal with my mail; I could use a secretary. The second round starts:

"What do you mean who? Don't be weird. Didn't you *see* him??? Straight back over your right shoulder!!!!"

I have to look; what else can I do? I think of certain tips I learned in Girl Scouts about poise. I cross my ankles. I hold a pen in my hand. I sit up as though I have a crown on my head. I swivel my head slowly, repeating to myself, *I could be Miss America.*

"Miss Mona Chang."

Horror raises its hoary head.

"Notes, please."

Mrs. Mandeville's policy is to read all notes aloud.

I try to consider what Miss America would do, and see myself, back straight, knees together, crying. Some inspiration. Cool Hand Luke, on the other hand, would, quick, eat the evidence. And why not? I should yawn as I stand up, and boom, the notes are gone. All that's left is to explain that it's an old Chinese reflex.

I shuffle up to the front of the room.

"One minute please," Mrs. Mandeville says.

I wait, noticing how large and plastic her mouth is. She unfolds a piece of paper.

And I, Miss Mona Chang, who got almost straight A's her whole life except in math and conduct, am about to start crying in front of everyone.

I am delivered out of hot Egypt by the bell. General pandemonium. Mrs. Mandeville still has her hand clamped on my shoulder, though. And the next thing I know, I'm holding the new boy's schedule. He's standing next to me like a big blank piece of paper. "This is Sherman," Mrs. Mandeville says.

"Hello," I say.

"*Non how a,*" I say. 60

I'm glad Barbara Gugelstein isn't there to see my Chinese in action.

"*Ji nu,*" I say. "*Shee veh.*"

Later I find out that his mother asked if there were any other Orientals in our grade. She had him put in my class on purpose. For now, though, he looks at me as though I'm much stranger than anything else he's seen so far. Is this because he understands I'm saying "soy sauce rice gruel" to him or because he doesn't?

"Sher-man," he says finally. 65

I look at his schedule card. Sherman Matsumoto. What kind of name is that for a nice Chinese boy?

(Later on, people ask me how I can tell Chinese from Japanese. I shrug. You just kind of know, I say. *Oy!*)

Sherman's got the sort of looks I think of as pretty-boy. Monsignor-black hair (not monk-brown like mine), bouncy. Crayola eyebrows, one with a round bald spot in the middle of it, like a golf hole. I don't know how anybody can think of him as orangeish; his skin looks white to me, with pink triangles hanging down the front of his cheeks like flags. Kind of delicate-looking, but the only truly uncool thing about him is that his spiral notebook has a picture of a kitty cat on it. A big white fluffy one, with a blue ribbon above each perky little ear. I get much opportunity to view this, as all the poor kid understands about life in junior high school is that he should follow me everywhere. It's embarrassing. On the other hand, he's obviously even more miserable than I am, so I try not to say anything. Give him a chance to adjust. We communicate by sign language, and by drawing pictures, which he's better at than I am; he puts in every last detail, even if it takes forever. I try to be patient.

A week of this. Finally I enlighten him. "You should get a new notebook."

His cheeks turn a shade of pink you mostly only 70 see in hyacinths.

"Notebook." I point to his. I show him mine, which is psychedelic, with big purple and yellow stick-on flowers. I try to explain he should have one like this, only without the flowers. He nods enigmatically, and the next day brings me a notebook just like his, except that this cat sports pink bows instead of blue.

"Pret-ty," he says. "You."

He speaks English! I'm dumbfounded. Has he spoken it all this time? I consider: Pretty. You. What does that mean? Plus actually, he's said *plit-ty,* much as my parents would; I'm assuming he means pretty, but maybe he means pity. Pity. You.

"Jeez," I say finally.

"You are wel-come," he says. 75

I decorate the back of the notebook with stick-on flowers, and hold it so that these show when I walk through the halls. In class I mostly keep my book open. After all, the kid's so new; I think I really ought to have a heart. And for a livelong day nobody notices.

Then Barbara Gugelstein sidles up. "Matching notebooks, huh?"

I'm speechless.

"First comes love, then comes marriage, and then come chappies in a baby carriage."

"Barbara!"

"Get it?" she says. "Chinese Japs." 80

"Bar-*bra,*" I say to get even.

"Just make sure he doesn't give you any *tea,*" she says.

Are Sherman and I in love? Three days later, I hazard that we are. My thinking proceeds this way: I think he's cute, and I think he thinks I'm cute. On the other hand, we don't kiss and we don't exactly have fantastic conversations. Our talks *are* getting better, though. We started out, "This is a book." "Book." "This is a chair." "Chair." Advancing to, "What is this?" "This is a book." Now, for fun, he tests me.

"What is this?" he says. 85

"This is a book," I say, as if I'm the one who has to learn how to talk.

He claps. "Good!"

Meanwhile, people ask me all about him. I could be his press agent.

"No, he doesn't eat raw fish."

"No, his father wasn't a kamikaze pilot." 90

"No, he can't do karate."

"Are you sure?" somebody asks.

Indeed he doesn't know karate, but judo he does. I am hurt I'm not the one to find this out; the guys know from gym class. They line up to be flipped, he flips them all onto the floor, and after that he doesn't eat lunch at the girls' table with me anymore. I'm more or less glad. Meaning, when he was there, I never knew what to say. Now that he's gone, though, I seem to be stuck at the "This is a chair" level of conversation. Ancient Chinese eating habits have lost their cachet; all I get are more and more questions about me and Sherman. "I dunno," I'm saying all the time. *Are* we going out? We do stuff, it's true. For example, I take him to the department stores, explain to him who shops in Alexander's, who shops in Saks. I tell him my family's the type that shops in Alexander's. He says he's sorry. In Saks he gets lost; either that, or else I'm the lost one. (It's true I find him calmly waiting at the front door, hands behind his back, like a guard.) I take him to the candy store. I take him to the bagel store. Sherman is crazy about bagels. I explain to him that Lender's is gross, he should get his bagels from the bagel store. He says thank you.

"Are you going steady?" people want to know.

How can we go steady when he doesn't have an ID 95 bracelet? On the other hand, he brings me more presents than I think any girl's ever gotten before. Oranges. Flowers. A little bag of bagels. But what do they mean? Do they mean thank you, I enjoyed our trip; do they mean I like you; do they mean I decided I liked the Lender's better even if they are gross, you can have these? Sometimes I think he's acting on his mother's instructions. Also I know at least a couple of the presents were supposed to go to our teachers. He told me that once and turned red. I figured it still might mean something that he didn't throw them out.

More and more now, we joke. Like, instead of "I'm thinking," he always says, "I'm sinking," which we both think is so funny, that all either one of us has to do is pretend to be drowning and the other one cracks up. And he tells me things—for example, that there are electric lights everywhere in Tokyo now.

"You mean you didn't have them before?"

"Everywhere now!" He's amazed too. "Since Olympics!"

"Olympics?"

"1960," he says proudly, and as proof, hums for 100 me the Olympic theme song. "You know?"

"Sure," I say, and hum with him happily. We could be a picture on a UNICEF poster. The only problem is that I don't really understand what the Olympics have to do with the modernization of Japan, any more than I get this other story he tells me, about that hole in his left eyebrow, which is from some time his father accidentally hit him with a lit cigarette. When Sherman was a baby. His father was drunk, having been out carousing; his mother was very mad but didn't say anything, just cleaned the whole house. Then his father was so ashamed he bowed to ask her forgiveness.

"Your mother cleaned the house?"

Sherman nods solemnly.

"And your father *bowed?*" I find this more astounding than anything I ever thought to make up. "That is so weird," I tell him.

"Weird," he agrees. "This I no forget, forever. *Fa-* 105 *ther* bow to *mother!*"

We shake our heads.

As for the things he asks me, they're not topics I ever discussed before. Do I like it here? Of course I like it here, I was born here, I say. Am I Jewish? Jewish! I laugh. *Oy!* Am I American? "Sure I'm American," I say. "Everybody who's born here is American, and also some people who convert from what they were before. You could become American." But he says no, he could never. "Sure you could," I say. "You only have to learn some rules and speeches."

"But I Japanese," he says.

"You could become American anyway," I say. "Like I *could* become Jewish, if I wanted to. I'd just have to switch, that's all."

"But you Catholic," he says.

I think maybe he doesn't get what means switch.

I introduce him to Mrs. Wilder's turkey pot pies. "Gross?" he asks. I say they are, but we like them anyway. "Don't tell anybody." He promises. We bake them, eat them. While we're eating, he's drawing me pictures.

"This American," he says, and he draws something that looks like John Wayne. "This Jewish," he says, and draws something that looks like the Wicked Witch of the West, only male.

"I don't think so," I say.

He's undeterred. "This Japanese," he says, and draws a fair rendition of himself. "This Chinese," he says, and draws what looks to be another fair rendition of himself.

"How can you tell them apart?"

"This way," he says, and he puts the picture of the Chinese so that it is looking at the pictures of the American and the Jew. The Japanese faces the wall. Then he draws another picture, of a Japanese flag, so that the Japanese has that to contemplate. "Chinese lost in department store," he says. "Japanese know how go." For fun, he then takes the Japanese flag and fastens it to the refrigerator door with magnets. "In school, in ceremony, we this way," he explains, and bows to the picture.

When my mother comes in, her face is so red that with the white wall behind her she looks a bit like the Japanese flag herself. Yet I get the feeling I better not say so. First she doesn't move. Then she snatches the flag off the refrigerator, so fast the magnets go flying. Two of them land on the stove. She crumples up the paper. She hisses at Sherman, "*This is the U.S. of A., do you hear me!*"

Sherman hears her.

"You call your mother right now, tell her come pick you up."

He understands perfectly. *I,* on the other hand, am stymied. How can two people who don't really speak English understand each other better than I can understand them? "But Ma," I say.

"Don't *Ma* me," she says.

Later on she explains that World War II was in China, too. "Hitler," I say. "Nazis. Volkswagens." I know the Japanese were on the wrong side, because they bombed Pearl Harbor. My mother explains about before that. The Napkin Massacre. "*Nanking,*" she corrects me.

"Are you sure?" I say. "In school, they said the war was about putting the Jews in ovens."

"Also about ovens."

"About both?"

"Both."

"That's not what they said in school."

"*Just forget about school.*"

Forget about school? "I thought we moved here for the schools."

"We moved here," she says, "for your education."

Sometimes I have no idea what she's talking about.

"I like Sherman," I say after a while.

"He's nice boy," she agrees.

Meaning what? I would ask, except that my dad's just come home, which means it's time to start talking about whether we should build a brick wall across the front of the lawn. Recently a car made it almost into our living room, which was so scary, the driver fainted and an ambulance had to come. "We should have discussion," my dad said after that. And so for about a week, every night we do.

"Are you just friends, or more than just friends?" Barbara Gugelstein is giving me the cross-ex.

"Maybe," I say.

"Come on," she says, "I told you *everything* about me and Andy."

I actually *am* trying to tell Barbara everything about Sherman, but everything turns out to be nothing. Meaning, I can't locate the conversation in what I have to say. Sherman and I go places, we talk, one time my mother threw him out of the house because of World War II.

"I think we're just friends," I say.

"You think or you're sure?"

Now that I do less of the talking at lunch, I notice more what other people talk about—cheerleading, who likes who, this place in White Plains to get earrings. On none of these topics am I an expert. Of course, I'm still friends with Barbara Gugelstein, but I notice Danielle Meyers has spun away to other groups.

Barbara's analysis goes this way: To be popular, you have to have big boobs, a note from your mother that lets you use her Lord & Taylor credit card, and a boyfriend. On the other hand, what's so wrong with being unpopular? "We'll get them in the end," she says. It's what her dad tells her. "Like they'll turn out too dumb to do their own investing, and then they'll get killed in fees and then they'll have to move to towns where the schools stink. And my dad should know," she winds up. "He's a broker."

"I guess," I say.

But the next thing I know, I have a true crush on 145 Sherman Matsumoto. *Mister* Judo, the guys call him now, with real respect; and the more they call him that, the more I don't care that he carries a notebook with a cat on it.

I sigh. "Sherman."

"I thought you were just friends," says Barbara Gugelstein.

"We were," I say mysteriously. This, I've noticed, is how Danielle Meyers talks; everything's secret, she only lets out so much, it's like she didn't grow up with everybody telling her she had to share.

And here's the funny thing: The more I intimate that Sherman and I are more than just friends, the more it seems we actually are. It's the old imagination giving reality a nudge. When I start to blush; he starts to blush; we reach a point where we can hardly talk at all.

"Well, there's first base with tongue, and first base 150 without," I tell Barbara Gugelstein.

In fact, Sherman and I have brushed shoulders, which was equivalent to first base I was sure, maybe even second. I felt as though I'd turned into one huge shoulder; that's all I was, one huge shoulder. We not only didn't talk, we didn't breathe. But how can I tell Barbara Gugelstein that? So instead I say, "Well there's second base and second base."

Danielle Meyers is my friend again. She says, "I know exactly what you mean," just to make Barbara Gugelstein feel bad.

"Like *what* do I mean?" I say.

Danielle Meyers can't answer.

"You know what I think?" I tell Barbara the next 155 day. "I think Danielle's giving us a line."

Barbara pulls thoughtfully on one of her pigtails.

If Sherman Matsumoto is never going to give me an ID to wear, he should at least get up the nerve to hold my hand. I don't think he sees this. I think of the story he told me about his parents, and in a synaptic firestorm realize we don't see the same things at all.

So one day, when we happen to brush shoulders again, I don't move away. He doesn't move away either. There we are. Like a pair of bleachers, pushed together but not quite matched up. After a while, I have to breathe, I can't help it. I breathe in such a way that our elbows start to touch too. We are in a crowd, waiting for a bus. I crane my neck to look at the sign that says where the bus is going; now our wrists are touching. Then it happens: He links his pinky around mine.

Is that holding hands? Later, in bed, I wonder all night. One finger, and not even the biggest one.

Sherman is leaving in a month. Already! I think, well, 160 I suppose he will leave and we'll never even kiss. I guess that's all right. Just when I've resigned myself to it, though, we hold hands all five fingers. Once when we are at the bagel shop, then again in my parents' kitchen. Then, when we are at the playground, he kisses the back of my hand.

He does it again not too long after that, in White Plains.

I invest in a bottle of mouthwash.

Instead of moving on, though, he kisses the back of my hand again. And again. I try raising my hand, hoping he'll make the jump from my hand to my cheek. It's like trying to wheedle an inchworm out the window. You know, *This way, this way.*

All over the world, people have their own cultures. That's what we learned in social studies.

If we never kiss, I'm not going to take it personally. 165

It is the end of the school year. We've had parties. We've turned in our textbooks. Hooray! Outside the asphalt already steams if you spit on it. Sherman isn't leaving for another couple of days, though, and he comes to visit every morning, staying until the afternoon, when Callie comes home from her big-deal job as a bank teller. We drink Kool-Aid in the backyard and hold hands until they are sweaty and make smacking noises coming apart. He tells me how busy his parents are, getting ready for the move. His mother, particularly, is very tired. Mostly we are mournful.

The very last day we hold hands and do not let go. Our palms fill up with water like a blister. We do not care. We talk more than usual. How much airmail is to Japan, that kind of thing. Then suddenly he asks, will I marry him?

I'm only thirteen.

But when old? Sixteen?

If you come back to get me. 170

I come. Or you can come to Japan, be Japanese.

How can I be Japanese?

Like you become American. Switch.

He kisses me on the cheek, again and again and again.

His mother calls to say she's coming to get him. I 175 cry. I tell him how I've saved every present he's ever given me—the ruler, the pencils, the bags from the bagels, all the flower petals. I even have the orange peels from the oranges.

All?

I put them in a jar.

I'd show him, except that we're not allowed to go upstairs to my room. Anyway, something about the orange peels seems to choke him up too. *Mis*ter Judo, but I've gotten him in a soft spot. We are going together to the bathroom to get some toilet paper to wipe our

eyes when poor tired Mrs. Matsumoto, driving a shiny new station wagon, skids up onto our lawn.

"Very sorry!"

We race outside. 180

"Very sorry!"

Mrs. Matsumoto is so short that about all we can see of her is a green cotton sun hat, with a big brim. It's tied on. The brim is trembling.

I hope my mom's not going to start yelling about World War II.

"Is all right, no trouble," she says, materializing on the steps behind me and Sherman. She's propped the screen door wide open; when I turn I see she's waving. "No trouble, no trouble!"

"No trouble, no trouble!" I echo, twirling a few 185 times with relief.

Mrs. Matsumoto keeps apologizing; my mom keeps insisting she shouldn't feel bad, it was only some grass and a small tree. Crossing the lawn, she insists Mrs. Matsumoto get out of the car, even though it means trampling some lilies-of-the-valley. She insists that Mrs. Matsumoto come in for a cup of tea. Then she will not talk about anything unless Mrs. Matsumoto sits down, and unless she lets my mom prepare her a small snack. The coming in and the tea and the sitting down are settled pretty quickly, but they negotiate ferociously over the small snack, which Mrs. Matsumoto will not eat unless she can call Mr. Matsumoto. She makes the mistake of linking Mr. Matsumoto with a reparation of some sort, which my mom will not hear of.

"Please!"

"No no no no."

Back and forth it goes: "No no no no." "No no no no." "No no no no." What kind of conversation is that? I look at Sherman, who shrugs. Finally Mr. Matsumoto calls on his own, wondering where his wife is. He comes over in a taxi. He's a heavy-browed businessman, friendly but brisk—not at all a type you could imagine bowing to a lady with a taste for tie-on sun hats. My mom invites him in as if it's an idea she just this moment thought of. And would he maybe have some tea and a small snack?

Sherman and I sneak back outside for another farewell, by the side of the house, behind the forsythia bushes. We hold hands. He kisses me on the cheek again, and then—just when I think he's finally going to kiss me on the lips—he kisses me on the neck.

Is this first base?

He does it more. Up and down, up and down. First it tickles, and then it doesn't. He has his eyes closed. I close my eyes too. He's hugging me. Up and down. Then down.

He's at my collarbone.

Still at my collarbone. Now his hand's on my ribs. So much for first base. More ribs. The idea of second base would probably make me nervous if he weren't on his way back to Japan and if I really thought we were going to get there. As it is, though, I'm not in much danger of wrecking my life on the shoals of passion; his unmoving hand feels more like a growth than a boyfriend. He has his whole face pressed to my neck skin so I can't tell his mouth from his nose. I think he may be licking me.

From indoors, a burst of adult laughter. My eyelids flutter. I start to try and wiggle such that his hand will maybe budge upward.

Do I mean for my top blouse button to come accidentally undone?

He clenches his jaw, and when he opens his eyes, they're fixed on that button like it's a gnat that's been bothering him for far too long. He mutters in Japanese. If later in life he were to describe this as a pivotal moment in his youth, I would not be surprised. Holding the material as far from my body as possible, he buttons the button. Somehow we've landed up too close to the bushes.

What to tell Barbara Gugelstein? She says, "Tell me what were his last words. He must have said something last."

"I don't want to talk about it."

"Maybe he said, Good-bye?" she suggests. "Sayonara?" She means well.

"I don't want to talk about it."

"Aw, come on, I told you everything about—"

I say, "Because it's private, excuse me."

She stops, squints at me as though at a far-off face she's trying to make out. Then she nods and very lightly places her hand on my forearm.

The forsythia seemed to be stabbing us in the eyes. Sherman said, more or less, *You will need to study how to switch.*

And I said, *I think you should switch. The way you do everything is weird.*

And he said, *You just want to tell everything to your friends. You just want to have boyfriend to become popular.*

Then he flipped me. Two swift moves, and I went sprawling through the air, a flailing confusion of soft human parts such as had no idea where the ground was.

It is the fall, and I am in high school, and still he hasn't written, so finally I write him.

I still have all your gifts, I write. *I don't talk so much as I used to. Although I am not exactly a mouse either. I don't care about being popular anymore. I swear. Are you happy to be back in Japan? I know I ruined everything. I was just trying to be entertaining. I miss you with all my heart, and hope I didn't ruin everything.*

He writes back, *You will never be Japanese.*

I throw all the orange peels out that day. Some of them, it turns out, were moldy anyway. I tell my mother I want to move to Chinatown.

"Chinatown!" she says.

I don't know why I suggested it.

"What's the matter?" she says. "Still boy-crazy? That Sherman?"

"No."

"Too much homework?"

I don't answer.

"Forget about school."

Later she tells me if I don't like school, I don't have to go every day. Some days I can stay home.

"Stay home?" In Yonkers, Callie and I used to stay home all the time, but that was because the schools there were *waste of time.*

"No good for a girl be too smart anyway."

For a long time I think about Sherman. But after a while I don't think about him so much as I just keep seeing myself flipped onto the ground, lying there shocked as the Matsumotos get ready to leave. My head has hit a rock; my brain aches as though it's been shoved to some new place in my skull. Otherwise I am okay. I see the forsythia, all those whippy branches, and can't believe how many leaves there are on a bush—every one green and perky and durably itself. And past them, real sky. I try to remember about why the sky's blue, even though this one's gone the kind of indescribable gray you associate with the insides of old shoes. I smell grass. Probably I have grass stains all over my back. I hear my mother calling through the back door, "Mon-a! Everyone leaving now," and "Not coming to say good-bye?" I hear Mr. and Mrs. Matsumoto bowing as they leave—or at least I hear the embarrassment in my mother's voice as they bow. I hear their car start. I hear Mrs. Matsumoto directing Mr. Matsumoto how to back off the lawn so as not to rip any more of it up. I feel the back of my head for blood—just a little. I hear their chug-chug grow fainter and fainter, until it has faded into the whuzz-whuzz of all the other cars. I hear my mom singing, "Mon-a! Mon-a!" until my dad comes home. Doors open and shut. I see myself standing up, brushing myself off so I'll have less explaining to do if she comes out to look for me. Grass stains—just like I thought. I see myself walking around the house, going over to have a look at our churned-up yard. It looks pretty sad, two big brown tracks, right through the irises and the lilies-of-the-valley, and that was a new dogwood we'd just planted. Lying there like that. I hear myself thinking about my father, having to go dig it up all over again. Adjusting. I think how we probably ought to put up that brick wall. And sure enough, when I go inside, no one's thinking about me, or that little bit of blood at the back of my head, or the grass stains. That's what they're talking about—that wall. Again. My mom doesn't think it'll do any good, but my dad thinks we should give it a try. Should we or shouldn't we? How high? How thick? What will the neighbors say? I plop myself down on a hard chair. And all I can think is, we are the only complete family that has to worry about this. If I could, I'd switch everything to be different. But since I can't, I might as well sit here at the table for a while, discussing what I know how to discuss. I nod and listen to the rest. ○

SEEING

1. What does Mona mean when she refers to herself as "ad-libbing" her "way through eighth grade"? How does Gish Jen play with chronology in her narrative? When—and with what effect(s)—does she switch back and forth between childhood and adult perspectives? How does she signal that switch through tone of voice and word choice? Please point to specific examples to verify your reading.

2. Comment on Jen's use of metaphor and analogy in her story, such as "My parents slide the question back and forth like a cup of ginseng neither one wants to drink" (para. 1). What connections does Jen establish among food, class, and ethnicity?

Delivering spontaneously; saying or performing without preparation.

WRITING

1. Recall an experience you've had with stereotypes: either your own incorrect assumption about someone or someone's incorrect assumption about you. Write the first draft of a narrative essay in which you recount the incident, the circumstances that prompted it, and the consequences and lessons you might reasonably draw from it.

2. How do you interpret Jen's title, "What Means Switch"? When and with what effects does she use the word *switch* throughout the piece? Write an essay in which you analyze the meanings of the word *switch* within Mona's experiences with race and class issues. As you consider the use of *switch* within Jen's story, you might want to speculate about the extent to which each of us can "switch" race, class, and nationality as Americans.

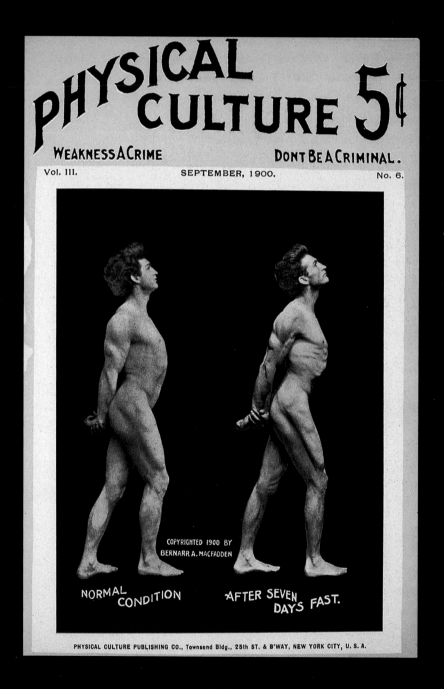

1900

HOW JOE'S BODY BROUGHT HIM FAME INSTEAD OF SHAME

I Can Make YOU A New Man, Too, in Only 15 Minutes A Day!

If YOU, like Joe, have a body that others can "push around"—if you're ashamed to strip for sports or a swim—then give me just 15 minutes a day! I'll PROVE you can have a body you'll be proud of, packed with red-blooded vitality! "*Dynamic Tension*." That's the secret! That's how I changed myself from a spindle-shanked, scrawny weakling to winner of the title, "World's Most Perfectly Developed Man."

Do you want big, broad shoulders—a fine, powerful chest—biceps like steel—arms and legs rippling with muscular strength—a stomach ridged with bands of sinewy muscle—and a build you can be proud of? Then just give me the opportunity to prove that "*Dynamic Tension*" is what you need.

"Dynamic Tension" Does It!

Using "*Dynamic Tension*" only 15 minutes a day,

in the privacy of your own room, you quickly begin to put on muscle, increase your chest measurements, broaden your back, fill out your arms and legs. Before you know it, this easy, NATURAL method will make you a finer specimen of REAL MANHOOD than you ever dreamed you could be! You'll be a New Man!

FREE BOOK

Send NOW for my FREE book. It tells about "*Dynamic Tension*," shows photos of men I've turned from weaklings into Atlas Champions, tells how I can do it for YOU. Don't put it off! Address me personally: Charles Atlas, Dept. 217B, 115 E. 23rd St., New York 10, N. Y.

Charles Atlas

—actual photo of the man who holds the title, "The World's Most Perfectly Developed Man."

How Relax-A-cizor Reduces the Size of your Waistline...

Effortless exercise does it while you REST!

What happened to your waistline? Have those belly muscles "stretched-out-of-shape"? And—you KNOW you need exercise but don't want to take the time.

NOW—there's a way! Now you can reduce the size of your abdomen and waistline . . . firm-up and tone those muscles with real exercise . . . while you REST at home! Or, do it at the office while you do your desk-work. About ½ hour a day is all the time it takes! Relax-A-cizor gives exercise WHILE YOU TAKE IT EASY!

▪ NOT A VIBRATOR ▪ NOT MASSAGE ▪ NOT A BICYCLE ▪ NOT A COUCH ▪ No weight loss! Relax-A-cizor does not cause or depend upon weight loss. Instead, it reduces SIZE by exercising and firming selected areas of muscles — and does this without effort. Doesn't make you tired; you REST while you use it. Watch TV. Take it easy — that's the Relax-A-cizor way.

▪ This is Relax-A-cizor being used with the abdominal belt. Slip it on and, in minutes, you're ready for your exercises while you REST!

Easy to use! Compact. All you do is put a pair of Relax-A-cizor pads on the body area you want reduced in size . . . twist a dial and, presto, you're exercising—really exercising—those muscles. Those abdominal muscles move 40 times a minute! 1200 times in a ½ hour! This concentrated, active exercise gives those waistline and abdominal muscles that "hold-you-in" a real workout!

Why Relax-A-cizor works. Many men lack good muscle tone because they don't get enough exercise. Relax-A-cizor exercises — but, without effort — such body areas as the waistline and abdomen 40 times a minute. This exercise firms and tones these muscles. Regular use causes these areas to reduce in size measurably to the extent these muscles lack tone because of insufficient exercise. And the less the muscle tone, the greater the degree of size reduction.

FOR WOMEN, TOO! Relax-A-cizor is the luxuriously effortless way to reduce the size of hips, waistline, abdomen and thighs. Relax-A-cizor beauty exercise tone and firm these muscles without a whit of work. Send coupon for free illustrated information.

OTHER USES, TOO: You'll use your Relax-A-cizor for restful, invigorating exercise of tense, tired muscles of shoulders, back, neck, arms and legs. Feels great!

FREE! Find out all about it. Send coupon TODAY and we'll mail you complete information and the free men's booklet "HOW TO REDUCE THE SIZE OF YOUR WAISTLINE." No cost. No obligation.

PRINCIPAL OFFICES: NEW YORK, NEW YORK, 575 Madison Ave., MU 8-4690/CHICAGO, ILL., 29 East Madison St., ST 2-5680/LOS ANGELES, CAL., 980 N. La Cienega Bl., OL 5-800. Available in Canada, Mexico City, Hong Kong, Manila, Milan *(foreign franchises available)*

RelaxAcizor®

©Relax-A-cizor 1967

ESQUIRE: JULY

Let us ask you something.
And tell us the truth.

Does it
matter to you
that if you skip a day
of running,
only
one person
in the world
will ever know?
Or
is that
one person
too many?

One less excuse to skip a day: the GEL-140™
Its substantial GEL® Cushioning System
can handle even the most mile-hungry feet.

asics

ALBERT BLISS

Albert Bliss originally published *Homeless Man Interviews Himself* in the 2001 issue of *Street News*—"the world's oldest active motivational homeless newspaper." Based in New York City, *Street News* is written, produced, and distributed by homeless people. Their mission is to "provide jobs and prevent homelessness." Bliss's article was later published in the September 2001 issue of *Harper's* magazine.

Bliss was born and raised in Newark, New Jersey. He began writing for *Street News* in 1996. Formerly a construction worker, he now travels around America, Canada, and Mexico spending time with other homeless people and writing about his experiences for homeless publications. According to the paper's editor, "Al prefers rescue missions to the public shelters, soup kitchens' food to panhandling, *Street News* to the *New York Times*."

Homeless Man Interviews Himself

Albert Bliss

Hello, my name is Albert Bliss. I am sitting on a long park bench across the street from Holy Apostles Soup Kitchen, located in Manhattan off Ninth Avenue on Twenty-sixth Street. I have just finished lunch and feel like interviewing myself. Since the interviewer and interviewee are the same person, I have split myself in half. I call the interviewer Mister Bliss and the interviewee Al.

MISTER BLISS: Please describe yourself.

AL: I am five feet ten inches tall and weigh 210 pounds. I am a homosexual, and I am HIV-negative. I like to smoke pot, but I am not a drug addict. I like to drink beer and often abuse the liquid. I like to loiter on park benches and talk to myself. I walk far distances. If there were a homeless marathon, I believe that I would take the gold in the long-distance walking event. Sometimes I walk around the border of Manhattan, starting at the Brooklyn Bridge, making my way north to the George Washington Bridge. It does not matter how long it takes. Last time it took me fifteen days.

MISTER BLISS: How long have you been homeless?

AL: Four years.

MISTER BLISS: Did you ever think you would be homeless?

AL: When I was a kid growing up in Newark, New Jersey, I saw homeless men all the time. I used to wonder, Where do they sleep, how do they get food, where do they go when they need to change their clothing?

  Some days I would see this older white man in Branch Brook Park. There was nothing special about him really. He was around fifty years old. He had short stumps for legs and always wore long baggy pants that he never cuffed. He had little hair and always tied a green neckerchief around his head. I thought of him as an Indian chief. I often hid behind a tree and watched the chief.

  Usually he was reading a discarded paper or riffling through a garbage can, drinking a beer from a big brown bottle or talking and answering himself as if he were two people. I never thought low of the chief because he was drinking a beer before school started. I knew there were reasons he did what he did, I just didn't know them. Other days, on my way home from school, I saw the chief chewing the rag and laughing with other trampy vagrants. Sometimes the poor men had a fire going in a park ash can, warming their hands and faces in winter. In the summertime they would cook hot dogs over the portable grill. I remember feeling jealous of their carefree lifestyle. No one to answer to and no rules to follow seemed to me like the best kind of life.

  Many years have passed. I'm forty-five years old now, but I never forget my homeless chief and his trampy friends from Branch Brook Park.

MISTER BLISS: Are you suggesting that the vagrant you spied on in a Newark park was a sort of hero during your adolescence?

AL: Yes.

MISTER BLISS: That's an interesting point of view. Most people would not think of a homeless idler as a worthy identification figure. Indeed, most New Yorkers would say that a city bum would be the worst role model a schoolchild could follow.

AL: Even though I was only twelve years old, I thought of these homeless riffraff as rugged individualists. I equated these men with great American pioneers I was studying in school, guys like Daniel Boone, Davy Crockett, and Jim Bowie. As I peeked at the men from behind that huge tree trunk I thought to myself, they had to be brave to camp outside, under the stars and moon every night. Though untidy and foul-mouthed, these sturdy outdoorsmen became my fearless real-life heroes. Of course I knew that they were poor and broken down. Of course I knew that they abused alcohol and didn't go to work. I was hiding behind the tree, but I wasn't hiding from the truth.

MISTER BLISS: Do you still consider "homeless riffraff" rugged individualists?

AL: Yes.

MISTER BLISS: Interesting.

AL: A man becomes a vagrant for different reasons. There are two groups of vagrants, basically. Both abuse drugs and drink but for different reasons. There's the vagrant who got frustrated and disgusted keeping up with the Joneses. These men got bored with the nine-to-five jig and now they drink and snort because there is nothing else to do. Then there is the other group of vagrants. These vagrants have had a serious one-to-one confrontation with meaninglessness. These men are cynical sourpusses, who dress like social losers and act defeated because they see no purpose to existence. This second group turns to substance abuse because life is pointless.

MISTER BLISS: What did you have for lunch?

AL: Hot dogs, beans, and salad. There was also a slice 20 of chocolate cake, but I gave that away.

MISTER BLISS: Would you please describe a typical day in the life of Albert Bliss?

AL: Yesterday I got up at 4:45—that's the time they throw the light switch at the rescue mission. I got dressed, straightened out my bunk-bed sheets, and folded the blanket. After I brushed my teeth I got in line. A hundred guys filed down three flights of stairs to the basement cafeteria. I ate a bowl of oatmeal, two buttered bagels, and drank hot tea. From six-thirty to ten-thirty, I waited at an employment agency for a per diem job, then took a spot at the end of Holy Apostle's soup line. After lunch I walked up to the Port Authority bus terminal and made a few bucks carrying travelers' luggage from Greyhound buses out to yellow cabs. I bought a bottle with the money I earned and drank some booze in Bryant Park. I chilled there until four o'clock and then made my move downtown. When I reached the mission I put my name on the lottery sheet for a bed, found a seat in the chapel, and waited for service to begin. What's the plan for today? Some jig as yesterday. Moving luggage from bus to cab. I need to make some coins.

MISTER BLISS: If food and shelter are free why do you need to work for money?

AL: I work to get jingle for liquor, cigarettes, and bus tickets. I like to travel. I also work per diem jobs to keep my mind off the "hot questions" of human life, like: Where do I come from? Who am I? Where am I going?

MISTER BLISS: Have these "hot questions" always 25 afflicted you?

AL: I used to keep myself busy, the way working people do, so that I would not be alone. Is this all there is? I tried to blot out the disturbing questions by working a full-time job. That did nothing to quell my anguish. I tried to distract myself by lifting barbells at a local gymnasium. That didn't work either. I did volunteer projects. But the relentless questioning of my inner tyrant persisted.

MISTER BLISS: Is it true that you purposely seek chaos in order to forget the painful questions?

AL: Yes, that's right. When I reach a big city, I can't despair over any answers to life's big problems. I need to be fearless and resourceful. When I'm broke and hungry and night is falling fast I must find my way to safety.

MISTER BLISS: You refer to street people as fearless. Could you explain?

AL: A neglected aspect of the homeless lifestyle is a 30 street man's persistent awareness of death. Street bums are brave individuals because they risk their lives, whether on the road or in their home state. A peaceful vagrant can do a face-to-face with a box blade as he stands in line with his food tray at Bowery Mission cafeteria. The homeless brother sleeping off a drunk in L.A.'s MacArthur Park can turn up strangled to death. A poor man waiting to get a bed at New Orleans's Ozanam Inn might suddenly find himself fighting for his life. At any time, at any place, the bad can go down and—poof! Constant danger is the homeless man's shadow.

MISTER BLISS: Well, we have come to the end of this interview. I want to thank you for your time and answers.

AL: Thank you. ○

SEEING

1. What message(s) about homelessness does Albert Bliss convey in this interview with himself? What, according to Bliss, are the two types of "vagrant" experiences? Based on the evidence in this interview, which category might Bliss identify with? Point to specific evidence to verify your response.

2. What are the effects of Bliss's use of a "split personality" in this interview? How does he use the split personality technique to convey his message? How would you characterize the voice of the interviewer? of the interviewee? What techniques does Bliss employ to establish each? In what ways are they similar or different?

WRITING

1. Prepare to conduct an interview of—and by—yourself. First, give your interviewer and interviewee a name and an identity, as Bliss does. Next, choose a specific journal or publication in which your interview will be published: a college newspaper or a national magazine or an online publication, for example. Then, write a letter to the editor in which you persuade the editor to authorize you to write the interview with yourself.

2. This interview by and with Albert Bliss originally appeared in an issue of *Street News*, a publication written and produced by homeless people. It then appeared in *Harper's* magazine, and now in this book on writing. Write an essay in which you explore how Bliss's interview might be read differently in each of these contexts. How would encountering Bliss's interview in each type of publication alter your reading experience and your overall impression of its effectiveness?

Homeless Man
Interviews Himself
Albert Bliss

Visualizing Composition
Purpose

Writers often respond to an initial impulse to explore a subject by articulating an idea about it. Thinking about *purpose* means converting that interest into a desire to say something specific about that subject. In effect, purpose gives intellectual shape and form to writing.

"I can't decide. I'm having a brand identity crisis."

Marisa Acocella, **"I Can't Decide"**

Purpose is the reason for writing—the intention that motivates and controls why and how we write. Purpose also provides a sense of direction for writing; we write with a goal in mind, with an end in view. Having a clear purpose for writing serves as a beacon that guides us along a path toward a specific compositional destination.

Each time you write, ask yourself what purpose you want your writing to serve. Is your essay meant, for example, to describe, to narrate, to explain, to convince, or to per-suade? What response(s) do you want your writing to evoke in the reader? What conse-quences do you want your writing to produce? Being able to articulate your purpose in writ-ing requires that you be clear about exactly what you are trying to accomplish.

Some of the most common purposes of expository writing are: to define, to classify, to illustrate, to compare and contrast, to draw analogies, to analyze, or to establish cause-and-effect relationships. If your purpose in writing is to convince an audience that a specific claim or proposition is verifiable with supporting evidence, then you are writing an argument and you are seeking to earn your readers' assent. If your purpose is to persuade, then you seek to dispose your audience to think and act in accordance with your will; you seek to earn their consent. Advertisements offer the most common examples of persuasion in American culture.

When the purpose of an essay is stated directly, it is often called the *thesis statement*. Although the thesis statement expresses what you are trying to achieve in writing, it does not explain fully your reasons for saying it. Your essay will be stronger—and the writing process easier—if you have a clear goal and thesis statement in mind at the outset.

Examine carefully the cartoon reprinted here. What purpose(s) can you identify in the image of the young woman holding up a sneaker to a salesman and saying, "I can't decide. I'm having a brand identity crisis"? What details does the cartoonist, Marisa Acocella, emphasize in order to underscore her purpose? Write the first draft of an argumentative essay in which you set out to convince your readers that Acocella has achieved her compositional purpose.

ART SPIEGELMAN >

Art Spiegelman was born in
Stockholm, Sweden, in 1948 and
moved with his parents to the
borough of Queens in New York
City when he was 3 years old. By
the age of 14 he had created a
satire magazine, and when he
was 15 he was selling drawings
to the Topps Chewing Gum
Company. Spiegelman is the
only person to win the Pulitzer
Prize for fiction for a comic book,
Maus (1991), a World War II fable
about the Holocaust. It was
based on the experience of his
parents, who survived the Nazi
death camps. In the comic book
the Germans are portrayed as
cats, the Jews as mice, and the
Poles as pigs.

Spiegelman sees nothing odd
about addressing a very weighty
subject in what had been a very
light medium. Comics are his
form of communication—the
only way, he says, that he knows
how to tell a story. They are also
his medium for understanding,
for "trying to understand myself
and trying to understand other
things." In the process, he has
expanded the breadth of what
can be done with drawings and
visual images, and he has almost
single-handedly shown that
comics can be of interest to serious readers. Spiegelman serves
as editor (along with Françoise
Mouly) and contributor in his
latest book, *Strange Stories for
Strange Kids* (2001), the second
in a two-volume series of illustrated fairytales and stories.

Art Spiegelman, **Mein Kampf, 1996** >

I WAS JUST ANOTHER BABY-BOOM BOY...

I GREW UP IN QUEENS...

I LOVED COMIX...

MY PARENTS SURVIVED AUSCHWITZ.

IT'S ALL A MATTER OF RECORD: I MADE A COMIC BOOK ABOUT IT... YOU KNOW...THE ONE WITH JEWISH MICE AND NAZI CATS.

ME(IN)ST(RUGGLE)PF

I STILL PROWL THE MURKY CAVERNS OF MY MEMORY, BUT NOW I FEEL LIKE THERE'S A 5,000-POUND MOUSE BREATHING DOWN MY NECK!

...REMEMBERING THOSE WHO REMEMBERED THE DEATH CAMPS IS A HARD ACT TO FOLLOW.

YOU'VE GOTTA BOIL EVERYTHING DOWN TO ITS ESSENCE IN COMIX...

REPRESSED MEMORIES

IT'S A GREAT MEDIUM FOR ARTISTS WHO CAN'T REMEMBER MUCH ANYWAY.

EROTIC MEMORIES

NEUROTIC MEMORIES

"WRITE WHAT YOU KNOW" IS THE FIRST COMMANDMENT IN ALL THE MANUALS.

BUT IT'S KIND OF A PROBLEM FOR ME... I DON'T REALLY KNOW ANYTHING!

INTRAUTERINE MEMORIES

CHILDHOOD MEMORIES

I ONCE SAW A BOOK WHOSE TITLE SUMMED IT ALL UP: "MEMOIRS OF AN AMNESIAC."

...BUT I CAN'T REMEMBER WHO WROTE IT OR EVEN IF I EVER READ IT.

CAPTAIN VIDEO

COOTIE

CAREERS

STAMPS

I WAS JUST ANOTHER BABY-BOOM BOY...

Fort Tryon Park c. 1956

SNAPSHOTS ILLUMINATE MY PAST LIKE FLARES IN THE DARKNESS...

FAMILY ALBUM

ALTHOUGH OFTEN THEY ONLY HELP ME REMEMBER HAVING SEEN THE PHOTOS BEFORE!

MAN, I LOVED MY CISCO KID OUTFIT. I WANTED TO BE A COWBOY BECAUSE I LIKED THE WAY THEY DRESSED.

I WORE IT TILL IT WAS WAY TOO SMALL FOR ME AND I'D WORN IT THROUGH AT THE KNEE,

AND THAT HOWDY DOODY PUPPET— IF I COULDN'T BE A COWBOY I WAS WILLING TO SETTLE FOR PUPPETEER... OR CARTOONIST. MY PARENTS —

PAPA! PAPA!

SHH! NOT RIGHT NOW, DASH! PAPA'S BUSY SOLILOQUIZING.

BUT PAPA! WE WERE WATCHING "KING KONG," AND IT WAS SCARY!...

MY PARENTS DIED BEFORE I HAD ANY KIDS.

IT'S OKAY... IT WAS ONLY A STORY!

SNF... HE WAS CLIMBING ON THE BUILDING AND TH'THEY KILLED HIM!

Dashiell, 1995

I WISH KING KONG JUST ATE THE GIRL...

THEN THERE WOULDN'T BE ANY TROUBLE!

THE KNEE ON DASH'S SUPERMAN PAJAMAS IS RIPPED.

DASH IS FOUR YEARS OLD, AND HIS SISTER IS ALMOST NINE. (TWO OF THEIR GRANDPARENTS SURVIVED AUSCHWITZ.)

SEEING

1. How would you describe the subject of this work of comic art? What does Spiegelman reveal about his personal history, his work, and his artistic sensibility in this selection? What expectations of—and cultural associations with—the narrator does the first line of *Mein Kampf* establish? What attributes does being "just another baby-boom boy" conjure?

2. What is the effect of the repetition of the first line: "I was just another baby-boom boy"? How does the juxtaposition of the snapshot in the second instance change your reading of the line? Comment on Spiegelman's use of the two snapshots. How do they provide contrast to the illustrations? To what extent do they blend in with the illustrations?

WRITING

1. " 'Write what you know' is the first commandment in all the manuals," writes Spiegelman. Create a mini self-portrait by choosing several snapshots of yourself from different periods in your life and writing brief descriptions to accompany—and to serve as glosses on—each of these photos. You might focus on descriptions of your experience at the moment captured in the photograph, or you might present your thinking about the photos in retrospect. Finally, place these photos in a sequence, thereby creating your own version of comic art.

2. What does Spiegelman mean when he says, "You've gotta boil everything down to its essence in comix"? To what extent do you agree with this assessment of the medium? Choose a comic from a local paper, magazine, or web site. Write an argumentative essay in which you support or refute Spiegelman's assertion, drawing on the comic you've chosen as evidence to confirm each of your assertions.

MOYRA DAVEY

"My photographs fall into a tradition of documentary objectivity," says Moyra Davey, "in that they are very much about the thing depicted . . . close-ups of the historical vignettes you find on American money; a newsstand on which you can read all the little hand-made signs a vendor has put up; book shelves blanketed with dust, etc. But I also try and have the photographs speak to more abstract ideas such as time, history, entropy, and the poignancy of certain human behaviors and proclivities like hoarding and collecting."

Davey's photographs have appeared in *Harper's*, *Grand Street*, *Documents*, and the *New York Times*. For three years her photography "took a back seat" to her role as the editor of *Mother Reader: Essential Writings on Motherhood* (2001), an anthology of essays, memoirs, and stories about motherhood by women writers. "I don't want to sound too overblown about this," said Davey in an interview, "but my strongest feeling about *Mother Reader*, and that's partly what's implied by the title, is that it is a book for readers, people who believe that the written word can change and save lives." Moyra Davey currently lives and works in New York City.

Moyra Davey, **The City**

SEEING

1. Moyra Davey's image presents a nontraditional take on the self-portrait by using such ordinary objects as books or a desk top to convey a sense of self-identity. What do you notice when you examine the objects presented in this image of a desk top? Which object attracts your attention first? Which holds your attention the longest? Explain why. What relationship does Davey establish between and among the objects shown? For example, does she convey any sense of hierarchy in arranging them? What perspective and attitude does she establish through the size, shape, and color of the objects presented? What overall sense of identity is embodied in these objects?

2. Recall more specifically your reaction to the objects presented in this photograph. For example, how did your eye move as you viewed the objects? At what point did you begin to draw inferences from what you observed? What were those inferences? How would you characterize the overall impression created by Davey's photograph? Comment on the appropriateness and significance of the title, *The City*.

WRITING

1. Make a list of the objects that are most important for you to have access to when you are writing. Make some notes about the significance of each. If you were to produce a composite portrait of yourself using these objects, which ones would you include? Why? How would you arrange them on your desk? Write an expository essay in which you explain how, taken as a whole, these objects can be said to embody a sense of your identity to someone who doesn't know you well.

2. The next time you look at your desk—or at the place where you do most of your writing and reading—try to re-see this space with the powerful simplicity of doing a "double take." Choose one object on which to focus your attention. You might want to photograph it as well. Make a series of observations that demonstrate your responsiveness to the object and convey the sense that you see it in a changed way—as a newly understood expression of your own identity. Then write a descriptive essay in which you present the object in great detail—in order to promote your readers' appreciation of how the object might be viewed as an expression of your identity.

Looking Closer
Self-Fashioning

Americans are continually reinventing themselves, whether they are inspired by infomercials, makeovers on talk shows, or ads for the hottest line of clothing. Whether we consider ourselves "fashion victims" or "trend setters," each of us creates and expresses identities through our physical appearance and by associating ourselves with particular objects, roles, and fashion images and statements. How do you create an identity for yourself? How do you choose to represent your personal style?

The selections that follow express different approaches to embodying identity. Cindy Jackson chose to reshape herself—through a series of nineteen operations that took her to **"Cindy Jackson 1998"**—into the literal embodiment of the classic Barbie Doll. As both the subject and artist of her work portraying memorable characters, Cindy Sherman began as an undergraduate (as *untitled #8* highlights) to reinvent herself in the identity of others. Yet the supermodel RuPaul, America's most popular man in women's clothing and the self-proclaimed "Queen of All Media," remains "comfortable" representing either gender. The photographer Nikki S. Lee provides revealing glimpses into the ways in which American teenagers draw their self-identity from traditional and iconoclastic roles. And Joe Queenan's **"Skin Game"** and Lynn Johnson's *Nose Piercing* offer glimpses into the significance of the tattoo and body piercing within the different spaces of personal and public life.

The Skin Game

Joe Queenan.

The Skin Game

Joe Queenan

MY FATHER DIED ON A FRIDAY EVENING IN DECEMBER 1997. This was a bad day for him, a bad day for me and a bad day for the tattoo world. Like many World War II vets, my father sported several hideous tattoos. Each bicep was adorned with crude blue markings that were a testament not only to how much he must have been drinking the night in Frisco he got them but also to how much the tattooist must have been drinking. Judging from the dermal carnage, it looked as if a one-eyed Maltese loan shark had ripped open my father's arms with a backhoe, carved a crude image of a heart and arrow, stilettoed a few words with a rusty penknife, filled up the gaping holes with a gallon of toxic waste, and stitched the whole mess back together with piano wire. Ostensibly, the tattoos symbolized Dad's affection for his mother and someone named Eileen (my mother's name was Agnes), but in the end they seemed more like testimonials to the anesthetizing powers of Jack Daniel's.

Leaving the hospital after saying good-bye to my father for the last time, I could not help remarking upon this matter. I told my younger sister Mary Ann what a shame it would be that when Dad's body was cremated, the tattoos would be cremated too. The world would be diminished by their passing, for they symbolized a way of looking at life that the rest of us were not likely to see again. This attitude was a mixture of youthful bravado, working-class insolence,

and the aforementioned fondness for alcohol, fused together in the kind of unrehearsed streets-of–North Philadelphia insouciance that has all but vanished from this preening, calculating society. Dad and his friends were boys who were going off to fight a war. They drank a lot. They smoked a lot. Inevitably, they got tattoos.

Not that I envied him or his tattoos. No, from the time I was old enough to pronounce the word *tattoos*, I thought they were stupid. At first this was because I took to heart the Catholic Church's teaching that the body is the temple of the Lord and that any self-imposed mutilation (with the possible exception of ritual flagellation) is anathema in the eyes of God. Then, between the ages of 9 and 11, I briefly contemplated a life of crime and wisely decided that easily identified body markings would be a major impediment to my success. But perhaps the most compelling reason I never seriously thought about paying some well-traveled drunk to mutilate my body was that tattoos immediately identified you as a member of the working class, and from an early age I'd decided that the industrial proletariat was going to have to go on without me. When the nuns would ask what we wanted to be when we grew up, most of my classmates in parochial school would say, "I want to be a fireman" or "I want to be a nurse" or "I want to be a truck driver." But when it came my turn to reply, I would beam: "I want to be a member of the bourgeoisie." And the bourgeoisie and tattoos didn't mix.

In the decades between grade school and my father's death, my attitude toward tattoos never wavered. Tattoos were fine if you were a sailor or a biker or a jock or a serial killer, but they really had no place in the rarefied world of satire, my chosen profession. Although I respected my father and his tattoos and the society that produced people like my father and their tattoos, I respected them in the same way I respected the people who built Stonehenge. If it made you happy to drag gigantic rocks all the way from Wales to southern England just so you could arrange them in some weird post-Jurassic chronometric pattern, hey, be my guest. But don't ask me to get involved. Ditto tattoos.

On December 19, 2000, the third anniversary of 5 my father's death, I was jostled from my sleep by an ominous specter. At first I thought it must be the Four Horsemen of the Apocalypse, but, no, it was Dad. Although the flickering light engulfing his body made it hard to determine his facial expression, I could see that he was wearing the same hospital gown he'd been wearing the night of his death, with the tattoos fully visible. As I rubbed the sleep from my eyes, he pointed to the tattoo on his left arm.

"What do you think of it?" he asked.

"It's great," I replied. "Very classy. I've always admired it."

"So why don't you have one?"

"For the same reason you haven't read Schopenhauer, Dad. You have your tastes, and I have mine. We've been through this a thousand times."

My father's steely expression never changed. 10

"Honor thy father," he intoned, pointing at the tattoo on the right shoulder. "Get one."

And then he vanished into the abyss.

Dad's nocturnal visitation was quite a jolt. For one, he hadn't asked about anybody else in the family. Two, he hadn't mentioned the Phillies' perennially horrible off-season maneuvers. Three, he was no longer smoking. One thing was clear: If Dad, who didn't like to travel, had come all the way back from the grave to talk about tattoos, there must be a reason for it. Perhaps there was some unwritten law in the next world that a tattooed man could not report to his eternal resting place until his son had inherited his tattoos. Assuming this was the case, I immediately suspended all my philosophical antipathy toward body markings and began shopping for a tattoo. I did not want one, I did not need one, and I certainly did not think that a tattoo was going to advance my career. But if it would help out Dad Up There, I would get one. A small one.

Tattoo shopping proved to be a distressing experience. Once the preserve of motorcycle gangs, hardened criminals, and men who had seen action in conflicts both foreign and domestic, tattoos began to lose their primordial symbolic value once people like Cher started getting them. As tattoo shops surfaced in suburban malls across the country, and as the term *body art* began to geyser into the lexicon of the hoi polloi, it became apparent that tattoos were slowly losing their power to daunt, shock, or amaze. But more important, they were rapidly being stripped of their traditional connotations as emblems of blue-collar lunacy, alcohol abuse, and temporary insanity. More and more, they were becoming the province of middle-class wannabes, commuters, and show-offs.

This much became clear when I made my initial 15 foray into the world of storefront self-mutilation. Eyeballing the people drifting in and out of the tattoo parlors on St. Mark's Place in New York's East Village, I was struck by how few sailors, bikers, felons, or bona fide urban-swamp trash seemed to be included in the clientele. Most of the people had a depressingly generic appearance. Punks who got to the party twenty-five years too late. Overdressed Jersey thuglets. Surly college kids. Feisty Smurfs. Iconoclastic grad students. And one or two people who actually looked like sous-chefs.

"Sous-chefs!" hissed my father when I apprised him of my findings that evening, when he made the second of his visits. "God-damn sous-chefs!"

"That's right, Dad: sous-chefs. The world of tattoos has really changed since your era; it's not like the good old days during the war. These days, housewives get tattoos. Schoolteachers get tattoos. And because of a statewide ban on body art (since lifted), I hear that a day-care center up in Boston held a tattoo party for the entire staff. A day-care center! Believe me, Dad, tattoos have been utterly stripped of all meaning as cultural semaphores."

I was hoping he would take the hint. It had always been obvious that I thought tattoos were gross; now I was suggesting that I thought they were frivolous. Dad thought about this for a second, then shook his head.

"I still want you to get a tattoo. You're my only son!"

"But Dad!"

"Get a tattoo!!!"

And then, as was to become of his pattern, he vanished into the night.

For the next week, we went back and forth like this every evening. I would go to a tattoo emporium during the day and present a crudely drawn picture of my Dad's tattoos. Invariably, a man who looked as if he'd just let Hieronymus Bosch use his forearms and neck as an easel would quote me a price. It was usually around $150. Then a world-weary young woman would suggest that I come back the next day and ask for "Scott."

"They've got people named Scott doing tattoos these days, Dad!" I would fume at my father's specter that evening. "And if Scott's not in, they recommend Erik. Or Reynaldo. Oh, how the mighty are fallen!"

"Jesus, I'll say," Dad would fret. "What ever happened to Shanghai, Butch, Fritz the Greek, and Mickey Three-Thumbs?"

"Your guess is as good as mine, Pop. You have no idea what it's like out there. It's enough to make you swear off tattoos forever. By the way, did you get a chance to watch that tape of Queen Latifah's show I made for you?"

"I did."

"Did you see the woman named Shelica with the tattoo on her shoulder? The one who can't get any dates because men think her standards are too high? Is that what you're asking me to do? You want me to go around looking like a woman named Shelica? Say it ain't so, Dad."

He thought about it for a minute.

"Stop making excuses."

"I'm not making excuses. But you're not being reasonable. Customer-service reps at Kinko's have tattoos. Stand-up comics have tattoos. Assistant producers at daytime shows on the Food Network have tattoos, usually reading 'Only the Strong Survive.' Believe me, Dad, the thrill is gone."

Despite what I felt were irrefutable arguments against contemporary body art, he refused to budge from his position. It was a man's duty to write a book, plant a tree, and have a son. It was a son's duty to get a tattoo when his father told him to. There was no room for further discussion.

One day I was walking down Avenue A when a fat man whose face was covered with tattoos strolled past. I had just stopped by a tattoo parlor filled with computers and fax machines and run by a guy who looked like Elvis Costello, only with white socks, when Queequeg himself came ambling into my life. Now very much a habitué of *mondo tattoisto*, I engaged the illustrated man in conversation. I asked him if he'd gotten all his tattoos at one time, and he said no. I asked him if he'd gotten the job done locally, and he said no. I asked him if he was finished tattooing his face, and he said no. He really wasn't all that chatty a guy, and he strolled away before I'd worked up the nerve to ask him what happened to facial tattoos as you got older and fatter and the crown of thorns on Jesus' head started spreading to your ears. But I was thankful for the tête-à-tête, because he'd provided me with plenty of ammunition when I confronted my father that evening.

"Tattoos are like drugs, Dad. You start with a couple of puffs of marijuana, and before you know it you're hooked on heroin. If I start out by getting a little tattoo on my shoulder, I know that I'll end up with a picture of Christ crucified—with Mary Magdalene, the Sanhedrin, the Pharisees, the holy of holies, the Knights Templars, and the entire Roman Empire—tattooed all over my face. I have an addictive personality."

"Get the tattoo, Joe. Stop beating around the bush." 35

"You have no idea what you're asking me to do, Dad. Every bozo in America is getting a tattoo these days. Believe me, it's not a badge of honor anymore. If you want me to do something that will test my manhood and serve as an undying memorial to your spirit, let me pluck out my toenails or cut off one of my fingers or undergo genital mutilation. But don't ask me to get a tattoo. Pain I can deal with. Humiliation is a whole other thing."

It was as if I were speaking to a brick wall.

"Get a tattoo," he said. "Tomorrow. Get a tattoo or you will have to deal with me and all the powers of hell."

And saying this, he vanished into the ether.

I spent another long day wandering around the 40 East Village. Although the tattoo parlors I visited said that they would prefer an artist's rendering of the image I wanted, they said they could work with my crude drawing. But they stressed that because the technological infrastructure of tattooing had evolved so much since Pearl Harbor, it would not be possible to make tattoos as primitive and ugly as the ones my father had. I briefly flirted with the idea of mentioning that to Dad but decided such high-tech banter was probably over his head. Glumly, I headed home.

That night, right on time. Dad emerged from the mist at five past midnight. I decided I would take one last crack at changing his mind. If that didn't work, I'd throw in the towel and get a tattoo the following day.

"Dad, I know a female journalist who writes for *Esquire* who has a tattoo . . ."

"I don't care."

"I know a maître d' who has a tattoo," I ventured. "He's not even one of those pushy, intimidating maître d's who insist their hearts will shatter if you don't at least taste the *cassoulet avec confit de canard*."

"I still don't care . . ." 45

Backed into a corner, I played my ace in the hole. Producing the latest issue of *YM* magazine, I thrust it into my father's face. The cover featured the Backstreet Boys, clad in black leather. Two were doing the usual smile-on-demand thing. Two were waxing pouty. But way over there in the corner, all by himself, was the sultry, rebellious Backstreet Boy, decked out in his shades and orange hair and winsome Fu Manchu. He was the Maverick. He was the Loner. He was the scary Backstreet Boy. And on his crossed arms, stretching as far as the eyes could see, were tattoos in all shapes and sizes.

My dad studied the picture. He was obviously taken aback.

Shattered, in fact.

"Who does this guy think he is?" my father asked.

"*El Bado Dudo*." I replied. "And I can't vouch for 50 this, but I think one of the guys in 98° may also have a tattoo. Though obviously not one as intimidating and iconographically prepossessing as this one."

I could see that the magazine cover had left my father devastated. Nothing in life—or death—had prepared him for this moment. He looked like a little boy who'd just found out that there wasn't a Santa Claus or, worse, that Bobby Thompson knew Ralph Branca was throwing him a fastball on the next pitch because the Giants had been stealing the catcher's signals and relaying them to the batters all game. The cocksuckers.

Sadly, he handed back the magazine.

"I won't bother you anymore," he mumbled as he began to recede into the all-encompassing darkness. Then, just as his outline faded into complete obscurity, I heard him say the words I would treasure forever:

"You did the right thing, son. I'm proud of you."

I looked down at my shoulders, which had recently 55 come oh so close to complete mutilation in a tawdry, nonsurgical environment.

Then I looked down at the picture of the Backstreet Boys.

Thanks, guys.

I owe you one. ○

Cindy Jackson, 1973   Cindy Jackson, 1998

Cindy Sherman, **untitled #8**

I'm comfortable

being a MAN

Rockport

rupaul, drag superstar

be comfortable. uncompromise.® start with your feet.

Lynn Johnson, **Nose Piercing**

Nikki S. Lee, **The Skateboarders' Project (#8)**

Nikki S. Lee, **The Tourist Project (#9)**

JOE QUEENAN

Joe Queenan's latest book, *Balsamic Dreams: A Short but Self-Important History of the Baby Boomer Generation* (2001), might just say it all in the title. On page eleven of the chapter humorously entitled "J'Accuse," Queenan writes: "The single most damning, and obvious, criticism that can be leveled at Baby Boomers is, of course, that they promised they wouldn't sell out and become fiercely materialistic like their parents, and then they did." Queenan, a funny man and a prolific writer, was born in Philadelphia, Pennsylvania, and today lives in Tarrytown with his wife and children. An astute critic of American pop culture, he has written seven books. Formerly an editor at *Spy* and *Forbes* magazines, Queenan has had his work published in numerous publications, including the *New York Times*, the *New Republic*, *Cosmopolitan*, and *Playboy*.

CINDY JACKSON

Cindy Jackson was, in her own words, "a homely, dumpy farm girl in Ohio," but with the help of cosmetic surgery she transformed herself into a close facsimile of her personal model of perfection, the Barbie Doll. Between her high school graduation in 1973 and her public debut in 1993, Jackson underwent over nineteen operations to alter her face, breasts, and other parts of her body. The unusually narrow waist, large bust, and high arched eyebrows of the classic Barbie Doll are trademarks of Jackson's "living doll" look.

As the founder of the Cosmetic Surgery Network, Jackson spends her days promoting the power of "surgical enhancements," urging women to gain power and influence through improved looks. In a culture defined by physical perfection, she argues, beauty is a commodity that can be purchased like any other.

LYNN JOHNSON

Lynn Johnson's photographs appear regularly in *National Geographic*, *Life*, *Sports Illustrated*, and many of the world's leading publications. She has traveled to the ends of the globe, "eating rats with Vietcong guerillas," recording the lives of monks in Tibet, and climbing the radio antenna on top of Chicago's Hancock Tower—though she writes that some of her favorite assignments have been capturing ordinary people in extraordinary circumstances (a family struggling with AIDS, an athlete learning to compete with artificial legs, or musicians volunteering to play for the dying).

Among her numerous books are *Pittsburgh Moments*, her first, and *We Remember: Women Born at the Turn of the Century*, her most recent (1999). She has contributed to many of the *Day in the Life* series of books and to the groundbreaking social commentaries *Material World* (1994) and *Women in the Material World* (1997).

NIKKI S. LEE

Photographer Nikki S. Lee was born in 1970 in Kye-Chang, South Korea. Lee is best known for capturing images of herself while assuming various identities. *The Tourist Project* and *The Skateboarders' Project* are featured in her collection of self-portraits entitled *Projects* (2001). As the introduction to the collection explains, Lee "identifies a particular group in society and infiltrates it over a period of weeks or months. She will drastically alter her hair, her weight, her clothes," the intro continues. "More subtly, she will take on the mannerisms, the gestures, the way of carrying oneself characteristic of the group she has chosen. After entering into her new identity, she will hand her point-and-shoot camera to someone and ask to have a snapshot taken of her in the chosen milieu." Lee earned degrees in photography and fashion at New York University and the Fashion Institute of Technology, respectively. She currently lives and works in New York City.

CINDY SHERMAN

Cindy Sherman positions herself on both sides of her camera lenses, acting as photographer and photographed subject. In 1977 she began her work, continuing until she had produced sixty-nine photographs—a collection she called *Untitled Film Stills*, which the Museum of Modern Art acquired in 1995. Her goal is not for her audience to gaze at many pictures of herself but rather that they see their own selves in her portraiture. Onlookers might recognize themselves in the posture of the person in Sherman's photos or in the way the subject's hair falls across her face. Sherman's objective is to capture the many masks of femininity. She was born in 1954 in New Jersey and now lives and works in New York.

RUPAUL

According to supermodel RuPaul, "Whether we are at work or at play we are all wearing masks and playing roles all the time. Like I've always said, 'you're born naked and the rest is drag.'" Born Andre Charles in San Diego, RuPaul is today's most popular man in woman's clothing. The self-named "Queen of All Media" is a celebrity whose talents include singing, modeling, acting, and hosting his own TV talk show.

RuPaul's first album, *Supermodel of the World* (1993), topped the charts for several months. In 1998 he recorded a Christmas album that included new versions of popular classics, such as "RuPaul the Red Nosed Drag Queen" and "I Saw Daddy Kissing Santa Claus."

His autobiography, *Lettin It All Hang Out* (1995), was also a popular success and is now in its third printing.

SEEING

1. Joe Queenan has written an engaging account of his continued struggles with his father's penchant for tattoos. What is the nature of Queenan's resistance to following his father's lead into the tattoo parlor? List the substantive points he makes to justify his resistance. What arguments did he find himself vulnerable to? How did he overcome them? Despite his reluctance to have a tattoo, in what other ways does Queenan establish an identity for himself in this essay? What is your own attitude toward having a tattoo? What arguments can you make in support of—or in resistance to—having a tattoo? In what ways have you considered fashioning an identity for yourself?

2. Examine the additional visual accounts of self-fashioning presented in this Looking Closer section: two photographs of the same woman after nineteen operations to change her appearance, a photo of a young woman pretending to be someone else, a photo of a woman with a pierced nose looking into a mirror, an ad featuring a drag queen promoting a traditional line of shoes, and two photographs depicting teenage stereotypes. As you study each of these images, make detailed notes about the ways in which each photographer and artist engages in self-fashioning. Who among these "authors" of self-fashioning do you think succeeds most effectively? Explain why.

WRITING

1. Joe Queenan cites the Catholic Church as the source of his long-held belief "that the body is the temple of the Lord and that any self-imposed mutilation (with the possible exception of ritual flagellation) is anathema in the eyes of God" (para. 3). Trace the origins of one of your long-held beliefs, be it religious or secular. What were the circumstances that led you to adopt this belief? How did you fashion an identity for yourself that enabled you to incorporate this belief into your daily life? Write a narrative essay in which you recount the circumstances that led you to adopt—and perhaps reject—this belief. How did you succeed in fashioning a self-identity while responding to the pressure of this belief?

2. How would you respond to those who claim that body piercing is a form of self-mutilation, a danger to the person's health, and an expression of antisocial behavior that ought to be prohibited by law? What points would you make in defense of the right to pierce any part of the body one chooses? Write an argumentative essay in which you summon as much evidence as possible to argue one side of this issue.

377

Producing America

Chapter 5
Producing America

From its earliest existence as a fabled "New World," America has always been as much a place dreamed of—a site of hope and expectation—as it has been a real place to be lived in. This distinction—and, often, discontinuity—between potential and actual Americas has been one of the most traditional features of American culture.

The first book published about America written in English—Thomas Hariot's *A Briefe and True Report of the New Found Lande of Virginia* (1588)—was filled with extraordinary observations detailing the geography, natural resources, as well as the civilization of the inhabitants of the "New World." Commissioned by Sir Walter Raleigh, Hariot's *Briefe and True Report*, along with the watercolors of the artist John

White, lured generations of immigrants to this wondrous new land. In reality, the land they found was a far cry from that promised by Hariot's promotional pamphlet—actually quite inhospitable, unprofitable, and in many ways incomprehensible.

America has always been—and remains—a "storied land," a place in which it is increasingly difficult to separate hype from reality, copy from original, image from actual. In many instances, as several of the essays in this chapter illustrate, the simulated America appears more real in our imaginations than the real one.

Perhaps the most visible contemporary example of the notion of "producing America" is Disneyland. This simulated, miniature "land" provides visitors with a hyper-concentrated version of a "real" America: main street, friendly faces, fireworks. Such "produced" versions of America simplify and condense the American experience in order to make it replicable—and therefore purchasable. When you can buy it, representation does not exist at one remove from reality nor does it reproduce reality. It replaces it.

In virtually every respect, America is a constructed space. Often described as "Nature's nation," this country has been carved out by succeeding generations of settlers, each creating "clearings" in the landscape as they eagerly moved further and further westward, lured there by the extravagant promises of what America could produce for them. Such expansion generated unprecedented economic growth and fueled the rapid development of systems of mass production and consumption. By the beginning of the twentieth century, the U.S. Patent Office was issuing more patents to corporations than to individuals. As the pace of mass production accelerated, individuality became less valued, especially in matters of substance and style. What Ralph Waldo Emerson had once extolled as the virtues of "an original relation to the universe" were now challenged by corporate appeals to a commercialized, generic version of "you."

In more recent decades, the value of originality has decreased as profits generated by repetition and duplication rise. Foundational phrases such as "life, liberty, and the pursuit of happiness" are increasingly co-opted by advertising slogans coined by marketers. If the language and images of politics and culture once centered around concrete issues of country and identity, today they are generated by corporations whose bottom line is profit. In such an environment, authenticity and certainty can seem increasingly remote.

Andreas Gursky, **99 Cent,** 1999

As America becomes a space defined as much by Tommy Hilfiger as by history, the lines are blurring between high art and popular culture, between the news and entertainment. While movies such as—to name but a few—*The Patriot* and *Saving Private Ryan* appear to depend on history for their plots, they ultimately celebrate myths and stereotypes more than they actually document the past.

Maintaining a critical distance from such well-orchestrated productions of American culture has provoked heightened anxiety and insecurity about America's self-image as well as about individual identity in a culture dominated by objects. Figuring out what it means—in principle and practice—to be an American and an individual at the outset of the twenty-first century is no longer a simple assignment in reciting traditional political maxims. The widely varying social, political, and economic circumstances of contemporary experience within—and beyond—this nation's borders make this responsibility ever more challenging, and all the more essential.

What was described as a "culture of narcissism" in the 1970s might more accurately be characterized now as a "culture of consumption"—a culture increasingly mirrored in societies around the world. More and more dependent on whatever terms and images are widely distributed, contemporary individuals appropriate these values as they struggle to articulate personal identity and social ideals. Analyzing—rather than simply consuming—language and imagery that seek to *re*-produce America as a place and a way of living is an important responsibility for any citizen and student of America.

ANDREAS GURSKY

German photographer Andreas Gursky was born in Leipzig, Germany, in 1955 and has spent most of his life in Düsseldorf. His technique has ranged widely—from the documentary, which required the artist to train his lens on the subjects at hand and capture real moments, to the commercial in the early 1980s, which enabled him to play with electronic image processing. During the last decade, Gursky has emerged as one of the world's visionary artists with his large-scale studies of twentieth-century spaces. Photographs of placid family life and leisure sport gave way to images of big business, like the trading floors of international stock markets, and the fast-paced, expensive world of competitive and professional sports, such as the Olympic Games. By using abstract techniques from painting, Gursky's new work throws supermarkets, warehouses, and industrial plants into new light and makes a larger statement about the individual's relationship to the environment in an age of global capitalism. Like many of Gursky's other recent pieces, *99 Cent* offers insight about America and our consumer culture.

SEEING

1. Where is your eye drawn in this photograph? How would you respond differently to the image if you could see the faces of the people shopping in this cornucopia of products? How are the effects of the photograph reinforced by the sense of depth, color, and light? How does Gursky produce the effects we see in this photo? How does he position himself in relation to the scene? to the products presented? to consumerism and acts of consumption? Point to specific details to verify your response.

2. What overall impression of consumer culture does Gursky project in this photograph? What other traditional American values does he highlight here? What relationship does he articulate between people and products in this photograph? How might this scene be read as an example of producing American values?

WRITING

1. In a recent essay entitled "The Sameness of Things," *New York Times* architectural critic Paul Goldberger explains a fundamental paradox of the mass market: "It is the opposite of alchemy: money is made not by rendering each object more valuable but by rendering it less valuable and less rare, so that it can be owned by anybody." Write an expository essay in which you explain the extent to which Goldberger's claim can be applied to such merchandise depots as Costco, Sam's Club, Wal-Mart, and Target. Do you agree that making products more accessible makes them more desirable? Explain why or why not.

2. At another point in "The Sameness of Things," Goldberger asserts that it took "the convergence of several trends—homogenization, mass communication, and the arrival of a new, more visually sophisticated young professional class—to make design more marketable in the way that it has become today. Now class distinctions are pretty much besides the point." Write an essay in which you argue that Gursky's photograph offers graphic evidence to support Goldberger's claim.

TO TELEVISION

Robert Pinsky

Not a "window on the world"
But as we call you,
A box a tube

Terrarium of dreams and wonders.
Coffer of shades, ordained   5
Cotillion of phosphors
Or liquid crystal

Homey miracle, tub
Of acquiescence, vein of defiance.
Your patron in the pantheon would be Hermes   10

Raster dance,
Quick one, little thief, escort
Of the dying and comfort of the sick,

In a blue glow my father and little sister sat
Snuggled in one chair watching you   15
Their wife and mother was sick in the head
I scorned you and them as I scorned so much

Now I like you best in a hotel room,
Maybe minutes
Before I have to face an audience: behind   20
The doors of the armoire, box
Within a box—Tom & Jerry, or also brilliant
And reassuring, Oprah Winfrey.

Thank you, for I watched, I watched
Sid Caesar speaking French and Japanese not   25
Through knowledge but imagination,
His quickness, and Thank You, I watched live
Jackie Robinson stealing

Home, the image—O strung shell—enduring
Fleeter than light like these words we   30
Remember in, they too winged
At the helmet and ankles.

Matt Groening, **The Simpsons**

ROBERT PINSKY

Poet laureate, acclaimed translator, and distinguished critic of contemporary American verse, Robert Pinsky is committed to poetic diction while addressing a wide range of experience. "I would like to write a poetry which could contain every kind of thing, while keeping all the excitement of poetry."

Born in Long Branch, New Jersey (1940), Pinsky earned a B.A. from Rutgers University and a Ph.D. from Stanford. He has taught at the University of Chicago, Wellesley College, the University of California, Berkeley, and for the past decade at Boston University. He has won numerous fellowships and awards. His poetry has been collected in *The Figured Wheel: New and Collected Poems, 1966–1996* (1996) and, most recently, in *Jersey Rain* (2001). His criticism spans three decades and includes his widely celebrated *The Sounds of Poetry* (1997).

While poet laureate (1997–2000) Pinsky initiated the multimedia Favorite Poem Project. Americans were asked to submit and read out loud their favorite poems. Pinsky served as editor on two volumes of poetry from that project, most recently *Poems to Read: A New Favorite Poems Project Anthology* (2002).

In an introduction to the preceding poem Pinsky wrote, "I've got an interest in the idea of the ode, which I take to be a poem addressed to someone or some entity, involving epithets and so forth. This poem is called 'To Television'."

THE SIMPSONS

Originally created by cartoonist Matt Groening as shorts for television's *The Tracey Ullman Show* in 1987, *The Simpsons* was granted full status as a series on the Fox network in 1990. Known for its pop culture allusions, good-humored social satire, and famous guest voices, the show today enjoys the longest prime-time run of any animated television sitcom. The family—Homer, Marge, Bart, Lisa, and Maggie—lives in an "Anywhere, USA" town called Springfield where they spend their lives in close proximity to the television set; in fact, the opening "credits" of the show culminate with an always-different collision of the characters on the couch in front of the TV.

The Simpson family may be stereotypically "American," but their personalities and behaviors either exaggerate these stereotypes or reverse them in unexpected ways. The mother, Marge, is a housewife with an enormous blue "beehive" hairdo and a feminist sensibility; the father, Homer, is a nuclear safety technician who is more concerned with donuts and beer than with safety. The children, Bart, Lisa, and Maggie (ages 10, 8, and 1), usually seem smarter than their parents. The humor these characters create is slapstick, but the jokes also address current social issues, and the writing often conceals sophisticated social commentary—so the show is popular with both children and adults.

SEEING

1. Consider the phrases Robert Pinsky uses to refer to television in the first sentence of "To Television": "window on the world," "box," "tube," "terrarium of dreams and wonders." Identify the differences between and among these metaphors. What cultural functions do they suggest about television? In what ways is the Greek god Hermes an appropriate "patron" of television? In stanza 5, Pinsky begins to explore the importance of television in his own life. How do these anecdotes anticipate the final stanza? What comparison between words and images does Pinsky draw there? With what effect(s)?

2. What role is imagined for television in the domestic lives of the Simpsons? Does television bring the family closer together or move them farther apart? How does each member of the family feel about television? In what ways can you compare (or would you resist comparing) this scene with the moments and events in Pinsky's poem?

3. How do you think Pinsky's view of television differs from that of Matt Groening, creator of *The Simpsons?* How is the television as a physical object represented in the two texts: poem and cartoon? What role do you think the different media play in these different representations?

WRITING

1. On a simple level, Pinsky's poem is about one person's relationship to television. Consider carefully your associations with television: How much time do you devote to watching it? What role(s) did it play in your family life as you were growing up? When and how did you watch it as a youngster? Did you view it primarily as a means of entertainment? as a source of information? as an occasion for relaxing? as "background noise"? as a backdrop for studying? as a social, group, or solitary activity? as something else? Draft an essay in which you draw on personal anecdotes to analyze the role(s) television has played in your personal and intellectual development.

2. Rather than simply representing the issue of writing in the age of the image, these two selections also address the issue of living in the age of the image. In this sense, television has become a focal point—as well as a vehicle— for analyzing contemporary American culture. Because people often watch television programs together, they can serve as social events. They also serve as shared cultural references. Draft an essay in which you analyze not only how but also the extent to which television shows— and the television itself—have become part of our cultural landscape.

In Greek mythology Hermes brings messages; leads gods, heroes, and mortals; and guides souls to the Underworld. He is considered the god of travelers, businessmen, thieves, game-players, and storytellers. He wears wings on his hat and sandals and carries a staff with snakes entwined around it.

ROBERT PINSKY

Although best known as a poet, Robert Pinsky is also an astute observer of contemporary American culture and has written widely on that subject. In an interview on why he likes *The Simpsons*, Pinsky noted that "the most powerful television of my lifetime has been broadcast live, what the book industry would call 'nonfiction': sports events, trials, assassinations, funerals, wars, missions into space. What all of these spectacles have in common is that they are unpredictable. . . . Television has a unique power to bring the dynamic, potentially startling event into the viewer's private, intimate space, immediately." The following essay first appeared in the *New York Times* Sunday paper on November 5, 2000. (For more information on Pinsky, see p. 388.)

CREATING THE "REAL" IN BRIGHT YELLOW AND BLUE

Robert Pinsky

A new season of "The Simpsons" begins tonight, arousing the happy anticipation that is one of the pleasures of all "genre" works: a certain blend of coziness and anticipated surprise. Genres like the film noir, the 16th-century song and the mystery novel may arouse the expectation not of greatness but of excellence. A penetrating sitcom like "The Simpsons" teases its form, and cavorts inventively within that form, the way a poem by Thomas Campion sports through the rhymes and stanzas of English verse.

Without equating different arts, we can compare them, and maybe see a little further into them: how might television, and a witty fiction like "The Simpsons," be related to an art like poetry, or to mass media like the movies and radio? How does "The Simpsons" relate to the often witless nonfiction that is TV's latest vogue? My way of dealing with such questions is through the art I know best.

Poetry, as I have come to understand it, is a vocal art that is not necessarily a performing art. That is, the medium for a poem is the reader's breath, any reader's voice—not necessarily the voice of a wonderful performer, or of the poet. This location in the audience's body gives poetry its peculiar intimacy and its inherently human scale. By its nature, it is the opposite of a mass medium; one person is the medium. That scale is part of poetry's power as well as its limitation. Poetry is the form where a public tool, language, attains an extraordinary intimacy.

In an age of media on a mass scale, an art that is by its nature on an individual scale has a restorative value. We crave, profoundly, what it offers. (On the other hand, excessive piety about poetry is not helpful. In its long and glorious history, the "Ode to a Nightingale" and "Further in Summer Than the Birds" are exceptional; there have been many stupid, trivial poems. And television has produced brilliant works amid its great mountain ranges of dross.)

Mass art, just like poetry, can 5 be good or bad. And like poems, television shows arise partly from their medium's past—as Campion's grace is often part of his subject, "The Simpsons" is often about television itself, in ways that illuminate the nature of the video medium (at least as we've known it so far). Television's current phase—the so-called "reality" programming that might be called "sitcom verité"—can be seen as a deeply traditional flowering, rooted in the medium's history. Under its tacky Trader Vic's décor and vaguely New Age solemnity, "Survivor" echoes not only the party games of "Beat the Clock" in the 50's but the very nature of the tube. The same goes for "Who Wants to Be a Millionaire." Great poems achieve a new understanding of their vocal, intimate medium while respecting its nature—they vault beyond repetition of past formulas by understanding the art's history, in order to warp, adapt, or defy the old conventions in new ways. Possibly in television—mass rather than intimate, broadcast rather than vocal—excellence depends on skill in dealing with those same two elements: the medium's nature and its past.

Television is the literal medium. The quotation marks that programs like "Survivor" have grafted onto the word "reality" express this literalness, at the heart both of TV's genius and its worst banalities. We "see" a movie but we "watch" television: television makes us feel that we are watching something happen—really happen, inside that box. This literal quality affects even cartoons, and even the most cartoon-like, stylized sitcom worlds, as in "Gilligan's Island" or "The Beverly Hillbillies." We see even the most unreal material a little as if it were happening inside a terrarium, rather than projected on a flat movie screen. The movie screen, like the actual world, reflects light. But we watch the glowing television, the screen emitting light—and in the sitcoms, as with professional wrestling, the very corniness of the fakery makes it somehow real.

Perception of the real must be created. Every creative form may have its characteristic illusion, the source of its dream-power to touch the real. The great illusion of the movies is of a world larger, better or more extraordinary than real life: a giant ape clinging to the Empire State Building and batting at airplanes; a man dancing on the ceiling or in the rain; Dorothy prancing down the Yellow Brick Road with her unlikely friends; kids riding bikes through the air. Those cinematic images saturate and reveal our own world.

The illusion of radio has to do with the way a voice can recruit imagination, creating belief through the passageways of our ears. We collaborate to create Orson Welles's invaders from Mars, to visualize the urgently described horse race or prize-fight, the accepted or rejected appeal to our belief by Churchill or Roosevelt or Tokyo Rose, Paul Harvey, or Don Imus. The radio music or voice becomes the background audio that adds drama to, or ornaments, daily life.

But television's great defining images don't resemble the fantastic spectacle of King Kong, and the memorable television moments don't have the willed rhetorical focus, the persuasion of the president announcing an attack on Pearl Harbor or Howard Stern describing a woman's breasts. Television's great moments have had to do with presence, immediacy, unpredictability: Oswald wincing at Ruby's bullet; Carlton Fisk dancing his home run onto the right side of the Fenway foul pole; Joseph Welch shaming Joseph McCarthy; Richard Nixon and Charles Van Doren sweating; athletes in agonies

and ecstasies of struggle; funerals; congressional hearings; men on the moon or in a white Bronco; political conventions in the days before they were scripted and rehearsed.

Television's quintessential form, the situation comedy, has responded to and teased this aspect of the medium. The most successful sitcoms have played with television's literal quality: Lucy, in "reality" a far greater star than Ricky, forever schemes to get into show business, or invents ways to meet a guest star like Cesar Romero—in reality, a faded and secondary figure. In "Seinfeld," Jerry Seinfeld plays a character called Jerry Seinfeld, who is pitching a show about "nothing" along with a character called George Costanza, a co-author played by an actor named Jason Alexander, who does not represent Seinfeld's co-author Larry David, who in a new HBO show plays a Costanza-like character named Larry David.

The idea of a show about "nothing" means a structure that is not artificially unified around a single conflict and resolution. Loose and casually choppy in feeling, that structure is less like a linear whodunit or one-problem "Honeymooners" episode than like a day at the office or a party.

The illusion of a structure based on "reality," developed by cop shows like Steven Bochco's "Hill Street Blues" and hospital shows like "St. Elsewhere," may have its roots in the old variety genre, or in the talk show as created by Steve Allen, Ernie Kovacs, and Jerry Lester. (Or is the genealogy through the illusion-breaking monologues, framing the narrative, of George Burns and then Gary Shandling?) The quiz show, no matter how banal the form, no matter what scandals taint its history, cannot die because—like sports

programming—it offers predictable unpredictability. As with professional wrestling, even if it may be faked, it is faked before our eyes. With the reliability of "Cops" or a sporting event or Mike Wallace about to expose a corrupt businessman who thinks Mike is flattering him, the quiz show offers canned, reliable immediacy.

On the other hand, television, which is now sometimes scolded for exploiting or manipulating reality, has also been scolded for its extreme unreality. And the medium has always had a second face—a cartoon mask that flaunts its fabricated, flat, or synthetic nature. Children like the Saturday cartoons partly because they are pleasingly unreal. I know a 3-year-old who prefers the "smooth" parts of "Sesame Street" to the "bumpy" ones, meaning she likes the reduced, graphic world of the animations. Hanna-Barbera discovered that television's literalness can be flipped or played against, creating animated programs that rely on an improvised, pasted-together look, utterly unlike the sheen and fluidity of Tex Avery and other masters of theatrical-short animation.

That quick, visibly pasted-together kind of artifice is the obverse of the medium's documentary quality: there is the literalness of reportage, and there is the literalness of blatant, candid (but far from guileless) artificiality. Studies have shown that the commercials on cable and UHF stations work better—more successfully marketing household gadgets or local car dealerships—if the production values are deliberately kept down. As with a piece of cardboard that has "Half-Price Sale!" scrawled on it with a marker, the lack of polish suggests a spontaneous bargain, something authentic.

The Hanna-Barbera cartoons [15] and their successors exploit this principle in a way characteristic of television. Many sitcoms have made human actors as much like cartoons as possible: this is the charm of Gilligan and the many other sitcoms that could be described as cartoons with human actors, just as "The Simpsons" (and "The Flintstones" plodding before it) are animated sitcoms.

The most interesting sitcoms have played with this overlap between a cartoonish reality and something closer to life. "Seinfeld" episodes often involve the hyperbole of "cartoon" characters like Kramer and Newman seducing or invading the somewhat more literal reality of the more "normal" Jerry and Elaine. This pattern recalls "The Mary Tyler Moore Show," where the impossibly oafish anchorman Ted Baxter, played by Ted Knight, contrasted with the relatively sincere characters of Mary and Lou (Ed Asner), who dealt with "real" news and issues in a more sober manner. Edith Bunker's double nature as alternate sage and idiot presages Marge Simpson's. Television characters change their degree of reality, shifting their proportions of absurdity even within a single episode. We look at what is inside television's mysterious though familiar coffer with a strange tolerance.

This tolerance does not preclude recognizing that, however rarely, television sometimes rises to the level of art. The medium's best work in comedy has sometimes attained that level by exploring in a self-reflecting way television's peculiar relationship between the literal and the fake. Sid Caesar performed astonishing improvisations as part of live broadcasts—crying real tears in a comedy sketch! The "Monty Python" shows brilliantly parody documentaries, news, interviews. In one sketch, the characters begin to leave a building, and on the doorstep, in a medium-distance shot, say, astonished, "We're on film!," then return inside to be on tape again. It's a rare episode of "The Simpsons" that does not make fun, tellingly, of television comedy, or television stars, or—maybe most often—all of the above.

The three superlative programs I've mentioned—"Your Show of Shows," "Monty Python's Flying Circus," and "The Simpsons"—all achieve their excellence partly by being, for different reasons, writers' shows, or those of artists. Caesar was more artist than star, the Pythons were the writers of their show, and the Simpsons' voices remain excellent actors, not stars. The relative absence of stars allows an astonishing kind of imaginative freedom even within the restraints of a rigid, mass-medium format.

A marvelous episode of "The Simpsons" presents a biography of that troubled but durable family, revealing their offscreen feuds, substance abuse, contract disputes, reunions, comebacks. The episode goes beyond mere parody of the many show business biography programs, which are often simultaneously weepy and leering. Because of its toughness, because it coolly derides the sanctimonious clichés of a genre, the account of the Simpsons' off-camera lives is more moving than many "actual" biographies. The emotion I feel while laughing at the onstage, reluctant get-together of Homer, Marge, Bart, Lisa, and Maggie includes genuine feeling: sadness at the arc of celebrity, a sense of mortality and mortal limits, appreciation of endurance—a complicated mixture of amusement and sorrow. That emotional reality needs no quotation marks.

The familiar yet infinitely manip- [20] ulable characters, with their bright yellow complexions and royal blue hair, are sad and funny in their literal flatness. Balloonlike yet also human, they convey the complex play between the literal and the imagined, the fake and the genuine, that is a central vibration in life, and in television. "Animated," after all, is based on "anima" or "soul." A poem can move me with a kind of vibration between the plain, familiar fact of my own breath and the tremendous force of something both true and made-up, outside of me and before me. I feel something like that same vibration between kinds of reality in the little animated drawings and their voices—and in the voices of the guest stars who play themselves, reduced visually to cartoons—and I can believe that feeling because, to paraphrase Marianne Moore's formula about poetry, "The Simpsons" reveals the real toads in an imaginary garden. ○

SEEING

1. Pinsky claims that "television is the literal medium" (para. 6). Without consulting a dictionary, write down your definition of the word *literal*. Review Pinsky's essay carefully. Which of his uses of the word *literal* are consistent with your definition? Which ones aren't? Now check *literal* in a dictionary. How did Pinsky's use of the word go beyond the dictionary definition? How did yours?

2. Compare the structure of an episode of *The Simpsons* to the structure of Pinsky's article. Begin on a large scale, and then focus on more and more detailed comparisons. For example, you might start by comparing how the two works begin. Next, you might look at different tones that the two works adopt such as humor, irony, or misdirection. When and why does each choose to be ironic? What prevents this particular moment in *The Simpsons* from being slapstick? How valid did you judge the comparison to be? What differences between the two media (television and prose) made the comparisons easy? difficult? impossible? What can an episode of *The Simpsons* communicate that an article cannot? Why?

WRITING

1. Imagine what your day would have been like today if it were an episode of *The Simpsons*. Using their cast of characters (for example, Homer, Marge, Mr. Smithers, and Otto), write the first draft of a story or draw a series of pictures that show what happened to you today. What events from your day would make good material for a show? Which ones wouldn't? Use the events in your day to develop a social commentary about the world around you.

2. Pinsky quotes the poet Marianne Moore at the end of his article. She was invited by the Ford Motor Company to develop a name for a new car. Fascinated by the challenge, she proposed such names as the "Mongoose Civique," the "Pluma Piluma," and the "Dearborn Diamante." (Moore's correspondence with the Ford Motor Company can be found at <www.people.fas.harvard.edu/~hinshaw/truemmoore.html>.) Review the full list of names Moore proposed, and compare the resonances of these terms to the metaphoric language of her poems. What kinds of similarities can you identify between her poetry and her car names? What sounds does she like to use? Which images tend to reoccur? Use this comparison as the basis for writing an expository essay in which you explain and support a theory about the similarities and differences between writing poetry and developing brand names.

DAVID GRAHAM

When David Graham is taking a picture of the American landscape, he focuses on the quirky and the exotic aspects of the familiar—a faded real estate sign or a backyard laundry tree, to name two examples. His photographs are included in the collections of the Museum of Modern Art, the Philadelphia Art Museum, the Art Institute of Chicago, and the San Francisco Museum of Modern Art. When Graham goes on a cross-country journey in the great tradition of notable American road trippers like Lewis and Clark, or Jack Kerouac, he goes looking for roadside attractions impossible for Lewis and Clark to have imagined, and undoubtedly agitating to Kerouac. Graham thrives on such Americana as the biggest ball of thread, donut-shaped restaurants, and larger-than-life lumberjacks. He captures more than the lawn ornaments in the front yard of a doublewide trailer—he draws a sense of nostalgia, of the importance of simple things, and of the tenderness of American culture out of the shot as well. His three books of photographs are *American Beauty* (1987), *Only in America* (1991), and *Land of the Free* (1999). The four portraits shown here are taken from *Land of the Free*, a collection of portraits of people who, according to Graham, "feel free and at liberty to express themselves."

CREATING THE "REAL" IN
BRIGHT YELLOW AND BLUE
Robert Pinsky

David Graham, **Army Navy Game, Philadelphia, PA**

David Graham, **Mike Memphis Lepore as Elvis, Brooklyn, NY**

David Graham, **Frankie Nardiello, Chicago, IL**

David Graham, **Denise Marie Hill, Miss Bucks County, Penndel, PA**

SEEING

1. "I am a photographer of the American cultural landscape in all its nooks and crannies," wrote David Graham. "Whether it is a portrait, a picture of a backyard or a great sign someone has made, it all fits together." To what extent does each photograph shown here satisfy your expectations of the word *American*? Explain. What does Graham enable us to see in these photographs that we might not have previously noticed about American culture? In what ways do these images provide a commentary on the American cultural landscape?

2. How would you characterize Graham's photographic style? To what extent do you notice a consistent approach in terms of subject choice, framing, perspective, and overall tone? In what respects does the image of the young man, Frankie Nardiello, in his room differ from Graham's other photos reprinted here? With what effects? To what extent does his style remind you of the tone or quality used by other artists or writers included in this collection? Please point to specific examples.

WRITING

1. David Graham is known for capturing images of the bizarre and the quirky in American culture. Write a two-page portrait of a person or group you consider "quirky" in contemporary American experience. Please be sure to define your use of the word *quirky*.

2. Graham wrote the following about the photographs in his book *Land of the Free*: "These are pictures about people who feel free and at liberty to express themselves. Some of these expressions are subtle, almost happenstance; others are extreme, especially in the case of the photographs of impersonators. These people indulge their love for celebrities by assuming the outward appearance and mannerisms of their most favored famous person.... I feel that the strength of the statements made by these impersonators does a lot to inform our understanding of the rest of us and our dreams."

Write an essay in which you explain the extent to which Graham's statement can be applied to "Mike Memphis Lepore as Elvis, Brooklyn, NY" or other images of "impersonators" such as Cindy Sherman (p. 371), Nikki S. Lee (pp. 374–75), or Cindy Jackson (p. 370).

ANDREW SULLIVAN >

British-born (1963) Andrew Sullivan began his writing career while at Harvard University's Kennedy School of Government in the mid-1980s, and continued when he joined Margaret Thatcher's informal policy think tank, for which he wrote a paper called "Greening the Tories." He might as easily have been seen in tights as with a pen in hand, because he was as comfortable on stage as at a writing desk. Between advanced studies at Harvard in political science and acting, he found work writing for *The New Republic* and penning articles for the *Wall Street Journal*, the *Washington Post*, the *Daily Telegraph*, and *Esquire*, among others. Although he wrote a monthly column for *Esquire*, his most steady work continued to be with *The New Republic*, and while he was still in his twenties he became the magazine's editor. In this role Sullivan changed the pitch and tenor of the magazine, adding subjects such as a controversial stance on early intervention in Bosnia, affirmative action, and gay rights. Sullivan campaigned heavily for gay rights and published several books, essays, and a reader on political and social issues of homosexuality in America and abroad. His essay on the power the Declaration of Independence's phrase "the pursuit of happiness" still has on the global landscape is an example of his sharp, smart take on international politics. It was first published in *Forbes* magazine in November, 2001.

The Pursuit of Happiness: Four Revolutionary Words

Andrew Sullivan

It's a small phrase when you think about it: "the pursuit of happiness." It's somewhat overshadowed in the Declaration of Independence by the weightier notions of "life" and "liberty." In today's mass culture, it even comes close to being banal. Who, after all, doesn't want to pursue happiness? But in its own day, the statement was perhaps the most radical political statement ever delivered. And when we try and fathom why it is that the United States still elicits such extreme hatred in some parts of the world, this phrase is as good a place to start as any.

Take the first part: pursuit. What America is based on is not the achievement of some goal, the capture of some trophy, or the triumph of success. It's about the process of seeking something. It's about incompletion, dissatisfaction, striving, imperfection. In the late eighteenth century, this was a statement in itself. In the Europe of the preceding centuries, armies had gone to war, human beings had been burned at stakes, monarchs had been dethroned, and countries torn apart because imperfection wasn't enough. From the Reformation to the Inquisition, religious fanatics had demanded that the state enforce holiness, truth and virtue. Those who resisted were exterminated. Moreover, the power and status of rulers derived from their own perfection. Kings and queens had artists portray them as demi-gods. Dissenters were not merely troublemakers, they were direct threats to the perfect order of the modern state. This was a political order in which everything had to be perfectly arranged—even down to the internal thoughts of individual consciences.

Enter the Americans. Suddenly the eternal, stable order of divine right and church authority was replaced by something far more elusive, difficult, even intangible. Out of stability came the idea of pursuit. To an older way of thinking, the very idea is heretical. The pursuit of what? Where? By whom? Who authorized this? By whose permission are you off on some crazy venture of your own? Think of how contemporary Islamic fundamentalists must think of this. For them, the spiritual and intellectual life is not about pursuit; it's about submission. It's not about inquiry into the unknown. It's about struggle for the will of Allah. Since the result of this struggle is literally the difference between heaven and hell, there can be no doubt about what its content is, or the duty of everyone to engage in it. And since doubt can lead to error, and error can lead to damnation, it is also important that everyone within the community adhere to the same struggle—and extend the struggle in a fight against unbelievers.

Today, we find this religious extremism alien. But it was not alien to the American founders. The European Christians of the sixteenth and seventeenth centuries were not so different in their obsessiveness and intolerance from many Islamic fundamentalists today. And against that fundamentalist requirement for uniformity, the Founders of a completely new society countered with the notion of a random, chaotic, cacophonous pursuit of any number of different goals. No political authority would be able to lay down for all citizens what was necessary for salvation, or even for a good life. Citizens would have to figure out the meaning of their own lives, and search for that meaning until the day they died. There would be no certainty; no surety even of a destination. Pursuit was everything. And pursuit was understood as something close to adventure.

And then comes the even more radical part. 5 The point of this pursuit was happiness! Again, this seems almost banal to modern ears. But it was far from banal in the eighteenth century and it is far from banal when interpreted by the radical mullahs of political Islam. Here's the difference. Before the triumph of American democracy, governments and states and most philosophers viewed happiness as incidental to something else. For Christians, happiness was only achieved if you were truly virtuous. Happiness was the spiritual calm that followed an act of charity; the satisfied exhaustion after a day caring for others. For Aristotle, happiness was simply impossible without virtue. Happiness was an incidental experience while pursuing what was good and true. The idea of pursuing happiness for its own sake would have struck Aristotle as simple hedonism. The happiness someone feels drinking a cold beer on a hot day or bungee-jumping off a bridge was not a happiness he recognized. And for almost every pre-American society, other goals clearly had precedence over the subjective sense of well-being. Remember Cromwell's England? Or Robespierre's France? Or Stalin's Russia? They weren't exactly pleasure-fests. Again, in radical Islam today, American notions of happiness—choice, indulgence, whimsy, humor, leisure, art—always have to be subjected to moral inspection. Do these activities conform to religious law? Do they encourage or discourage virtuous behavior, without which happiness is impossible and meaningless? These are the questions human beings have always historically asked of the phenomenon we call happiness.

Not so in America. Here, happiness is an end in itself. Its content is up to each of us. Some may believe, as American Muslims or Christians do, that happiness is still indeed only possible when allied to virtue. But just as importantly, others may not. And the important thing is that the government of the United States take no profound interest in how any of these people define their own happiness. All that matters is that no-one is coerced into a form of happiness he hasn't chosen for himself—by others or by the state. Think of this for a moment. What America means is that no-one can forcibly impose a form of happiness on anyone else—even if it means that some people are going to hell in a hand basket. Yes, there have been many exceptions to this over the years—and America has often seen religious revivals, spasms of cultural puritanism, cultural censorship, and so on. But the government has been barred from the deepest form of censorship—the appropriation of any single religion under the auspices of the state. You can call this all sorts of things. In my book, it's as good a definition of freedom as any. But to others—countless others—it seems a callous indifference to the fate of others' souls, even blasphemy and degeneracy. This view is held by some Christian fundamentalists at home. And it is surely held by Islamic fundamentalists abroad. We ignore this view at our peril.

There are, of course, many reasons why America evokes hostility across the globe. There are foreign policies; there are historical failings. There is resentment of American wealth and power. There is fear of the social dislocation inherent in globalization. But there is also something far deeper. What we have forgotten is how anomalous America is in the history of the world. Most other countries have acquired identity and culture through ancient inheritance, tribal loyalty, or religious homogeneity. Even a country very like the United States, Britain, still has a monarchy and an established church. If you told the average Brit that his government was designed to help him pursue "happiness," he'd laugh. Other developed countries, like Germany, have succumbed to the notion of race as a purifying and unifying element. Many others, like Pakistan or India, cling to a common religious identity to generate a modicum of political unity. In none of these countries is "happiness" even a political concept. And in none of these places is the pursuit of something in and of itself an admirable goal, let alone at the center of the meaning of the state and Constitution.

And when the society which has pioneered this corrosively exhilarating idea of happiness becomes the most powerful and wealthy country on earth, then the risks of backlash increase exponentially. In the late eighteenth century Europeans could scoff at banal American encomiums to happiness as an amusing experiment doomed to failure. At the beginning of the twenty-first century, with the products of such happiness—from McDonald's to Starbucks to MTV—saturating the globe, foreigners can afford no such condescension. Happiness is coming to them—and moral, theological certainty is departing. In response to this, they can go forward and nervously integrate—as countries like China, South Korea, and Russia are attempting. Or they can go back, far, far back to a world where such notions of happiness were as alien as visitors from outer space.

Far, far back is where some in the Middle East now want to go. The roots of Islamic fundamentalism go back centuries and bypass many more recent, and more open, strains of Islam. And we are foolish if we do not see the internal logic of this move. The fundamentalist Muslims are not crazy. They see that other cultures are slowly adapting to the meme of the pursuit of happiness—from Shanghai to Moscow, from Bombay to Buenos Aires. They see that they are next in line. But they also see that such a change would deeply alter their religion and its place in society. So they resist. They know that simply accommodating piece-meal to slow change will doom them. So they are pulling a radical move—a step far back into the past, allied with a militarist frenzy and rampant xenophobia to buttress it. This move is the belated response of an ancient religious impulse to the most radical statement of the Enlightenment, which is why it is indeed of such world-historical importance. As I write I have no idea as to the conclusion of this new drama in world history—except that it will have ramifications as large and as lasting as the end of the Cold War.

What power four little words still have. 10 And what carnage they must still endure to survive. ○

SEEING

1. Although Sullivan subtitles his article "Four Revolutionary Words," he seems concerned principally with only two of the words: *pursuit* and *happiness*. Try and change the two words that he doesn't focus on—*the* and *of*—to different but similar words and see if his argument still holds. For example, which points would still make sense if the four words were "A Pursuit of Happiness"? or "The Pursuit *in* Happiness," or even "Some Pursuit *with* Happiness"? What does Sullivan leave out of his analysis of the United States by not examining the ignored words' contribution to the phrase?

2. Sullivan summarizes the attitudes of several cultures, religions, and times in a small number of words. How does he reduce such complexity to simplicity? What does this reduction enable him to do? Which conclusions would he not be able to draw from a more supple analysis? How much more (or less) convincing would his points be if they were supported by generalizations? Determine how accurate his characterizations are. For example, you might read more about "many Islamic fundamentalists today" and determine the extent to which they might be characterized by "obsessiveness and intolerance" (para. 4). Or you might read about Aristotle—to determine whether he thought "happiness was simply impossible without virtue" (para. 5).

WRITING

1. Choose another phrase from the Declaration of Independence—such as "all men are created equal" or "they are endowed by their Creator with certain unalienable Rights." Then write the first draft of an essay in which you use either phrase to summarize the hopes and aspirations of many Americans.

2. Sullivan claims that in the United States "no-one is coerced into a form of happiness he hasn't chosen for himself" (para. 6). Consider enslaved Africans. How do their narratives serve as a commentary on *coercion, happiness,* and *choice*? Alternatively, consider Native Americans, or women who weren't allowed to vote in national elections until 1920. Or people who are imprisoned now. Read several first-person accounts (diaries, eyewitness accounts, court documents, and the like), and identify what they say about *coercion, happiness,* and *choice* in the United States. Prepare the first draft of a response to Sullivan's argument, written from one of these points of view.

DIESEL

In 1978, clothes designer Renzo Rosso founded Diesel, with the hopes that a new type of clothing industry might be born. Today, Diesel has a large international market and a desire to dress the young independent consumer in clothes designed and marketed by a diverse and innovative staff. Diesel's mission statement: "Beginning as a company focused on making quality clothing, Diesel has become part of youth culture worldwide. It can legitimately claim to be the first brand to believe truly in the global village and to embrace it with open arms." Diesel does not view itself as merely a clothier, but also as a company whose ideas are expressed by the people who will choose the Diesel brand. The company's advertising is bold and brassy, and it is not afraid to celebrate America's love affair with consumerism.

Diesel ads have won many awards and accolades for their ironic and yet extremely successful sales model. The "Freedom" ad is a great example of this: "FREEDOM is a feeling you celebrate with the world. Let's visit the plastic surgeon and replace our arms with wings. This may cost a lot of money." According to Diesel's web site, the tele-tubby-like character in the middle of the ad is Diesel's mascot, Daniel.

Diesel, **Freedom is now sponsored by Diesel**

1. "In the fashion market, where there is ever-increasing choice, companies have realized it's not simply about the clothes on the rails. Branding now plays a major role in fashion as more labels than ever before compete in an already crowded market," wrote cultural critic Sarah Smith. This advertisement is part of an ad campaign Diesel calls "Successful Living." What is your overall impression of the ad? What thoughts and feelings does it evoke in you? Do you find it humorous? annoying? repulsive? something else? How would you describe the brand that Diesel is trying to promote with this ad? What qualities and ideas do the image and language convey? If not "clothes on the rails," what is Diesel attempting to sell here?

2. Take a moment to describe the compositional elements of this ad. Examine, for example, the ad's typeface, image selection, use of color, and word choice. How would you describe its tone and style? How do these compositional features work together to form an overall effect? What specific cultural references does this ad trade on?

1. How do you interpret the phrase "Freedom is now sponsored by Diesel"? What meanings does it elicit? How would the phrase read differently without the inclusion of the word *now*? Where else in American popular culture do you see and hear the word *freedom* invoked? Using Andrew Sullivan's essay "The Pursuit of Happiness" (see p. 400) as a model, write an essay in which you explain the meanings of the word *freedom* in American culture.

2. In a January 30, 2002, press release on this ad campaign, Diesel representatives wrote: "Diesel takes a shot at 'Corporate America' with the Spring/Summer 2002 'Happy Valley' advertising campaign. . . . Do you feel sad and depressed? Are you running out of Prozac? . . . Give a twist to your life and enter Diesel's Happy Valley! Excitement, joy, passion, pleasure, fun, romance, desire and more are now available for you to try, experience, enjoy and buy from Diesel, the worldwide sponsor of mankind's lightest emotions." To what extent do you agree that Diesel has taken a "shot at 'Corporate America'" with this ad? What aspects of corporate America are criticized here? To what extent is corporate America "free" to criticize itself? Spend some time on Diesel's web site, <www.diesel.com>, and familiarize yourself with Diesel's latest ad campaign. Then write an essay in which you assess the campaign as an effective marketing tool.

Visualizing Composition
Audience

Developing a practiced awareness of the person—or people—for whom a text is composed remains an essential ingredient in any successful act of composition. We most often call this person "the reader." Each of us who seeks to communicate some idea to an audience needs to decide who our intended readers are, to address their needs and expectations, and to assess the effects on them of the compositional choices we make.

When we talk about the writer's need to be sensitive to an audience, we are speaking not only about the writer's ability to analyze the needs and attitudes of readers but also the ability to anticipate and therefore to shape the readers' response. In effect, having a sense of audience is not only a matter of the writer's adapting his or her purpose to suit the expectations of readers; it is also a matter of the writer's knowing how to get readers to adapt themselves to his or her purpose.

Many students assume that they are writing solely to satisfy the expectations of their instructor. Yet, to write successful academic prose, students ought to practice frequently the skills not only of

Visa, **It's Your Life. How Do You Want To Spend It?**

accommodating the needs and expectations of actual readers but also of anticipating and actually directing the responses of implied readers. Such is the reader Nathaniel Hawthorne imagined in the Preface to his novel *The Marble Faun* (1858): "that one congenial friend—more comprehensive of his purposes, more appreciative of his success, more indulgent of his short-comings, and, in all respects, closer and kinder than a brother—that all sympathizing critic, in short, whom an author never actually meets, but to whom he implicitly makes his appeal, whenever he is conscious of having done his best." As Hawthorne suggests here, considering audience early in the writing process can be used heuristically to jump-start writing. Likewise, writers ought to avoid rigidity or premature closure in conceptualizing their audience, lest their ideas be stillborn.

Consider this advertisement for Visa credit cards. Who is the "you" being addressed? What attitudes and assumptions are embedded in the two sentences in this ad: "It's your life. How do you want to spend it?"? Write an expository essay in which you analyze the ability of the writer and designer of this ad not only to anticipate but also to manage the reader's response.

Photographer Joel Sternfeld captures Americans and American life in his full-color portraits and landscapes. Documenting both commercial objects in ancient-looking settings and age-old expressions on people wearing trendy clothes evokes subtle contradictions and Sternfeld's passion for presenting memory, place, and authentic Americana. His photos are timeless and yet undeniably modern; his work begins where the celebrated American photographer Walker Evans left off and inspires other contemporary photographers such as Andreas Gursky. The man in "A Young Man Gathering Shopping Carts" might be a Calvin Klein model, but he is standing in front of the generically named Foodtown supermarket. His large hands might be those of a farmer, yet he wears a button-down shirt and tie, although the tie is loose and his shirtsleeves are disheveled. Sternfeld's eye is especially adept at capturing these seeming visual contradictions.

Sternfeld was born in New York City in 1944. His photographs have appeared at exhibits in the Museum of Modern Art in New York, the Art Institute of Chicago, the Museum of Fine Arts in Houston, and the Fotomuseum in Winterthur, Switzerland. Sternfeld has received two Guggenheim fellowships and a Prix de Rome prize. His books include *Campagna Romana: The Countryside of Ancient Rome* (1992), *American Prospects* (1994), *On This Site* (1997), *Hart Island* (1998), *Stranger Passing* (2001), and *Walking the High Line* (2002).

Joel Sternfeld, **A Young Man Gathering Shopping Carts, Huntington, New York, July 1993**

SEEING

1. As you examine this image, identify which aspects of the photograph your eye is drawn to—and in roughly what sequence. Are you first drawn, for example, to the young man's body? to the shopping cart next to him? to the carts and stores in the background? How would you describe the mood captured in this photograph? What compositional choices help create this mood? Consider, for example, Sternfeld's use of color, how he has framed the image, the way he arranged the different elements in the photograph (the central figure, shopping carts, store signs, etc.).

2. Focus your attention for a moment on the young man. To what, specifically, is your eye drawn as you observe him? What features of his appearance strike you as most memorable? Explain why. What reasonable inferences might you make about the young man from your observations of him? How would you describe his body language in this photograph? Consider his posture, his facial expression, the positioning of his hands, the way he wears his clothes. What do you imagine he is thinking and feeling? What do you imagine he feels about having his picture taken? Explain why.

WRITING

1. The strip mall is one of the most common elements of the American built environment. Nearly every town and city in America includes a strip mall of some kind. Visit a strip mall and—as if you were visiting another country for the first time—spend some time observing and taking notes on the environment as a physical and social space. You might ask yourself some of the following questions: What are the dominant features of the visual landscape (colors, signs)? What patterns are there in the ways people use the space? Which spaces are more frequented than others? Which spaces seem more conducive to social interaction than others? Why? Write a descriptive essay in which you convey the overall qualities of the physical and social environment of the strip mall, based on your observations.

2. Sternfeld's photograph and Gursky's "99 Cent" (see p. 382) provide two views of supermarkets from different vantage points. What similarities or differences do you notice between them? What statements can you make about supermarkets as physical environments based on these two photographs? What do they suggest about the culture of modern shopping environments? Write an essay in which you compare and contrast the two photographs, paying special attention to such compositional elements and stylistic choices as color, repetition, and point of view.

JAMES B. TWITCHELL

Many Americans poke fun at themselves for heeding the call of consumerism. Many non-Americans view our love of things commercial and plastic with downright contempt and malice. James B. Twitchell studies the American Dream and our un-relenting quest for luxury and for things by going to the hubs of the shopping and spending cen-ters of the nation and simply ob-serving what goes on there, and who makes it all go. Then, when he comes home at the end of the day, he writes about it. Twitchell's essays and books on material culture are packed with humor, frank talk, and the reality of the impact popular culture has on America. He does not apologize for it, criticize it, or denounce it—he merely explains it.

Twitchell is a professor of English at the University of Florida and the author of many books, including *Adcult USA: The Triumph of Advertising in America* (1997); *Lead Us into Temptation: The Triumph of American Materi-alism* (2000); *20 Ads That Shook the World: The Century's Most Ground Breaking Advertising and How It Changed Us* (2001); and *Living It Up: Our Love Affair with Luxury* (2002). The essay "In Praise of Consumerism" first ap-peared in the August/September issue of *Reason* magazine.

James B. Twitchell

IN PRAISE OF CONSUMERISM

Sell them their dreams. Sell them what they longed for and hoped for and almost despaired of having. Sell them hats by splashing sunlight across them. Sell them dreams—dreams of country clubs and proms and visions of what might happen if only. After all, people don't buy things to have things. They buy things to work for them. They buy hope—hope of what your merchandise will do for them. Sell them this hope and you won't have to worry about selling them goods. –Helen Landon Cass

Those words were spoken some years ago by a female radio announcer to a convention of salesmen in Philadelphia. *The Philadelphia Retail Ledger* for June 6, 1923, recorded Ms. Cass' invocations with no surrounding explanation. They were simply noted as a matter of record, not as a startling insight.

There are two ways to read her spiel. You can read it like a melancholy Marxist and see the barely veiled indictment of the selling process. What does she think consumers are—dopes to be duped? What is she selling? Snake oil?

Or you can read it like an unrepentant capitalist and see the connection between consuming goods and gathering meaning. The reason producers splash magical promise over their goods is because consumers demand it. Consumers are not sold a bill of goods; they *insist* on it. Snake oil to the cynic is often holy water to the eager. What looks like exploiting desire may be fulfilling desire.

How you come down in this matter depends on your estimation of the audience. Does the audience manipulate things to make meaning, or do other people use things to manipulate the audience? Clearly, this is a variation of "I persuade, you educate, they manipulate," for both points of view are supportable. Let's split the difference and be done with it.

More interesting to me, however, is to wonder 5 why such a statement, so challenging, so revolutionary, so provocative in many respects was, in the early 1920s, so understandable, so acceptable, even so passé that it appears with no gloss. Why is it that when you read the early descriptions of capitalism, all the current bugaboos—advertising, packaging, branding, fashion, and retailing techniques—seem so much better understood?

And why has the consumer—playing an active, albeit usually secondary, part in the consumptive dyad of earlier interpretations—become almost totally listless in our current descriptions? From Thomas Hobbes in the mid-17th century ("As in other things, so in men, not the seller but the buyer determines the price") to Edwin S. Gingham in the mid-20th century ("Consumers with dollars in their pockets are not, by any stretch of the imagination, weak. To the contrary, they are the most merciless, meanest, toughest market disciplinarians I know"), the consumer was seen as participating in the meaning-making of the material world. How and why did the consumer get dumbed down and phased out so quickly? Why has the hypodermic metaphor (false needs injected into a docile populace) become the unchallenged explanation of consumerism?

I think that much of our current refusal to consider the liberating role of consumption is the result of who has been doing the describing. Since the 1960s, the primary "readers" of the commercial "text" have been the well-tended and -tenured members of the academy. For any number of reasons—the most obvious being their low levels of disposable income, average age, and gender, and the fact that these critics are selling a competing product, high-cult (which is also coated with its own dream values)—the academy has casually passed off as "hegemonic brainwashing" what seems to me, at least, a self-evident truth about human nature: We like having stuff.

In place of the obvious, they have substituted an interpretation that they themselves often call *vulgar* Marxism. It is supposedly vulgar in the sense that it is not as sophisticated as the real stuff, but it has enough spin on it to be more appropriately called Marxism *lite.* Go into almost any cultural studies course in this country and you will hear the condemnation of consumerism expounded: What we see in the marketplace is the result of the manipulation of the many for the profit of the few. Consumers are led around by the nose. We live in a squirrel cage. Left alone we would read

Wordsworth, eat lots of salad, and have meetings to discuss Really Important Subjects.

In cultural studies today, everything is oppression and we are all victims. In macrocosmic form, the oppression is economic—the "free" market. In microcosmic form, oppression is media—your "free" TV. Here, in the jargon of this downmarket Marxism, is how the system works: The manipulators, a.k.a. "the culture industry," attempt to enlarge their hegemony by establishing their ideological base in the hearts and pocketbooks of a weak and demoralized populace. Left alone, we would never desire things (ugh!). They have made us materialistic. But for them, we would be spiritual.

To these critics, the masters of industry and their henchmen, the media lords, are predators, and what they do in no way reflects or resolves genuine audience concerns. Just the opposite. The masters of the media collude, striving to infantilize us so that we are docile, anxious, and filled with "reified desire." While we may think advertising is just "talking about the product," that packaging just "wraps the object," that retailing is just "trading the product," or that fashion is just "the style of the product," this is not so. That you may think so only proves their power over you. The marginalized among us—the African American, the child, the immigrant, and especially the female—are trapped into this commodifying system, this false consciousness, and this fetishism that only the enlightened can correct. Legendary ad man David Ogilvy's observation that, "The consumer is no fool, she is your wife" is just an example of the repressive tolerance of such a sexist, materialist culture.

Needless to say, in such a system the only safe place to be is tenured, underpaid, self-defined as marginalized, teaching two days a week for nine months a year, and writing really perceptive social criticism that your colleagues can pretend to read. Or rather, you *would* be writing such articles if only you could find the time.

THE TRIUMPH OF STUFF

The idea that consumerism creates artificial desires rests on a wistful ignorance of history and human nature, on the hazy, romantic feeling that there existed some halcyon era of noble savages with purely natural needs. Once fed and sheltered, our needs have always been cultural, not natural. Until there is some other system to codify and satisfy those needs and yearnings, capitalism—and the culture it carries with it—will continue not just to thrive but to triumph.

In the way we live now, it is simply impossible to consume objects without consuming meaning. Meaning is pumped *and* drawn everywhere throughout the modern commercial world, into the farthest reaches of space and into the smallest divisions of time. Commercialism is the water we all swim in, the air we breathe, our sunlight and shade. Currents of desire flow around objects like smoke in a wind tunnel. . . .

This isn't to say that I'm simply sanguine about such a material culture. It has many problems that I have glossed over. Consumerism is wasteful, it is devoid of otherworldly concerns, it lives for today and celebrates the body. It over-indulges and spoils the young with impossible promises. It encourages recklessness, living beyond one's means, gambling. Consumer culture is always new, always without a past. Like religion, which it has displaced, it afflicts the comfortable and comforts the afflicted. It is heedless of the truly poor who cannot gain access to the loop of meaningful information that is carried through its ceaseless exchanges. It is a one-dimensional world, a wafer-thin world, a world low on significance and high on glitz, a world without yester-days.

On a personal level, I struggle daily to keep it at bay. For instance, I am offended by billboards (how do they externalize costs?); I fight to keep Chris Whittle's Channel One TV and all place-based advertising from entering the classroom; political advertising makes me sick, especially the last-minute negative ads; I contribute to PBS in hopes they will stop slipping down the slope of commercialism (although I know better); I am annoyed that Coke has bought all the "pouring rights" at my school and is now trying to do the same to the world; I think it's bad enough that the state now sponsors gambling, do they also have to support deceptive advertising about it?; I despise the way that amateur athletics has become a venue for shoe companies (why not just replace the football with the Nike swoosh and be done with it?); and I just go nuts at Christmas.

But I also realize that while you don't have to like it, it doesn't hurt to understand it and our part in it. We have not been led astray. Henry Luce was not far off when he claimed in a February 1941 editorial in *Life* magazine that the next era was to be the American Century: "The Greeks, the Romans, the English and the French had their eras, and now it was ours." Not only that, but we are likely to commandeer much of the 21st century as well.

Almost a decade ago, Francis Fukuyama, a State Department official, contended in his controversial essay (and later book) "The End of History?" that "the ineluctable spread of consumerist Western culture" presages "not just the end of the Cold War, or the passing of a particular period of postwar history, but the end of history as such: that is, the end point of mankind's ideological evolution." OK, such predictions are not new. "The End of History" (as we know it) and "the end point of mankind's ideological evolution" have been predicted before by philosophers. Hegel claimed it had already happened in 1806 when Napoleon embodied the ideals of the French Revolution, and Marx said the end was coming soon with world communism. What legitimizes this modern claim is that it is demonstrably true. For better or for worse, American commercial culture is well on its way to becoming world culture. The Soviets have fallen. Only quixotic French intellectuals and anxious Islamic fundamentalists are trying to stand up to it.

To some degree, the triumph of consumerism is the triumph of the popular will. You may not like what is manufactured, advertised, packaged, branded, and broadcast, but it is far closer to what most people want most of the time than at any other period of modern history.

TROLLOPE AND *THE JERK*

Two fictional characters personify to me the great divide: Augustus Melmotte, the protagonist of Anthony Trollope's 19th-century novel, *The Way We Live Now,* and Navin R. Johnson, the eponymous hero of Steve Martin's 1979 movie, *The Jerk.*

Melmotte, a Jew, comes from Paris to London with his daughter and his Bohemian wife. When the action of the novel is over and Augustus has committed suicide because he cannot fit in to proper Victorian society, wife and daughter head off to America—to San Francisco, to be exact. Trollope is always exact in letting you know that geography determines character. So too we know that Ruby Ruggles and her bumpkin brother belong at Sheep's Acres Farm and that Roger Carbury should preside over Carbury Hall. Sir Felix Carbury, fallen from grace, must go to Germany—there is no room for his kind, no club that will accept him. Mrs. Hurtle comes from San Francisco and in the end must return there.

Any Trollope lover worth his salt can tell you much about the protagonists simply by such comings and goings. These paths are the code by which our grandparents recognized, in Dominick Dunne's felicitous title, those who are "people like us": our kind/not our kind. The Victorian reading public needed such shorthand because *things* had no brand personalities—manners, places, sinecures—and bloodlines did. Salaries meant little, accomplishments even less. The central acts of *The Way We Live Now* are the attempts by Augustus Melmotte to buy a titled husband for his daughter and get a named estate for himself. He can't do it, of course—how silly to try, even if he is the "City's most powerful financier." In his world, meaning was generated through such social conventions as the abstract concept of bloodline, the value of patina, your club, owning land, acceptable in-laws, your accent, the seating chart for dinner, the proper church pew—all things Melmotte could never master. It was a stultifying system—a real old-boy network, but one that to Trollope still worked. It was a system presided over by chummy squires, comfortable gentlemen, and twinkling clerics.

Compare that to the world of *The Jerk*. Here, the story is held together by the running joke that when Navin R. Johnson is being the most idiotic, he is really being the most savant. After a series of misadventures, Navin amasses a fortune by inventing a way to keep eyeglasses from slipping down the nose (the "Opti-grab"). He wins the hand of his sweetheart, buys incredibly gauche gold chains, swag lamps, outrageous golf carts, and ersatz Grecian mansions. Surrounded by things, he is finally happy. But then—curses!—he loses his possessions as a google-eyed litigant wins a class-action lawsuit because the Opti-grab has made many wearers cross-eyed. Navin's wife is distraught. She bursts into tears. "I don't care about losing the money, it's losing all this stuff."

Navin, as innocent as he is honest, says he doesn't really care about these things, he knows who he is without possessions. His sense of self is certainly not tied to the material world. "I don't want stuff . . . I don't need anything," he says to her as he starts to leave the room in his pajamas. He sees an old ashtray. "Except this ashtray, and that's the only thing I need is this," he says, as he leans over to pick it up. Navin walks to the door. "Well, and this paddle game and the ashtray is all I need. And this, this remote control; that's all I need, just the ashtray, paddle game, and this remote control."

Navin is growing progressively more frantic in vintage Steve Martin fashion. He is in the hall now, pajamas down around his knees and his arms full of stuff. "And these matches. Just the ashtray, paddle ball, remote control, and these matches . . . and this lamp, and that's all I need. I don't need one other thing . . . except this magazine." We hear him gathering more things as he disappears down the hall. Navin, jerk enough to think he needs nothing, is sage enough not to leave home without a few of his favorite things.

Augustus Melmotte, certified world-class financier, is forever kept at bay. He never achieves his goal and finally commits suicide. Navin R. Johnson, certified consumer jerk, achieves (if only for a while) the objects of his heart's desire. He finally becomes a bum on Skid Row, true, but a bum who at least can try it all over again. In a consumerist culture, the value-making ligatures that hold our world together come from such conventions as advertising, packaging, branding, fashion, and even shopping itself. It is a system presided over by marketers who deliver the goods and all that is carried in their wake. It is a more democratic world, a more egalitarian world, and, I think, a more interesting world.

That said, commercialism can be a stultifying system too, and wasteful. It would be nice to think that this eternally encouraging market will result in the cosmopolitanism envisioned by the Enlightenment philosophers, that a "universalism of goods" will end in a crescendo of hosannas. It would be nice to think that more and more of the poor and disenfranchised will find their ways into the cycle of increased affluence without contracting "affluenza," the "disease" of buying too much. It would be nice to think that materialism could be heroic, self-abnegating, and redemptive. It would be nice to think that greater material comforts will release us from racism, sexism, and ethnocentricism and that the apocalypse will come as it did at the end of Shelley's *Prometheus Unbound,* leaving us "Sceptreless, free, uncircumscribed . . . Equal, unclassed, tribeless, and nationless . . . Pinnacled dim in the intense inane."

But it is more likely that the globalization of capitalism will result in the banalities of an ever-increasing, worldwide consumerist culture. Recall that Athens ceased to be a world power around 400 B.C., yet for the next three hundred years Greek culture was the culture of the world. The Age of European Exposition ended in the mid-20th century; the Age of American Markets—Yankee imperialism—is just starting to gather force. The French don't stand a chance. The Middle East is collapsing under the weight of dish antennas and Golden Arches. The untranscendent, repetitive, sensational, democratic, immediate, tribalizing, and unifying force of what Irving Kristol calls the American Imperium need not result in a Bronze Age of culture, however. In fact, who knows what this Pax Americana will result in? But it certainly will not produce what Shelley had in mind.

We have been in the global marketplace a short time, and it is an often scary and melancholy place. A butterfly flapping its wings in China may not cause storm clouds over Miami, but a few lines of computer code written by some kid in Palo Alto may indeed change the lives of all the inhabitants of Shanghai.

More important, perhaps, we have not been led into this world of material closeness against our better judgment. For many of us, especially when young, consumerism is not against our better judgment. It *is* our better judgment. And this is true regardless of class or culture. We have not just asked to go this way, we have demanded. Now most of the world is lining up, pushing and shoving, eager to elbow into the mall. Woe to the government or religion that says no.

Getting and spending have been the most passionate, and often the most imaginative, endeavors of modern life. We have done more than acknowledge that the good life starts with the material life, as the ancients did. We have made stuff the dominant prerequisite of organized society. Things "R" Us. Consumption has become production. While this is dreary and depressing to some, as doubtless it should be, it is liberating and democratic to many more. ○

SEEING

1. How does James Twitchell define consumerism? Summarize the points he offers in "praise" of consumerism. To what extent does he balance his praise with criticism? What are his critiques of the phenomenon? What is the overriding point of Twitchell's essay? Which points of praise and critique do you find most convincing? Explain why.

2. What examples does Twitchell use to illustrate his points in this piece? What similarities do you find among them? How effective are these examples—individually and taken as a whole—in furthering the main point of Twitchell's argument? Consider the connections he establishes between historical examples and modern-day phenomena. How might you strengthen or extend these links?

WRITING

1. "You are what you buy," or so the saying goes. Create a log of the purchases you make in a three-day period, keeping an exact record of the items you buy and their cost. Using this journal as a snapshot of your "life" as a consumer, write an expository essay in which you explain what your spending habits reveal about you.

2. "Sell them their dreams. Sell them what they longed for and hoped for and almost despaired of having," said Helen Landon Cass to a group of salesmen in 1923. Twitchell claims that Cass's words are as pertinent to contemporary commercial culture as they were then. Consider carefully the nature of the advertising appeals made to you each day. To what extent do you find the approach Cass identifies to be still operative in the advertisements you encounter on a daily basis? Choose one such contemporary ad that sells "dreams and hope" rather than goods, and write an expository essay in which you explain what the ad is selling and how.

James B. Twitchell

IN PRAISE OF CONSUMERISM

Visualizing Context
A Culture of Consumption

Palmolive, **I Pledge Myself**, 1943

Advertisements are so ubiquitous that it is difficult to imagine daily life without them. The most recent estimates suggest that the "average" American sees, reads, or listens to nearly three thousand commercial messages each day. They confront us everywhere: on the road, in our homes, at work, on vacation, and now even in our classrooms.

The business of advertising is to invent memorable—and enduring—relationships between people and products. What has remained distinctive about advertising over the centuries of its history is the apparent paradox of its aim: to build lasting associations between an individual product and massive numbers of buyers. To achieve this goal, advertisers employ language and graphics designed to be readily accessible and immediately persuasive. It should be no surprise to most Americans that ads sometimes outlive the products they promote.

Helen Landon Cass's call in 1923 to advertisers to "Sell [consumers] their dreams. Sell them what they longed for and hoped for and almost despaired of having" (see p. 411) is as pertinent today as it was when she made it. Despite noticeable changes in social standards and expectations from one generation to the next, advertisements frequently repeat certain themes and concerns. As such, they offer a remarkably sensitive portrait of the collective hopes and aspirations, fears and anxieties of any—and every—generation of Americans.

Consider, for example, the accompanying advertisement for Palmolive Soap, first printed in 1943. What special features of its use of language and illustration do you notice? As soon as you are confident that you understand what the ad is selling and how, find a recent ad on the same subject. What specific features of this ad do you notice?

Write an expository essay in which you compare and contrast the effective use of language and image in these two advertisements. After you have established the continuities of theme, style, and design between the ads, you should explain which one you judge to be more effective.

GUILLERMO GÓMEZ-PEÑA

Among the most popular performance artists of his generation, Guillermo Gómez-Peña has made the shifting border between Mexico and the United States his native land. Raised in Mexico City, where he was born in 1955, Gómez-Peña emigrated to the United States in 1978 and lived for many years in the Tijuana/San Diego area. It was here that his eclectic "border sensibility," expressed in English, Spanish, Spanglish, journalism, radio, poetry, and live mixed-media performance, first captured public attention. Challenging the traditional folkloric icons of Mexican culture as well as contemporary Chicano political forms, Gómez-Peña exposes the stereotypes in every culture. A frequent contributor to National Public Radio as well as to Latino Radio USA, he received a MacArthur fellowship in 1991. Gómez-Peña's book *Warrior for Gringostroika* was published in 1993, and in 1997 his book *The New World Border* received the American Book Award.

Guillermo Gómez-Peña, **Authentic Cuban Santeria**

SEEING

1. What do you first notice when you examine the photograph of Guillermo Gómez-Peña's *Authentic Cuban Santeria?* Keep track of your eye movement as you view these two figures. Which features of each character call for your attention? Which ones hold your eye the longest? Explain why. What relationship(s) does Gómez-Peña establish between the two characters depicted in this photograph? What gestures are emphasized by each? With what effect(s)? What perspective and attitude does Gómez-Peña establish by positioning each figure within a frame and in relation to each other? What overall "statement(s)" does he make by doing so?

2. Identify the ways in which Gómez-Peña conveys a sense of authenticity in this photograph. Point to specific examples to support each of your assertions. Comment on his use of irony in the photograph and in his use of the Spanish word *Santeria*. For example, identify and comment on the points he makes by presenting "authentic" costumes along with the props of a fast-food culture.

WRITING

1. Read the excerpt from W.E.B. DuBois's *The Souls of Black Folk* (p. 563). Summarize in one paragraph the features of his vision of racial equality. Then create a list of the ways in which the photograph of Guillermo Gómez-Peña as *Authentic Cuban Santeria* illustrates DuBois's idea of "double consciousness." Write an essay in which you argue that the character Gómez-Peña presents here reflects the fundamental ideas embedded in DuBois's idea of double consciousness.

2. Consider the ways in which "authenticity" is reflected not only in racial and ethnic terms but also in class differences in contemporary American experience. Develop a list of the range of associations you make between "authenticity" and each of these social categories. How is authenticity made a matter of language—of specific vocabulary and ways of talking? Write an expository essay in which you explain the socioeconomic, cultural, and regional differences involved in defining authenticity in contemporary American society.

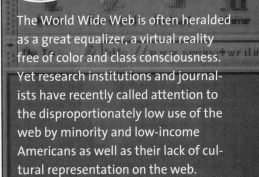

www   Re: Searching the Web

The World Wide Web is often heralded as a great equalizer, a virtual reality free of color and class consciousness. Yet research institutions and journalists have recently called attention to the disproportionately low use of the web by minority and low-income Americans as well as their lack of cultural representation on the web.

Concurrently, an increasing number of sites are addressed to particular ethnic groups. For example, NetNoir <www.netnoir.com> aims "to be the #1 Black interactive on-line community in the world" by providing a space for black-oriented news, social interaction, and links to black businesses. LatinoNet <www.latinoweb.com> promises a Latino Cyber Space Community in order to "empower the Latino community."

Choose a web site devoted to an ethnic or racial group. What are its announced—or implied—aims? How does it cater to a particular audience? What visual and verbal techniques does it use to envision American culture for this audience? Comment on its effectiveness.

Now consider the ways in which you can compare entering this ethnic neighborhood in a city or a town. Describe the experience of entering an ethnic neighborhood—as either an insider or an outsider. Write an expository essay in which you compare and contrast the ways in which entering a web site devoted to a particular ethnic group is similar to—or different from—actually walking into an ethnic neighborhood.

Shane Young, **Carol Gardner and Bumper Sticker Wisdom, 1995**

CAROL GARDNER

Author Carol Gardner spent two years touring the United States in the 1990s, seeking out interesting bumper stickers and talking with their owners. To her, bumper stickers are a form of advertising for the individual, a way to announce who you are and what you believe. Her book, *Bumper Sticker Wisdom* (1995), takes a close look at American culture and introduces the people behind the "one-liners." Whether the bumper sticker is humorous, thought provoking, or even risqué, the message behind it is often an expression of what Americans find important. In our post–September 11 environment, for example, people have used bumper stickers to demonstrate their patriotism or make a statement. Gardner's book is both fun and thought provoking, and the bumper stickers are downright hilarious.

SEEING

1. After examining this photograph, would you characterize your initial reaction to the image as surprised? engaged? disinterested? disappointed? something else? Please explain. What details do you notice about the ways in which Carol Gardner presents herself in this photo? Where have you seen similar poses and postures in other aspects of American culture? How relevant are these other sources to your reading of this photograph? To what extent do the statements made on each of the bumper stickers reinforce—or undercut—your overall impression of Gardner? Which bumper sticker comes closest in your judgment to representing the woman most adequately? Explain why.

2. Consider the choices that the photographer made in organizing this photograph. What overall effects are produced, for example, from the ways in which the photographer frames the photo? Comment on the contrast the photographer establishes between the position of Gardner and the placement of the bumper stickers on the station wagon. In what ways does Gardner's appearance reinforce—or subvert—the effects of the photo? Consider, for example, the placement of her hands and legs. What would have been the effect, for example, if she had been positioned standing next to the car?

WRITING

1. Imagine that you saw these bumper stickers on a car but no one was near it. How would you characterize the political and social sensibility expressed in these statements? Based on the cumulative effect(s) of these declarations, what would you expect the owner of the car to look like? Write an expository essay in which you explain how bumper stickers offer a compact and reliable form of personal identity.

2. Consider carefully the kind of writing printed on T-shirts. In what ways are the messages there different from—or similar to—those printed on bumper stickers? Which venue do you judge to be more effective in announcing one's political and/or social views? Write an essay in which you compare and contrast the likely impact of making statements on your own shirts or car.

CHARLES M. YOUNG
Born in Wisconsin, Charles M. Young received his master's degree in journalism from Columbia University in 1975. Young has been first and foremost a music critic and a writer whose offbeat and often satirical features for magazines like *Rolling Stone* and *Musician* covered the underground music scene in the 1970s and 1980s. His career changed, however, in the 1990s when he began to expand his focus and penned pieces on Noam Chomsky, Howard Zinn, and Ralph Nader. At the same time, the magazines and journals he was writing for were transforming themselves along with him. Instead of printing interviews with famous musicians and articles about their fame and lifestyles, these publications were including pieces on unknown musicians and on famous people who were not previously known for their musical zeal. Young began focusing on more obscure subject matter such as "losing," what it is like to be a middle-aged guitar player, and what happens at an extreme snowboarding competition in Alaska. Young still stays true to his musical roots, however. He has recently written music reviews for *The Atlantic*, and he·writes two album reviews every month for *Playboy*. "Losing: An American Tradition" was first published in *Men's Journal*.

LOSING: AN AMERICAN TRADITION

Charles M. Young

JUST NORTH OF THE NORTH END ZONE OF Blackshear Stadium at Prairie View A&M University in Texas is an unmarked grave.

"We buried last season," said Greg Johnson, the Prairie View Panthers' coach, during a break in football practice. "In March, just before the start of spring practice, we had them write down everything they didn't like about the past—being 0–9 last season, the record losing streak. We used the example of Superman, this guy that nobody could stop unless you got him near some green kryptonite. We asked them, 'Well, what's your green kryptonite? What is it that keeps you from doing what you need to do in the classroom and on the football field? Is it a female? Is it your friends? Is it a drug? Is it alcohol? Lack of dedication? Not enough time in the weight room? You got a nagging injury that you didn't rehab?' Whatever they wanted to bury, they wrote it down on a piece of paper. And the last thing we did, we looked at the HBO tape. The segment that Bryant Gumbel did on us for *Real Sports*, where they laughed at us and ridiculed us as the worst team in the country—'How does it feel to be 0–75 since 1989?' or whatever it was at that point. I said, 'That's the last we'll ever see of that tape,' and I put it in a big plastic trash bag with the paper. We took it to a hole I had dug near the gate, and we threw it in. All the players and all the coaches walked by. Some of them

kicked dirt on it, some of them spit on it. Some of them probably thought I was crazy. I said, 'This is the last time we're going to talk about last year. This is the last time we're going to talk about the losing streak. The past is dead, and anything that's dead ought to be buried. It's history. It's gone.' "

That took place in September 1998, when Prairie View's NCAA-record losing streak stood at 0–77. Now skip ahead to the postgame interviews of the January 9, 1999, AFC playoff game, in which the Denver Broncos beat the Miami Dolphins 38–3. Shannon Sharpe, the Broncos' tight end, called Miami's Dan Marino a "loser." Universally, this was viewed as a mortal insult, far beyond the bounds of acceptable trash talk.

"I cringed when I read that," said Mike Shanahan, the Broncos' coach. "I was really disappointed. Dan Marino's no loser."

So Sharpe, much humbled (and probably at Shanahan's insistence), groveled after the next Denver practice: "In no way, shape, or form is Dan Marino a loser. Dan, if I offended you or your family, your wife, your kids, your mother or father, your brothers or sisters, I apologize. I stand before you and sincerely apologize. I would never disrespect you as a person."

Which is odd. Football, along with every other major sport, is constructed to create losers. On any given game day, half the teams win, and half the teams lose. By the end of the playoffs, exactly one team can be called a winner, while thirty other teams are, literally, losers. So given that 96.7 percent of the players in the NFL can't help but be losers, why should calling somebody a loser be considered such an egregious violation of propriety that the guy who won must debase himself in public for pointing out that the guy who lost, lost?

Consider *Patton*, winner of the 1971 Academy Award for Best Picture and a favorite of coaches, team owners, and politicians ever since. It opens with George C. Scott standing in front of a screen-size American flag in the role of General George S. Patton, giving a pep talk to his troops. Using sports imagery to describe war (mirroring the sportswriters who use war imagery to describe sports), Patton delivers a succinct sociology lesson: "Americans love a winner, and will not tolerate a loser. Americans play to win all the time. I wouldn't give a hoot in hell for a man who lost and laughed. That's why Americans have never lost, and will never lose a war—because the very thought of losing is hateful to Americans."

Which is a view of most Americans that's shared by most Americans. Certain women of my acquaintance refer to men who score low on the Multiphasic Boyfriend Potentiality Scale as losers. *Cosmopolitan* has run articles on how to identify and dump losers before they have a chance to inseminate the unwary.

In *Jerry Maguire*, Tom Cruise suffers his worst humiliation when he spots his former girlfriend dating a rival agent at a *Monday Night Football* game. She makes an L with her fingers and mouths, "Loser."

In *American Beauty*, Kevin Spacey announces during his midlife crisis: "Both my wife and daughter think I'm this gigantic loser." 10

In *Gods and Monsters*, Lolita Davidovich, playing a bartender, dismisses the possibility of sex with her sometime lover, played by Brendan Fraser: "From now on, you're just another loser on the other side of the bar."

In *200 Cigarettes*, set in the ostensibly alternative subculture of Manhattan's Lower East Side, Martha Plimpton works herself into a state of despair considering the idea that no one will come to her New Year's Eve party. Then, considering an even worse possibility, she weeps: "All the losers will be here!"

At the real-life sentencing last February of Austin Offen for bashing a man over the head with a metal bar outside a Long Island night club, Assistant District Attorney Stephen O'Brien said that Offen was "vicious and brutal. He's a coward and a loser." Offen, displaying no shame over having crippled a man for life, screamed back: "I am not a loser!"

In his book *Turbo Capitalism: Winners and Losers in the Global Economy*, Edward Luttwak equates losing with poverty and observes that Americans believe that "failure is the result not of misfortune or injustice, but of divine disfavor."

I could list a hundred more examples, but you get the point. 15

Shannon Sharpe, in using the word *loser*, implied that Dan Marino was: unworthy of sex or love or friendship or progeny, socially clueless, stupid, parasitical, pathetic, poverty-stricken, cowardly, violent, felonious, bereft of all forms of status, beneath all consideration, hated by himself, hated by all good Americans, hated by God. And Dan Marino is one of the best quarterbacks ever to play football.

I was standing on the sideline during a Prairie View Panthers practice one scorching afternoon when a large boy on his way to class stopped to watch for a moment. Someone pointed him out to Coach Johnson and suggested that the boy be recruited for the team. "No, he was out last year, and he quit," said Johnson. "He has female tendencies. He looks like Tarzan and plays like Jane."

Johnson didn't say that *to* the boy, but suddenly my unconscious was barfing up all kinds of post-traumatic stress disorder from my own athletic experience. The next day in his office, I asked Johnson about football as an initiation rite in which aspiring Tarzans get all the Jane beaten out of them.

"That's just an old coach saying," he said. "If I had my druthers, I'd cut a kid open and look at his heart.

You never can tell just what tempo it's beating at until you put them in the heat of battle. Football is a test of manhood, a test of who has the biggest *cojones*. Win, lose, or draw, all my guys got great big *cojones*, 'cause they fight when they know the odds are against them."

Johnson's coaching record has ranged from 0–11 [20] as an assistant at Tennessee Tech to winning a couple of championships as a head coach at Oklahoma's Langston University. Feeling the need to migrate out of his "comfort zone," he came to Prairie View for the '97 season, becoming the fourth coach during the losing streak.

Back on the sideline, Anthony Carr, a sophomore cornerback from Houston, told me: "All these people put the streak in your mind. We say that's the past, but when everybody reminds you, it's hard to forget."

One of the lamest clichés in football, I said, was that it's so hard to repeat as champion because the other teams get so fired up to play you. In my experience, they got a lot more fired up to pulverize someone they knew they could pulverize—the incentive being that if you lose to the last-place team, you're worse than the worst.

"Yeah, nobody wants to lose to us. The other team is going to catch it. We've been called the laughing stock of the nation. That hurts. And it will hurt somebody to lose to the laughing stock of the nation."

Josh Barnes, a 165-pound junior quarterback returning from knee surgery, said he had chosen Prairie View to "make history" by breaking the losing streak. "My freshman year was tough. Southern beat us 63–0, Jackson State beat us 76–20. It hurt me. I hate losing. The cynicism was terrible. We heard it from everybody: 'Yawl suck!' If you have any pride, it's hard to take."

"A lot of people say losing builds character. I got [25] enough character for several lifetimes," said Michael Porter, a running back who graduated in 1997. At Jefferson Davis High School in Houston, he lost every game for three years, and at Prairie View, he lost every game for four years. He is now coaching football at his old high school. "It's hard to keep kids on the team when it's losing. It's hard to keep fans in the stands. But I just loved the game. I loved the spotlight. I didn't love losing. You never get used to that. Never. Ever."

So how did he keep going when he was getting crushed 60–0 in the fourth quarter?

"You got to have a nut check. Either I'm going to get whipped like a girl, or I'm going to come out like a man and get on with it. You may be winning on the scoreboard, but I'm going to whip your ass on the next play. It's war, man. That what it is—and it's not for everybody. This is no girlie sport."

When I was losing football games in college, it seemed like the worst thing you could call somebody was a pussy.

"Oh yeah. You don't want to be called a pussy on the field. I remember the times they'd be calling us the Prairie View Pussy Cats, and maybe some names even worse than that. It was a bad situation, having your organization ridiculed all the time. And you really hated it when it happened on campus. But it's all about manhood. Football forces you to be mature, to be disciplined, everything a man should be."

Later, I asked Coach Johnson if there was anything [30] to learn from losing.

"You learn what's wrong, and then you do the opposite. These kids will win even if they lose, because they're going to get their degree. Football helps keep them focused. Every kid wants discipline and structure and a chance to be special. When the world is telling them, 'You're not gonna be nothin',' football gives them a chance to prove themselves."

But maybe most people don't want to find out how good they are. If you give something a complete effort and fail, it would be logical to conclude that you are a loser. An incomplete effort offers the appeal of an excuse.

"Yeah, that's the real loser concept," said Johnson. "That's something you say on the porch with your wino buddies: 'Yeah, if I hadn't beat up that girl when I was sixteen, I'd still be playing football. If I hadn't taken that first drink or that first hit of marijuana, I'd be a star.' That's a penitentiary story."

The literal truth is, I may not be the worst college football player of all time. I've claimed that occasionally in the course of conversation, but I may be only the worst college football player of 1972. I was definitely the worst player on the Macalester College Scots of St. Paul, Minnesota, and we lost all of our games that season by an aggregate score of 312–46. The team went on to win one game in each of the following two seasons (after I graduated), then set the NCAA record with fifty straight losses. So, strictly speaking, the losing streak wasn't my fault. I do think I made a huge contribution to the atmosphere of despair and futility that led to the losing streak. I think that as Prairie View was to the '90s, Macalester was to the '70s. But in the final analysis, I think that over two decades at both schools, some athlete may have failed more than I did.

I may therefore merely be one of the worst, a weaker distinction that makes me even more pathetic than whoever it is who can make the case for sole possession of the superlative—if someone wants to make that case. No one, though, can question my credentials for at least a display in the Hall of Failure. In my junior year, on a team with barely enough players for one string, I was the only guy on third string. The coach wouldn't put me in the game even when the other team was winning by six touchdowns. In my senior year, we got a new head coach who had a terrifying policy: "If you practice, you play." And I did play in every game on the kickoff team, often getting a few additional minutes at strong safety after the game was hopelessly lost. The opposing third-string quarterback would throw a couple of touchdowns over my head just so I could feel as mortified as the rest of the team.

I got injured once. I came in too high to tackle a halfback and he drove his helmet into the left side of my chest. When I took off my shoulder pads in the locker room later, I was surprised to discover that I had a hemorrhaged pectoralis major muscle, which looked like a large, purple, female breast. To this day, when I am in the company of big American men and they compare their unstable knees, necrotic hips, herniated disks, cracked vertebrae, tilted atlas bones, arthritic shoulders, and twisted fingers, I can't make my wounded tit, as it was called back then, work even as a joke. No matter how I phrase it, they exchange "that guy's pathetic" looks. If your football injury made you look like Marilyn Manson, it definitely won't get you into the club of manly heterosexuals.

As many manly writers and equally manly psychologists have asserted, manhood is something you supposedly win. Females are simply born to womanhood. Males must wrest their manhood from some other male in a trial-by-fire ritual, the hottest of which in America is football.

I failed. I'm a loser.

Losing puts you in the center of a vast vacuum, where you are shunned by your own teammates, scorned by spectators, avoided by your friends. It's a lot like smelling bad. Nobody wants to talk about it in your presence.

Losing is hard to write about, too. Writing was why I went out for football, because the football players I knew had the best stories. I played two seasons. In my junior year, we won just one game, and the coach played me a total of sixty-three seconds over ten games. The losing wasn't quite mine, since I wasn't playing much, and the psychological distance made it possible to write a lot, mostly about stuff other than the actual games, because I didn't want to hurt the feelings of anyone on the team.

In my senior year, though, the shame became mine. Playing every game as a strong safety, I was supposed to line up about seven yards deep over the tight end. I could never figure out who the tight end was. The enemy huddle would break, and all I could see was this undifferentiated mass of enemy uniforms. "Strong left!" I would yell, which was part of my job. Our middle linebacker would turn around and hiss, "Strong right, you fucking idiot!"

In a chronic state of embarrassment, I wrote very little. The one long article I wrote was mostly about a

Ping-Pong game I played with a sexually ambiguous linebacker named Wally. (If I won, I got to spend the night with his girlfriend; if he won, he got to spend the night with me.) I beat Wally, and suddenly the words began to flow in the brief absence of humiliating defeat, in the brief presence of a different sport, one in which we could make a farce out of the cult of achieved masculinity. Not that I could articulate that insight at the time, but that's what we were doing. Farce is the only refuge for losers.

A couple weeks after I left PVU, the Panthers won a football game, 14–12, against Langston University, ending the losing streak at eighty. The campus erupted in a victory celebration that was typical of the orgiastic outpourings that people all over the world feel entitled to after an important win. I was happy for them. I felt bad for Langston, having to carry the stigma of losing to the losers of all time.

There being virtually no literature of losing, I became obsessed with reading books about winning, some by coaches and some by self-help gurus. All of them advised me to forget about losing. If you want to join the winners, they said, don't dwell on your past humiliations. Then I thought of George Santayana's dictum: "Those who forget the past are condemned to repeat it." So if I remembered losing, I'd be a loser. And if I forgot losing, I'd be a loser. Finally, I remembered a dictum of my own: "Anybody who quotes George Santayana about repeating the past will soon be repeating even worse clichés."

That Christmas, my local Barnes & Noble installed 45 a new section called "Lessons from the Winners." Publishers put out staggering numbers of books with "win" in the title (as they do with *Zen and Any Stupid Thing*), and they make money because there's a bottomless market of losers who want to be winners. Almost all of these books are incoherent lists of aphorisms and advice on how to behave like a CEO ("Memorize the keypad on your cell phone so you dial and drive without taking your eyes off the road"). Most of these books are written by men who have made vast fortunes polluting the groundwater and screwing people who work for a living, and these men want to air out their opinions, chiefly that they aren't admired enough for polluting the groundwater and screwing people who work for a living. I thought of the ultimate winner, Howard Hughes, who was once the richest man in the world, who had several presidents catering to his every whim, who stored his feces in jars. I got more and more depressed.

Maybe I was just hypnotized by my own history of failure, character defects, and left-wing politics. Maybe what I needed was a pep talk. Maybe what I needed was Ray Pelletier, a motivational speaker who has made a lot of money raising morale for large corporations and athletic teams. Pelletier, a member of the National Speakers Association Hall of Fame, wrote a book, *Permission to Win*, that Coach Johnson had recommended to me. Basically an exhortation to feel like a winner no matter how disastrous your circumstances happen to be, the book deals with losing as a problem of individual psychology. I asked Pelletier if the thought that the emphasis American culture places on competition was creating vast numbers of people who, on the basis of having lost, quite logically think of themselves as losers.

"I don't think you have to think of yourself as a loser," he said. "I think competition causes you to reach down inside and challenges you to be at your very best. The key is not to beat yourself. If you're better than I am and you're more prepared to play that day, you deserve to win. I have no problem with that. Every time I give a presentation, I want it to be better than the last one. I want to be sure I'm winning in everything that I do."

Yeah, but wasn't there a difference between excellence and winning?

"No, that's why I say that if I get beat by a team that's more talented, I don't have a problem with that."

When one guy won, was he not inflicting defeat on 50 the other guy?

"No. I'll give you an example. The first time I worked with a female team before a big game. I was getting them all riled up and playing on their emotions, telling them how they deserved this win and how they worked really hard. A rah-rah, goose-pimple kind of speech. Just before we went on the court, the point guard said, 'Can I ask a question? Haven't the girls in the other locker room worked really hard, too? Don't they deserve to win, too?' "

Pelletier then veered off into a discussion of how the game teaches you about life, of how his talks are really for fifteen years down the line when your wife leaves you, or the IRS calls for an audit, or you can't pay your mortgage. I asked him how he replied to the point guard in the locker room.

"I said, 'Absolutely the other team deserves to win, too. What we have to do is find out if we can play together tonight as a team.' See, that's the biggest challenge facing corporate America today. We talk about teamwork but we don't understand the concept of team. Most of us have never been coached in anything. We've been taught, but not coached. There's a big difference. Great coaches challenge you to play at your best. The key is, you're in the game, trying to better yourself."

But Bill Parcells, the former coach of the Jets, is famous for saying that you are what the standings say you are . . .

"Winning is playing at your best. Do you know the number-one reason why an athlete plays his sport? Recognition. Once you understand that, everything else becomes easy. Lou Holtz says that win means 'What's Important Now.' "

That's just standard practice in books about winning, I told him. They redefine the word to include all human behavior with a good connotation. In *The Psychology of Winning*, Dr. Denis Waitley writes that winning is "unconditional love." Winning could hardly be a more conditional form of love. You are loved if you win, and scorned if you lose.

"I don't believe that."

If athletes play for recognition, don't they want to be recognized as winners? And if you've lost, won't you be recognized as a loser?

"I don't think they're labeled that way."

By the press? By the fans?

"To me, unconditional love is an aspect of winning. The problem is that you and I have not been trained to think positively. In one of my corporate seminars, I ask people to write down all the advantages there are to being negative. I want them to think about it seriously. It's an exercise that can take fifteen or twenty minutes, and then they have the 'Aha!' There is no advantage to negative thinking. None. And yet the biggest problem we face in America is low self-esteem."

Low self-esteem has its uses, though. Whenever you see a couple of male animals on a PBS nature special duking it out for the privilege of having sex with some female of the species, one of the males is going to dominate and the other male is either going to die or get low self-esteem and crawl off making obsequious gestures to the winner. The evolutionary value is obvious: Fight to the death and your genes die with you; admit you're a loser and you may recover to fight again or find another strategy for passing on your genes through some less selective female. Species in which one alpha male gets to have sex with most of the females—elephant seals are a good example—need a lot of low self-esteem among the beta males for social stability.

With 1 percent of the population possessing more wealth than the bottom 95 percent, the American economy operates a lot like a bunch of elephant seals on a rock in the ocean. And it simply must mass-produce low self-esteem in order to maintain social stability amidst such colossal unfairness.

According to the World Health Organization, mood disorders are the number-one cause worldwide of people's normal activities being impaired. In the United States alone, the WHO estimates, depression costs $53 billion a year in worker absenteeism and lost productivity. While that's a hell of a market for Ray Pelletier and the National Speakers Association, which has more than three thousand people giving pep talks to demoralized companies and sports teams, doled-out enthusiasm is a palliative, not a curative. In fact, demoralization is a familiar management tool; the trick is creating just enough. Too much and you have work paralysis, mass depression, and suicide. Too little and you have a revolution. Ever hear a boss brag that he doesn't *have* ulcers, he *gives* them? He's making sure his employees are demoralized enough to stay in their place.

Consider the book *Shame and Pride*, by Dr. Donald L. Nathanson, a psychiatrist and the executive director of the Silvan S. Tomkins Institute in Philadelphia. Starting in the mid-1940s, Dr. Tomkins watched babies for thousands of hours and made a convincing case that humans are born preprogrammed with nine "affects"—potential states of emotion that can be triggered by a stimulus or memory. These affects are: interest-excitement, enjoyment-joy, surprise-startle, fear-terror, distress-anguish, anger-rage, dis-smell (*dissmell* is similar to *distaste*, but related to the sense of smell), disgust, and shame-humiliation. These affects "amplify" an outside stimulus or memory to give you an increase in brain activity that eventually becomes full-blown emotion.

Until recent years, shame was the "ignored emotion" in psychology. But a few people, Nathanson most prominently, built on Tomkins and discovered the key to . . . well, not quite everything, but an awful lot. According to Tomkins and Nathanson, shame erupts whenever "desire outruns fulfillment." An impediment arises to the two positive affects (interest-excitement and enjoyment-joy), and suddenly your eyes drop, your head and body slump, your face turns red, and your brain is confused to the point of paralysis. This is observable in babies and in adults. This is also observable in the NFL, exquisitely so after the regular season, when the coaches of the teams that don't make the playoffs are ritually humiliated at press conferences. A variation on the theme, often seen in losing coaches who manage to keep their jobs for another season, is the compensatory jutting chin and the disdainful stare, both directed at the press and usually accompanied by promises to examine every aspect of the organization and by pronouncements about "recommitment to winning." Players in this state of shame often attack journalists verbally,

and sometimes physically. Sportswriters, who in general demand that losing competitors exhibit lots of shame for dramatic purposes and who reinforce the savage lie that losers aren't man enough to win, keep the system in place even as they complain about it.

So I called up Nathanson and asked if he had any thoughts about why athletes get so upset when they are called pussies.

"One of the major tasks of childhood is the formation of gender identity, the shift from saying, 'I'm a kid,' to saying, 'I'm a boy,' or 'I'm a girl,' " he replied. "I don't think anyone gets over the shame we have of not being adequately identified by the right gender. We see a lot of that worry in adults, in the drive for perfection of the body through plastic surgery and steroids. People don't just wish to be someone else anymore, they buy it. Men also face the problem of 'Am I masculine enough?' In Blake Edwards's remarkable movie *Victor/Victoria*, Alex Karras says something to the effect that a lot of men go into football because they want to undo any worry that they're not adequately masculine. Men are concerned that they'll be called not just female, but female genitalia. I don't think any of this is trivial, because of the risk of violence when someone is shamed in public. Sports are an analog of what goes on in everyday life, and it's amazing what people get away with on the so-called field of honor."

Sports events are often described as a morality play, I said, but there's nothing moral about it. Sports decide who will participate in power and who will be humiliated.

"That's understandable when you recognize that our sense of place in society is maintained by shame. Keeping people in their place is maintaining them at certain levels of shaming interaction at which they can be controlled. This issue of winning and losing, it throws us. It defines our identity, doesn't it?"

Calling someone a loser is probably the worst insult in the United States today.

"If you're calling someone that, the person must live in a perpetual state of shame. The only way he can live with himself is to have massive denial, disavowal of his real identity. He has to make his way in the world somehow, and he can't walk around constantly thinking of himself as a loser. Yet if someone in our eyes is a loser and he refuses to admit it, this is narcissism. He has an identity that can't be sustained by consensual validation."

Is there some value in competition, in creating all these losers?

"When you're young and you're learning and it's just a bunch of guys playing a game, that's not shame. That's just figuring out that Billy is faster than Johnny. When parents and schools and bureaucracies start getting involved and demanding wins, then it gets pathological."

Playing for the Chicago Bears, the Philadelphia Eagles, and the Dallas Cowboys from 1961 to 1972, Mike Ditka was All-Pro five times as a tight end, won an NFL championship with the Bears in 1963, won Super Bowl VI with the Cowboys, and was elected to the Hall of Fame. As the coach of the Bears from 1982 to 1992, he won Super Bowl XX with an 18–1 team generally acknowledged as one of the greatest ever and was named Coach of the Year twice. As the coach of the New Orleans Saints for the past three seasons, he had a 15–33 record and is now most vividly remembered for flipping off the fans and grabbing his crotch during and after an especially inept defeat. (He was fined $20,000.) I asked him if he thinks that football fans are inherently interested in the game, or in the hallucination of power they get when their team wins?

"They relate to the winning. Well, you can't say they aren't interested in the game. They watch the game. But the excitement comes from winning."

When football players snap at journalists in the locker room after a loss . . .

"That's only human nature. They probably snap at their wives when they get home, too. Are you saying, Does losing bother people? Sure it does. It's no different from a guy at IBM who loses a sale to a competitor. You just don't like to lose. Most people want to be associated with winning. When you work your butt off and don't get the results you want, you might be a little short-tempered as a coach. That's only life. But that's no different than any other segment of life. Football parallels society, period."

I've noticed that the worst thing you can call somebody in the United States is a loser.

"No. The word *quitter* is the worst thing you can call somebody. Lemme ask you something: If two teams play all year, and they reach the Super Bowl, the one that loses is a loser? Come on.

"I don't like the term. . . . It's not fair. I think as long as you compete and you do your best, if the other team is better, I don't think you really lose. I think you lose when you quit trying."

The problem with declaring a quitter to be a lower form of dirt than a loser is that you're still stigmatizing almost everybody. Studies indicate that up to 90 percent of children drop out of organized competitive sports by the age of fifteen. Extrapolating from my own experience, I would guess that they don't enjoy feeling like losers so that the jocks can feel like winners. Since they associate intense physical activity with feeling rotten, they grow up having problems with obesity and depression, both of which have become epidemic in the United States.

As Mike Ditka would say, it's not fair. But I think there's a way out. And I think that Alfie Kohn has seen it. Kohn, an educational philosopher, has helped inspire the opposition to standardized tests, an especially pernicious form of competition. His first book, *No Contest: The Case Against Competition,* cites study after study demonstrating that competition hinders work, play, learning, and creativity in people of all ages. (In fact, there is almost no evidence to the contrary in the social sciences.) The book is wonderfully validating for anyone who ever had doubts about the ostensible fun of gym class and spelling bees. I told Kohn that in my experience, people get unhinged when you question the value of making other people fail.

"Absolutely. It calls into question America's state religion, which is practiced not only on the playing field but in the classroom and the workplace, and even in the family. The considerable body of evidence demonstrating that this is self-defeating makes very little impression on people who are psychologically invested in a desperate way in the idea of winning. The real alternative to being number one is not being number two, but being able to dispense with these pathological ratings altogether. If people accepted the research on the destructiveness of competition, you wouldn't see all these books teaching how to compete more effectively. I hear from a lot of teachers and parents whose kids fall apart after losing in spelling bees and awards assemblies, and they feel dreadful about it. The adults start to think, *Hmm, maybe competition isn't such a good thing, at least for those kids.* It took me years to see that the same harms were being visited upon the winners. The kids who win are being taught that they are good only to the extent that they continue to beat other people. They're being taught that other people are obstacles to their own success, which destroys a sense of community as effectively as when we teach losers that lesson. And finally, the winners are being taught that the point of what they are doing is to win, which leads to diminished achievement and interest in what they are doing. What's true for kids is also true for adults. It's not a problem peculiar to those who lose. We're all losers in the race to win."

I'm very blessed that way. I didn't have the perspective to spell it out like Alfie Kohn, but I've known I was a total loser since my first college football practice. I've admitted it here publicly, and I am free. You, you're probably holding on to some putrefying little shred of self-esteem, denying that you're a loser in a country inhabited by Bill Gates and 260 million losers. You're still hoping to beat your friend at racquetball and make him feel as bad as you do when you lose, still looking to flatten some rival with just the right factoid in an argument, still craving the sports car in the commercial that accurately announces, "There's no such thing as a gracious winner." Give up, I say. Join me. Losers of the world, unite! You have nothing to lose but your shame. ○

SEEING

1. Why does Young call losing an American tradition? According to him, what kinds of things make losing traditional? Who has participated (historically and currently) in the tradition? How does losing get passed on from one generation to another? To what extent might the title be read another way—as advice on how to lose an American tradition? How does Young show the reader how to change her or his traditional relationship to losing? What must happen for America to "lose" its attitude toward losing?

2. Read "The Pursuit of Happiness" by Andrew Sullivan (p. 400). What effects do the different subject matters have on the writing strategies that both Sullivan and Young use? How is writing about pursuing happiness different from writing about attaining "loserdom"? Which author has the more difficult writing assignment? Explain why. Who works harder to justify his position? What stylistic changes would be required to write effectively about other emotional states—such as disgust, fear, or hope?

WRITING

1. One of Young's strongest arguments for reconceiving losing in American society is that almost everyone loses. As he puts it, we live "in a country inhabited by Bill Gates and 260 million losers" (para. 85). Write a list of your own greatest moments as a loser: your worst sports moment, your most embarrassing fall, your lowest grade. Now find out how many of those moments have been shared by the greatest winners in our culture. For example, Albert Einstein famously failed out of school. Former president George Bush vomited on the prime minister of Japan. What does it say about our notions of winners and losers that these people who have excelled, still fail?

2. How do other cultures or historical periods deal with losing and winning? Pick a particular competitive event in another country—for example, a political election or a soccer match. Read at least five different articles leading up to the event, describing it, and analyzing its aftermath. How do the authors characterize the competitive elements of the event? What kinds of metaphors do they use? Compare this characterization of winning and losing to a similar American event. What differences do you find? What similarities? Which characterization do you think was better? Write an essay supporting your claim.

Tracy Moffatt, **Fourth #4, 2001**

1957

1993

NEAL GABLER

Hollywood shapes our views of American life, and Neal Gabler knows how and why this happens. It is show business that makes the world turn around, but the seemingly harmless glitz and glam also form the fabric of modern American culture, and Gabler is not afraid to add his voice to those who debate the merits of an entertainment-driven society. Gabler, a media critic, historian, and television commentator, has written several books on the subject, including *An Empire of Their Own: How the Jews Invented Hollywood* (1989); *Winchell: Gossip, Power and the Culture of Celebrity* (1995); and *Life the Movie: How Entertainment Conquered Reality* (2000).

Gabler is a senior fellow at the Norman Lear Center at the University of Southern California, Annenberg, and he is a frequent contributor to *Jewish World Review*. Gabler has taught at his alma mater, the University of Michigan, and at Pennsylvania State University; he has also been a cultural historian appearing on *Good Morning America* and a commentator on the PBS broadcast *Sneak Previews*. Gabler has also served as chair of the nonfiction panel of the National Book Awards.

Inside Every Superhero Lurks a Nerd

Neal Gabler

You can attribute the record-breaking $114 million gross of *Spider-Man* last weekend to many factors—hype, branding, superb timing before the deluge of summer blockbuster hits. But none of these seem to explain the rabid enthusiasm with which the film has been greeted, especially by teenagers, or the way it has almost immediately entrenched itself in the popular culture.

To understand that phenomenon, one may have to look beyond the shilling and marketing to the movie's content. *Spider-Man* exists at the nexus and confluence of two fundamental American rites: adolescence and moviegoing.

When Stan Lee and Steve Ditko of Marvel Comics created Spider-Man in 1962, they revised the standard superhero mythology—the protagonist had to come from another planet, like Superman, or be a rich, handsome do-gooder, like Batman, for whom crime-busting is a way to avenge his parents' deaths. And they relocated it in adolescence.

At the comic book's inception, their hero, Peter Parker, is a dorky American teenager beset with adolescent doubts and fears. He has to navigate the terrifying world of high school, where he is dismissed by the popular kids as a "bookworm" and ignored by the girl he worships. But when he is bitten by an irradiated spider (in the comic) or a genetically altered spider (in the movie) and is suddenly endowed with superpowers, he achieves the ultimate adolescent dream. He is transformed from an outcast into the toughest kid in the school. No wonder teenagers respond.

Everyone knows how strongly this idea resonates, not just because most adults have experienced adolescent powerlessness themselves, but because it offers an awful reminder of Columbine, Colo., where two alienated teenage outcasts took revenge on their more popular classmates in a bloody high school rampage.

Operating from the same impulse, *Spider-Man* takes the sense of powerlessness in its audience and displaces it onto the screen, providing catharsis. In effect, it is the sunny antidote to teenage alienation, the other side of Columbine. What makes the movie all the more effective is that in Tobey Maguire's diffident, self-effacing performance, viewers aren't given the idea that inside every nerd there lurks a superhero—the basic thrust of Superman—as much as the idea that inside every superhero there lurks a nerd. Spider-Man, c'est moi!

In saying this, one could just as easily be talking about the movies generally. Whatever else American films do, the most popular ones are almost always about wish fulfillment, and the great stars, from Jimmy Cagney to Marlon Brando to Clint Eastwood, are the ones with whom viewers can identify and through whom they can transcend themselves. They empower the audience.

This is one reason that movies appeal so profoundly to teenagers. The movies hit them where they

live—in their own state of desperation and doubt. Movies don't just
provide them with escape, as the
conventional wisdom would have
it. They give teenagers the exhila-
ration of hope through the illusion
of power. So when *Spider-Man*
takes wish fulfillment and provides
a teenage protagonist, it is combining two powerful elements: a
primary source of moviegoing pleasure with a primary means of
audience identification. In a way, it
makes *Spider-Man* a movie about
the things that make movies
intoxicating.

But if *Spider-Man* exists at the junction of adolescent dreams and the
Hollywood dream machine, it also
exists at another junction where
adolescence and American culture
converge: responsibility. One of the
great American conundrums has
been how to reconcile the nation's
much-vaunted frontier individualism with a sense of community necessary for a functioning society. Fit-
tingly for a country as young as
America, this is one of the great adolescent problems as well. Adolescence is the period where one must
move from youth to maturity, which
means adjusting individual needs
and desires to the larger world.

While *Spider-Man* is about 10
teenage dreams of power, it is also
about that adjustment. Spider-
Man's nemesis in the film, the
Green Goblin, is a rich industrialist
who conducts an experiment on
himself to win a government contract and then discovers that along
with chemically induced superpowers, he has acquired a malevolent
streak he cannot control. He is the
personification of irresponsible
self-interest—an adult who hasn't
grown up.

At first, Peter Parker himself, like
a typical self-involved teenager, uses
his superpowers to try to get money
to buy a car to win the attentions of
the girl he loves. It is only when,
through a quirk of fate, he realizes
that his failure to use his superpowers for good can have awful consequences that he takes seriously his
Uncle Ben's injunction: with power
comes responsibility.

This idea, too, taps into one of the
deepest satisfactions of moviegoing.
Hollywood movies invariably celebrate individualism. Indeed, the
star system is a tribute to it. But
what makes a hero truly heroic—
and what gives the audience its
kick—is not simply that he stands
alone. Villains, after all, often stand
alone. It is that he deploys his individualism for the larger good,
which is how the movies reconcile
the American problem of self and
society. Superman, Batman, and
now Spider-Man, not to mention
John Wayne, Arnold Schwarzenegger, and the Rock, are all non-
pareil individualists who serve the
community and do what in movies
the community itself seems incapable of doing—namely, acting. Or
put another way, they are both
cool and good.

As with wish fulfillment, *Spider-
Man* is not only an example of this
pleasure of watching responsibility
in action, it is about accepting responsibility. Peter Parker enters
the adult world by avenging evil,
taking the audience vicariously
with him. He gives teenage viewers
the high of public service.

In this way, the film once again
self-reflexively reinforces one of
the joys of moviegoing generally
with the specific concerns of its
viewers. It may well be that *Spider-
Man* is raking in all that dough because it is both so faithful to the
genetic roots of the movies and so
sensitive to the needs of its target
audience, teenagers who want to
feel better about themselves. In
short, it is the movie that modern
Hollywood was designed to make
for the audience Hollywood was designed to deliver it to. ○

SEEING

1. According to Neal Gabler, what is there about Spider-Man (the character and the film) that resonates so deeply with teenagers? Why has the movie so easily "entrenched itself in the popular culture"? To what extent do you agree with Gabler's assessments of the film's popularity? To what do *you* attribute the record-breaking success of *Spider-Man*?

2. How convincing do you find Gabler's overarching argument about the film? What additional, supporting arguments does he articulate in this essay? In your judgment, where—and to what extent—do these arguments succeed or fall short? Where—and how effectively—does Gabler use specific examples to support each of his arguments? What additional examples might you include to strengthen or refute them?

WRITING

1. How common is the notion that "inside every superhero there lurks a nerd" in contemporary popular American culture? Where else, besides Superman, do you find evidence of this "belief"? Choose some work of writing—a song, television show, movie, cartoon, or advertisement (to name a few possibilities). Write a two-page essay explaining how this work relies on characters "with whom viewers can identify and through whom they can transcend themselves" (para. 7).

2. Consider the terms *individuality* and *responsibility* in contemporary American culture. Where do you see these terms invoked in politics, in advertising, or in popular entertainment? To what extent are they associated with specifically American characteristics or values? How? Choose one such cultural document, and write an essay in which you analyze the use of one or both of these terms to appeal to American audiences. Please be sure to identify the purpose of focusing on the term(s) as well as to comment on the effectiveness of using them.

NAOMI HARRIS >

A Canadian printmaker turned photographer, Naomi Harris recently spent two years in Miami—after winning the Agfa International Prize for Young Photojournalism—photographing the retirees of the Haddon Hall Hotel. She saw a certain stereotypical regularity in the way the elderly are photographed—always in black and white, and always in some degree of despair. Harris changed that by taking pictures in the broad daylight and pastel brights of Miami Beach, and she captured the elderly in a more upbeat and positive way. She is hoping to publish the resulting collection, "Haddon Hotel—Where Living Is a Pleasure" in a book or on a web site.

Harris's work has been published in the *London Telegraph Magazine*; *Nerve*; *Shift* magazine; and the *Observer*, among others. She currently lives and works in New York City. The "Makeover" was first published in the November 12, 2000 issue of the *New York Times Magazine*.

1. Paul Viaros outside his Toronto home. John Kenyon, the location manager, scouted for a month for the right Greek house. "When you find it, you know," he says.

2. Viaros signs the contract with Kenyon before the crew—armed with the directive of taking everything Greek and "turning it up to 11"—arrived.

5. A power line is removed to make way for the shot. "Somebody's got a lot of power and money to remove a pole," says Doug Buchanan of Toronto Hydro.

6. Buchanan, who refers to Toronto as Hollywood North, oversees the removal of the pole, which will sit in the Hydro yard until the shoot ends.

9. Having sodded the original Viaros driveway, the production team added a new one, complete with ersatz garage.

10. The fully prepped house, ready for its close-up. Not knowing it was being used in a movie, a neighbor commented, "What, wasn't it Greek enough before?"

Naomi Harris, **The Makeover**

3. Kenyon (left) and Kei Ng, the art director, made the house look bigger to match the interiors, which were shot elsewhere.

4. Sodding the driveway to expand the lawn. "This was not a large job," says Jim Peters, the landscaper. A large job is 200 trees and 3,000 tons of dirt.

7. A new facade goes up. Viaros says that it was only after the first visit that the location manager said "to remove the driveway, then the pole, then the facade. . . ."

8. Viaros already had plans for a real second floor, but he likes this one better. "Now I have a problem," he says. "What do I use: my design or the movie company's?"

11. At last, the scene as planned in Nia Vardalos's semiautobiographical script. She's happy that the house was made to look funny but not like a cartoon.

12. Home, sweet home. Now Paul Viaros's daughters, who had been embarrassed by all the hubbub, can stop pretending they don't live here.

SEEING

1. Scriptwriter Nia Vardalos was happy that the house used in *My Big Fat Greek Wedding* was "made to look funny but not like a cartoon," writes Naomi Harris. To what extent do you agree with Nia Vardalos's characterization? What is typically Greek about Paul Viaros's house—in its original and Hollywood versions?

2. Examine carefully the nature of the makeover of Viaros's house. Create a catalogue of the changes made to the house and surrounding grounds. What elements of the house were emphasized and altered? What new elements were added? How does Harris encourage her readers to respond to the phrase "Home, sweet home" in the final frame? Why will Paul Viaros's daughters now be able to stop pretending they don't live here?

WRITING

1. Choose a house or apartment that you are familiar with. Imagine that you have been asked by a Hollywood studio for permission to use it as the set for a film focusing on the lives of college students. Develop an imaginary concept for the film, and then write a two-page plan for making over your apartment or house, Hollywood style. What elements of the space would you choose to highlight or change? Why?

2. The "makeover" craze on day-time talk shows and late-night advertisements is not a recent invention; it is the most recent version of a long tradition in popular American culture, examples of which are printed in this book. Note, for example, the type of transformative effects promised by products such as Charles Atlas's "Dynamic Tension" in the 1940s (see advertisement, p. 351). Consider also the images of Cindy Jackson (see p. 370), the woman who underwent a series of nineteen cosmetic surgeries to transform herself into her personal model of perfection, the Barbie doll. Write an expository essay in which you explore the similarities and differences between any two of these variations on the "makeover" in American culture.

 Talking Pictures

Naomi Harris's photographs of the house used in *My Big Fat Greek Wedding* demonstrate a process used in television and film on a regular basis: enhancing and manipulating "real" homes and locations for use on screen. In this case, the filmmakers focused on exaggerating the features of a "typical" Greek-American home.

From the caricatures of blacks on *Amos 'n' Andy* to the portrayals of angst-ridden Jewish mothers on *Seinfeld*, racial and ethnic stereotyping has long been a staple of television and movie humor. What more recent portrayals of various American ethnic groups do you find on television and in film? To what extent are these portrayals stereotypical? From one of these media, choose a character or scene that relies on ethnic or racial identity as a source of humor. What is the nature of the stereotype, and on what does the humor rely? Write an expository essay in which you discuss the relation of humor to matters of ethnic stereotypes of a particular race.

Looking Closer
Marketing Cool

LOOK-LOOK

Cool Like Me
Donnell Alexander

No Logo:
Taking Aim at the
Brand Bullies
Naomi Klein

According to Teen Research Unlimited, American teenagers spent an estimated $105 billion and influenced their parents to spend an additional $48 billion in 2001. Given these stakes, advertisers and the entertainment and fashion industries are more invested than ever in tapping into the pulse of youth cultures around the nation—and the globe. "Cool hunters" like Dee Dee Gordon and Sharon Lee (interviewed in **"Look-Look"**) provide companies with frequent reports on fashion and social and cultural trends before they become labeled and marketed as such.

In **"No Logo,"** cultural critic Naomi Klein claims that "the history of cool in America is really...a history of African-American culture...for many of the superbrands, cool hunting simply means blackculture hunting." In **"Cool Like Me,"** Donnell Alexander argues that "Cool has a history and cool has a meaning," one that is inextricably bound to the African American experience. Each of the images in this unit offers a provocative vantage point from which to view cool: **Lauren Greenfield**'s photograph shows a Beverly Hills high school rap band taping a music video; Phat Farm's advertisement *Classic American Flava* shows urban cool in a stereotypically suburban setting; and Adbusters' *Tommy: Follow the Flock* provides a humorous double-take on a line of clothing that has managed to wear well across the demarcations of American class, ethnicity, and race.

Cool Like Me

Donnell Alexander

I read fashion magazines like they're warning labels telling me what not to do.

When I was a kid, Arthur Fonzarelli seemed a garden-variety dork.

I got my own speed limit.

I come when I want to.

I maintain like an ice cube in the remote part of the freezer.

Cooler than a polar bear's toenails.

Cooler than the other side of the pillow.

Cool like me.

Know this while understanding that I am in essence a humble guy.

I'm the kinda nigga who's so cool that my neighbor bursts into hysterical tears whenever I ring her doorbell after dark. She is a new immigrant who has chosen to live with her two roommates in our majority-black Los Angeles neighborhood so that, I'm told, she can "learn about all American cultures." But her real experience of us is limited to the space between her Honda and her front gate; thus, much of what she has to go on is the vibe of the surroundings and the images emanating from the television set that gives her living room a minty cathode glow. As such, I'm a cop-show menace and a shoe commercial demigod—one of the rough boys from our 'hood and the living, breathing embodiment of hip hop flava. And if

I can't fulfill the prevailing stereotype, the kids en route to the nearby high school can. The woman is scared in a cool world. She smiles as I pass her way in the light of day, unloading my groceries or shlepping my infant son up the stairs. But at night, when my face is visible through the window of her door lit only by the bulb that brightens the vestibule, I, at once familiar and threatening, am just too much.

Thus being cool has its drawbacks. With cool come assumptions and fears, expectations and intrigue. My neighbor wants to live near cool, but she's not sure about cool walking past her door after dark. During the day, she sees a black man; at night what she sees in the shadow gliding across her patio is a nigga.

Once upon a time, little need existed for making the distinction between a nigga and a black—at least not in this country, the place where niggas were invented. We were just about all slaves, so we were all niggas. Then we became free on paper yet oppressed still. Today, with as many as a third of us a generation or two removed from living poor (depending on who's counting), niggadom isn't innate to every black child born. But with the poverty rate still hovering at around 30 percent, black people still got niggas in the family, even when they themselves aren't niggas. Folks who don't know niggas can watch them on TV, existing in worlds almost always removed from blacks. Grant Hill is black, Allen Iverson is a nigga. Oprah interviewing the celebrity du jour is a black woman; the woman being hand-cuffed on that reality TV show is a nigga.

The question of whether black people are cooler than white people is a dumb one, and one that I imagine a lot of people will find offensive. But we know what we're talking about, right? We're talking about style and spirit and the innovations that those things spawn. It's on TV; it's in the movies, sports and clothes and language and gestures and music.

See, black cool is cool as we know it. I could name 15 names—Michael Jordan and Chris Rock and Me'shell Ndegeocello and Will Smith and bell hooks and Li'l Kim—but cool goes way back, much further than today's superstars. Their antecedents go back past blaxploitation cinema, past Ike Turner to Muddy Waters, beyond even the old jazz players and blues singers whose names you'll never know. Cool has a history and cool has a meaning. We all know cool when we see it, and now, more than at any other time in this country's history, when mainstream America looks for cool we look to black culture. Countless new developments can be called great, nifty, even keen. But, cool? That's a black thang, baby.

And I should know. My being cool is not a matter of subjectivity or season. Having lived as a nigga has made me cool. Let me explain. Cool was born when the first plantation nigga figured out how to make animal innards—massa's garbage, hog maws and chitlins—taste good enough to eat. That inclination to make something out of nothing and then to make that something special articulated itself first in the work chants that slaves sang in the field and then in the hymns that rose out of their churches. It would later reveal itself in the music made from cast-off Civil War marching-band instruments (jazz); physical exercise turned to public spectacle (sports); and street life styling, from pimps' silky handshakes to the corner crack dealer's baggy pants.

Cool is all about trying to make a dollar out of 15 cents. It's about living on the cusp, on the periphery, diving for scraps. Essential to cool is being outside looking in. Others—Indians, immigrants, women, gays—have been "othered," but until the past 15 percent of America's history, niggas in real terms have been treated by the country's majority as, at best, subhuman and, at worst, an abomination. So in the days when they were still literally on the plantation they devised a coping strategy called cool, an elusive mellowing strategy designed to master time and space. Cool, the basic reason blacks remain in the American cultural mix, is an industry of style that everyone in the world can use. It's finding the essential soul while being essentially lost. It's the nigga metaphor. And the nigga metaphor is the genius of America.

Gradually over the course of this century, as there came to be a growing chasm of privilege between black people and niggas, the nature of cool began to shift. The romantic and now-popular image of the pasty Caucasian who hung out in a jazz club was one small subplot. Cool became a promise—the reward to any soul hardy enough to pierce the inner sanctum of black life and not only live to tell about it but also live to live for it. Slowly, watered-down versions of this very specific strain of cool became the primary means of defining American cool. But it wasn't until Elvis that cool was brought down from Olympus (or Memphis) to majority-white culture. Mass media did the rest. Next stop: high fives, chest bumps, and "Go girl!"; Air Jordans, Tupac, and low-riding pants.

White folks began to try to make the primary point of cool—recognition of the need to go with the flow—a part of their lives. But cool was only an avocational interest for them. It could never be the necessity it was for their colored co-occupants. Some worked harder at it than others. And as they came to understand coolness as being of almost elemental importance, they began obsessing on it, asking themselves, in a variety of clumsy, indirect ways: Are black people cooler than white people and, if so, why?

The answer is, of course, yes. And if you, the reader, 20 had to ask some stupid shit like that, you're probably white. It's hard to imagine a black person even asking the question, and a nigga might not even know what you mean. Any nigga who'd ask that question certainly isn't much of one; niggas invented the shit.

Humans put cool on a pedestal because life at large is a challenge, and in that challenge we're trying to cram in as much as we can—as much fine loving, fat eating, dope sleeping, mellow walking, and substantive working as possible. We need spiritual assistance in the matter. That's where cool comes in. At its core, cool is useful. Cool gave bass to 20th-century American culture, but I think that if the culture had needed more on the high end, cool would have given that, because cool closely resembles the human spirit. It's about completing the task of living with enough spontaneity to splurge some of it on bystanders, to share with others working through their own travails a little of your bonus life. Cool is about turning desire into deed with a surplus of ease.

Some white people are cool in their own varied ways. I married a white girl who was cooler than she ever knew. And you can't tell me Jim Jarmusch and Ron Athey and Delbert McClinton ain't smooth.

There's a gang of cool white folks, all of whom exist that way because they've found their essential selves amid the abundant and ultimately numbing media replications of the coolness vibe and the richness of real life. And there's a whole slew more of them ready to sign up if you tell 'em where. But your average wigger in the rap section of Sam Goody ain't gone nowhere; she or he hasn't necessarily learned shit about the depth and breadth of cool, about making a dollar out of 15 cents. The problem with mainstream American culture, the reason why irony's been elevated to raison d'être status and neurosis increasingly gets fetishized, is its twisted approach to cool. Most think cool is something you can put on and take off at will (like a strap-on goatee). They think it's some shit you go shopping for. And that taints cool, giving the mutant thing it becomes a deservedly bad name. Such strains aren't even cool anymore, but an evil ersatz-cool, one that fights real cool at every turn. Advertising agencies,

record-company artist-development departments, and over-art-directed bars are where ersatz-cool dwells. What passes for cool to the white-guy passerby might be—is probably—just rote duplication without an ounce of inspiration.

The acceptance of clone cool by so many is what makes hip hop necessary. It's what negates the hopelessness of the postmodern sensibility at its most cynical. The hard road of getting by on metaphorical chitlins kept the sons and daughters of Africa in touch with life's essential physicality, more in touch with the world and what it takes to get over in it: People are moved, not convinced; things get done, they don't just happen. Real life doesn't allow for much fronting, as it were. And neither does hip hop. Hip hop allows for little deviation between who one is and what one can ultimately represent.

Rap—the most familiar, and therefore the most emblematic, example of hip hop expression—is about the power of conveying through speech the world beyond words. Language is placed on a par with sound and, ultimately, vibes. Huston Smith, a dope white guy, wrote: "Speech is alive—literally alive because speaking is the speaker. It's not the whole of the speaker, but it is the speaker in one of his or her living modes. This shows speech to be alive by definition. . . . It possesses in principle life's qualities, for its very nature is to change, adapt, and invent. Indissolubly contextual, speaking adapts itself to speaker, listener, and situation alike. This gives it an immediacy, range, and versatility that is, well, miraculous."

Which is why hip hop has become the most insidiously influential music of our time. Like rock, hip hop in its later years will have a legacy of renegade youth to look back upon fondly. But hip hop will insist that its early marginalization be recognized as an integral part of what it comes to be. When the day comes that grandmothers are rapping and beatboxing as they might aerobicize now, and samplers and turntables are as much an accepted part of leisure time as channel surfing, niggas will be glad. Their expression will have proven ascendant.

But that day's not here yet. If white people were really cool with black cool, they'd put their stuff with our stuff more often to work shit out. I don't mean shooting hoops together in the school-yard as much as white cultural institutions like college radio, indie film, and must-see TV. Black cool is banished to music videos, sports channels, and UPN so whites can visit us whenever they want without having us live right next door in the media mix. Most of the time, white folks really don't want to be part of black cool. They just like to see the boys do a jig every once in a while.

At the same time, everyday life in black America is not all Duke Ellington and Rakim Allah. Only a few black folks are responsible for cool. The rest copy and recycle. At the historical core of black lives in this country is a clear understanding that deviation from society's assigned limitations results in punitive sanctions: lynching, hunger, homelessness. The fear of departing from the familiar is where the inclination to make chitlins becomes a downside. It's where the shoeshine-boy reflex to grin and bear it was born. Black rebellion in America from slave days onward was never based on abstract, existentialist grounds. A bird in the hand, no matter how small, was damn near everything.

Today, when deviation from normalcy not only goes unpunished but is also damn near demanded to guarantee visibility in our fast-moving world, blacks remain woefully wedded to the bowed head and blinders. Instead of bowing to massa, they slavishly bow to trend and marketplace. And this creates a hemming-in of cool, an inability to control the cool one makes. By virtue of their status as undereducated bottom feeders, many niggas will never overcome this way of being. But, paradoxically, black people—who exist at a greater distance from cool than niggas—can and will. That's the perplexity of the cool impulse. As long as some black people have to live like niggas, cool, as contemporarily defined, will live on. As long as white people know what niggas are up to, cool will continue to exist, with all of its baggage passed on like, uh, luggage. The question "Are black people cooler than white people?" is not the important one. "How do I gain proximity to cool, and do I want it?" is much better. The real secret weapon of cool is that it's about synthesis. Just about every important black cultural invention of this century has been about synthesizing elements previously considered antithetical. MLK merged Eastern thought and cotton-field religious faith into the civil rights movement. Chuck Berry merged blues and country music into rock 'n' roll. Michael Jordan incorporated the old school ball of Jerry West into his black game. Talk about making a dollar out of 15 cents.

Out in the netherworld of advertising, they tell us [30] we're all Tiger Woods. He plays the emblematic white man's game as good as anyone. Well, only one nigga on this planet gets to be that motherfucker, but we all swing the same cool, to whatever distant ends. The coolness construct might tell us otherwise, but we're all handed the same basic tools at birth; it's up to us as individuals to work on our game. Some of us have sweet strokes, and some of us press too hard, but everybody who drops outta their mama has the same capacity to take a shot. ○

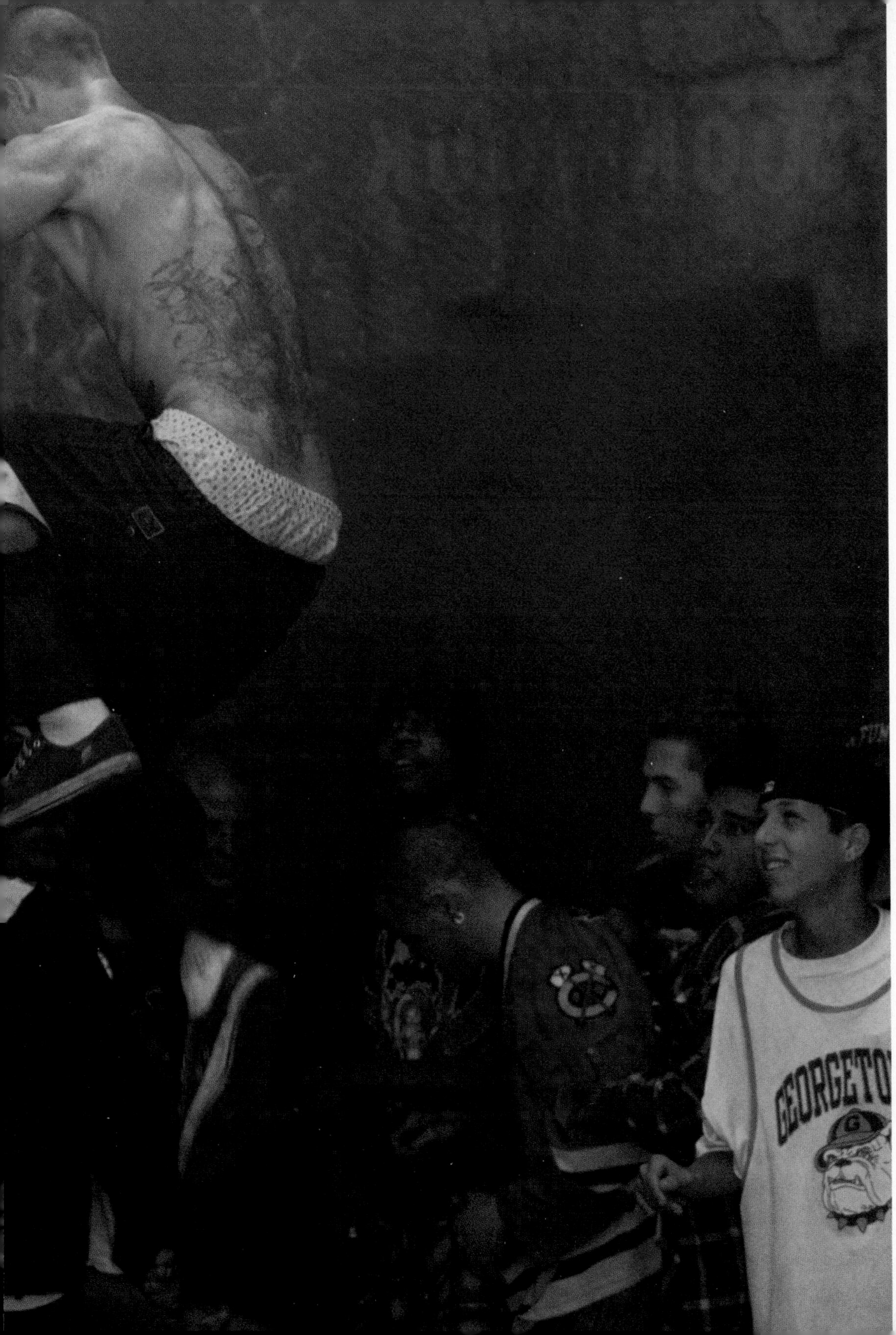

LOOK-LOOK

Dee Dee Gordon and Sharon Lee

WHAT IS LOOK-LOOK?

GORDON: What is it? What is Look-Look? We actually have two different sides of our company. We do consulting with companies on youth culture... and about youth, more significantly, from all over the world.

SO WHAT DOES THAT MEAN, SHARON, IN TERMS OF WHAT THE ELEMENTS OF YOUR COMPANY ARE?

LEE: The company is really about providing the most accurate, ongoing real-time resource about what we think is a very important subculture of this world–and we identify it as youth culture. We live in an adult-centered view of the world. And there's this teeming, very exciting, vibrant subculture going on that's got its own identity, its own thoughts, and issues that we don't have a resource to try to understand. So if you wanted to know more about it...we're providing that bridge. First of all, we think it's valid enough to have its own resource. There's so much great information happening....

WHAT ARE SOME OF YOUR PROJECTS? HOW DO YOU CREATE THIS BRIDGE?

GORDON: We have correspondents out in the field who report on what's going on. They do various different things. They have kids complete surveys. They go out and they find kids who report on certain things that are happening in their area, who will take pictures, who will take a videotape. They send all that stuff in. We look at it. We compile it. We look for trends and themes that are happening through all the information, and that's the stuff that we put on our website.

We also do consulting projects for people. So we look at a product, say, a movie or something. We'll see how can we make this relevant to youth, and we go about finding new and interesting ways of doing that, by using all of our kids to tell us how to do it.

WHAT IS A CORRESPONDENT?

GORDON: A correspondent is a person who has been trained by us to be able to find a certain type of kid, a kid that we call a "trendsetter" or an "early adopter." This is a kid who looks outside their own backyard for inspiration, who is a leader within their own group. These kids are really difficult to find. So this correspondent goes out and finds and identifies these chart-setting kids. They interview them. They get them interested in what we do. They hire them to do work for us. Let's say they're a music expert. They can report on music. Or if they're expert in sports, they can report on that, or just take pictures about that new sport. They get a bunch of kids who can do that in their area and they monitor and manage those kids. . . .

SO YOU HAVE A GROUP OF KIDS, NOT JUST CORRESPONDENTS, BUT ALSO THE RESPONDENTS, RIGHT? HOW MANY KIDS ARE UNDER YOUR UMBRELLA?

GORDON: You have about 10,000 kids, maybe a little bit more than that. And that's not just the United States. We also work in Europe and in Japan. We have about 500 kids who we call corre-

spondents . . . who make sure that we always have new and interesting people joining our group.

SHARON, WHEN YOU HAVE THESE KIDS OUT THERE LOOKING FOR STUFF, WHAT STUFF ARE YOU LOOKING FOR? WHAT KINDS OF THINGS ARE YOU HOPING THAT KIDS ARE GOING TO BRING BACK TO YOU?

LEE: We actually don't direct them. The great thing about why we call them correspondents is that, in the traditional sense of correspondent, they have a digital camera around their neck, they have a laptop with them, and they're living in the culture, as opposed to being outside the culture. So they're open to the things that are really happening in their lives. Rather than assigning them, "Well, we want to know about this," really we're just great listeners and great editors of information.

They will say, "Oh, I just saw this group of girls wearing this type of jeans and, oh my God, it's fabulous. And here's a photo and here's what I think of it. And here's what me and my friends think of it." The judgment of whether it's important or not really comes from them. What we hope for from them is that insight, that they have their eyes and their ears open to what's going on in their culture to see it in, take a photo of it, give us a story. So it could be something that they're doing. "My friends and I are doing this type of activity. We're hanging out playing old video games," as opposed to the new hi-tech ones. "We're collecting them. We're going to flea markets and we're buying them for five dollars and we're taking them home and doing that." Or, "We're having this type of party."

It's giving insight into what's real and not packaged, so it feeds itself. What we do here is we're really the mechanism to filter that information and use that, so we can say, "Well, this is what's really going on," versus what you think is going on....

WHAT IS THE INTERNET ASPECT OF WHAT YOU GUYS DO?

LEE: The Internet is this great resource for both the kids and us. It's a vital link to the whole concept of what we believe in, that the youth culture is constantly moving. Most researchers take the perspective, "Oh, we'll go out there in the field," which happens maybe once or twice or three times in a year. "We'll get the information from that, and that'll be enough." And the reason why we think it's not is that teenagers, young people, use the Internet as such an everyday part of life, and it's such a resource for them. Communication, spreading ideas, learning about things that the speed with which information travels has just accelerated to such a degree that you really need that online real time resource to say, "This is what's going on." It's moving faster and faster and faster.

And the other part of it is that we can reach out to so many more people, instantly, globally. It's this global network of our community of correspondents, respondents, and us, and we're able to communicate so much more efficiently.... The Internet part of it makes all of that so much more efficient and so much easier, because they can just come into our network, decide they want to be a correspondent... and then the information gets loaded up so much quicker of the people who are interested. ○

CLASSIC AMERICAN FLAVA

No Logo: Taking Aim at the Brand Bullies

Naomi Klein

HIP-HOP BLOWS UP THE BRANDS

As we have seen, in the eighties you had to be relatively rich to get noticed by marketers. In the nineties, you have only to be cool. As designer Christian Lacroix remarked in *Vogue*, "it's terrible to say, very often the most exciting outfits are from the poorest people."

Over the past decade, young black men in American inner cities have been the market most aggressively mined by the brandmasters as a source of borrowed "meaning" and identity. This was the key to the success of Nike and Tommy Hilfiger, both of which were catapulted to brand superstardom in no small part by poor kids who incorporated Nike and Hilfiger into hip-hop style at the very moment when rap was being thrust into the expanding youth-culture limelight by MTV and *Vibe* (the first mass-market hip-hop magazine, founded in 1992). "The hip-hop nation," write Lopiano-Misdom and De Luca in *Street Trends*, is "the first to embrace a designer or a major label, they make that label 'big concept' fashion. Or, in their words, they 'blow it up.'"

Designers like Stussy, Hilfiger, Polo, DKNY, and Nike have refused to crack down on the pirating of their logos for T-shirts and baseball hats in the inner cities and several of them have clearly backed away from serious attempts to curb rampant shoplifting. By now the big brands know that profits from logo-wear do not just flow from the purchase of the garment but also from people seeing your logo on "the right people," as Pepe Jeans' Phil Spur judiciously puts it. The truth is that the "got to be cool" rhetoric of the global brands is, more often than not, an indirect way of saying "got to be black." Just as the history of cool in America is really (as many have argued) a history of African-American culture—from jazz and blues to rock and roll to rap—for many of the superbrands, cool hunting simply means black-culture hunting. Which is why the cool hunters' first stop was the basketball courts of America's poorest neighborhoods.

The latest chapter in mainstream America's gold rush to poverty began in 1986, when rappers Run-DMC breathed new life into Adidas products with their hit single "My Adidas," a homage to their favorite brand. Already, the wildly popular rap trio had hordes of fans copying their signature style of gold medallions, black-and-white Adidas tracksuits, and low-cut Adidas sneakers, worn without laces. "We've been wearing them all our lives," Darryl McDaniels (aka DMC) said of his Adidas shoes at the time. That was fine for a time, but after a while it occurred to Russell Simmons, the president of Run-DMC's label Def Jam Records, that the boys should be getting paid for the promotion they were giving to Adidas. He approached the German shoe company about kicking in some money for the act's 1987 Together Forever tour. Adidas executives were skeptical about being associated with rap music, which at that time was alternately dismissed as a passing fad or vilified as an incitement to riot. To help change their minds, Simmons took a couple of Adidas bigwigs to a Run-DMC show. Christopher Vaughn describes the event in *Black Enterprise:* "At a crucial moment, while the rap group was performing the song ["My Adidas"], one of the members yelled out, 'Okay, everybody in the house, rock your Adidas!'—and three thousand pairs of sneakers shot in the air. The Adidas executives couldn't reach for their checkbooks fast enough." By the time of the annual Atlanta sports-shoe Super Show that year, Adidas had unveiled its new line of Run-DMC shoes: the Super Star and the Ultra Star—"designed to be worn without laces."

Since "My Adidas," nothing in inner-city branding 5 has been left up to chance. Major record labels like BMG now hire "street crews" of urban black youth to talk up hip-hop albums in their communities and to go out on guerrilla-style postering and sticker missions. The L.A.-based Steven Rifkind Company bills itself as a marketing firm "specializing in building word-of-mouth in urban areas and inner cities." Rifkind is CEO of the rap label Loud Records, and companies like Nike pay him hundreds of thousands of dollars to find out how to make their brands cool with trend-setting black youth.

So focused is Nike on borrowing style, attitude and imagery from black urban youth that the company has its own word for the practice: bro-ing. That's when Nike marketers and designers bring their prototypes to inner-city neighborhoods in New York, Philadelphia, or Chicago and say, "Hey, bro, check out the shoes" to gauge the reaction to new styles and to build up a buzz. In an interview with journalist Josh Feit, Nike designer Aaron Cooper described his bro-ing conversion in Harlem: "We go to the playground and we dump the shoes out. It's unbelievable. The kids go nuts. That's when you realize the importance of Nike. Having kids tell you Nike is the number one thing in their life—number two is their girlfriend." Nike has even succeeded in branding the basketball courts where it goes bro-ing through its philanthropic wing, P.L.A.Y. (Participate in the Lives of Youth). P.L.A.Y. sponsors inner-city sports programs in exchange for high swoosh visibility, including giant swooshes at the center of resurfaced urban basketball courts. In tonier parts of the city, that kind of thing would be called an ad and the space would come at a price, but on this side of the tracks, Nike pays nothing, and files the cost under charity.

TOMMY HILFIGER: TO THE GHETTO AND BACK AGAIN
Tommy Hilfiger, even more than Nike or Adidas, has turned the harnessing of ghetto cool into a mass-marketing science. Hilfiger forged a formula that has since been imitated by Polo, Nautica, Munsingwear (thanks to Puff Daddy's fondness for the penguin logo), and several other clothing companies looking for a short cut to making it at the suburban mall with inner-city attitude.

Like a depoliticized, hyper-patriotic Benetton, Hilfiger ads are a tangle of Cape Cod multiculturalism: scrubbed black faces lounging with their windswept white brothers and sisters in that great country club in the sky, and always against the backdrop of a billowing American flag. "By respecting one another we can reach all cultures and communities," the company says. "We promote . . . the concept of living the American dream." But the hard facts of Tommy's interracial financial success have less to do with finding common ground between cultures than with the power and mythology embedded in America's deep racial segregation.

Tommy Hilfiger started off squarely as white-preppy wear in the tradition of Ralph Lauren and Lacoste. But the designer soon realized that his clothes also had a peculiar cachet in the inner cities, where the hip-hop philosophy of "living large" saw poor and working-class kids acquiring status in the ghetto by adopting the gear and accoutrements of prohibitively costly leisure activities, such as skiing, golfing, even boating. Perhaps to better position his brand within this urban fantasy, Hilfiger began to associate his clothes more consciously with these sports, shooting ads at yacht clubs, beaches and other nautical locales. At the same time, the clothes themselves were redesigned to appeal more directly to the hip-hop aesthetic. Cultural theorist Paul Smith describes the shift as "bolder colors, bigger and baggier styles, more hoods and cords, and more prominence for logos and the Hilfiger name." He also plied rap artists like Snoop Dogg with free clothes and, walking the tightrope between the yacht and the ghetto, launched a line of Tommy Hilfiger beepers.

Once Tommy was firmly established as a ghetto 10 thing, the real selling could begin—not just to the comparatively small market of poor inner-city youth but to the much larger market of middle-class white and Asian kids who mimic black style in everything from lingo to sports to music. Company sales reached $847 million in 1998—up from a paltry $53 million in 1991 when Hilfiger was still, as Smith puts it, "Young Republican clothing." Like so much of cool hunting, Hilfiger's marketing journey feeds off the alienation at the heart of America's race relations: selling white youth on their fetishization of black style, and black youth on their fetishization of white wealth.

SELL OR BE SOLD

After almost a decade of the branding frenzy, cool hunting has become an internal contradiction: the hunters must rarefy youth "microcultures" by claiming that only full-time hunters have the know-how to unearth them—or else why hire cool hunters at all? Sputnik warns its clients that if the cool trend is "visible in your neighborhood or crowding your nearest mall, the learning is over. It's too late.... You need to get down with the streets, to be in the trenches every day." And yet this is demonstrably false; so-called street fashions—many of them planted by brandmasters like Nike and Hilfiger from day one—reach the ballooning industry of glossy youth-culture magazines and video stations without a heartbeat's delay. And if there is one thing virtually every young person now knows, it's that street style and youth culture are infinitely marketable commodities.

Besides, even if there was a lost indigenous tribe of cool a few years back, rest assured that it no longer exists. It turns out that the prevailing legalized forms of youth stalking are only the tip of the iceberg: the Sputnik vision for the future of hip marketing is for companies to hire armies of Sputnik spawns—young "street promoters," "Net promoters" and "street distributors" who will hype brands one-on-one on the street, in the clubs and on-line. "Use the magic of peer-to-peer distribution—it worked in the freestyle sport cultures, mainly because the promoters were their friends.... Street promoting will survive as the only true means of personally 'spreading the word.'" So all arrows point to more jobs for the ballooning industry of "street snitches," certified representatives of their demographic who will happily become walking infomercials for Nike, Reebok, and Levi's.

By fall 1998 it had already started to happen with the Korean car manufacturer Daewoo hiring two thousand college students on two hundred campuses to talk up the cars to their friends. Similarly, Anheuser-Busch keeps troops of U.S. college frat boys and "Bud Girls" on its payroll to promote Budweiser beer at campus parties and bars. The vision is both horrifying and hilarious: a world of glorified diary trespassers and professional eavesdroppers, part of a spy-vs.-spy corporate-fueled youth culture stalking itself, whose members will videotape one another's haircuts and chat about their corporate keepers' cool new products in their grassroots newsgroups. ○

DONNELL ALEXANDER

Donnell Alexander (b. 1967) is a staff writer for ESPN online magazine, where his work explores the intersections of popular culture, sports, and entertainment.

Throughout his career, Alexander has examined topics ranging from what suit to wear on NBA draft day to the life of security guards. As a former staff writer for *LA Weekly*, he covered that city's booming hip-hop music scene as well as the O.J. Simpson trial.

Alexander's work confronts head-on the preconceptions readers have of topics associated with the culture of African American men. Speaking with an insider's ease, Alexander has developed a style that is at once articulate, rigorous, and highly metaphorical.

DEE DEE GORDON AND SHARON LEE

Dee Dee Gordon and Sharon Lee are the women who founded Look-Look, a group that sends consultants to retail and manufacturing companies to discuss the trends and patterns of youth culture. Their consultants get their knowledge from Look-Look's correspondents, who in turn go right into the streets and homes of today's youth to learn what is cool and what is not. These correspondents are almost always young people who Look-Look has trained, because Look-Look believes that there is no one better to ask about youth culture than youth itself.

NAOMI KLEIN

In January 1999, Naomi Klein's book *No Logo: Taking Aim at the Brand Bullies* was published, amidst the hoopla surrounding the riots in Seattle, Washington, during the World Trade Association meeting. Klein's book, which she had spent four years researching and writing, addresses many of the issues of the dangers of corporate globalization. Protesters soon noticed her book and began urging Klein to take up their cause more fully, which she did when she began a forum for them on the Internet at <www.nologo.org>. Since then she has been touring around the world, giving lectures and lending her support for those who stand with her against corporate globalization. Klein, a Canadian citizen, was born in Montreal in 1970.

ADBUSTERS

Based in Vancouver, British Columbia, Adbusters Media Foundation is a consortium of artists, activists, and merry pranksters who love to make fun of commercial America. The magazine *Adbusters* has a circulation of about 85,000; these readers probably feel the same way its writers and artists do—that the physical, mental, and spiritual well-being of humankind is threatened by the global economy and big brand corporations. Adbusters' mission is serious, but its articles and artwork are also funny because they use humor to expose the underlying messages in corporate advertising, as in this spoof of a Tommy Hilfiger ad.

PHAT FARM

Phat Farm brings hip-hop inspired clothing to the suburbs and farmlands of America. One of the company's lines of baggy pants and terry button-downs is called Classic American Flava, which is classic by hip-hop standards, but the polo shirts offered at Phat Farm are interesting to contrast with the polo shirt made famous by Ralph Lauren. The founder of Phat Farm, Russell Simmons (b. 1958), is a friend of designer Tommy Hilfiger, who has been credited with bridging the unlikely gap between the tailored, preppy look of designers like Ralph Lauren and modern urban sportswear. Simmons (called Rush by those who know him) is the mogul behind Rush Communications, a conglomerate that includes a record label (Def Jam), a management company (Rush Artist Management), a clothier (Phat Farm), a movie production house (Def Pictures), television shows ("Def Comedy Jam" and "Russell Simmons' Oneworld Music Beat"), a magazine (*Oneworld*), and an advertising agency (Rush Media Co.).

Cool Like Me
Donnell Alexander

No Logo:
Taking Aim at the
Brand Bullies
Naomi Klein

LOOK-LOOK

LAUREN GREENFIELD

Lauren Greenfield (b. 1966) got the job any photojournalist would die for: a *National Geographic* photographer. She began her work at the prestigious magazine as an intern, after starting her career while an undergraduate student at Harvard University. In 1993, *National Geographic* backed her on a documentary project she planned upon moving near Los Angeles, California; it was the first time the magazine had ever given such a grant. Called *Fast Forward: Growing Up in the Shadows of Hollywood*, this collection of photographs about LA-area kids won Greenfield many awards and much recognition, and it also led to a book by the same name. The photographs from this portfolio and others have been published in *Time*; *Newsweek*; *Vanity Fair*; *Life*; *Harper's*; and the *New York Times Magazine*. Greenfield continues to win awards such as Young Photographer of the Year, and she has received the National Press Photographers/ Nikon Sabbatical Grant.

SEEING

1. Donnell Alexander's "Cool Like Me," Naomi Klein's "No Logo," and the interview with the owners of Look-Look offer varying perspectives on how the notion of cool is produced and consumed in contemporary American culture. What central arguments does each text make? How does each one define the term cool? What similarities and differences do you notice between and among their approaches to the ways in which cool and youth culture are generated and marketed? What is *your* definition of cool, and how is it similar to—or different from—the definitions of cool within these texts?

2. Consider each of the images in this unit: Lauren Greenfield's photograph, the ad by Phat Farm, and the Adbusters spoof on Tommy Hilfiger ads. Which of these images would you characterize as cool? Explain why. Which ones wouldn't qualify as cool? Why? Explain your reasoning with specific evidence from each image. What strategies and compositional choices do you find successful in each? Which strategies are less successful? How might you revise them, and with what effect(s)?

WRITING

1. Alexander claims that evidence of cool exists everywhere in American popular culture. "We all know cool when we see it, and now, more than at any other time in this country's history, when mainstream America looks for cool we look to black culture" (para. 15). Choose an example of cool—a musician, a celebrity, an athlete, or a style of dress, to name a few possibilities—or something that passes for cool (what Alexander calls "cool clone") in mainstream American culture. Write an essay in which you pursue Alexander's explanation of the relationship between black culture and cool. Explain why you think your subject is "authentic" cool or "wanna-be."

2. Naomi Klein argues in "No Logo" that "like so much of cool hunting, Hilfiger's marketing journey feeds off the alienation at the heart of America's race relations: selling white youth on their fetishization of black style, and black youth on their fetishization of white wealth" (para. 10). Write an essay in which you argue in support of or refute Klein's statement by analyzing carefully a current Hilfiger advertisement.

Reading Icons

Chapter 6
Reading Icons

The peace sign. The happy face. The four-leaf clover.

Glimpse at them for a split second, and you know exactly what they mean. Because right behind every powerful icon lies a powerful idea.

A little over a century ago, we set out with what we considered to be some pretty powerful ideas:

Build cars to be fast. (We set land speed records that would last for half a century.)

Safe. (Developments in crumple zones, antilock brakes, and restraint systems have helped make all cars safer.)

Innovative. (The pioneering spirit that drove Karl Benz to patent the first three-wheel motor carriage still guides everything we do today.)

And, just as important, beautiful. (Museums throughout the world have placed our cars in their permanent collections.)

Our symbol has stood for all of these things for over a hundred years.

We look forward to the next.

What makes a symbol endure?

Mercedes-Benz, **What Makes a Symbol Endure?**

Open any newspaper or magazine, or simply turn on the television, and you will immediately encounter everything and everyone heralded as an *icon*—from blue jeans, Tupperware, the Nike swoosh, and pickup trucks to Michael Jordan, Barbie, and Martin Luther King. The cultural commentator Russell Baker complains that the current overuse of the term has escalated to "epidemic" proportions. If we casually assign great leaders, celebrities, clothing labels, and automobiles iconic status, what then might we say the term *icon* has come to mean? And what reasonable inferences might we draw from our fascination with the term?

Perhaps the oldest association of the word is with the religious representation of a sacred figure. The word has also been used historically in natural history to refer to an illustration of a plant or animal, and in rhetoric to indicate a simile. This range in the use of the term—from the sacred and religious to the scientific and technical—has not only endured but expanded to the secular and the mundane.

At its most mundane, the word *icon* suggests a recognizable image or representation—something that stands for something else. In this sense, one thing acts as a substitute or symbol for another. The signs for men and women on doors to public restrooms, for example, are pictorial symbols that convey or represent information about which door to use, in the same way that thumbnail graphics on our computer screens tell us how to quickly open certain programs or files. In such instances, icons communicate specific meanings.

Icon is also used to identify certain individuals who are the objects of attention and devotion, people who have taken on the status of an idol. Michael Jordan has been elevated to this status for basketball, as has Elvis Presley for rock and roll. When we say that Michael Jordan is an icon, we suggest that his image has worked its way into American culture so deeply that it now represents not only all the excitement of watching professional basketball but also the American values of working hard, succeeding, and reaping the rewards.

Cultural commentator Aaron Betsky has described objects, people, and events as lenses through which to examine American culture. He sees much in the new proliferation of icons, calling them "magnets of meaning onto which we can project our memories, our hopes, and our sense of self," and observing that "part of our twentieth-century loss of faith has been a loss of the kind of icons that are unapproachable, semi-divine apparitions, and yet icons are all around us."

Corporate logos everywhere—in advertisements and on designer clothing—have extended the range of associations for the word icon. Perhaps without even knowing it, we are quite versed—and invested—in the vocabulary of corporate icons: We immediately recognize the McDonald's arches, the Nike swoosh, and the Mercedes-Benz symbol. American advertising agencies want consumers to grant iconic status to the products they promote for their corporate clients. Market research conducted by these ad agencies suggests that when their creative efforts succeed, commercial icons can and do sell products.

In the selections that follow, you will encounter a wide range of American icons. If icons are "sound bites" (to use Holly Brubach's term), then what is lost and gained in the process of representing complicated ideas through streamlined symbols? As you continue to develop your skills of seeing and writing, consider the ways in which each of the following writers and artists provides a double take on the nature and the meaning of the term icon. How do these multiple perspectives differ from, alter, or contribute to your own understanding of—and experience with—icons in contemporary American culture?

Most people tell us, "Don't touch the icon," but we're taking a calculated risk to contemporize our products.
– Marty Thrasher, president of Campbell Soup, on the redesign of the Campbell Soup can, 1995

MERCEDES-BENZ

Carl Benz assembled his first automobile in Mannheim, Germany, in 1886, and Gottlieb Daimler, maker of the Mercedes (a car named for his young daughter), assembled his a few years later. In the economic slump following World War I the companies were forced to merge, creating in 1927 the company known as Mercedes-Benz. Having manufactured "The Car with the Star" for more than 100 years (with temporary forays into military aircraft design), Mercedes-Benz is known for its engineering innovations and high-quality construction. With its headquarters today in Stuttgart, Germany, Mercedes-Benz is a division of the Daimler-Chrysler Group, Europe's largest industrial manufacturer. The company employs over 199,000 people at more than 50 production and assembly plants.

SEEING

1. Review each of the twenty-nine images depicted in this advertisement. How many can you identify immediately? Which ones do you consider to be icons? Why? Why not? What do the images have in common? In what ways do they differ? What aspects of contemporary American life do they represent? Are any significant aspects omitted? If so, please identify those and explore the possible reasons for their omission.

2. Consider the ad copy that accompanies the images. After identifying three of the icons, the speaker in the advertisement reassures us not only that we can identify the images in "a split second" but also that we "know exactly what they mean. Because right behind every powerful icon lies a powerful idea." What is the powerful idea behind each of the icons shown? What reasonable inferences about the Mercedes-Benz automobile might you draw from the "powerful ideas" the copy claims are associated with the symbol that represents the car?

WRITING

1. The advertisement says: "Our symbol has stood for all of these things for over a hundred years." Does it seem reasonable to infer that the speaker seems to equate the word *symbol* with the word *icon?* If so, why? If not, why not? How does the final line of the advertisement—"What makes a symbol endure?"—influence your reasoning? To what extent is your response a reaction to the layout of the ad, which places this question alongside the ornament that appears on the hoods of Mercedes-Benz cars? Does the text of the ad suggest a distinction between the icon (the Mercedes-Benz automobile) and the symbol (the hood ornament) chosen to represent it?

List all the meanings of *icon* that you can think of. Draft an essay in which you assert that *icon* and *symbol* are (or aren't) terms that can be used interchangeably when talking about the images represented in contemporary culture.

2. In a 1996 article, *Investor's Business Daily* observed "that the automobile is a presence in our lives from birth until death, and the car has become a subject second only to love in our popular culture." Do you agree that the car serves as an icon for America? Write an essay in which you identify *the* American icon and explain why you've chosen it, giving specific cultural examples.

Grant Wood, **American Gothic**

THE GEOGRAPHY OF THE IMAGINATION
Guy Davenport

A GEOGRAPHY OF THE IMAGINATION WOULD EXTEND the shores of the Mediterranean all the way to Iowa.

Eldon, Iowa—where in 1929 Grant Wood sketched a farmhouse as the background for a double portrait of his sister Nan and his dentist, Dr. B. H. McKeeby, who donned overalls for the occasion and held a rake. Forces that arose three millennia ago in the Mediterranean changed the rake to a pitchfork, as we shall see.

Let us look at this painting to which we are blinded by familiarity and parody. In the remotest distance against this perfect blue of a fine harvest sky, there is the Gothic spire of a country church, as if to seal the Protestant sobriety and industry of the subjects. Next there are trees, seven of them, as along the porch of Solomon's temple, symbols of prudence and wisdom.

Next, still reading from background to foreground, is the house that gives the primary meaning of the title, *American Gothic*, a style of architecture. It is an example of a revolution in domestic building that made possible the rapid rise of American cities after the Civil War and dotted the prairies with decent, neat farmhouses. It is what was first called in derision a balloon-frame house, so easy to build that a father and his son could put it up. It is an elegant geometry of light timber posts and rafters requiring no deep foundation, and is nailed together. Technically, it is, like the clothes of the farmer and his wife, a mail-order house, as the design comes out of a pattern-book, this one from those of Alexander Davis and Andrew Downing, the architects who modified details of the Gothic Revival for American farmhouses. The balloon-frame house was invented in Chicago in 1833 by George Washington Snow, who was orchestrating in his invention a century of mechanization that provided the nails, wirescreen, sash-windows, tin roof, lathe-turned posts for the porch, doorknobs, locks, and hinges—all standard pieces from factories.

We can see a bamboo sunscreen—out of China by way of Sears Roebuck—that rolls up like a sail: nautical technology applied to the prairie. We can see that distinctly American feature, the screen door. The sash-windows are European in origin, their glass panes from Venetian technology as perfected by the English, a luxury that was a marvel of the eighteenth century, and now as common as the farmer's spectacles, another revolution in technology that would have seemed a miracle to previous ages. Spectacles begin in the thirteenth century, the invention of either Salvino degl'Armati or Alessandro della Spina; the first portrait of a person wearing specs is of Cardinal Ugone di Provenza, in a fresco of 1352 by Tommaso Barisino di Modena. We might note, as we are trying to see the geographical focus that this painting gathers together, that the center for lens grinding from which eyeglasses diffused to the rest of civilization was the same part of Holland from which the style of the painting itself derives.

Another thirteenth-century invention prominent in our painting is the buttonhole. Buttons themselves are prehistoric, but they were shoulder-fasteners that engaged with loops. Modern clothing begins with the buttonhole. The farmer's wife secures her Dutch Calvinist collar with a cameo brooch, an heirloom passed down the generations, an eighteenth-century or Victorian copy of a design that goes back to the sixth century B.C.

She is a product of the ages, this modest Iowa farm wife: she has the hair-do of a mediaeval madonna, a Reformation collar, a Greek cameo, a nineteenth-century pinafore.

Martin Luther put her a step behind her husband; John Knox squared her shoulders; the stock-market crash of 1929 put that look in her eyes.

The train that brought her clothes—paper pattern, bolt cloth, needle, thread, scissors—also brought her husband's bib overalls, which were originally, in the 1870s, trainmen's workclothes designed in Europe, manufactured here for J. C. Penney, and disseminated across the United States as the railroads connected city with city. The cloth is denim, from Nîmes in France, introduced by Levi Strauss of blue-jean fame. The design can be traced to no less a person than Herbert Spencer, who thought he was creating a utilitarian one-piece suit for everybody to wear. His own example was of tweed, with buttons from crotch to neck, and his female relatives somehow survived the mortification of his sporting it one Sunday in St. James Park.

His jacket is the modification of that of a Scots [10] shepherd which we all still wear.

Grant Wood's Iowans stand, as we might guess, in a pose dictated by the Brownie box camera, close together in front of their house, the farmer looking at the lens with solemn honesty, his wife with modestly averted eyes. But that will not account for the pitch-fork held as assertively as a minuteman's rifle. The pose is rather that of the Egyptian prince Rahotep, holding the flail of Osiris, beside his wife Nufrit—strict with pious rectitude, poised in absolute dignity, mediators between heaven and earth, givers of grain, obedient to the gods.

This formal pose lasts out 3000 years of Egyptian history, passes to some of the classical cultures—

Etruscan couples in terra cotta, for instance—but does not attract Greece and Rome. It recommences in northern Europe, where (to the dismay of the Romans) Gaulish wives rode beside their husbands in the war chariot. Kings and eventually the merchants of the North repeated the Egyptian double portrait of husband and wife: van Eyck's Meester and Frouw Arnolfini; Rubens and his wife Helena. It was this Netherlandish tradition of painting middle-class folk with honor and precision that turned Grant Wood from Montparnasse, where he spent two years in the 1920s trying to be an American post-Impressionist, back to Iowa, to be our Hans Memling.

If Van Gogh could ask, "Where is my Japan?" and be told by Toulouse-Lautrec that it was Provence, Wood asked himself the whereabouts of his Holland, and found it in Iowa.

Just thirty years before Wood's painting, Edwin Markham's poem "The Man with the Hoe" had pictured the farmer as a peasant with a life scarcely different from that of an ox, and called on the working men of the world to unite, as they had nothing to lose but their chains. The painting that inspired Markham was one of a series of agricultural subjects by Jean François Millet, whose work also inspired Van Gogh. A digging fork appears in five of Van Gogh's pictures, three of them variations on themes by Millet, and all of them are studies of grinding labor and poverty.

And yet the Independent Farmer had edged out the [15] idle aristocrat for the hand of the girl in Royal Tyler's "The Contrast," the first native American comedy for the stage, and in Emerson's "Concord Hymn" it is a battle-line of farmers who fire the shot heard around the world. George III, indeed, referred to his American colonies as "the farms," and the two Georges of the Revolution, Hanover and Washington, were proudly farmers by etymology and in reality.

The window curtains and apron in this painting are both calico printed in a reticular design, the curtains of rhombuses, the apron of circles and dots, the configuration Sir Thomas Browne traced through nature and art in his *Garden of Cyrus,* the quincunxial arrangement of trees in orchards, perhaps the first human imitation of a phyllotaxis, acknowledging the symmetry, justice, and divine organization of nature.

Curtains and aprons are as old as civilization itself, but their presence here in Iowa implies a cotton mill, a dye works, a roller press that prints calico, and a wholesale-retail distribution system involving a post office, a train, its tracks, and, in short, the Industrial Revolution.

That revolution came to America in the astounding memory of one man, Samual Slater, who arrived in Philadelphia in 1789 with the plans of all Arkwright's, Crompton's, and Hargreaves's machinery in his head, put himself at the service of the rich Quaker Moses Brown, and built the first American factory at Pawtucket, Rhode Island.

The apron is trimmed with rickrack ribbon, a machine-made substitute for lace. The curtains are bordered in a variant of the egg-and-dart design that comes from Nabataea, the Biblical Edom, in Syria, a design which the architect Hiram incorporated into the entablatures of Solomon's temple—"and the chapiters upon the two pillars had pomegranates also above, over against the belly which was by the network: and the pomegranates were two hundred in rows round about" (1 Kings 7:20) and which formed the border of the high priest's dress, a frieze of "pomegranates of blue, and of purple, and of scarlet, around about the hem thereof; and bells of gold between them round about" (Exodus 28:33).

The brass button that secures the farmer's collar [20] is an unassertive, puritanical understatement of Matthew Boulton's eighteenth-century cut-steel button made in the factory of James Watt. His shirt button is mother-of-pearl, made by James Boepple from Mississippi fresh-water mussel shell, and his jacket button is of South American vegetable ivory passing for horn.

The farmer and his wife are attended by symbols, she by two plants on the porch, a potted geranium and sansevieria, both tropical and alien to Iowa; he by the three-tined American pitchfork whose triune shape is repeated throughout the painting, in the bib of the overalls, the windows, the faces, the siding of the house, to give it a formal organization of impeccable harmony.

If this painting is primarily a statement about Protestant diligence on the American frontier, carrying in its style and subject a wealth of information about imported technology, psychology, and aesthetics, it still does not turn away from a pervasive cultural theme of Mediterranean origin—a tension between the growing and the ungrowing, between vegetable and mineral, organic and inorganic, wheat and iron.

Transposed back into its native geography, this icon of the lord of metals with his iron sceptre, head wreathed with glass and silver, buckled in tin and brass, and a chaste bride who has already taken on the metallic thraldom of her plight in the gold ovals of her hair and brooch, are Dis and Persephone posed in a royal portrait among the attributes of the first Mediterranean trinity, Zeus in the blue sky and lightning rod, Poseidon in the trident of the pitchfork, Hades in the metals. It is a picture of a sheaf of golden grain, female and cyclical, perennial and the mother of civilization; and of metal shaped into scythe and hoe: nature and technology, earth and farmer, man and world, and their achievement together. ○

GRANT WOOD

For many Americans, Grant Wood's painting *American Gothic* (1930) is as familiar as the *Mona Lisa*. The problem is, no one has ever known definitively what to make of it. Are the two people in the picture father and daughter, or husband and wife? Are their dour faces meant to be real representations of midwestern folks, or is Wood poking fun at rural Americans? Grant Wood never helped to resolve the controversy. He called himself a "Regionalist," a term used by artists who drew simple, rural portraits in contrast with the Realism movement of urban portraiture most popular in the 1920s and 1930s.

What is known is that Grant Wood was born in 1891 in Iowa and spent most of his life there, dying at age 50 in 1942. In the 1920s he made his way to Eldon, Iowa, where he first saw the house that stands in the background of *American Gothic*. He was taken with the Gothic-style windows and sketched the house on a piece of paper. Later he asked his sister Nan and his dentist, Dr. B. H. McKeeby, to pose as the couple in the picture.

Wood began his career as an artist when he was 14 years old. Later he traveled to Europe to study art, returning to Iowa to teach it in several high schools. In 1927 he received a commission from the city of Cedar Rapids to design a large stained glass window for the Veterans Memorial Building. He spent two years designing it in the fifteenth century Northern Gothic style he admired, and it is likely that this project drew him to the house he painted in *American Gothic*.

GUY DAVENPORT

An author of poems, homoerotic short stories, essays, and critical reviews, and a painter and longtime professor of English at the University of Kentucky, Guy Davenport seems to have done it all. In 2001, one year after his retirement, Davenport was honored with the University of Kentucky Libraries Medallion for Intellectual Achievement for his contribution to American and world literature.

An early immersion in the classics along with an interest in homoeroticism and pop culture forms the backdrop to many of his poems and short stories. Davenport is most fond of painting still lifes but he has also worked in other styles and mediums. Davenport has said, "the prime use of words is for imagery: my writing is drawing."

Davenport was born in 1927 and began his teaching career at the University of Kentucky in 1963. He has published over a dozen books of his writings and art, most recently a collection of essays on the art of the still life, *Objects on a Table, Harmonious Disarray in Art and Literature* (1999). The preceding excerpt is from *The Geography of the Imagination*, a collection of essays published in 1981. Davenport has been the recipient of the prestigious O. Henry Award for short stories, the 1981 Morton Douwen Zabel award for fiction from the American Academy and Institute of Arts and Letters, translation awards from PEN and the Academy of American Poets, the Leviton-Blumenthal Prize for poetry, and the 1990 MacArthur fellowship.

SEEING

1. Grant Wood's *American Gothic* may or may not be an image familiar to you. In either case, take a few moments to examine it with fresh eyes. What is your overall impression of this painting? of its use of detail, color, and tone? What responses does it evoke? Which aspects of the painting stand out most prominently to you? In what ways might the painting be said to be a quintessential expression of American identity? What, in effect, gives it the status of a cultural icon?

2. Summarize the extent to which Guy Davenport's reading of the painting enhances or changes your understanding and appreciation of it. In his essay, Davenport focuses on the cultural/historical aspects of each element in the painting. How might you supplement his analysis by focusing on the compositional elements of the painting? To what extent does Jane Yolen's poem about the painting supplement or distract you from the particularities of Davenport's reading? Cite specific examples to validate your response.

WRITING

1. Jane Yolen's poem "Grant Wood: American Gothic" offers a set of directions to guide the viewer's response to this iconic painting. In contrast to Davenport's essay, what alternate point of view of the painting does Yolen's poem provide? Summarize the structure of her poem. What relationship can you establish between the first three parts of the poem (lines 1–5, 6–9, and 10–11) and its final two lines? What do you notice about the structure of these two final lines? How does the final line depend for its meaning on the penultimate line? Write the first draft of an expository essay in which you explain how the final two lines of the poem do—or do not—encapsulate its meaning.

2. Choose a painting—one you are already familiar with, or one you find in this or another book or at a museum or gallery or on the web. Write an essay in which you engage in a close reading of the painting, using Guy Davenport's essay as a model. Focus on several key elements of the painting, and provide your readers with the historical, cultural, or social meaning of each element.

GRANT WOOD:
AMERICAN GOTHIC
Jane Yolen

Do not dwell on the fork,
the brooch at the throat,
the gothic angel wing
of window pointing toward
a well-tended heaven.   5
Do not become
a farmer counting cows
as if the number of the herd
defines you.
Look behind the eyes,   10
to see who looks out at you.
We are not what we own
We own what we would be.

Visualizing Context
The Culture of the Copy

Gordon Parks, **American Gothic**

Americans have long been fascinated with copies, duplicates, and replicas of all sorts—be they counterfeits, mannequins, decoys, or, more recently, digital images, photocopies, or even instant replays. Few works of American art are as celebrated—or as reproduced, imitated, or parodied—as Grant Wood's *American Gothic*. Viewing this painting might remind some of the immortal words of the legendary baseball star and hero of American folklore, Yogi Berra: "It's *déjà vu* all over again."

As Guy Davenport remarks in his analysis of Wood's *American Gothic*, this image has taken on an identity and status to which we have become "blinded by familiarity and parody." Like the *Mona Lisa*, *American Gothic* has been so often reproduced on T-shirts, postcards, and coffee mugs, as well as referenced—or alluded to—in the work of numerous painters, artists, and writers, that it has assumed the status of an American cultural icon. Few works of American art are as celebrated—and less understood.

Consider, for example, Gordon Parks's photograph. What specific elements does Parks repeat? With what effect(s)? How does he play off the tone and overall qualities of Grant Wood's painting?

Using the library and the web as research sources, identify other artists and writers who have sought to reproduce the central image and distinguishing features of Wood's *American Gothic*. Then write an expository essay in which you demonstrate the extent to which Wood's image changes in the specific cultural contexts in which it is reproduced. Show how the original cultural and historical significance of the painting changes—to make room for new cultural associations and meanings expressed by different generations.

ADBUSTERS >

"We want a new media environment, one without a commercial heart and soul," asserts the Media Foundation, and producing *Adbusters,* a nonprofit magazine, is one of their core tactics. This Canadian magazine boasts an international circulation of 85,000, and two-thirds of its subscribers live in the United States. *Adbusters* is perhaps best known for its "spoof ads" in which designers manipulate corporate advertisements in subtle but humorous ways, provoking us to rethink the messages and assumptions of the ads we encounter every day.

The magazine also features criticism of corporate advertising campaigns and reports on international activist campaigns, as well as its own annual campaigns such as "Buy Nothing Day" and "TV Turnoff Week." "Ultimately," say the editors, "*Adbusters* is an ecological magazine, dedicated to examining the relationship between human beings and their physical and mental environment."

Mark Kingwell wrote "Ten Steps to the Creation of a Modern Media Icon" for the Winter 1998 edition of *Adbusters*. Kingwell is a witty cultural and media critic and a political theorist who has written many books, including: *Marginalia: A Cultural Reader* (1999) and *The World We Want: Virtue, Vice and the Good Citizen* (2000). He currently teaches philosophy at the University of Toronto.

Ten Steps to the Creation of a Modern Media Icon

MARK KINGWELL

1 "Icon" is from the Greek *eikon,* which means "image," which is everything: The name of a camera. The word for all those little point-and-click pictures on your computer screen. Greek and Roman Orthodox religious objects. Little oil paintings of saints with elaborate gold panel coverings. Anybody who represents something to someone somewhere. The image that gives a debased Platonic suggestion of reality without ever being it. So create an image—one the cameras, and therefore we, will love.

2 The image must be drastically beautiful or else compellingly ugly. It must, for women, show a smooth face of impenetrable maquillage and impeccably "tasteful" clothing (Chanel, Balenciaga, Rykiel; not Versace, not Moschino, definitely not Gauthier), a flat surface of emotional projection, the real-world equivalent of a keyboard emoticon. Icon smiling at the cheering crowds: :-). Icon frowning bravely at diseased child or crippled former soldier in hospital bed: :-(. Icon winking slyly at the crush of press photographers as she steps into the waiting limousine: ;-). There should be only one name, for preference a chummy or faux-intimate diminutive: Jackie, Di, Barbra. Sunglasses are mandatory whenever the ambient light rises above building-code-normal 250-foot candles. These can be removed or peered over to offer an image of blinking vulnerability. Or else the image should be, in men, so overwhelmingly tawdry and collapsed, preferably from some high-cheekbone peak of youthful beauty, that it acquires a can't-look-away magnetism, the sick pull of the human car wreck. (The only exceptions: (1) Athletes—Tiger, Michael—whose downy smoothness and transcendental physical abilities offer a male counterpoint that is almost female in appeal; they are the contraltos of the icon chorus. And (2) actors, whose malleable faces are so empty of particular meaning as to be innocent of intelligence.) Folds of leathery skin, evidence of drug use and chain-smoking, the runes of dissipation etched on

the pitted skin of hard living—they all have them. Johnny Cash, Mick Jagger, Leonard Cohen, Kurt Cobain, Chet Baker, late Elvis: the musician in ruins, the iconic face as crumbling stone monument. Basic black attire is effective but must be Armani, never Gap. This suggests wisdom and sexual power, deep and bitter knowledge of the world—but with dough. The face need never change, its very stasis a sign of rich inner troubles. Sunglasses are superfluous. They smack of effort.

3 There must be a narrative structure that bathes the icon in the pure light of the fairy tale or morality play. Beautiful princess beset by ugly siblings or nasty step-mother. Lovely rich girl mistakes the charisma of power for true character. Overweening ambition turns simple boy into gun-toting, pill-popping maniac. Feisty rebel takes on the establishment of (circle one) Hollywood/big business/government/rock music/professional sports. Prodigy singled out for great things at an early age by psycho father. Indispensable words in the story: "trapped," "betray," "tragic," "love," "promise" (as both verb and noun), "happiness" (always without irony), "fame" (always with venom), and "money" (never spoken). The details of the story may change, but the overarching structure cannot: you can improvise and elaborate, but never deviate. Sometimes a new story (thrill-happy slut consorts with swarthy and disreputable jet-setter) will be temporarily substituted for an old one that no longer applies (virginal bride is unloved by philandering husband). We can't be sure which story will win out until . . .

4 Death. Already, at step four? Yes, absolutely, for iconography is very much a postmortem affair. The death ends the life but does not quite complete it: that is the business of story-tellers and their audience, the cameras and their lights. Death is just the beginning. It should be, if possible, violent, messy and a bit mysterious. Unwise confrontations with fast-moving industrial machines—sports cars, airplanes, cargo trucks, high-speed trains, bullets. Accidents are good, having as they do an aura of adventitious innocence,

followed closely in order of preference by murder, assassination, execution, and suicide. If suicide it must be either a gun or an overdose of illicit drugs, usually in colorful and nasty combination: alcohol and barbiturates, crack and benzedrine, heroin and anything. In all cases, the death is "shocking" and "tragic," though in neither instance literally.

5 Now, an outbreak of hysterical mourning, baseless and all the more intense for being so. (Nobody feels so strongly about someone they actually know.) Extended retrospectives on television. Numerous panel discussions and attempts to "make sense," to "assess the life," to "provide context." Long broadcasts of the funeral or memorial service complete with lingering, loving shots of weeping crowds. Greedy close-ups of the well-known people in attendance, the bizarre fraternity of celebrity which dictates that those famous for being born in a certain family have everything in common with those famous for signing pop tunes or throwing a ball in a designated manner. News agencies and networks must spend a great deal of money sending a lot of people somewhere distant to cover the death. They must then justify that expense with hours and hours of coverage. We must see images of the iconic face, beautiful or ruined, over and over and over. "Ordinary" people must be shown, on the media, insisting that the media have nothing to do with their deep feelings of loss. They must say that they "felt they knew him (her)," that "she (he) was like a member of the family." This keeps them happy and ensures that no larger form of public participation— say, protesting a tax hike or program cut, resisting a corporate takeover—will ever cross their minds as possible, let alone desirable.

6 A small backlash must gather strength, a token gesture of cultural protest that, in pointing out the real faults and shortcomings of the dead icon, unwittingly reinforces the growing "larger-than-life" status of the image. This is the culture's way of injecting itself with a homeopathic inoculation, introducing a few strains of mild virus that actually beef up the dominant media

antibodies. Those who have the temerity to suggest that the dead icon was not all he (she) is thought to be will be publicly scorned, accused of cynicism, insulted at dinner parties, but secretly welcomed. The final storyline of the icon-life will now begin to set, rejecting the foreign elements as dead-ends or narrative spurs, or else accepting them as evidence that the icon was "after all" human—a suggestion that, in its very making, implies the opposite. The media coverage will fall into line in telling this story because individual producers and anchors will be unable to imagine doing otherwise. Tag-lines and feature-story titles will help set the narrative epoxy for good, providing catchy mini-stories for us to hang our thoughts onto. Quickie books with the same titles will begin to appear—things like Icon X: Tragic Ambition or Icon Y: Little Girl in Trouble. The producers and anchors must then claim that they are not creating this tale, simply "giving the people what they want." Most people will accept this because to do otherwise would hurt their brains.

7 The image will now be so widely reproduced, so ubiquitously mediated on television, at the supermarket, in the bookstore, that it seems a permanent feature of the mediascape, naturalized and indispensable. It will now begin its final divorce from the person depicted. Any actual achievements—touchdowns thrown, elections won, causes championed—fall away like the irrelevancies they are. The face (or rather, The Face) looms outward from glossy paper, T-shirts, fridge magnets, posters, Halloween masks and coffee mugs. Kitschification of the image is to be welcomed, not feared. It proves that the icon is here to stay. The basic unit of fame-measurement is

of course, as critic Cullen Murphy once argued, the warhol, a period of celebrity equal to fifteen minutes. Kitsch versions of the image augers well: we're talking at least a megawarhol icon or better (that's 15 million minutes of fame, which is just over 10,400 days, or about 28.5 years—enough to get you to those standard silver-anniversary retrospectives). No kitsch, no staying power: a 100 kilowarhols or less, a minicon.

8 There follow academic studies, well-meaning but doomed counter-assessments, sightings, and cameo appearances of the icon on a Star Trek spinoff series or as an answer on Jeopardy. People begin to claim they can commune with the spirit of the dead icon across vast distances of psychic space. Conspiracy theories refuse to be settled by overwhelming evidence of a boringly predictable chain of events involving a drunk driver, too much speed, and unused seatbelts. Or whatever.

9 Television retrospectives every decade, with a mid-decade special at 25 years. The final triumph of the image: entirely cut off now from its original body, it is free-floating and richly polysemous. Always more surface than depth, more depiction than reality, the icon now becomes pure zero-degree image, a depicted lifestyle without a life, a face without a person, a spiritual moment without context or meaning. In other words, the pure pervasive triumph of cultural exposure, a sign lacking both sense and referent. In still other words, the everything (and nothing) we sought all along: communion without community.

10 Now, for a religious experience, just point and click. ○

SEEING

1. What do you think Kingwell's purpose is in writing this piece? What central ideas do you imagine he wants to leave his readers with? What points about the state of icons in contemporary American culture does he attempt to convey? To what extent do you think he is successful?

2. Comment on the compositional strategies Kingwell employs in this essay. You might, for example, consider the significant advantages and disadvantages of the ten-part structure. Consider, as well, the fact that Kingwell references very few icons specifically in this piece. Why might he have chosen this technique? How does it contribute to the overall points he makes?

WRITING

1. Review the icons pictured in the advertisement for Mercedes-Benz (see p. 464). To what extent does each icon in the ad satisfy Kingwell's criteria for a modern media-icon? Explain why. To what extent would Kingwell consider the images pictured in the Mercedes-Benz ad worthy of the term *icon*? Although Kingwell focuses on celebrities in his essay, how might his arguments apply to the other types of icons? Write an essay in which you choose one of the icons in the Mercedes-Benz ad and argue for or against its status as a modern-media icon, according to Kingwell's criteria.

2. Invent a person, place, or thing that you might imagine turning into a modern media-icon, using Kingwell's criteria. Your subject might be something completely outlandish or entirely plausible. Write a persuasive essay in which you draw on Kingwell's ten steps to propose a plan for creating an icon.

ANDY WARHOL >

Born Andrew Warhola to Czech immigrant parents in Pittsburgh, Pennsylvania, the artist now known simply as "Warhol" (1928–1987) began collecting movie-star photographs and autographs as a young child. This fascination with all things glamorous helped fuel his successful career as a commercial fashion artist in New York in the 1950s.

By 1963 Warhol was at the center of the American pop art movement, which sought to erase the boundary between fine art and popular culture. By painting Campbell's Soup can labels on canvas and installing a sculpture of Brillo boxes, Warhol proposed an aesthetic in which the machine-made image competed with the hand-made for significance, and "image" very often was the subject itself. This was especially explicit in his paintings of Marilyn Monroe, which were based on a publicity "headshot." Warhol reproduced, altered, and transformed her face into a series of brightly colored semi-abstract icons.

Warhol's studio loft in Greenwich Village became known as "The Factory," a meeting place for New York's avant-garde. Here Warhol created experimental films such as *Sleep* (1963) and *Chelsea Girls* (1966). Of this work he said, "All my films are artificial, but then everything is sort of artificial. I don't know where the artificial stops and the real starts."

Large Triple Elvis, 1963

The Twenty Marilyns, 1962

SEEING

1. What shared characteristics can you identify in these two Warhol paintings? What does the artist gain—and lose—by repeating images of these American icons? How does Warhol use color in each painting? What is the overall effect of putting these separate paintings together on a single page?

2. What is unique about each of these paintings? What features of Marilyn Monroe's fame, for example, does Warhol emphasize? Why do you think he chooses to show Elvis as a pistol-packing cowboy? What role does each repetition play in each painting? Please remember to point to specific aspects of each painting when formulating your response. For each painting, identify a distinct message that you see Warhol making—along with any cultural values you can read in the paintings as a group.

WRITING

1. Given what you have observed in these paintings, what role do you think originality and uniqueness play in Warhol's aesthetics? What cultural virtues and values seem to be privileged in his art? Draft an expository essay in which you explain the relationship between the subjects and techniques of Warhol's paintings and the rise of American mass production in the decades following World War II. What role does duplication play in Warhol's painting and in that culture?

2. Compare and contrast Warhol's depiction of Marilyn Monroe with the other rendition of her as an American icon in this chapter. (See the poem by Sharon Olds on p. 483 and the second 1991 Madonna photo on p. 509.) Then draft an argumentative essay in which you build a convincing case that one of these "images" of Monroe is more memorable than the other. Please be sure to validate each of your assertions by pointing to specific evidence in the text you choose to discuss.

SHARON OLDS

Born in San Francisco in 1942, Sharon Olds attended Stanford and Columbia Universities. In 1980 she published her first book of poems, *Satan Says,* which won the first award given by the San Francisco Poetry Center. Her second book of poems, *The Dead and the Living* (1983), was the Lamont Poetry Selection for that year and also won the National Book Critics Circle Award. Since then, Olds has authored five books of poetry and has contributed to numerous literary journals and magazines.

Olds recently named Lucille Clifton, Brenda Hillman, Seamus Heaney, and Rita Dove among the writers who have influenced her. "It's just wonderful," Olds explained, "that every writer is shaped, and the poems are shaped, by so many things: by the life, by the mind and the spirit of the writer, so that you read a poem and know who wrote it. By where they're from, by being right here, to hear people's voices in the sense of their style as well as their physical region of the country."

Olds teaches poetry workshops at New York University, where she is chair of the Creative Writing Program, and in the University's program at Goldwater Hospital for the severely physically disabled on Roosevelt Island in New York. Named New York State poet in 1998–2000, she is currently working on a new collection of poems.

THE DEATH OF MARILYN MONROE

Sharon Olds

The ambulance men touched her cold
body, lifted it, heavy as iron,
onto the stretcher, tried to close the
mouth, close the eyes, tied the
arms to the side, moved a caught   5
strand of hair, as if it mattered,
saw the shape of her breasts, flattened by
gravity, under the sheet,
carried her, as if it were she,
down the steps.   10

These men were never the same. They went out
afterwards, as they always did,
for a drink or two, but they could not meet
each other's eyes.

Their lives took   15
a turn—one had nightmares, strange
pains, impotence, depression. One did not
like his work, his wife looked
different, his kids. Even death
seemed different to him—a place where she   20
would be waiting,
And one found himself standing at night
in the doorway to a room of sleep, listening to
a woman breathing, just an ordinary
woman   25
breathing.

SEEING

1. What are the implied effects of Marilyn Monroe's death on the men in the poem? How do you interpret the last sentence of Sharon Olds's poem? What do you make of the phrase "just an ordinary/woman/breathing"? What is the effect of the line breaks in the final three lines of the poem?

2. "The Death of Marilyn Monroe" tells a story about the intersection of ordinary people and celebrities. What larger insights does the poem prompt you to make about the ways in which we turn celebrities into icons?

WRITING

1. Consider carefully the title of Sharon Olds's poem, "The Death of Marilyn Monroe." We immortalize icons and celebrities through images, songs, and stories. But does a celebrity ever really die? Periodically we hear people proclaim that Elvis is not dead, and in fact in the public arena he may be more alive than ever. Do celebrities achieve greater iconic status in death? Choose a celebrity who died relatively recently. (Princess Diana, Frank Sinatra, and Kurt Cobain might serve as examples.) Write an argumentative essay in which you argue for—or against—the proposition that celebrities are granted an even greater iconic status after they die.

2. Both Olds's poem and Andy Warhol's painting *The Twenty Marilyns* feature representations of Marilyn Monroe. Write an essay in which you compare these two different representations and try to account for their differences.

www   Re: Searching the Web

The Citizens Flag Alliance is an organization devoted to a single purpose: "to persuade the Congress of the United States to propose a constitutional amendment to protect the American flag from physical desecration, and send it to the states for ratification"; its web site can be found at www.cfa-inc.org/index.html. The author of The Flag-Burning Page <www.indirect.com/www/warren/flag.html>, on the other hand, describes his site as "a standing protest to any amendment to the U.S. Constitution which would allow Congress or the States to pass laws against flag-burning laws that the Supreme Court has already said are unconstitutional."

Spend some time exploring the substance and spirit of what is presented at each of these web sites. Which aspects of the debate on desecration of the flag does each web site emphasize? Consider the evidence each presents to support a particular point of view. Does each rely more on visual or verbal texts to make the case for—or against—laws banning flag-burning activities? To what extent does each site provide new evidence—or angles—on the debate?

Use an Internet search engine to explore other web sites devoted to the debate about representations of the flag. In what ways do these other sites extend, complicate, or enrich your understanding of the public debate surrounding the flag-burning issue?

HOLLY BRUBACH >
A former style editor for the *New York Times Magazine,* Holly Brubach has written on topics as diverse as luggage and architecture. According to one critic, she is "a writer who could make a safety pin sound interesting."

Brubach's writing on the style scene goes far beyond fashion predictions to analyze the advertising strategies behind such phenomena as "heroin chic" or to examine the changing images of feminine identity—from both academic and popular perspectives.

In her book *Girlfriend: Men, Women, and Drag* (1999) with photographer Michael James O'Brien, Brubach examines drag (men dressing in women's clothing) as a conjunction of many issues concerning sex and gender. The book surveys the various "drag scenes" in major cities around the world. Brubach writes, "Drag is a subject capable of triggering ferocious responses in a wide variety of people. There are men (both straight and gay) who abhor drag for its flamboyant display, who find it alarming that the transition from masculine to feminine can be made so easily."

Brubach has won numerous awards for her journalism, and she has worked as staff writer for the *Atlanta Times* and the *New York Times,* as a fashion columnist, and as a style editor for the *New York Times Magazine.* A native of Pittsburgh, she now divides her time between New York and Milan.

Holly Brubach

Heroine

It's the '90s, and the pantheon we've built to house the women in our minds is getting crowded. **Elizabeth Taylor, Eleanor Roosevelt, Oprah Winfrey, Alanis Morissette, Indira Gandhi, Claudia Schiffer, Coco Chanel, Doris Day, Aretha Franklin, Jackie Onassis, Rosa Parks**—they're all there, the dead and the living side by side, contemporaneous in our imaginations. On television and in the movies, in advertising and magazines, their images are scattered across the landscape of our everyday lives.

Their presence is sometimes decorative, sometimes uplifting, occasionally infuriating. The criteria for appointment to this ad hoc hall of fame that takes up so much space in our thoughts and in our culture may at first glance appear to be utterly random. In fact, irrespective of their achievements, most of these women have been apotheosized primarily on the basis of their ability to appeal to our fantasies.

An icon is a human sound bite, an individual reduced to a name, a face and an idea; Dale Evans, the compassionate cowgirl. In some cases, just the name and an idea suffice. Few people would

recognize Helen Keller in a photograph, but her name has become synonymous with being blind and deaf to such an extent that she has inspired an entire category of jokes. Greta Garbo has gone down in collective memory as an exalted enigma with a slogan about being alone. Asking a man if that's a gun in his pocket is all it takes to invoke Mae West. Catherine Deneuve's face, pictured on a stamp, is the emblem of France. Virginia Woolf has her own T-shirt. Naomi Campbell has her own doll. Celebrity being the engine that drives our culture, these women have been taken up by the

Worship
the age of the female icon

media and made famous, packaged as commodities and marketed to a public eager for novelty and easily bored.

Many worthy women are acknowledged for their accomplishments but never take on the status of an icon. Many women are acknowledged as icons but for one reason or another are absent from the pages of this special issue, which is by no means comprehensive. The sheer number of icons now in circulation makes any attempt to catalogue them all impossible. Of the women included here, who they are—or were—is in some respects not nearly as significant as what they've come to stand for. Kate Axelrod, the 11-year-old on our cover, stands not only for the girls of her generation, whose identities are in the formative stages, but for women of all ages, who tend to regard themselves as works in progress.

Our icons are by no means exclusively female, but the male ones are perhaps less ubiquitous and more accessible. The pedestals we put them on are lower; the service they are called on to perform is somewhat different.

Like women, men presumably look to icons for tips that they can take away and apply to their lives. The men who are elevated to the status of icons are the ones who are eminently cool, whose moves the average guy can steal. They do not prompt a fit of introspection (much less of self-recrimination), as female icons often do in women. What a male icon inspires in other men is not so much the desire to be him as the desire to be accepted by him—to be buddies, to shoot pool together, to go drinking. I have all this on good authority from a man of my acquaintance who insists that, though regular guys may envy, say, Robert Redford for his ability to knock women dead, what they're thinking as they watch him in a movie is not "Hey, I wonder if I have what it takes to do that, too," but "I wonder if Redford would like to hang out with me."

Whereas women may look at an icon like Raquel Welch, whose appeal is clearly to the male half of humanity, and ask themselves, "If that's what's required to appeal to a man, have I got it, or can I get it?" (The thought of hanging out with

487

Welch—going shopping together or talking about boyfriends—would, I think it's safe to say, never cross most women's minds.)

An entire industry, called fashion, has grown up around the business of convincing women that they need to remake themselves in someone else's image: makeup and clothes and other products are presented not as alterations but as improvements. The notion of appearance and personality as a project to be undertaken is inculcated early on. A man may choose to ignore certain male icons; a woman has no such luxury where the great majority of female icons are concerned. She must come to terms with them, defining herself in relation to them—emulating some, rejecting others. In certain cases, a single icon may exist for her as both an example and a reproach.

Our male icons are simply the latest entries in a tradition of long standing, broad enough in any given era to encompass any number of prominent men. But the current array of female icons is a recent phenomenon, the outgrowth of aspirations many of which date back no more than 100 years.

What were the images of women that informed the life of a girl growing up 200 years ago? It's hard for us to imagine the world before it was wallpapered with ads, before it was inundated with all the visual "information" that comes our way in the course of an average day and competes with real people and events for our attention. There were no magazines, no photographs. In church, a girl would have seen renderings of the Virgin Mary and the saints. She may have encountered portraits of royalty, whose station, unless she'd been born an aristocrat, must have seemed even more unattainable than that of the saints. There were picturesque genre paintings depicting peasants and chambermaids, to be seen at the public salons, if anyone thought to bring a girl to them. But the most ambitious artists concentrated on pagan goddesses and mythological women, who, being Olympian, inhabited a plane so lofty that they were presumably immune to quotidian concerns. History and fiction, for the girl who had access to them, contained tales of women whose lives had been somewhat more enterprising and action-packed than those of the women she saw around her, but her knowledge of most women's exploits in her own time would have been limited to hearsay: a woman had written a novel, a woman had played hostess to one of the greatest philosophers of the age and discussed ideas with him, a woman had disguised herself as a man and gone to war. Most likely, a girl would have modeled herself on a female relative, or on a woman in her community. The great beauty who set the standard by which others were measured would have been the one in their midst—the prettiest girl in town, whose fame was local.

Nineteenth-century icons like Sarah Bernhardt and George Sand would have imparted no more in the way of inspiration; their careers were predicated on their talents, which had been bestowed by God. It was Florence Nightingale who finally provided an example that was practicable, one to which well-born girls could aspire, and hundreds of women followed her into nursing.

Today, the images of women confronting a girl growing up in our culture are far more diverse, though not all of them can be interpreted as signs of progress. A woman who in former times might have served as the model for some painter's rendering of one or another pagan goddess is now deployed to sell us cars and soap. The great beauty has been chosen from an international field of contenders. At the movies, we see the stories of fictional women brought to life by real actresses whose own lives have become the stuff of fiction. In the news, we read about women running countries, directing corporations, and venturing into outer space.

The conditions that in our century have made possible this proliferation of female icons were of course brought on by the convergence of advances in women's rights and the growth of the media into an industry. As women accomplished the unprecedented, the press took them up and made them famous, trafficking in their accomplishments, their opinions, their fates. If, compared with the male icons of our time, our female icons seem to loom larger in our culture and to cast a longer shadow, perhaps it's because in so many cases their stories have had the urgency of history in the making.

When it comes to looking at women, we're all voyeurs, men and women alike. Does our urge to study the contours of their flesh and the changes in their faces stem from some primal longing to be reunited with the body that gave us life? Women have been the immemorial repository of male fantasies—a lonesome role that many are nonetheless loath to relinquish, given the power it confers and the oblique satisfaction it brings. The curiosity and desire inherent in the so-called male gaze, deplored for the way it has objectified women in art and in films, are matched on women's part by the need to assess our own potential to be found beautiful and by the pleasure in putting ourselves in the position of the woman being admired.

Our contemporary images of women are descended from a centuries-old tradition and, inevitably, they are seen in its light. Women have often been universalized, made allegorical. The figure who represents Liberty, or Justice, to say nothing of Lust or Wrath, is a woman, not a man—a tradition that persists: there is no Mr. America. The unidentified woman in innumerable paintings—landscapes, genre scenes, mythological scenes—transcends her circumstances and becomes Woman. It's the particular that is customarily celebrated in men, and the general in woman. Even our collective notions of beauty reflect this: a man's idiosyncrasies enhance his looks; a woman's detract from hers.

"I'm every woman, it's all in me," Chaka Khan sings, and the chords in the bass modulate optimistically upward, in a surge of possibility. Not all that long ago, the notion that any woman could be every woman would have been dismissed as blatantly absurd, but to our minds it makes evident sense, in keeping with the logic that we can be anything we want to be—the cardinal rule of the human-potential movement and an assumption that in America today is so widely accepted and dearly held that it might as well be written into the Constitution. Our icons are at this point sufficiently plentiful that to model ourselves on only one of them would seem arbitrary and limiting, when in fact we can take charge in the manner of Katharine Hepburn, strut in the way we learned by watching Tina Turner, flirt in the tradition of Rita Hayworth, grow old with dignity in the style of Georgia O'Keeffe. In the spirit of post-modernism, we piece our selves together, assembling the examples of several women in a single personality— a process that makes for some unprecedented combinations, like Madonna: the siren who lifts weights and becomes a mother. We contemplate the women who have been singled out in our culture and the permutations of femininity they represent. About to move on to the next century, we call on various aspects of them as we reconfigure our lives, deciding which aspects of our selves we want to take with us and which aspects we want to leave behind. o

SEEING

1. Holly Brubach defines the modern icon as a "human sound bite, an individual reduced to a name, a face and an idea" (para. 3). How does she argue that the nature and impact of human icons have changed over time? What other definitions of the term *icon* does she work with in this essay? What sources does she draw on? What evidence does she use to substantiate each of her claims? Where, in your judgment, does her reasoning seem to fall short?

2. What distinctions does Brubach draw between the ways in which women and men relate to female and male icons, respectively? How do her assertions resonate with—or differ from—your own experience with male and female icons? Choose a particular cultural icon to illustrate your point. The editors of the *New York Times Magazine* had to choose certain female icons to include as illustrations for Brubach's article (not shown here). Which ones would you choose to illustrate "Heroine Worship"? Explain why.

WRITING

1. Reread the following passage several times, until you feel comfortable dealing with its substance and implications for self-identity: "we piece our selves together, assembling the examples of several women in a single personality—a process that makes for some unprecedented combinations, like Madonna: the siren who lifts weights and becomes a mother" (para. 16). Consider carefully the ways in which you "piece [yourself] together" and especially the ways in which you rely in this process on connecting your identity to the role model(s) and heroes/heroines in your own life. Draft an essay in which you account for the role of male or female icons in establishing your identity.

2. Over 200 years ago, Brubach argues, a young woman most likely "would have modeled herself on a female relative, or on a woman in her community" (para. 10). Explain how the current era of "visual information" has changed our relationship to the role of icons, models, and celebrities in American culture, citing as examples the male and female icons *you* find most important.

I was looking for an American
symbol. A Coca-Cola bottle or a
Mickey Mouse would have been
ridiculous, doing anything with
the American flag would have been
insulting, and Cadillac hubcaps
were just too uncomfortable.

– Lizzy Gardiner on her choice of the American
Express gold card to wear to the 1995 Academy
Awards, where she accepted an Oscar for best
costume design.

Visualizing Composition
Metaphor

Lemon.

This Volkswagen missed the boat.

The chrome strip on the glove compartment is blemished and must be replaced. Chances are you wouldn't have noticed it; Inspector Kurt Kroner did.

There are 3,389 men at our Wolfsburg factory with only one job: to inspect Volkswagens at each stage of production. (3000 Volkswagens are produced daily; there are more inspectors than cars.)

Every shock absorber is tested (spot checking won't do), every windshield is scanned. VWs have been rejected for surface scratches barely visible to the eye.

Final inspection is really something! VW inspectors run each car off the line onto the Funktionsprüfstand (car test stand), tote up 189 check points, gun ahead to the automatic brake stand, and say "no" to one VW out of fifty.

This preoccupation with detail means the VW lasts longer and requires less maintenance, by and large, than other cars. (It also means a used VW depreciates less than any other car.)

We pluck the lemons; you get the plums.

Metaphor remains one of the most productive aids to writing effectively. *Metaphors* surface frequently in everyday conversation, and many of us use them so often that we're not always conscious of doing so. Consider, for example, the metaphors many undergraduates use to talk about attending school: The language and images used are drawn from prison ("What time are you free?" "How long do you have to go?"); taking a course is described in terms of suffering from a disease ("What do you have this semester?").

Many textbooks on writing urge inexperienced writers to regard metaphor as a feature of style—as a means to enliven the writer's prose during revision. Metaphor can—and should—play such a role in any writer's compositional efforts; but it can also function equally effectively during the earliest phase of the writing process, when the writer sets out to generate ideas about a subject as well as to create a structure for that prose.

By enabling us to articulate—and clarify—concepts and images of one subject in terms of another, metaphor can help us understand and appreciate new connections that may lead to new insights about a subject. In the language of advertising, metaphor is frequently used to persuade us that one thing is another—to establish memorable rhetorical relationships between people and products. Consider, for example, one of the most famous advertisements in American corporate and cultural history—Volkswagen's *Lemon*. This ad heralded a revolution in American advertising by labeling the pictured Volkswagen a "lemon," a negative metaphor to use in connection with purchasing a car.

Examine carefully the most recent issue of your favorite magazine, concentrating on the use of metaphor in the advertising printed in it. Then write an expository essay in which you explain fully the various functions that metaphor serves in one advertisement in this issue. What compositional purposes—and effects—does metaphor highlight in this ad?

Metaphor operates as an implied comparison (for example, "Her mind is a high-speed computer") and can be distinguished from simile, which works by means of an explicit comparison linked by the use of *like* or *as* ("Her brain moves as quickly as a high-speed computer.").

TIBOR KALMAN

Born in Budapest, Tibor Kalman (1949–1999) moved to the United States at the age of 7. He grew up in Poughkeepsie, New York, and attended New York University. In 1979 he founded the design firm M&Co and attracted clients ranging from MTV and the Talking Heads to the Museum of Modern Art. M&Co's aesthetic was in direct opposition to the "slick" corporate styles of the day, and Kalman is widely known for establishing an offbeat and often humorous design vocabulary that critiques the dishonesty and superficiality of most corporate public relations and advertising. Kalman left M&Co to edit *Colors,* a magazine launched by Benetton, and he used this platform to engage in new forms of media activism, especially concerning racism. The following images first appeared in a *Colors* issue devoted to race as part of a feature called What If . . .

Kalman critiques modern society because, as he explains, our economic system "tries to make everything look right. . . . But . . . when you make something no one hates, no one loves it." Thus Kalman is "interested in imperfections, quirkiness, insanity, and unpredictability. That's what we really pay attention to anyway." A retrospective monograph, *Tibor Kalman: Perverse Optimist* (1998), is what he calls an "almanac of oddities." His other books include *Chairman* (1997).

SEEING

1. How did you respond to the altered images of Michael Jackson, Arnold Schwarzenegger, Spike Lee, and Queen Elizabeth? What response does each photograph elicit from you? How does each photograph challenge your assumptions about what familiar public figures should look like? Which image do you find most—and least—plausible? Explain why.

2. Comment on Tibor Kalman's choices in manipulating the skin color, hair style, and eyes of each public figure. In what ways does each of these images seem more striking, more contrived, or more realistic than others you've seen of public figures? Do you find Kalman's images humorous? satiric? ironic? some combination of these? Please clarify and explain. What, in effect, do you think he is trying to accomplish? Explain the extent to which you think he is successful.

WRITING

1. Kalman has employed computer technology to "switch" the racial identity of these public figures. Imagine that you were able to assume a different racial identity. Which would you choose? Why? What would be the consequences of doing so? How might your daily life be different as a result? Write the first draft of a comparison/contrast essay in which you imagine the impact such a change would have on the spirit and substance of your daily life—on campus or beyond.

2. Choose one of these photographs and write an essay in which you explain what Kalman's manipulation of the image of this public figure suggests about the role of race in that person's public life. How much does the public identity of each person portrayed here depend on his or her racial identity?

TOM PERROTTA

Tom Perrotta is the author of *Bad Haircut: Stories of the Seventies* (1994), *The Wishbones* (1997), and *Joe College* (2000), but he may be best known for *Election: A Novel* (1998), a darkly funny story about a suburban New Jersey high school election that became a Paramount movie starring Matthew Broderick and Reese Witherspoon. All of Perrotta's stories and novels deal with the experiences of adolescence. Although his characters are sometimes exaggerated, as is the protagonist of *Election*, oftentimes they reveal how real-life teens perceive their world as it is presented to them by pop icons, such as Britney Spears.

"My literary generation seems to have been defined by a group of virtuoso postmodernists in the David Foster Wallace school. I feel less affinity with those writers than I do with the realists of the previous generation.... I'm committed to making fiction out of 'ordinary' experience and to telling stories in a way that will make them accessible to a large audience."

Perrotta has taught expository writing at Harvard University but ceased teaching and writing novels to work on writing and selling his screenplays. He also has two television pilots in development. The *Washington Times* called him "a writer to watch," and *Newsweek* heralded him as "one of America's best-kept literary secrets." He lives in Belmont, Massachusetts. "The Cosmic Significance of Britney Spears" first appeared in the December 2001 edition of *GQ* magazine.

The Cosmic Significance of Britney Spears

Tom Perrotta

She is our most famous singing virgin, this nymphet hottie who admits she's "All about sit-ups" and has the most adorable abs in the universe to prove it. But there's more to Britney than that, isn't there? Isn't there?

Like a lot of other people, I had trouble concentrating on my work in the days after the September 11 terrorist attacks. I found it hard to focus on anything unrelated to the tragedy, hard to convince myself that what I was doing really mattered. In my case, this fairly common emotional response was exacerbated by the fact that I happened to be writing an essay about Britney Spears. The truth is, even in what now seem to have been the idyllic, clueless days preceding one of the bloodiest events in American history, I was having a certain amount of difficulty taking my subject seriously. Britney, after all, is the kind of person who can look straight into the camera, as she did in her recently televised *MTV Diary*, and tell the world, without any trace of irony, "I'm all about sit-ups."

This isn't to say she's not a likable person. I mean, what's not to like about Britney? Millions of kids think she's great, she loves her family and her totally cute world-famous boyfriend, and by all accounts she remains the sweet, God-fearing, down-to-earth southern girl she was brought up to be, miraculously unchanged by global megastardom. Plus, she looks hot in really tight pants, and you can't say that about everyone. All those sit-ups paid off, apparently.

So the question isn't whether we *like* Britney. Of course we *like* her. At least we *would* like her if we hung out with her on the patio of her $3 million dream house in the Hollywood Hills and chowed down on hot dogs and cookie-dough ice cream (her favorite foods, according to www.adoredcelebrities.com, though a recent *Rolling Stone* profile shows her snacking on steamed soybeans). The real question is: Do we need to think about Britney? Does the fact that she's currently one of the biggest pop stars in the universe, a one-name trademark on par with Oprah and Madonna, make her by definition a figure of sociological significance? Or is Britney a phenomenon of such mind-numbing simplicity that she's the pop-culture equivalent of a stealth bomber, zooming cheerfully below the radar of thoughtful analysis?

It would be easy enough to write her off as just another teen idol, one in the never-ending progression of Debbies and Tiffanys the entertainment industry has been selling to American kids ever since Annette Funicello first donned her mouse ears. Then we wouldn't have to think about her at all.

On the other hand, some of the most important and revealing cultural figures of the past half century first came to our attention disguised as pop stars—think Michael Jackson, whose ghoulishly altered face tells a mythic and terrible story about race and celebrity in America. So shouldn't we consider the possibility that Britney is more than just the latest teenage wonder, the obligatory icon on this year's school lunchbox? What if she's an era-defining superstar, one of those very lucky, once-or-twice-in-a-decade figures whose job it is to tell us who we are and where we're going? Maybe she has more in common with more iconic artists like Elvis Presley or Madonna or Kurt Cobain than we ever gave her credit for. At the very least, the comparisons are instructive.

Britney and Elvis

Am I the only guy in America who doesn't lust for Britney? In a purely theoretical sense, I appreciate her aerobically engineered body and her eagerness to flash a little thong. But there's something disconcertingly childish about her persona, some willful refusal to acknowledge her own sexuality that makes it hard for me to join Bob Dole and his dog in their slack-jawed worship of this girl.

As Elvis did before her, Britney presents herself to the world as a divided personality—shy and self-effacing in private, shockingly bold in public. Unwilling or unable to acknowledge a contradiction between her avowed religious piety and her uninhibited onstage sexuality, Britney at first defended herself not by raising the flag of sexual empowerment à la Madonna but by denying any impure intent, much as Elvis did a half century earlier. "I'm not trying to be sexy," Elvis used to claim, responding to questions about his provocatively jiggling leg. "It just automatically wiggles like that." Similarly, Britney professed bewilderment when challenged about her famously neither-here-nor-there outfits. "All I did was tie up my shirt!" she told a reporter, in reference to the sexy schoolgirl-strumpet outfit she wore in the video for ". . . Baby One More Time," which brought her to the attention of many middle-aged pedophiles. "I'm wearing a sports bra under it."

It's really not such a stretch to think of Britney and Elvis as distant celebrity cousins. They both grew up in humble circumstances in the Deep South (Elvis in Mississippi and Tennessee, Britney in Louisiana), with strong attachments to their doting mothers. Like Elvis, Britney makes a point of ritually invoking her loyalty to her small-town roots even as success calls her away from home. Elvis could have been speaking for both of them when he said, "Them people in New York and Hollywood are not going to change me none."

For Britney, being southern is a powerful personal identity, one she frequently mentions. "I'm from the South," she said in a recent profile, "so I'm a very open person." Her aesthetic tastes and moral values seem clearly rooted in the region: Her fondness for frilly, floral-patterned furniture; her sweet disposition and unfailing good manners; the prayer diary she keeps by her bed; her public declarations of chastity until marriage; and her brief stint at Parklane Academy, a private Christian school in Missisippi.

What being southern is not for Britney—and this is where she parts company decisively with Elvis—is a musical identity. Nothing in her songs, not a single geographical reference or vocal inflection, marks her as hailing from America's richest musical region, the cradle of the blues, the home of country music, zydeco, and rockabilly. Britney's music is the musical equivalent of a big-budget Hollywood action movie; you don't need to understand English, let alone be conversant with the musical traditions of the Missisippi Delta, to enjoy the multimedia juggernaut that is Britney.

The South, of course, is far less a separate and culturally unique region in Britney's day than it was in Elvis's. By the time Britney was old enough to listen to the radio, authentic country music had pretty much been homogenized out of existence; all that was left was the high hair and cowboy hats. Until her most recent album, Britney wrote almost none of her material; her sound was created by Swedish producer Max Martin. "I'm so lucky to work with Max," she says in *Heart to Heart*, the unintentionally revealing autobiography she cowrote with her mother, Lynne. "He knows not only what will make a great song but also what I will love singing."

Elvis didn't write his own material, either, and he too was deeply indebted to a shrewd producer, Sam Phillips of Sun Records. Yet there seems to be little doubt that the 18-year-old Elvis was a musical innovator, a naive singer who somehow created a new synthesis of blues and country music, fusing the two dominant musical forms of his childhood—one black, the other white—that were constantly rubbing up against each other in the streets and on the radios in the segregated South but rarely mixing. Everyone involved in the early Sun sessions bears witness to the feeling of something totally unexpected being born, some-

thing no one had heard before, and that Elvis was the source. Elvis created himself out of the materials at hand; Britney had a musical identity imposed on her that she gratefully accepted. Britney is, and was always intended to be, a familiar and easily consumable product, appealing to a wide swath of humanity without first belonging to an actual place or community or individual consciousness. If Elvis is the particular that became universal, Britney is the universal that was never particular.

Britney and Madonna

I do believe religion and eroticism are absolutely related. And I think my original feelings of sexuality and eroticism originated in going to church.
—Madonna

I don't think I could ever look at how lucky I am now and not think that God had a hand in it.
—Britney Spears

When I first saw *Truth or Dare* in 1991, I remember feeling sorry for Madonna's brother and sisters and grateful I didn't have to contend with such a formidable sibling. I lent some of these sentiments to Tammy Warren, the Madonna-obsessed lesbian teenager in my novel *Election*: "I tried to imagine what it would be like to be a member of her family, how hard it would be to keep your spirits up, to wake up in the morning and actually believe you have a life worth living."

In *Truth or Dare*, Madonna portrays herself as an unapologetic celebrity monster—vain, self-obsessed, willing to mock and humiliate anyone who crosses her path, including her father and a childhood friend desperate for her approval. At that moment in her career, Madonna indulged her egotism without shame, daring you to deny that you would have behaved any differently in her place.

Britney poses no such challenge to her fans or the people around her. At least in her *MTV Diary*,

Britney emerges as the anti-Madonna, the celebrity without an ego. She seems to want so little from her fame and fortune: She is holding off on the sex for now and is mostly indifferent to the money. Like the rest of us, she makes do with simple pleasures, seeming almost erotically disheveled after a ride on a roller coaster, deriving real satisfaction from the shot she sinks at a charity basketball game, getting choked up at her father's birthday party. She's just so pleasant and thoughtful; she wouldn't want to do or say anything that might upset anyone.

Considering their wildly different attitudes toward stardom, it's intriguing to note how often Britney refers to Madonna as a role model. Madonna successfully navigated the treacherous transition from lightweight pop singer, catering to preteen tastes and drag queens, to major artist with a loyal adult following. Over and over, Britney and her management invoke Madonna when trying to imagine a strategy for overcoming the built-in obsolescence of the teen pop star. "I admire the way Madonna always reinvents herself," Britney says in *Heart to Heart*. "I think that's one reason she's managed to stay a success for so long while other artists have fizzled out."

The superficial bond between the two performers is intensified by the fact that they occupy the same highly charged spot on the pop-culture spectrum, that narrow band where spirituality and sexuality intersect. This isn't to say they share the same attitudes about religion or sex ("I just think it's important to fuck what you want to fuck and not feel shame about it," Madonna once remarked). But simply to notice this peculiar connection between our most famous singing virgin and our most famous singing bad girl is to confront a highly revealing irony: Britney may be more conventionally devout in her personal life, but Madonna is far and away the more religiously engaged artist of the pair.

Over the years, Madonna has spoken frequently, and at times thoughtfully, about her religious upbringing, joking about her name but also connecting the Catholic concepts of sin and guilt with her own interest in sexual transgression. But even if Madonna had a different first name and never said a word about her background, the fact that she had grown up Catholic would be obvious to anyone familiar with her body of work in the '80s.

On the other hand, we know Britney is religious only because she tells us (and tells us and tells us), though to be honest, her theology seems to begin and end with gratitude toward the good Lord for making her such a big friggin' star. If we were deprived of magazine profiles and publicity materials and had access only to Britney's CDs and videos, we'd have no idea that she's a devout Baptist who attends church regularly or holds stricter ideas about sexual morality than the average pop singer. Britney specializes in featherweight love songs, her persona shifting from breathless little girl ("Dear Diary") to apologetic tease ("Oops! . . . I Did It Again"). Though a determined critic might be able to infer a desire to set sexual boundaries from some of the lyrics, her videos and live performances move strenuously in the opposite direction: They're all about breaking limits and showing midriff—from the whiff of pedophilia in ". . . Baby One More Time" to her notorious nude bodysuit at the 2000 MTV Video Music Awards.

Some observers admire Britney for this ability to simultaneously inhabit the roles of nice girl and sexpot. "I like the way that she refuses to have any truck with virgin-or-whore stereotypes, how her Christianity sits perfectly happily alongside her breasts," wrote Julie Burchill in the *Guardian*. Others suspect her of being a hypocrite: "She and Justin Timberlake look a little close," sniffed teen actress Kirsten Dunst in a recent profile. "Maybe she is [a virgin]. I don't know." For most of us, though, Britney is simply unreadable. What does she mean when she says she's "not that innocent"? That she's lying to the public and running around behind her mama's back? That she has an elastic definition of what constitutes sexual relations, like Bill Clinton or one of those junior-high blow-job queens who've found their own ways of circumventing the virgin/whore dichotomy? Or does she mean something much more innocent than that? Your guess is as good as mine.

All I really know is that Madonna always seems deadly serious about what she's doing or saying, whereas Britney always seems as if she's kidding around. Her surprisingly lame Jungle Jane–themed performance at this year's MTV Video Music Awards is a good case in point. If Madonna performed a song called "I'm a Slave 4 U" and choreographed it with sexy multicultural dancers, vaguely Egyptian overtones, and a finale that included a huge yellow serpent, you'd immediately know that she was trying to make some kind of allegorical statement about sex, sin, and power and that these were issues she'd thought about in some sustained way and had put to the test in her private life. But when Britney does it, all you can say is, "Hey, cool, there's Britney holding a fat snake."

Britney and Cobain

When Nirvana burst onto the scene in the early '90s, they struck a lot of people as something new under the sun. And while it's true they represented a stark departure from the hair-metal poseurs then dominating the rock world, they were immediately familiar to anyone who, like me, had gone to a working-class high school in the late '70s. They were burnouts, sullen stoners who cut class, got high in the bathroom, and didn't get along with the gym teachers. That they were outcasts was part of the point—rock 'n' roll was supposed to be the music of losers, the means by which they were allowed to engineer their own redemption.

I recently spent a day switching between Britney Spears's *Heart to Heart* and *Heavier Than Heaven*,

Charles R. Cross's new biography of Kurt Cobain. The effect was disorienting, like leaving a birthday party at Chuck E. Cheese to visit a friend in a mental hospital. Britney is a relentlessly upbeat and utterly inoffensive person who believes that "there's nothing . . . as good as a cold glass of iced tea on a hot summer day or the smell of fresh-cut grass in the backyard." Cobain was the kind of guy who kept a pet rat (which he accidentally stepped on and killed), named his first band Fecal Matter, and had fantasies about being raped by Chef Boyardee.

And yet, for all the vast psychic distance between them, Britney and Cobain are fated to be forever linked in our national consciousness as the opposing bookends of the 1990s, poster children for a schizoid decade. There's Cobain on the left, mumbling and unshaven, representing a gloomy time of war and recession. And there's Britney on the right, the official superstar of the late-'90s boom, the chipper emblem of a fat, happy country bubbling over with irrational exuberance.

Kurt Cobain's childhood prepared him well to be the spokesman for an unhappy era. A sensitive and gifted kid, he grew up in a hardscrabble logging town that was a breeding ground for dysfunction and suicide. Between the ages of 15 and 19, he lived, according to his biographer, "in ten different houses, with ten different families," at one point crashing in a cardboard box on a friend's porch. A high school dropout who worked as a janitor, dishwasher, and carpet installer, Cobain suffered from a mysterious stomach ailment that left him in chronic pain and that he later claimed to be self-medicating with his heroin habit.

Given his lifelong intimacy with pain, abandonment, and failure, it's probably not surprising that the enormous commercial success of Nirvana left Cobain feeling isolated and bewildered, at the mercy of alien forces. He responded by embracing the identity of junkie, and once he'd chosen this path, nothing could divert him from it. He was the rare rock star who seemed genuinely uncomfortable with the idea of being rich and famous and well loved, as if it were a betrayal of who he was and where he'd come from.

Britney, of course, has no such qualms with fame—she was raised for success, in the same way that Cobain seems to have been raised for unhappiness. Her life story consists of one triumph piled on top of another, each at an absurdly young age: She wins a *Star Search* competition at 10, is picked to be a Mouseketeer at 11, signs a recording contract at 15, has a number one record at 17, and so on.

In fact, Britney and her mom are sensitive to the appearance that it's all come a little too easily. They devote a considerable amount of energy in *Heart to Heart* to establishing Britney's bona fides as an artist who has suffered for her success, but the best they can come up with is an almost comical series of incidents that barely qualify as hardships under the loosest of definitions: Most distressing was the inconvenient knee injury she incurred during a video shoot shortly after the release of her first album. Britney had to cancel several TV appearances (including one on Jay Leno!) while recuperating from arthroscopic surgery; her career was momentarily stalled. "It threw us all for a loop," Lynne Spears writes. "But this time it was her mountain to climb alone."

Music provided Kurt Cobain with a desperately needed outlet for transforming pain into art. For Britney, though, therapy and self-expression are beside the point; her music serves primarily as a vehicle for advancing her career, and she talks about her craft with a cool, professional distance. "I have an amazing team of writers, musicians, and producers," she notes in her book, "and they are churning out great songs for me." As a performer, Britney resembles a young Olympic athlete more than she does an artist—she seems at times to have no inner life at all, only a burning desire to master the task at hand: "I will practice and practice a move in front of a mirror, over and over again—ten, twenty, a hundred times— until I'm happy with it." It's precisely the purity and intensity of her youthful ambition that made Britney such a potent symbol of the late '90s. The whole point of the new-economy boom was that you could be rich and powerful right now, while you were still young and good-looking— you didn't have to wait your turn to climb the corporate ladder. If you took the right risks with the right attitudes, the rewards would flow. And it worked. At least for a few years it did. By the turn of the millennium, there was no longer a distinction between youth culture and grown-up culture; youth culture was American culture, and right there at this high-achieving pinnacle of the late '90s was Britney.

The big question for Britney right now isn't whether she can make a Madonna-like transition into adult stardom but whether her moment hasn't already passed. Quite suddenly, the boom is over. The '90s are gone. Recession is knocking, and the country is at war. America has an inner life again; our demons have returned from vacation. It looks as if we may soon start casting around for someone capable of giving voice to a new mood of pain and uncertainty, and it's fair to assume that that someone's probably not going to look or sound a helluva lot like Britney. ○

BRITNEY GOES TO COLLEGE?

Julie L. Nicklin

Britney Spears sings that she is not a girl but not yet a woman on her current single, which may mean she's just about ready for college. "I've really, really been thinking about it," the 20-year-old teen idol told *Entertainment Weekly* this month.

So what advice would a savvy admissions counselor give to the Mouseketeer turned superstar, who has been home-schooled since the age of 9? Here's the take of Steven Antonoff, president of his own firm in Denver and a former admissions dean at the University of Denver.

Q. How can Ms. Spears make herself more attractive to colleges?
A. She has to develop more skills beyond her singing. If she studied spiders in the Arctic, or if she wrote children's books, she'd have a better chance of getting in. She should sing at leper colonies because it shows her caring.

Between tour dates, she should take some college classes online from Stanford and MIT to show her interest in intellectual things. She should write an essay about how great it is to be humble, or read the dictionary daily and show some understanding of *Beowulf*. She should donate all of her profits to charity because colleges want community service and people who care. She should be seen in magazines reading.

She should lose the midriff—unless she's interested in Brown or Wesleyan, because they're interested in diversity of all sorts. She has to be "well rounded"—that's the buzz-word. She can't be pointed.

Q. What colleges would she have the best shot of getting into?
A. The big rah-rah places—Texas, Michigan, Virginia—because she's very peppy and has lots of enthusiasm and lots of zip and spirit. A big sports program would be good—Stanford, maybe Duke or UCLA. Not too intellectually challenging, where her personal qualities would shine. Maybe Pepperdine—she could be one of the Barbies on Malibu Beach. I don't see her in a small liberal-arts college. I don't think there's enough going on for her. She needs a place where there's a balance between academic and social—a good sorority system would be good.

I don't think she'd want to attend the University of Chicago, because the intellectual discussions might be off-putting to her. The University of Florida at Gainesville might be a good fit. She could be near the others at Disney World.

Q. What courses should she take?
A. "The Art of Superficiality" might be in sync with her. A course on "People Are More Than Goody-Two-Shoes." A good course on defining one's self. I think she's, on the one hand, wanting to be the all-American girl and, on the other hand, wanting to be the sexpot. A good psychology course on self-concept would be good.

Q. What major would be a good fit for her?
A. She's going to have lots and lots of money, so maybe an economics major. Perhaps even international relations or political science. She's well known around the world, and if she did slow down in her singing career, maybe she could be an influence in the world for good in 20 or 30 years. Fashion design might be good. Let her develop a line of midriffery clothes. She might even want to think about music. She might have more range than she knows. Classical music might be the ticket for her.

Q. What should she look for in a roommate?
A. She would need to be able to handle lots of clothes, Top 40 on the radio. The roommate has to be tough—a woman who's going to be all right with all the adulation that comes to Britney. I think Britney would like someone who is kind of star-struck. She might need a little reinforcement in who she is and how great she is. ○

SEEING

1. What is the "cosmic significance" of Britney Spears? What features of an icon does she exemplify? When does Perrotta take her seriously? When does he resist taking her seriously? With what effect(s)? Explain why you were convinced, or not convinced, that writing an article about Britney Spears matters "in the days after the September 11 terrorist attacks."

2. What is the difference between sarcasm and irony? Look up both words, and after you understand the distinctions between these concepts, review Perrotta's article carefully to identify—and comment on—several examples of each. After you have completed this exercise, choose an example of each and convert a sarcastic example into an ironic one, and vice versa. Which is easier to transform into the other? Why? Now look at Caitlin Donovan's photograph of the Britney Spears Live from Las Vegas concert poster, and find examples of sarcasm and irony in it. What is the difference between visual irony and visual sarcasm? Compare the two. Which ironic elements in the image are ironic elements in the article? sarcastic elements? How do visual sarcasm and irony differ from verbal sarcasm and irony?

WRITING

1. The section of Perrotta's essay in which he compares Britney Spears to other pop stars has a simple structure. First he tells how they are alike, and then he tells how they are different. Following the same structure, make your own list of pop stars with whom you can compare Britney Spears. For example, you might compare her with Lauryn Hill, Jennifer Lopez, or Mandy Moore. Or you might compare her with Billie Holiday, Bessie Smith, or Ma Rainey—or even Eminem, ODB, or DMX. Write an essay in which you compare and contrast Spears with another icon in American popular music.

2. According to Perrotta, Britney Spears is "a potent symbol of the late '90s" in the United States (para. 30). Find out about a young, female pop star from another decade and/or another country, and show how she is or is not a symbol of her time and nation. Choose an era or an area that you don't know much about. For example, you might compare Britney Spears's career in North America with Shakira's career in South America. Or you could find pictures and recordings of Jenny Lind, who was an immensely popular star in England and the United States in the late nineteenth century.

The
Cosmic Significance
of Britney Spears

Tom Perrotta

Caitlin Donovan, **Defaced Britney Spears poster, New York City subway**

Retrospect:
Madonna, 1982–2002

1982

1985

1995

1996

1991

1991

1993

98

1999

2002

TV

Talking Pictures

One of the most important aspects of extending and enriching the marketing success of any product is developing a widely recognized and well-respected corporate logo. Paul Rand, one of the most influential graphic designers of the twentieth century, identified several criteria for measuring the effectiveness of a logo. "The effectiveness of a logo," he said, "depends on (a) distinctiveness, (b) visibility, (c) useability, (d) memorability, (e) universality, (f) durability, (g) timeliness."

Now turn your attention to any readily recognizable logo you have seen recently on television. What do you notice about the design of this logo that strikes you as especially effective? Why? Measure the success of this logo against Paul Rand's criteria.

As you work your way through each of these criteria, please be sure to validate each assertion you make about the logo's effectiveness by pointing to specific evidence in the nature—and implied significance—of the logo. Write an analytical essay in which you use Rand's criteria to assess the effectiveness of the logo you have chosen to discuss.

TOURÉ

Not many people can claim to be an African American staff writer for *Rolling Stone*. In fact, only Touré can claim that distinction, and he is the first in the magazine's history. In 2002 he published his first book, a collection of stories and observations called *The Portable Promised Land*. Touré infuses these stories with mystical though realistic portrayals of black America in the technological age. The form of each story varies considerably—as does his tone, which at times mimics the hip-hop rhythms that seem to guide each line.

Still, Touré's most recognizable writing to date is his nonfiction. Touré and Dale Earnhardt Jr., one of NASCAR's biggest rising stars, seem an unlikely coupling, but Touré formed a bond with the storytelling racecar driver when exploring Earnhardt Jr.'s obsession with Kurt Cobain. Although Cobain, the former lead singer for the rock band Nirvana, brought the two men together initially, Touré returned to do a second story (entitled "Inherit the Wind") for *Rolling Stone* when the young driver's legendary father, Dale Earnhardt Sr., was killed in a race.

Born in Boston, Touré now lives in Brooklyn and writes for *The New Yorker*, the *New York Times*, and *The Village Voice*. "Kurt Is My Co-Pilot" first appeared in *Rolling Stone* and was included in *The Best American Sports Writing* (2001).

Kurt Is My Co-Pilot

Touré

Step on it! It's in the high-test blood
—B.C.

ale Ernhardt Jr. is pretty good at telling a story. He's telling one now about the thing that changed his life.

"Up until I was fourteen or fifteen, I was real short, and I was kind of an Opie," Junior begins. He's twenty-five now. "I wore Wranglers and cowboy hats and fished and raced around on boats and listened to country music. Then one day changed it all." He's telling this while standing behind the bar in the nightclub he built in the basement of his Mooresville, North Carolina, home. The basement club is dimly lit with purple neon and has tall black stools, mirrored walls, a cooler large enough for eleven cases of Bud, and a framed poster of Kurt Cobain.

"I was a junior in high school, and I went to a buddy's house, and this song came on MTV," he says. "We was gittin' ready to go do some shit, and he's like, 'Man, dude, this song is kickass! Let's just sit here and listen to it 'fore we leave.' And I sit down, and, man, when it was over with I was fuckin' blown away. It was 'Teen Spirit,' by Nirvana. It fit my emotions. I was tired of listenin' to my parents, I was tired of livin' at home, I didn't know what I was gonna do, I didn't have any direction. The fact that Kurt Cobain could sit there and scream into that mike like that give you a sense of

relief. And the guitar riffs, and the way Dave Grohl played the drums? It was awesome." Dale was, that moment, pulled from the good-ol'-boy path and rebaptized by rock & roll.

He went out and bought Nirvana's *Nevermind*. "I couldn't really get anybody else to dig Nirvana like I dug it," he remembers, "and I never heard nobody else listenin' to it in the high school parking lot. When I was listenin' to Nirvana, I felt like I was doin' somethin' wrong. But I didn't care. I'd just sit there and turn it up."

Nirvana led to Pearl Jam, which led to Smash 5 Mouth, Tupac, Third Eye Blind, JT Money, Moby, Mystikal, Matthew Good Band, Busta Rhymes, and Primus. ("That was my first moshing experience. That was awesome.") According to Carlos Santana, "Sound immediately rearranges the molecular structure of the listener." Junior is a prime case study.

"When I was twelve or thirteen, Dad's races came on the country station," Junior says. Dad is Dale Earnhardt Sr., widely considered to be one of the three best drivers in the history of stock-car racing. "And I 'member sittin' there playin' with Matchbox cars on the floor. I had the perfect little bedroom with the perfect toys and the perfect friend up the road who always played every day I wanted to play and played all day till I couldn't play anymore, and I thought everybody fished, everybody listened to country, and everybody lived in a cool house on a lake, and it was sunny all the time.

"Then I got my driver's license and I was able to buy music and listen to it on my own, and you hear the words and you think, 'Man, I never thought about that.' I never really was rebellious against my parents. I never really thought the government was fucked up. I never really paid much attention to the schools suckin'. Up until I was sixteen, I thought every cop up and down the road was just happy and glee, and now you hear these songs and you're like, 'Is that the case? Is that what's goin' on?' You don't learn from anywhere else."

Junior followed Dad into big-time stock-car racing, and now, in a sport filled with good ol' boys, he's known as the rock & roll driver. That's him in the red number 8 Budweiser Chevrolet Monte Carlo in the NASCAR Winston Cup Series, facing off against heavyweights like Jeff Gordon, Dale Jarrett, Tony Stewart, and Dale Sr. In seven starts since February, Junior is ranked first among rookies and eighteenth overall. On April 2nd, he won his first big race, the DirecTV 500. He has now won more than $600,000 this season, but the numbers don't show that Junior is also a fan favorite. People see in him a kid from the MTV generation invading one of America's most stubborn subcultures. A kid like you, maybe, who on Monday, Tuesday, and Wednesday does little or nothing—fixes up the house, plays paint ball and Sega NFL2K with the guys, surfs the Net, hangs with best friend T-Dawg (his mom still calls him Terrell), and watches videos on MTV, BET, and MuchMusic, a Canadian channel. A kid who gets to the racetrack and thinks, "Can't wait to get home so I can fuck off some more."

(Apparently, fuckin' off actually helps him on race days. "The thing about drivin' race cars is mental," he says. "How long can you concentrate? How long can you focus? And if you don't focus good and you cain't be in deep thought for a long time, then you're not gonna be very good at it. The

things I do every day prepare me for that. When you're on the computer playin' a game or on the Play-Station whippin' your buddy's ass in Knockout Kings, you gotta be on top of it.")

When not fuckin' off, Junior is raisin' hell, as in gettin' in one of his cars and peelin' the tires, every gear wide-ass open (read: goin' real fast). He's got a Corvette he won that he almost never drives. He's got a Chevy Impala with a global-positioning system, a VCR, and TV screens in the front and back. He's got a hulking red four-door Chevy pickup truck with a monster stereo system, and, if you lift the back seats, on top of where the bass amps are hidden, there is this skull-and-crossbones design that Skippy from Freeman's Car Stereo etched in there without Junior even askin', and the darn thing lights up when you push a button on a keypad, but no one knows that, 'cause Junior ain't one to show off. And then there's the breathtaker: a mint-condition midnight-blue 1969 Camaro with an exposed grille on the hood and an oversize finger-thin steering wheel and a gearshift shaped like a bridge and a top-of-the-line Alpine stereo. Junior bought this piece of art for a mere $12,000.

Junior eases into the piece of art and floats down the road to get some pizza from Pie in the Sky. "When I got this," he says, "I took it out and thought, 'This thing has no fire.'" He added a new transmission, a new aluminum-head Corvette engine, and a 2,500-rpm stall converter that allows you to shift and keeps the piece of art from changing gears until it reaches 2,500 rpm. Now the thing runs pretty awesome.

"It's real stiff and hard and doesn't have the handlin' package like a new car," Junior says, cruising at a leisurely forty miles an hour on the thin, desolate Carolina road. "So you gotta really know what you're doin', have your hands on the wheel at all times and stuff." The piece of art is loud, the engine rumbles and gurgles and practically drowns out the stereo, but the ride is cool, and he turns *Dr. Dre 2001* up way loud and it still sounds crisp. "I like Dr. Dre," Junior says. "He's got a good attitude. I saw him on that VH1 deal, that *Behind the Music*, and that really give you an idea of who he was. I mean, he enjoys success. I mean, that's kinda the way I've tried to be. There's a lot of money comin' in, and there's a lot of talk about how good the future is gonna be and how much is gonna happen, and I'm excited about it, but I don't wanna be molded or changed. I wanna be able to go back to $16,000 a year and be O.K. I wanna be able to still realize the value of a dollar bill. And I think that's what Dr. Dre's done. He's still maintained his coolness and not turned into a big jerk."

Junior pulls back on the shifter and says, "Check this out." The engine seems to constrict slowly, tightening like a coil, roaring and snarling as if it is angry at us, and then, after three slow seconds of build, the engine growling louder all the time, it reaches 2,500 rpm and there's a loud *pop!* like a gun, and we slingshot off, leaping in a millisecond from forty miles per hour to eighty—like light speed in the *Millennium Falcon* or something—and suddenly we're flying down the backstretch, zipping past cows and tractors and horses and go-carts as the malevolent funk of Dr. Dre booms out the window: *Nowadays, everybodywannatalk, liketheygot sumpintosay, but nuttincomesout whentheymovetheirlips, justabunchagibberish, and motherfuckersack liketheyforgotaboutDre....* It sounds so alien in this Waltons-ish country town, like music from another planet. And Junior is cool with both.

Vegas two days later, a Friday, is cloudless blue sky, heavy wind, a lot of sun. Out at the Motor Speedway, it's qualifying day for Sunday's race, the CarsDirect.Com 400. The fifty-five guys vying for the forty-three spots in the race go out one at a time, tearing around the track as fast as they can. Today's top twenty-five finishers are guaranteed spots in the race, their starting positions based on their qualifying speeds.

The hours before qualifying are for practice. [15] Crews work on their cars, send the driver out for a lap or two around the track so he can judge what adjustments are needed, and then tinker some more. Junior has spent years working on cars, so he's really good at feeling what they're doing and at communicating to his crew what will make the car go faster. After laps, the guys—Favio, B, Brendan, Keith, Jeff, and Tony Jr.—jump all over the car, soldering, clipping, pouring, cramming like in the minutes before a final exam, wrenching, wiping, welding, tweaking the $250,000 beast, $50,000 engine, and $6,000 transmission, turning the engine into "a time bomb," as Steve Crisp, Junior's manager, calls it. "All loose and sloppy and about to all fall to hell."

Whereas Sunday is about being consistently fast for four straight hours, qualifying is one lap of brute strength and balls-out sheer speed—so the qualifying engine isn't made to last. For example, to improve the aerodynamics, they tape over the car's every hole and crack. But this makes the engine very hot—hence, a time bomb. Another example: Just before Junior gets in the car, there'll be a little portable heater linked up to the oil tank to get the oil up around two hundred degrees. "The hotter the oil, the thinner it is and the faster you can go," Crisp says. "It's like runnin' with Vaseline 'tween your cheeks. If you're lubed up, you can really haul ass."

At 11:00 A.M., after four practice laps, Junior is the eighth-fastest qualifier. At a quarter past noon, after fifteen laps, he has fallen to sixteenth place, but he isn't worried. The tires haven't been changed all morning, and at high speeds tires wear down very fast, making them crown, which means your contact with the ground lessens and you can't grab the track—try to turn at 140 miles an hour on crowned tires and you'll think you're on ice. At one o'clock, the crew finally throws on stickers (new tires), and Junior beats around the big oval like there's a killer on his tail, finishing practice with the day's fastest lap, faster than the next guy by more than three-tenths of a second, a monster lead in this business.

When at last it's time for the qualifying lap, Favio and the guys wheel the Chevy out to the track. Soon after, Junior joins them. As he walks down pit road, the Allman Brothers' "Midnight Rider" is booming on the track's loudspeakers, and twenty thousand fans are in the stands cheering, and Junior, with his impeccable military-school posture, the red and black race suit snug on his long, slender body, the blazing sun gleaming off the silver on his racing shoes, the black wraparound shades and the stubble and the chiseled chin and the movie-star cheekbones, shit, Junior looks like gotdamn Steve McQueen.

He slides into the doorless beast, straps on his crimson skull-and-crossbones helmet, pulls on his black gloves and goggles, then screws on the steering wheel, which sits about a foot and a half from his face, so close that he can't slide in or out of the beast without unscrewing it, so close so that he can drive using his forearm muscles instead of his back and shoulder muscles. There is only one seat (roll bars are where the passenger seat would be), and that seat is form-fitted to Junior's body like shrink-to-fit jeans. There are gauges for water, oil, and fuel, and a tachometer to register rpms, but no speedometer, because it doesn't matter how fast you're going, just that you're going faster than everyone else. There is a thin rearview mirror about two feet wide, and a clear tube Junior can suck on to get water, and on Sunday there will also be a black tube stuck down into his suit to blow cool air, because the car's interior gets up around 100 degrees, and sometimes, during the summer, 130. One more thing: All the teams paste decals of headlights and brake lights onto their cars to heighten the illusion that they're driving the same sort of car that Bob has out in the driveway.

Ironically, stock-car racing is the most popular form of racing in America because it seems to be the most pedestrian. Back in the sixties, guys bought regular Chevelles or Dodge Chargers, yanked out the passenger seats, threw in some roll bars, and went racing. Nowadays the cars are constructed by the race teams themselves—I actually saw someone bending and molding a big piece of sheet metal into a door—and they're nothing like any car you can buy from Chevy. But Junior's "Chevy" shows up on TV, shaped like the car Bob owns, with headlights and brake lights—which doesn't even make sense, because why would a race car need headlights? They drive during the day!—and Bob says to himself, "Hey, that car's just like mine," or, even better, "Hey, that's like the Chevy down at the dealership. Think I'll go get me one." You think Bob doesn't think like that? One of the oldest sayings in racing is: Win on Sunday, sell on Monday.

Early this morning, all the drivers pulled numbers to determine the order of qualifying. Junior drew a two. When his turn comes, he flicks the lever to start the engine, and the beast cackles loudly, then begins to ripple and roar as if it were a lion growling through clenched teeth, or a gigantic, demented bowl of Rice Krispies snap-crackle-popping in a fury. A NASCAR official drops his arm, and Junior steps on the gas and flies off like a low-slung comet, sounding like the humming of a six-foot-long hornet an inch from your ear, and when the lap is over and the speed is flashed on the board—172.216 mph, a new track record—the crowd thunders. He has bested the old record—correction, demolished it—by more than two miles an hour.

He parks, and his team runs over to celebrate. "When ya drove into the corner," says a breathless Favio, "ya went all the way wide open! We didn't think you was gonna lift! The whole pit road just sit and looked at ya, amazed!" (Translation: "It seemed as though you took that first corner without braking—an impossibility! We though you'd never get off the gas! You the man, baby!")

Junior jumps out of the car, ecstatic. "It doesn't matter if we git the pole [position]," he says, beaming like a kid getting good presents at Christmas. "That was awesome!"

But when ESPN and local TV rush over to get a comment, he mutes his excitement: "The car handled real good. I don't know if it'll stand up as far as the pole goes, but it'll be up there somewhere toward the front. My expectations at the first of the week were to come in here and make the top twenty-five, and that hasn't changed."

After the cameras disappear, Junior says, "I don't wanna sit here and go, 'Whoo-hoo!' and then get beat, and have everyone go, 'What an as hole.' " [25]

And sure enough, his track record lasts about six minutes. Ricky Rudd tops him by three-tenths of a second.

Junior looks down the track and sees his father walking onto pit road for his qualifying run. "There's Dad," he says. "Let's go talk to him. A hundred bucks says my daddy give me shit for gittin' beat. He don't say, 'Nice goin'.' He'll say, 'Why'd you get beat?' "

Junior jogs down the track and catches his old man. Before Junior can say a word, Dad ribs him in a barbed but loving tone, "What happened? Why ain't ya first? What'd ya do wrong?"

"I don't know," Junior says with a laugh. Photographers snap wildly behind them.

"What should I do?" Dad says as another car [30] flies by. "What were ya doin'?"

Junior says, "Run deep, brake hard, turn left." It was about the most smartass thing he could say without being rude.

"Run deep, brake hard?" Dad laughs. Terry Labonte, another top driver, is walking by. Dad grabs Labonte's arm and says, "Listen to him," then turns back to Junior. "How ya get 'round there, now?"

"Run deep, brake hard, turn left."

The veterans laugh. "He don't even know how he did it!" Dad says. There is a pause. Then Dad pats Junior on the shoulder, silently saying, "Good job."

A little later, Junior is back in his trailer, watching [35] other cars qualify on ESPN2. No one beats Ricky Rudd, and only one other driver, Scott Pruett, beats Junior. At the press conference for the top three qualifiers, a reporter asks about Junior's relationship with his father.

"Well," Junior says, "durin' practice and qualifyin' it was 'Dad, car owner.' " Junior actually races for Dale Earnhardt Inc., in a car owned by Dad, although the car Dad races doesn't actually belong to him, because he's still loyal to Richard Childress, the man who put him in a race car long before he could buy one himself. "He's all, 'How's it goin'? We need to get faster. We need to do this, we need to do that,' " Junior says. "Then when the race starts, it's diff'rent. Last week at Rockingham, we were goin' into Turn Three. I was on the inside of Jeff Gordon and got loose [lost control] goin' into the corner, and I slammed into him. About a straightaway and a half later, Dad went by shakin' his finger out the window at me. I guess that was where the father was goin', 'You'd better watch it. You'd better straighten up.' "

After the press conference, Junior is asked, If you were leading on the last lap and Dad was right behind you, would Dad use one of his legendary tricks to spin you out and take the checkered flag for himself? Junior doesn't pause: "He would do what it took to win."

In the 1940s, in North Carolina, South Carolina, Georgia, Tennessee, and Virginia, there were some good ol' boys fresh from the war with a little money, a little training in how to service military planes and jeeps, and a talent for brewing moonshine. They made their outlaw liquor in hidden stills in the woods and got it to the dance halls, speakeasys, and bootleggers in cars big enough to carry a hundred gallons of the stuff—maybe seven hundred pounds—and still fast enough to outrun the cops: Ford or Pontiac sedans with killer engines and real stiff suspensions—liquor cars. Racing's first superstar, Junior Johnson, was a moonshiner. He could always outrun the cops, until they got radios.

Sometimes some good ol' boys would get together and brag about who had the fastest liquor car, and if the braggin' got too loud, they'd pick a Sunday, head out to some deserted field, plow out an oval, and race. Thus was born American stock-car racing, now the country's most popular spectator sport—bigger than football or baseball or basketball, bigger even than professional wrestling. On any of thirty-six weekends a year, as many as 150,000 people or more show up to watch NASCAR at the tracks, and many millions more watch on TV. "In the South," says Crisp, a natural comedian, "ya see stock cars everywhere—from the time you're a little kid to the time you're put in the grave, you're gonna be around a stock-car track. Hell, ya can't sling a dead cat 'thout hittin' a shop."

In the late forties, the National Association for Stock Car Auto Racing was founded. It presided over a sport where the track and the stands and everything in between were filled with good ol' boys. Crisp describes the average fan: "He hunts, his dad taught him to hunt, and his dad taught him to hunt. He drinks Jack Daniel's and Maker's Mark. He listens to Hank Williams. He loves his huntin' dog and his pickup truck, and he married his high school sweetheart, and he lives in the town he grew up in, or a stone's throw away. He puts God first and then his family, then his truck."

Dale Earnhardt Jr. has a pickup truck, loves dogs, and maintains a certain down-homeness about him, but Junior ain't no good ol' boy. For example, he hates to hunt. He's got a story about that, too: "My dad's always been a deer hunter. He loves that shit. He took me a coupla times. I went out there and sat in a tree stand all freakin' day. And it's great to sit there and think about shit and reflect back on what's been happenin' with ya, but, really, it's just a waste of a day. Just pissin' it away.

"After a while, a deer walked out there, and I shot the hell out of it. You shoot him right in the chest, and it's s'posed to go right into his heart. When I saw it, I thought, 'Dad's gonna like this.' And then I'm like, 'Man *I* don't like it.' The only ex-

citement I got out of it was seein' him bein' excited, but I didn't enjoy sittin' there all day, and I didn't enjoy havin' to drag it over to the truck and pickin' it up and throwin' it in there and then sit there watchin' him skin it and gut it—and that pissed away all night, so there went a day and a night! So the next time I went in a deer stand, I'm like, 'I ain't shootin' shit, 'cause I got shit to do tonight.' So then I'm like, 'What am I doin' up here?' I got down and never went back."

Stock-car racing is still dominated by good ol' boys, though Junior is part of a class of new blood, some of whom aren't from the South—Matt Kenseth from Wisconsin, Tony Stewart from Indiana—and some Southerners who aren't good ol' boys, a titanic shift in the cultural direction of NASCAR. Imagine the NBA beginning to be dominated by white guys.

"There's a lot of drivers within this age group that are diff'rent," Junior says. "It's just the way things are goin', and NASCAR's not immune to it. Even the image is something more modern. Just look at the TV coverage. Ten years ago, when they'd go to break, it'd be some fiddle banjo-pickin' music. And now it's this jammin' rock music. Somebody somewhere said, 'Hey, let's change it.'"

But things change slowly. It's not easy to refuse all the cultural stimuli around in favor of another drummer's beat. Sure, Junior hates to hunt, but there, mounted on the wall of his living room, are the head and neck of a deer.

On Friday night, the Speedway is quiet and empty, and around ten Junior heads out for a walk around the track and another story. "I'd just started drivin' my late-model car," he says. The late-model series is the lowest rung of organized stock-car racing. "We had this shitbox of a car, and we was racin' at this track with all the big dawgs." The Speedway's rock-concert bright lights are on. The only sound, besides our feet on the concrete, is the muffled snarl of dirt-track racing half a mile away.

"My crew chief was an old-timer everyone knew, named Gary Hargett, and he ordered a brand-new car for me from Rick Townsend, the most popular car builder. And we were so excited. So we git to the track, and Gary's like, 'Man, we ordered that car, when you think you're gonna git on it?' Rick's like, 'Well, we're behind. It's gonna be a couple months 'fore we even start on it. You guys should get it midway through the season.' And then he says, 'By the way, where's your driver at?' And I was standing a little ways away, and Gary's like, 'He's over there.' And Rick says, 'Boy don't look like much. Looks like he barely know how to get out of the rain.'

"So we started the race 'bout midpack and beat our way up through there, and two laps to go I came up on Rick's house car runnin' second. And I drilled him straight in the ass, man! Right in the fuckin' ass, and turned him sideways and went past him and finished second in the race. They don't do that here, but that's how we do back home. After the race, Rick come up to Gary and said, 'That was pretty awesome. We'll start on your shit Monday.' And Rick's been a good friend ever since. But I always remembered what Rick said, and everywhere I go, when I walk into a room with people I don't know, I assume they look at me and say, 'He don't look like much.' That's kept me real humble and small-time."

Junior was born in Concord, North Carolina, an hour's drive from his house in Mooresville. His parents separated when he was two or three, and he and his older sister, Kelly, were raised by his mother in a small mill house until Junior, at six, awoke to a fire in the kitchen. Everyone ran out, the house burned down, and nothing was ever the same. Mom handed over custody of her kids to Dale Sr. and moved to Norfolk, Virginia. "She didn't have the means to git us another house or take care of us," Junior says, "so she said, 'Man, your dad's doin' good, and he can put ya in school, so this is the best thing for ya.' I was just like, 'Are my toys here?' " She still lives in Norfolk and works as

a loader for UPS. Junior has seen her once or twice a year since he was six, but she calls often. "She puts forth a lot of effort in our relationship," he says, and talks happily of her plan to retire and move back to the Charlotte area within the next year. "She's awesome."

When Junior arrived in his dad's custody, racing was a very small sport. "The tracks they raced at were shit holes," Junior says. "If you got fifty thousand fans there, you were lucky." Dad was away a lot of the time, so Junior was raised by his stepmom, Teresa. "When he and Kelly were growin' up," Dale Sr. says, "I was workin' and racin' and goin' all the time."

"We'd go upstairs and sit down on the couch," Junior says, "and he'd be sittin' there watchin' TV in the recliner, and you ask him a question and he wouldn't hear you. You rarely even get a response. He was so in his racin' thing, you could hardly sometimes have a conversation with him, 'cause his mind was on what he was thinkin' about." It's been suggested by people who know them that Junior became a driver to get his father's attention. Both deny it. But there seems to be a kernel of truth to it.

Dad grew up at the track, watching his father, Ralph, a champion stock-car driver in the fifties. Dale drove his black number 3 Chevy to a record-tying seven Winston Cup season championships. Called the Man In Black and the Intimidator, he's the consummate winner with a questionable reputation, like the Bill Laimbeer Detroit "Bad Boy" Pistons or the Lyle Alzado Oakland Raiders. But winning wins company, so he's also one of the most revered drivers in the history of the sport.

He took his winnings to Mooresville and built a giant palace of a racing shrine, perhaps the greatest ever constructed by NASCAR money, lovingly called the Garage Mahal. There are security guards in cowboy boots and red button-down shirts that say DALE EARNHARDT INC., surrounded by corporate offices for DEI's 160 employees, all of Dad's trophies, old winning cars preserved for public view, and big glass display cases for the tuxedos he wore to the Winston Cup banquets during his championship seasons and the gowns worn by his wife and the cute pink polka-dot toddler's dress sported by their daughter Taylor and pictures of Ralph Earnhardt and all the commercials Dad and Junior have made and a gift shop with all sorts of souvenirs—spoons, toy bears, pins, watches, shirts, robes, beer steins, shot glasses, tiny model cars (all of which earned Junior around $2 million last year), and, this just in, a Dale Earnhardt Monopoly set. The game pieces include a car, a checkered flag, and a helmet. Earnhard's face is on the money. He's the first individual to have a Monopoly set made around him. The shop's best-selling item, the clerks say, is a decal you can affix to your car to give the impression you bought it at the old man's dealership.

As all of this was being built, Junior was at Mitchell Community College in Statesville, North Carolina, getting a degree in automotives, and then at his father's dealership working as a grease monkey for $180 a week. "I got to where I could do an oil change in eight minutes," he says. "I was really proud of that."

Then one Saturday night in Myrtle Beach, South Carolina, he raced his late-model car: "It was $1,000 to win and 100 to 150 fans, but it didn't matter. It was kickass, man! It was like buildin' a freakin' remote-control car and goin' to where everybody else went to play with it. I learned everything—how to save your tires, pace yourself, not wreck your car, communicate with your team, motivate 'em to work—you got volunteer guys, and you gotta be able to get 'em to work or they're gonna go to the track and drink up the sodas. And that's just people skills."

In time, he moved up to the Busch Series—which is like the supercharged minors to the Winston Cup's majors—was season champ in '98 and '99, and graduated to the Winston cup. "But growin' up as a kid, I didn't try to drive race cars,

so I know inside that it's not a live-or-die thing. I'm a little more three-dimensional than, 'Oh, drivin's kickass.' Drivin' is fun, but that's not the ultimate high. Right now, I'd rather be home. I'd much more enjoy kickin' it on my couch."

At ten o'clock Sunday morning, Junior is in his trailer with Crisp and his trailer driver, Shane, eating Corn Pops, listening to Pink Floyd's *The Wall*, arguing about racing movies. The race is just over an hour away, and there is about as much tension in the air as there is in your house before you drive to the 7-Eleven for milk.

"*The Last American Hero* is real redneck-y," Crisp says of the film many consider the best ever made on racing.

"But it's the only racin' movie that's about racin'," Junior says, "I didn't like *Le Mans*," he said of the Steve McQueen classic. "They were just raisin' hell and racin' cars. There's no dialogue. It's just racin' and sittin'. It didn't have a plot."

"*Heart Like a Wheel* is uncool," Shane says of the Bonnie Bedelia film, "'cause they had it like she's gittin' her ass beat by her boyfriend."

"What about *Days of Thunder*?" someone asks about the Tom Cruise movie. All at once everyone says, "Sucked!"

"*Grand Prix* kicks ass," Crisp says.

"Here's *Le Mans*," Junior says. "A bunch of people sittin' aroun' for five minutes. Then, all of a sudden, snap, they're racin', then, snap, they're all sittin' around. No dialogue whatsoever. It's like someone actually followed the guy around, filmin' him."

"Yeah," Shane says. "It was realistic."

"Yeah, it was real," Junior says, "but it didn't have a plot and shit like *Grand Prix*. Who was the guy in *Grand Prix*?"

"James Garner," everyone says.

"I like that guy," Junior says.

"The girl liked him in *Grand Prix*," Shane says.

"'Member? And her husband got in a wreck and she turned out to be a bee-itch!" Crisp says as though he were Snoop Dogg. The room crumbles in hysterics. "She was a big *beeee*-itch! A biznitch!"

There is no pre-race ritual, no discussion of strategy, no prayer, no psyching. It seems strange. Junior is moments away from the event that defined his week, and, more, is about to spend four hours risking his life, and he seems largely unconcerned. You don't do anything special before you go out to race?

Junior looks puzzled, as if the idea of doing something special had never occurred to him.

"I think ya do a lot of soul-searching," Shane says. "I don't think you notice it, but you usually walk around in a daze."

"One thing I do," Junior says, "is, when I walk out the trailer door, I don't wait up for people."

"His mind is already there," Shane says.

"I go at my pace. Real fast."

"Almost to the point where if ya didn't know him, you'd think he was rude," Crisp says.

"It would wear me out to psych myself up all mornin'," Junior says. "I pray to God before the race. I don't pray to win. I say, 'When it's over, can I go the next five days till the next race with a content, satisfied attitude so I can live comfortably and not be all down on myself on a bad finish all week? 'Cause if I finish bad, I'm depressed as hell for the next week."

That's it? C'mon! You could die today!

With childlike innocence, Junior says, "Ya think?" Everyone laughs.

"Nah, man. It's safe as hell in there. All that paddin' in there, how I'm buckled in there, all the bars and things? Dude, man, that car is bulletproof."

But no one is shooting at you. Seriously, man, this is worse than boxing. You must know that.

"Yeah, sometimes guys get cocked just right. That's the way it is. There's things in there your head can hit, and if it hits it just right you could be permanently injured. But guys normally walk away."

Suddenly he turns to Crisp. "You know what I wanna do? When they do driver introductions? I wanna say somethin' into the mike like, 'I gotta say hi to my friend Chester McGroovy. Get well soon!'"

Then Junior says, "Last week we were drivin' up to the racetrack, and there were all these people campin' outside, thousands of people, and I'm like, 'That's what the fuck I'd like to be doin'.' That's fun! Just raisin' hell at the racetrack with your buddies, drinkin' beer, campin' out, watchin' the race. No pressure, man. I mean, you don't get no money, but, shit, you're havin' a good time. It'd be fun. And I'll never get to do that."

He pauses. "When I turn seventy, that's what I'm gonna do. Go campin' and park outside the track and sit there and drink beer and just raise hell and aggravate all the fuckin' rednecks with all this rock & roll music." ○

SEEING

1. This essay appeared in *Rolling Stone*, a magazine devoted to contemporary, popular music. What is an article about a race car driver doing in a magazine about music? How does Touré connect Earnhardt Jr.'s life to music? Where in the essay do music and cars or racing come together? What changes might Touré have made if he had written the article for a car magazine such as *Car & Driver*? What about a food magazine such as *Gourmet*? *Essence*? *Vogue*?

2. Touré never explicitly tells his readers what he thinks of Dale Earnhardt Jr., but he manages to make his opinion clear in the essay. Why doesn't Touré say what he thinks more directly? How does he imply his views without making them explicit? Find at least four different strategies that Touré uses to show the reader how he feels about Earnhardt Jr. Which ones are the most effective for communicating Touré's point of view? Which ones are the least effective? Why?

WRITING

1. How accurate is the stereotype of "A kid like you" (para. 8)? Make a survey that asks which of the activities from "fixes up the house" to "gets to the racetrack and thinks, 'Can't wait to get home so I can fuck off some more'" are typical of your group. Have at least five of your friends fill out the survey. How many "yes" responses are there? How many "no" responses? Calculate the overall percentage of "yes" responses to find out how close you and your friends are to that stereotype. Then write an expository essay in which you explain what characteristics you would need to add to the list in order to make it more accurately describe your life.

2. Why write an article about a 25-year-old whose favorite thing to do is being at home "kickin' it" on his couch? With all the important things that are happening in the world every day, what makes this article worth the time it took you to read it? Write an expository essay explaining why this article is important. Consider questions such as the following: Who does this article seek to reach? What can this article teach by focusing on Earnhardt Jr. that an article with a more serious subject couldn't teach? How does Touré's informal style enable him to elegantly explore subjects that could only be written about in the most awkward manner by way of more formal prose?

Kurt Is My Co-Pilot
Touré

DAVID BUTOW

Although the New York–born Butow's career as a photographer has taken him all over the world, he works for *U.S. News & World Report* primarily out of his home in Los Angeles. After graduating from the University of Austin in 1987, Butow took pictures for several Los Angeles newspapers and began freelancing in 1992 when he covered the Los Angeles riots. And the people of Los Angeles continue to be the focus of his art: "I think one of the great things about taking pictures in L.A. is the interesting juxtapositions that you get. The huge variety of people, culturally speaking, and also the contrast between the rich and the poor is very interesting in L.A. . . . Because of the entertainment industry and all the people who want to get into show biz, you have a lot of flamboyant people who would look completely out of place in Chicago or maybe even New York."

Butow's photographs have appeared in magazines and newspapers worldwide, including *Life* and the *New York Times*. His coverage of the secretive world of Saddam Hussein was honored in a solo exhibit at the Visa Pour L'Image annual photojournalists' convention in Perpignan, France. The full photographic essay, dated September 11, 2000, appeared in *U.S. News & World Report*. One year later the World Trade Center twin towers went down, and Butow was there to capture the moments of the terrible aftermath. *Hollywood Walk of Fame* was taken in Los Angeles in 2001.

David Butow, **Hollywood Walk of Fame, Los Angeles, September 30, 2001**

SEEING

1. Which of the objects and figures in the store window are recognizable to you? Which ones are not? Take a moment to identify them. Which ones qualify as American icons in your judgment? Why? What generalizations, if any, can you make about these objects as a group? To what extent can you identify an overarching theme of this display? How would you characterize it? How would you re-title this photograph?

2. How might this window display help draw customers into a store that offers passport photos? What mood does the display foster? What sort of shopping environment does it create? What sorts of customers do you think it would appeal to? How would you describe the display's composition? Consider the selection and placement of the objects.

WRITING

1. How would you "read" this window display differently if you saw it used by a national chain store? Consider how it might function as a display for a store like the Gap, Urban Outfitters, Saks Fifth Avenue, or Target. How about an American chain store abroad? How might you interpret the message, mood, and overall effect of the display differently in each context? What assumptions about the intent and message of the display would the differing contexts provoke? Choose any national chain store, and write an essay in which you compare and contrast how the same window display would read differently in a national chain store as opposed to a local shop as captured in Butow's photograph.

2. Material culture studies examines the values, ideas, attitudes, and assumptions of a society through the physical objects it produces. What insights about American culture do the artifacts in this display offer? Choose one of the objects in this display, and research the origins and history of the figure, concept, or phenomena it represents. How might it have ended up portrayed as an object or piece of memorabilia in such a window display as this? Write an essay in which you explain the history and cultural significance of the object you've chosen.

Looking Closer
The Stars and Stripes

Few symbols are as recognizable as the American flag, and few stir emotions as strong. The flag is ubiquitous. It flies on government buildings, but it also decorates front lawns, T-shirts, and bumper stickers. Americans encounter the flag not only in official ceremonies and at sports events, but in all kinds of "everyday" situations—in advertisements for weekend sales, on doormats, as well as on clothing and commercial packaging, especially so in the aftermath of September 11, 2001. Indeed, it is difficult to spend a day in this country without seeing the flag.

The Stars and Stripes evokes passionate responses—from patriotism to violence to tears—and the feelings about our right to burn this symbol are no less passionate. The **Majority Opinion** of the United States Supreme Court, by Justice William Brennan Jr., and the **Dissenting Opinion** by Chief Justice William Rehnquist articulate the two sides of this complicated issue; and a range of images— Jesse Gordon's Op-Art **"What Is America?";** Matt Groening's cartoon **"Pledging the Flag";** a **Plateau Indian bag;** and a mural from Sunnyside, Queens—suggests how central this symbol is in American life.

"freedom"

— Yen, Vietnam

"money"

— Frankie, Queens

"imperialism"

— Aaron, New York City

"diversity"

— Karine, New York City

"religious freedom"

— Dhananjay, India

"plastics"

— Ian, Canada

"possibility"

— Raymond, St. Kitts

"choice"

— Melissa, New York City

"ignorance"

— Devo, Kansas City

"my adopted country"

— Sister Mary, England

"needs healing"

— Elijah, South Carolina

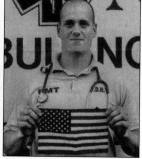

"hope"

— Pat, Staten Island

"open minded"
— Isaac, Brooklyn

"jazz"
— Valerie, Connecticut

"ketchup"
— Constantino, Greece

"original ideas"
— Charles, New York City

"business"
— Adaib, Yemen

"consumerism"
— Silvia, Barcelona

"fun"
— Nobuhisa, Japan

"lost opportunities"
— Dan, Seattle

"excess"
— Katherine, Boston

"sundar (beautiful)"
— Sharada, India

"everything"
— Larry, Puerto Rico

"ahhhh!"
— Jadah and Joziah, New York City

Wednesday

Everybody has flags out. Homes, businesses. It's odd: You never see anybody putting out a flag, but by Wednesday morning there they all are. Big flags, small flags, regular flag-size flags. A lot of home-owners here have those special angled flagholders by their front door, the kind whose brace takes four Phillips screws. And thousands of those little hand-held flags-on-a-stick you normally see at parades—some yards have dozens all over as if they'd some-how sprouted overnight.

. . .

The point being that on Wednesday here there's a weird accretive pressure to have a flag out. If the purpose of a flag is to make a statement, it seems like at a certain point of density of flags you're making more of a statement if you *don't* have one out. It's not totally clear what statement this would be. What if you just don't happen to have a flag? Where has everyone gotten these flags, especially the little ones you can put on your mailbox? Are they all from July 4th and people just save them, like Christmas ornaments? How do they know to do this? Even a sort of half-collapsed house down the street that everybody thought was unoccupied has a flag in the ground by the doorway.

—David Foster Wallace

MAJORITY OPINION OF THE U.S. SUPREME COURT IN *TEXAS V. JOHNSON* (1989)

Justice William J. Brennan Jr.

AFTER PUBLICLY BURNING AN AMERICAN FLAG as a means of political protest, Gregory Lee Johnson was convicted of desecrating a flag in violation of Texas law. This case presents the question whether his conviction is consistent with the First Amendment. We hold that it is not.

While the Republican National Convention was taking place in Dallas in 1984, respondent Johnson participated in a political demonstration dubbed the "Republican War Chest Tour." . . .

The demonstration ended in front of Dallas City Hall, where Johnson unfurled the American flag, doused it with kerosene and set it on fire. While the flag burned, the protestors chanted, "America, the red, white, and blue, we spit on you." After the demonstrators dispersed, a witness to the flag burning collected the flag's remains and buried them in his backyard. No one was physically injured or threatened with injury, though several witnesses testified that they had been seriously offended by the flag burning.

Of the approximately 100 demonstrators, Johnson alone was charged with a crime. The only criminal offense with which he was charged was the desecration of a venerated object in violation of Texas Penal Code Ann. Sec. 42.09 (a)(3) (1989) ["Desecration of a Venerated Object"]. After a trial, he was convicted, sentenced to one year in prison and fined $2,000. The Court of Appeals for the Fifth District of Texas at Dallas affirmed Johnson's conviction, but the Texas Court of Criminal Appeals reversed, holding that the State could not, consistent with the First Amendment, punish Johnson for burning the flag in these circumstances. . . .

STATE ASSERTED TWO INTERESTS

To justify Johnson's conviction for engaging in symbolic speech, the State asserted two interests: preserving the flag as a symbol of national unity and preventing breaches of the peace. The Court of Criminal Appeals held that neither interest supported his conviction.

Acknowledging that this Court had not yet decided whether the Government may criminally sanction flag desecration in order to preserve the flag's symbolic value, the Texas court nevertheless concluded that our decision in West Virginia Board of Education v. Barnette, 319 U.S. 624 (1943), suggested that furthering this interest by curtailing speech was impermissible.

The First Amendment literally forbids the abridgement only of "speech," but we have long recognized that its protection does not end at the spoken or written word. . . .

Especially pertinent to this case are our decisions recognizing the communicative nature of conduct relating to flags. Attaching a peace sign to the flag, Spence v. Washington, 1974; saluting the flag, Barnette, and displaying a red flag, Stromberg v. California (1931), we have held, all may find shelter under the First Amendment. . . . That we have had little difficulty identifying an expressive element in conduct relating to flags should not be surprising. The very purpose of a national flag is to serve as a symbol of our country; it is, one might say, "the one visible manifestation of two hundred years of nationhood." . . .

Pregnant with expressive content, the flag as readily signifies this nation as does the combination of letters found in "America."

The Government generally has a freer hand in restricting expressive conduct than it has in restricting the written or spoken word. . . . It may not, however, proscribe particular conduct because it has expressive elements. . . . It is, in short, not simply the verbal or nonverbal nature of the expression, but the governmental interest at stake, that helps to determine whether a restriction on that expression is valid.

The State offers two separate interests to justify this conviction: preventing breaches of the peace, and preserving the flag as a symbol of nationhood and national unity. We hold that the first interest is not implicated on this record and that the second is related to the suppression of expression. . . .

We thus conclude that the State's interest in maintaining order is not implicated on these facts. The State need not worry that our holding will disable it from preserving the peace. We do not suggest that the First Amendment forbids a state to prevent "imminent lawless action." And, in fact, Texas already has a statute specifically prohibiting breaches of the peace, Texas Penal Code Ann. Sec. 42.01 (1989), which tends to confirm that Texas need not punish this flag desecration in order to keep the peace.

If there is a bedrock principle underlying the First Amendment, it is that the Government may not prohibit the expression of an idea simply because society finds the idea itself offensive or disagreeable. . . .

We have not recognized an exception to this principle even where our flag has been involved. In Street v. New York, 394 U.S. 576 (1969), we held that a state may not criminally punish a person for uttering words critical of the flag. . . .

Nor may the Government, we have held, compel [15] conduct that would evince respect for the flag. . . .

We never before have held that the Government may insure that a symbol be used to express only one view of that symbol or its referents. . . . To conclude that the Government may permit designated symbols to be used to communicate only a limited set of messages would be to enter territory having no discernible or defensible boundaries.

WHICH SYMBOLS WARRANT UNIQUE STATUS?

Could the Government, on this theory, prohibit the burning of state flags? Of copies of the Presidential seal? Of the Constitution? In evaluating these choices under the First Amendment, how would we decide which symbols were sufficiently special to warrant this unique status? To do so, we would be forced to consult our own political preferences, and impose them on the citizenry, in the very way that the First Amendment forbids us to do.

There is, moreover, no indication—either in the text of the Constitution or in our cases interpreting—that a separate juridical category exists for the American flag alone. Indeed, we would not be surprised to learn that the persons who framed our Constitution and wrote the Amendment that we now construe were not known for their reverence for the Union Jack.

The First Amendment does not guarantee that other concepts virtually sacred to our nation as a whole—such as the principle that discrimination on the basis of race is odious and destructive—will go unquestioned in the marketplace of ideas. We decline, therefore, to create for the flag an exception to the joust of principles protected by the First Amendment.

We are fortified in today's conclusion by our con- [20] viction that forbidding criminal punishment for conduct such as Johnson's will not endanger the special role played by our flag or the feelings it inspires. . . .

A REAFFIRMATION OF PRINCIPLES

We are tempted to say, in fact, that the flag's deservedly cherished place in our community will be strengthened, not weakened, by our holding today. Our decision is a reaffirmation of the principles of freedom and inclusiveness that the flag best reflects, and of the conviction that our toleration of criticism such as Johnson's is a sign and source of our strength.

The way to preserve the flag's special role is not to punish those who feel differently about these matters. It is to persuade them that they are wrong. . . .

We can imagine no more appropriate response to burning a flag than waving one's own, no better way to counter a flag-burner's message than by saluting the flag that burns, no surer means of preserving the dignity even of the flag that burned than by—as one witness here did—according its remains a respectful burial. We do not consecrate the flag by punishing its desecration, for in doing so we dilute the freedom that this cherished emblem represents. ○

DISSENTING OPINION IN *TEXAS V. JOHNSON* (1989)

Chief Justice William H. Rehnquist

IN HOLDING THIS TEXAS STATUTE UNCONSTITU-
tional, the Court ignores Justice Holmes's familiar
aphorism that "a page of history is worth a volume of
logic." For more than 200 years, the American flag
has occupied a unique position as the symbol of our
nation, a uniqueness that justifies a governmental
prohibition against flag burning in the way respondent Johnson did here.

At the time of the American Revolution, the flag
served to unify the 13 colonies at home while ob-
taining recognition of national sovereignty abroad.
Ralph Waldo Emerson's Concord Hymn describes
the first skirmishes of the Revolutionary War in
these lines:

> By the rude bridge that arched the flood,
> Their flag to April's breeze unfurled,
> Here once the embattled farmers stood,
> And fired the shot heard round the world.

In the First and Second World Wars, thousands of
our countrymen died on foreign soil fighting for the
American cause. At Iwo Jima in the Second World
War, United States Marines fought hand to hand
against thousands of Japanese. By the time the
marines reached the top of Mount Suribachi, they
raised a piece of pipe upright and from one end flut-
tered a flag. That ascent had cost nearly 6,000 American lives. . . .

The flag symbolizes the nation in peace as well as in
war. It signifies our national presence on battleships,
airplanes, military installations and public buildings
from the United States Capitol to the thousands of
county courthouses and city halls throughout the
country. . . .

No other American symbol has been as universally honored as the flag. In 1931 Congress declared
"The Star Spangled Banner" to be our national anthem. In 1949 Congress declared June 14th to be
Flag Day. In 1987 John Philip Sousa's "The Stars and
Stripes Forever" was designated as the national
march. Congress has also established "The Pledge of
Allegiance to the Flag" and the manner of its deliver-
ance. . . . all of the states now have statutes prohibiting the burning of the flag. . . .

The result of the Texas statute is obviously to deny one in Johnson's frame of mind one of many means of "symbolic speech." Far from being a case of "one picture being worth a thousand words," flag burning is the equivalent of an inarticulate grunt or roar that, it seems fair to say, is most likely to be indulged in not to express any particular idea, but to antagonize others. . . .

The Texas statute deprived Johnson of only one rather inarticulate symbolic form of protest—a form of protest that was profoundly offensive to many—and left him with a full panoply of other symbols and every conceivable form of verbal expression to express his deep disapproval of national policy. . . .

But the Court today will have none of this. The uniquely deep awe and respect for our flag felt by virtually all of us are bundled off under the rubric of "designated symbols" that the First Amendment prohibits the Government from "establishing." But the Government has not "established" this feeling; 200 years of history have done that. The Government is simply recognizing as a fact the profound regard for the American flag created by that history when it enacts statutes prohibiting the disrespectful public burning of the flag.

The Court concludes its opinion with a regrettably patronizing civics lecture, presumably addressed to the members of both houses of Congress, the members of the 48 state legislatures that enacted prohibitions against flag burning, and the troops fighting under that flag in Vietnam who objected to its being burned: "The way to preserve the flag's special role is not to punish those who feel differently about these matters. It is to persuade them that they are wrong."

The Court's role as the final expositor of the Constitution is well established, but its role as a platonic guardian admonishing those responsible to public opinion as if they were truant school children has no similar place in our system of government. . . .

Even if flag burning could be considered just another species of symbolic speech under the logical application of the rules that the Court has developed in its interpretation of the First Amendment in other contexts, this case has an intangible dimension that makes those rules inapplicable.

A country's flag is a symbol of more than "nationhood and national unity." It also signifies the ideas that characterize the society that has chosen that emblem, as well as the special history that has animated the growth and power of those ideas. . . .

So it is with the American flag. It is more than a proud symbol of the courage, the determination and the gifts of nature that transformed 13 fledgling colonies into a world power. It is a symbol of freedom, of equal opportunity, of religious tolerance and of good will for other peoples who share our aspirations. . . .

The value of the flag as a symbol cannot be measured. Even so, I have no doubt that the interest in preserving that value for the future is both significant and legitimate. . . . The creation of a Federal right to post bulletin boards and graffiti on the Washington Monument might enlarge the market for free expression, but at a cost I would not pay.

Similarly, in my considered judgment, sanctioning the public desecration of the flag will tarnish its value—both for those who cherish the ideas for which it waves and for those who desire to don the robes of martyrdom by burning it. That tarnish is not justified by the trivial burden on free expression occasioned by requiring that an available, alternative mode of expression—including uttering words critical of the flag—be employed.

The ideas of liberty and equality have been an irresistible force in motivating leaders like Patrick Henry, Susan B. Anthony, and Abraham Lincoln, schoolteachers like Nathan Hale and Booker T. Washington, the Philippine Scouts who fought at Bataan, and the soldiers who scaled the bluff at Omaha Beach. If those ideas are worth fighting for—and our history demonstrates that they are—it cannot be true that the flag that uniquely symbolizes their power is not itself worthy of protection from unnecessary desecration. ○

THE SATURDAY EVENING

POST

MAY 29, 1943   10¢

BEGINNING—A NEW
KELLAND SERIAL
Heart on Her Sleeve

EDGAR SNOW
REPORTS ON GERMAN
ATROCITIES

ERN! ...2001... PINK SMITH ...

JESSE GORDON

Jesse Gordon is a writer and film-maker who lives in New York City. The twenty-four photos shown here were among thirty-five that appeared in an Op-Art piece in the *New York Times* on July 3, 2000. The question posed to those photographed was "What is America?"

DAVID FOSTER WALLACE

By the age of 34, David Foster Wallace had already written his second novel, become a professor at Illinois State University, and attracted a cult-like band of followers. There aren't many writers who can produce a successful 1,079-page novel in less than three years. *Infinite Jest* (1996) offers a sad portrayal of a post-millennial, nostalgic America through the eyes of the twenty- and thirty-somethings living in a halfway house and at a tennis academy.

Wallace's other writing has appeared in many publications, including literary magazines, *Harper's*, *The New Yorker*, *Esquire*, and the *New York Times Magazine*. This quote is from "The View from Mrs. Thompson's Backyard," an essay published in the October 2001 issue of *Rolling Stone*.

WILLIAM H. REHNQUIST

Chief Justice William H. Rehnquist has been a member of the Supreme Court since 1971 and Chief Justice of the United States since 1986. He served with the Army Air Corps during World War II, and then graduated from Stanford Law School in 1952. President Richard Nixon appointed him assistant attorney general in 1969. Two years later he joined the Supreme Court.

For nearly thirty years Chief Justice Rehnquist has anchored the Court's conservative wing. In the Texas flag-burning case he voted with the minority to uphold the constitutionality of the law and wrote a dissenting opinion.

PLATEAU INDIAN BAG

Measuring 11 × 10 inches, this bag might have been used to carry tools, personal items, or sacred objects in the late nineteenth- or early twentieth century by the Plateau Indians, who inhabited eastern Washington, Oregon, and Idaho. The bag was most likely made from Native tanned hide, glass beads, and commercial cloth binding acquired through trading with Europeans. The bag is pictured in *The Flag in American Indian Art* (1993) by Toby Herbst and Joel Kopp with the following caption: "The tableau of cowboys/settlers versus Indians was acted out innumerable times in real life as well as in Wild West shows, frontier days, fairs, and rodeos, and would have been a well-known scene to the native craftworker."

WILLIAM J. BRENNAN JR.

Justice William J. Brennan (1906–1997) was one of the most influential justices of the United States Supreme Court in the twentieth century. He served on the nation's highest court for thirty-three years, from 1956 until he retired in 1990 at the age of 84. Justice Brennan often fashioned the legal arguments that persuaded a majority of justices in difficult and controversial cases.

The *Texas v. Johnson* case is an excellent example. In 1984, while the Republican National Convention was taking place in Dallas, Gregory Lee Johnson burned an American flag as a statement of protest against the policies of the Reagan administration. He was arrested and convicted under a Texas law that made it a crime to desecrate the flag. The case reached the Supreme Court in 1989, and Justice Brennan wrote for a bare 5-to-4 majority overturning Johnson's conviction and upholding his right to burn the American flag as an exercise of his constitutionally protected freedom of speech.

MATT GROENING

America's most visible cartoonist and animator, Matt Groening (pronounced as "groaning") was born in Portland, Oregon, in 1954. He worked in a sewage treatment plant, as a chauffeur, and as a ghostwriter before his "Life in Hell" comic strip (featuring two rabbits because, as he says, "they are easy to draw") earned him international acclaim as a cartoonist. In 1990 Groening launched *The Simpsons* on the Fox network; it soon became the most successful animated prime-time series in television history.

NORMAN ROCKWELL

"Without thinking too much about it in specific terms, I was showing the America I knew and observed to others who might not have noticed." Norman Rockwell achieved his goal through an unequaled ability to capture the looks and gestures of Americans in every imaginable setting. Born in New York City in 1894, Rockwell attended the New York School of Art at the age of 14 and never looked back. He began to draw magazine covers, and at age 22 he did his first cover for *The Saturday Evening Post*, the magazine that found a home on more coffee tables than any magazine today. Forty-seven years later, Rockwell drew his last of 321 covers for the *Post*. He created "Rosie the Riveter" for the *Post* in 1943.

MURAL, SUNNYSIDE, QUEENS

As part of the post–September 11 culture, many forms of public art emerged, some as outdoor murals, recapturing the sense of the civic emotion that was evident just after the attack on the World Trade Center. Three artists, who identify themselves as Erni, Smith, and Lady Pink, created a block-long mural on a wall facing the Long Island Expressway in Sunnyside, Queens. Lady Pink, who was a pioneering graffiti artist in the late 1970s, often includes the image of a large-eyed woman in her work, and it is seen in this mural as a deity who watches over the firemen at Ground Zero. The artwork powerfully conveys the sense of overwhelming patriotism and unity felt by many New Yorkers at that time.

SEEING

1. What do you notice about each of the images and verbal texts in this section? Explain how the American flag is represented and/or appropriated in each. Compare and contrast, for example, the way in which the flag is used in the photographs in Jesse Gordon's Op-Art photo essay with its use in the cartoon by Matt Groening. In what respects might the creator of each image be said to engage in an act of persuasion—to prompt readers to take a particular course of action or accept a particular point of view? How might these actions or views be fundamentally different? How are the strategies used in each instance similar? different?

2. In his account of the majority decision in *Texas v. Johnson* (1989), Supreme Court Justice William J. Brennan Jr. wrote, "Pregnant with expressive content, the flag as readily signifies this nation as does the combination of letters found in 'America'" (para. 9). Many representations of and discussions about the flag in this section comment on what the flag "stands for" in American culture. Choose two of these renditions of the American flag in contemporary popular culture. What social, cultural, and/or historical versions of America does each suggest?

WRITING

1. Since 1989, when the United States Supreme Court ruled that a person may not be prosecuted for burning the American flag as a peaceful political protest, the issue of whether the flag should receive special protection under the law has remained hotly debated. Write an essay in which you build an argument to determine whether the American flag should be protected, and to what extent and under what circumstances. Draw on the essays and images in the preceding pages to support your argument.

2. The debate over the legality of flag burning involves one of the most precious rights of Americans: freedom of speech. Go to the annual index of a local or national newspaper, and identify another controversy that focuses on interpreting the rights guaranteed under the First Amendment to the Constitution (such as the right to protest outside an abortion clinic or the right to buy pornographic materials). Then write an expository essay in which you account for the ways in which the nature and extent of this issue is similar to—or different from—the debate over burning the American flag.

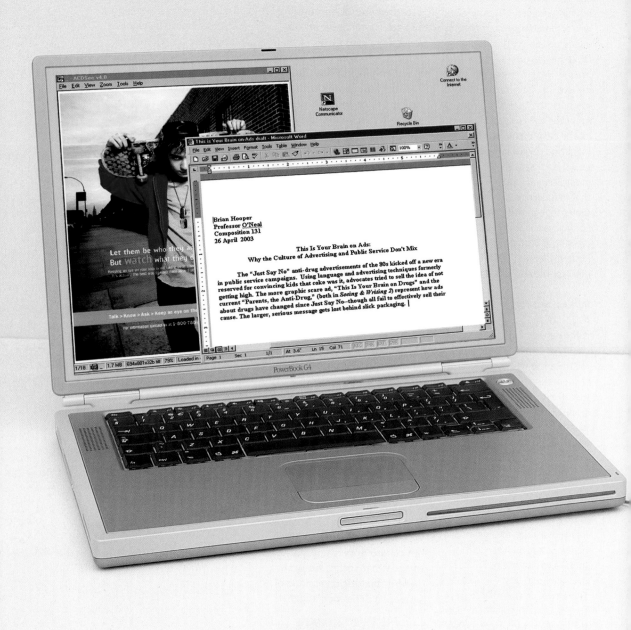

Challenging Images

Chapter 7
Challenging Images

We have chosen the title "Challenging Images" to illustrate in the visual and verbal selections that follow the different descriptive meanings of the word "challenging." In its most unequivocal sense, *challenging* functions as an adjective to project complexity and difficulty as well as to imply a subject that requires focused and sustained attention. This subject may be a topical issue (say, a proposal to resolve the political conflict in the Middle East) or some perennial issue (such as the death penalty or abortion) that requires us to articulate and perhaps put into practice our most deeply rooted convictions and beliefs.

Challenging is also a verb form that can be said to characterize the intellectual work you have been practicing

Barbara Kruger, **Untitled**

throughout *Seeing & Writing 2*. In this sense *challenging* images requires deliberate and purposeful intellectual activity and highlights the contested nature of that thinking and writing. In effect, images become the opponent of the mind at work using language—much in the way that a challenge is an invitation to compete, be it at a sport or an argument.

In contemporary America, images and words challenge each other for our attention. In the competition (some would call it a battle) between words and images, images seem to be winning, or so media pundits would have us believe. Images dominate more public space—on the front pages of newspapers and the covers of magazines, as well as on television, movie, and computer screens, and on roadside signs and sides and tops of buildings—than ever before.

Images play an increasingly important role in what we know—and how we learn—about current events. In fact, more Americans get their news from TV than from a newspaper, with each televised story accompanied by a stream of moving images on the screen: a student dissident halting a line of tanks outside Beijing's Tiananmen Square, a nation's sense of security shattered by the indelible image of twin towers collapsing. The list of such enduring images grows longer each year. As media critic Neil Postman has observed, "We are now a culture whose information, ideas, and epistemology are given form by television, not by the printed word."

You have come of age at a time when images play a prominent role in determining American values and assumptions—and thus a time when questioning what we see is more important than ever before. More of us spend our leisure time, for example, visually engaged by flipping through TV channels, watching movies, or surfing the web. Even when we are not looking at images in the public media, we record and sometimes even plan significant personal and private events around the photographs and home videos they will yield.

In a similar vein, an unprecedented influx of information, data, news, and stories is pouring into our lives at an incredible rate. Rapidly advancing computer and digital technologies now make copying, sending, and disseminating images increasingly speedy and accessible. Just as the invention of

The impact of television on our culture is indescribable. There's a certain sense in which it is nearly as important as the invention of printing.
– *Carl Sandburg, 1955*

the printing press facilitated the widespread distribution of print and required people to develop verbal literacy, today more and more people have to demonstrate another kind of literacy, a visual literacy—the ability to read, understand, and act on the information conveyed in powerful contemporary images.

The language of constructing images has infused itself in the public consciousness. We hear of politicians who hire consultants to perfect their public "images." We speak of improving our own "self-image." We might even say that Americans now have become more accustomed to looking at—and thinking about— images of things than the things themselves. For example, we can now walk through a replica of the streets of downtown New York City in Las Vegas, encounter "virtual" friends on the web, or watch a war being conducted "live" on television, whether that war is being fought on the other side of the globe or down the street.

Differentiating between image and reality has never been easy, but the question now is whether it's even possible. Cultural commentators such as Neal Gabler argue that it isn't: "Everywhere the fabricated, the inauthentic and the theatrical have gradually driven out the natural, the genuine and the spontaneous until there is no distinction between real life and stagecraft. In fact, one could argue that the theatricalization of American life is the major cultural transformation of our era. Devoured by artifice, life is a movie." The "real" events we watch on TV are what the social historian Daniel Boorstin calls "pseudo-events," events that have been crafted or framed solely for media presentation—and audience reception. At the same time that Americans are arguably more removed from real experience, we are nonetheless more obsessed with determining whether something is real or fake. Advertisers capitalize on the desire for the "authentic": authentic "stonewashed jeans" and "Coke: the real thing," for example.

More often we accept the image as our medium of choice. One example of the way in which we're becoming accustomed to working with a representation of reality in our daily lives involves the computer. When we sit in front of a monitor screen, mouse in hand, navigating a piece of software, what we're working with is a designed interface—an image, a

> Images show us a world but not the world itself. Images are not the things shown but are representations thereof: representations.
> – Richard Leppert, 1996

> The assumption that seeing is believing makes us susceptible to visual deception.
> – Kathleen Hall Jamieson, 1992

representation of the workings of the computer. In fact, computer sales-people join cultural commentators in questioning whether computer screens will ultimately replace books as the principal format by which we read. Already book sales are decreasing, and students are demonstrating only marginal progress in reading and writing proficiency.

Meanwhile we channel surf, rapidly scanning dozens of images in a few seconds, or we click from icon to icon. How do those processes differ from reading from left to right on a page? Computers have given new meaning to the term *multitasking* for millions of workers who must shift back and forth among windows on their computer screen or simultaneously talk on the phone, type, and wait for a web page to download. How does multitasking change the way in which we can be expected to read? and the ways in which we think and write?

Today writers must think like designers and designers like writers. If you're writing text for a web page, how do the visual aspects of text design—your ability to use hypertext—change the way you write as well as the content itself? If you are writing an article for a magazine or newspaper, how do space and design constraints affect your writing style and content? How might you write an article differently if you knew a photograph or illustration were to accompany it? In more general terms, how—and to what extent—should university curricula adjust to the changing nature of reading and writing to help students become more confident and articulate readers and writers?

Some scholars have noted that rather than simply propelling us forward in a linear way, rapidly advancing computer technology is also drawing on past ideas. Voice recognition software, for example, might allow us to return to the oral tradition of using our voices to create and record. And Scott McCloud reminds us (see p. 636) that ancient civilizations have long integrated the visual and verbal in their communication systems—think of Mandarin or Arabic characters. What consequences do you think the new "age of the image" has for writing and reading? We invite you to explore this question, and to form and revise your own judgments, as you critically read the authors and artists in this chapter.

BARBARA KRUGER

Barbara Kruger has been making cultural and political statements with her bold graphic images for over three decades. Combining black and white "found" photographs with powerful red-letter slogans, Kruger appropriates the techniques of advertising and circulates her work on billboards, posters, matchboxes, and postcards.

More than a dozen years as a designer and photo editor for Condé Nast publications gave Kruger an insider's view of how the media can manipulate the public. "To those who understand how pictures and words shape consensus," she writes, "we are unmoving targets waiting to be turned on and off."

In the early 1980s Kruger focused on feminist issues, as in one work that combines the phrase "We don't need another hero" with an image of a little boy showing his muscles. Most recently, Kruger's concerns have focused on the media.

Her writing is collected in *Remote Control: Power, Cultures and the World of Appearances* (1993), and her graphic work can be seen in *Love for Sale: The Words and Pictures of Barbara Kruger* (1996). Of her work as an artist, she writes, "I want to be on the side of pleasure and laughter and to disrupt the dour certainties of pictures, property, and power."

SEEING

1. What exactly do you think Barbara Kruger is trying to say in this piece? The copy gives us one message—does the image reinforce or subvert the words? How does Kruger manipulate the saying "a picture is worth a thousand words"? How do you interpret "worth" in this phrase? What might "worth" mean? to whom? in what context? What importance do you attach to "more" here? What significance does Kruger attach to it? How would you characterize the relationship of words to illustration in this image?

2. How would you describe Kruger's style? Comment on the effects of the choices she has made in type face and size, the position of language in relation to illustration, and the use of color. How many different images within an image can you identify here? From where does Kruger draw these images? More generally, what cultural references does she evoke? How might this image be read as a product of the culture of the 1990s?

WRITING

1. Think carefully about the phrase "a picture is worth more than a thousand words." With what experiences do you associate this expression? What patterns can you identify between and among these experiences? Are they, for example, personal experiences? more public in nature? something else? Explain. Write the first draft of an essay in which you argue for—or against—the applicability of this phrase to the circumstances of your own life.

2. Having studied Kruger's image carefully, please turn now to Andrew Savulich's news photographs (p. 268). Examine the role Savulich's brief descriptive titles play in establishing the impact of his photos. How do even these brief descriptions affect your understanding of his photographs? How might you interpret Savulich's photographs if the titles were worded differently? Draft an essay in which you compare and contrast the different impact of combining images and text in the work of Barbara Kruger and Andrew Savulich.

LOOKING AT THE UNBEARABLE

Susan Sontag

FIRST OF ALL, IT'S A SERIES—THOUGH NOT A narrative. A sequence (of images, and their captions) to be read. In its original state, something like a book: loose pages, a portfolio. In reproduction, invariably a book.

Easy to imagine more plates. Indeed, to the eighty published in the first edition of 1863, in Madrid by the Royal Academy of San Fernando, later editions invariably include at least two more plates, clearly intended for the series but which were rediscovered after 1863.

Easy to imagine fewer plates, too. How few? How do they kill thee? Let me count the ways.

Would one image be enough? (*The Disaster of War?*) No.

How to look at, how to read, the unbearable? 5

The problem is how not to avert one's glance. How not to give way to the impulse to stop looking.

The problem is despair. For it is not simply that this happened: Zaragoza, Chinchón, Madrid (1808–13). It *is* happening: Vucovar, Mostar, Srebrenica, Stupni Do, Sarajevo (1991–).

What to do with the knowledge communicated, shared by these images. Emerson wrote: "He has seen but half the universe who has never been shown the house of pain." It seems optimistic now to think that the house of pain describes no more than half the universe.

The images are relentless, unforgiving. That is, they do not forgive us—who are merely being shown, but do not live in the house of pain. The images tell us we have no right not to pay attention to the crimes of this order which are taking place right now. And the captions—mingling the voices of the murderers, who think of themselves as warriors, and the lamenting artist-witness—mutter and wail.

Although Goya himself may not have written the 10 captions (anyway, they're not in his hand), it's thought that whoever did them took the phrases from the artist's notes.

They are meant—images and captions—to awaken, shock, rend. No reproduction in a book comes close in sheer unbearableness to the impact these images have in the original 1863 edition. Here in the words of some of the captions is what they show:

One cannot look at this.
This is bad.
This is how it happened.
This always happens.
There is no one to help them.
With or without reason.
He defends himself well.
He deserved it.
Bury them and keep quiet.
There was nothing to be done and he died.
What madness!
This is too much!
Why?
Nobody knows why.
Not in this case either.
This is worse.
Barbarians!
This is the absolute worst!
It will be the same.
All this and more.
The same thing elsewhere.
Perhaps they are of another breed.
I saw it.
And this too.
Truth has died.
This is the truth.

No se puede mirar. / Esto es malo. / Así sucedió. / Siempre sucede. / No hay quien los socorra. / Con razon ó sin ella. / Se defiende bien. / Lo merecia. / Enterrar y callar. / Espiró sin remedio. / Que locura! / Fuerte cosa es! / Por qué? / No se puede saber por qué. / Tampoco. / Esto es peor. / Bárbaros! / Esto es lo peor! / Será lo mismo. / Tanto y mas. / Lo mismo en otras partes. / Si son de otro linage. / Yo lo vi. / Y esto tambien. / Murió la verdad. / Esto es lo verdadero.

Francisco Goya, **Qué Hai Que Hacer Mas? (What More Can Be Done?)**

Francisco Goya, **No Hay Quien los Socorra (There Is No One to Help Them)**

SUSAN SONTAG

Sontag's essay, "Looking at the Unbearable," about Francisco Goya's "Disasters of War" series was excerpted from *Transforming Vision: Writers on Art* (1994), a lavishly illustrated book that matches up well-known writers with artists whose works appear in the Art Institute of Chicago. Previously published poems, essays, and short stories by such writers as Saul Bellow, Carl Sandburg, and Delmore Schwartz are included in this volume, along with pieces (like Sontag's) that were written exclusively for this book. For more on Susan Sontag, see p. 300.

FRANCISCO GOYA

Francisco Goya was born in northern Spain in 1746 and found success as a painter at a relatively young age. He was appointed painter to the king of Spain in 1786 and court painter in 1789, the year of the French Revolution, a defining event in his life and work. Goya produced the "Disasters of War" series in response to the atrocities committed on both sides during the Napoleonic invasion of Spain and the Spanish War of Independence (1808–1814). Goya died in 1828 in France, where he had exiled himself after seeing that Spain would not return to a liberal government. The series of etchings was not published until 1863.

Goya is known as "The Father of Modern Art" for his innovative technique, his satirical etchings, and his belief in the primacy of the artist's vision over tradition. In his long career (he painted until his death at age 82) he excelled at many genres of painting ranging from portraiture to landscape, but it is his later work that ensured his place as a revolutionary artist whom artists today still credit as an influence. In his later work he eschewed classical themes, choosing instead to portray the harsh realities of the turbulent social and political world around him. For his uncompromising vision some scholars locate the beginnings of nineteenth-century realism in his work. By the end of his life his paintings had evolved a uniquely personal style (he executed a series of paintings on the walls of his house titled "Black Paintings") and reflected his increasing bitterness at humanity's folly and violence toward each other.

SEEING

1. Susan Sontag's essay on the series of etchings by Francisco Goya was first published in *Transforming Vision*, a collection of essays by major American writers on paintings and sculptures on display in the Art Institute of Chicago. Based on her essay, what would you say most attracted Sontag's eye—and mind—to these works by Goya? What does she say about the interrelation between image and words? What language does she offer, if any, to enable herself and others to "look at," "to read," and to think and write about "the unbearable"?

2. What does Sontag identify as the overarching challenge of looking at these works of art? What reaction(s) did these images evoke in you as you saw them for the first time? Where was your eye drawn as you studied these images? To what extent did you want to avert your gaze from the images? Or was it more a matter of averting your attention from the meaning of the images? from something else? Please explain, and support each point you make with detailed references to—and analyses of—specific aspects of Goya's images. To what extent do you find yourself endorsing—or resisting—Sontag's point that the images are "unforgiving"?

WRITING

1. In paragraph 8, Sontag observes: "What to do with the knowledge communicated, shared by these images." What do you make of the fact that Sontag places a period—rather than a question mark—at the end of this sentence? She then immediately cites Emerson's famous passage about "the house of pain." Reflect on the line she quotes from Emerson here. To what extent might it be applied to your own response to viewing Goya's images? Write an essay in which you argue for—or against—drawing on this line from Emerson to characterize your own response(s) to Goya's images of unbearable suffering.

2. At another point in her essay, Sontag observes: "The images tell us we have no right not to pay attention to the crimes of this order which are taking place right now." Choose one conflict and, in the first draft of an essay, discuss the ways in which different news media (Internet, TV, newspaper, magazine, radio) address "looking at the unbearable."

NICK HORNBY

Nick Hornby (b. 1958) is a born and bred Londoner. An international best-selling author, this former English teacher continues to live and work in the North London neighborhood where he grew up—the better to be near his beloved football club, Arsenal, the subject of his breakthrough memoir, *Fever Pitch* (1992). Hornby's other books include *High Fidelity* (1995), *About a Boy* (1999), and *How to Be Good* (2002). Two of his books, *High Fidelity* and *About a Boy*, have been made into Hollywood feature films—which is not surprising because his books seem to resonate well with American audiences: "I think there's always been that strain of American writing that wants to write simply and accessibly, but intelligently."

Hornby's books are suffused with references to pop culture. He says: "It seemed obvious to me that popular culture is an important part of all our lives and it should have some kind of reflection in the books we are reading. I've never understood why people didn't describe or just mention what TV programmes people were watching; I've always suspected it's something to do with having an eye on posterity."

In addition to writing novels, Hornby finds the time to write critical pieces about other artists—he writes about pop music for the *New Yorker*, and he contributed this piece on Richard Billingham to *Writers on Artists* (2001), a collection of essays by well-known writers on famous artists first published in the now-defunct *Modern Painters* magazine.

Richard Billingham

Nick Hornby

However enthusiastic you felt about Charles Saatchi's traveling exhibition "Sensation," much of it was unlikely to detain you for long. I don't mean that in any pejorative sense, or at least, I don't think I do: presumably there are critics who would argue that any successful work of art should provoke at least a break in a gallery visitor's stride, and that therefore works such as Sarah Lucas's *Au naturel* (the one with the dirty mattress, and his'n'hers melons, bucket, banana, and oranges) are comprehensive failures. You see it coming, as it were, from the other side of the room; you snort—with existential and aesthetic despair, if you are Brian Sewell, or with amusement, if you are a normal person—and you move on. I don't have a problem with that. For a few seconds I loved *Au naturel,* which means that I loved it more than I have loved other works that demanded much more of me and turned out not to repay the effort.

Even if they do nothing else—although actually they do plenty else—the photographs of Richard Billingham do detain you. You might not want to be detained; you might think, when you see his pictures of his battered, bewildered, distressed, and alcoholic father Raymond, and

of Elizabeth, his enormous, tattooed mother, that you'd rather wander off and look at something funnier, or more beautiful, or less real (and despite the proliferation of blood and pudenda and intestines elsewhere in "Sensation," nobody could describe the show as sober). But you can't. Wandering off is simply not an option, not if you have any curiosity at all: there is too much to think about, too much going on, too much narrative.

The first thing to think about is the rights and wrongs of these pictures, because anyone who has ever had parents of any kind, let alone parents like Billingham's, would wonder whether it were possible to justify snapping their moments of distress and plastering them all over the walls of the Royal Academy. You could argue that Billingham is unfortunate that he is a photographer: the immediacy of his medium seems to expose people in a way that writing never can. Tobias Woolf, Mary Karr, Blake Morrison, Tim Lott, and Katherine Harrison, among many others, have all displayed and analyzed their parents' crises and failings in recent years, but prose mediates and transforms, creates a distance even while trying to tell you things about a character's innermost soul. It's only writing, in other words, whereas photography is real life. But of course that is one of the tricks Billingham plays on you, because part of his art is to strip distances away, to convince you that this is life unmediated—an artistic device in itself.

Spend enough time with these pictures and eventually you realize that their complexity and empathy answers any of the questions you might ask of them and their creator: there's nothing exploitative going on here. Empathy is not to be confused with sentimentality, however: whatever else it is, Billingham's work is not sentimental. One of the most striking photographs in the "Sensation" exhibition shows Raymond sitting on the floor by the lavatory, his eyes cast down so that he seems to be in a state of philosophical and weary self-acceptance. His fly is undone, the soles of his sneakers are facing the lens; the toilet seat is broken, and some indistinct bodily waste—puke? blood?—is trickling down the outside of the bowl. It was never going

to be a pretty picture, but Billingham's pitiless, neutral gaze doesn't overweigh it, and consequently it is allowed to take its place in the ongoing narrative of his parents' life together.

It takes some talent, and some nerve, to be able to do this, and it is Billingham's impeccable judgment that impresses one first of all. It would have been easy for the artist to let these pictures become self-pitying—what sort of childhood and young adulthood is possible in this domestic climate?—but they are not: there is too much tolerance. Nor are they angry, hectoring, or loud. Even the pictures depicting violence, a violence born, presumably, out of alcohol and despair, don't succeed in turning the collection into a campaign about this or a plea to the government for that.

It is hard to be definitive about how Billingham pulls this off, but his insistence on giving Raymond and Elizabeth, his two leads, equal attention is certainly wise, because then these

Richard Billingham, **Untitled, 1994**

Richard Billingham, **Untitled, 1995**

pictures become the portrait of a marriage as much as an analysis of social despair or urban alienation, and the artist is at pains to show that this marriage has its moments of calm domesticity and evidently peaceable companionship, as well as all the other stuff. Elizabeth sitting over a jigsaw (a brilliantly realized shot, this, with the jigsaw pieces, Elizabeth's floral print dress, and her tattoos coming together in an orchestrated riot of synthetic color); Raymond and Elizabeth sitting watching TV on the sofa, a roast dinner on their laps, gravy down their fronts, the family pets in between them; even the spectacular shot of Ray hurling the cat violently through the air is a strangely matter-of-fact, life-goes-on moment. Given their context, these photos are rich and strange.

But there is blood on the walls in this household, and Billingham shows it to us—quite literally, in the case of one photograph, which depicts a thin claret trickle apparently emerging from one of those cutesy mass-produced portraits

of a mannequin that you used to be able to buy in Boots. There is more action here than one might expect to find in a selection of family snapshots: three of the pictures in Billingham's "Sensation" selection deal with violence or its immediate aftermath, and the changes of clothes alert you to the fact that this is not a sequence, but simply part of an ongoing domestic pattern. That Billingham was able to take the pictures at all is a clear indication that physical abuse is an organic part of the day; Raymond and Elizabeth would, presumably, have preferred their spats to take place away from their son's lens, but in the end were unable to stop themselves.

There is an inherent and perverse fascination, of course, in seeing grown people knock lumps off each other, and the fascination in this case is intensified by Elizabeth's obviously immense physical power. In one picture the couple are resting after what must have been a particularly vehement disagreement. Elizabeth has a bloody nose. Ray's scars are around his eye, and there

Richard Billingham, **Untitled, 1994**

is a sense that this match has ended in a score draw—Elizabeth even appears to be offering Raymond a paper hankie in a gesture of concern and reconciliation. In the rest, however, there is no doubt who the victor has been or will be. Perhaps the saddest photo of the lot is of an angry Elizabeth, fist raised, threatening her utterly defeated and understandably trepidatious partner: it is the closest Billingham comes to direct articulation of despair, if only because Raymond's expression has, for once, not been neutralized by the blank mask of drink, and we can see him clearly. Even when he is out of his head and toppling head first towards the floor, there is no indication of feeling, and maybe, you can't help reflecting, it's better that way.

"This book is about my close family," Billingham writes on the dustjacket of his book *Ray's a Laugh*. "My father Raymond is a chronic alcoholic . . . My mother Elizabeth hardly drinks but she does smoke a lot. She likes pets and things that are decorative. My younger brother Jason was taken into care when he was 11 but is now back with Ray and Liz again." There is a tone to these words that could be mistaken for blankness, just as the photographs could seem blank if one couldn't be bothered to look at them hard enough, but actually this collection is much, much warmer than that: it is clearly about love. Richard Billingham, one would hazard, loves his parents, but they are not loveable, not in the most straightforward sense of the term. Hence the careful neutrality of tone, the refusal to allow his lens to become clouded with pity or anger or disgust: he knows that enough of his audience will feel those things anyway and that actually the truth is a lot more complicated. The last picture in the "Sensation" exhibition shows Raymond and Elizabeth cuddling on the bed, and it's a kind of optimistic ending to an unsettling, extraordinary show—until you see Raymond's eyes, focusing somewhere in the middle distance, and you wonder what he has seen. ○

Richard Billingham, **Untitled, 1995**

SEEING

1. How does your reading of Billingham's photographs compare to Nick Hornby's? Which aspects of Billingham's photographs stand out to Hornby? to you? What qualities do these photographs convey to you: violence, empathy, sympathy, love, pain, or something else? Point to specific words and phrases to verify each of your claims. What, in your judgment, is challenging or confrontational about these images? To what extent do you see narrative in them? To what extent do you find Billingham's gaze "neutral," as Nick Hornby describes it?

2. If Billingham's photographs were not printed with this essay, how clear an image would Hornby's writing give you of the photographs? What examples and descriptions does Hornby use to support his analysis? How much contextual information does he include? What overall impression of Billingham's photographs does Hornby leave us with, and what strategies does he employ to achieve that effect?

WRITING

1. What does Hornby mean when he says, "the first thing to think about is the rights and wrongs of these pictures." What ethical issues do the photographs raise? What other artistic or commercial images do you know that have raised similar issues? Imagine you are the curator of a major museum. Write a two-page essay in which you identify the ethical issues raised by Billingham's work and argue for or against displaying them at your institution.

2. "Billingham's photographs may be innocent," wrote art critic Lara Grieve, "but they are undoubtedly truthful. He took so many shots that his family stopped noticing, and, although we see them through his camera lens, they are without artifice." Do you consider Billingham's photographs to be *artistic* or *documentary*? something in between? What is the difference? To what extent are those terms useful distinctions? Write an essay in which you argue that Billingham's photographs are either more artistic, more documentary, or something else entirely.

Richard Billingham
Nick Hornby

SUSAN BORDO

An archeologist of the culture of the body, Susan Bordo has helped bring "body studies" to the forefront of feminist intellectual debate. She writes, "The body is a powerful symbolic form, a surface on which the central rules, hierarchies and even metaphysical commitments of a culture are inscribed, and thus reinforced."

Bordo's best known book, *Unbearable Weight: Feminism, Western Culture and the Body,* was nominated for a Pulitzer Prize and named a notable book of 1993 by the *New York Times.* In it she explores women's relationships to food, desire, and power. She is also the author of *The Flight to Objectivity: Essays on Cartesianism and Culture* (1987) and the co-editor of a collection of essays entitled *Gender/Body/ Knowledge* (1989). The subjects of her numerous articles range from anorexia and cosmetic surgery to Hollywood's leading men and the impact of contemporary media. Her work on cultural analysis is exemplified by *Twilight Zones: The Hidden Life of Cultural Images from Plato to O.J.* (1997), from which the following essay is drawn. She turned her attention to the male body in *The Male Body: A New Look at Men in Public and Private* (1999), a work she describes as "a personal exploration of the male body from a woman's point of view."

Born in 1947, Bordo is Professor of English and Women's Studies at the University of Kentucky, where she holds the Singletary Chair of Humanities.

Never Just Pictures

Susan Bordo

BODIES AND FANTASIES

When Alicia Silverstone, the svelte nineteen-year-old star of *Clueless,* appeared at the Academy Awards just a smidge more substantial than she had been in the movie, the tabloids ribbed her cruelly, calling her "fatgirl" and "buttgirl" (her next movie role is Batgirl) and "more *Babe* than babe."[1] Our idolatry of the trim, tight body shows no signs of relinquishing its grip on our conceptions of beauty and normality. Since I began exploring this obsession it seems to have gathered momentum, like a spreading mass hysteria. Fat is the devil, and we are continually beating him—"eliminating" our stomachs, "busting" our thighs, "taming" our tummies—pummeling and purging our bodies, attempting to make them into something other than flesh. On television, infomercials hawking

Figure 1 *All our mothers needed to diet.*

---

1. I give great credit to Alicia Silverstone for her response to these taunts. In *Vanity Fair* she says, "I do my best. But it's much more important to me that my brain be working in the morning than getting up early and doing exercise. . . . The most important thing for me is that I eat and that I sleep and that I get the work done, but unfortunately . . . it's the perception that women in film should look a certain way" ("Hollywood Princess," September 1996, pp. 292–294). One wonders how long she will manage to retain such a sane attitude!

miracle diet pills and videos promising to turn our body parts into steel have become as commonplace as aspirin ads. There hasn't been a tabloid cover in the past few years that didn't boast of an inside scoop on some star's diet regime, a "fabulous" success story of weight loss, or a tragic relapse. (When they can't come up with a current one, they scrounge up an old one; a few weeks ago the *National Inquirer* ran a story on Joan Lunden's fifty-pound weight loss fifteen years ago!) Children in this culture grow up knowing that you can never be thin enough and that being fat is one of the worst things one can be. One study asked ten- and eleven-year-old boys and girls to rank drawings of children with various physical handicaps; drawings of fat children elicited the greatest disapproval and discomfort, over pictures of kids with facial disfigurements and missing hands.

Psychologists commonly believe that girls with eating disorders suffer from "body image disturbance syndrome": they are unable to see themselves as anything but fat, no matter how thin they become. If this is a disorder, it is one that has become a norm of cultural perception. Our ideas about what constitutes a body in need of a diet have become more and more pathologically trained on the slightest hint of excess. This ideal of the body beautiful has largely come from fashion designers and models. (Movie stars, who often used to embody a more voluptuous ideal, are now modeling themselves after the models.) They have taught us "to love a woman's pelvis, her hipbones jutting out through a bias-cut gown . . . the clavicle in its role as a coat hanger from which clothes are suspended."[2] (An old fashion industry justification for skinniness in models was that clothes just don't "hang right" on heftier types.) The fashion industry has taught us to regard a perfectly healthy, nonobese body such as the one depicted in figure 1 as an unsightly "before" ("Before CitraLean, no wonder they wore swimsuits like that"). In fact, those in the business have admitted that models have been getting thinner since 1993, when Kate Moss first repopularized the waif look. British models Trish Goff and Annie Morton make Moss look well fed by comparison,[3] and recent ad campaigns for Jil Sander go way beyond the thin-body-as-coat-hanger paradigm to a blatant glamorization of the cadaverous, starved look itself.* More and more ads featuring anorexic-looking young men are appearing too.

The main challenge to such images is a muscular aesthetic that *looks* more life-affirming but is no less punishing and compulsion-inducing in its demands on ordinary bodies. During the 1996 Summer Olympics—which were reported with unprecedented focus and hype on the fat-free beauty of muscular bodies—commentators celebrated the "health" of this aesthetic over anorexic glamour. But there is growing evidence of rampant eating disorders among female athletes, and it's hard to imagine that those taut and tiny Olympic gymnasts—the idols of preadolescents across the country—are having regular menstrual cycles. Their skimpy level of body fat just won't support it. During the Olympics I heard a commentator gushing about how great it was that the 1996 team was composed predominantly of eighteen- and nineteen-year-old women rather than little girls. To me it is far more disturbing that these nineteen-year-olds still *look* (and talk) like little girls! As I watched them vault and leap, my admiration for their tremendous skill and spirit was shadowed by thoughts of what was going on *inside* their bodies—the hormones unreleased because of insufficient body fat, the organ development delayed, perhaps halted.

2. Holly Brubach, "The Athletic Esthetic," *The New York Times Magazine*, June 23, 1996, p. 51.

3. In early 1996 the Swiss watch manufacturer Omega threatened to stop advertising in British *Vogue* because of *Vogue's* use of such hyperthin models, but it later reversed this decision. The furor was reminiscent of boycotts that were threatened in 1994 when Calvin Klein and Coca-Cola first began to use photos of Kate Moss in their ads. In neither case has the fashion industry acknowledged any validity to the charge that their imagery encourages eating disorders. Instead, they have responded with defensive "rebuttals."

* For reasons of copyright, we are unable to reproduce the Jil Sander advertisement shown in Bordo's essay [eds.].

Is it any wonder that despite media attention to the dangers of starvation dieting and habitual vomiting, eating disorders have spread throughout the culture?[4] In 1993 in *Unbearable Weight* I argued that the old clinical generalizations positing distinctive class, race, family, and "personality" profiles for the women most likely to develop an eating disorder were being blasted apart by the normalizing power of mass imagery. Some feminists complained that I had not sufficiently attended to racial and ethnic "difference" and was assuming the white, middle-class experience as the norm. Since then it has been widely acknowledged among medical professionals that the incidence of eating and body-image problems among African American, Hispanic, and Native American women has been grossly underestimated and is on the increase.[5] Even the gender gap is being narrowed, as more and more men are developing eating disorders and exercise compulsions too. (In the mid-eighties the men in my classes used to yawn and pass notes when we discussed the pressure to diet; in 1996 they are more apt to protest if the women in the class talk as though it's their problem alone.)

The spread of eating disorders, of course, is not just about images. The emergence of eating disorders is a complex, multilayered cultural "symptom," reflecting problems that are historical as well as contemporary, arising in our time because of the confluence of a number of factors.[6] Eating disorders are overdetermined in this culture. They have to do not only with new social expectations of women and ambivalence toward their bodies but also with more general anxieties about the body as the source of hungers, needs, and physical vulnerabilities not within our control. These anxieties are deep and long-standing in Western philosophy and religion, and they are especially acute in our own time. Eating disorders are also linked to the contradictions of consumer culture, which is continually encouraging us to binge on our desires at the same time as it glamorizes self-discipline and scorns fat as a symbol of laziness and lack of willpower. And these disorders reflect, too, our increasing fascination with the possibilities of reshaping our bodies and selves in radical ways, creating new bodies according to our mind's design.

The relationship between problems such as these and cultural images is complex. On the one hand, the idealization of certain kinds of bodies foments and perpetuates our anxieties and insecurities, that's clear. Glamorous images of hyperthin models certainly don't encourage a more relaxed or accepting attitude toward the body, particularly among those whose own bodies are far from that ideal. But, on the other hand, such images carry fantasized solutions *to* our anxieties and insecurities, and that's part of the reason why they are powerful. They speak to us not just about how to be beautiful or desirable but about how to get control of our lives, get safe, be cool, avoid hurt. When I look at the picture of a skeletal and seemingly barely breathing young woman in figure 2, for example, I do not see a vacuous fashion ideal. I see a visual embodiment of what novelist and ex-anorexic Stephanie Grant means when she says in her autobiographical novel, *The Passion of Alice,* "If I had to say my anorexia was about any single thing, I would have said it was about living without desire. Without longing of any kind."[7]

Now, this may not seem like a particularly attractive philosophy of life (or a particularly attractive body, for that matter). Why would anyone want to look like death, you might be asking. Why would anyone want to live without desire? But recent articles in

5

4. Despite media attention to eating disorders, an air of scornful impatience with "victim feminism" has infected attitudes toward women's body issues. Christina Hoff-Sommers charges Naomi Wolf (*The Beauty Myth*) with grossly inflating statistics on eating disorders and she poo-poos the notion that women are dying from dieting. Even if some particular set of statistics is inaccurate, why would Sommers want to deny the reality of the problem, which as a teacher she can surely see right before her eyes?

5. For the spread of eating disorders in minority groups, see, for example, "The Art of Integrating Diversity: Addressing Treatment Issues of Minority Women in the 90's," in *The Renfrew Perspective,* Winter 1994; see also Becky Thompson, *A Hunger So Wide and So Deep* (Minneapolis: University of Minnesota Press, 1994).

6. See my *Unbearable Weight* (Berkeley: University of California Press, 1993).

7. Stephanie Grant, *The Passion of Alice* (New York: Houghton Mifflin, 1995), 58.

both *The New Yorker* and the *New York Times* have noted a new aesthetic in contemporary ads, in which the models appear dislocated and withdrawn, with chipped black nail polish and greasy hair, staring out at the viewer in a deathlike trance, seeming to be "barely a person." Some have called this wasted look "heroin chic": ex-model Zoe Fleischauer recalls that "they wanted models that looked like junkies. The more skinny and fucked-up you look, the more everybody thinks you're fabulous."[8]

Hilton Als, in *The New Yorker,* interprets this trend as making the statement that fashion is dead and beauty is "trivial in relation to depression."[9] I read these ads very differently. Although the photographers may see themselves as ironically "deconstructing" fashion, the reality is that no fashion advertisement can declare fashion to be dead—it's virtually a grammatical impossibility. Put that frame around the image, whatever the content, and we are instructed to find it glamorous. These ads are not telling us that beauty is trivial in relation to depression, they are telling us that depression is beautiful, that being wasted is *cool*. The question then becomes not "Is fashion dead?" but "Why has death become glamorous?"

Freud tells us that in the psyche death represents not the destruction of the self but its return to a state prior to need, thus freedom from unfulfilled longing, from anxiety over not having one's needs met. Following Freud, I would argue that ghostly pallor and bodily disrepair, in "heroin chic" images, are about the allure, the safety, of being beyond needing, beyond caring, beyond desire. Should we be surprised at the appeal of being without desire in a culture that has invested our needs with anxiety, stress, and danger, that has made us craving and hungering machines, creatures of desire, and then repaid us with addictions, AIDS, shallow and unstable relationships, and cutthroat competition for jobs and mates? To have given up the quest for fulfillment, to be unconcerned

Figure 2 *Advertising anorexia?*

with the body or its needs—or its vulnerability—is much wiser than to care.

So, yes, the causes of eating disorders are "deeper" [10] than just obedience to images. But cultural images themselves *are* deep. And the way they become imbued and animated with such power is hardly mysterious. Far from being the purely aesthetic inventions that designers and photographers would like to have us believe they are—"It's just fashion, darling, nothing to get all politically steamed up about"—they reflect the designers' cultural savvy, their ability to sense and give form to flutters and quakes in the cultural psyche. These folks have a strong and simple motivation to hone their skills as cultural Geiger counters. It's called the profit motive. They want their images and the products associated with them to sell.

The profit motive can sometimes produce seemingly "transgressive" wrinkles in current norms. Recently

8. Zoe Fleischauer quoted in "Rockers, Models, and the New Allure of Heroin," *Newsweek*, August 26, 1996.

9. Hilton Als, "Buying the Fantasy," *The New Yorker*, October 10, 1996, p. 70.

designers such as Calvin Klein and Jil Sander have begun to use rather plain, ordinary-looking, un-madeup faces in their ad campaigns. Unlike the models in "heroin chic" ads, these men and women do not appear wasted so much as unadorned, unpolished, stripped of the glamorous veneer we have come to expect of fashion spreads. While many of them have interesting faces, few of them qualify as beautiful by any prevailing standards. They have rampant freckles, moles in unbeautiful places, oddly proportioned heads. Noticing these ads, I at first wondered whether we really were shifting into a new gear, more genuinely accepting of diversity and "flaws" in appearance. Then it suddenly hit me that these imperfect faces were showing up in clothing and perfume ads only and the *bodies* in these ads were as relentlessly normalizing as ever—not one plump body to complement the facial "diversity."

I now believe that what we are witnessing here is a commercial war. Clothing manufacturers, realizing that many people—particularly young people, at whom most of these ads are aimed—have limited resources and that encouraging them to spend all their money fixing up their faces rather than buying clothes is not in their best interests, are reasserting the importance of body over face as the "site" of our fantasies. In the new codes of these ads a too madeup look signifies a lack of cool, too much investment in how one looks. "Just Be," Calvin Klein tells us in a recent CK One ad. But looks—a lean body—still matter enormously in these ads, and we are still being told *how* to be—in the mode which best serves Calvin Klein. And all the while, of course, makeup and hair products continue to promote their own self-serving aesthetics of facial perfection. ○

SEEING

1. Susan Bordo reports that "The spread of eating disorders . . . is not just about images. The emergence of eating disorders is a complex, multilayered cultural 'symptom,' reflecting problems that are historical as well as contemporary" (para. 5). Identify as many problems as possible that may have caused the spread of eating disorders. In what ways has the power of mass imagery exacerbated this problem?

Later in paragraph 5, Bordo links eating disorders to "the contradictions of consumer culture, which is continually encouraging us to binge on our desires at the same time as it glamorizes self-discipline and scorns fat as a symbol of laziness and lack of willpower." Read carefully the advertisements in several widely circulated women's magazines. What visual and verbal strategies do the advertisers use to encourage readers to fantasize about reshaping their bodies and selves in radically new ways?

2. In paragraph 7, Bordo discusses the "heroin chic" ads of recent years. Along with her own interpretation, she provides several different readings of the messages and the cultural significance projected in these ads. Which analysis do you find most convincing? Why? What is your reading of these ads? Where would you position your analysis in relation to the others? What aspects of the ads does your reading attend to that the others do not?

WRITING

1. In the opening paragraph, Bordo reminds us that "On television, infomercials hawking miracle diet pills and videos promising to turn our body parts into steel have become as commonplace as aspirin ads." Choose an infomercial and examine it carefully. What appeals and promises does it trade on? What strategies do its producers use to induce viewers to buy the product? Write an expository essay in which you analyze the nature of the success of this infomercial. What recommendations, if any, would you offer to support— or resist—an effort to regulate more carefully the claims made by the promoters of these goods and services?

2. In the final paragraph, Bordo reports that clothing manufacturers are "reasserting the importance of body over face as the 'site' of our fantasies." Review some advertisements aimed at young people, especially those with limited financial resources. Write an essay in which you assess the "new codes" of values projected in these ads. What conclusions, however tentative, do you draw about the cultural implications of shifting the "site" of beauty from the face to the body?

W.E.B. DUBOIS

William Edward Burghardt DuBois, born in Massachusetts in 1868, was the guiding intellectual light behind the establishment of the modern movement for the rights of African Americans. He was the first African American to earn a doctorate from Harvard University, and in 1909 he co-founded the National Association for the Advancement of Colored People (NAACP). He was the author of many works on slavery and "color," including the ground-breaking *The Souls of Black Folk* (1903), from which this excerpt is taken, and *Color and Democracy* (1945).

The critic Saunders Redding once described *The Souls of Black Folk* in these words: "it not only represented a profound change in its scholar-author's view of what was then called the 'Negro Problem,' but heralded a new approach to social reform on the part of the American-Negro people—an approach of patriotic, non-violent activism."

DuBois was a life-long champion of radical political activism as a method of social change. He joined the Communist Party in 1961 and at the age of 91 moved to Ghana, where he died in 1963 after becoming a naturalized citizen.

Never Just Pictures
Susan Bordo

Double Consciousness

W.E.B. DuBois

... THE PROBLEM OF THE TWENTIETH CENTURY is the problem of the colorline. . . .

After the Egyptian and Indian, the Greek and Roman, the Teuton and Mongolian, the Negro is a sort of seventh son, born with a veil, and gifted with second-sight in this American world—a world which yields him no true self-consciousness, but only lets him see himself through the revelation of the other world. It is a peculiar sensation, this double-consciousness, this sense of always looking at one's self through the eyes of others, of measuring one's soul by the tape of a world that looks on in amused contempt and pity. One ever feels his two-ness,—an American, a Negro; two souls, two thoughts, two unreconciled strivings; two warring ideals in one dark body, whose dogged strength alone keeps it from being torn asunder.

The history of the American Negro is the history of this strife,—this longing to attain self-conscious manhood, to merge his double self into a better and truer self. In this merging he wishes neither of the older selves to be lost. He would not Africanize America, for America has too much to teach the world and Africa. He would not bleach his Negro soul in a flood of white Americanism, for he knows that Negro blood has a message for the world. He simply wishes to make it possible for a man to be both a Negro and an American, without being cursed and spit upon by his fellows, without having the doors of Opportunity closed roughly in his face.

Work, culture, liberty,—all these we need, not singly but together, not successively but together, each growing and aiding each, and all striving toward that vaster ideal that swims before the Negro people, the ideal of human brotherhood, gained through the unifying ideal of Race; the ideal of fostering and developing the traits and talents of the Negro, not in opposition to or contempt for other races, but rather in large conformity to the greater ideals of the American Republic, in order that some day on American soil two world-races may give each to each those characteristics both so sadly lack. We the darker ones come even now not altogether empty-handed: there are to-day no truer exponents of the pure human spirit of the Declaration of Independence than the American Negroes; there is no true American music but the wild sweet melodies of the Negro slave; the American fairy tales and folk-lore are Indian and African; and, all in all, we black men seem the sole oasis of simple faith and reverence in a dusty desert of dollars and smartness. ○

SEEING

1. In "Double Consciousness," what points does DuBois enumerate in his compelling account of the consequences of the segregated identity of African Americans? Based on what DuBois says here—as well as on other sources known to you—what restrictions (legal, social, educational, political, and psychological) did African Americans encounter in their daily experience in this nation at the time DuBois wrote *The Souls of Black Folk?* Concentrate briefly on paragraph 2. What language can you point to here that makes DuBois's argument most convincingly?

2. Examine the advertisement for Cream of White cereal. In what ways does it exemplify DuBois's point about seeing oneself in terms of "the eyes of others"? To what extent might you defend—or argue against—the proposition that this ad pits "two souls, two thoughts, two unreconciled strivings; two warring ideals in one dark body" (para. 2)? How would you characterize the depiction of the child in this ad? the "uncle"? Comment on the reasonableness of applying DuBois's point of "double consciousness" to the overall relationship between the child and the "uncle." What inferences might you draw from this advertisement about the state of race relations in the United States during the first several decades of the twentieth century?

WRITING

1. Seeing oneself in terms of "the eyes of others" remains an ongoing problem for virtually every member of any nonwhite racial and ethnic group in the United States. Pick up the most recent issue of a popular magazine, one addressed to as broad a base of the American reading public as possible. *Time, Newsweek, U.S. News & World Report* are a few possibilities. Review the nature of the racial and ethnic identities projected in the magazine's editorial and advertising content. Now do the same for a magazine circulated primarily among a specific ethnic or racial audience. *Essence* is one example. Write an essay in which you compare and contrast the representation of a specific minority group in magazines with different targeted audiences. What differences do you notice? What are the implications of these graphic differences?

2. Reread the final paragraph of DuBois's statement on double consciousness, especially its final line. What does DuBois mean when he calls "black men . . . the sole oasis of simple faith and reverence in a dusty desert of dollars and smartness"? Write an expository essay in which you explore the meaning as well as the significance for American cultural history of this assertion. Be sure to validate each of your points with a detailed analysis of specific evidence.

Double Consciousness

W.E.B. DuBois

"GIDDAP, UNCLE"

Painted by Edw. V. Brewer for Cream of Wheat Co.   Copyright 1921 by Cream of Wheat Co.

Edward V. Brewer, **Cream of Wheat**

Retrospect:
Reel Native Americans

1910

1929

1990

1998

Kenneth Cole, **Think you have no privacy? You're not alone.**

KENNETH COLE

The son of a shoe manufacturer, Kenneth Cole (b. 1954) grew up in Great Neck, Long Island. He worked for his father after graduating from Emory University and in 1982 set out to start his own shoe company. He did not have a lot of money when he started out, but he had some designs and he had European banks backing him if he could only get off on the right foot. He debuted his first collection of ladies' footwear from the back of a 40-foot tractor trailer (borrowed from a trucker friend and allowed to park in mid-town Manhattan only after Cole applied for a parking permit to shoot a film titled *The Birth of a Shoe Company*) during New York's annual footwear show. The film was never made, but Cole Productions, Inc., sold 40,000 pairs of shoes over two days and the highly successful fashion company was born.

Today Kenneth Cole has grown into one of the country's largest fashion companies, expanding into men's and women's clothing and accessories. Cole is known for incorporating catchy, sometimes humorous, and sometimes serious slogans in its national ad campaigns and was one of the first fashion companies to address the AIDS crisis directly. Kenneth Cole has received numerous awards for raising public consciousness on social issues such as AIDS, homelessness, and gun violence. He has been a National Board Member of AmFAR (The American Foundation for AIDS Research) since 1985 and the HELP U.S.A. Homeless project since its inception in 1987.

SEEING

1. Kenneth Cole is a widely circulated and well-known brand name for clothing and accessories. What do you make of the fact that the advertisement doesn't clearly show any Kenneth Cole products? In what ways does it *not* work like most of the ads you see and read? In what ways is the ad similar to—and different from—other ads? Based on the "information" presented in this ad, what would you expect Kenneth Cole products to look like? For example, what would make a Kenneth Cole belt different from another brand's belt?

2. Compare this ad to the "Anti-Drug" ad on page 590. To what extent does each ad place the viewer in a different position (watched/watcher)? How effectively would these ads work if the viewer's position were switched? What kind of emotions does each ad bring out? Fear? Paranoia? Concern? Comment on the nature and extent of the similarities and differences in how the ads evoke these emotions.

WRITING

1. Re-create the scene in the advertisement by fogging up a window while a friend stands on the other side ready to read what you write. What have you written? What does your friend notice about the writing? How do you go about making your writing easily readable to the person on the other side? Writing so that it makes sense to your friend, rewrite the ad's text. How does your reversed writing compare with the ad's text? Look closely at the letters in the ad—their shape, thickness, angles, and the spaces in between them. How can you determine from which side of the mirror the letters in the ad were written? What evidence supports your judgment? In the ad's context, why does it matter from which side the letters were written?

2. Who is Kenneth Cole? Go to the library, search the Internet, and/or visit the company's web site to find out more about Kenneth Cole. How would it change the ad's meaning if Kenneth Cole were simply a brand name? What significance would you attach to a circumstance in which a brand-name representative were to leave a message on your bathroom mirror? What kind of person do you imagine—and know—him to be? Write an expository essay in which you determine the extent to which you can offer some judgments of his personality based on how he represents himself in the advertisement.

KATHARINE MIESZKOWSKI
Katharine Mieszkowski is a senior
writer for *Salon*'s Technology and
Business section, and she is a
columnist for the *San Francisco
Bay Guardian*. Between 1997 and
2000 she wrote for *Fast Company*, a glossy, hi-tech business
magazine, and was the Boston-
based national magazine's Bay
Area correspondent. Living in San
Francisco makes it easy for her to
cover nearby Silicon Valley, and
her commentaries and essays
about the World Wide Web stem
from her interest in and interaction
with the Internet since its earliest
beginnings. In 1994 she joined
Women's Wire, the pioneering
Internet company for women,
now Women.com Networks.
Mieszkowski has also contributed
to *Ms. Magazine*, *On Magazine*,
Slate, the *San Francisco Chronicle*,
the *San Jose Mercury News*, and
the *Financial Times*. She can also
be heard on National Public
Radio's "All Things Considered."
The essay "Nowhere Left to Hide"
was first published on Salon.com.

Nowhere Left to Hide

Katharine Mieszkowski

June 18, 2001 | Decked out in full riot gear, a police battalion storms a women's jail
cell. "Ladies, you're gonna step out single file, one at a time, stand a gainst the wall!"
bellows an officer. The cops wear Army boots and helmets. They carry batons and
shields. They look like they're prepared to quell rampant mayhem in the streets.
Instead, they're entering a secure women's holding cell, supposedly to search for
contraband.

Viewed through the small streaming-video frame on a computer monitor the female
inmates look poor, fat and nonplussed as they file out of the cell and stand splayed
against the "wall," which is actually a window in the men's holding cell. Hands
above their heads against the window, they face the male inmates through the glass.
The men immediately flock closer to gawk and taunt.

A "shakedown" at the Madison Street Jail in Maricopa County in Phoenix has begun.

"Put your hands on the glass! Ladies, keep your hands on the wall at all times," yells
another officer, as female cops pat down the women and the riot police search the
now empty women's cell.

The pat-down spectacle is apparently too much for the male inmates behind the
glass watching the free show. "They flashing me! They flashing too much of what
they ain't got," complains one of the women. On our computers, we can't see what

5

she sees, but it's not hard to imagine. She sasses back through the window: "Hey, where's your boyfriend at, baby? Are you your bitch?"

Getting arrested in Maricopa County can make you a star—a star in a sick webcam drama that turns the inside of a local jail into a worldwide freak show for any voyeur with a Web connection. Since July 2000, the county jail's four cameras have served up live images of the facility's search area, the men's and women's holding cells and the pre-intake area. The images are hosted on Crime.com, a site now owned by USA Networks and started by the co-founder of the reality TV show *Cops*. Bonus scenes include the shakedown video, which the site bills as "Special Ops," a two-minute low-budget movie that provides extra titillation for Web-enabled prying eyes.

Watching the video provides the same kind of fascination as a train wreck, but the legality of the world's first jail webcam has come under fire. On May 24, Middle Ground Prison Reform, a nonprofit in Tempe, Ariz., filed suit on behalf of the tens of thousands of inmates who have been incarcerated in the jail since the webcams started rolling on Crime.com. Middle Ground is seeking class-action status for the suit and a whopping $1.375 billion in damages.

"These people's images are being used on a commercial Web site without their permission and, in most cases, without their knowledge," says Donna Leone Hamm, co-founder of Middle Ground. "We're saying: 'Take the webcams down. You can leave the cameras up for security, fine, you're allowed to do that. But you have to take them off the Web site. That is an inappropriate invasion of privacy.'"

Privacy? In a jail? Sheriff Joe Arpaio, the publicity-seeking head of Madison Street Jail, thinks there is no such thing. He characterizes the lawsuit as frivolous and vows: "This is a great program. I'm not going to back down."

The billion-dollar case of the sheriff and his rogue webcams hinges on a single issue: 10 What rights do prisoners in a county jail have to their own images? But it also raises a scarier question: What rights do any of us have to our own images these days? Is your image property you own or something you give up by venturing out in public?

As surveillance by security cameras, in every public space from airports to parking garages to convenience stores, becomes the norm, one estimate suggests that we're each taped an average of 30 times a day. Women seeking abortions are alarmed to discover that their images as they enter a clinic might be broadcast on the Web. Football fans attending this year's Super Bowl in Tampa, Fla., were surprised to learn that their images not only had been recorded but had been compared with a database of known criminals using new "biometric" face-recognition technology.

Compounding the problem, video cameras are getting cheaper and smaller. Privacy experts predict that it won't be long before security cameras are networked. Can Big Brother–style tracking of individuals' whereabouts be far behind?

In the early days of the Web, exhibitionists like Jenni of Jennicam couldn't wait to webcast their lives to the world. But like it or not, we're all becoming more like Jenni every day. For as perversely fascinating as it may be to peek in on the spectacle at the Madison Street Jail, we may have more in common with the inmates than we'd like to think.

From "Snooper Bowl" football fans in Florida to ferry passengers in Rhode Island, surveillance subjects are starting to realize that they don't control the dissemination of their own images. In April, a local businessman in Block Island, R.I., moved his webcam, which had been aimed at the island's only ferry, after the company operating the ferry threatened to sue, complaining that passengers could be identified from the images. The webcam owner backed down to avoid a costly lawsuit.

He may have jumped the gun. According to legal experts, in most states there are no legal grounds to object to your image being captured in a public place, unless it's a place with an "expectation of privacy," like a bathroom stall. Shari Steele, executive director of the Electronic Frontier Foundation, a nonprofit civil liberties organization, explains: "People are putting cameras in all sorts of public facilities. They're everywhere. We, as a society, have just decided that that's acceptable." But is what Arpaio, the self-proclaimed "Toughest Sheriff in America," doing acceptable? The hugely popular sheriff has gained notoriety around the country for an array of harsh practices, for some of which he has already been sued. He brags it costs just 40 cents a day to feed one of his inmates, while it costs $1.15 to feed one of the jail dogs. He serves inmates green baloney sandwiches, makes them wear pink underwear and houses them in tents outdoors in the 115-degree Arizona heat. He lets the inmates watch only two channels—the Food Channel, so they can drool at the gourmet cooking, and the Weather Channel so they can see all the other places around the country where it's not so damn hot. In one case, the county's insurance company paid out $8 million to the family of a man who died in a restraining chair while in custody at the jail.

Arpaio says the jail webcam is just a sign that he and his officers have nothing to hide: "It's there to let the whole world know that we're doing nothing wrong. I'm tired of my officers being accused of killing people." But Eleanor Eisenberg, executive director of the Arizona Civil Liberties Union, says that the public's right to know doesn't justify the constant presence of the webcams: "The public's right to know is adequately taken care of by the existence in our jail, and virtually every other jail in the country, of video surveillance cameras that are internal and make a record: That record is a public record."

Middle Ground's Hamm even suggests that the "shakedown," which is marketed on the sites as the first one in four years at the jail, is "a staged event for the webcam. . . . It's a titillating opportunity for the viewers to see something other than prisoners standing around doing nothing. It wasn't exciting enough, so they had to stage something."

Sheriff Arpaio denies the accusation that the shakedown was staged. His position is that there is a punitive purpose for his 24-hour reality show. "Johns picking up prostitutes can wave to their wives on the Web, and drunk drivers can wave to their employers," brags Arpaio. "That might deter that segment of society." He thinks that subjecting detainees to the public eye of the Web might make petty criminals think twice before they strike again.

The only problem is, many of the people caught in the jail webcam haven't been convicted of anything. They're "pretrial detainees," says Eisenberg, many of them unable to make bail. "The people in the booking area where the webcams [are] not only haven't been convicted of a crime but haven't been charged with a crime yet. . . . He is acting as the judge, jury and the entire justice system without the authority to do that."

"Really all this is is a way to humiliate people who have been arrested," says Cara Gotsch, public policy coordinator for the ACLU's National Prison Project in Washington. [20]

And what about those of us who haven't been arrested? What about those of us buying a Coke at the minimart, or sitting on a bench in a public park, or hanging out at a ballgame? The webcam at Madison Street Jail may seem like an outlandish and absurd mockery, but it can also be seen as merely the leading edge of a campaign to invade privacy unthinkable in the days before the Internet and omnipresent video cameras.

Evan Hendricks, editor and publisher of *Privacy Times*, sees the aggregation of images over time from the webcams at Madison Street Jail as a real threat to inmates' rights. "You could set up your computer so you could automatically check this jail cam, and you could be downloading images off of it, and later you could apply facial-recognition technology and make a database of everyone who has been arrested at that Arizona jail."

Such a database might be extremely valuable to local employers screening the people they hire. As Hendricks explains, while conviction information becomes a part of the public record, arrest information does not, and that's where the webcam changes the rules. "This whole thing is a potential end run around the traditional privacy that's developed for arrest information," says Hendricks.

Technology that can match faces to names is neither futuristic nor far-fetched, as the Super Bowl fans discovered. Nineteen "matches" were found when images of their faces were captured and compared with face-recognition technology against thousands of images of wanted criminals provided by the FBI, Secret Service and local police.

Executives at Viisage, which provided the face-recognition technology used at the [25] Super Bowl this year, are puzzled by all the fuss about the filming of football fans, whose images were compared with thousands of images of wanted criminals provided by the FBI, Secret Service and local police. Tom Colatosti, Viisage's CEO, says: "The average person is on a surveillance camera 30 times a day. When you go to a gas station, in an elevator, in a parking lot, shopping mall, ATM, Dunkin' Donuts, 7-Eleven, highway— surveillance is a part of our everyday life." And let's not forget casinos and banks and airports and border crossings.

"All the uproar is about the potential of what could happen," Colatosti says, by which he means the potential for databases of images to be used to track an individual from place to place. "That doesn't happen, because the images are not stored, and secondly, apart from [providing] good copy [for reporters] and paranoia, who would want to track your face? I can tell you that law enforcement has enough images in the database without cluttering it up with useless images of some fan going to a football game."

But privacy experts like Phil Agre, an associate professor of information studies at UCLA and co-editor of "Technology and Privacy: The New Landscape," says that while that kind of tracking hasn't happened yet, it's coming. "As soon as face recognition goes prime time, the world changes instantaneously overnight. You walk past a store and you get junk mail from that store. You walk into the store and the salesperson mysteriously knows your name. People going into business, selling files of who has been where—a market springs up. I'm not saying the consequences are all bad—it has law enforcement and crime protection as well as Big Brother kind of consequences."

Already, throughout the borough of Newham in London, 300 cameras monitor the streets looking for known criminals. "If you institute this properly, you can get the support of the public," says Frances Zelazny of Visionics, the company that makes the face-recognition technology used in Newham. "You always have the fringe, but in general this is a neighborhood where people feel afraid."

But is it worth it to trade a fear of crime for a fear of being watched? The EFF's Steele believes that as people become more aware of how their images are being captured and used, there will be a backlash: "I do suspect that people are going to kind of grab back their privacy rights at some point, but we're not there yet."

Hendricks also thinks that there will be a backlash to the intrusion, but by then the 30 cameras won't just be everywhere—they'll be hooked together: "These cameras will be integrated into a network just the way that computers were by the Internet."

There are some small efforts to combat the proliferation of this style of public broadcasting. In Arizona, state Rep. Gabrielle Giffords recently introduced legislation that would require notification of video surveillance in public places, but the bill languished in committee and then was superseded by another bill (which also died) that would have created a committee to study the issue. Giffords plans to reintroduce the legislation next session.

Still, for now it seems that we have as much control over our images in public spaces as do the inmates of Madison Street Jail. "If you're in a public place, you don't have much defense, unless your image is being used for commercial purposes," says Thomas Coleman, author of "It's Mine, Not Yours! Take Back Your Personal Information and Privacy." And if there used to be no easy way for the images from the cameras in the Madison Street Jail to make it into your living room, now there's an easy way for your own image to go places that you can't even picture. ○

SEEING

1. Mieszkowski asks: "Is your image property you own or something you give up by venturing out in public?" (para. 10). How does she answer the question in the article? Based on her writing, what answer would you give? Find evidence in her writing to support each of your assertions.

2. What is Mieszkowski's opinion about organizations that record people's public images? What techniques does she use to imply what she thinks without directly stating her opinion? Find one paragraph where Mieszkowski's opinion is especially obvious but unspoken. Rewrite the paragraph so that no one can tell what the author's opinion is on the subject, and then compare the two paragraphs. Which one is more fun to read? Why?

WRITING

1. Watch a "live" sports event for at least a half hour. Instead of looking at the competitors, look at the audience. Try to focus on one or two people and observe them carefully. Write down as many details as you can about what they are wearing, how they act, who they are with, and so on. After the game, draft a short biography of the people you observed. Try to explain who they are, what their life is like, and why they are at the game. For the last paragraph, offer a written speculation about how they would respond if they knew that someone was giving their images such attention.

2. Photographic metaphors tend to be violent. You *take* someone's picture. Images are *captured*. "That's a great *shot*." If you speak another language, write down all the ways that people talk about taking pictures in that language. How are that language's metaphors similar to the ones used in English? To what extent are they different? In what ways do the differences affect how people in that culture think about taking pictures? If you don't speak another language, interview someone who does. Write an essay in which you compare and contrast how the interviewee's language is used to describe taking photographs with how your own language is used, and then answer the above questions.

"You have the right to remain silent. Anything you say may be used against you in a court of law, newspapers, periodicals, radio, television, all electronic media, and technologies yet to be invented."

Re: Searching the Web

Since Katharine Mieszkowski wrote "Nowhere Left to Hide," the events of September 11, 2001, have increased the demand for and development of digital technology that captures and analyzes images. Face- and fingerprint-recognition technology used at airports and for access to other public spaces is heralded as a necessary preventative measure by some and as a dangerous infringement on civil liberties by others. The issue of surveillance and privacy on the Internet—where the interactive nature of the medium makes tracking individual habits effortless—raises still other privacy debates. Once downloaded, for example, software called "spyware" tracks the web sites you visit, records how long you spend on each page, gathers personal data, and then sends back a user profile to marketing companies that automatically serve up carefully targeted ads.

Go to a news site with a focus on technology such as Wired News <www.wired.com>, the *Washington Post's* tech news section <www.technews.com>, or an organization devoted to online privacy such as the Online Privacy Alliance <www.privacyalliance.org> or the Privacy Foundation <www.privacyfoundation.org/resources/webbug.asp>. Gather as much reliable information as you can on spyware or another current issue in privacy related to Internet usage, such as "web bugs." Then write an essay in which you argue for or against the use of spyware or similar software.

KARAL ANN MARLING

Karal Ann Marling (b. 1943) is a professor of American studies and art history at the University of Minnesota. She has been a visiting professor at various universities, including Harvard and the University of Wyoming.

Marling's many books include *Iwo Jima: Monuments, Memorials and the American Hero* (1991); *As Seen on TV: The Visual Culture of Everyday Life in the 1950s* (1994), which was awarded a 1995 Minnesota Book Award for History; *Graceland: Going Home with Elvis* (1997); *Designing Disney's Theme Parks: The Architecture of Reassurance* (1997); and *The Colossus of Roads: Myth and Symbol along the American Highway* (2000).

The Karal Ann Marling Collection of Papers on New Deal Art Programs, a collection of photocopies of correspondence, publications, and newspaper clippings created by and about the original federal programs (1916–1949), resides at the Case Western Reserve University Library site. "In this atmosphere in which the Taliban and other fundamentalists are screaming that there is something decadent, corrupt, and deeply horrible about American media and pop culture," said Marling in a recent interview, "it might behoove Americans to reexamine some of them. We're looking at these objects that are products of our commercial culture, whether it's the movies or Coca-Cola bottles that are the images America carries abroad." "They Want Their Mean TV" first appeared in the *New York Times* in 2002.

They Want Their Mean TV

Karal Ann Marling

The traditional network tv season peters out every spring shortly before the school year does, and from where this professor sits, television has been O.K. this year—a B or a B-plus. But why trust me? I'm in that pathetic demographic nobody pays any attention to—the "early geezers" that advertisers write off or consign to a bleak celebration of incontinence products and denture cleaners beginning with the nightly news.

For what it's worth, though, I thought life was rosy on the major-network prime-time dramas that I follow, much to the amusement of my cable-savvy students. Except when somebody's contract expired, necessitating an off-camera exit via brain tumor, *E.R., N.Y.P.D. Blue, West Wing,* and my other old favorites were satisfying because the formula guarantees speedy resolution of all life's problems. At the end of the hour, the Constitution, common sense, or good science has restored order. Life goes on, with a reassuring feeling that things always turn out fine in a nation governed by laws, rules, and human kindness.

But for that other group of viewers, the younger ones, the channel-surfers, the 56 percent of American kids with sets in their own bedrooms—my students and their siblings!—must-see TV apparently doesn't cut it. They're made of sterner stuff; they tell me they prefer to troll on the dark end of the dial, where the larger numbers appear and where the bottom-feeders play.

Where, for instance, *Jackass* subjected a guy wearing a cup to a series of kicks and whams in his most tender area courtesy of his so-called friends. "Don't try this at home!" read the disclaimers, aimed at preventing seventh-grade fans from maiming one another just for the fun of it. (Despite the copious disclaimers, copycats have been injured, seriously in at least one case. Undeterred, the show—now in reruns—will spawn a major motion picture this summer.) Or where the syndicated *Blind Date* has couples engage in meanspirited postmortems about each other, for a scintillating balance of sex and verbal violence. Dating shows are a particularly rich vein of this modern maliciousness: *Change of Heart, Dismissed, Elimidate Deluxe.*

And there is worse lurking in between the home shopping pitches and the infomercials for devices to refill your printer's ink cartridges: an unbridled meanness that represents the flip side of the entertainment of optimism purveyed to those who follow *E.R.* But why? What have we of the Geritol set done wrong?

It is no news that humiliation—other people's discomfort—is pleasurable stuff. Back in the "golden age" of TV, inane game shows like *Beat the Clock* made human contestants do stupid pet tricks for prizes, long before David Letterman applied the idea to poodles and parakeets. The Nielsen ratings for the second week of May show that this meanness has begun to creep into the major networks' prime-time lineups. The most recent incarnation of *Survivor* was in seventh place (behind *E.R.* and *Law and Order*), with *Fear Factor* and *The Amazing Race* in the top 50.

These so-called "reality" shows are about watching ordinary—albeit cute-in-a-swimsuit—people sweat, fret, scream, scheme, eat bugs, and diss one another in nastily amazing ways. And the younger members of the Nielsen families seem to look on with real interest, or with the same sort of horrified fascination that makes local TV stations speed to the scene of traffic accidents. They admit to loving the insect-eating and the trash-talking. They're mesmerized by the cable aesthetic, though a little puzzled, too. Why do the "contestants" do it? For the exposure, say some, with dreams of minor stardom in mind. For the money. For the fun?

I think reality TV may be symptomatic of a broader trend toward cultural nastiness that crept up on us with the advent of Jerry, Maury, Ricki, Montel, and the other professional talkers who specialize in bleeping and screaming, as "guests" are subjected to verbal assaults from former spouses or secret gay admirers. (In the notorious Jenny Jones case, an actual off-camera murder ensued.) The tears and curses and venomous exchanges make any outlandish soap opera plot pale by comparison. But the question remains: What makes Americans watch? Is it a kind of bizarre revival of slapstick, a banana-peel joke raised to a surreal pitch? Is it an offshoot of the politics of accusation, exposé, sleaze, and attack ads that dominated the Clinton years? Is Monica Lewinsky the mother of Fox? Is this what TV is all about for today's undergraduates?

The fact that the panels of combatants aren't stars in full makeup is important: it's easier to wish ill to an un-pretty, un-famous face with missing teeth and acne scars. There's a class bias at work, too. Clearly, these shrieking, incest-ridden families are not our kind of people. They're "trailer trash," with home-bleached hair and cheap nose jobs: Tonya Harding and Paula Jones, who recently duked it out on Fox (only because the courts wouldn't let Amy Fisher appear), don't have Ivy League diplomas and they don't shop at Talbots. And voyeurs everywhere can feel superior to Paula—whereas it's not so easy to put on airs in the televised presence of, say, Jennifer Aniston or Sarah Jessica Parker.

Coinciding with the end of the TV season have come the results of an opinion poll conducted by the New York–based research group Public Agenda. Of the 2,013 respondents, 70 percent decried the collapse of courtesy and respect for others in real life, out there on the highway where road rage prevails, in public places where trumpeting one's private business into cell phones is the norm, and on sidewalks where the elderly and the infirm are routinely mowed down by the hurrying mob. The adults polled were quick to blame television for what they saw as a surge in bad behavior, and it is hard to disagree after an evening of "hilarious" home videos, with a studio audience in stitches when the bride trips and splats into the wedding cake. Or when Dr. Phil, the TV psychologist, rivets the attention of Oprah's followers by telling overweight guests that they really want to be that way. It's all their fault, in other words; they're dumb and lazy. Meanness in the name of pop psychology is still meanness, even if Dr. Phil smiles like a crazed alligator while calling down anathema on the unhappy people who seek his help.

The medium might be the real message here: nasty television produces nasty audiences. The undergraduates I teach often behave in what we fogeys regard as a boorish manner, reminiscent of the resi-

dents of the *Big Brother* house. They wear their hats indoors. They chomp noisily on snacks during class. They fiddle with their backpacks, snicker with their friends, let their cell phones ring and their watches beep away the quarter hours. Now, none of this is meant to be irritating or disrespectful; indeed, they are indignant if I point out that I'm not a TV set but a sensate, hardworking professor who is looking right at them. They have forgotten that a lecture is not a spectacle, a talk show minus commercials (a surprising number have to answer a call of nature about 20 minutes into a 50-minute class). That life is not viewed in one's living room, where mindless activity—rustling, ribpoking—rather than quiet attention seems to be the norm.

It's unconsidered spectatorship, I think, that fosters the birth of these good-natured barbarians in my lecture hall. The young are perpetual onlookers to their own lives, thanks to TV: they have no responsibility for the yelling and the bloodshed—no stake in the mayhem, which makes it all too easy to enjoy wickedness from a distance. Merely watching things happen absolves the viewer of any responsibility for them. Those are somebody else's troubles on the screen, and, as such, of no real consequence to the kid with the bag of Doritos in the third row of my morning class, the lumpy kid with the Minnesota Twins cap on backward. The hurts of the chubby lady talking to Dr. Phil are no more real than the agonies of Wile E. Coyote, flattened by a steamroller. It's all TV. In a culture of images, we watch and we judge, and call for a pizza and wings, delivered. With a mouthful of Doritos, it is hard to empathize.

At the same time, the genteel, predictable, feel-good fare offered by the major networks (with more

to come next season, to calm post-9/11 trauma) is not of much interest to Generation Y or Z, or so their members tell me. For the clear-eyed young, the familiar dramatic conventions of conflict and resolution offer neither comfort nor stimulus: even in the bosom of the university, life is tougher than that, less predictable, and pretty nasty—at opposite poles from old-fashioned, denture-wearing, *Leave It to Beaver* TV-land, where everything turns out fine every time the clock ticks off another hour between 8 p.m. and 11 p.m. If questioned closely, my students will confess a passion for *I Love Lucy* reruns. They hate *Friends*, but they like the fact that the solutions to the problems posed every episode by Lucy's zany insistence on a show-biz career are so bogus. They like the fact that Lucy will forever go on stuffing chocolates down her dress and making herself sick on patent medicine—that her life will always be a mess, until she divorces Desi, dies, and finally turns up in a highly rated CBS special emceed by her children.

Ever since Newton Minow, the F.C.C. chairman, called much of television a "vast wasteland" in 1961, Americans have been blaming it indiscriminately for every social ill, from the rise of the hippies to the bad manners of people who talk in movie theaters. But old-fashioned hourlong drama can, perhaps, be indicted for being so predictable, so formulaic, so comfortable that young viewers go looking for a little edge—and wind up in the clutches of Mean TV, Naked TV, Innuendo TV, Splat TV, and the other channels where passing gas is a mark of sophisticated drollery. Meanwhile, the fogeys nod off over their glasses of constipation remedy, believing that it's prime time in America, so everything must be fine. ○

1. What does the word *tone* mean when used to describe writing rather than sound? Describe and characterize Marling's overall tone in this article. Where does she change her tone? (Point to specific words and phrases to verify your reading.) Why does she change it where she does? How does her overall tone affect the argument? Which parts of the argument would have been less effective if they had been written in a different tone? Why? Which parts would have been more effective in a different tone? Why?

2. How many different styles of humor can you identify in Marling's piece? Find examples of ironic, sarcastic, deadpan, glib, and dry humor. What does Marling's use of humor contribute to the overall effect of the essay? Do you think humor helps make her argument more effective? Why or why not?

1. Imagine yourself as one of the students that Marling describes. For example, imagine that you're in her class as the student eating Doritos, or the student with a hat on backwards. Write a response from that student to Professor Marling. How would the student defend himself or herself? What types of behavior would the student attribute to Marling's own television-watching habits (and those she had as a child)?

2. Read Gerard Jones's "Killing Monsters" (see p. 582). Then write an essay in which you compare and contrast Jones's and Marling's positions on the effect television has on young people. How would Jones respond to some of Marling's points? How would Marling respond to some of Jones's? Choose a few passages—one from each writer—that strongly oppose each other. Write a brief argument that supports one passage over the other. For example, you might compare Jones's belief that violent imagery gave him a fantasy self who is "unhesitating and effective in action" (para. 4) with Marling's belief that television makes young people "perpetual onlookers to their own lives" (para. 12).

Visualizing Composition
Point of View

Whether we are responding to what someone else has written or generating our own prose, the question of point of view has always been at the center of effective reading and writing: From whose "eye" do we see the story being told or the points being made in an argument? This fundamental question leads to two other aspects of point of view that deserve special attention from writers and readers:

1. What is the *perspective* from which a story is told or a line of reasoning is developed?
2. What particular *bias* is immediately evident—or eventually surfaces—in that perspective?

Most of us can recall the moments in our high school English class when our teacher first directed our attention to thinking about how narrative is structured in works of fiction. Many of us still carry a useful distinction when responding to reading fiction: An author writes a story; someone else—a narrator—tells the story.

On the surface, determining a writer's point of view seems relatively simple: Pay attention to the writer's use of pronouns. For example, personal narrative is distinguished by the writer's "I"—be it an autobiographical essay (such as Judith Ortiz Cofer's "The Story of My Body" on p. 314) or a work of literary fiction, such as Mark Twain's *Huckleberry Finn* or J. D. Salinger's *Catcher in the Rye*. In these two classic novels, a character narrates the story from a distinctive first-person point of view. Yet, not all first-person narrators need be the central figure in the narrative. (Consider, for example, Marlow in Joseph Conrad's novels *The Heart of Darkness* and *Lord Jim*.)

Other writers rely on third-person narration to tell their story: "she said," "he did," "they decided," and the like. This point of view is usually limited to the perspective of a single character and can involve exploring the mind of that character. A more all-encompassing perspective is called omniscient point of view: The author creates a narrator who stands, almost godlike, outside the people and events being described and occupies an "all-seeing" position. In such instances, the narrator not only can observe and describe the action but also can see into the minds of the characters and account for what motivates them.

As you think about point of view in your own writing, you should also consider how your perspective has a particular built-in bias. We are using "bias" here to signal the preference(s) or inclination(s) that surface in writing, especially ones that inhibit impartial judgment. As

you read and revise your drafts, attending to the bias of your point of view can be one of the most effective means of strengthening your credibility and increasing the impact of your writing. The basic compositional purpose of point of view is simple enough: Establish a clear and consistent point of view, and attend to the prejudices built into it.

Carefully examine the advertisements reprinted here. What points of view can you identify in the exchanges among a bottle of vodka and a tomato and an orange? What perspective and bias are evident in the point of view from which each character speaks? Prepare the first draft of what you envision could be the next ad in this sequence, one in which you use playful banter to convince your audience that buying Wolfschmidt's vodka will improve their social lives.

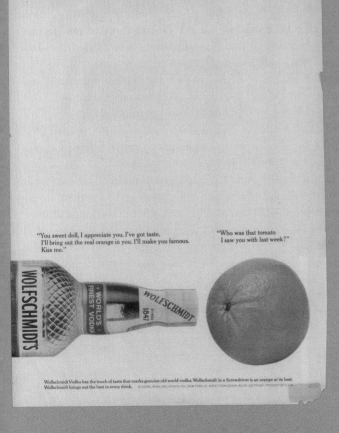

"You sweet doll, I appreciate you. I've got taste. I'll bring out the real orange in you. I'll make you famous. Kiss me."

"Who was that tomato I saw you with last week?"

Wolfschmidt Vodka has the touch of taste that marks genuine old world vodka. Wolfschmidt in a Screwdriver is an orange at its best. Wolfschmidt brings out the best in every drink.

GERARD JONES >
As a former comic writer and artist, Gerard Jones collaborated on many iconic comics such as *Batman, Spider-Man, Superman,* and the *Green Lantern.* He also developed his own line of heroes and villains (Ultraforce, Prime, The Trouble with Girls, and The Haunted Man, to name a few) and has adapted Japanese comics and cartoons for the English-speaking world. Many of his fictional characters serve as the basis for a dazzling array of paraphernalia from simple books to 3-D video games marketed across the globe.

More recently, he has made a name for himself by describing why it is that children respond so readily to violent toys and imaginative games. His book *Killing Monsters: Why Children Need Fantasy, Superheroes, and Make Believe Violence* (2002, in which the essay reprinted here first appeared) directly tackles this issue, but his previous books, *The Beaver Papers* (1984), *Honey I'm Home: Sitcoms Selling the American Dream* (1993), and *The Comic Book Heroes* (1996), have also touched on this subject. To this end, he has also appeared on television and radio news programs including "Nightline" with Ted Koppel, NPR's "Fresh Air" with Terry Gross, and the BBC World News. His articles have appeared in *Harper's,* the *New York Times,* the *Boston Globe,* and other publications. Today he is working with other children's advocates and media experts to develop an organization to help understand and harness the power of entertainment for the benefit of children.

KILLING MONSTERS

GERARD JONES

At thirteen I was alone and afraid. Taught by my well-meaning, progressive, English-teacher parents that violence was wrong, that rage was something to be overcome and cooperation was always better than conflict, I suffocated my deepest fears and desires under a nice-boy persona. Placed in a small, experimental school that was wrong for me, afraid to join my peers in their bumptious rush into adolescent boyhood, I withdrew into passivity and loneliness. My parents, not trusting the violent world of the late 1960s, built a wall between me and the crudest elements of American pop culture.

Then the Incredible Hulk smashed through it.

One of my mother's students convinced her that Marvel Comics, despite their apparent juvenility and violence, were in fact devoted to lofty messages of pacifism and tolerance. My mother borrowed some for me, thinking they'd be good for me. And so they were. Not because they preached lofty messages but because, beneath their literary ambitions, they were juvenile. And violent.

The character who caught me, and freed me, was the Hulk: overgendered and undersocialized, half-naked and half-witted, raging against a frightened world that misunderstood and persecuted him. Suddenly I had a fantasy self to carry my stifled rage and buried desire for power. I had a fantasy self who *was* a self: unafraid of his desires and the world's disapproval, unhesitating and effective in action. "Puny boy follow Hulk!" roared my fantasy self, and I followed.

I followed him to new friends—other sensitive geeks chasing their own inner 5 brutes—and I followed him to the arrogant, self-exposing, self-assertive, super-heroic decision to become a writer. Eventually, I left him behind, followed more sophisticated heroes, and finally my own lead along a twisting path to a career and an identity. In my thirties, I found myself writing action movies and comic books. I wrote some Hulk stories and met the geek-geniuses who created him. I saw my own creations turned into action figures, cartoons, and computer games. I talked to the kids who read my stories. Across generations, genders, and ethnicities I kept seeing the same story: people pulling themselves out of emotional traps by immersing themselves in violent stories. People integrating the scariest, most fervently denied fragments of their psyches into fuller senses of selfhood through fantasies of superhuman combat and destruction.

I have watched my son living the same story—transforming himself into a bloodthirsty dinosaur to embolden himself for the plunge into preschool, a Power Ranger to muscle through a social competition in kindergarten. In the first grade, his friends started climbing a tree at school. But he was afraid: of falling, of the centipedes crawling on the trunk, of sharp branches, of his friends' derision. I took my cue from his own fantasies and read him old *Tarzan* comics, rich in combat and bright with flashing knives. For two weeks he lived in them. Then he put them aside. And he climbed the tree.

But all the while, especially in the wake of the recent burst of school shootings, I heard pop psychologists insisting that violent stories are harmful to kids, heard teachers begging parents to keep their kids away from "junk culture," heard a guilt-stricken friend with a son who loved *Pokémon* lament, "I've turned into the bad mom who lets her kid eat sugary cereal and watch cartoons!"

That's when I started the research.

"Stories are how we learn what it is to be human," says Diane Stern, a clinical psychologist and mother of two boys. "And it's through stories about behavior that's normally forbidden to them that children can experience and accept the parts of themselves we don't normally allow them to. For a child always told to behave, stand in line, do his homework, treat people nicely, contain his anger, hide his fear, stories of violence and destruction can be a tremendous relief. Every piece of entertainment is a story, and while we don't usually do whatever we heard someone else did in a story, hearing it or seeing it helps us better understand other people and the other sides of ourselves. Every story makes us more complete."

Stern is one of the many psychologists and educators I've been consulting over 10 the past four years in developing my Art and Story Workshops, in-class programs to help young people improve their self-knowledge and sense of potency through storytelling. They've helped me learn a great deal about the ways in which children use stories, including violent ones, to meet their emotional and developmental needs—and the ways in which adults can help them use those stories healthily.

I've found that every aspect of even the trashiest pop-culture story can have its own developmental function. Pretending to have superhuman powers helps children conquer the feelings of powerlessness that inevitably come with being so young and small, even in the most child-centered homes. The dual-identity concept at the heart of many superhero stories helps kids negotiate the conflicts between the inner self and the public self as they work through the early stages of socialization. Identification with a rebellious, even destructive, hero helps children learn to push back against a modern culture that cultivates fear and teaches dependency.

At its most fundamental level, what I call *creative violence*—head-bonking cartoons, bloody videogames, playground karate, toy guns—gives children a tool to master their rage. Children will feel rage. Even the sweetest and most civilized of them, even those whose parents read the better class of literary magazines, will feel rage. The world is uncontrollable and incomprehensible; mastering it is a terrifying, enraging task. Rage can be an energizing emotion, a shot of courage to push us to resist greater threats, take more control, than we ever thought we could. But rage is also the emotion our culture distrusts the most. Most of us are taught early on to fear our own. Through immersion in imaginary combat and identification with a violent protagonist, children engage the rage they've stifled, come to fear it less, and become more capable of utilizing it against life's challenges.

I knew one little girl who went around exploding with fantasies so violent that other moms would draw her mother aside to whisper, "I think you should know something about Emily. . . ." Her parents were separating, and she was small, an only child, a tomboy at an age when her classmates were dividing sharply along gender lines. On the playground she acted out "Sailor Moon" fights, and in the classroom she wrote stories about people being stabbed with knives. The more adults tried to control her stories, the more she acted out the roles of her angry heroes: breaking rules, testing limits, roaring threats.

Then her mother and I started helping her tell her stories. She wrote them, performed them, drew them like comics: sometimes bloody, sometimes tender, always blending the images of pop culture with her own most private fantasies. She came out of it just as fiery and strong, but more self-controlled and socially competent: a leader among peers, the one student in her class who could truly pull boys and girls together.

I worked with an older girl, a middle-class "nice girl," who held herself together 15 through a chaotic family situation and a tumultuous adolescence with gangsta rap.

In the mythologized street violence of Ice-T, the rage and strutting of his music and lyrics, she found a theater of the mind in which she could be powerful, ruthless, invulnerable. She avoided the heavy drug use that sank many of her peers, and flowered in college as a writer and political activist.

I'm not going to argue that violent entertainment is harmless. I think it has helped inspire some people to real-life violence. I am going to argue that it's helped hundreds of people for every one it's hurt, and that it can help far more if we learn to use it well. I am going to argue that our fear of "youth violence" isn't well-founded on reality, and that the fear can do more harm than the reality. We act as though our highest priority is to prevent our children from growing up into murderous thugs—but modern kids are far more likely to grow up too passive, too distrustful of themselves, too easily manipulated.

We send the message to our children in a hundred ways that their craving for imaginary gun battles and symbolic killings is wrong, or at least dangerous. Even when we don't call for censorship or forbid *Mortal Kombat*, we moan to other parents within our kids' earshot about the "awful violence" in the entertainment they love. We tell our kids that it isn't nice to play-fight, or we steer them from some monstrous action figure to a pro-social doll. Even in the most progressive households, where we make such a point of letting children feel what they feel, we rush to substitute an enlightened discussion for the raw material of rageful fantasy. In the process, we risk confusing them about their natural aggression in the same way the Victorians confused their children about their sexuality. When we try to protect our children from their own feelings and fantasies, we shelter them not against violence but against power and selfhood. ○

SEEING

1. According to Jones, violent media is good for which children? Look for evidence to identify the type of young people whom Jones has in mind. What kinds of children do you imagine from these indications? Looking at Jones's examples, why does violent imagery help these youngsters? What kinds of children do not fit Jones's stereotype? What would Jones say about violent media's effect on these other young people?

2. Describe the effect that violent comic books had on Jones as a young teenager. What generalization does he extrapolate from his personal experience? Does he rely only on his (and his son's) experience to buttress his argument? What evidence does Jones use to support his conclusion that violent media can be good for people? Do you find his argument convincing?

WRITING

1. Keep a note pad and a pencil with you for a day. Starting in the morning, make a mark every time you see a violent image in some kind of media (television, newspaper, magazine, video game, web site, etc.). At the end of the day, count how many violent images you have encountered. How many of those images do you think were good for you in the way(s) that Jones says they are? Just for fun, multiply your number by 7. That's how many violent images you typically encounter in a week. Multiply by 365. That's how many you encounter in a year. Now write an expository essay in which you explore the relationship between violent images seen and crimes committed. How many images do you think are necessary to be seen before the therapeutic effect Jones argues for takes effect? What do the rest do?

2. In his essay, "Inside Every Superhero Lurks a Nerd" (p. 439), Neal Gabler argues that movies are about "wish fulfillment" and the great film stars "are the ones with whom viewers identify and through whom they can transcend themselves." Write an essay in which you compare and contrast Gabler's characterization of the appeal of Spider-Man to Jones's assertions about the developmental functions of stories in pop-culture. In what ways do their arguments overlap? How do they differ? What research and anecdotal evidence does each author use to support his claim?

KILLING MONSTERS
GERARD JONES

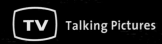

TV Talking Pictures

When movie-goers watched the characters in *ET: The Extra-Terrestrial* (1982) munching on Reese's Pieces, the candy's sales shot up by 65 percent and the brand became a household name. Since then, the nature of product placements in TV and film has become more and more sophisticated. As one media critic put it, "Nowadays, the movie and TV industries are molding products, logos, and slogans into the very building blocks of popular culture—often without audiences realizing it." In Steven Spielberg's film *Minority Report* (2002), for example, the actor Tom Cruise drives a futuristic Lexus developed for the movie by Toyota. "I've been driving a Lexus SUV," commented Spielberg, "and I thought Lexus might be interested in holding hands with us and going into a speculative future to see what the transportation systems and cars would look like on our highways in 50 years."

Watch a few hours of prime-time TV or a feature-length film. How many brand name products can you identify? How often is each product shown? Which kinds of products seem to be displayed more often than others? To what extent do you notice a relationship between the type of product placement and the anticipated audience? To what extent would you characterize these product placements as "successful"? Why or why not? Write an expository essay in which you identify and analyze the nature of the product placements in a specific TV show or film.

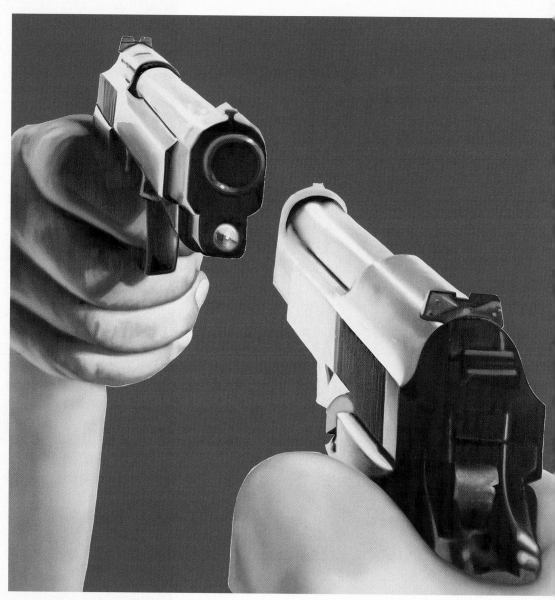

James Rosenquist, **Professional Courtesy,** 1996

JAMES ROSENQUIST

James Rosenquist (b. 1933) made a name for himself by combining popular and easily recognizable images with contemporary military and mechanical hardware. His work first gained notoriety when he showed *President Elect*, in which sex and automobile imagery are layered over John F. Kennedy's face, during Kennedy's election campaign year. In 1965 he made the 26-meter-wide picture *F-111*, which was shown worldwide and is still considered to be his signature work. This brightly colored panorama features images of an adorable blonde-haired girl under an industrial hair dryer, an angel food cake, tinned spaghetti, the words "U.S. AIR FORCE," a nuclear explosion, and a Firestone tire, all pasted across the length of an F-111 fighter plane.

In the introduction to his book *Target Practice* (from which the painting shown here is taken) Rosenquist wrote, "I want to illustrate the stark look and confrontation of a handgun. . . . Young people are confused by the way guns are depicted in the movies and on television. It shows the hero being shot, getting up, brushing himself off, and then going on to act in another movie—becoming an even bigger star. The reality of being shot is really death forever and a big flame usually comes out of a real gun. These paintings are intended to be nondecorative and oblique. I hope they question the idea of who really is the target."

Rosenquist's paintings reside permanently in such major collections as the Guggenheim Museum and the Chicago Art Institute among many others.

SEEING

1. How would you characterize the overall effect of this painting? What aspects of it is your eye most drawn to? Why? Rosenquist's painting measures 4 feet by 4 feet. What does this considerably reduced reproduction gain or lose by virtue of its size when compared with the original? What kinds of shapes, colors, and details become more or less important as the image becomes larger or smaller? Why? How does reducing the size of the painting change its impact on the viewer? Which aspects of the painting would you need to change to make the smaller image have the same impact as the original painting?

2. Rosenquist characterizes the series of paintings that includes *Professional Courtesy* in the following terms: "These paintings are intended to be nondecorative and oblique." What does he mean by each of these words, and especially in this context? Under the headings "nondecorative" and "oblique," list specific features in the painting that would justify each adjective as an appropriate characterization of it. Consider, for example, color, shape, style, and relations between and among these elements.

WRITING

1. A commonplace saying is that "Every picture tells a story." What story does Rosenquist's painting tell? Imagine that the painting is a photograph. Write the first draft of a narrative that tells the story of how the picture came to be. Make your story as realistic as possible, and account for such obvious features as the two guns, the two hands, the red background, as well as less obvious aspects of it: the shadows, the position of the photographer, and so on.

2. In everyday language, "professional courtesy" normally means being helpful to someone who works in the same field. In what ways does the painting play with this meaning? How do the historical meanings of the words connect with the current meaning of the painting? For example, the word *professional* comes from the word *profess*, which is made up of the Greek prefix *pro* (which indicated motion from a source to a target) and *phatos* (which can be translated as "claim" or "statement"). A professional is like a gun, then, because whereas a gun shoots bullets, a professional produces expert statements. Write an expository essay in which you account for how the two sets of meaning (historical and current) work together to enrich the painting's message and significance.

Office of National Drug Control Policy, **Tommy**

OFFICE OF NATIONAL DRUG CONTROL POLICY

The White House Office of National Drug Control Policy (ONDCP) is a branch of the Executive Office of the President. The ONDCP was born out of the Anti-Drug Abuse Act of 1988, and its aim is to establish policies, priorities, and objectives for the country's drug control program in order to reduce illicit drug use, manufacturing, and trafficking; drug-related crime and violence; and drug-related health consequences. The director of ONDCP, also known as the nation's "Drug Czar," controls the National Drug Control Strategy, which directs the nation's anti-drug efforts and puts in place a program, a budget, and guidelines for cooperation among federal, state, and local entities.

Print advertisements like this one are sponsored by the National Youth Anti-Drug Media Campaign, which is an arm of the ONDCP. These ads and other similar public service messages are broadcast on <www.mediacampaign.org> and can be translated into Spanish, Cambodian, Chinese, Korean, and Vietnamese. The George W. Bush administration formulated the message illustrated by the "Tommy" ad that parent-to-child communication is the key to keeping kids off drugs.

SEEING

1. This advertisement presents the seemingly contradictory idea that surveillance is compatible with individual freedom. How does the picture work to make this idea seem reasonable? Why would the parents of this boy agree that keeping an eye on him is still letting him be himself? What is there about the boy in the picture that lets the viewer know he needs someone to watch him? What details indicate that the boy might be in danger of becoming a drug user?

2. Compare the use of colors in the picture to the use of colors in the text. For example, consider orange. Why is the word *watch* the same color as the logo on the right side of the boy's jacket and the highlight band around "Talk > Know > Ask >..."? In other words, how does the use of that particular color tie those particular elements together? Also, look at contrasting colors like the bright colors of the boy's shirt and jacket in contrast with the gray color of the street. How do the contrasts contribute to the advertisement's message?

WRITING

1. Imagine that you're this boy's parent. Write an expository essay in which you describe how you would go about watching him. Create a detailed surveillance schedule that includes as many ways of monitoring him as you can envision. Let your imagination flow. You can imagine such activities as phone tapping, e-mail monitoring, hiring informers, and the like. How might thinking of your child as someone you need to keep an eye on change your relationship with him for the better? for the worse?

2. What are the laws governing children's rights to privacy? What kinds of things can be done without a child's permission? What kinds of things cannot be done? How do the laws change as the child grows into a teenager? Which of them do you think are justified? You might use a search engine to find an advocacy group (such as the Electronic Privacy Information Center at <http://epic.org>) that offers information on these issues. Write the first draft of an argumentative essay in which you advocate for specific changes in the current law.

Visualizing Context
History Repeats Itself

No other public service announcement is perhaps more famous than the television spot created and sponsored by the Partnership for a Drug Free America in 1987. Directed by Joe Pytka, this advertisement has achieved iconic status within the advertising industry. The advertisement features contrasting images of the brain—in a normal state and on drugs. "This is your brain," a confident voice announces over the image of a brain at rest. As we watch an egg being fried in a pan, the voiceover solemnly intones: "This is your brain on drugs."

In 2001, the Partnership issued an updated remake of the "This is your brain" spot entitled *Frying Pan*. The new advertisement features actor Rachael Leigh Cook destroying an entire kitchen with a frying pan—a demonstration of the effects of heroin addiction. "This is what happens to you, your friends and family when you're taking heroin," declares the voiceover.

Partnership for a Drug Free America, **This Is Your Brain on Drugs**

This historical context informs the "Tommy" anti-drug ad by the Office of National Drug Control Policy reprinted on page 590. As you examine this ad carefully, identify the approaches the Partnership has taken toward communicating its message to a new generation of young people. How—and to what extent—have its core message, rhetorical strategies, techniques, and methods changed over the past few decades?

The Office of National Drug Control Policy maintains a comprehensive web site <www.mediacampaign.org>, where you can view and study its latest anti-drug commercials and print advertisements. Choose two different advertisements from this site. Write an expository essay in which you compare and contrast the message and rhetorical strategies and techniques used in the two ads. To what specific audience (age, socioeconomic group, ethnic group, etc.) is each advertisement addressed? Which do you judge more successful? Explain why. (You might consider, for example, comparing and contrasting an advertisement targeted toward caregivers with one addressed to teenagers.)

SEBASTIÃO SALGADO >

"More than ever, I feel that the human race is one. There are differences of color, language, culture, and opportunities, but people's feelings and reactions are alike. People flee wars to escape death, they migrate to improve their fortunes, they build new lives in foreign lands, they adapt to extreme hardship. . . ." Brazilian photojournalist Sebastião Salgado begins his book *Migrations: Humanity in Transition* (2000) with these lines that almost needlessly express what the reader is about to see. Working only in black and white images, which lend dignity and grace to serious subjects, Salgado has a reputation for capturing the downtrodden in his camera lens in a way that makes his subjects suddenly impossible to ignore.

Born in 1944 in Brazil, Salgado trained as an economist, earning a doctorate from the University of Paris in 1971. After borrowing his wife's camera on a trip to Africa, Salgado switched careers and began working as a photojournalist in 1973. Since then he has spent his entire professional life chronicling the existence of the poor and dispossessed around the world. He has published many collections of his work, most recently *The Children: Refugees and Migrants* (2000) and *Terra: Struggle of the Landless* (1997). Sebastião Salgado has been twice named Photographer of the Year by the International Center of Photography. He was appointed a UNICEF (United Nations International Children's Emergency Fund) special representative in 2001. Salgado currently resides in Paris, France, with his family.

Sebastião Salgado, **São Paulo, Brazil,** 1996
This photograph shows abandoned babies playing on the roof of a FEBEM center in the Pacaembu district of São Paulo against a backdrop of middle-class apartment buildings. Some 430 children live here, 35 percent of whom were found abandoned on city streets; the others were delivered at the center by parents no longer able to care for them. According to FEBEM, the proportion of abandoned children in the city long averaged 10 percent, but has recently risen sharply.

Sebastião Salgado, **Southern Sudan,** 1993

Both the government and the rebels try to capture boys and force them to fight in the civil war tearing apart southern Sudan. So, from an early age, the youths are sent away by their families. They leave in groups, by neighborhoods or villages, and head for northern Kenya to become refugees in camps run by the United Nations. Traveling through southern Sudan, I frequently came across groups of young boys, dishevelled and hungry, half-hiding out of fear, sometimes just resting on their long treks south.

Sebastião Salgado, **Bombay, India,** 1995
A pipeline carrying drinking water to more prosperous districts of Bombay passes through the shanty-town of Mahim, not far from the city's airport. Most of Bombay's inhabitants live in slums, many of them embedded in middle-class neighborhoods.

Sebastião Salgado, **Galang Island, Indonesia,** 1995
At the entrance of the detention camp on Galang Island, Indonesia, stands a copy of the Statue of Liberty, with the dove of freedom in one hand and flowers in the other. Sculpted by a refugee, it symbolizes the desire to go to the United States and live the American dream.

Sebastião Salgado, **State of Roraima, Brazil,** 1998
The majority of the territory of the State of Roraima has one of the oldest geological formations of the world. The deforestation by settlers and cattle ranchers has provoked erosion on a disastrous scale.

SEEING

1. These photographs are part of a series entitled *Migrations: Humanity in Transition.* Yet, they seem to conjure up images beyond migration, humanity, or transition. What rationale can you articulate about why the pictures that don't seem to be about these concepts are included in Salgado's series? What does the picture of deforestation, for example, have to do with humanity? What does the picture of the water pipeline have to do with migration? the Statue of Liberty with transition?

2. Identify all the features that the photographs have in common. Make a list of simple observations that are true about each of the photographs. Using what you know about drawing reasonable inferences from simple observations, what reasonable (that is, supported by evidence) inferences about Salgado as a photographer might you draw from these images? Based on the evidence you have here, what does a scene need to attract his eye? How does he like to compose his shots? What is the typical Salgado photograph like? How do Salgado's captions impact your reading of his photographs?

WRITING

1. Take a series of photographs, draw a series of pictures, or write a few short stories that you would—and could—entitle *Migrations: Humanity in Transition.* Then write an expository essay in which you explain the appropriateness of this title to the works you have created.

2. Nobody's family started in America. (Even Native Americans immigrated thousands of years ago.) Chart your own family's migrations as far back as you can. Talk to your parents, grandparents, aunts, uncles, and other relatives to find out how many countries your family has moved through in the past. When you have found what seems to be a "home" country or countries—that is, when you can't trace your family's migration patterns further—read a history about the region(s). Then write an expository essay in which you explain the ways in which your family's migration has contributed to who you are, the foods you like, your attitudes, and so on.

MICHAEL KIMMELMAN ›

Michael Kimmelman is chief art critic for the *New York Times.* Although an art critic himself, he is also curious about how artists view art. This curiosity led him to invite prominent artists such as Cindy Sherman and Lucian Freud to various museums and then to let them wander throughout the galleries and see where their interests took them, asking them questions and discussing art all along the way. The result was Kimmelman's book *Portraits: Talking with Artists at the Met, Modern, Louvre, and Elsewhere* (1998), and in its pages artists from Francis Bacon to Balthus shared their views on the art in famous museums.

As for his own view on art, Kimmelman says: "I refuse to bow to the enormous pressure in America to accept the old Puritan idea that art is a therapeutic occupation, and that if it is not somehow good for us then it isn't really good art. I think that on some level art is profoundly a frivolous thing and also completely indispensable."

Kimmelman is an accomplished pianist and was a finalist in the Van Cliburn International Piano Competition held in 1999. This essay appeared in the *New York Times* in 2000. Kimmelman lives and works in New York City.

150TH ANNIVERSARY: 1851–2001

The Assignment Is to Get the Story, but the Image Can Rise to Art

Michael Kimmelman

On the days just after, we paused, many of us, to look at the photographs of the events that had seemed to rush by on the streets and on our televisions. We woke up, hoping it wasn't true, to check with the newspapers whose still images of the smoking towers and fleeing people confirmed what had happened. They gave us a chance, which we reluctantly needed, to grasp the unimaginable by stopping time, as still images do. Instead of the same endless video loop of jets going into the World Trade Center towers that we had watched on Sept. 11, until it had almost become a blur, we saw details:

We saw the tiny figure of a man standing on the edge of a gaping hole that looked like a broken-tooth grimace, where the first plane had just crashed into the north tower, an inferno behind him, nowhere to go, one arm raised. (To shade his eyes? To signal for help?) We saw the photograph by Shannon Stapleton, of Reuters, of five dust-covered rescue workers carrying out the Rev. Mychal F. Judge, a Fire Department chaplain, who had just died in a rain of debris while ministering to victims when the towers collapsed, a modern-day Pietà. And we saw the photograph by Richard Drew of the Associated Press, maybe the most excruciating and indelible of all the images that ran in the *Times,* of a man tumbling headfirst from the north tower.

We saw these photographs, and since then, even against our will, we have not been able to forget them. They may or may not be the most horrific images of any atrocities we have seen, but they can seem as if they are the most horrific at this moment because these are our buildings and our streets and our families and our lives. In their immediate aftermath, it is impossible to imagine the photographs ever fading from anybody's memory or losing their national symbolism.

BEAUTY, PERHAPS, BUT RARELY ART

The magnitude of that event enhanced the urgency of the photographs, but it did not automatically raise their status. In photojournalism the balance isn't easily tipped from the utilitarian picture, which delivers information quickly, efficiently, even deeply affectingly, to a work of art, which delivers more than information. It is rarely just a question of the scale of the recorded subject or the intention of the photographer. All photojournalists hope their best pictures are good enough to be considered art, but most of the time they don't succeed. They can't.

The task of conveying news, an 5 honorable and complicated job, generally relegates the picture, like the event it records, to ephemera. The picture may be complete and even beautiful in its way. It may go so far as to shape history and therefore endure, like Eddie Adams's unforgettable photograph of the South Vietnamese police commander shooting a Vietcong prisoner. But the picture does not transcend its event, which is where the art comes in.

This transcendence entails a novel composition, an expression, the echo of some previous images we have seen, maybe in museums or books, which are stored in our memories as archetypes and symbols, so that the photograph, by conscious or unconscious association and special variation, is elevated from the specific to the universal.

Often this is just a fluke of fate, a result of an accident, serendipity. Or rather it is the serendipity of good photographers who by nature seem to have the uncanny instinct to be in the right spot at the right moment.

It wasn't many years ago that readers scanning photographs in the *New York Times* over breakfast could expect a lean diet of single-column black-and-white head shots accompanying the news. The Gray Lady was gray back then, and it wasn't just that she hadn't made the leap yet to color (almost a century after color photography's invention, but who's counting).

Now, the world having rapidly changed, this newspaper, like most newspapers, has gradually changed with it. In the age of the Internet and television, papers including the *Times* have had to think differently. The reading public is more accustomed to looking at pictures, which doesn't just mean that it is more comfortable getting information from them. It means that people are smarter about how pictures work: the belief that facts were whatever appeared through a viewfinder seems quaint in our digital age. So a more visually shrewd populace expects a more visually sophisticated menu of the day's events over its coffee and toast.

This proliferation of competing 10 images and the acuteness of public attention to visual culture permit fresh latitudes (within the bounds of truth). Look at the front page of Aug. 3, 2001, the 51,834th number of the *Times,* an average day before Sept. 11, and you will see two photographs. One, above the fold, is a fairly straightforward spot-news shot of Radislav Krstic, a Bosnian Serb general, on crutches, in The Hague, where he was found guilty of genocide. Below is a picture by Ruth Fremson of the *Times,* apropos of nothing much except summertime: it shows a boy, arms out, face heavenward, standing before a wall of electric fans that belong to an artwork at the P.S. 1 Contemporary Art Center in Queens.

The weather photograph is one of the oldest journalistic clichés, but here it is turned into something akin to the famous Cartier-Bresson image, a surreal masterpiece of a Spanish boy, eyes skyward, arms out, as if in ecstasy. Cartier-Bresson excluded from his picture the ball the boy had tossed and was waiting to catch. One ordinary truth yielded to a deeper one about joy and transcendence. That is how art works. Now look at the two photographs on the front page. Which sticks in your mind?

Notwithstanding its formerly gray reputation, the *Times* has published hundreds of memorable pictures, documenting not just history but the history of photomechanical reproduction, from the first photographs ever published in the newspaper—credit-card-size head shots of Stephen A. Douglas and John Bell on Sept. 6, 1896—through what must be the most memorable photographs ever taken: stills from the video transmissions of the Apollo 11 moon landing, published on July 21, 1969. By then, most readers had already seen these pictures on television, the newly dominant medium.

In between was the photograph that Richard E. Byrd claimed to be the first aerial shot of the North Pole, transmitted via radio from London to New York. It appeared under a banner headline with the lead article on the front page of May 29, 1926, and not once, not twice, but three times it was stated in the headline and subheadings that the photograph, which is hard to make out, had been radioed from London. This was as much a technological marvel, and thus news, as the fact that Byrd had taken a picture near the pole from an airplane.

But none of those historic photographs are art. The *Times* published plenty of artful photographs, too: Ernest Sisto's vertiginous view from atop the Empire State Building looking down at the wreckage made by a bomber that had crashed into the 78th and 79th floors (published July 29, 1945), a memorable image, even considering what happened to the twin towers; Gilles Peress's sprinting rioters in Belfast on May 5, 1981, the day Bobby Sands died after a hunger strike; Sebastião Salgado's series of firefighters and oil workers in Kuwait (June 9, 1991); and Meyer Liebowitz's Weegee-like picture of the dead Umberto Anastasia in the barbershop of the Park Sheraton Hotel after his gangland-style rubout—although when the photograph appeared on Oct. 26, 1957, the body was cropped out in keeping with a policy of weighing the gory content of such photographs against their importance as news (an equation that has been altered somewhat with color printing).

Some of Dorothea Lange's classic Depression-era photographs of migrant families in California also appeared in the newspaper, including one of a mother holding two children beside a makeshift shelter made of canvas sheets roughly stretched between a beat-up car and a tent—an image doubly interesting today because if you look at the *Times*'s original copy, you see that it was touched up, with the faces drawn in to make them reproduce more clearly. Nobody thought much about airbrushing in the days before digital technology. Paradoxically, tinkering, now that it is so easy to do, is not done, because everyone is more sensitive to its ramifications.

Two photographs, both unconnected to Sept. 11, and therefore perhaps a little easier to see clearly, sum up the current state of the art of photojournalism. One, by Stephen Crowley of the *Times,* is from the last presidential campaign and appeared on Jan. 22, 2000: Gov. George W. Bush is shown behind the lunch counter in a drugstore in Grinnell, Iowa, pretending to wait on customers for the benefit of news cameras, which you see beyond the counter. In the foreground a woman looks peevishly away, toward something out of the picture. The image bespeaks artifice and alienation—but wittily, turning a mundane event into a symbol of modern American political life.

The other photograph, by Alan Chin, on assignment for the *Times,* shows mourners around the dead body of Ali Paqarizi, a 19-year-old Albanian killed by a Serb booby trap. It depicts not Paqarizi's formal military funeral, but what happened that day in his family's living room, where his mother, surrounded by grieving women, cried over her son's corpse. The picture captures not the public display of political defiance, but its root: the private despair that is the outcome of war.

The formal geometry of this image, with the semicircle of mourners, is locked in place by the horizontal body of the dead man in his striped shroud and by the vertical axis of his mother's foreshortened arm, his impassive mask set against her explicit grief. As a document of human expression it achieves what good art achieves on a basic level. The purpose of a newspaper photograph, after all, is to amplify a story in ways that words can't. This picture, which appeared on Oct. 29, 1998, with an article about the funeral of a young man in a town in Serbia that most readers have never heard of, speaks for itself insofar as it articulates the larger meaning of the conflict in the Balkans and, most important, of suffering generally. It is proof not only that art imitates life but that life, when captured in the most profound news photograph, is art. ○

SEEING

1. What does Michael Kimmelman see in "art" photographs that he doesn't see in other photographs? Make a list of all the things that an art photograph should do and be, according to the article. How would you rank the items on the list? Which characteristics do you think are not necessary to include in a working definition of a photograph as art? Which characteristics would you judge to be essential? Explain why.

2. Find a passage in which Kimmelman describes an art photograph and one in which he talks about a photograph that he doesn't think is art. How does his language change between the two? What kinds of words does he use when he describes art photographs? What about the nature of his sentences? Do they become less artistic when he's writing about photographs he considers not to be art? Are they more artistic when he writes about art photographs?

WRITING

1. Pick a photograph in this book that you think qualifies as an art photograph, whether or not Kimmelman would agree with you. Then draft a letter to Kimmelman, explaining why you think the picture should be viewed as art. Please make sure to respond to the points he makes in his article.

2. Kimmelman argues that Eddie Adams's photograph of a South Vietnamese police commander shooting a Vietcong prisoner is "unforgettable," but that "the picture does not transcend its event" (para. 5). Use an Internet search engine to locate a copy of Adams's photograph and compare and contrast it with another photograph drawn from the Vietnam War that you feel does transcend the event. Write an expository essay in which you explain why the photograph transcends the chronological limitations of the event whereas that of the execution does not. Pay special attention to the compositional details and the structural aspects of each picture. Other than the subject matter, what makes one picture "art" whereas the other just conveys information?

Looking Closer
The Ethics of Representation

Is seeing really believing? Photographs may never have been the documents of "truth" that they initially were assumed to be, and now the growing accessibility of digital technology has made it possible for even home-computer users to alter the look of a holiday portrait. Doctoring family snapshots may seem benign, but what are the ethics of enhancing or altering news photographs?

As Mitchell Stephens describes in **"Expanding the Language of Photographs,"** magazines and advertisers have a history of enhancing and manipulating photographs. George Hunt's **"Doctoring Reality"** is evidence that photo-doctoring has long been a staple of government propaganda. And a hoax photo distributed on the Internet, *Newsweek* magazine's enhancement of **"Bobbi and Kenny McCaughey,"** and the U.S. Postal Service's revision of a 1920 photograph of **"William Hopson"** provoked new occasions for this debate. In **"Ethics in the Age of Digital Photography,"** John Long underscores how easily—and frequently—such manipulations of images can occur at a time when digital imagery is widely available and understood by the general public.

What standards should be used for the images designed to report news and information? What role do words and captions play in the debate? To what extent should such images be labeled? And in what manner? These and other complicated ethical questions surround the use of technologies to enhance, store, and recombine information.

Ethics in the Age of Digital Photography

John Long

EXPANDING THE LANGUAGE OF PHOTOGRAPHS
Mitchell Stephens

A PHOTO ON THE FRONT PAGE OF *NEW YORK Newsday* on Feb. 16, 1994, showed two well-known Olympic ice skaters, Tonya Harding and Nancy Kerrigan, practicing together. By the standards of the tabloid war then raging in New York City (a war *New York Newsday* would not survive), this shot of Harding and the fellow skater she had been accused of plotting to assault did not seem particularly incendiary. But there was something extraordinary about this photograph: The scene it depicted had not yet taken place. Harding and Kerrigan, as the paper admitted in the caption, had not in fact practiced together. A computer had stitched together two separate images to make it appear as if they already had.

Newsday was certainly not the first publication to have taken advantage of techniques that allow for the digital manipulation of photographs. In 1982, for example, a *National Geographic* computer had nudged two pyramids closer together so that they might more comfortably fit the magazine's cover. In July 1992, *Texas Monthly* had used a computer to place the head of then-Gov. Ann Richards on top of the body of a model riding a Harley-Davidson motorcycle. But you had to be an expert on pyramids to figure out what *National Geographic* had done, and you had to miss a fairly broad joke to take umbrage with *Texas Monthly*. *New York Newsday*'s editors had fiddled with photos featuring two of the most talked-about individuals of the day, and they weren't joking. The results of their efforts were clearly visible on newsstands all over Manhattan.

Defenders of journalism's accuracy and reliability quickly grabbed their lances and mounted their steeds: "A composite photograph is not the truth," Stephen D. Isaacs, then acting dean of the Columbia Graduate School of Journalism, thundered. "It is a lie and, therefore, a great danger to the standards and integrity of what we do." The dean of the S. I. Newhouse School of Public Communication at Syracuse University, David M. Rubin, concluded that "*New York Newsday* has taken leave of its ethical moorings."

This front-page photo in a major daily seemed to announce that craven journalists had found a powerful new way to debase themselves: computer reworkings of photographs.

Others of us, however, heard a different announcement on that winter day in 1994: *Newsday*'s rather ordinary-looking attempt to further exploit an unpleasant, mostly unimportant story, we believed, was an early indication that news images might finally be coming of age.

To understand the significance of *New York Newsday*'s digital manipulation of this photograph, it is first necessary to acknowledge all the other ways photographs are manipulated. Photographers choose angles, making sure, for example, that the crowd of reporters isn't in the shot. They use filters, adjust contrast and vary depth of field. They frame and crop, and routinely transform reds, blues and yellows into blacks, grays and whites. Aren't these distortions of sorts?

It is also necessary to acknowledge the ways in which we manipulate language. Words are routinely arranged so that they describe events that are not currently occurring, as in the sentence: "Nancy Kerrigan and Tonya Harding will practice together." Words are even deployed in tenses that describe events that likely will not or definitely will not occur: "She might have won the gold medal." And words frequently speak of one thing as if it were another: Despite its proximity to New York harbor, *New York Newsday* did not literally possess "ethical moorings." Deans Isaacs and Rubin, for all their devotion to journalistic integrity, probably did not grab lances or mount steeds. In their efforts to approach the truth, words regularly depart from the literal truth.

In fact, words have gained much of their strength through speculation, negation, hypothesizing and metaphor through what, by Dean Isaacs's definition, might qualify as lies. In the first century and a half of their existence, photographic images, on the other hand, have been held back by their inability to speak of what will be, what might be and what won't be; their inability to present something as if it were something else. "Pictures," the theorist Sol Worth wrote dismissively in 1975, "cannot depict conditionals, counter-factuals, negatives or past future tenses." Well, now they can. Alert observers of journalism learned that on Feb. 16, 1994.

The above-board computer manipulation of photographs will give responsible journalists—those with their ethical moorings intact—a powerful new tool. Sometimes the results will be fanciful: an image of Bill Clinton and Newt Gingrich arm wrestling, perhaps. Sometimes such computer-altered photographs will be instructive: They might picture, for example, how that plane should have landed. Such reworked photos will allow us to peek, however hazily, into the future: showing not just how Harding and Kerrigan might look together on the ice but how that new building might change the neighborhood. They will also allow us to peek into the past: portraying, with photographic realism (not, as in TV reenactments, with clumsy actors), how a crime might have been committed. The idea should be to clarify, not to pretend.

For news photographs will not come of age by 10 hoodwinking those who look at them. That must be emphasized. Before digital editing and digital photography, harried photographers occasionally rearranged backgrounds or restaged scenes; adept photo editors, armed with a thick black pencil, occasionally added hair where there was too little or subtracted a chin where there were too many. Computers make such attempts to deceive much easier but no more conscionable. There is no doubt that they have been used for such purposes already. *Time* magazine's surreptitious digital darkening of O.J. Simpson's face on its cover later in 1994 may qualify as an example. But *New York Newsday*'s Harding-Kerrigan photo was labeled as a "composite." "Tomorrow, they'll really take to the ice together" the paper explained on that front page, though not in as large type as we journalism professors would have liked.

Here is a standard journalism deans might more reasonably champion: Digitally manipulated photographs must not be used as a tool for deceiving. They must be labeled, clearly, as what they are. (Let's take a hard line on this, initially at least: no lightening of a shadow, no blurring of an inconvenient background without some sort of acknowledgment.) But the potential these photographs offer as a tool for communicating honestly must not be suppressed.

With the aid of computers, photographic images will be able to show us much more than just what might present itself at any one time to a well-situated lens, as words tell us about much more than just what is, at any one time, literally the case. And computers will be able to work this magic on moving as well as still photographic images, on television news video as well as newspaper and magazine photographs.

None of this should be that hard to imagine. The computer-produced graphics that increasingly illustrate print and television news stories have been perpetrating clever and effective reimaginings of reality for many years now: politicians' faces matched with piles of dollar bills, the affected states jumping out of maps, items flying in and out of shopping carts. And all this has been happening without attracting the ire of the defenders of journalism's integrity.

The notion that news photographs themselves—not just cartoon-like graphics—are subject to these new types of alteration will take some getting used to. The labels will have to be very clear, their type very large—particularly at the start. For we have been in the habit of accepting photography as what one of its inventors, William Henry Fox Talbot, called "the pencil of nature." That was always something of a misperception. Now, if we are to take advantage of the great promise of digital technology, we'll have to wise up.

For computers are going to expand our control 15 over this pencil dramatically. Journalists will have unprecedented ability to shape the meanings their photographs, not just their sentences, can communicate. Their pictures will approach issues from many new directions. The language of photojournalism will grow. And that is good news for those who struggle to report with images. ○

Ethics in the Age of Digital Photography

John Long

Two disclaimers need to be stated before we begin:

1. My purpose is not to give answers. My purpose is to provide you with a vocabulary so you can discuss the ethical issues that may arise when using computers to process photographs. I also want to present the principles I have found helpful when trying to make decisions of an ethical nature. I do not expect everyone to agree with me. I want you to think about the issues and arrive at your own conclusions in a logical and reasoned manner.

2. The advent of computers and digital photography has not created the need for a whole new set of ethical standards. We are not dealing with something brand new. We merely have a new way of processing images, and the same principles that have guided us in traditional photojournalism should be the principles that guide us in the use of the computers. This fact makes dealing with computer-related ethics far less daunting than if we had to begin from square one.

We have many problems in journalism today that threaten our profession and in fact threaten the Constitution of our country. Photo-ops, lack of access to news events, rock show contracts, yellow tape, and bean counters are just a few. Everyone has a spin; everyone wants to control the news media. We are under attack from all sides.

One of the major problems we face as photojournalists is the fact that the public is losing faith in us. Our readers and viewers no longer believe everything they see. All images are called into question because the computer has proved that images are malleable, changeable, fluid. In movies, advertisements, TV shows, magazines, we are constantly exposed to images created or changed by computers. As William J. Mitchell points out in his book *The Reconfigured Eye, Visual Truth in the Post-Photographic Era* we are experiencing a paradigm shift in how we define the nature of a photograph. The photograph is no longer a fixed image; it has become a watery mix of moveable pixels, and this is changing how we perceive what a photograph is. The bottom line is that documentary photojournalism is the last vestige of the real photography.

Journalists have only one thing to offer the public and that is CREDIBILITY. This is the first vocabulary word I want you to remember, and the most important. Without credibility we have nothing. We might as well go sell widgets door to door since without the trust of the public we cannot exist as a profession.

Our credibility is damaged every time a reputable news organization is caught lying to the public, and one of the most blatant and widely recognized cases was the computer enhancement of the *Time* magazine cover photo of O. J. Simpson. *Time* took the mug shot of Simpson when he was arrested and changed it before using it on their cover. They would not have been caught if *Newsweek* had not used the same photo on their cover photo just as it had come from the police. The two covers showed up on the news stands next to each other, and the public could see something was wrong.

Time darkened the handout photo, creating a five o'clock shadow and a more sinister look. They darkened the top of the photo and made the police lineup numbers smaller. They decided Simpson was guilty so they made him look guilty. (There are two issues here: one is a question of photographic ethics and the other is a question of racial insensitivity by *Time* in deciding that blacker means guiltier. The black community raised this issue when the story broke, and [it] needs to be the subject of another article. My concern is with the issue of photographic ethics.)

In an editorial the next week, *Time's* managing editor wrote, "The harshness of the mug shot—the merciless bright light, the stubble on Simpson's face, the cold specificity of the picture—had been subtly smoothed and shaped into an icon of tragedy." In other words, they changed the photo from what it was (a document) into what they wanted it to be. *Time* was making an editorial statement, not reporting the news. They presented what looked like a real photograph and it turned out not to be real; the public felt deceived, and rightly so. By doing this, *Time* damaged their credibility and the credibility of all journalists.

In order to have a rational, logical discussion of ethics, a distinction needs to be drawn between ethics and taste. Ethics refers to issues of deception, or lying. Taste refers to issues involving blood, sex, violence, and other aspects of life we do not want to see in our morning paper as we eat breakfast. Not everyone defines taste-ethics this way, but I find it useful. Issues of taste can cause a few subscription cancellations and letters to the editor, but they tend to evaporate in a few days. Ethics violations damage credibility, and the effects can last for years. Once you damage your credibility, it is next to impossible to get it back.

The photo of the dead American soldier being dragged through the streets of Mogadishu raises issues of taste, not issues of ethics. This photo is a fair and accurate representation of what happened in Somalia that day. (I hesitate to use the word "truthful." Truth is a loaded concept, open to personal interpretation. What is true for one person may not be true for another. I prefer to use the terms "fair and accurate." These terms are more precise, though not completely without debate over their meaning.)

If we are to use this photo, a photo that is ethically 10 correct but definitely of questionable taste (no one wants to see dead American soldiers in the newspaper), we need to have a compelling reason. Earlier I mentioned I would give you some principles that I find useful, and this is the first: If the public needs the information in the photo in order to make informed choices for society, then we must run the photo. We cannot make informed choices for our society unless we have access to fair and accurate information. A free society is based on this right. It is codified in our country as the First Amendment. We have to know what is happening in our towns, in our country, in our world, in order to make decisions that affect us as a society. The First Amendment does not belong to the press, it belongs to the American people. It guarantees all of us the right to the fair and accurate information we need to be responsible citizens.

We needed to see the dead soldier in the streets so we could make an informed choice as a country as to the correctness of our being in Somalia. Words can tell us the facts, but photos hit us in the gut. They give us the real meaning, the deep and emotional impact of what was happening much better than words can. As a society we decided that we needed to leave that country.

I feel bad for the family of the soldier, but sometimes the needs of the many outweigh the needs of the few, or the one. In our country, we have the right to our privacy (usually the Sixth Amendment is cited) but we also have to live together and act collectively. This need is addressed by the First Amendment: "Congress shall make no law respecting an establishment of religion, or prohibiting the free exercise thereof; or abridging the freedom of speech or of the press; or the right of the people peaceably to assemble, and to petition the government for a redress of grievances."

Honest photographs can have an ethical dimension when it concerns the personal ethics of the photographer. Did the photographer violate some ethical standard in the process of making the picture?

For example, take the very famous photo of the young child dying in Sudan while a vulture stands behind her, waiting. It was taken by Kevin Carter, who won a Pulitzer Prize for the photo (a photo that raised a lot of money for the relief agencies). He was criticized for not helping the child; he replied there were relief workers there to do that. After receiving his Pulitzer, Kevin Carter returned to Africa and committed suicide. He had a lot of problems in his life but, with the timing of the sequence of events, I cannot help thinking there is a correlation between his photographing the child and his suicide.

This is the kind of choice all journalists will face 15 sometime in [their] career; maybe not in the extreme situation that Carter faced, but in some way, we all will be faced with choices of helping or photographing. Someday we will be at a fire or a car accident and we will be called upon to put the camera down and help. It is a good idea to think about these issues in advance because when the hour comes, it will come suddenly and we will be asked to make a choice quickly.

Here is the principle that works for me. It is not a popular one and it is one that many journalists disagree with, but it allows me to sleep at night. If you have placed yourself in the position where you can help, you are morally obligated to help. I do not ask you to agree with me. I just want you to think about this and be prepared; at what point do you put the camera down and help? At what point does your humanity become more important than your journalism?

It is time to get back to the theme of this report— the ethics involved with the use of computers to process images.

I like the *Weekly World News*. It provides a constant source of photos for these discussions about ethics. One of the more famous front pages shows a space alien shaking hands with President Clinton. It is a wonderful photo, guaranteed to make the career of any photographer who manages to get an exclusive shot of this event.

We can laugh at this photo, and I have no real problem with the *Weekly World News* running such digitally created photos because of the context of where this photo is running. This is the second of the vocabulary words I want to give you: CONTEXT. Where the photo runs makes all the difference in the world. If this same photo ran on the front page of the *New York Times*, it would damage the credibility of the *Times*. In the context of *Weekly World News*, it cannot damage their credibility because that newspaper does not have any credibility to begin with (it seems we need to create a new set of terms when we can refer to the *Weekly World News* and the *New York Times* both as newspapers).

Context becomes a problem when we find digitally 20 altered photos in reputable publications, and there have been many. For example, the cover of *Texas Monthly* once ran a photo of then Governor Ann Richards astride a Harley-Davidson motorcycle. It came out that the only part of the photo that was Ann Richards was her head. The body on the motorcycle belonged to a model, and the head of the governor was electronically attached to the model.

On the credit page in very small type, the editors claimed they explained what they had done and that this disclosure exonerated them. They wrote:

Cover photograph by Jim Myers
Styling by Karen Eubank
Accessories courtesy of Rancho Loco, Dallas; boots courtesy of Boot Town, Dallas; motorcycle and leather jacket courtesy of Harley-Davidson, Dallas; leather pants by Patricia Wolfe
Stock photograph (head shot) by Kevin Vandivier / Texastock

In the first place this was buried on the bottom of a page very few people look at, in a type size few over 40 can read, and was worded in a way as to be incomprehensible.

Secondly, my feeling is that no amount of captioning can forgive a visual lie. In the context of news, if a photo looks real, it better be real. This photo looked real, but it was a fake. We have an obligation to history to leave behind us a collection of real photographs. This photo of Ann Richards entered into the public domain, and on the day she lost her re-election bid, AP ran the photo on the wire for its clients. AP had to run a mandatory kill when they were informed it was not a real photo.

Janet Cooke was a reporter at the *Washington Post* who won a Pulitzer Prize in 1981 for a story she wrote about an eight-year-old heroin addict named Jimmy. The Prize was taken back and she was fired when it was discovered that she [had] made up the story. Can you imagine if the *Post* put a disclaimer in italics at the end of the story when it first ran, that said something along these lines: "We know this exact kid does not exist, but we also know this kind of thing does happen and so we created this one composite kid to personalize the story. Even though Jimmy does not exist, you can believe everything else we wrote." The *Post* would have been the laughing stock of the industry, and yet this is what *Texas Monthly* is doing by captioning away a visual lie. You have to have the same respect for the visual image as you have for the written word. You do not lie with words, nor should you lie with photographs.

In one of the early Digital Conferences, the Reverend Don Doll, S.J., pointed out that there are degrees of changes that can be done electronically to a photograph. There are technical changes that deal only with the aspects of photography that make the photo more readable, such as a little dodging and burning, global color correction, and contrast control. These are all part of the grammar of photography, just as there is a grammar associated with words (sen-

tence structure, capital letters, paragraphs) that make it possible to read a story, so there is a grammar of photography that allows us to read a photograph. These changes (like their darkroom counterparts) are neither ethical nor unethical—they are merely technical.

Changes to content can be Accidental or Essential [25] (this is an old Aristotelian distinction)—Essential changes change the meaning of the photograph, and Accidental changes change useless details but do not change the real meaning. Some changes are obviously more important than others. Accidental changes are not as important as Essential changes, but both kinds are still changes.

If you had a photograph of a bride and groom and removed the groom, this would constitute an Essential change because it would change the meaning of the photograph. (In fact, there are companies that will provide this service if you get a divorce. I guess the wedding book would end up looking like the bride got all dressed up and married herself.)

In the two photos of the ladies on the parade float,* the photo on the left has a set of wires running behind the ladies. In the photo on the right, the lines have been removed. It takes only a few seconds with the cloning tool in PhotoShop to remove these lines. Removing the lines is an Accidental change, a change of meaningless details. If we had changed the flag to a Confederate flag, or removed a couple of the ladies, this would have changed the meaning of the photo and it would have been an Essential change. But if we just remove the lines, what is the big deal? Who is harmed? As far as I am concerned, we are all harmed by any lie, big or small.

I do not think the public cares if it is a little lie or a big lie. As far as they are concerned, once the shutter has been tripped and the MOMENT has been captured on film, in the context of news, we no longer have the right to change the content of the photo in

*For reasons of space and copyright, we are unable to reproduce these two photos.

any way. Any change to a news photo—any violation of that MOMENT—is a lie. Big or small, any lie damages your credibility.

The reason I get so adamant when I discuss this issue is that the documentary photograph is a very powerful thing, and its power is based on the fact that it is real. The real photograph gives us a window on history; it allows us to be present at the great events of our times and the past. It gets its power from the fact that it represents exactly what the photographer saw through the medium of photography. The raw reality it depicts, the verisimilitude makes the documentary photo come alive. Look at the photo of Robert Kennedy dying on the floor of the hotel in California; look at the works of David Douglas Duncan or the other great war photographers; look at the photo of Martin Luther King martyred on the balcony of a motel in Memphis. The power of these photographs comes from the fact they are real moments in time captured as they happened, unchanged. To change any detail in any of these photographs diminishes their power and turns them into lies. They would no longer be what the photographer saw but what someone else wanted the scene to be. The integrity of the Moment would be destroyed in favor of the editorial concept being foisted, as is the case in the O. J. Simpson *Time* cover.

There have been many cases of digital manipulation over the past 20 years or so, the first of note being the famous pyramids cover of *National Geographic* in 1982. *National Geographic* had a horizontal photo of the pyramids in Egypt and wanted to make a vertical cover from it. They put the photo in a computer and squeezed the pyramids together—a difficult task in real life but an easy task for the computer. They referred to it as the "retroactive repositioning of the photographer" (one of the great euphemisms of our age), saying that if the photographer had been a little to one side or the other, this is what he would have gotten. The photographer was not 10 feet to the right and he did not get the photo they wanted, so they created a visual lie. They damaged their credibility, and (as I said before) taste

issues have a short life span, ethics issues do not go away. Here we are almost 20 year later, and we are still talking about what *Geographic* did.

Sports Illustrated recently produced a special edition for Connecticut on the UConn National Championship basketball season. In one photo, they showed a star player, Ricky Moore, going up for a lay-up with another player, Kevin Freeman, in the frame. They also used the same photo on the cover of the regular edition of the magazine, cropped tighter but with Kevin Freeman removed. I guess he cluttered up the cover, so he was expendable.

The point I want to make here is that if *Sports Illustrated* had not used the same photo twice, they would not have been caught. The computer allows for seamless changes that are impossible to see, and if you shoot with an electronic camera, you do not even have film to act as a referent. How many times has *Sports Illustrated* or *Time* or *Newsweek* or any of a long list of newspapers and magazines changed a photo and we the reading public not known about it? This is the Pandora's box of the computer age.

It is not just in the computer that photographers and editors can lie. We can lie by setting up photos or by being willing partners to photo ops. These things are as big, if not bigger, threats to our profession as the computers. The *L. A. Times* ran a photo of a fireman dousing his head with water from a swimming pool as a house burned in the background. In doing preparations for contest entries, they discovered that the photographer had said to the fireman something along the lines of, "You know what would make a good photo? If you went over by the pool and poured water on your head." The photo was a set-up. It was withdrawn from competition, and the photographer was disciplined severely.

This is as much a lie as what can be done in Photo-Shop. Neither is acceptable.

"A Day in the Life" series of books has a long history of manipulated covers. In *A Day in the Life of California*, for example, the photo was shot on a gray day as a horizontal. The hand came from another frame; the surfboard was moved closer to the surfer's head, and the sky was made blue to match his eyes. They had about 30,000 images to pick from and could not find one that looked like California to them, so they had to create an image—an image of what they wanted California to look like.

The list can go on for pages: *Newsweek* straightened the teeth of Bobbi McCaughey, the mother of the septuplets; *Newsday* ran a photo supposedly showing Nancy Kerrigan and Tonya Harding skating together a day before the event really happened; *People* ran a photo of famous breast cancer survivors made from five separate negatives; the *St. Louis Post Dispatch* removed a Coke can from a photo of their Pulitzer Prize winner. This just scratches the surface. How many cases have not become known? The cumulative effect is the gradual erosion of the credibility of [the] entire profession, and I am not sure we can win this war. We are being bombarded from all sides, from movies, television, advertisements, the Internet, with images that are not real, that are created in computers, and documentary photojournalism is the victim.

We may be in a death-struggle, but the end is worth fighting for. Real photos can change the hearts and minds of the people. Real photographs can change how we view war and how we view our society. Vietnam is a prime example. Two photos sum up that war: the Nick Ut photo of the girl burned by napalm running naked down the street and the Eddie Adams photo of the man being executed on the streets of Saigon. These photos changed how we perceived that war. They are powerful, and they get their power from the fact that they are real Moments captured for all time on film.

No one has the right to change these photos or the content of any documentary photo. It is our obligation to history to make sure this does not happen. ○

"and you think your [sic] having a bad day at work!!
Although this looks like a picture taken from a Hollywood movie, it is in fact a rea
photo, taken near the South African coast during a military exercise by the British
Navy. It has been nominated by National Geographic as 'THE photo of the year'."

Newsweek

December 1, 1997 · $2.95

'We're Trusting in God'

The Amazing McCaughey Septuplets

Gambling With Fertility Drugs

Bobbi and Kenny McCaughey

POSTMARK
AMERICA

MITCHELL STEPHENS

Mitchell Stephens teaches journalism and mass communications at New York University. An acclaimed commentator on both the history and practice of journalism, he has written on the topic for various newspapers and has also published several journalism textbooks. His general-interest publications include *A History of the News* (1996) and *The Rise of the Image and the Fall of the Word* (1998). In the latter work he challenges the belief that "visual" information is eroding the intelligence of the news audience, arguing instead that future viewers will become as adept at reading the subtleties of moving pictures and images as they now are at understanding the nuances of language.

NEWSWEEK

Bobbi and Kenny McCaughey were thrust into the national spotlight when they became the parents of septuplets in 1997. When *Newsweek* touched up its cover photograph of the couple, making Mrs. McCaughey's teeth appear straighter and whiter, it furthered the national debate on the ethics of altering photographs. *Newsweek*'s enhancement became glaring when *Time* printed a similar, unaltered image of the couple on its cover the very same week. "The photo we decided to use had a considerable shadow over her mouth," explained Richard M. Smith, *Newsweek*'s president and editor in chief. "The editors decided to lighten and improve the picture. In the process of doing that, the technical people went too far."

GEORGE HUNT

Anthropologist Franz Boas and photographer George Hunt were members of a late-nineteenth-century expedition designed to study and record indigenous cultures of the North Pacific, which were facing increasing westernization. While cameras provided an ideal tool for capturing daily life and cultural practices, the still-cumbersome technology created ample opportunities for staging or manipulating "authentic" culture. This photograph, featured in an American Museum of Natural History exhibition, shows Boas (left) and Hunt (right) preparing a backdrop for a photograph of a cedar bark weaving by a Kwakiutl woman.

JOHN LONG

John Long was the National Press Photographers Association Ethics co-chair and past president (1989–1990), and he has a firm grasp on the principles by which he believes photojournalists need to adhere. "Each day when you step out onto the street, remember that you have been granted a sacred trust to be truthful. You have the responsibility to produce only honest images. You have no right to set up pictures; you have no right to stage the news; you have no right to distort the facts. Your fellow citizens trust you. If you destroy the credibility of your work, *even in small ways*, it destroys the credibility of your newspaper or TV station in the eyes of the people you are covering." Today Long is a photojournalist for the *Hartford Courant*.

HOAX PHOTO

This photograph, labeled as National Geographic's "Photo of the Year," circulated in emails and on the internet from August 2001 until August 2002, when National Geographic officially declared it a hoax in a statement posted on their web site. The photograph was a composite of a U.S. Air Force photograph of an HH-60G Pave Hawk helicopter taken by Lance Cheung near San Francisco's Golden Gate Bridge and a photograph of a breaching great white shark taken by South African photographer Charles Maxwell. "I'd like to make contact with the person who did this," said Maxwell, "not to get him or her into trouble, but because it's a lot of fun and it is a good job. However, I must make clear that I would not like to see this happen to one of my photographs again. It is wrong to take images from a web site without permission."

Ethics in the Age of Digital
Photography
John Long

U.S. POSTAL SERVICE

William "Big Bill" Hopson served as an air-mail pilot in the 1920s. Before his death in a plane crash in 1928, he submitted a photograph of himself for Postal Service records. "Enclosed please find photo of bum pilot," he wrote. The U.S. Postal Service recently featured his photograph on the cover of a Postmark America brochure (a catalog of apparel, gifts, and collectibles) as well as on an Air Mail sweatshirt. The Postal Service chose to make one change to the original image: a cigarette has been airbrushed out of Hopson's right hand. Seen by some as a valuable contribution to antismoking campaigns and others as an example of dangerous tampering with an historical document, the choice remains controversial.

SEEING

1. In "Expanding the Language of Photographs," Mitchell Stephens draws a distinction between *Time*'s manipulation of Simpson's image and *Newsday*'s composite image of Harding and Kerrigan. The former, Stephens argues, is unethical and the latter is not. To what extent do you agree with Stephens? What are the ethics involved in each case? What was manipulated in each instance, and how? Did the editors act ethically in each instance? Why or why not? In your view, is an image used as "cover art" not subject to the same standards as a news photograph?

2. Here is what one critic said after the Kerrigan/Harding photo was printed: "Different standards applied to photographic and textual evidence, indicating that photographs have a lower status in the editorial hierarchy. Whereas *Time*'s editors would presumably never consider rewriting a quotation from O.J. Simpson, attempting to say it better for him, they evidently felt fewer qualms about altering the police photograph in order to lift . . . 'a common police mug shot to the level of art, with no sacrifice to the truth.'"

Do you agree with this distinction—and with its implications? To what extent do you think *Newsweek*'s enhancement of the McCaugheys' photograph was unethical? Should *Newsweek* have labeled the image as a "photo-illustration"?

WRITING

1. Stephens makes a comparison between manipulating photographs and words in journalism. Like photographs, words are equally subject to being shaped and edited.

Compare and contrast a news photo and a written report of the same event. How is the event framed visually and verbally? What did the photographer and writer/editor choose to include? to omit? How would you compare the overall point of view and tone of a photograph with the same aspects of a verbal description of the same event? Draft an essay in which you argue for—or against—the assertion that visual and verbal material are held to the same standards of evidence in journalism.

2. Draft an argumentative essay in which you agree or disagree with Stephens's proposed standard for labeling manipulated news photos: "Digitally manipulated photographs must not be used as a tool for deceiving. They must be labeled, clearly, as what they are. (Let's take a hard line on this, initially at least: no lightening of a shadow, no blurring of an inconvenient background without some sort of acknowledgment.)" (para. 11).

Appendix A
On the Theory and Practice of Seeing

As visual images have become increasingly integrated into our lives, the call to define the term *visual literacy* has grown louder. What does it mean to be visually literate? How exactly do we see? How should we train ourselves to see clearly and read images analytically? How do images affect us? How are images different from or similar to words? How are visual images the products of their cultural contexts? Scholars and cultural commentators in the fields of art history, science, social history, design, and literary and cultural studies have responded to these questions in dozens of studies.

Appendix A presents two fundamental theoretical works: the first essay in John Berger's *Ways of Seeing*, and the sixth chapter (entitled "Show and Tell") in Scott McCloud's *Understanding Comics: The Invisible Art*.

Of his book *Ways of Seeing*, John Berger writes in a note to the reader, "The form of the book has as much to do with our purpose as the arguments contained within it." The same might be said of Scott McCloud's illustrated "essay."

Each of these selections uses text and images to present theories on both *how we see* and *how visual images have been seen* throughout history. You are encouraged to use these texts to re-examine any of the visual and verbal selections presented in *Seeing & Writing 2*.

JOHN BERGER

John Berger was born in 1926 in London, where he attended Central School of Art and Chelsea School of Art. Known primarily as an art critic and social historian, Berger is also a distinguished novelist, artist, poet, essayist, Marxist critic, screenwriter, translator, and actor. He has published more than eight works of fiction and fifteen works of nonfiction, along with numerous articles and screenplays, during a remarkably prolific career. His novel *G: A Novel* won the Booker Prize in 1972.

Berger began his career as an artist and drawing teacher. While exhibiting his work at local galleries in London, he also wrote art criticism for British journals. Beginning with *Permanent Red: Essays in Seeing* (1960), Berger focused his criticism on the broad issues of seeing as a social and historical act. He introduced a mixed-media approach—combining poetry, photography, essays, and criticism—to the field of art criticism in books such as *Ways of Seeing* (1972), *About Looking* (1980), and *Another Way of Telling* (1982). His most recent work, *Photocopies* (1995), offers a series of personal vignettes from the past several decades. Berger currently lives and works in a small French peasant community.

The selection printed here is the first essay in *Ways of Seeing*, which was based on a BBC television series.

Ways of Seeing

John Berger

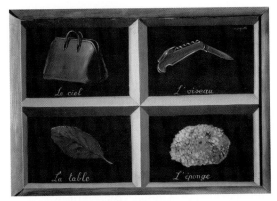

The Key of Dreams by Magritte (1898–1967).

SEEING COMES BEFORE WORDS. THE CHILD LOOKS and recognizes before it can speak.

But there is also another sense in which seeing comes before words. It is seeing which establishes our place in the surrounding world; we explain that world with words, but words can never undo the fact that we are surrounded by it. The relation between what we see and what we know is never settled. Each evening we *see* the sun set. We *know* that the earth is turning away from it. Yet the knowledge, the explanation, never quite fits the sight. The Surrealist painter Magritte commented on this always-present gap between words and seeing in a painting called *The Key of Dreams.*

The way we see things is affected by what we know or what we believe. In the Middle Ages when men believed in the physical existence of Hell the sight of fire must have meant something different from what it means today. Nevertheless their idea of Hell owed a lot to the sight of fire consuming and the ashes remaining—as well as to their experience of the pain of burns.

When in love, the sight of the beloved has a completeness which no words and no embrace can match: a completeness which only the act of making love can temporarily accommodate.

Yet this seeing which comes before words, and can 5 never be quite covered by them, is not a question of mechanically reacting to stimuli. (It can only be

thought of in this way if one isolates the small part of the process which concerns the eye's retina.) We only see what we look at. To look is an act of choice. As a result of this act, what we see is brought within our reach—though not necessarily within arm's reach. To touch something is to situate oneself in relation to it. (Close your eyes, move round the room and notice how the faculty of touch is like a static, limited form of sight.) We never look at just one thing; we are always looking at the relation between things and ourselves. Our vision is continually active, continually moving, continually holding things in a circle around itself, constituting what is present to us as we are.

Soon after we can see, we are aware that we can also be seen. The eye of the other combines with our own eye to make it fully credible that we are part of the visible world.

If we accept that we can see that hill over there, we propose that from that hill we can be seen. The reciprocal nature of vision is more fundamental than that of spoken dialogue. And often dialogue is an attempt to verbalize this—an attempt to explain how, either metaphorically or literally, "you see things," and an attempt to discover how "he sees things."

In the sense in which we use the word in this book, all images are manmade [see below]. An image is a sight which has been recreated or reproduced. It is an appearance, or a set of appearances, which has been detached from the place and time in which it first

made its appearance and preserved—for a few moments or a few centuries. Every image embodies a way of seeing. Even a photograph. For photographs are not, as is often assumed, a mechanical record. Every time we look at a photograph, we are aware, however slightly, of the photographer selecting that sight from an infinity of other possible sights. This is true even in the most casual family snapshot. The photographer's way of seeing is reflected in his choice of subject. The painter's way of seeing is reconstituted by the marks he makes on the canvas or paper. Yet, although every image embodies a way of seeing, our perception or appreciation of an image depends also upon our own way of seeing. (It may be, for example, that Sheila is one figure among twenty; but for our own reasons she is the one we have eyes for.)

Images were first made to conjure up the appearance of something that was absent. Gradually it became evident that an image could outlast what it represented; it then showed how something or somebody had once looked—and thus by implication how the subject had once been seen by other people. Later still the specific vision of the image-maker was also recognized as part of the record. An image became a record of how X had seen Y. This was the result of an increasing consciousness of individuality, accompanying an increasing awareness of history. It would be rash to try to date this last development precisely. But certainly in Europe such consciousness has existed since the beginning of the Renaissance.

No other kind of relic or text from the past can 10 offer such a direct testimony about the world which surrounded other people at other times. In this respect images are more precise and richer than literature. To say this is not to deny the expressive or imaginative quality of art, treating it as mere documentary evidence; the more imaginative the work, the more profoundly it allows us to share the artist's experience of the visible.

Yet when an image is presented as a work of art, the way people look at it is affected by a whole se-

ries of learnt assumptions about art. Assumptions concerning:

Beauty
Truth
Genius
Civilization
Form
Status
Taste, etc.

Many of these assumptions no longer accord with the world as it is. (The world-as-it-is is more than pure objective fact, it includes consciousness.) Out of touch with the present, these assumptions obscure the past. They mystify rather than clarify. The past is never there waiting to be discovered, to be recognized for exactly what it is. History always constitutes the relation between a present and its past. Consequently fear of the present leads to mystification of

Regents of the Old Men's Alms House by Hals (1580–1666).

Regentesses of the Old Men's Alms House by Hals (1580–1666).

the past. The past is not for living in; it is a well of conclusions from which we draw in order to act. Cultural mystification of the past entails a double loss. Works of art are made unnecessarily remote. And the past offers us fewer conclusions to complete in action.

When we "see" a landscape, we situate ourselves in it. If we "saw" the art of the past, we would situate ourselves in history. When we are prevented from seeing it, we are being deprived of the history which belongs to us. Who benefits from this deprivation? In the end, the art of the past is being mystified because a privileged minority is striving to invent a history which can retrospectively justify the role of the ruling classes, and such a justification can no longer make sense in modern terms. And so, inevitably, it mystifies.

Let us consider a typical example of such mystification. A two-volume study was recently published on Frans Hals.[1] It is the authoritative work to date on this painter. As a book of specialized art history it is no better and no worse than the average.

The last two great paintings by Frans Hals portray the Governors and the Governesses of an Alms House for old paupers in the Dutch seventeenth-century city of Haarlem. They were officially commissioned portraits. Hals, an old man of over eighty, was destitute. Most of his life he had been in debt. During the winter of 1664, the year he began painting these pictures, he obtained three loads of peat on public charity, otherwise he would have frozen to death. Those who now sat for him were administrators of such public charity.

The author records these facts and then explicitly 15 says that it would be incorrect to read into the paintings any criticism of the sitters. There is no evidence, he says, that Hals painted them in a spirit of bitterness. The author considers them, however, remarkable works of art and explains why. Here he writes of the Regentesses:

> Each woman speaks to us of the human condition with equal importance. Each woman stands out with equal

clarity against the *enormous* dark surface, yet they are linked by a firm rhythmical arrangement and the subdued diagonal pattern formed by their heads and hands. Subtle modulations of the *deep*, glowing blacks contribute to the *harmonious fusion* of the whole and form an *unforgettable contrast* with the *powerful* whites and vivid flesh tones where the detached strokes reach *a peak of breadth and strength.* [Berger's italics]

The compositional unity of a painting contributes fundamentally to the power of its image. It is reasonable to consider a painting's composition. But here the composition is written about as though it were in itself the emotional charge of the painting. Terms like *harmonious fusion, unforgettable contrast,* reaching *a peak of breadth and strength* transfer the emotion provoked by the image from the plane of lived experience, to that of disinterested "art appreciation." All conflict disappears. One is left with the unchanging "human condition," and the painting considered as a marvellously made object.

Very little is known about Hals or the Regents who commissioned him. It is not possible to produce circumstantial evidence to establish what their relations were. But there is the evidence of the paintings themselves: the evidence of a group of men and a group of women as seen by another man, the painter. Study this evidence and judge for yourself.

1. Seymour Slive, *Frans Hals* (Phaidon, London).

The art historian fears such direct judgement:

> As in so many other pictures by Hals, the penetrating characterizations almost seduce us into believing that we know the personality traits and even the habits of the men and women portrayed.

What is this "seduction" he writes of? It is nothing less than the paintings working upon us. They work upon us because we accept the way Hals saw his sitters. We do not accept this innocently. We accept it in so far as it corresponds to our own observation of people, gestures, faces, institutions. This is possible because we still live in a society of comparable social relations and moral values. And it is precisely this which gives the paintings their psychological and social urgency. It is this—not the painter's skill as a "seducer"—which convinces us that we *can* know the people portrayed.

The author continues:

> In the case of some critics the seduction has been a total success. It has, for example, been asserted that the Regent in the tipped slouch hat, which hardly covers any of his long, lank hair, and whose curiously set eyes do not focus, was shown in a drunken state. [below]

This, he suggests, is a libel. He argues that it was a fashion at that time to wear hats on the side of the head. He cites medical opinion to prove that the Regent's expression could well be the result of a facial paralysis. He insists that  the painting would have been unacceptable to the Regents if one of them had been portrayed drunk. One might go on discussing each of these points for pages. (Men in seventeenth-century Holland wore their hats on the side of their heads in order to be thought of as adventurous and pleasure-loving. Heavy drinking was an approved practice. Etcetera.) But such a discussion would take us even farther away from the only con-frontation which matters and which the author is determined to evade.

In this confrontation the Regents and Regentesses stare at Hals, a destitute old painter who has lost his reputation and lives off public charity; he examines them through the eyes of a pauper who must nevertheless try to be objective; i.e., must try to surmount the way he sees as a pauper. This is the drama of these paintings. A drama of an "unforgettable contrast."

Mystification has little to do with the vocabulary [20] used. Mystification is the process of explaining away what might otherwise be evident. Hals was the first portraitist to paint the new characters and expressions created by capitalism. He did in pictorial terms what Balzac did two centuries later in literature. Yet the author of the authoritative work on these paintings sums up the artist's achievement by referring to

> Hals's unwavering commitment to his personal vision, which enriches our consciousness of our fellow men and heightens our awe for the ever-increasing power of the mighty impulses that enabled him to give us a close view of life's vital forces.

That is mystification.

In order to avoid mystifying the past (which can equally well suffer pseudo-Marxist mystification) let us now examine the particular relation which now exists, so far as pictorial images are concerned, between the present and the past. If we can see the present clearly enough, we shall ask the right questions of the past.

Today we see the art of the past as nobody saw it before. We actually perceive it in a different way.

This difference can be illustrated in terms of what was thought of as perspective. The convention of perspective, which is unique to European art and which was first established in the early Renaissance, centres everything on the eye of the beholder. It is like a beam from a lighthouse—only instead of light travelling outwards, appearances travel in. The conventions called those appearances *reality*. Perspective makes the single eye the centre of the visible world. Everything converges on to the eye as to the vanishing point of infinity. The visible world is arranged for the spectator as the universe was once thought to be arranged for God.

According to the convention of perspective there is no visual reciprocity. There is no need for God to

situate himself in relation to others: he is himself the situation. The inherent contradiction in perspective was that it structured all images of reality to address a single spectator who, unlike God, could only be in one place at a time. After the invention of the camera this contradiction gradually became apparent.

I'm an eye. A mechanical eye. I, the machine, show you a world the way only I can see it. I free myself for today and forever from human immobility. I'm in constant movement. I approach and pull away from objects. I creep under them. I move alongside a running horse's mouth. I fall and rise with the falling and rising bodies. This is I, the machine, manoeuvring in the chaotic movements, recording one movement after another in the most complex combinations.

Freed from the boundaries of time and space, I coordinate any and all points of the universe, wherever I want them to be. My way leads towards the creation of a fresh perception of the world. Thus I explain in a new way the world unknown to you.[2]

The camera isolated momentary appearances and in so doing destroyed the idea that images were timeless. Or, to put it another way, the camera showed that the notion of time passing was inseparable from the experience of the visual (except in paintings). What you saw depended upon where you were when. What you saw was relative to your position in time and space. It was no longer possible to imagine everything converging on the human eye as on the vanishing point of infinity.

This is not to say that before the invention of the camera men believed that everyone could see every-

Still from *Man with a Movie Camera* by Vertov (1895–1954).

thing. But perspective organized the visual field as though that were indeed the ideal. Every drawing or painting that used perspective proposed to the spectator that he was the unique centre of the world. The camera—and more particularly the movie camera—demonstrated that there was no centre.

The invention of the camera changed the way men saw. The visible came to mean something different to them. This was immediately reflected in painting.

For the Impressionists the visible no longer presented itself to man in order to be seen. On the contrary, the visible, in continual flux, became fugitive. For the Cubists the visible was no longer what

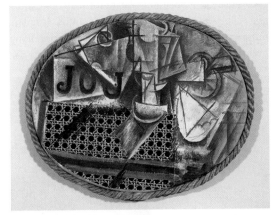

Still Life with Wicker Chair by Picasso (1881–1973).

2. This quotation is from an article written in 1923 by Dziga Vertov, the revolutionary Soviet film director.

confronted the single eye, but the totality of possible views taken from points all round the object (or person) being depicted [*Still Life with Wicker Chair*, p. 627].

The invention of the camera also changed the way in which men saw paintings painted long before the camera was invented. Originally paintings were an integral part of the building for which they were designed. Sometimes in an early Renaissance church or  chapel one has the feeling that the images on the wall are records of the building's interior life, that together they make up the building's memory—so much are they part of the particularity of the building [below].

The uniqueness of every painting was once part of the uniqueness of the place where it resided. Sometimes the painting was transportable. But it could never be seen in two places at the same time. When the camera reproduces a painting, it destroys the uniqueness of its image. As a result its meaning changes. Or, more exactly, its meaning multiplies and fragments into many meanings.

This is vividly illustrated by what happens when a painting is shown on a television screen. The painting enters each viewer's house. There it is surrounded by his wallpaper, his furniture, his mementos. It enters the atmosphere of his family. It becomes their talking point. It lends its meaning to their meaning. At the same time it enters a million other houses and, in each of them, is seen in a different context. Because of the camera, the painting now travels to the spectator rather than the spectator to the painting. In its travels, its meaning is diversified.

One might argue that all reproductions more or less distort, and that therefore the original painting is still in a sense unique. Here [right] is a reproduction of the *Virgin of the Rocks* by Leonardo da Vinci.

Having seen this reproduction, one can go to the National Gallery to look at the original and there discover what the reproduction lacks. Alternatively one can forget about the quality of the reproduction and simply be reminded, when one sees the original, that it is a famous painting of which somewhere one has already seen a reproduction. But in either case the uniqueness of the original now lies in it being *the original of a reproduction*. It is no longer what its image shows that strikes one as unique; its first meaning is no longer to be found in what it says, but in what it is.

This new status of the original work is the perfectly rational consequence of the new means of reproduction. But it is at this point that a process of mystification again enters. The meaning of the original work no longer lies in what it uniquely says but in what it uniquely is. How is its unique existence evaluated and defined in our present culture? It is defined as an object whose value depends upon its rarity. This market is affirmed and gauged by the price it fetches on the market. But because it is nevertheless "a work

Church of St. Francis of Assisi.

Virgin of the Rocks by Leonardo da Vinci (1452–1519). Reproduced by courtesy of the Trustees, The National Gallery, London.

Before the *Virgin of the Rocks* the visitor to the National Gallery would be encouraged by nearly everything he might have heard and read about the painting to feel something like this: "I am in front of it. I can see it. This painting by Leonardo is unlike any other in the world. The National Gallery has the real one. If I look at this painting hard enough, I should somehow be able to feel its authenticity. The *Virgin of the Rocks* by Leonardo da Vinci: it is authentic and therefore it is beautiful."

To dismiss such feelings as naive would be quite wrong. They accord perfectly with the sophisticated culture of art experts for whom the National Gallery catalogue is written. The entry on the *Virgin of the Rocks* is one of the longest entries. It consists of fourteen closely printed pages. They do not deal with the meaning of the image. They deal with who commissioned the painting, legal squabbles, who owned it, its likely date, the families of its owners. Behind this information lie years of research. The aim of

of art"—and art is thought to be greater than commerce—its market price is said to be a reflection of its spiritual value. Yet the spiritual value of an object, as distinct from a message or an example, can only be explained in terms of magic or religion. And since in modern society neither of these is a living force, the art object, the "work of art," is enveloped in an atmosphere of entirely bogus religiosity. Works of art are discussed and presented as though they were holy relics: relics which are first and foremost evidence of their own survival. The past in which they originated is studied in order to prove their survival genuine. They are declared art when their line of descent can be certified.

Virgin of the Rocks by Leonardo da Vinci (1452–1519). Louvre Museum.

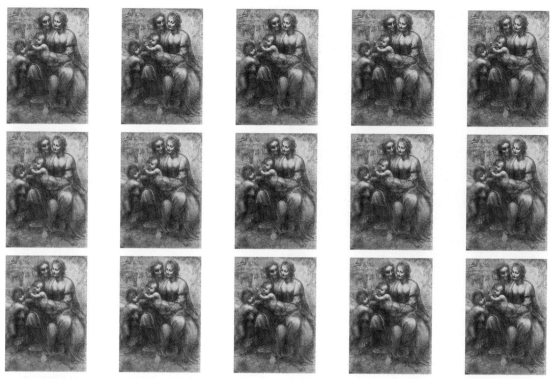

The Virgin and Child with St. Anne and St. John the Baptist by Leonardo da Vinci (1452–1519). Reproduced by courtesy of the Trustees, The National Gallery, London.

the research is to prove beyond any shadow of doubt that the painting is a genuine Leonardo. The secondary aim is to prove that an almost identical painting in the Louvre is a replica of the National Gallery version [see bottom, p. 629].

French art historians try to prove the opposite.

The National Gallery sells more reproductions of Leonardo's cartoon of *The Virgin and Child with St. Anne and St. John the Baptist* [above] than any other picture in their collection. A few years ago it was known only to scholars. It became famous because an American wanted to buy it for two and a half million pounds.

Now it hangs in a room by itself. The room is like a chapel. The drawing is behind bullet-proof perspex. It has acquired a new kind of impressiveness. Not because of what it shows—not because of the meaning of its image. It has become impressive, mysterious, because of its market value.

The bogus religiosity which now surrounds original works of art, and which is ultimately dependent upon their market value, has become the substitute for what paintings lost when the camera made them reproducible. Its function is nostalgic. It is the final empty claim for the continuing values of an oligarchic, undemocratic culture. If the image is no longer unique and exclusive, the art object, the thing, must be made mysteriously so.

The majority of the population do not visit art museums. The following table [right] shows how closely an interest in art is related to privileged education.

The majority take it as axiomatic that the museums are full of holy relics which refer to a mystery which excludes them: the mystery of unaccountable wealth. Or, to put this another way, they believe that original masterpieces belong to the preserve (both materially and spiritually) of the rich. Another table indicates what the idea of an art gallery suggests to each social class.

Venus and Mars by Botticelli (1445–1510). Reproduced by courtesy of the Trustees, The National Gallery, London.

In the age of pictorial reproduction the meaning of paintings is no longer attached to them; their meaning becomes transmittable: that is to say it becomes information of a sort, and, like all information, it is either put to use or ignored; information carries no special authority within itself. When a painting is put to use, its meaning is either modified or totally changed. One should be quite clear about what this involves. It is not a question of reproduction failing to reproduce certain aspects of an image faithfully; it is a question of reproduction making it possible, even inevitable, that an image will be used for many different purposes and that the reproduced image, unlike an original work, can lend itself to them all. Let us examine some of the ways in which the reproduced image lends itself to such usage.

Reproduction isolates a detail of a painting from the whole. The detail is transformed. An allegorical figure becomes a portrait of a girl [see left].

When a painting is reproduced by a film camera it inevitably becomes material for the film-maker's argument.

National proportion of art museum visitors according to level of education: Percentage of each educational category who visit art museums

	Greece	Poland	France	Holland
With no educational qualification	0.02	0.12	0.15	—
Only primary education	0.30	1.50	0.45	0.50
Only secondary education	0.5	10.4	10	20
Further and higher education	11.5	11.7	12.5	17.3

Source: Pierre Bourdieu and Alain Darbel, *L'Amour de l'art,* Editions de Minuit, Paris 1969, Appendix 5, table 4.

Of the places listed below which does a museum remind you of most?

	Manual workers	Skilled and white collar	Professional and upper managerial
	%	%	%
Church	66	45	30.5
Library	9	34	28
Lecture hall	—	4	4.5
Department store or entrance hall in public building	—	7	2
Church and library	9	2	4.5
Church and lecture hall	4	2	—
Library and lecture hall	—	—	2
None of these	4	2	19.5
No reply	8	4	9
	100 (n = 53)	100 (n = 98)	100 (n = 99)

Source: As left, Appendix 4, table 8.

Procession to Calvary by Breughel (1525–1569).

A film which reproduces images of a painting leads the spectator, through the painting, to the film-maker's own conclusions. The painting lends authority to the film-maker. This is because a film unfolds in time and a painting does not. In a film the way one image follows another, their succession, constructs an argument which becomes irreversible. In a painting all its elements are there to be seen simultaneously.

The spectator may need time to examine each element of the painting but whenever he reaches a conclusion, the simultaneity of the whole painting is there to reverse or qualify his conclusion. The painting maintains its own authority.

Paintings are often reproduced with words around them.

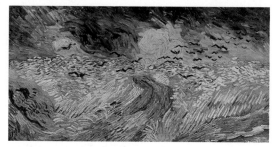

Wheatfield with Crows by Van Gogh (1853–1890).

This is a landscape of a cornfield with birds flying out of it. Look at it for a moment. Then see the painting below.

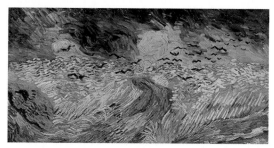

This is the last picture that Van Gogh painted before he killed himself.

It is hard to define exactly how the words have changed the image but undoubtedly they have. The image now illustrates the sentence.

In this essay each image reproduced has become 50 part of an argument which has little or nothing to do with the painting's original independent meaning. The words have quoted the paintings to confirm their own verbal authority. . . .

Reproduced paintings, like all information, have to hold their own against all the other information being continually transmitted [see top, p. 633].

Subject and significance in Titian's *Death of Actaeon*

Heritage exploits the authority of art to glorify the present social system and its priorities.

The means of reproduction are used politically and commercially to disguise or deny what their existence makes possible. But sometimes individuals use them differently [see top, p. 634].

Adults and children sometimes 55 have boards in their bedrooms or living-rooms on which they pin pieces of paper: letters, snapshots, reproductions of paintings, newspaper cuttings, original drawings, postcards. On each board all the images belong to the same language and all are more or less equal within it, because they have been chosen in a highly personal way to match and express the experience of the room's inhabitant. Logically, these boards should replace museums.

What are we saying by that? Let us first be sure about what we are not saying.

We are not saying that there is nothing left to experience before original works of art except a sense of awe because they have survived. The way original works of art are usually approached—through museum catalogues, guides, hired cassettes, etc.—is not the only way they might be approached. When the art of the past ceases to be viewed nostalgically, the

Consequently a reproduction, as well as making its own references to the image of its original, becomes itself the reference point for other images. The meaning of an image is changed according to what one sees immediately beside it or what comes immediately after it. Such authority as it retains, is distributed over the whole context in which it appears [below].

Because works of art are reproducible, they can, theoretically, be used by anybody. Yet mostly—in art books, magazines, films, or within gilt frames in living-rooms—reproductions are still used to bolster the illusion that nothing has changed, that art, with its unique undiminished authority, justifies most other forms of authority, that art makes inequality seem noble and hierarchies seem thrilling. For example, the whole concept of the National Cultural

EVERY JACKET CARRIES A GOVERNMENT HEALTH WARNING.

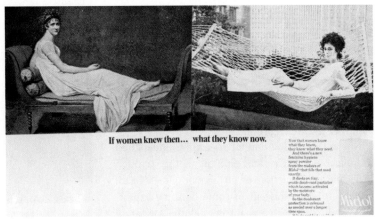

If women knew then... what they know now.

works will cease to be holy relics—although they will never re-become what they were before the age of reproduction. We are not saying original works of art are now useless.

Original paintings are silent and still in a sense that information never is. Even a reproduction hung on a wall is not comparable in this respect for in the original the silence and stillness permeate the actual material, the paint, in which one follows the traces of the painter's immediate gestures. This has the effect of closing the distance in time between the painting of the picture and one's own act of looking at it. In this special sense all paintings are contemporary. Hence the immediacy of their testimony. Their historical moment is literally there before our eyes. Cézanne made a similar observation from the painter's point of view. "A minute in the world's life passes! To paint it in its reality, and forget everything for that! To become that minute, to be the sensitive plate . . . give the image of what we see, forgetting everything that has appeared before our time . . ." What we make of that painted moment when it is before our eyes depends upon what we expect of art, and that in turn depends today upon how we have already experienced the meaning of paintings through reproductions.

Nor are we saying that all art can be understood spontaneously. We are not claiming that to cut out a magazine reproduction of an archaic Greek head, because it is reminiscent of some personal experience, and to pin it to a board beside other disparate images, is to come to terms with the full meaning of that head.

The idea of innocence faces two ways. By refusing to 60 enter a conspiracy, one remains innocent of that conspiracy. But to remain innocent may also be to remain ignorant. The issue is not between innocence and knowledge (or between the natural and the cultural) but between a total approach to art which attempts to relate it to every aspect of experience and the esoteric approach of a few specialized experts who are the clerks of the nostalgia of a ruling class in decline. (In decline, not before the proletariat, but before the new power of the corporation and the state.) The real question is: to whom does the meaning of the art of the past properly belong? To those who can apply it to their own lives, or to a cultural hierarchy of relic specialists?

Woman Pouring Milk by Vermeer (1632–1675).

The visual arts have always existed within a certain preserve; originally this preserve was magical or sacred. But it was also physical: it was the place, the cave, the building, in which, or for which, the work was made. The experience of art, which at first was the experience of ritual, was set apart from the rest of life—precisely in order to be able to exercise power over it. Later the preserve of art became a social one. It entered the culture of the ruling class, whilst physically it was set apart and isolated in their palaces and houses. During all this history the authority of art was inseparable from the particular authority of the preserve.

What the modern means of reproduction have done is to destroy the authority of art and to remove it—or, rather, to remove its images which they reproduce—from any preserve. For the first time ever, images of art have become ephemeral, ubiquitous, insubstantial, available, valueless, free. They surround us in the same way as a language surrounds us. They have entered the mainstream of life over which they no longer, in themselves, have power.

Yet very few people are aware of what has happened because the means of reproduction are used nearly all the time to promote the illusion that nothing has changed except that the masses, thanks to reproductions, can now begin to appreciate art as the cultured minority once did. Understandably, the masses remain uninterested and sceptical.

If the new language of images were used differently, it would, through its use, confer a new kind of power. Within it we could begin to define our experiences more precisely in areas where words are inadequate. (Seeing comes before words.) Not only personal experience, but also the essential historical experience of our relation to the past: that is to say the experience of seeking to give meaning to our lives, of trying to understand the history of which we can become the active agents.

The art of the past no longer exists as it once did. 65 Its authority is lost. In its place there is a language of images. What matters now is who uses that language for what purpose. This touches upon questions of copyright for reproduction, the ownership of art presses and publishers, the total policy of public art galleries and museums. As usually presented, these are narrow professional matters. One of the aims of this essay has been to show that what is really at stake is much larger. A people or a class which is cut off from its own past is far less free to choose and to act as a people or class than one that has been able to situate itself in history. This is why—and this is the only reason why—the entire art of the past has now become a political issue. ○

Many of the ideas in the preceding essay have been taken from another, written over forty years ago* by the German critic and philosopher Walter Benjamin.

His essay was entitled The Work of Art in the Age of Mechanical Reproduction. *This essay is available in English in a collection called* Illuminations *(Cape, London, 1970).*

---

* Now over seventy years ago [eds.].

SCOTT MCCLOUD

"When I was a little kid I knew exactly what comics were," Scott McCloud writes in his book *Understanding Comics: The Invisible Art* (1993). "Comics were those bright, colorful magazines filled with bad art, stupid stories and guys in tights." But after looking at a friend's comic book collection, McCloud became "totally obsessed with comics" and in the tenth grade decided to become a comics artist.

In 1982, McCloud graduated with a degree in illustration from Syracuse University. "I wanted to have a good background in writing and art and also just liberal arts in general because I thought that just about anything can be brought to bear in making comics." Later McCloud worked in the production department of DC Comics until he began publishing his two comic series, "Zot!" (1984) and later "Destroy!!"

In *Understanding Comics*, a caricature of McCloud leads readers through an insightful study of the nature of sequential art by tracing the history of the relationship between words and images. "Most readers will find it difficult to look at comics in quite the same way ever again," wrote cartoonist Garry Trudeau of McCloud's work. Recently McCloud has been working with comics in the digital environment. His web site is at <www.scottmccloud .com>. "Show and Tell" is the sixth chapter in *Understanding Comics.*

SHOW AND TELL

Scott McCloud

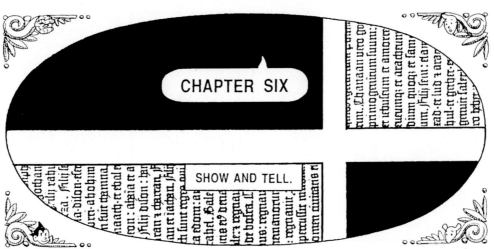

CHAPTER SIX

SHOW AND TELL.

THIS IS MY ROBOT.

WHAT CAN YOU *TELL* US ABOUT YOUR ROBOT, TOMMY?

WELL, UH... I LIKE IT 'CAUSE... 'CAUSE, UH...

IT'S GOT ONE OF *THESE* THINGS.

WHAT IS *THAT*, TOMMY?

138

139

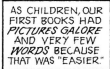

140

MEANWHILE, WORDS AND *MOVING* PICTURES HAVE HALF THE WORLD IN THRALL TO THEIR CHARMS, BUT MUST STRUGGLE TO MAKE *THEIR* POTENTIAL UNDERSTOOD.

WORDS AND PICTURES ARE AS POPULAR AS EVER, BUT THIS WIDESPREAD FEELING THAT THE COMBINATION IS SOMEHOW *BASE* OR *SIMPLISTIC* HAS BECOME A *SELF-FULFILLING PROPHECY.*

THE ROOTS OF THIS ATTITUDE RUN PRETTY *DEEP.*

AS NEAR AS WE CAN TELL, PICTURES *PREDATE* THE WRITTEN WORD BY A *LARGE MARGIN.* HERE ARE SOME BIG HITS FROM THE GOLDEN AGE OF CAVE PAINTING, ABOUT 15,000 YEARS AGO.

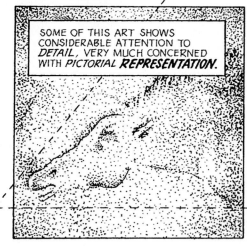

SOME OF THIS ART SHOWS CONSIDERABLE ATTENTION TO *DETAIL,* VERY MUCH CONCERNED WITH PICTORIAL *REPRESENTATION.*

BUT OTHERS WERE VERY *ICONIC,* ACTING AS *SYMBOLS* RATHER THAN PICTURES-- MORE LIKE A *PRIMITIVE LANGUAGE!*

141

AS MENTIONED IN OUR *LAST CHAPTER,* THE EARLIEST *WORDS* WERE, IN FACT, *STYLIZED PICTURES.*

AS SEEN, MOST OF THESE EARLY WORDS STAYED *CLOSE BY* THEIR PARENTS, THE *PICTURES.*

IT DIDN'T TAKE *LONG,* THOUGH-- RELATIVELY SPEAKING-- BEFORE ANCIENT WRITING STARTED TO BECOME MORE *ABSTRACT.*

SOME WRITTEN LANGUAGES SURVIVE TO THIS DAY, BEARING TRACES OF THEIR ANCIENT PICTORIAL HERITAGE.

* SEE PAGE 129.

142

143

*IN ILLUMINATED MANUSCRIPTS, FOR EXAMPLE.

FACSIMILE DETAILS OF PORTRAITS BY DURER
(1519) REMBRANDT (1660) DAVID (1788) AND INGRES
(1810-15).

144

FACSIMILE OF JEAN-BAPTISTE-CAMILLE COROT'S "A VIEW NEAR VOLTERRA" (1838).

John Keats   1819
Ode on a Grecian Urn

1

Thou still unravish'd bride of quietness,
  Thou foster-child of silence and slow time,
Sylvan historian, who canst thus express
A flowery tale more sweetly than our rhyme:
What leaf fring'd legend haunts about thy shape
  Of deities or mortals, or of both,
    In Tempe or the dales of Arcady?
  What men or gods are these? What maidens loth?
What mad pursuit? What struggle to escape?
  What pipes and timbrels? What wild ecstasy?

FIRST STANZA OF KEATS' POEM.

BY THE EARLY 1800's, WESTERN ART AND WRITING HAD DRIFTED ABOUT AS FAR APART AS WAS *POSSIBLE.*

ONE WAS OBSESSED WITH *RESEMBLANCE, LIGHT* AND *COLOR,* ALL THINGS *VISIBLE...*

...THE *OTHER* RICH IN *INVISIBLE* TREASURES, SENSES, EMOTIONS, SPIRITUALITY, PHILOSOPHY...

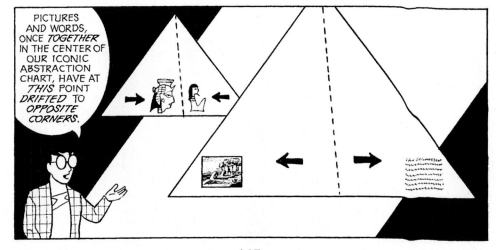

PICTURES AND WORDS, ONCE *TOGETHER* IN THE CENTER OF OUR ICONIC ABSTRACTION CHART, HAVE AT *THIS* POINT *DRIFTED* TO *OPPOSITE CORNERS.*

145

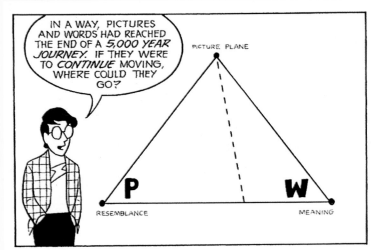

IN A WAY, PICTURES AND WORDS HAD REACHED THE END OF A *5,000 YEAR JOURNEY.* IF THEY WERE TO *CONTINUE* MOVING, WHERE COULD THEY GO?

PICTURE PLANE

P

W

RESEMBLANCE

MEANING

FOR *PICTURES,* THERE WAS ONLY *UP!*

IMPRESSIONISM SENT WESTERN ART TOWARD THE *ABSTRACT VERTEX,* BUT IN A WAY THAT *CLUNG* TO WHAT THE *EYE* SAW.

P

IMPRESSIONISM, WHILE IT COULD BE THOUGHT OF AS THE FIRST *MODERN* MOVEMENT, WAS MORE A *CULMINATION* OF THE *OLD,* THE *ULTIMATE STUDY* OF *LIGHT* AND *COLOR.*

FACSIMILE DETAIL OF "A SUNDAY AFTERNOON ON THE ISLAND OF LA GRANDE JATTE" BY GEORGES SEURAT.

SOON AFTER CAME THE *EXPLOSION!* EXPRESSIONISM, FUTURISM, DADA, SURREALISM, FAUVISM, CUBISM, ABSTRACT EXPRESSIONISM, NEO-PLASTICISM, CONSTRUCTIVISM.

EVERY WHICH WAY BUT *BACKWARDS!*

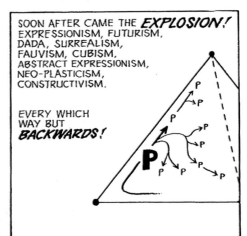

P

STRICT REPRESENTATIONAL STYLES WERE OF LITTLE IMPORTANCE TO THE NEW SCHOOLS. *ABSTRACTION,* BOTH ICONIC AND *NON*-ICONIC MADE A SPECTACULAR *COMEBACK!*

FACSIMILE DETAILS OF PORTRAITS BY PICASSO, LEGER AND KLEE.

MONDRIAN A LA McCLOUD.

SOME ARTISTS HEADED *UPWARD* TO THE *SUMMIT* OF THE PICTURE PLANE, WANTING NEITHER *RESEMBLANCE* NOR EXTERNAL *"MEANING."*

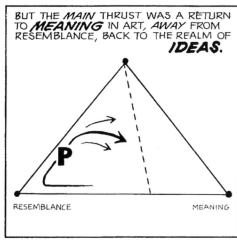

BUT THE *MAIN* THRUST WAS A RETURN TO *MEANING* IN ART, *AWAY* FROM RESEMBLANCE, BACK TO THE REALM OF *IDEAS.*

P

RESEMBLANCE   MEANING

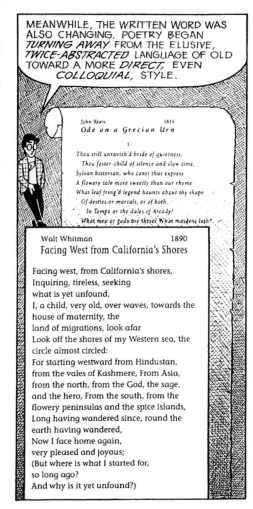

MEANWHILE, THE WRITTEN WORD WAS ALSO CHANGING. POETRY BEGAN *TURNING AWAY* FROM THE ELUSIVE, *TWICE-ABSTRACTED* LANGUAGE OF OLD TOWARD A MORE *DIRECT,* EVEN *COLLOQUIAL,* STYLE.

John Keats   1819
Ode on a Grecian Urn

1

Thou still unravish'd bride of quietness,
   Thou foster-child of silence and slow time,
Sylvan historian, who canst thus express
   A flowery tale more sweetly than our rhyme:
What leaf fring'd legend haunts about thy shape
   Of deities or mortals, or of both,
      In Tempe or the dales of Arcady?
What men or gods are these? What maidens loth?

Walt Whitman   1890
Facing West from California's Shores

Facing west, from California's shores,
Inquiring, tireless, seeking
what is yet unfound,
I, a child, very old, over waves, towards the
house of maternity, the
land of migrations, look afar
Look off the shores of my Western sea, the
circle almost circled:
For starting westward from Hindustan,
from the vales of Kashmere, From Asia,
from the north, from the God, the sage,
and the hero, From the south, from the
flowery peninsulas and the spice islands,
Long having wandered since, round the
earth having wandered,
Now I face home again,
very pleased and joyous;
(But where is what I started for,
so long ago?
And why is it yet unfound?)

IN PROSE, LANGUAGE WAS BECOMING EVEN MORE DIRECT, CONVEYING MEANING *SIMPLY* AND *QUICKLY,* MORE LIKE *PICTURES.*

"MEANING" WAS NOT *ABANDONED* BY *ANY MEANS,* BUT AUTHORS WERE DEFINITELY MOVING *LEFT*--

W

-- AND HEADED FOR A *COLLISION!*

P

W

RESEMBLANCE   MEANING

147

DADA POSTER FOR THE PLAY "THE BEARDED HEART"

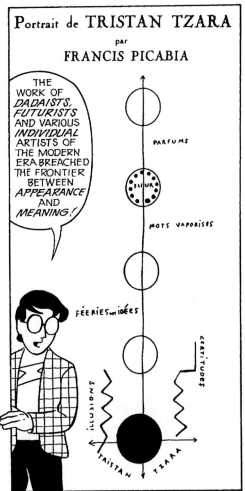

THE WORK OF *DADAISTS*, *FUTURISTS* AND VARIOUS *INDIVIDUAL* ARTISTS OF THE MODERN ERA BREACHED THE FRONTIER BETWEEN *APPEARANCE* AND *MEANING!*

FACSIMILE OF "ORIENTAL SWEETNESS" (1938) BY PAUL KLEE.

PAINTINGS INCREASINGLY TOOK ON *SYMBOLIC*, EVEN *CALLIGRAPHIC*, MEANINGS...

WHILE SOME ARTISTS ADDRESSED THE IRONIES OF WORDS AND PICTURES *HEAD-ON!*

148

AND IN *POPULAR* CULTURE THE TWO FORMS COLLIDED *AGAIN AND AGAIN* WITHOUT ANY PRETENSES OF *"HIGH"* ART.

NOWHERE IS THIS COLLISION MORE THOROUGHLY EXPLORED THAN THE MODERN COMIC. AND IT'S NOT A RECENT OBSESSION.

LET'S GO BACK TO THE EARLY 1800'S BEFORE ANY OF THIS HAPPENED, WHEN WORDS AND PICTURES HAD DRIFTED AS FAR APART AS *POSSIBLE.*

UP TO THAT POINT, *EUROPEAN BROADSHEETS* HAD OFFERED *REMINDERS* OF WHAT WORDS AND PICTURES COULD DO WHEN COMBINED.

BUT AGAIN IT WAS *RODOLPHE TÖPFFER* WHO FORESAW THEIR *INTERDEPENDENCY* AND BROUGHT THE FAMILY *BACK TOGETHER* AT LAST.

M. CRÉPIN ADVERTISES FOR A TUTOR, AND MANY APPLY FOR THE JOB.

I'M SURE THAT THESE IDEAS WERE THE *FURTHEST THING* FROM TÖPFFER'S MIND WHEN HE PUT *PEN TO PAPER*--

--BUT THE FACT THAT THE MODERN COMIC WAS BORN JUST AS ART AND WRITING WERE PREPARING TO CHANGE DIRECTION IS AT LEAST *INTRIGUING.*

AND PERHAPS THIS COMMON THREAD OF *UNIFICATION* DID GROW OUT OF A *SHARED INSTINCT* OF THE DAY...

...AN INSTINCT WHICH SAID THAT WE HAD REACHED THE END OF A *LONG JOURNEY* AND THAT IT WAS TIME AT LAST TO *HEAD FOR HOME.*

TRANSLATION BY E. WIESE.

149

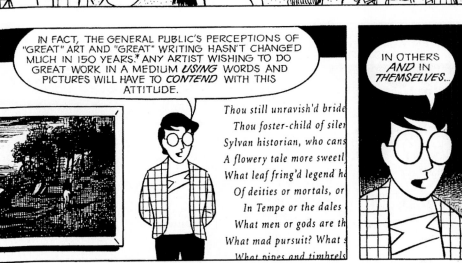

* NOT AS MUCH AS WE LIKE TO
THINK IT HAS, ANYWAY.

THE ART FORM OF COMICS IS MANY CENTURIES OLD, BUT IT'S *PERCEIVED* AS A RECENT INVENTION AND SUFFERS THE CURSE OF *ALL* NEW MEDIA,

THE CURSE OF BEING JUDGED BY THE STANDARDS OF THE OLD.

EVER SINCE THE INVENTION OF THE WRITTEN WORD, NEW MEDIA HAVE BEEN *MISUNDERSTOOD*.

CAREFUL, JACOB! IF YOU KEEP DOING THIS, YOU'LL STOP USING YOUR *MEMORY!*

EACH NEW MEDIUM BEGINS ITS LIFE BY IMITATING ITS *PREDECESSORS*. MANY EARLY MOVIES WERE LIKE FILMED *STAGE PLAYS*, MUCH EARLY *TELEVISION* WAS LIKE *RADIO WITH PICTURES* OR *REDUCED MOVIES*.

FAR TOO MANY COMICS CREATORS HAVE NO HIGHER GOAL THAN TO MATCH THE ACHIEVEMENTS OF OTHER MEDIA, AND VIEW ANY CHANCE TO *WORK* IN OTHER MEDIA AS A *STEP UP.*

AND *AGAIN,* AS LONG AS WE VIEW COMICS AS A *GENRE* OF WRITING OR A *STYLE* OF GRAPHIC ART THIS ATTITUDE MAY *NEVER* DISAPPEAR.

151

WORDS AND PICTURES IN COMBINATION MAY NOT BE MY *DEFINITION* OF COMICS, BUT THE COMBINATION HAS HAD *TREMENDOUS INFLUENCE* ON ITS *GROWTH.*

com·ics (kom'iks)**n.** ... form, used with a singula... Juxtaposed pictoria... ...er images in deliberate... ...ence, intended to conve... ...on and/or to produ... response in t... **2.** Superheroes... costumes, figh... villains who want... ...e world, in violent s... ...use.

A HUGE RANGE OF HUMAN EXPERIENCES CAN BE *PORTRAYED* IN COMICS THROUGH EITHER WORDS OR PICTURES.

AS A RESULT--AND DESPITE ITS MANY *OTHER* POTENTIAL USES -- COMICS HAVE BECOME *FIRMLY IDENTIFIED* WITH THE ART OF *STORYTELLING.*

AND *INDEED,* WORDS AND PICTURES HAVE *GREAT* POWERS TO TELL STORIES WHEN CREATORS FULLY EXPLOIT THEM *BOTH.*

DADA
BIOGRAPHY
HORROR
ROMANCE
SURREALISM
BLANK VERSE
HISTORICAL FICTION
EPIC POETRY
FOLK TALES
SOCIAL ALLEGORY
EROTICA
MYSTERY
ADAPTATIONS
RELIGIOUS TOPICS
STREAM OF CONSCIOUSNESS
SATIRE

SEQUENTIAL ART

AND SO FAR, WE'VE ONLY SEEN THE *TIP OF THE ICEBERG!*

AS CHILDREN, WE "SHOW AND TELL" *INTERCHANGEABLY,* WORDS AND IMAGES COMBINING TO TRANSMIT A *CONNECTED SERIES OF IDEAS.*

IT'S GOT ONE OF *THESE* THINGS

THE DIFFERENT WAYS IN WHICH WORDS AND PICTURES CAN *COMBINE* IN COMICS IS VIRTUALLY *UNLIMITED.*

BUT LET'S TRY TO BREAK IT DOWN INTO SOME DISTINCT *CATEGORIES.*

152

FIRST, WE HAVE THE **WORD SPECIFIC** COMBINATIONS, WHERE PICTURES *ILLUSTRATE*, BUT DON'T SIGNIFICANTLY *ADD* TO A LARGELY *COMPLETE* TEXT.

WE STUMBLED BACK TO THE APARTMENT SHORTLY BEFORE DAWN, *VOMITING* EVERY 20 YARDS.

JUDY GAVE ME HER KEYS AND SMILED.

THE *UNITED STATES CONSTITUTION* WAS ADOPTED BY THE *SECOND CONTINENTAL CONGRESS* IN 1787 AND PUT INTO EFFECT IN 1789.

THEN THERE ARE **PICTURE SPECIFIC** COMBINATIONS WHERE WORDS DO LITTLE MORE THAN ADD A *SOUNDTRACK* TO A VISUALLY TOLD SEQUENCE.

HE DID IT!

MMM... MMM...

AND, OF COURSE, **DUO-SPECIFIC** PANELS IN WHICH BOTH WORDS AND PICTURES SEND ESSENTIALLY THE *SAME* MESSAGE.

GRIM-FACED, GEORGE LIFTED HIS LOLLYPOP.

*B*UT THE CAPTAIN'S MIGHTY BLOW *MISSES* ITS INTENDED TARGET!

BLAST! HE *DODGED* MY PUNCH AND I STRUCK THIS *BRICK WALL!*

HA! I DODGED YOU!

I FEEL SO *SAD!*

...THOUGHT AMY.

153

ANOTHER TYPE IS THE **ADDITIVE** COMBINATION WHERE WORDS *AMPLIFY* OR *ELABORATE* ON AN IMAGE OR *VICE VERSA.*

MY HEAD FEELS LIKE A *SMASHED PUMPKIN!*

HOW D'YA LIKE MY *NEW THREADS,* BABE?

IS THIS THE SAME *JUPITER* OF MY YOUTH?

IN **PARALLEL** COMBINATIONS, WORDS AND PICTURES SEEM TO FOLLOW VERY DIFFERENT COURSES--WITHOUT *INTERSECTING.*

"TALKED TO *BILL* YET?"

"*SALLY* DID. *WHY?*"

"THE *TEST RESULTS* CAME BACK. ALL *NEGATIVE.*"

"*REALLY?* THAT'S *GREAT!*"

WELL...

PEPPER.

CEREAL.

MILK. BUTTER.

LIGHT BULBS.

STILL ANOTHER OPTION IS THE **MONTAGE** WHERE WORDS ARE TREATED AS INTEGRAL *PARTS* OF THE PICTURE.

CASH FLOW PUBL. BOTTOM LINE ANNUAL REPORT

HAPPY!

154

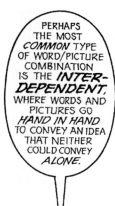

155

156

WHEN *PICTURES* CARRY THE WEIGHT OF CLARITY IN A SCENE, THEY FREE WORDS TO EXPLORE A WIDER AREA.

LET'S SAY I SHOW YOU A WOMAN WALKING ACROSS THE STREET IN THE RAIN, BUYING A PINT OF ICE CREAM AND EATING IT IN HER APARTMENT--

--ALL IN *PICTURES.*

157

WHEN A SCENE SHOWS YOU ALL YOU *"NEED"* TO KNOW, LIKE *THIS* ONE, THE LATITUDE FOR **SCRIPTING** GROWS *ENORMOUSLY.*

I MAY BE ALONE LIKE THIS FOR A VERY LONG TIME.

IT COULD BECOME AN *INTERNAL MONOLOGUE.*

(INTERDEPENDENT)

PERHAPS SOMETHING WILDLY *INCONGRUOUS*

"MISSION CONTROL, MISSION CONTROL, DO YOU READ ME?"

(PARALLEL)

MAYBE IT'S ALL JUST A BIG *ADVERTISEMENT!*

YOU'LL *Love* THE TASTE!

(INTERDEPENDENT)

OR A CHANCE TO RUMINATE ON *BROADER TOPICS.*

THIS IS THE WAY THE WORLD ENDS...

THIS IS THE WAY THE WORLD ENDS...

(INTERDEPENDENT)

158

ON THE *OTHER* HAND, IF THE **WORDS** LOCK IN THE *"MEANING"* OF A SEQUENCE, THEN THE *PICTURES* CAN REALLY TAKE OFF.

SAME SCENE NOW, BUT THIS TIME ALL IN *WORDS!*

I CROSSED THE STREET TO THE CONVENIENCE STORE. THE RAIN SOAKED INTO MY BOOTS.

I FOUND THE LAST PINT OF CHOCOLATE CHOCOLATE CHIP IN THE FREEZER.

THE CLERK TRIED TO PICK ME UP. I SAID *NO THANKS.* HE GAVE ME THIS CREEPY LOOK...

I WENT BACK TO THE APARTMENT--

--AND FINISHED IT ALL IN AN HOUR.

ALONE AT LAST.

159

NOW, ONE COULD JUST *COMBINE* THE *PICTURES* FROM PAGE 157 WITH THE WORDS FROM PAGE 159 --

--BUT WHAT ARE SOME *OTHER* OPTIONS?

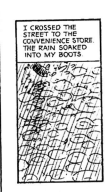

IF THE ARTIST WANTS TO, HE/SHE CAN NOW SHOW ONLY *FRAGMENTS* OF A SCENE.

(WORD SPECIFIC)

OR MOVE TOWARD GREATER LEVELS OF *ABSTRACTION* OR *EXPRESSION*.

THE CLERK TRIED TO PICK ME UP. I SAID *NO THANKS*. HE GAVE ME THIS CREEPY LOOK...

(AMPLIFICATION)

PERHAPS THE ARTIST CAN GIVE US SOME IMPORTANT *EMOTIONAL* INFORMATION.

I WENT BACK TO THE APARTMENT--

(INTERDEPENDENT)

OR SHIFT AHEAD OR BACKWARDS IN TIME.

--AND FINISHED IT ALL IN AN HOUR.

ALONE AT LAST.

(WORD SPECIFIC)

160

HOWEVER MUCH WE MAY *CHART* THESE THINGS, THEY'RE ALL *ULTIMATELY* BEST LEFT TO THE CREATOR'S *INSTINCTS.*

THE MIXING OF WORDS AND PICTURES IS MORE *ALCHEMY* THAN SCIENCE.

SOME OF THE SECRETS OF THOSE *FIRST* ALCHEMISTS MAY HAVE BEEN LOST IN THE ANCIENT PAST.

BUT WE HAVE SOME POWERFUL MAGIC RIGHT HERE IN THE *20TH CENTURY, TOO!*

THE RICHNESS OF MODERN LANGUAGE IS AN *IRREPLACEABLE COMMODITY!*

THIS IS AN *EXCITING TIME* TO BE MAKING COMICS, AND IN MANY WAYS I FEEL VERY *LUCKY* TO HAVE BEEN BORN WHEN I WAS.

STILL, I DO FEEL A CERTAIN *VAGUE LONGING* FOR THAT TIME OVER *50* CENTURIES AGO --

-- WHEN TO TELL WAS TO *SHOW* --

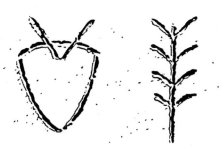

-- AND TO SHOW WAS TO *TELL.*

161

Appendix B
On Reading Visual and Verbal Texts

Many writers create pictures with words; many artists convey a complicated idea in a single image; and, increasingly, many people use words and images in combination to create meaning. As you become better readers of the diverse texts in *Seeing & Writing 2* and better writers, we hope that you also will become more conversant with the distinctions between types of texts and among the different genres. The following eight groups of suggestions offer possible strategies for helping you begin to approach a range of verbal and visual texts: images, essays, advertisements, poetry, paintings, photographs, short stories, and mixed media.

Reading an Image

Seeing & Writing 2 features many different types of images, including photos, ads, paintings, prints, and film stills and frames. The following gives general guidelines for reading and making meaning of various kinds of images.

Determine the initial source of the image. In some cases, images that appear to be photos are actually stills or frames from films. This means that the shot is cut from a larger whole, which might change the meaning (e.g., the stills from *Pocahontas* and *Smoke Signals* in Chapter 7, p. 567). In other cases, images that appear to be photos may be paintings (e.g., Alfred Leslie's *Television Moon* in Chapter 1, p. 88). In other cases, images are clearly photos or paintings.

Viewers should consider the context and construction of each image. In looking at a movie still, it is important to have an understanding of the film, as this is probably assumed by the artist. You should also be aware of the different limitations and opportunities available to photographers as opposed to painters. Photographers can and often do enhance and transform their shots, but initially they begin with an image that captures a specific and finite moment in time. Painters may capture the mood of a moment, but not with the click of a shutter. A photographer is expected, on some level, to be "true" to his or her subject; a painter is not. Thus, when a photographer alters the image, the reader should ask why—as she should when a painter attempts to exactly re-create life.

Determine what is the figure and what is the background. These are terms from Gestalt theories of visual organization. They are useful in determining the most important object in an image. The figure is what draws the viewer's attention; the background is its immediate context. Just as a story might have a protagonist, a visual image has a figure—what the viewer should follow through the narrative of the image. This figure might be a building, a person, or an object. The background is all else.

Often the viewer's eye works almost unconsciously to find the figure in a visual image. For example, it is fairly easy to determine that the figure in Mark Peterson's *Image of Homelessness* (p. 155) is the homeless man in the appliance box. The viewer intuits this information because in many ways the photo is a standard, centered portrait. However, in an image like Andreas Gursky's *99 cent* (pp. 382–83), it might take a moment to think through what the figure is. Depending on how the viewer defines the figure, he or she may read the photo quite differently.

Determine the narrative of the image. Every image is communicating something to the viewer. Our culture is driven by narrative, driven by a desire to draw connections. Those who study visual perception and literacy even refer to people as *homo significans*—"meaning makers." So, the easiest way to first read an image is to determine its story, its message. What are the denotative and connotative meanings of the objects, people, and places within the image? Where are the items in the image placed in relationship to each other? In our drive to make meaning, we often connect elements that are in close proximity and establish relationships between or among them. This is just as true for objects (e.g., the merchandise in David Butow's photo in Chapter 6, p. 521) as it is for people (e.g., the people sitting around the table in Tina Barney's photo on p. 215). Viewers, just like readers, prefer an interpretation that offers closure.

Because viewers come from different backgrounds and read with different perceptions, the narrative of an image may be perceived differently by different viewers. In some cases, such as with images we think of as "art," these varying perspectives add depth to a reading. However, in other cases, such as with images we think of as "ads," the varying perspectives can destroy a product. For example, Miranda Lichtenstein might be quite pleased if a variety of viewers were to find a variety of narratives in her *Untitled #9* (pp. 166–67). But if some viewers were to read the Rockport image (p. 372) as a parody of masculinity rather than as a paean to it, the Rockport ad agency might soon find itself out of a job.

Break the image into visual fields, looking for focal points. Images direct a viewer's eyes. Some aspects of the image draw our attention, whereas others recede. Our initial impulse is to focus on the center of an image because it offers balance, but often an artist shifts the viewer's focus through the use of color, light, or line. If the viewer can locate the composition's focal point (or points), this can serve as a clue to interpreting the image. It might help first to divide an image by finding its horizontal or diagonal line. Sometimes this line is self-evident, as in Richard Misrach's *Waiting, Edwards Air Force Base* (p. 177), where it is an actual horizon. At other times this line is not as self-evident but still present, as in the bicycle ad (p. 67), where it is the textual line "Save Money—Save Time—Save Temper." Such lines direct the viewer's attention, leading it up or down or across, and they also provide smooth movement within an image, which is crucial for the visual perception of most viewers.

If the viewer's initial reaction is to stare at the center of an image, then the artist must have some reason for fighting this impulse. The viewer should think about how the focal point (its position, its composition, its identity) helps to construct the meaning of the image. For example, in Raghubir Singh's photo *Durga Puja Immersion* (p. 198), the viewer can try to focus on a statue that is slightly off-center, but the crowd at another statue at the right edge of the picture captures the viewer's eye, creating a sense of movement and drawing the viewer into the activity.

Look for patterns of color, shape, or shadow in the image. Viewers organize information by establishing relationships of similarity, by looking for patterns. And patterns may be established by repeating a color or a shape, by repeating the use of light or dark. Just as a writer might use alliteration or rhyming to draw a reader's attention to connections in a poem, a visual artist uses repetition to draw a viewer's eye. The question is, "Why is my eye being drawn in this way?" The pattern may hint at the image's meaning—or part of that meaning—or it may be a pattern wholly imposed by a viewer longing for closure.

Advertising images rely heavily on repeated patterns to convey and then hammer home their message. So, for example, a viewer can easily find a repetition of color in the 1953 Roadmaster ad (p. 68). The color red links the bike, the AMF and Roadmaster logos, the slogan, the star, the package under the tree, the boy's pajamas, the curtain, and the boy's hair. In the end, the message is simple: Christmas = Roadmaster. Yet patterns are not exclusively the domain of commercial art. Instead, they may be traced within one painting, like the red in Carmen Lomas Garza's *Tamalada* (p. 212), or across a series of images to determine an artistic style, like the intense color saturation of Raghubir Singh's photos (pp. 198–99).

Look for visual manifestations of metaphor, metonymy, or symbolism. Visual artists employ many of the same devices that verbal artists use. Thus, when a viewer considers an image, he or she should look for metaphor, metonymy, and symbol. Whereas readers frequently find metaphor, viewers frequently find metonymy. The concept of "part for whole" is particularly well suited to a visual medium. Thus, an artist might show only a fragment of a larger object in order to send a message to a reader. For example, in David Butow's photograph (p. 521), he shows only a storefront window. We do not need to see the entire store in order to understand what is being represented. In addition, this section is cut from the whole and now stands as an aesthetic object, which a standard storefront window would not.

Viewers should also look for symbolic images, often referred to as cultural icons. A culture often has a visual shorthand language, and within this language certain images have specific, shared meanings: for example, the American flag, a cowboy, Elvis Presley, Marilyn Monroe. These symbolic images may be used in a way that is true to their accepted cultural currency or in a way that subverts this cultural meaning. For example, the Graphis image entitled *Man Turning into a Barcode* (p. 56) plays on our cultural understanding of the bar code. Such codes mark commercial products, track inventory, and encode prices. So, when a person turns into a bar code, what happens to him? He is now a product, a piece of inventory just like, say, a bottle of mouthwash.

Remember that a complete reading should account for all design elements that were within the control of the artist. Viewers should remember that all images are composed. The elements within them are like the elements in a poem. When a reader analyzes a poem, she accounts not just for the language of the poem but also for the capitalization, the punctuation, the arrangement into lines and stanzas, and so on. When a viewer analyzes an image, she should think about it in essentially the same way, asking the following questions about its design:

— Is there any obvious distortion in the image (things taller, smaller, flatter, fatter, brighter, darker, etc.)? How does this distortion relate to or shape the meaning of the image?

— Is there anything only partially within the frame of the image? Why?

— What is the perspective of the image? Is the viewer placed above the image, below it, or at the same level? How is this related to the meaning of the image?

— What is the size of the image? Is it a miniature or a magnification? How does this relate to the message?

An active reader remembers how the artist has chosen to present his or her final image: photo or painting, watercolor or oil, black and white or color. These statements hold true for painters, graphic designers, and photographers. For example, one of the most popular contemporary photographers, Lorna Simpson, often dramatically enlarges her photos and has them printed to feltboard. In this case, a viewer wishing to read the images needs to also account for the manner in which a photo printed on felt is very different from a photo printed to glossy paper. The picture of the painting by Chuck Close that is reproduced in this textbook (p. 118) is small; but in a museum a viewer looking at a painting by Close would see a massive work, usually 7 feet by 8 feet. The size of this work is crucial to reading it.

Reading an Essay

Each essay in *Seeing & Writing 2* is part of a larger whole—a textbook—composed of written and visual texts. Each essay should be read not only for what it says but also for how it is laid out (how words and images are distributed) and how it fits into the entire chapter. What inferences can be made about *Seeing & Writing 2* from the way the texts are presented? Looking at essays as physical objects can be an important step in seeing (and developing one's own) written texts with a fresh eye.

The core activity of reading an essay involves being a careful observer, first getting the facts straight through a series of precise observations.

— Exactly what happens in the essay? What process occurs between the opening and the closing paragraphs?

— Where does the voice of the essay originate? (Who is speaking?) In what tone does the voice speak? What kind of language does it use?

— Where does the essay take place? What details are given to help the reader visualize the world of the essay?

— What images or ideas predominate? What patterns or shifts in images or ideas occur during the course of the essay?

— What is the purpose of the text? Is it to describe, to argue, to tell a story, to explain, to compare—or a combination of these?

The more accurate and plentiful a reader's observations are about a given text, the more opportunities there will be to construct and defend meaningful inferences.

Reading an Advertisement

There are many examples of advertisements in *Seeing & Writing 2*, spanning a wide range of products and pitches from throughout the twentieth century. The advertisement as a genre has probably existed for as long as the market economy has; a combination of words and pictures is used for a single purpose, no matter the product—to entice consumers to buy. Because ads often must make their points in a page or two, they combine visual and verbal strategies to shape the most powerful message possible in the briefest amount of space. Most of us encounter more advertisements in a day than any other kind of text; the following questions will facilitate critical reading of these texts.

What is foregrounded in the frame of the advertisement? Where is the viewer's eye drawn first? In the Coca-Cola advertisement at the beginning of Chapter 2 (p. 127), the bottle of Coke in the bottom half of the frame and the word *America* in the top half are roughly equal in drawing our attention. Our eye goes only secondarily to the rest of the print on the page. Thus, the association of Coca-Cola with America is made visually.

How much of the advertisement's message is delivered through words and how much through images? What is the proportion of one to the other? In the 1998 Murray bicycle ad (p. 69), most of the message is conveyed through the image: a man and a woman, a few feet away from two bicycles, gaze into the distance from a coastal vista. The text, overwhelmed by the picturesque view, appeals to Americans' love of freedom and downplays the importance of place: Place is not important. It's the freedom that counts. Of course, place is important; otherwise the couple would have been presented at a far less interesting place. By the time the readers get to the text, they have taken in the striking image and will probably not compare the two for any possible contradictions.

Are the connotations of the language congruent with the connotations of the images? The image of RuPaul dominates the advertisement on page 372 of Chapter 4; the Rockport trademark takes a background position in the upper righthand corner of the frame. The central printed assertion. "I'm comfortable being a MAN," draws our eye. In this case the small print "drag superstar" at the bottom and the larger print "I'm comfortable . . ." at the top create a tension between the image of the well-dressed, masculine man and the implied questioning of his gender identity.

In what ways does the advertisement appeal to a specific type of viewer? The purpose of advertisements is to market something to a particular audience. The Visa advertisement in Chapter 5 (p. 406), with a young man holding a guitar, clearly has a youthful appeal.

What is the underlying logic of the advertisement? What does it suggest? This logic is created by the pairing of the image and the product. In Diesel's *Freedom Is Now* advertisement (p. 404), for example, the underlying logic is that as a customer of the Diesel brand you participate in the outlook and lifestyle of the carefree, nonconformist couple pictured.

Reading a Poem

Poetry is one of the oldest and most complicated forms of verbal texts. Generally it can be defined as any rhythmical or metrical composition distinguished by a creative use of verbal tools. Historically governed by strict rules of form, style, diction, and meter, poets have created memorable texts within the poetic tradition by carefully deploying such tools as words, phrases, sounds, sentence structures, figurative language, imagery, and ideas. The rules governing poetry today are much more loose, but readers generally know a poem when they see it: a short text with set line breaks. Because poets' language has to be more economical than that of prose writers, every word in a poem can be packed with multiple meanings. Many people argue that poetry is meant to be experienced as much as it is meant to be read. The questions that follow will help readers who are unfamiliar with this complicated and sometimes difficult genre.

How does the poem look on the page? A reader doesn't need a detailed knowledge of poetics to make careful observations about a poem's shape—its length, the arrangement of lines, or any other visual detail. In "Edward Hopper and the House by the Railroad (1925)" by Edward Hirsch, (p. 131), the length of the stanzas and the placement of the stanzas on the page suggest a balanced structure, which is fitting since the poem describes a house.

Who is the speaker of the poem? Although readers often feel mystified by poems, if they imagine the speaker they may get some clues. In Marge Piercy's "Imaging," for example (p. 336), it is a woman speaking for her body. Her language attempts to heal the split between her body and her mind.

What kinds of images are present in the poem? The poem "Imaging" by Marge Piercy (p. 336) starts with many images that tell the reader what her body is not: "a dress," "a coat," "a house," "a suit of armor," "a lump of meat in which I nuzzle like a worm." By listing these diverse inanimate things the speaker's body is not, the poet evokes in the reader a sense of what her body might be: something active, something alive. In the final stanza, Piercy uses metaphor again, this time to suggest what her body is: "this angel I meet on my back . . . dark as the inside of the moon," an image that is very different from those in the opening stanza, powerful precisely because it is difficult to categorize and impossible to visualize.

What does the poem sound like? Poems are made for breath and air, and often reading them aloud aids in understanding. This can be a way to investigate the tone of a poem as a means to discovering its meanings. Reading aloud Sharon Olds's poem "The Death of Marilyn Monroe" (p. 483) may illustrate, for example, how the speaker's breath is essential. The single-word lines that end the poem depend upon a single breath for each line. In this way, the reader is connected to the "ordinary woman" breathing in the poem's conclusion.

What is the world of the poem like? Does it have a setting? Is it in a landscape? Does it have characters? Different poems foreground different elements. Lucille Clifton's poem "When I Go Home," for example (p. 213), takes place in the memory of the speaker's "home." Elements of this home include her mother ("alive again and humming"), the smell of bread dough, the feel of linoleum, and the way her mother held the house "together with her song." In short, the memory of the home her mother created is her home.

Reading a Painting

Each painting in *Seeing & Writing 2* is part of a visual genre that shares certain conventions and goals. Painting, along with sculpture, has historically been associated with high art and the individual style and vision of the artist; one of the oldest visual genres, it has developed through many schools of representative and abstract styles of expression. The following questions will help you read paintings in a meaningful way even if you have no previous experience in studying the genre conventions of painting.

What is the style of painting? A viewer doesn't need to be well versed in art history to determine whether a painting is more or less realistic. To begin reading a painting, he or she must understand what the painter wants to convey: a realistic depiction of a person, place, or thing; a purely personal impression of it; or something in between. For example, Edward Hopper's *House by the Railroad* (p. 130) is clearly recognizable as a house by a railroad even though Hopper imbues the painting with a haunting feeling and a strong sense of isolation.

What is the tone of the painting? Just as a writer uses words, a painter uses color and light. Thus a painting might be airy and inviting, with little shading and bright colors. An example is Carmen Lomas Garza's *Tamalada* (p. 212), which conveys a sense of family togetherness with little complication. Alternatively a painting might be dark and foreboding, with lots of shadow and dark shades. An example is Andy Warhol's *Large Triple Elvis, 1963* (p. 480).

What is the size of the painting? In an illustrated textbook, the size of an original painting is quite difficult to discern. However, an image's size makes a significant impression on a viewer. Consider the images by Chuck Close and Tim Gardner that are included in this textbook (pp. 118–19, 79–82). Seen in a museum, Close's painting is nearly five times as large as Gardner's—although in Close's work we see only a head and in Gardner's we see an entire person. An artist often uses size to convey a message. For example, during the Renaissance loved ones gave each other small miniature portraits to wear on garments to indicate intimate relationships. The size permitted this message to be shared.

How does the subject of the painting relate to the manner in which the artist depicts it? Like all art, paintings can affect the way their viewers see the world. For example, through his depiction of the American West, Albert Bierstadt shaped the world's view of this part of America—as both reality and myth. In *Among the Sierra Nevada Mountains, California, 1868* (pp. 142–43) Bierstadt's approach to his subject is reverential, and he expects his audience to share this feeling because the grandeur of nature is worthy of their respect. In contrast, Gardner plays with his audience's expectations of painting and photography by re-creating candid photographs in watercolor paintings (pp. 79–82).

What perspective is used in the painting? The perspective situates the viewer and can be used to convey or negate depth. For example, in *House by the Railroad* (p. 130), Edward Hopper relies on perspective to create a sense of isolation. In contrast, many primitive or folk art styles of painting, such as the one used by Carmen Lomas Garza (p. 212), eschew perspective and offer simple, flat images. These underscore a sense of primitive purity and honesty. Readers should also be alert to paintings that add depth where one might not expect it (e.g., the reflections in the window in Richard Estes's *Central Savings,* p. 54) or deny depth where one does expect it (e.g., the images of Elvis and Marilyn Monroe in Warhol's paintings, pp. 480–81). Often, these works use perspective to add an extra layer of meaning.

Reading a Photograph

Like the paintings, the photographs in *Seeing & Writing* 2 are part of a visual genre that shares certain conventions and goals. This genre has existed for a little over a century and is commonly recognized as setting the standard for realistic representation, replacing painting as the most accurate means of recording an image. Generally, photographs can be divided into one of two broad categories: documentary photographs, such as those that accompany a news story, that seek to accurately show what a person, place, or event actually looks like; and creative photographs, such as advertising or artistic photos, in which the person, place, event, or photograph has been staged to some degree in order to achieve a certain effect. The Looking Closer section for Chapter 7, "The Ethics of Representation" (pp. 603–619), examines the blurring of the lines between these two types of photographs. The following questions will help you interpret photographs even if you are unfamiliar with the genre conventions of photography.

Is the photo a news, commercial, or art image? The distinctions are becoming increasingly blurred, but a reader should still understand the initial purpose of the photo if only to get a sense of its context. For example, viewers may be expected to spend only a few seconds scanning a newspaper photo but minutes or hours studying an art photo in a gallery. A photographer's beliefs about how the image will be received by an audience affect the way in which he or she composes the image. Viewers might consider how Adbusters' *Tommy: Follow the Flock* (p. 459) differs dramatically from James Nachtwey's photo of Ground Zero (p. 274) largely because of their contexts and purposes: One spoofs advertising, the other presents a historic moment.

Is the photo in black and white or color? Black and white photos, such as Andrew Savulich's snapshots (pp. 268–71), hold a documentary connotation. Often these may be news photos, and the simplicity of black and white (initially a limitation of the printing press) conveys a sense of straightforward truth. Other photos may not be news images but are associated with the same connotations, such as Guillermo Gómez-Peña's *Authentic Cuban Santeria* (p. 418). Color photos may more accurately reflect the images we associate with real life, but often they are regarded as commercial.

Does the image in the photo seem to have been altered in any way? Photography seems like an art that captures exactly what the photographer sees: a moment in time. However, it is easy to airbrush out cosmetic defects, rearrange subjects, enhance colors and shading, or add digital effects. Often these changes are difficult to discern. Viewers should consider the purpose of a photo when asking whether effects might have been added and how to interpret their use. For example, a model in an ad or fashion editorial is unlikely to appear "as is," and most readers understand that the model's image will be modified before it is published. However, fewer readers expect that news images, such as that of the flag-raising on Iwo Jima (p. 226), will be altered.

How is the image framed in the photo? Just like text on a page, an image in a photo might be centered, offset to the left, or offset to the right. Traditionally a straight, centered shot has been used for portraits. Offset shots are often used to suggest motion by drawing the viewer's eye along a horizontal or diagonal line, as in Raghubir Singh's *Durga Puja Immersion* (p. 198). Sometimes these images also suggest entrapment by crowding the subject against one of the photo's edges. In addition, photos have a vertical axis that can either open up or close down an image. If a photographer heavily shades the top of an image it can appear to be pressing down on the photo subject, whereas if the image is bright, the effect can be the opposite. For example, William Eggleston's *Untitled* (pp. 64–65) offers an imposing top element that crowds the composition.

How is the photo cropped? Often what is left out of a photo is as important as what is included in it. A photo may have been cropped (or cut) to eliminate elements that would distract from the subject or to refocus the subject. For example, Joe Rosenthal's picture (p. 226) has focused the viewer's attention on the flag-raising as a symbol of victory by eliminating anything distracting.

Reading a Short Story

The short story spans works such as biblical narratives and Chaucer's tales, and it gained ground especially in the twentieth century as a dominant literary genre. Generally a short story can be defined as a brief fictional prose narrative; the term is often applied to any work of narrative prose fiction that is shorter than a novel. A short story is usually a connected narrative that has an identifiable plot, structure, characters, setting, and point of view. Short stories are usually easier to read than other verbal texts. The following questions will help you think critically about the formal elements of the story.

What is the point of view of the story? Who is the narrator, and from what perspective is he or she speaking? In "Nebraska" (p. 171), Ron Hansen tells the story from the third person point of view. The story's omniscient narrator describes the people and things that populate a small Nebraska town. The narrator's knowledge of the town suggests that he is a citizen, but his knowledge of people's thoughts and feelings makes him less of a character and more of a device.

What is the setting of the story? Where does it take place? What are the characteristics of that place? Eudora Welty's "The Little Store" (p. 134) takes place in Jackson, Mississippi, and as the title suggests, the store is the setting. This location becomes emblematic of the lives that play out in the small community during the narrator's childhood. As Welty states, "We weren't being sent to the neighborhood grocery for facts of life, or death. But of course those are what we were on the track of, anyway" (para. 30).

Who are the characters in the story? To whom is the story happening? How are the characters affected? The very short story "Viewfinder" by Ethan Canin (p. 297) has few characters—primarily the narrator and his wife. However, it is about characters that are not present—his mother and grandmother. The story is about the narrator's realization that a photograph he has always treasured is not of his mother but of his grandmother. What he thought was his very clear memory of the day and place in the photograph turns out to be faulty. He questions, "My God, you're right. How could that have happened?" (para. 4). Indeed, the family history embodied in family snapshots may not be "true" as we remember.

What happens in the story? What is the main action? What happens in "I Stand Here Ironing" by Tillie Olsen (p. 73) is simple and profound. As she irons a dress, the narrator's thoughts dwell upon her troubled daughter and how her family has arrived at its present situation. The story's action does not move beyond the woman's ruminating as she irons.

What are the significant images in the story? How do things look? Eudora Welty's "The Little Store" (p. 134) is about what a child sees and fails to see. Although Welty's descriptions utilize the five senses, some of the most revealing involve sight. The description of the cheese being "as big as a doll's house" (para. 16) firmly puts readers in the child's point of view. The narrator's descriptions provide readers with a sense of character as well as a sense of place.

What changes or transformations occur (or fail to occur) during the course of the narrative? In Gish Jen's "What Means Switch" (p. 339) the title gives clues about possible transformations. What kind of switching is central to the story? In a narrative about changing ethnic identity, the Chinese American character Mona asserts that her Japanese friend, Sherman, "doesn't get what means switch" (para. 111) when she tries to tell him he can become an American, too. Mona has already "switched"; Sherman does not. Instead, he returns to Japan.

Reading Mixed Media

Mixed media is generally used to describe the work of contemporary artists who employ unusual combinations of material to achieve a desired effect (sometimes appealing to senses of smell, taste, and touch as well as sight). Materials used in the texts in *Seeing & Writing 2* that are labeled as mixed media include wood, "found" ordinary objects, photographs, newspapers, videos, and other unusual or unexpected building blocks combined and presented in extraordinary ways. (*Mixed media* is often used when a piece doesn't fall into a "pure" category such as painting or photography.)

What material has been used in the creation of the work? Why might the artist have used this particular combination of materials? Often the original source of some part of the artwork—text from a newspaper, for example—has been deliberately chosen to make a particular point and must be considered in reading the work as a whole. The artist Sally Mankus (not represented in *Seeing & Writing 2*), for example, lifts rust, carbon, and marking from charred surfaces (mainly bakeware). She writes that "objects (pans, pot lids, napkins, etc.) and materials (rust, carbon) used are so common they become symbols in a universal language."

Is any part of the work a "found" object? Mixed media works often include "found" objects, that is, things that have been incorporated into an original piece or simply appropriated for art. When artists use found objects, they are commenting on the role of these products within our culture. For example, Pepón Osario's *Badge of Honor* (pp. 90–91 and 93) includes actual posters of basketball players and suggests how such figures can become father figures.

Is the work realistic, or is it abstract and impressionistic? Any work of art falls along this spectrum. For example, Duane Hanson's *Tourists* (p. 295) is so realistic that many museum visitors may fail to understand it is a sculpture. In part, this realism is the message. We know these people and immediately recognize their qualities. In contrast, Pepón Osario's *Badge of Honor* (pp. 90–91 and 93) is not as realistic. Instead, the exaggerated opulence of the boy's room invites viewers to contrast it with the father's stark cell.

If the work is three dimensional, what does the third dimension add to the piece? Unless otherwise enhanced, photography and painting are primarily two-dimensional media. Most mixed media offers viewers a third dimension, which might make the work tactile or might add realism. For example, Duane Hanson's *Tourists* would not have the same impact of automatic recognition ("I've seen that couple!") if it were just a photo of tourists.

If the work includes text, what is the relationship between the text and the image/body of the piece? Mixed media pieces sometimes take the form of a collage of image and text. The text comments on the work, helping to frame the viewer's reading. For example, Barbara Kruger's *Untitled* (p. 541) foregrounds the word *picture*—which describes both the work itself and the subject of the work. Yet because the viewer's eye is probably first drawn to the word, not the image, *Untitled* may be offering another interpretation to the viewer: A word can supersede an image.

Glossary

abstract art visual art that explores meaning through shape, color, and texture rather than a realistic representation of scenes or objects.

abstract expressionism an abstract art movement in which the act of expressing emotions was considered as important as the resulting work. Abstract expressionists applied paint rapidly to the canvas, believing that the spontaneity of this technique released creativity.

ad-libbing speaking or performing spontaneously, without preparation.

allusion an indirect, brief, or casual reference to a person, place, event, object, or artwork. Allusion draws on a body of images or stories shared by the audience and allows a short phrase to bring up a whole set of associated information. In "What Means Switch" (p. 339), Gish Jen uses allusions to ski areas, department stores, and "the burning bush" to convey her belonging in Scarsdale.

ambiguity the potential for being reasonably understood in more than one way. Both literature and the visual arts use ambiguity to express the inherent richness and complexity of the world. In advertising, ambiguity can be used to create deception without actually lying.

analogy use of a comparison to extend knowledge of something new by its similarity to something already known. Analogy can be explanatory, as in comparing ice skating with in-line skating. Comparing the "war on drugs" with Prohibition is an example of using analogy to further an argument.

analysis the process of breaking something complex into its parts, examining each part and the relations among the parts, and coming to a better understanding of the whole. An analytical essay reconstructs the whole in an orderly way to facilitate understanding.

argument a claim advanced with its supporting reasons, or evidence. The claim addresses a single point ("the town should fund a night school"). The reasons may be facts ("25 percent of high school students in this town drop out without graduating") or values ("everyone deserves equal treatment"), but they must lead logically to the conclusion without intellectual dishonesty. In an argument essay, the claim is the thesis statement; it is presented early and followed by a summary of the argument. Each of the reasons is then developed, with supporting information where it is needed. In addition to advancing sufficient reasons to support its claim, a good argument assesses and refutes claims opposed to it. An effective argument essay takes into account the audience's values and knowledge base.

assertion a claim or statement of belief. To be useful in discourse, an assertion needs supporting evidence. An unsupported assertion is merely an expression of opinion.

assumption a claim accepted without the necessity of proof or other support. While assumptions are necessary devices in all arguments, many faulty arguments depend on assumptions that, once accepted, require the acceptance of the conclusions. Analysis of an argument should always include a clear statement of its assumptions.

audience the intended recipient of a communication or work of art. In "Learning to See" (p. 238), Barry Lopez identifies audience as an essential part of the photographer's artistic act of "seek[ing] intimacy with the world and then endeavor[ing] to share it." Audiences differ as to their values, assumptions, knowledge bases, needs, desires, tastes, and styles. Having a clear picture of the intended audience is an essential task for a writer.

brainstorming recording thoughts as they occur, with no regard for their relation to each other. When writers brainstorm, they often leap from one thought to another without exploring the connections between ideas. Brainstorming unleashes creativity by temporarily removing the censor or editor that restricts us to considering only what we already know.

cause and effect an analysis that focuses on why something happens (cause) and what happens as a result (effect). Explorations of cause and effect can be quite complex since some events have many contributing causes, not all of them close to the event itself. Unless a causal mechanism is demonstrated, the mere association of events (coincidence) is not grounds for concluding a cause and effect relationship.

character the combination of features or qualities that distinguishes a person, group, or object from another; a person (or occasionally an animal or inanimate object) in a literary or dramatic work.

claim a statement made with the intention that it be accepted as true. In an argument essay, the claim is expressed as the thesis statement.

classification the act of sorting things based on shared characteristics. The characteristics can be physical (the class of all round things), social (the class of middle income people), personal (the class of things I don't like), and so on. The items in one class may or may not also belong to other classes. When Sherman Alexie (p. 251) applies the newly discovered concept of "paragraph" to the reservation, to the houses around his, and to each of his family members, he is classifying the broad world into categories whose relationships can be explored and understood.

cliché a figure of speech or a graphic expression that has lost its capacity to communicate effectively because of overuse. A cliché fails in two ways: first, because the point of figurative language is to convey something more richly than literal words can, and second, because the empty phrase is like a dead space. Because a

sentence that uses cliché was not worth writing carefully, it probably is not worth reading carefully. To avoid cliché, use figures of speech that arise from concrete, specific experience. Picture in your mind what you want the reader to see and make sure your language calls that picture up effectively.

color in seeing, color is seeing the different ranges of the electromagnetic spectrum that are reflected by pigments or transmitted by light. In art, the use of color is a deliberate choice. In writing, color is adding emotional content to a factual account, a technique that is sometimes considered distorting.

comic a story told in drawings, hand-lettered dialogue, and very short bits of written narrative. Not all comics are intended to be funny; Art Spiegelman's "Mein Kampf" (p. 360) is a comic fable based on his parents' experience at Auschwitz.

compare and contrast a systematic exploration of the ways in which two or more things are alike and the ways in which they are different. A writer might use this technique to show that two apparently dissimilar things are alike in some important way or to point out important differences between two related things.

composition the act of arranging parts so that they form a meaningful or pleasing whole. A written or graphic composition requires thought and planning of the sequential or spatial relationship of its elements to produce this meaningful unity. See each chapter's "Visualizing Composition" for explanations and illustrations of specific elements of composition: "Close Reading" (p. 54), "Tone" (p. 196), "Structure" (p. 266), "Purpose" (p. 358), "Audience" (p. 406), "Metaphor" (p. 492), and "Point of View" (p. 580).

connotation the associations and emotional impact carried by a word or phrase in addition to its literal meaning. A minivan, an SUV, and a Volkswagen Bug are all vehicles, but specifying one of them as a character's means of transportation tells us about more than just the cubic feet of interior capacity.

context the part of a text or statement that surrounds a particular word or image and helps determine its meaning; the interrelated conditions within which something exists or occurs (historical, cultural, and environmental setting). Context is essential to the full understanding of a text or event. See each chapter's "Visualizing Context" for further illustration and explanation of context.

contrast to make use of strong differences in art or in argument. Advertising often uses contrast by pointing out the differences between a product and its competitors.

critical reading the act of analyzing, interpreting, and evaluating verbal or graphic text. A critical reading of a text includes close reading, note taking, contextualizing, rereading, and connecting. Most texts provoke some emotional response; critical reading explores this emotional response rather than simply accepting it as true.

critical thinking the practice of subjecting claims to close examination and analysis.

cropping make smaller by cutting so that some of the original photo is lost. Cropping is part of the photographer's act of framing an image.

deduction in logic, a form of argument in which *if* the premises are true, then the conclusion *must be* true as well. To dispute a conclusion arrived at using deduction, you must show that at least one of the premises is false. (Compare with "Induction.")

definition an explanation of the meaning of a word, phrase, or concept. A definition essay is an extended exploration both of the class to which something belongs and of the ways it differs from other things in that class.

demographic statistical characterization of a population by age, marital or household status, education, income, race, ethnicity, and so on, used for planning and marketing purposes.

description an account of an event, object, person, or process. A writer uses description to convey a vivid and accurate mental image to the reader. Description requires attention to sensory details—sights, smells, sounds, tastes, touch. *Subjective description* includes an account of the writer's inner experience of the thing being described.

design to work out the plan for an event, object, or process. Design combines purpose with an understanding of the ways things work. It marks the difference between a random collection and a purposeful composition.

diction stylistic choice of words and syntax, as between high (educated and formal) and low (ordinary and popular), between abstract and concrete, between specific and general. In "The Little Store" (p. 134), Eudora Welty uses a distinctively southern diction: "[W]here our house was when I was a child growing up in Jackson, it was possible to have a little pasture behind your backyard where you could keep a Jersey cow, which we did. My mother herself milked her." In "Cool Like Me" (p. 446), Donnell Alexander alternates street diction—"I'm the kinda nigga who's so cool that my neighbor bursts into hysterical tears whenever I ring her doorbell after dark"—with more conventional usage—"But her real experience of us is limited to the space between her Honda and her front gate."

digital imaging creating or altering images electronically. Before the use of digital imaging, photographic evidence was considered a reliable record of events. Since digital technology can generate quite realistic images of things that have no real-world counterpart, photographs have lost this status.

documentary photography photography that pays close attention to factual detail. Although it captures an image of what actually is, it still uses such compositional techniques as framing and cropping. Documentary photography often has a social commentary intent, but not always. The photographers Moyra Davey (p. 363), Mario Testino (p. 306), and James Nachtwey (p. 274) each have a particular sense of what the form is about.

draft a preliminary or intermediate version of a work. A first draft forges the results of research, planning, note taking, brainstorming, and freewriting into the beginning of a cohesive whole. Further drafts refine the thesis, improve the organization, and add transitions.

emphasis bringing increased attention to a point or element to convey its importance. Repetition and prominent placement add emphasis, as do the use of italics, larger type, color, and bold contrast.

euphemism an expression used in place of a word or phrase that is considered harsh or unpleasant—for example, using *passed away* for *died.*

evidence information presented in support of a claim. To be convincing, the information must be from a reliable source and adequately documented.

exposition an essay that explains difficult material. In addition to analysis, exposition uses familiar illustrations or analogies. K. C. Cole's "A Matter of Scale" (p. 111) is an example of exposition.

figurative language language that is not literally true but is used to express something more richly and effectively than literal language can. In "Seeing" (p. 94), Annie Dillard calls an island *tear-shaped*, conveying in two words an image that would require a much longer physical description if described literally.

font the design of lettering used in text. Fonts can be formal, elegant, traditional, modern, casual, silly, or purely functional. Choice of font is a subtle but critical design element.

found objects ordinary objects, not originally intended as art, that are found, chosen, and exhibited by an artist.

framing to construct by fitting parts into a whole; to design, shape, construct; to put into words, to formulate; to contrive the evidence against an innocent person; to enclose in, or as if in, a frame. Framing is one of the compositional elements of a photo or other graphic image.

freewriting also called *nonstop writing,* a strategy in which the writer writes without pausing to consider grammar, sentence structure, word choice, and spelling.

graphic design the application of design principles to articles intended for commercial or persuasive purposes. Virtually every printed or broadcast item encountered—packaging, signage, sets and backdrops, book covers, magazines—has been graphically designed to maximize the effectiveness of its message.

graphic elements separate pieces that are assembled into a whole in a graphic composition.

high art art whose techniques require formal education and whose purpose is primarily aesthetic. In contrast, *craft* may be decorative but is mainly functional, and *folk* or *popular art* requires little formal training.

hyperbole an obvious and intentional exaggeration—for example, using *starving* for *hungry.*

hypothesis an explanation that accounts for the known facts and makes further predictions that logically must be true if the explanation is true. These predictions can be tested, and the hypothesis is disconfirmed if they are false.

identity a unified, persistent sense of who a person uniquely is; the inner experience of one's self.

idiom a style of expression peculiar to an individual or a group. Idiomatic expressions may make no sense literally—for example, "to have it in for someone" or "to give someone a piece of your mind."

illustration / illustrative essay a design or picture in a print medium used to explain the text.

image a thing that represents something else; a symbol, an emblem, a representation. Also, the picture called into a reader's mind by a writer's use of descriptive or figurative language.

induction method of reasoning from experience, from observed facts to a generalized pattern; scientific reasoning is inductive. *Inductive generalization* is the conclusion that the next item in a series will be like the items already observed. The strength of an inductive conclusion depends on the size of the sample observed and the uniformity of the sample.(Compare with "Deduction.")

inference an intellectual leap from what one sees to what those details might suggest; a conclusion drawn from available facts. An interpretation of a text is an inference, a conclusion about what the text means based on detailed observations about it.

installation a planned, deliberate arrangement of art works in a space.

invention the development of a device or process not previously in use.

irony a humorous aspect of writing that calls attention to the difference between the actual result of a sequence of events and the expected result; an expression that says one thing while intending to convey its opposite.

layout the process of arranging printed or graphic material on a page; the overall design of a page, including such elements as type size, typeface, titles, and page numbers.

media the methods by which things are transmitted; in particular, the mass media—newspapers, magazines, movies, television and radio broadcasts, and recordings—that transmit ideas and images to the culture at large.

medium the material or technique used by an artist; by extension, the material or technique that carries a message, including print and airwaves.

metaphor a word or phrase that means one thing but is used to describe something else in order to suggest a relationship between the two; an implied comparison. "America . . . is the taste of ice-cold Coca-Cola" uses metaphor to create an association of homeland, national culture, and one brand of soft drink. See "Visualizing Composition: Metaphor" (p. 492) for more examples.

metonymy a figure of speech in which one word or phrase substitutes for another closely associated with it—for example, *Washington* for *U.S. government.*

mixed media using two or more media in one composition, as in a collage, a sound and light show, or a combination of sculptures and plantings.

narrative a verbal or graphic account of the events of a story. More than just a listing of occurrences, narrative provides a cohesive unity to a description of events.

narrator the person telling a story, from whose point of view it has cohesive unity. The narrator can be a character in the story or an observer who takes no part in the action.

observation the act, practice, or power of noticing; a comment or remark based on something observed. In rhetoric, an observation is a neutral statement supported by specific evidence about something in a text.

ode a formal poem in praise of something noble.

parody a mocking imitation that exaggerates some quality in the original. Parody is used to entertain,

unlike satire, whose general purpose is to stimulate reform.

personification a metaphor in which something non-human is given human attributes. In "Edward Hopper and the House by the Railroad (1925)" (p. 131), Edward Hirsch gives a house a facial expression, feelings, and even the moral capacity to do "something against the earth."

perspective the physical or figurative point from which the artist or writer sees the subject; also, the effect of that standpoint on what the writer or artist sees and conveys. The size, relation, and even existence of both physical and conceptual things seem different depending on where, in relation to a scene, one stands to observe.

persuasion the act or process of moving someone to a decision or a position.

photo-essay a collection of photographs composed to develop a point or a theme in the manner of a written essay.

photojournalism reporting on events through the use of photographs.

point of view the angle of vision, the perspective from which writers and artists see—and present—a subject. This perspective may be expressed—simply and literally—as the physical stance they establish in viewing a subject. In writing, point of view may also be revealed through the tone of voice, or attitude, that the writer expresses in addressing a subject. See "Visualizing Composition: Point of View" (p. 580) for more examples.

pop art an art movement that used familiar images from the mass culture to blur the distinction between high art and popular expression. Andy Warhol (p. 480) is an example of a Pop artist.

portfolio a collection representative of an artist's work; in particular, a collection of closely related images. See the portfolios of Tim Gardner (p. 79), Richard Misrach (p. 176), Andrew Savulich (p. 268), Peter Rostovsky (p. 325), David Graham (p. 395), Tibor Kalman (p. 494), and Sebastião Salgado (p. 594) for examples of this kind of representation.

portraiture a posed representation of specific person or group of persons. In additional to showing a physical likeness, portraits convey the subject's personality. Historically, portraits included clothing, jewelry, and settings that showed the subject's relative social standing.

premise a statement that forms the basis of an argument and leads to the conclusion; one of the reasons why a claim should be accepted.

public art art that is paid for with tax dollars, installed in public places, and intended for a wide audience. The Vietnam Memorial in Washington, D.C., is an example of public art.

purpose the goal a writer has in mind; the effect a writer intends to have on the audience. A writer's purpose is the *why* behind the text. See "Visualizing Composition: Purpose" (p. 358) for more examples.

representation a depiction, portrayal, or reproduction that brings a thing or person to mind.

revise the act of rewriting an initial draft of a text, towards a final version. Revising includes both large-scale revisions such as restructuring or rewriting and smaller-scale revisions such as editing for grammar and syntax.

rhetoric writing or speaking for the purpose of communication or persuasion, with attention to audience and purpose; the principles, technical terms, and rules developed for the practice of rhetoric.

satire a literary composition that criticizes vice through the use of ridicule. Satire is a form of political speech whose intent is to provoke change.

simile a figure of speech that compares two unlike things using the words *like, as, as if,* or *as though.* In "Seeing" (p. 94), Annie Dillard uses simile when she writes that a drawing "looked as though five shining, real quarter horses had been corraled by mistake with a papier-mâché moose."

staged photography a work in which the photographer arranges the elements of a picture deliberately, in contrast to a candid shot or a documentary photograph.

stereotype an uncritical generalization, which can be either positive or negative. The word *stereotype* comes from the form or mold used by artisans to create a repeating pattern. To hold a stereotyped idea of a population is to act as if all of its members were stamped out of a mold instead of being complex, highly variable individuals.

still life a form of painting that represents a composed arrangement of ordinary objects. The act of making art out of the ordinary challenges the viewer to look more deeply and carefully at the everyday.

structure the way in which the parts in a system are put together; the planned framework of a piece of writing. See "Visualizing Composition: Structure" (p. 266) for more examples.

style a writer's distinctive way of using words to achieve particular effects. Style includes diction, syntax, figures, imagery, and tone.

syllogism a valid argument containing two premises and a conclusion. If both premises are true, then the conclusion is true. But if one of the premises is false, there is no way to judge the conclusion.

symbolism the use of something tangible, material, or visible to stand for and express what is intangible, spiritual, or invisible—for example, the eagle standing for the qualities that make up U.S. national culture.

syntax the study of the rules whereby words or other elements of sentence structure are combined to form grammatical sentences; the pattern of formation of sentences or phrases in a language. Syntax implies a systematic, orderly arrangement.

texture as an element of art, the surface feel—smooth, rough, soft, and so on. The texture may be actual or simulated.

thesis statement an explicit statement of the purpose of an essay; in an argument essay, the claim that is being advanced and will be supported.

tone the feelings conveyed by the writer's choice of words. In "No Place Like Home" (p. 157), David Guterson conveys disapproval with his choice of descriptive words—"expensive mountain bikes," "conspicuously devoid of gas stations." See "Visualizing Composition: Tone" (p. 196) for more examples.

typography the design, style, and arrangement of printed material. Careful choice of fonts establishes tone. The relative sizes of fonts; use of color, italics, and bold; and the arrangement of blocks of text and white space guide a reader's attention. Digital technology has made typography options widely available and has increased the effectiveness of text as a communication.

vsual literacy the ability to read and write in a purely visual medium; the ability to decode the meaning delivered by visual texts, as through design, typography, and images.

voice the sound of the text in the reader's mind, as well as the sense of the person it conveys. Voice results from the distinctive blend of diction and syntax, the resulting rhythms and sounds, and the use of images and idioms. A voice that is natural and authentic sounds consistent to the reader, but a voice that is put on gives itself away in false notes.

Rhetorical Table of Contents

ACKNOWLEDGMENTS (continued from copyright page)

Tillie Olson. "I Stand Here Ironing." From *Tell Me a Riddle*, by Tillie Olsen. Introduction by John Leonard. © 1956, 1957, 1960, 1961 by Tillie Olsen. Used by permission of Dell Publishing Group, a division of Random House, Inc.

George M. Whitesides. "Compact Disc." From *On The Surface of Things: Images of the Extraordinary in Science* by Felice Frankel and George M. Whitesides. © 1997. Reprinted by permission of Chronicle Books, LLC, San Francisco.

Larry Woiwode. "Ode to an Orange." Originally published in Harper's. Copyright © 1985 by Larry Woiwode. Reprinted by permission of Donadio & Olson, Inc.

Visual Texts

Untitled #2. Courtesy Tracey Baran, 1999.

Self-Portrait. Courtesy Chuck Close.

Seascape. Courtesy Michael Collins.

Milk Drop Coronet. © Harold & Esther Edgerton Foundation, 1999. Courtesy of Palm Press, Inc.

Untitled, by William Eggleston. Courtesy Cheim & Read, New York.

Central Savings, by Richard Estes. Courtesy of The Nelson-Atkins Museum of Art, Kansas City, Missouri. (Gift of the Friends of Art) F75-13.

Refrigerator. © 1999, Roe Etheridge.

Compact Disc. Courtesy Felice Frankel.

Aspirin Self-Portrait. Courtesy Tom Friedman.

Untitled photos, by Tim Gardner. Courtesy 303 Gallery, New York.

1920 Cycle Trades of America *Ride a Bicycle* poster ad. Courtesy Gaslight Ad Archives, Commack, NY.

Roadmaster Bicycles. © 1999 Brunswick Corporation. *Roadmaster* is a registered trademark which is used by the express permission of Brunswick Corporation. 1953 ad Courtesy Gaslight Ad Archives, Commack, NY.

Television Moon. © Alfred Leslie. Reprinted by permission.

The place is not important. It's the freedom that Counts. Murray Bicycles, 1998.

1886 Columbia Bicycle ad poster. Litho by Forbes Company, Boston. Collection of the New York Historical Society.

Badge of Honor, by Pepón Osorio. Courtesy Ronald Feldman Fine Arts, New York.

A Kitchen Scouring Pad, by David Scharf. © Photo Researchers, Inc.

Chapter 2

Verbal Texts

Lucille Clifton. "When I Go Home." From *A Place Called Home: Twenty Writing Women Remember* by Mickey Pearlman, editor. © Lucille Clifton. Reprinted by permission of the author.

Marita Golden. "A Sense of Place." Copyright © 2000 Marita Golden. Reprinted by permission of the PEN/Faulkner Foundation and Bloomsbury Publishing.

David Gutterson. "No Place Like Home: On the Manicured Streets of a Master-Planned Community." Originally appeared in *Harper's Magazine*, November 1992. Copyright © 1992 by David Gutterson. Reprinted by permission of Georges Borchardt, Inc. for the author.

Ron Hansen. "Nebraska." First published in Atlantic Monthly Press, 1998. Copyright © 1998 by Ron Hansen. Used by permission of Grove/Atlantic, Inc.

Edward Hirsch. "Edward Hopper and the House by the Railroad." From *Wild Gratitude* by Edward Hirsch. Copyright © 1985 by Edward Hirsch. Reprinted by permission of Alfred A. Knopf, a division of Random House, Inc.

Tony Hiss. Excerpt from *The Experience of Place* by Tony Hiss. Copyright © 1990 by Tony Hiss. Used by permission of Alfred A. Knopf, a division of Random House, Inc.

David Ignatow. "My Place." From *Against the Evidence* by David Ignatow. Reprinted by permission of University Press New England.

Pico Iyer. "Why We Travel." First published in *Salon Travel*. Copyright © 2000 by Pico Iyer. Reprinted by permission of the author.

Erica Jong. From "Coming Home to Connecticut."

Chang-rae Lee. "Coming Home Again." First appeared in *The New Yorker*, 1996. Copyright © 1996 by Chang-rae Lee. Reprinted by permission of International Creative Management, Inc.

Norman Mailer. From "Three Minutes or Less." Reprinted with permission.

Scott Russell Sanders. "Homeplace." From *Staying Put* by Scott Russell Sanders. Copyright © 1993 by Scott Russell Sanders. Reprinted by permission of Beacon Press, Boston.

Eudora Welty. "The Little Store." From *The Eye of the Story: Selected Essays and Reviews* by Eudora Welty. Copyright © 1975 by Eudora Welty. Reprinted by permission of Random House, Inc.

Visual Texts

Ericsson advertisement. Reprinted with permission.

Family in Kitchen. Photo by Tina Barney. Courtesy of Janet Borden, Inc.

Among the Sierra Mountains, 1868. Photo by Albert Bierstadt, National Museum of American Art, Washington, DC/Art Resource, N.Y.

Tamalada. Artist Carmen Lopez Garza. Photo: Wolfgang Dietze. Collection of Lenoila Ramierz, Don Ramon's Restaurant, San Francisco, CA. Reprinted by permission.

The Far Side by Gary Larson. © 1991 Farworks, Inc. All Rights Reserved. Used with permission.

Untiled # 9. Courtesy Miranda Lichtenstein.

Richard Misrach portfolio. Courtesy Robert Mann Gallery, New York.

House by the Railroad, 1925, by Edward Hopper. The Museum of Modern Art, New York. Given anonymously. Copyright The Museum of Modern Art/Licensed by SCALA/Art Resource, NY.

Mr. Lee's House, The Hill, 1991. Margaret Morton. From *Fragile Dwelling* by Margaret Morton (New York: Aperture, 2000). © Margaret Morton. Reprinted by permission.

Image of Homelessness. Photo courtesy Mark Peterson.

Rancho Seco Nuclear Plant, Sacremento, CA 1983. Photo John Pfahl. Courtesy Janet Borden, Inc.

Durga Puja Immersion and *Diwali Day Pilgrims*. © Raghubir Singh.

Taylor Hall Parking Lot, Kent State University, Kent, OH, May 1994. Copyright © Joel Sternfeld.

65 East 125th Street, Harlem. Courtesy Camilo José Vergara.

Storekeeper. Eudora Welty Collection, Mississippi Department of Archives & History.

Chapter 3

Verbal Texts

Sherman Alexie. "The Joy of Reading and Writing: Superman and Me." Reprinted by permission of the author.

Dorothy Allison. "This Is Our World." From *DoubleTake Magazine*, Summer, 1998. Copyright © 1998 by Dorothy Allison. Reprinted by permission of Frances Goldin Literary Agent, Inc.

Ethan Canin. "Viewfinder." Originally titled, "Vivian, Fort Barnwell " by Ethan Canin. First published in *DoubleTake*. Copyright © 1998 by Ethan Canin. Reprinted by permission of the author.

Don DeLillo. "In the Ruins of the Future: Reflections on terror, loss and time in the shadows of September." Copyright © 2001 by Don DeLillo. First published in *Harper's Magazine*. Reprinted by permission of the Wallace Literary Agency, Inc.

Barry Lopez. "Learning To See." From *About This Life*, by Barry Lopez (Vintage Books, a Division of Random House, 1998). Copyright © 1998 by Barry Lopez. Used by permission of Alfred A. Knopf, a division of Random House, Inc. and Sterling Lord Literistic, Inc.

N. Scott Momaday. " The Photograph." From *The Man Made of Words*. By N. Scott Momaday. Copyright © 1997 by N. Scott Momaday. Reprinted by permission of St. Martin's Press, Incorporated.

James Nachtwey. "Ground Zero." From *American Photo*, 13.1 January/February 2002. Reprinted by permission.

Joe Rosenthal. "Flag Raising on Iwo Jima, February 23, 1945." From *Faces of the 20th Century: Master Photographers and Their Work*, Abbeville Press.

Susan Sontag. "On Photography." From "In Plato's Cave" in *On Photography* by Susan Sontag. Copyright © 1977 by Susan Sontag. Reprinted by permission of Farrar, Straus and Giroux, LLC.

Sarah Vowell. "Shooting Dad." From *Take the Cannoli: Stories from the New World* by Sarah Vowell. Copyright © 2000 by Sarah Vowell. Reprinted by permission of Simon & Schuster Adult Publishing Group.

Visual Texts

3 Cent Iwo Jima Stamp. AP/Wide World Photos.

Flag Raising, World Trade Center, 2001. Associated Press photograph by Thomas E. Franklin.

Ashleigh, 13, with her friend and parents, Santa Monica. Courtesy Lauren Greenfield Photography.

Tourists. Photo by Duane Hanson. Courtesy of National Galleries of Scotland.

Malayan Tapir, London 1992. From *Zoo*, by Britta Jaschinski. © 1996 Phaidon Press Ltd.

Here Is New York. © 2001 Jeff Mermelstein, *New York Times*. All Rights Reserved.

Meander Along the Green River, Aerial View, Gray Canyon, Utah. © 1993 William Neill/www.WilliamNeill.com.

Front Page New York Times, September 11, 2001. © The New York Times. Reprinted by permission.

Kalkan, Turkey. © Martin Parr/Magnum Photos, Inc. Reprinted by permission.

Crushed Car. Photograph by James Nachtwey. From *American Photo*, 13.1 January/February 2002. Reprinted by permission.

Superbowl XXXVI. Associated Press photograph by David J. Phillip, 2002.

Marines Raising Flag on Mount Suribachi, Iwo Jima. Photo by Joe Rosenthal. From *Faces of the 20th Century: Master Photographers and Their Work*, Abbeville Press.

Andrew Savulich portfolio. Courtesy Andrew Savulich.

Witnessing a Dreadful Moment in History. Photograph by Patrick Witty.

Strangers. Photographs by Shizuka Yokomizo. Courtesy Cohan Leslie and Brown, NY.

Chapter 4

Verbal Texts

Albert Bliss. "Homeless Man Interviews Himself." Copyright © by *Harper's* magazine. Reproduced from the September issue by special permission. All Rights Reserved.

Bruce Bower. "Average Attractions." From *Science News* 12, May, 1990. pp. 298–99. Reprinted with permission from Science Service, the weekly newsmagazine of science. Copyright 1998.

Jacinto Jesús Cardona. "Bato Con Khakis." From *Heart to Heart: New Poems* by Jacinto Jesús Cardona. © 2001 Jacinto Jesús Cardona. Reprinted by permission of Chili Verde Press.

Judith Ortiz Cofer. "The Story of My Body." From *The Latin Deli: Prose & Poetry* by Judith Ortiz Cofer. Copyright © 1993 by Judith Ortiz Cofer. Reprinted by permission of The University of Georgia Press.

Gish Jen. "What Means Switch." From *Who's Irish*, by Gish Jen. Copyright © 1999 by Gish Jen. Reprinted by permission of the Alfred A. Knopf, a division of Random House, Inc.

Marge Piercy. "Imaging." From *Mars and Her Children* by Marge Piercy. Copyright © 1992 by Middlemarsh, Inc. Reprinted with permission of Alfred A. Knopf, Inc, a division of Random House.

Joe Queenan. "The Skin Game." From *GQ* magazine, May 2001 issue. Copyright © 2001 Joe Queenan. Reprinted by permission.

Visual Texts

I Can't Decide. © The New Yorker Collection 1998 Marisa Accocella from: cartoonbank.com. All Rights Reserved.

Asics ad. © Asics Tiger Corporation, 1998. Reprinted by permission.

The City. Photograph by Moyra Davey.

Cindy Jackson. © Cindy Jackson Ltd. <www.cindyjackson.com>. Reprinted by permission.

Nose Piercing. Courtesy Lynn Johnson, photographer. Courtesy Aurora & Quanta Productions.

Your body is a battleground, 1989. Photo by Barbara Kruger. Collection: Eli Broad Family Foundation, Santa Monica. Courtesy: Mary Boone Gallery, New York.

The Skateboarders' Project (#8), The Tourist Project (#9). Copyright Nikki S. Lee, courtesy Leslie Tonkonow Artworks & Projects, New York.

Bato Con Khakis, by César A. Martínez. From *Heart to Heart*, ed. Jan Greenberg and Harry N. Abrams, 2001.

Grace Under Duty. Photograph by Shirin Neshat. From *Women Artists in the 20th & 21st Century*.

I'm Comfortable Being a Man Rockport Rupaul ad. Reprinted with permission of Rupaul, The Rockport Company, Inc. and Lorenzo Agius, Photographer.

Portfolio by Peter Rostovsky. From *Cabinet Magazine*, Winter 2001 issue.

Untitled #8. Photograph by Cindy Sherman. Courtesy Cindy Sherman and Metro Pictures.

Mein Kampf. Comic art by Art Spiegelman. From *New York Times Magazine*, May 12, 1996. © The New York Times.

Doubles, Lima and *Shalom and Linda, Paris.* Reprinted for and on behalf of Mario Testino/Art Partner, NY.

Chapter 5

Verbal Texts

Donnell Alexander. "Cool Like Me." First published in *Utne Reader*, November/December 1997. Reprinted by permission of the author.

Neil Gabler. "Inside Every Superhero Lurks a Nerd." From the *New York Times*, May 12, 2002. © The New York Times Company, Inc. Reprinted by permission.

Dee Dee Gordon and Sharon Lee. "Look-Look." Interview on *Frontline.* <www.pbs.org>. Reprinted by permission.

Naomi Klein. Excerpt from "No Logo: Taking Aim at the Brand Bullies." Copyright © 1999 by Naomi Klein. Reprinted by permission of Picador ® St. Martin's Press, Inc. All Rights Reserved.

Robert Pinsky. "To Television." Reprinted by permission of the author. "Creating the 'Real' in Bright Yellow and Blue" from the *New York Times*, November 5, 2000. Copyright © The New York Times Company, Inc. Reprinted with permission.

Andrew Sullivan. "The Pursuit of Happiness: Four Revolutionary Words." © 2002. First published on the Internet at <www.andrewsullivan.com>. Reprinted with permission of the Wylie Agency.

James B. Twitchell. "In Praise of Consumerism." From *Lead Us Into Temptation*, by James B. Twitchell. Copyright © 1999 by James B. Twitchell. Reprinted with permission of Columbia University Press.

Charles M. Young. "Losing: An American Tradition." From *Men's Journal*, April 2000. Copyright © 2000 by Men's Journal, LLC. All Rights Reserved. Reprinted by permission.

Visual Texts

Follow the Flock, Tommy Hilfiger. Image courtesy <www.adbusters.org>. 2001. Photograph by David Butow.

Freedom ad. Courtesy Diesel.

Palmolive ad. Courtesy Gaslight Ad Archives, Commack, NY.

Portfolio by David Graham. Reprinted with permission.

Scott, 16, Beverly Hills. © 2002 Lauren Greenfield/VII.

The Simpsons. Matt Groening TM & © 20th Century Fox/Courtesy Everett Collection.

99 Cent. Photograph by Andreas Gursky. Courtesy Mathew Marks Gallery, New York. © 2001 Andreas Gursky.

The Makeover. Photographs by Naomi Harris. From the New York Times Magazine. © The New York Times.

Fourth #4, 2001. Photo by Tracy Mofatt. Courtesy Paul Morris Gallery, 465 W. 23rd Street, New York, NY 10011.

Classic American Flava ad. Courtesy Phatfarm.

Projecting Family Values. Courtesy Photofest.

Authentic Cuban Santeria. Caption: "Authentic Cuban Santeria and El Aztec High-Tech Welcome Columbus with ritual offerings." © 1990. The collaborations of Guillermo Gómez-Peña and Coco Fusco explore the notions of "authenticity" and the artificial construction of ethnic identity by the mainstream. From the project "Norte/Sur," Mexican Museum, San Francisco. Photo by Christina Taccone.

A Young Man Gathering Shopping Carts. From *Stranger Passing* by Joel Sternfeld. Copyright © 2001 Joel Sternfeld.

It's Your Life ad. Courtesy Visa.

Carol Gardner and Bumper Sticker Wisdom. Photograph by Shane Young, from *Bumper Sticker Wisdom*, by Carol Gardner. Courtesy AP/Wide World Photos.

Chapter 6

Verbal Texts

Holly Brubach. "Heroine Worship." From *The New York Times Magazine*, November 24, 1996. Copyright © 1996 by The New York Times Company, Inc. Reprinted by permission.

Guy Davenport. "The Geography of the Imagination by Guy Davenport." Copyright © 1991 by Guy Davenport. Reprinted by permission.

Mark Kingwell. "Ten Steps to the Creation of a Modern Media Icon." Courtesy Adbusters, Winter 1998.

Julie L. Nicklin. "Britney Goes to College?" From the *Chronicle of Higher Education*, February 15, 2002. Reprinted with permission.

Sharon Olds. "The Death of Marilyn Monroe." From *The Living and the Dead* by Sharon Olds. Copyright © 1983 by Sharon Olds. Reprinted by permission Alfred A. Knopf, a Division of Random House, Inc.

Tom Perrotta. "The Cosmic Significance of Britney Spears." From *GQ* magazine, December 2001. Copyright © Tom Perorotta, 2001. Reprinted courtesy of GQ Magazine.

Touré. "Kurt Is My Co-Pilot." From *Rolling Stone*, May 11, 2000. © 2000 Rolling Stone LLC. All Rights Reserved. Reprinted by permission.

David Foster Wallace. From "The View from Mrs. Thompson's Backyard." Courtesy *Rolling Stone*, October 2001.

Jane Yolen. "Grant Wood: American Gothic." Copyright © 2001 by Jane Yolen. First appeared in *Heart to Heart*, published by Harry N. Abrams, edited by Jan Greenburg. Reprinted by permission of Curtis Brown, Ltd.

Visual Texts

Madonna, 1982–1998. Archive Photos; A/P World Wide Photo; Corbis; Kim Kulish/*Los Angeles Daily News* and Popperfoto.com. Reprinted by permission.

Hollywood Walk of Fame, September 10, 2001, by David Butow. © David Butow/Corbis Saba

Life In Hell. © 1985 by Matt Groening.

Lizzy Gardiner, 1995 Academy Awards. Photo © Dan Groshong/SYGMA. Courtesy American Express/Sandra Marsh Management.

Tibor Kalman portfolio. From *Colors Magazine*, #4, "Race." Reprinted by permission.

American Indian Beaded Bag: Flags, Eagle, & Shield. Courtesy of Joel & Kate Kopp, American Hurrah Archive, NY.

Mercedes-Benz ad. Courtesy of Mercedes-Benz USA, Inc. Montvale, NJ., A Daimler Chrysler Company. <www.mbusa.com>.

American Gothic. Photograph by Gordon Parks. Courtesy Gordon Parks/Corbis.

Rosie the Riveter. Painting by Norman Rockwell. Courtesy The Picture Desk.

Elvis Presley and *Marilyn Monroe.* © 2000 Andy Warhol Foundation for the Visual Arts/ARS, New York and the Andy Warhol Foundation, Inc./Art Resource, NY.

Madonna 2002. Courtesy Warner Music.

American Gothic. Painting by Grant Wood.

Index of Verbal and Visual Texts

A NOTE ON THE TYPE

Seeing & Writing 2 was designed by Michael Rock and Katie Andresen of 2x4, New York City, using a mixture of historical and contemporary typefonts. Chapter heads, headnotes, and questions appear in two Dutch faces: Lucas de Groot's *TheSans* (1994); and *Caecilia* (1990), a slab serif by Peter Matthias Noordzij. Heads for the text selections are set in *Electra* (1935–49), which was drawn by the great American designer William Addison Dwiggins. The primary text font is *Minion* (1989) by Robert Slimbach.

www.seeingandwriting.com

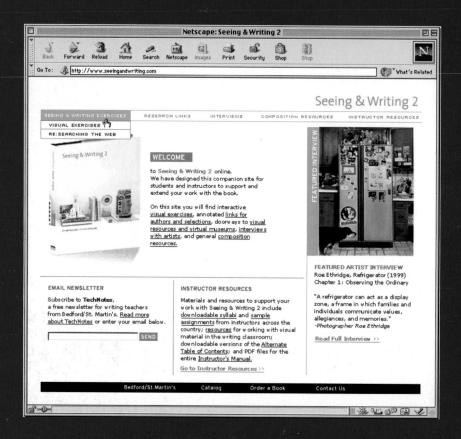

Visit the *Seeing & Writing 2* companion web site for materials to supplement the text including interactive exercises, annotated links for authors and selections, research links, interviews with artists, and general composition resources. Resources for instructors include sample syllabi, additional projects and assignments from instructors around the country, and downloadable course material.